STARTING POINT

An Introduction to the Dialectic of Existence

Robert Denoon Cumming

The University of Chicago Press
Chicago and London

THE UNIVERSITY OF CHICAGO PRESS, CHICAGO 60637
THE UNIVERSITY OF CHICAGO PRESS, LTD., LONDON

Library of Congress Cataloging in Publication Data
Cumming, Robert Denoon, 1916–
Starting point.
1. Existentialism. 2. Existentialism in literature.
3. Dialectic. I. Title.
B819.C8   142′.7   78–16317
ISBN 0–226–12347–2

ROBERT DENOON CUMMING is Frederick J. Wood-
bridge Professor of Philosophy at Columbia University. He has been a Fulbright Professor at the
University of Paris and was awarded a Rockefeller
fellowship in political and social thought and a
senior fellowship from the National Endowment
for the Humanities. He is the editor of *The
Philosophy of Jean-Paul Sartre* and the author of
*Human Nature and History: A Study of the De-
velopment of Liberal Political Thought.*

For Charlie

*Whether he would ever become a philosopher he
did not know. . . . With quiet solemnity he decided
he would start.*

*The dialectic of the starting point must be
made clear.*

—JOHANNES CLIMACUS

Contents

PART IV

CONCLUDING

PART V

POSTSCRIPT

Preface

That I shall be preoccupied with philosophy as a genre will come as no great surprise to those who have been previously exposed to philosophy. A philosopher often spends more time fretting about what he is up to than being up to it. But I have tried to write too for those not previously exposed, so I am also preoccupied with the philosophical problem of how one is introduced to philosophy.

In a mere preface even a philosopher, it might be assumed, could be more expeditious and not step on his own feet. Yet a preface is a starting point which may pose problems, if the philosophy to be presented is dialectical. Resort to dialectic is often prompted by a philosopher's dissatisfaction with conventional arrangements, whether in the real world or in previous philosophies. Here as elsewhere a distinguishing characteristic of philosophy as a genre is the generality of its scope: the conventional arrangements with which the philosopher is dissatisfied may be moral, artistic, political, economic. . . . The list might be extended indefinitely and could include a preface, which is a conventional arrangement (or prearrangement) enabling the writer to come together with his prospective reader and reach some preliminary understanding. Yet philosophers who have worried about philosophy and its conventions as a genre have rarely worried over their own prefaces.

An exception is Hegel, who protests in the most formidable of all philosophical prefaces that nothing consequential can be accomplished in a preface. "It is conventional," he announces in the first sentence of the preface to his *Phenomenology*, "to give some anticipatory explanation in a preface of the end the writer has set before himself in the work, of the circumstances which have occasioned it, and of the relations in which he believes it should be seen to earlier or contemporary treatments of the same subject." Such general prefatory remarks, Hegel argues, cannot be adapted to a work in philosophy without going "counter to its end." They "cannot be accepted as the way in which philosophical truth is to be presented." Generalizations may seem acceptable because of the generality of scope we associate with philosophy—or, as Hegel puts it, "because the medium for philosophy is essentially the universal which includes within itself the particular." But he argues that the relations of inclusion are complicated and dynamic as well as teleological, so that the philosopher is relaxing his grasp of these relations when he anticipates in a prefatory, preliminary fashion "the end or final conclusions." Such a fashion is a mere formality, whereas the conformity of form to content should be organic. Unfortunately this argument against prefaces cannot be dealt with in a mere preface, since Hegel feels the same misgiving about an introduction, with its conventional pretense of "leading" the reader from outside philosophy "into" philosophy. And I am writing an introduction.

The earlier treatment of the problem of a preface or an introduction, in relation to which I believe mine should be seen, is provided by Kierkegaard, who often sees his own treatment in relation to Hegel's. Probably Hegel's misgiving was a factor which encouraged Kierkegaard to make a dialectical countermove: philosophy itself Kierkegaard sees as merely prefatory or introductory, for he is convinced that it is not possible for one individual (the reader) to share significantly the "end" another individual (the writer) "sets before himself"—to revert to Hegel's terminology. Thus Kierkegaard regards Hegel's promise of "final conclusions," if only we would patiently follow out the detailed development of his philosophy, not as philosophically justifiable conduct but as "seduction"—a "leading" of the reader "astray" from the final conclusions which he can reach only from his own experience.

There is an ambiguity here. Conventionally a preface or an introduction is prefatory or introductory *for* a reader as well as *to* the subject that will be treated, just as a "convention" itself can be both a "coming together" of individuals as well as their implicit mutual "understanding" regarding some subject. (Some of the characteristics of a "convention" in both these senses will be explored in the present work, as will also be the way in which a philosopher can take dialectical advantage of such ambiguities.) But the prominence the relation between writer and reader gains with Kierkegaard's countermove to Hegel depends on the collapse of the conventional distinction between the dimensions of the "to" and the "for": in Kierkegaard there is a respect in which the subject to which one is introduced by philosophy is the individual one might become, and another respect in which the subject of Kierkegaard's philosophy, by virtue of his very effort to communicate it, must be expanded to include his relation to his reader.

With this relation brought to the fore, Kierkegaard regularly tries to come to some preliminary understanding with his reader in his prefaces. In fact the collapse of the conventional distinction is illustrated by his ironic work, *Prefaces*, which is entirely composed of prefaces. In its preface he (or rather his pseudonym) concedes to Hegel that "a preface in relation to a book is something without significance." His "desire is to have written a book," but his wife regards the prospect of his going public by becoming an actual writer as "open infidelity," so he is confined to prefaces. Kierkegaard himself had problems with actuality and openness, and he never married, though he was briefly engaged—a merely prefatory relation, it might seem. Yet it was one he had a great deal to say about, for his virtual reduction of the subject matter of philosophy to one's relation to oneself and to others is further illustrated by the extent to which he manipulates ironically, in opposition to Hegel, conventional arrangements for personal relations: not only "engagement" and "seduction" but also "marriage," which he sometimes construes as the final conclusive Hegelian fashion in which one comes into actual relation with the whole history of humanity. Kierkegaard himself decides instead to become an individual.

Kierkegaard is probably again outmaneuvering Hegel's arrangements when he entitles his major philosophical work, in which he tries to come to some final understanding with his reader, *Concluding Unscientific Postscript*. A preface is etymologically a matter of what one "says before." Yet Hegel's preface to the *Phenomenology* was not written "before" but "after" the work itself—like most prefaces. It was in effect not a preface but a postscript. What was "last" for the writer becomes "first" for his reader.

In general the relation between "first" and "last" (if Hegel will permit a prefatory explanation) is a dialectically pivotal relation. For the time being it can be illustrated by turning from the first paragraph of Hegel's preface to the last, where Hegel explains that "the individual, in keeping with the scientific nature of philosophy, must forget himself." Hegel has come full circle from the problem in the first paragraph of "the way in which philosophical truth is to be *presented*" to the problem of its *reception*. The relation which has finally emerged (and may justify in retrospect the writing of the preface as dealing with a problem separable from the work itself) is "The Writer's Relation to His Public." This public, along with the writer's relation to it, Hegel finds has developed in his time, and in a manner which he doubtless also finds in keeping with

the scientific nature of philosophy. But this development leaves us
with an apparent contradiction: in spite of Hegel's initial discounting
of prefaces in favor of the actual work, the final conclusion of his preface
suggests that the actual work to which this preface is a preface is itself,
not just his work as an individual; but in the sense that this is the case,
it is also merely prefatory to what the work must actually become: "We
must be confident that it is of the nature of truth to prevail by finding
expression when its time has come," that "the truth never finds a public
not ripe to receive it, and also that the individual needs this outcome
in order to demonstrate the truth of what is until then merely a matter
of his solitary concern and to experience the confidence that what at the
start belongs only to a particular individual is something universal." This
transition is for Hegel an *Aufhebung*, which I shall later explain when
I deal with Kierkegaard's effort to subvert it.

But for the present let us linger with the apparent contradiction. In
the first paragraph the reader, in keeping with the scientific nature of
philosophy, has to wait patiently for particulars and the relations between
them to develop. But in the last paragraph the individual in his particularity is to be discounted as merely a starting point, even when that
individual happens to be the writer. He must now wait upon the reception of the work, granted that he should not have to wait too long,
since the public is "ripe." Instead of being confined to the preface, "the
writer's relation to his public" would comprehend Hegel's entire work,
if he did not "forget himself" and allow the public to take over, allied
as it is with the truth.

I am not suggesting that the conclusion of Hegel's preface is inconsistent
with the way he started out. Hegel is only being dialectical, as he also is
when he argues in a preface against prefaces. He is saved from inconsistency by presupposing the distinction, which I have indicated Kierkegaard will liquidate: particulars in Hegel's first paragraph do not refer
specifically to particular individuals, nor are the relations between these
particulars specifically personal relations.

In the present work I shall be considering the effect on the scientific
nature of philosophy of the refusal of Kierkegaard and certain other
philosophers, each in his own way, to forget himself as an individual
and surrender his solitary concern to some public demonstration of the
truth. Inasmuch as this refusal also has an effect on his relation to his
readers, some prefatory comment on this relation has seemed justified.
Hegel distressed most of his successors (including these philosophers) by
the fact that he was on such confident speaking terms with the Absolute
and its "final conclusions." But what are we to make of his confidence
in the public, which is a universal that also holds its ingredient particu-

lars in a complex but firm embrace? How strictly are we to take his developmental and organic metaphor "ripe" when it applies not only to his philosophy as a whole but also to the public as a whole? What philosopher today can anticipate in his preface so conjoint a fruition?

Hegel does allow us some discrimination. At the very moment of transition when he with his philosophy becomes a spokesman for the public, he also recognizes that "at this juncture the public must be distinguished from those who take it upon themselves to be its representatives and spokesman." Hegel is referring to professional colleagues who will be his reviewers. His confidence is, rather, in the public itself in some higher sense.

Today professional philosophers are no longer expert in higher senses. Nor do they pretend to represent and speak for the public; by and large they speak to each other and write for each other. And their public can hardly be said to be ripening. It is just aging. History (in Hegel's phrase) is going on behind their backs and determining the destiny of their own profession: its younger generation, like Kierkegaard's pseudonym (though marriage is less Hegelian a threat than it once was), can only write prefaces to the books they would some day have written, were they not instead to be frozen out of the profession by the elimination of teaching careers. At the same time, vested philosophical interests are being frozen in by the permanent tenure enjoyed by the middle-aged. This state of affairs is of course not restricted to philosophy; and if one were a Michel Foucault, one might probe for the invisible strategy which institutionalized power is inflicting on humanity by so disposing of the humanities.

At any rate, this state of affairs has been (in Hegel's recipe for a "conventional" preface) among the "circumstances which have occasioned" the present work and dictated the way I would "come together" with my readers. I have skirted dominant philosophical controversies, except where they lay directly in my path, and I have not attempted to protect my own flanks. I have attempted instead to exhibit certain issues raised by philosophy as a genre in a manner which might pick up some readers who are sufficiently unprofessional to be interested in a dialectic designed to adapt this genre to the concern of the individual with himself and his personal relations. I am not arguing that this is necessarily what philosophy should be about. I am only observing that today, for better or worse, a certain intellectual sensitivity in this area seems to survive increasing indifference to more broadly conceived ideologies as well as to the aloof abstractness of most professional philosophy. It is of course true that talented philosophers have supplied trenchant analyses of such personal problems as abortion (e.g., in terms of a woman's right to control her own body), but to isolate a right can be a way of abstracting from personal relations without which the problem might not have been posed.

Finally, I am not claiming that a dialectical philosophy animated by the individual's concern with himself and personal relations is very novel. This is a concern of Socrates in many Platonic dialogues, and each of these dialogues is likely to be named after some other individual whose character, way of life, and relation to Socrates would give him some stake as an interlocutor in the subject treated.

Yet after all that has happened since Plato's time to render philosophy a professional discipline, it may seem that the issue raised by my attempt is the outrage of popularization. This issue I take up in the introduction proper. But the real risk is minimal, since I have not spared the reader the weariness of a long, sustained argument or a close textual analysis forbiddingly buttressed by footnotes.

In making this attempt my most valued interlocutor has been Charles Cumming. Not only did he catch numerous errors, but he was also persistent in discovering stretches that were obscure and required rewriting if I was to expect readers to continue reading. He himself did continue and completed his criticism of the manuscript the day before his operation for a brain tumor. This is his book.

Some readers have already been able to trace a certain debt to Jacques Derrida. There are also differences. But I have deferred any attempt to come to grips with him—if that were possible.

David Hoy and Calvin Schrag read the manuscript and offered encouragement as well as suggestions which I have tried to take into account. The manuscript has meantime undergone extensive revision, so that it will be difficult for me to saddle either of them with any responsibility for its present shortcomings. Some of the discussion of Sartre's "Marxism" herein has appeared previously in *Political Theory* under the title "This Place of Violence, Obscurity and Witchcraft."

Any one who has tried, without much success, to keep track of Sartre's occasional writings must acknowledge a debt to the diligence and acumen of Michel Contat and Michel Rybalka for their bibliography with citations. I am also grateful for the notes to the Danish collected works of Kierkegaard and for the superb editing of *Husserliana*. All this might have been cheerfully taken for granted, were it not necessary to register disappointment—nay, fury—as successive volumes of Heidegger's lectures, etc., come out in his German collected works unannotated and without critical apparatus. If only it had been possible, as with Husserl, to smuggle Heidegger's manuscripts across the border to Louvain!

Note on References and Translations

The reader may sometimes be interested in the context of my citations, so I refer to editions in English when these are reasonably reliable and available. The translations themselves are usually my own.

In citing Kierkegaard, I sometimes follow an interpolated Danish term with its German equivalent, since his terminology oftens reflects Hegelian philosophical usage. The terms can be distinguished, for Danish nouns are no longer capitalized since the spelling reform of 1948. But I have not otherwise modernized Kierkegaard's spelling. References to Kierkegaard's journals and other papers are to the Heiberg/Kuhr edition, but most of the entries should be locatable in English when an index and collation are provided with the publication of volume 7 of the Hong translation. When biographical information is relevant for the interpretation of my quotation, I cite one of the standard biographies.

Hegel's *Encyclopaedia Logic* is cited as *Encyclopaedia*, pt. 1, in order to avoid confusion with his *Science of Logic*, which is cited as *Logic*. References to *Phenomenology* are to Hegel's *Phenomenology of the Spirit*; references to *Perception* are to Merleau-Ponty's *Phenomenology of Perception*. Citations of Heidegger's *Being and Time* refer to the German pagination, which is retained in the English translation.

Situations followed by a volume number refers to the collected essays of Sartre in French. These references should not be confused with citations of *Situations* without a volume number or citations of *Life/ Situations*, also without a volume number, both of which are English editions of some of these essays.

References to *Sartre* are to my anthology, *The Philosophy of Jean-Paul Sartre*.

Introduction

The Vagabond

Philosophy is . . . the renewed experience of its own starting point.
—Merleau-Ponty

STARTING OUT

The first question a philosopher faces is where to start. It is the first question anyone faces when he becomes aware of some disarray in his experience and decides to take the initiative in order to bring matters under control. Or perhaps what should be acknowledged first is that wherever one starts, there will be ensuing implications. The particular experience that is allowed to come to the forefront of one's concern tends to impose its significance by soliciting some kind of treatment. This treatment can never be kept entirely ad hoc; it tends to carry over in treating other experiences that turn up. If compulsion is then felt to meet some standard of consistency or coherence, the performance to this extent approximates the philosophical. A sense of this compulsion is almost anyone's experience, and one way in which he may approach becoming a philosopher. "Where you started out, there you will remain" is a pronouncement of the poet Hölderlin, but it is cited by Heidegger for its philosophical relevance.[1]

The question of starting point is at least as old as Aristotle. It can be said to be at least as old as philosophy, if the claim can be made that philosophy itself started with Aristotle, inasmuch as he was the first thinker to distinguish what he called "first philosophy" from other scientific disciplines. For one way he distinguished it was as the science of first principles (*archai*).[2] But his starting point in a sense eludes us. *Archē* was an ordinary Greek word which can be translated by our "starting point." Did it become for Aristotle also a term whose technical status should be respected by translating it instead as "principle"? What we cannot get behind here is the discrepancy between our ordinary usage (and the ordinary experiences we count on it to convey) and philosophical technicalities, especially if it is the case (as Heidegger argues) that, when

1

the Romans provided us with such technical translations as *principium* for the Greek *archē*, their translations failed to preserve the original experiences with which Greek philosophy started out.[3]

This failure may have been crucial, insofar as modern philosophy has never entirely emancipated itself from a terminology deriving from Latin.[4] But loss of contact with experience is a recurrent philosophical episode: a starting point imposes its significance by hardening into a principle; but then it is forgotten why the philosopher once started out where he did. Indeed a philosophy is only recognized to have lost contact with experience when there is some concomitant summons to renewed experience. But even when the renewal itself takes philosophical form, it is not the renewal of the original experience; a renewed experience can never quite be the original experience.

With the summons to renewal the previously prevailing philosophy may be denounced as "scholasticism." Yet something else happens in the modern period besides this denunciation. With respect to philosophical principles, the intimate association slackens that held in the case of *archē* between the notion of "starting out" and the notion of "remaining in control." (In Greek an *archōn* [ruler] occupies first place by exercising both initiative and control.) Thus when Heidegger answers the question *What is Philosophy?* by attempting to renew the experience of the way it started out with the Greeks, he has to insist,

> We must understand the word *archē* in its full sense. It designates the "where" that something starts out "from." But this "from where" is not left behind in the process of starting out; the *archē*, rather, becomes . . . that which controls.[5]

To regain the full sense of this process of starting out (and thereby what philosophy is), Heidegger has to turn back to the Greeks or to the poetry of Hölderlin, who had already turned back to the Greeks. For as we all know, the area where philosophical principles still exercise control has shrunk as various specialized scientific disciplines have acquired their own autonomy. Whatever philosophy is today, it is no longer "first philosophy" or "the science of first principles," for the sciences are no longer disciplines within its sway. Where philosophy once "started out" the sciences no longer "remain."

Today where philosophy still exercises control, it is to a considerable extent only over the performances of philosophers. It has tended to become increasingly professional during our own century. The English philosopher who was initially perhaps the most influential in encouraging many philosophers to resign themselves to this state of affairs was G. E. Moore, whose attachment to principles is signalized by his title *Principia Ethica*. How he started out is suggested by his candid comment:

I do not think that the world or the sciences would ever have suggested to me any philosophical problems. What has suggested philosophical problems to me is things which other philosophers have said about the world or the sciences.[6]

Yet some of us may still feel that the impulse with which a philosopher starts out ought not to be just some professional scruple about what other philosophers have said. Only we are no longer likely to denounce such scruples as "scholasticism"; nowadays a summons to renewed experience is more likely to be the demand that his "starting point" should be "existential."

Ending Up

So far the history I have outlined is tediously familiar. Now the plot thickens. With our reaction against the professionalization of philosophy, we have let ourselves in for an ambiguity. In promoting a starting point not confined to what philosophers have already said, we may feel we are appealing directly to experience. But we have nonetheless adopted a technical philosophical term to characterize this appeal. What, after all, is an "existential" experience? There are a good many technicalities that we shall have to go into before we can have much confidence in our answer. Since we are on less familiar ground than before, let us adjust our perspective, for we now need a history of philosophy's loss of control rather different from the one that has already been outlined.

If we have adopted the term "existential" to indicate where we think a philosopher should in some sense start, the availability of the term illustrates quite another issue—where a philosophy may end up. Presumably a philosopher attempts to maintain control by respecting (as I have mentioned) some standard of consistency or coherence until he reaches the conclusion of his argument or analysis. But the conclusion a philosopher reaches is not always the end of his philosophy. A philosophy is not its history. It is often betrayed in a fashion which is roughly opposite to the way it is betrayed when it becomes the merely professional affair which has to do with what other philosophers have already said: however spontaneous the initiative with which a philosopher may have started out, if the philosophy gains widespread acknowledgment, its impact is blunted as it encounters what would have been thought had its influence never been exerted. The philosophy no longer controls the use to which it is being put.[7] Thus it can end up by equipping the amateur with some philosophically irresponsible commonplace. "Existential" is a notorious example, for it has attained a popularity not accorded any other technical philosophical term in recent years, except possibly "alienation," which has been closely associated with existentialism and suggests that initiative and control have been lost to "others."[8]

ALIENATION

It is rather striking that existentialism should have ended up in this fashion, since it puts such a premium on initiative—on the "authenticity" of having one's own experiences. ("Authenticity" is another term that has been widely popularized.) Kierkegaard, the first existentialist, started out his major work, *Concluding Unscientific Postscript*, by proclaiming that he is proceeding *proprie Marte*—that is, "on his own initiative without the help of others."[9] And he employed this slogan or variations thereon elsewhere in his writings. Usually it is assumed that existentialism is a philosophy of life and that its requirements are intended for us to live by. But Kierkegaard's proclamation illustrates that existentialism also requires us to be "existential" when we do philosophy, and this requirement has a considerable range of implications which it will be the main concern of my exposition to explore.

For the present I am only selecting some of the more obvious implications. I shall disregard the specific loss of initiative and control by philosophy in general to the sciences.[10] As the "Unscientific" suggests in the title of Kierkegaard's major work, existentialists are often capable of turning their backs on the sciences. This attitude I shall deal with in my postscript, since it brings criteria to bear that are not specific to existentialism. The question as to how an existential philosophy should end up will have to wait until we see in part IV the way an existentialist himself visualizes reaching a conclusion and how he proposes to exercise an influence.

All I am emphasizing now is that professionalization and popularization are both peculiarly threats to the way a philosopher, if he is an existentialist, would maintain his initiative and control in order to avoid "alienation" and achieve "authenticity." The fact that Hegel was a professor of philosophy irritated Kierkegaard and was the brunt of much of his satire. He was even more hostile toward professors at the University of Copenhagen, many of whom were not even Hegelians. Thus his animosity was directed not just against particular professors of a particular persuasion but against the Professor as such. And there was the added bitterness of reflecting that his philosophy, in spite of its repudiation of professors, would end up as their legacy:

> I shall leave behind me, intellectually speaking, considerable capital; and yes, I know too who will be my heir—that figure so very distasteful to me, he who until now has inherited and will continue to inherit all

that is best: the Scholar, the Professor. . . .
Addendum:

   And even if the Professor should happen to read this, it will not
give him pause . . . ; this too will be made the subject of a disquisition.
And again this observation, if the Professor should chance to read, it
will not give him pause; no, this too will be made the subject of a
disquisition.[11]

Another possible subject of a professorial disquisition is how scornful
Kierkegaard might be of an introduction to existentialism. For he feared
the popularizer even more than the professor. He welcomed Schopen-
hauer's definition of journalists as "renters out of opinions" and then
went on to explain;

   He shows that, whereas in outward matters most people would be
   ashamed to wear a second-hand hat or coat, it is not the same in matters
   of the spirit. Here practically everybody goes about in cast-off clothing. . . . "It is every man's duty," the journalists say, "to have an
   opinion."[12]

Let it then be clear from the outset that it would be existentially degrading for me to supply anyone with an opinion regarding existentialism so
that he could add it to the list of items he knows what to think about.[13]

<h2 style="text-align:center">RENEWAL</h2>

   It should have become clear too that the question of starting point in
existentialism is not simply a problem of deciding how to exercise the
initiative supplied by the impetus of one's own experience. It can be the
more complicated problem of renewing a philosophical impetus that has
slackened or been lost—most obviously to the professor or popularizer. I
have alluded to Heidegger's effort to renew philosophy in relation to
the Greek experience of the way it started out. He is concerned in some
sense to return to the starting point of philosophy, the Pre-Socratics.
Kierkegaard is concerned in another sense to return to a Socratic starting
point. Merleau-Ponty generalizes, "Philosophy is . . . the renewed experience of its own starting point."[14]

   But why, we are tempted to ask, impede one's own existential initiative
by dragging in historical references to other philosophers—to the way the
Pre-Socratics or Socrates started out or, in our own case, to the way
Heidegger, Kierkegaard, etc., started out? One minor consideration is that
the effort at renewal is not "historical" in the usual professorial or
scholarly sense that would exclude initiative of one's own.[15] When
Heidegger invites us "to re-cover [*wieder-holen*] the starting point of our

historical-spiritual existence," it is "in order to transform it into the new starting point [*in den anderen Anfang*]" which will be our own. He explains that "a starting point is not recovered when it is reduced to something past and now known which needs merely be imitated; rather, the starting point must become the point from which we start out again more *originally* [*ursprünglicher*] with all the strangeness, darkness, insecurity that attend a true starting out."[16]

Less intimidating is Kierkegaard's undertaking to renew the Socratic starting point. He starts out as a philosopher with a dissertation on *The Concept of Irony with Constant Reference to Socrates*. Kierkegaard's references to Socrates remain constant throughout his career, until he finally requests as "an inscription for my grave *That Single Individual*." He comments that "this category has been used only once before . . . in a decisively dialectical way by Socrates."[17] The principle at stake at once in Socrates' irony and his individualism is "self-knowledge," inasmuch as his fundamental irony was his demonstration, by his cross-questioning of others, that unlike them, he knew that he knew nothing.

It is plausible to suppose that self-knowledge is a prerequisite for meeting the existential requirements of initiative and control. But then Kierkegaard envisages the following predicament: "These words ["Know yourself"] have frequently been torn loose from the complex of Ideas to which they belong and have long wandered like a vagabond through literature unchallenged." His own dealing with the principle of self-knowledge in the dissertation is an attempt to rescue it from vagabondage and "to bring it back to its native ground."[18]

This rescue operation provides a point of entry, and perhaps a model, for an introduction to existentialism. We can try to renew the way in which existentialism started out and rescue the term "existential" from vagabondage. The popularization of this term in America has loosened it from the control of the philosophical complex of ideas to which it natively belonged on the Continent. And serious philosophical control has never been regained here, where there has been no influential philosopher who could (or perhaps would want to) qualify as an existentialist.

TRANSPLANTATION

The fact that we allow an erstwhile technical term to become "vagabond" probably indicates something about American culture. We often seem to relish our ideas loose. Perhaps philosophy itself is not integral to the fabric of our culture. One can refer without apology to American literature and even to the American language, but not with very much confidence to American philosophy. With the exception of pragmatism, no influential philosophies have been initially native American. They have been transplanted here.

Kierkegaard enforces the requirement of a "native ground" in one's life as well as in philosophy. In his earliest appraisal of how he should start out in life, he notes that "it is first of all necessary to be planted in the ground where one really belongs."[19] Thus his use of the metaphor with respect to irony can be regarded as its extension from the personal experience of the individual. Such personification of a concept seems to be the earliest and most rudimentary form taken in Kierkegaard's existential attempt to relate what is personal to what is conceptual. The relation between these two levels is prima facie what the existentialist is attempting and will require considerable exploration later. Another already available illustration of the attempt is the double title of the dissertation, which itself starts out by personifying the concept: "It is with Socrates that the concept of irony enters the world. Concepts like individuals have their histories. . . . But . . . they retain a kind of homesickness for their native place."[20]

In the first chapter I shall allow the homesick concept "existential" to regain its native place. But let me now pause to examine its American transplantation. Norman Mailer, for example, has gone on what he reports were *Existential Errands*. That they were merely "errands" suggests that "existential" can indeed be loosened from the control of any full-fledged philosophy. (Such control would doubtless be felt by Mailer as bondage.) Let us examine one instance of Mailer's usage. The liberation of certain buildings by students at Columbia in 1968 he commends as "existential" because "these kids went out and did something they had never done before, and they did not know how it was going to turn out."[21]

Here "existential" may not embody exactly the Socratic principle of self-knowledge, though there is perhaps a certain self-satisfaction taken in ignorance. Mailer would seem to be commending the actual experience of initiating a resolute action, untrammeled by previous experience or knowledge. One might wish for more precision, for philosophers (especially since Kant) have frequently treated the problem of acting on insufficient knowledge. But in Mailer's case the lack of precision seems to go not only with indifference to philosophical constraints but also with the premium placed on acting. This suggests that existentialism can be identified as some kind of romantic activism. But here too more precision seems needed to obtain a philosophically distinguishable position. Romantic activism is old hat and could be labeled "Napoleonic" as readily as "Maileresque," for Napoleon was the most eminent romantic figure (as far as I am aware) to elevate action explicitly to the level of principle by taking it as his starting point: "Act first and then see what happens" ("Agir et puis on voit").

WILD LEAP

Iris Murdoch describes more subtly the exuberance of an existential act when she defines existentialism as "freedom . . . to 'fly in the face of the facts,' " as "escaping from science by a wild leap of the will."[22] Here too knowledge is irrelevant, for commitment yields a sense of exaltation that supersedes the need for knowledge.

The popular use of "existential" is not so loose as to conceal a certain inconsistency that prompts reconsideration. On one hand there is, as my examples have illustrated, a stress on the actual experience of taking the initiative, commiting oneself by acting, as if the experience were self-authenticating. On the other hand, how does this manifestation of "authenticity" jibe with the equally popular notion that "existential" commitment involves responsibility for what one has done? Presumably an experience cannot remain actual for long, but fades; sooner or later one must come down from a wild leap. Thus this mystique about commitment and action which passes for existentialism in America and England is at best an oversimplification, betraying the disappearance of a surrounding philosophical complex of ideas. Since Mailer and Murdoch are novelists, it may be sufficient for the present to cite Sartre's description in one of his novels of an individual who has acted:

> He is free. He has acted, and now he can't go back: It must seem strange to him to feel behind him an unknown act, which he has already almost ceased to understand and which will turn his life upside down.[23]

The performance described seems fairly close to what Mailer was commending as "existential" and would seem to illustrate what Murdoch identifies as existentialism. But it is clear in the context of the novel that Sartre is not endorsing the action in question, which is an engagement to get married. Under certain circumstances Sartre might not disapprove of marriage, but the prospective groom is a homosexual (something which Sartre would of course not disapprove of), and his other performances are evidence of what Sartre would diagnose as "self-deception." In short, what we are presented with here is not the behest to take the initiative and commit oneself by acting but a description of the dangerous fascination the actual experience of performing an action can have. Should this example of an engagement to get married seem a rather inconsequential action, the reader can check out Sartre's portrayal of the anti-Semite as a man who is fascinated with the prospect of becoming irresistibly a man of unmitigated action—"pitiless rock, furious torrent, devastating lightning."[24]

NATIVE GROUND

In Sartre's *Nausea*, which was published in 1938 (i.e., long before Sartre was dubbed an "existentialist"), there is what might well be taken as a satire *avant la lettre* of what I am classifying as American existentialism. The Autodidact is expounding his humanism to Sartre's protagonist:

> "A few years ago I read a book by an American writer called *Is Life Worth Living*? Isn't that the question you are raising?"
>
> Of course not [I say to myself]; that is not the question. But I don't want to explain.
>
> "In conclusion," the Autodidact says, consolingly, "he comes out for an optimism of the will. Life has a meaning, if one in fact wants to give it one. One must first of all act, throw oneself into some undertaking. If then one reflects, the die is already cast. One is committed [*engagé*]. I don't know what you think about this, sir?"
>
> "Nothing," I say.[25]

This put-down is, I believe, Sartre's protagonist speaking for Sartre.

But we cannot entirely neglect American existentialism, since "native ground" is something which existentialists themselves seem to cherish. At least Kierkegaard and Heidegger do, rather strenuously.[26] So before returning the term "existential" to the control of the philosophical "complex of ideas" to which it belonged in Europe, I might speculate briefly upon how its implications became simplified and popularized in America. When existentialism first came to general public attention in America after World War II, it arrived enhanced by the almost mythical prestige of the Resistance in France to the German occupation. By the 1950s American intellectuals were beginning to become politically apathetic. Yet one thing some intellectuals never became entirely apathetic about was their apathy. Having lamented the end of ideology and the lack of commitment and responsibility in their lives, they felt starved for significance and wanted to pack a wallop. They read French existentialists or saw Sartre's plays. Contemplating lonely acts of daring, they felt unused moral muscles flex; contemplating politically dirty hands, they felt twinges of political vigor as existentialism administered momentary relief from the sense of their own political flabbiness. Thus existentialism became interpreted almost exclusively as some kind of mystique about stripping for action, some kind of unmotivated behest for the individual to commit himself. It became the excitement that would be felt if one actually did something and became involved—*engagé*.

In the 1960s many of these American intellectuals did in fact become politically involved. "Existential" then became a vogue word. To wind up with another example besides the Columbia episode, as interpreted by Mailer, women's liberation discovered that the country was occupied by men. Thus Mary Ellman uses the term "existential" when in *Thinking about Women* she dismisses with mock disdain sperm as "jostling masses, swarming out on signal like a crowd of commuters." But while they stick together, "the ovum travels singly . . . in a kind of existential loneliness."[27]

Notes

1. *On the Way to Language*, p. 7.
2. *Metaphysics* 982b.
3. *Poetry, Language, Thought*, p. 23.
4. Taking as my theme Montesquieu's "It is impossible to leave the Romans behind" (*Spirit of the Laws*, bk. 11, chap. 13), I have dealt in *Human Nature and History* with some distorting translations of Greek political philosophy into Latin and traced the continued modern influence of the Romans even in the political arena, where men are often presumed most sensitive to their immediate interests.
5. *What Is Philosophy?* p. 81. In *The Essence of Reasons* Heidegger renews the way philosophy started out by starting with Aristotle's doctrine of *archai* in the *Metaphysics*. The fact that he translates *archē* as *Grund*, which in turn is rendered by the English translators as "reason," suggests something of the range of ambiguity surrounding the concept of "starting point." For the sense in which a *Grund* is a starting point, see chap. 2, n. 68 below.
6. *The Philosophy of G. E. Moore*, p. 14.
7. Heidegger recalls how Nietzsche, "the most quiet and shiest of men . . . endured the agony of having to scream." But his scream has become "no more than a commonplace," which proliferates "in the uncountable profusion of books on the state of the world" (*What Is Called Thinking*, pp. 48–49).
8. Let me present some of the evidence for the history of the term "alienation" which Walter Kaufmann has compiled. Although "Hegel used the term frequently," it did not appear in German or English indices to his works. Neither did it appear in Sidney Hook's widely read *From Hegel to Marx* (1936). However, "in the fifties a few refugees from Germany and Austria naturalized 'alienation' in the United States." The way had been prepared by Lukács's publication of *Der junge Hegel* in 1948 (Lucács had been influenced by Kierkegaard), by Marcuse's *Reason and Revolution: Hegel and the Rise of Social Theory* in 1941 (Marcuse had been a student of Heidegger's), and by the translation of Camus's *L'étranger* in 1942 (Camus had a somewhat random acquaintance with Kierkegaard's and Heidegger's writings). During the 1950s appeared *The Human Condition* of Hannah Arendt, who had been influenced by Heidegger as well as by Jaspers, and the writings of Paul Tillich, a disciple of Heidegger's. What was most crucial of course was the publication of Marx's early manuscripts. These were translated in 1961 by Erich Fromm, and Kaufmann refers to the term "alienation" as "a meeting place . . . for Marxism and existentialism." He points out, "Lukács had tried to make his

early existentialist leanings respectable by appealing to the young Marx. In the United States Marx was made more appealing by attempts to show that he had much in common with existentialism" (introduction to Richard Schacht, *Alienation*, pp. xv–xxi). There are numerous surveys dealing with alienation, and I shall make no attempt here to deal with the term as such.

9. P. 6. I have abbreviated Kierkegaard's formula, which derives from Cicero. See *Philosophical Fragments*, p. 153.

10. It may be that this threat of impotency has most troubled contemporary philosophers. But it is frequently diagnosed, and prescriptions for its cure are widely available. In any case, the contributions of existentialism to the philosophy of science most recognized philosophers of science would regard as negligible.

11. *Papirer*, X⁴ A 628, 629.

12. *Papirer*, XI² A 58. As disseminators of opinions the journalist and the professor are collaborators: "Those with ideas . . . accomplish absolutely nothing. During their lives their words are drowned in the drivel of their time, and after their death they are drowned in the drivel of professors" (XI² A 438). For Heidegger's and Sartre's conception of "talk," see chap. 8 below.

13. It is true that Sartre undertook a popular vindication of existentialism, first as a public lecture, then as the book *Existentialism Is a Humanism*, which was widely circulated and eagerly accepted as an introduction to existentialism. But Sartre himself has long since largely disowned it. See Contat, 1:133.

14. *Perception*, p. xiv. I am not implying that these returns and renewals are the same procedure with all the philosophers I shall be interpreting, only that there are certain respects in which the movements in question are comparable.

15. Heidegger warns, "Few are experienced enough in the difference between a subject for scholarship and a matter for thought" (*Poetry, Language, Thought*, p. 5).

16. *Introduction to Metaphysics*, p. 32; italics in original. This forbidding prospect even leaves us somewhat insecure with the humdrum term "starting point" itself. The German verb *fangen* has the more energetic sense of "taking hold of," "catching on to," "capturing." The obvious alternative translation, "beginning," is even less able to convey much sense of "strangeness," etc. "Start" does at least suggest a "setting in motion" or a "setting out on a journey," or a "rupture" with what has gone on before, and we shall discover later that all three metaphors are pertinent renderings for existential initiative. Kierkegaard's *begyndelse* is cognate with our "beginning," but when he uses the term philosophically he often has Hegel's *Anfang* in mind.

17. *Papirer*, VIII A 482; *Reference to Socrates* is further justified as a historical starting point "inasmuch as prior to Socrates the self did not exist" (*Irony*, p. 202) and so was not available for "knowledge."

18. *Irony*, p. 202. Capitalizing "Ideas" is Hegelian usage. One of the implications of "Constant" in the dissertation title is that Socratic irony has to be rescued from its confusion with romantic irony. Thus "Hegel was infatuated with the form of irony nearest him" (romantic irony), and this infatuation "distorted his apprehension of the concept" (ibid., p. 282). See chap. 1, n. 47 below.

19. *Papirer*, I A 72. I am quoting from a letter which Kierkegaard wrote when he was twenty-two. The organic metaphor is not just romantic nature loving. Kierkegaard is writing to a natural scientist (Peter Wilhelm Lund, a relative by marriage), ostensibly replying to a letter from Brazil detailing the scientist's hunt for paleontological specimens, and the first possible career for himself that Kierkegaard dismisses in the letter is natural science. The sequel to this letter is a series of journal entries (the earliest of consequence) in which Kierkegaard continues to reflect on starting out in life and does seek the bosom of nature. Indeed they were written during a prolonged excursion into the country which provided the occasion for such reflections. The mature postromantic Kierkegaard largely reserved organic metaphors for the stage of immediacy and for women whom he assigned to this stage (see pp. 274, 405 below.) Fifteen years after this early letter he again compared his life with Lund's (see p. 35 below).

It is usually assumed that Kierkegaard never mailed this letter (see Lowrie, *Kierkegaard*, 1:107). His failure to do so can be considered an adumbration of the difficulty of communication which he later faced explicitly, and the letter fits easily into the sequence of journal entries.

20. *Irony*, p. 47. For the context, see p. 41 below. Kierkegaard may be toying with the romantic and Hegelian notion that the Greeks felt "at home" in the world as members of a community, instead of feeling "alienated" as moderns do, who are "separated" from each other. If Kierkegaard is toying, he is being ironical, for he construes Socrates' "Know yourself" as meaning "Separate yourself from others" (p. 202). Thus to restore this concept to its "native place" is to restore it to a separate individual, and indeed to the individual whose irony Kierkegaard regarded as responsible for the disintegration of the Greek community into separate individuals, alienated from each other.

21. For this citation from Mailer, I am indebted to Benjamin De Mott, *Supergrow*, pp. 168–69. Is it necessary to add that I am only illustrating a fairly standard use of the term "existential"? I am not endorsing Mailer's wholesale assessment of the students' motivation.

22. *The Sovereignty of Good*, p. 27.

23. *The Age of Reason*, p. 295.

24. *Anti-Semite and Jew*, p. 54.

25. *Nausea*, p. 112.

26. Here the most relevant fervor is the way Kierkegaard and Heidegger cherish their native language, while Sartre indulges in a variety of French literary styles. Kierkegaard felt "bound to my mother tongue, . . . bound as Adam was to Eve because there was no other woman, bound because it has been impossible for me to learn any other language. . . . But I am also glad to be bound to a mother tongue . . . which does not groan when it is caught up in the expression of a difficult thought; . . . a tongue which is responsive and emotional when the right lover knows how to arouse in a manly fashion the feminine passion of the language" (*Stages*, pp. 440–41; observe that Kierkegaard personifies his language just as he does irony). "With respect to its possibilities for thinking," Heidegger compares German with Greek as "at one and the same time the most powerful and the most spiritual of languages" (*Introduction to Metaphysics*, p. 47). Hegel, whom I shall also be quoting, had fervent feelings about German too. Inadequate as the gesture may be as a concession to their fervor, demanding as it may seem in an introduction, I shall sometimes interpolate and explain terms in Danish, German, and French. I hope these interpolations will serve as slightly more than a reminder that English is not the native language of existentialism and that this is a matter of some philosophical significance.

27. Quoted in De Mott, p. 228.

Part I

Existence

———

"ekstasis." 1. Any dislocation or displacement. 2. Distraction of mind. 3. A trance.—Liddell and Scott, "Greek-English Lexicon" (abbreviated)

1

The Philosophical Movement

The vocation of the philosopher . . . concerns only the structure of movement that belongs to the work, as it works itself out in him.—Heidegger

COHERENCE

I am returning "existential" from the vagabondage of its lonely American travels and errands to the original complex of ideas to which it belonged in Europe. But arrangements must be made for this return trip. What is the difference between a complex of ideas which is philosophical and the hodgepodge of ideas which enjoy a popular intellectual vogue? Presumably some measure of coherence or structure that holds the complex together. I brought up coherence at the outset as a criterion which is usually applied in assessing the thought of an individual. But we must stretch it to apply to a complex embracing the thought of more than one individual. For the technical term "existence" is not the coinage of any one philosopher; existentialism is a philosophical movement. Will the criterion of coherence stretch that far? And even if there are philosophical movements which can satisfy this criterion without stretching it out of shape, can we be confident that existentialism is one of them? These are questions which will have to be answered if we are to restore the term "existence" to its complex of ideas.

Unfortunately we shall soon find that philosophical movements have no well-assured philosophical status today. Hence some argument is needed on behalf of recognizing their general significance. If the reader would protest that preliminaries are being unduly prolonged, if he would prefer to unwrap my interpretation of existentialism and regard it only as an interpretation of existentialism itself, so be it. But then he also risks missing the general significance I have attached to the issue of starting point. On one hand I have argued that this issue is of *general* significance, since anyone must start with some problem, and whatever it is, the treatment it solicits will have ensuing implications if one tries to be coherent. On the other, I argued that the issue undergoes a *par-*

15

ticularly significant elaboration in existentialism. Similarly, I shall argue in the present chapter that a philosophical movement is of more *general* significance than is usually acknowledged and that existentialism is a *particularly* significant illustration.

The question of coherence, which was raised in connection with the starting point issue, is of course also larger than existentialism and its distrust of opinionating by professors and journalists. Most thinking is a matter of being sucked into the proliferation of opinions, so that one's mind almost ceaselessly munches away evaluating this and that while barely distinguishing this from that. But do we really want to reduce the history of thought to two such widely separated extremes—at one extreme individuals who happen to exhibit in their thinking initiative, integrity, and coherence and at the opposite extreme the diffusion, the debris, of the influence of such individuals, along with other vagabond thoughts? I shall argue that between these extremes a place can sometimes be claimed for a philosophical movement.

Once the question of where an individual philosopher starts out is put together with the question of where his philosophy ends up, if it becomes influential, we have tentatively circumscribed the scope of a philosophical movement. Yet we are still involved with the question of starting point, which now has to be reformulated. Although it may be exhilarating to visualize a philosopher (especially if he is oneself) starting out spontaneously with his own existential initiative, we have seen that not even the leading existentialists actually started out without reference to what other philosophers had said. Pick up any piece of philosophical writing and you will usually observe that, however straightforwardly the philosopher may seem to start out with an experience (or with some problem he makes out of it), a turn of phrase with which he selects this experience or treats this problem will manifest his allegiance to (or dissent from) some philosophical movement. Even when a philosopher simply starts out as a tenacious disciple of another philosopher, this relation itself is an embryonic philosophical movement, granted that the movement may also turn out to be abortive. An introduction to a philosophical movement can accordingly also serve as an introduction to philosophy, for we are dealing with the way in which almost any individual is introduced to philosophy.

Isms

Although philosophical movements would thus seem a notable feature of philosophical experience, the concept of a philosophical movement not only has little philosophical standing today, but it has not been subject to any very explicit analysis, either. I doubt if any philosopher's list of the forty most significant works in Anglo-American philosophy written in the twentieth century would include one on a philosophical movement; and even if it did, the work would most probably rehash the successive contributions by the philosophers involved to the treatment of some specifiable problems rather than focus on the overall general structure of the movement itself. It often seems assumed that there should not be any such general structure—only the specific requirements of the specific problems. Anything more general in its pretensions would only get in the way of their treatment, and disdain is accordingly expressed for philosophical movements as such. "Drat isms," as Gilbert Ryle an (influential figure in one of these movements) has put it.[1]

One can sympathize with this reaction when one is confronted by the sweep of such a title as *Sartre's Existentialism, as Related to Vitalism, Humanism, Mysticism, Marxism*. Yet does one want to assume that some single philosopher has a virtual monopoly of the truth or of whatever procedures may be available for attaining it? But he still develops his philosophy under the pressures of the objections (or perhaps merely the performances) of other philosophers whose philosophies he finds sufficiently akin to be relevant to his own. And even if one should grant him a monopoly, one's relation to him, as I have already noted, itself constitutes an incipient philosophical movement.

Alternatively, if the assumption of a monopoly of truth seems rather unlikely, can one move toward the truth by reconciling all philosophers? This is an implausible prospect: it is not just that many philosophical movements are almost invincibly sectarian but, rather, that such efforts at large-scale reconciliation as there are seem wishy-washy compared with the incisiveness with which issues can be formulated within the confines of a single movement.

I am not assuming that existentialists march shoulder to shoulder. In fact my focus will shift eventually to the issues on which they differ. But one cannot begin here: what has to be demonstrated first is that, in spite of these differences, the philosophers in question constitute a philosophical movement. In other words, only if I can bring out first the significant measure of coherence that their movement exhibits are the differences likely to permit incisive formulation—at least more incisive than is usually possible with philosophers who are unmanageably far apart.

Yet philosophical movements today often receive merely casual and unphilosophical interpretations. Their salient themes may be sketched as nebulous features of intellectual history instead of as efforts to grapple with the specific issues that perplexed the philosophers themselves. Or the movement may be dissolved into some pervasive climate of opinion.

Or, if its development does retain some contours, the interpretation may allow these to be shaped entirely by presumed pressures of social and economic or other circumstances.

Nevertheless, we do identify as "a philosophy" what can be attributed to a succession or school of philosophers, almost as readily as we attribute this identification to a succession of works by an individual philosopher as well as to a single one of his works. Differences can still be discriminated, as they can when we attribute the same "style" to a succession or school of artists almost as readily as to a succession of works by an individual artist and to one of his works. We can determine the traits of a style without necessarily also explaining them by reference to social and economic circumstances. Indeed one trouble with such explanations is not that they are misconceived but that the traits—whether of a style or of a philosophy—that they would explain as the discernible effects of these circumstances are themselves inaccurately described. It would have been safer to have begun by describing these effects more carefully. Then one could be more hopeful of accuracy in probing for the relevant circumstances.

PHILOSOPHICAL METHOD

When a philosopher expresses his disdain for philosophical movements by dratting isms, he may merely be embattled and unable to survey the battlefield. But often, as I have hinted, he is simply trying to retain an innocent eye; he is starting out with some problem that he is trying to treat in its own specific terms. Among the issues that then become less obvious and largely neglected are those of philosophical method. These are more likely to emerge (as I suggested at the outset) when one is aware of selecting a particular problem for treatment rather than another and of the implications of the way it lends itself to treatment carrying over in the treatment of other problems. When Gilbert Ryle and others convened in France to exhibit to their Continental colleagues (some of whom were existentialists) the philosophical movement they represented (labeled "analytic philosophy" or "the Oxford School"), there was no meeting of minds. One explanation was that

> the continental questioners wished to discuss matters which are rarely discussed in Oxford and usually thought to be a waste of time. . . . For the questioners naturally wanted to bring the discussion to matters of *methodology*, to the philosophical justification of the procedures of the [analytic] school. And this is not a popular subject of discussion at Oxford.[2]

The respondents accordingly defended their ad hoc treatment of specific problems by adopting "the stance of the inarticulate gardener with a green thumb being interrogated by the agronomist—"I just plants it and it grows."

The Oxford philosophers in question were not exactly "inarticulate." One reason for their indifference to French questioning was their conviction that they were themselves speaking the lingua franca of philosophy. If anything had been expressed in another philosophical idiom that might be worth saying, they assumed that it could be translated into the analytic idiom in order for it to become clear what was meant. The more respectable "Anglo-American" expositions of Continental philosophy have been such translations. One of the perversities of the present introduction will be the effort to retain the original Continental idiom.

PERSPECTIVES

Making this effort does not mean that I am posing as a Continental philosopher any more than I am writing for a Continental audience. Although I am concerned with matters of methodology, I shall not deal with the perspective of "the end of philosophy" to which it is fashionable to fit these matters on the Continent. In the nineteenth century Hegel announced the end of art, and his dialectic moved on then to a higher stage, religion, and finally to the highest, philosophy. In the next generation Feuerbach announced the end of religion; in the next, Marx announced the end of philosophy. All these announcements have been frequently repeated, for the end has often been temporarily postponed. Sartre, for example, has sometimes been dubbed "the last philosopher."[3]

One of the concomitants of "the end of philosophy" perspective, whether Marxist or positivistic or Heideggerian or Derridaian is an effort to demonstrate the homogeneity of what has come to an end, in order that it may be acknowledged to have come, or to be coming, to an end in its entirety. Thus there is a temptation to argue that certain general assumptions or characteristics are shared by all the philosophies that compose the history of philosophy. And there is a corresponding tendency to downgrade the significance of the specific differences between philosophies and philosophical movements.

Such a large-scale and sometimes rather apocalyptic perspective does not reflect the pace at which philosophical thinking can actually be carried on.[4] My effort here is not to fit any perspective over the entire history of philosophy. I am adopting the middle-range perspective of a philosophical movement. But even this modest perspective requires cautious propping up; to assume that a philosophical movement may exhibit sufficient coherence to be worthy of philosophical investigation is not to assume that different movements are necessarily similar in structure or that any one movement necessarily demands only one type of analysis. Bring back the earlier comparison between a philosophical movement and an artistic style: we attribute the same "philosophy" (as we attribute the same "style") to successive works of a single individual and to one of his works. Now there can be controversy over the traits of the philosophy (as there can be over the traits of a style) which are controlling features of successive works. And what type of analysis best brings out what is distinctive about these traits can be controversial too. Such controversies are legitimate insofar as they are illuminating. All that I am trying to put beyond controversy is that a philosophical movement, like an artistic style, is one way in which experience attains a significant measure of both coherence and articulation.

ANNEXATION

However, before we can analyze existentialism as a specimen of a philosophical movement, we need to decide if it is amenable to such an analysis. A tempting convenience in considering existentialism as a specimen is that we need not bog down in debate as we would in the case of many other philosophical movements) over the individual philosopher with whom existentialism started. As I have already assumed, it started with Kierkegaard. This still leaves open the question of what other philosophers should be taken into account as belonging to the movement which Kierkegaard started but never heard of.

Indeed, if he can be taken at his word, it is unlikely that he had any interest in starting a philosophical movement. He regarded it as an "aberration of our time to found parties, form schools, maintain solidarity, etc.," and concluded that "for the sake of truth one must stress the opposite as strongly as possible." We have already observed how he stressed the opposite, by starting out "on his own initiative without the help of others" and remaining "the single individual."[5] Heidegger, whom I shall argue is in effect the second founder of existentialism, is just as rebuffing as Kierkegaard: "When we hear of a school of philosophy, the character of [philosophical] questioning is misunderstood."

Kierkegaard's career ended with a series of polemical pamphlets in which his attack on Hegelianism was transformed into the *Attack on Christendom*. In the pamphlets that have been compiled under this title, he dissociated himself from the established Danish church. After his death at the age of forty-two, neither the establishment nor his supporters knew quite what to do with Kierkegaard. The dean of the cathedral was disposed to refuse him Christian burial. When it did take place, Kierkegaard's nephew demanded the right to speak, over the protest of the dean, and he denounced the official proceedings: "Only by a trick has the church annexed him and tried to steal him after his death." He quoted Kierkegaard: "Whoever does not take part in the official worship of God has certainly committed one sin the less." When he had finished speaking, the dean pointed out that an unordained individual was not allowed to make a speech in a cemetery, and there was an outcry—"He is desecrating holy places."

Some days after the funeral, the nephew published a pamphlet continuing Kierkegaard's attack. His half brother adds,

> It was only a weak echo of Soren Kierkegaard. He soon realized that he was not equal to the task. Excited and overdriven as he was, he decided to follow his Master into death. When his father unexpectedly called on him one morning in his apartment, he found him almost unconscious, with severed veins. . . . With tender nursing, he gradually came to himself. . . . He later . . . built up a considerable practice as a skillful and respected doctor.[6]

After the funeral there were others who decided to leave the established church in order to launch a new religious movement. But the movement petered out.

It was only in the twentieth century, long after Kierkegaard's death, that philosophers too tried to steal him. He became annexed to existentialism as the founder of the movement, and the question of "whether he would ever become a philosopher" was answered by his having become an "existential philosopher." Thus Sartre insists, "If we are to understand the present day ambitions of existentialism and its function, we must go back to the time of Kierkegaard."[7] Existentialism may then seem merely to illustrate how, without his ever intending it, an individual's philosophy can become a philosophical movement. But a philosophical movement is not necessarily (indeed is rarely) a matter of the intentions of the philosopher who can be interpreted as having started it.

A MONSTROUS HOAX

However, there is a more serious difficulty in pushing an interpretation of existentialism as a philosophical movement. If Kierkegaard did not suspect that he was an existentialist, some of his followers are certain that he was not. Walter Lowrie, for example, rounded out his career of dedication to the translation of Kierkegaard by bristling with disparagement of

Sartre. Lowrie was incensed that the label "existentialism" should have become affixed to both their philosophies. He was convinced that, when one has "heard in the very words of Kierkegaard what he understood by 'existence,' one must feel bewildered by the claim that Sartre is his legitimate successor." So he suspects "a monstrous hoax" and concludes that "between these two men there is hardly enough likeness to make it easy to define the difference."[8] To mention only the most obvious unlikenesses, Kierkegaard was a strenuous theist and a political reactionary, while Sartre is just as strenuously an atheist and committed to political revolution. In fact so many unlikenesses of this sort permeate the existentialist movement that it has to be admitted that anyone who prefers chewing existentialists for the varied flavors of their opinions will hardly relish my effort to get at the more fundamental philosophical traits of the movement to which I shall claim they belong.

The burden of proof will be on me. Philosophers have been as disinclined as the theologian Lowrie to credit existentialism with the coherence that would seem to be requisite to its constituting a philosophical movement. Alasdair MacIntyre observes;

> That two writers both claim to be existentialists does not seem to entail their agreement on any cardinal point. . . . Any formula sufficiently broad to embrace all the major existentialist tendencies would necessarily be so . . . vague as to be vacuous.[9]

A. J. Ayer offers a comparable observation with respect to the leading representatives of existentialism: "There are so many points on which they disagree that it is doubtful if any one of them would regard himself as belonging to a movement which included all the others."[10] What then is there left to say about existentialism as a philosophical movement except

> 'Tis all in peeces, all cohaerance gone:
> All just supply, and all Relation.

EXISTENTIAL ANALYTIC

If we are to persist in the attempt to deal with existentialism as a philosophical movement, the most plausible procedure might seem to be to trace the history of its development, by taking up in their sequence the different philosophers who are usually assigned to the movement. We would be tracing "connections of dependency and influence . . . from one writer to another," as does MacIntyre, who suggests that we might try to see them as belonging to "the same family tree."[11] But unfortunately a family tree ramifies, especially one that goes back to the middle of the nineteenth century, and thus is not a very encouraging model for a philosophical movement, if some coherence or structure is a relevant criterion for considering a movement philosophical.

It will be safer to restrict the number of philosophers to be taken into account. The most straightforward way of deciding who are to be "looked upon" as the "leading representatives" of existentialism is to pick out those who have exercised the most influence as philosophers. For this is a matter easily determined statistically by counting the number of copies of the works each existentialist has sold, say, in the last twenty years and the number of works written about him by other philosophers or historians of philosophy. The count would yield a sample of four: Kierkegaard, Heidegger, Sartre, Merleau-Ponty. The statistical argument for restricting the list to these four is that there is no fifth candidate who would come close to any of them in the philosophical influence he has exercised.[12] At the same time the differences among them are more than complicated enough to put the notion of belonging to a single philosophical movement under sufficient strain for testing.

The first complication has already been encountered: although Kierkegaard has to be taken in some sense as the starting point of existentialism, his influence was kept in cold storage for more than half a century after his death. There is a second complication—the fact that Heidegger's "existential analytic" in *Being and Time* (1927) has certainly been a more important influence on the development of contemporary existentialism than any of Kierkegaard's own works. (*Being and Time* has even been an important influence on the interpretation of Kierkegaard himself.) Thus it would not be amiss to argue that Heidegger rather than Kierkegaard was the founder of existentialism. To defy chronology in this fashion is not necessarily to lose one's sense of direction philosophically. Following a philosophical development through chronologically can lull one into taking what turns up next for granted, so that one fails to attend to the distinctively philosophical exigencies that may hold the movement together or, alternatively, to the distinctively philosophical incongruities that indicate it is in danger of coming apart.

The third complication we encounter is more serious than the fact that Kierkegaard was the founder of a movement he never heard of. Heidegger vehemently denies that he is an existentialist. It is striking that this denial antedates Sartre's existentialist interpretation of *Being and Time* in his own *Being and Nothingness* (1943). In 1937 Heidegger had written, "My philosophical effort . . . cannot be categorized as philosophy of existence. . . . The question which I am concerned with is not the existence of man."[13]

Heidegger may have been the more disconcerted by Sartre's *Being and Nothingness* because it attained its vogue at a time when he himself was not permitted to publish in Germany as a result of his period of membership in the Nazi party. After Sartre had categorized both their positions as atheistic existentialism in *Existentialism Is a Humanism* (1946), Heidegger arranged to have a *Letter on Humanism* (1947) published in Switzerland. In it he repudiated as humanism Sartre's existentialism, along with the latter's existentialist interpretation of *Being and Time*.[14] However, our concern for the present is not to do justice to Heidegger's own philosophy in its own terms but to accord him the place his "existential analytic" has earned in the development of existentialism, whether Heidegger liked it or not.

PHENOMENOLOGICAL EXISTENTIALISM

There is a fourth and more intricate complication still to be faced. To respect distinctively philosophical exigencies is presumably to credit existentialism with that kind of sustained effort at coherence which is known as the application of a philosophical method. Now in *Being and Time* Heidegger labels his method "phenomenological." Sartre and Merleau-Ponty by and large retain this label for their methods. But the coherence we would demand of any intellectual performance that can pass muster as philosophical hardly seems assured by its borrowing its method from another philosophical movement.

In short, if we are to deal with contemporary existentialism, we have to cope not just with one movement but with two—with the phenomenological movement as well as existentialism. (Contemporary existentialism is often more fully characterized as "phenomenological existentialism" or "existential phenomenology.")

Thus with existentialism we should be prepared to take into account not only its founder, Kierkegaard, but also the founder of phenomenology, Husserl; and we shall then encounter the full complexity that is a result of the conflation of these two movements. While Heidegger repudiated an existentialist interpretation of *Being and Time* with all the authority he commanded by virtue of its paramount influence on existentialism, Husserl lent all the authority he commanded as the founder of phenomenology to repudiate *Being and Time* as not phenomenology but existentialism.

Indeed it would be all too easy to demonstrate that these two movements are intrinsically incompatible and could not possibly be conflated. Existentialism one would expect to deal with the problem of existence (whatever this may turn out to be), but Husserl explicitly abstracts from this problem in order to deal exclusively with what he identifies as "essences"—for example, with what an act of consciousness or of perception essentially is as such, whether or not anything exists corresponding to what one is conscious of in performing the act. The antithesis between essence and existence has been about as firmly implanted in the philosophical tradition as any distinction could be.

The apparent incompatibility between the two movements can be put more concretely. The *Logical Investigations* (1900–1901) was Husserl's first distinctively phenomenological work. The first investigation starts out with a definition of the "sign" as a vehicle of "meaning." The definition assumes its methodological significance when taken together with the assertion that the "meaning" can be analyzed whether or not it refers to anything that really exists. We can depart from chronology and allow Kierkegaard to protest in one of the aphorisms of *Either/Or*;

> What the philosophers say about reality is often as disappointing as a sign you see in a shop window, which reads: PRESSING DONE HERE. If you brought your clothes to be pressed, you would be deceived, for only the sign is for sale.[15]

PHILOSOPHICAL EXIGENCIES

It should not be supposed that such apparent incompatibilities are simply due to imprecision of thought on the part of either movement or to one philosopher's lack of familiarity with another's thinking. G. E. Moore's misgivings about features of Russell's philosophy persisted, though he would seem to have had ample opportunity to resolve them in private conversation. A more general point has been well put by Jean Beaufret:

> A characteristic of the history of thought is that the great philosophers have talked more about each other the less they were acquainted. Moreover, they were rarely acquainted, not more than a dozen of them in 2,000 years. When Descartes died, Leibniz was only a child, and he died ten [*sic*] years before Kant's birth. . . Schelling and Hegel, although their first works were published while Kant was still alive, seemed to consider him as belonging to another age. . . . Yet the whole thing began with Aristotle's lengthy training by Plato, who himself had spent ten years in Socrates' company. But if Aristotle speaks of Plato, it is without indicating what exactly those eighteen years meant to him that he spent with his master, whose favorite student he was, according to tradition. Plato and Aristotle: the link between them remains for us an enigma. No less enigmatic for us is Heidegger's relation to Husserl, in spite of the fact that their dialogue went on for years, as doubtless did Aristotle's and Plato's.[16]

To this appraisal I would add some evidence of the difficulties philosophers can encounter in even becoming aware of their philosophical
affinities. In 1929, the year that Sartre completed his graduate work and
two years before Merleau-Ponty completed his, neither of them bothered
to attend Husserl's lectures at the Sorbonne. In 1931 Sartre published
his first philosophical work in a short-lived magazine (*Bifur*), where there
also appeared the first French translation of Heidegger. With regard
to this translation Simone de Beauvoir comments on herself and Sartre,
"We weren't interested; we didn't understand a word of it." She does
list their lively and extensive intellectual interests at this time but observes, "We paid no particular attention to Kierkegaard's "Diary of the
Seducer.' "[17] This was the first work of Kierkegaard's translated into
French. In short it was possible for Sartre to reach the mature age of
twenty-seven (and Merleau-Ponty was almost as old) without having yet
begun to understand, or even having any interest in understanding, the
philosophers whose influence would become decisive for them.

In 1933–34 Sartre did attend lectures in Freiburg for a while. But
when after the war Heidegger had trouble in remembering his by then
famous student, he finally identified him as "the Frenchman who had
always confused him with Husserl."[18] And this was at the time the
"dialogue" between Husserl and Heidegger had completely broken down.
Sartre's only postwar meeting with Heidegger was apparently a disaster.
One must conclude that a philosophical movement is not a matter of
obvious temperamental or cultural affinities but, rather, what I have
referred to broadly as satisfying certain philosophical exigencies.

CROSS-PURPOSES

I am anxious to be less enigmatic than Beaufret, and I prefer to stress
the cross-purposes that seem to govern the relations between philosophers,
even when they can be assigned to the same movement. Cross-purposes
seem to be at stake when Husserl complains that objections to his position
which he attributes to Heidegger are "based . . . fundamentally upon the
fact that my phenomenology is misinterpreted backwards from a level
which it was its very purpose to overcome."[19] Husserl is complaining that
Heidegger conducts his analysis at the level of human existence, which
he had overcome by arriving at the transcendental level of consciousness
as such. The cross-purposes could be further illustrated by the fact that
Husserl's complaint against Heidegger comes close in its formulation to
the latter's complaint against Sartre. In fact Husserl's usual formulation
for Heidegger's attempt to base phenomenology upon an analysis of

human existence is the ugly charge of "anthropologism." And Sartre eventually, in his *Critique of Dialectical Reason,* will characterize his analysis as philosophical "anthropology."

I am not trying to confirm some of my reader's worst suspicions about philosophers. I am only trying to sharpen up the question as to whether the philosophers in question should be regarded as composing a philosophical movement, and to make clear that the philosophers themselves have not managed to straighten out the issues between them to each others' mutual satisfaction.

The mere fact that philosophers who have been prominently involved in the development of existentialism are so often at cross-purposes is not itself sufficient to disqualify existentialism as a philosophical movement. The mating or mismating of initially divergent movements (such as existentialism and phenomenology) is a recurrent undertaking in the history of philosophy. Of course the cross-purposes indicate that a philosophical movement does not exhibit the same kind of coherence as an individual philosophy. It certainly does not approximate a logical deduction, not even a very relaxed logical deduction. But still it is some kind of drawing out of implications.

What kind of coherence existentialism exhibits as a movement must remain to be seen. But the present point is that cross-purposes are a seemingly ineradicable feature of the way philosophizing goes on, even within a philosophical movement. What is unusual in the history of philosophy is the case I mentioned initially in which one philosopher is plainly and simply the disciple of another philosopher. In the more usual case, a philosophy starts out influenced by competing philosophers or philosophical movements, at least to the extent of accepting some of the criticisms which are brought forward. There are likely to be implicit in these criticisms criteria that demand a different treatment of problems.

Archaeology

There is one obvious respect in which the apparent incompatibility of phenomenology and existentialism does not leave us totally without recourse. It so happens that there is one philosophical problem that Husserl does share with the existentialists—the problem of starting point. At forty-five Husserl describes himself as "still a miserable beginner." He criticizes traditional philosophies as lacking the "seriousness of a first beginning."[20] Indeed before Heidegger, in his attempt to define philosophy, brooded over the term *archē*, Husserl would have liked to be able to revive it in order to designate his own undertaking not "phenomenology"

but "archaeology"—that is, "the science of starting out" or of "principles."
Unfortunately the label had already been preempted by a rather different
discipline, so Husserl had to be satisfied with *First Philosophy*, with its
reminiscence of Aristotle's definition as "the science of first principles."[21]
But Merleau-Ponty did not hesitate to use the label in quotes, and now
that Foucault has boldly dropped the quotes, there is no good philosophical reason why the present volume should not be entitled *An Introduction
to Archaeology*.

Thus far I have only considered Kierkegaard's Socratic starting point.
But later we shall see that after the dissertation he started out all over
again in *Johannes Climacus*, before finally reaching in *Either/Or* the
starting point to which he continued to attach his "authorship." Although Husserl denounces existentialism as "bathos," his own struggle to
make a fresh start betrays the depth of his own feeling:

> At some point, after prolonged efforts, the clarity we have yearned
> for seems in the offing. We think that the most superb results are so
> close that we need only reach out. All the problems seem to be re-
> solved; our critical sense mows down contradictions one after another.
> And now only a final step remains. We are about to take it, and begin
> with a self-conscious "therefore," and then we suddenly discover a
> point that is obscure [but] which continues to loom larger. It grows to
> a monstrous size, swallowing up all our arguments and reanimating
> the contradictions which have just been overcome. The corpses come
> back to life; they leer, they snicker. The work and the struggle start
> all over again.[22]

What Husserl requires of his reader—his prospective follower in the
phenomenological movement—is readiness to join in this struggle: "Only
he who is himself struggling to reach a starting point," Husserl felt, could
respond to his undertaking and "say to himself, *Tua res agitur*."[23]

In spite of the fact that Husserl shares the problem of starting point
with existentialists, he never recognizes his problem in their treatment.
He fails to respond to their treatment by saying to himself what he ex-
pects of his own reader, "This is my own undertaking at stake here, too."
Husserl's failure to respond means that existentialism and phenomenology
are at cross-purposes at the precise juncture where the problem on which
I shall be focusing arises.

But for the present it is only necessary to recognize that the task of
delineating the relation between existentialism and phenomenology is
less a matter of observing family resemblances than of adjudicating cross-
purposes. Accordingly, in lieu of MacIntyre's family tree, I offer the following crude diagram:

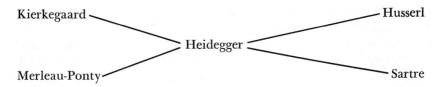

In this diagram I have carefully kept apart the founders of existentialism and of phenomenology; Kierkegaard exercised no influence whatsoever on Husserl. The diagram next brings out what I have already indicated—that Heidegger's *Being and Time* has been the major channel for the conflation of Kierkegaard's influence with Husserl's. But the problem of the relation between existentialism and phenomenology receives further illustration from the relation between Sartre and Merleau-Ponty. On my diagram I have placed Merleau-Ponty on the same line as Husserl. This is not just by way of recognizing that Merleau-Ponty gave Husserl's texts (including his manuscripts before they were published) closer study than Sartre ever did. Although both Merleau-Ponty and Sartre are phenomenological existentialists, there are respects in which Merleau-Ponty's method is more distinctively phenomenological than Sartre's. Indeed his major work is entitled *The Phenomenology of Perception*. On my diagram Sartre is on the same line as Kierkegaard. This is not just by way of recognizing that Sartre has been more interested in Kierkegaard than has Merleau-Ponty and, unlike Merleau-Ponty, has actually written on him. There are respects in which Sartre's method resembles Kierkegaard's more than it does Merleau-Ponty's. Thus the principle of contradiction evoked by the title of Kierkegaard's *Either/Or* is also implicit in the pairing of contradictory terms in the title of Sartre's major existential work, *Being and Nothingness*.

Since the relation between existentialism and phenomenology is complicated, I am postponing until a sequel to this introduction any investigation of the phenomenological method as such. And since the most methodologically significant differences between our philosophers are associated with the conflation of existentialism and phenomenology, it is also in this sequel that I shall deal with the substantive differences. My postponement of the phenomenological method does not mean, however, that I shall at present restrict myself to following out what I have described as the existentialist axis in the diagram. Indeed I shall deal with all our philosophers except Husserl as sharing the same existential traits. In this way I am attempting to demonstrate a measure of coherence for the existentialist movement as a whole, *including* the phenomenological existentialists. One reason for making this attempt is to counter the presumption that the adoption of the phenomenological method has lent contemporary existentialism a coherence it would not otherwise have attained. The phenomenological method, I should explain, enjoys much more philosophical esteem than existentialism. But my claim is that phenomenological existentialism as well as existentialism exhibits traits of a method which Kierkegaard characterizes as "dialectical." Once I have sorted out these dialectical traits, it will be possible to distinguish from them the purely phenomenological traits of Husserl's method and to take into account the differences between Kierkegaard and his successors, all of whose methods blend dialectical with phenomenological traits. Cognoscenti may be alarmed at these differences which I am for the present disregarding. But I do not believe that the differences are sufficient to impede my attempt to establish the coherence of existentialism as a movement.

EXPERIENCE

I consider that the attempt is worthwhile not in spite but because of the mixture of methods in existential phenomenology. For the mixture is not capricious. Let us make the broad assumption that the subject matter to which the philosopher applies his method is experience. The dialectical and phenomenological methods are philosophical refinements of different ways in which we do in fact try to get at the meaning of our experience and in particular to determine how we should start out doing so. From the very start the method applied by the philosopher extracts different implications from experience. Now it so happens that German is equipped with two terms for experience, one of which has been exploited by Husserl and the other by Heidegger. Briefly considering the different implications that have been extracted from these two terms may help relieve the largely schematic character of my preliminaries, granted that one cannot make much philosophical progress with just two terms. Husserl's preferred term for "experience," as he gets at its meaning with his phenomenological method, is *Erlebnis*. Its root, *leben*, permits an emphasis on experience as lived. The French often translate the term as *le vécu*; in English "lived experience" is sometimes used. In the setting of the application of the phenomenological method, this emphasis requires one to start out with experience as *immediately* experienced—that is, to determine what it means by removing the accretions that tend to encroach from prevailing interpretations of experience which go beyond what is immediately experienced.

Heidegger deliberately reverts to the more traditional German term for "experience," *Erfahrung*. The verb *erfahren* can mean "to come to know," and Heidegger associates it etymologically with *fahren*, which means "to journey." Experience in this sense can be construed in terms of the process of development by which it acquires its meaning through its interpretation in relation to other experiences, so that the implications of where we started out emerge only in retrospect. Interpretation cannot then be eliminated from an experience: its meaning, which enables us to identify it, is a matter of interpretation.

This rough comparison is perhaps sufficient to suggest why the dialectical method has to be taken up in this introductory volume, even in order to deal with phenomenological existentialism. It would be impossible to combine phenomenologically a phenomenological with a dialectical method, since the phenomenological appeal to immediate experience is designed to eliminate interpretations that have come between us and our experience, including those upheld by previous philosophers. But a dialectical method (at least as illustrated by such philosophers as Plato, Aquinas, Hegel, and Kierkegaard) canvasses previous interpretations. Thus it is only dialectically that Husserl's phenomenology can be combined with existentialism.

INFLUENCE

Let us now return to my diagram. There will be an inclination to construe what I am attempting simply as a tracking down of influences. But here the diagram is misleading. Hegel is not included, though I am not denying the pervasiveness of his influence on the development of existentialism.[24] But the interpretation of Hegel varies so much from one existentialist to another that I would have to reconstruct a different Hegel to bring out the character of his influence in each case. The reconstruction itself would be of some intrinsic philosophical interest only in the cases of Kierkegaard and Heidegger, and their Hegels are hopelessly discrepant. So Hegel's influence would not provide a manageable framework for tracing the development of existentialism.

Other lines of influence are missing from my diagram. Husserl influenced both Sartre and Merleau-Ponty directly, as well as indirectly via Heidegger. But neither Sartre nor Merleau-Ponty could have elaborated his own philosophy under the joint influence of Husserl and Heidegger without having had Heidegger's assistance in misinterpreting his relation to Husserl; for Heidegger had presented his *Being and Time* as if its method were still phenomenological and consistent with what Husserl had undertaken. Finally, Merleau-Ponty both was influenced by Sartre and reacted against his influence, while himself exercising (perhaps especially after his death) some influence on Sartre. Although these missing lines of influence will have to be taken into account in the sequel to this volume, along with the specific differences separating our philosophers, the diagram can serve to map out their relations for the present.

As soon as I have sorted out most of the general traits of existentialism, I shall pay the close textual attention to Kierkegaard that he deserves, not just because Wittgenstein is supposed to have identified him as by far the greatest philosopher of the nineteenth century, nor just because he is credited with being the founder of existentialism, but mainly because he employs (in contrast to his successors) a purely dialectical method which can be opposed in the sequel to Husserl's purely phenomenological method. I shall pay considerably more attention to Sartre than to Merleau-Ponty. Sartre is more familiar; most readers are likely to have a nodding acquaintance with his literary works, if not his philosophy. More important, he is (as I have indicated) more of an existentialist than Merleau-Ponty, so that he provides a clearer illustration of the movement that I am now attempting to delineate. Merleau-Ponty will assume more of a role in the sequel, not only because his method is more phenomenological than Sartre's but also because in the course of his philosophy's development he was more conscious of the differences separating them than Sartre, until Merleau-Ponty finally drew these differences to his attention.

CHRONOLOGY

In dealing with Heidegger in this volume, I shall be much less concerned to do justice to his own philosophy (as I have already admitted) than to its pivotal place in the development of existentialism. I shall accordingly sometimes turn first to his philosophy to illustrate traits of the movement. But since his philosophy is more difficult than the others, I shall sometimes ease the way to the consideration of some trait by picking an illustration from another philosopher. My readiness to ignore chronology is due to my preoccupation with the exigencies of existentialism as a distinctive philosophical movement instead of with "connections of dependency and influence," except insofar as they yield clues to the exigencies.

But even these connections sometimes defy chronology. The postwar vogue of Kierkegaard, Sartre, and Merleau-Ponty encouraged more attention than even these philosophers themselves had paid to Hegel, Husserl, and Heidegger, until philosophical interest in this earlier trio finally eclipsed the vogue of the later trio. Thus Kierkegaard, Sartre, and Merleau-Ponty became in effect for the present generation in French philosophy (and to a considerable extent elsewhere) an introduction to these predecessors, who have almost entirely dislodged them.

This quirk in the history of philosophy I respect for several reasons. First of all the history of philosophy *is* quirky, and historians too often try to pull it out straight as if an account of what really was at stake should exhibit evidence of linear progress toward our present culmination. Furthermore, I am not only reproducing an introduction—"a leading up to"—which has been roughly the way philosophy has evolved in France (and this evolution has had considerable influence elsewhere), but I am also producing an introduction in the ordinary sense, in which the easier precedes the more difficult. Hegel is more difficult than Kierkegaard; Husserl and Heidegger are more difficult than Sartre and Merleau-Ponty, for the later philosophers in each case go in for what is at best an over-simplified interpretation of their predecessors. The existentialists can thus provide a simpler introduction to the predecessors who have suc-ceeded them in influence but who in fact attained most of their present influence outside Germany only after existentialism had prepared the way for them.

Of course I would not use the existentialists for this introductory purpose were their own philosophies without intrinsic merits. Their over-simplifications, even their misinterpretations, are enmeshed in genuine philosophical issues which were not raised (or not in the same way) by their predecessors. And they help compose the philosophical movement which I have been arguing has its own interest as such, quite aside from the individual merit of each of the philosophers involved.

Let me illustrate another way in which it is hard to determine the channel along which an influence flows. When I disregarded chronology by suggesting that it would not be amiss to argue that Heidegger rather than Kierkegaard was the founder of existentialism, I was not denying that Kierkegaard influenced Heidegger; indeed he exercised much more influence on the "existential analytic" of Heidegger's *Being and Time* than on Sartre's *Being and Nothingness*. (I have already mentioned that Kierkegaard's direct influence on Merleau-Ponty was minimal.) In making my suggestion I was recognizing that Heidegger so transmuted whatever he took over from Kierkegaard as to constitute almost a new starting point for existentialism as a movement.

Even when influence is more easily traced, it is still influence only because the influenced respond. A comment by Merleau-Ponty provides a good example of how a philosophy, through the response to it, gains the momentum which makes it a movement. Merleau-Ponty recalls how he and others (Sartre in particular) had "the impression on [first] reading Husserl or Heidegger not so much of encountering a new philosophy as of recognizing what they had been waiting for."[25] Ideally we should allow for the influence of what they had been waiting for on how they were influenced by what they read and on their tendency to misread Husserl and Heidegger as proponents of the same "new philosophy." But in fact what they had been waiting for remained elusive until it was precipitated by what they read.

RETROSPECT

Elusiveness takes another form when the "new philosophy" is no longer new. Just as the prospects the philosophers themselves initially entertained disappear into the movement they can eventually be recognized to compose, so this recognition is altered in retrospect by succeeding redeployments in philosophy. Thus most of the features of existentialism that I shall select for attention are issues that have already been selected by succeeding philosophical movements—that is, by structuralists, poststructuralists, and hermeneutic phenomenologists. They are features which have either been disputed (e.g., the existentialist preoccupation with starting point or origin, the initiative assigned to the individual as the subject who in some sense constitutes this starting point or origin) or handled in a quite different way (e.g., the significance of metaphor and the relation between philosophy and literature). To this extent I shall be offering a retrospective interpretation of existentialism.[26] But I shall try in the present volume to carry out the interpretation of such features as I have listed without much benefit of hindsight, especially since most of the later developments, when they do impinge on their predecessors, are quarrels over the viability of the phenomenological method and will therefore become more relevant in the sequel.

Need I stress here what should be obvious? If one is to deal with a philosophical movement, one must wait until it has run its course, as existentialism now seems to have done. It then acquires, I am arguing, a new philosophical interest—as a philosophical movement. As such it has for the time being (if one can trust the *Zeitgeist*) more or less exhausted a certain range of philosophical options, just as a succession of artists may exhaust for the time being the possibilities of a certain style. But philosophy is not the addition of the opinions that find their way into print in this year's articles, and it should not hustle to keep up with future shock—the devil take the hindmost. Philosophers and philosophical movements regularly lose favor and are put to one side before the options they select or stumble upon are fully exploited. This is one reason they are subject to renewal. After all, existentialism itself is in part of a renewal of interest in a long neglected philosopher, Kierkegaard. And Kierkegaard himself had compared his undertaking to that of a relative who was a paleontologist: "It occurred to me today how like his life mine is. He lives in Brazil, lost to the world, lost in his search for antediluvian fossils, while I live away from the world lost in my excavations of Christian ideas."[27]

Even when renewal is not in prospect, a significant retrospect is usually possible from the perspective of later developments. For the significance of any succeeding development is likely to be seen (at least by the time it has in turn run its course) to have been in some measure its reaction against predecessors.

In any case there is a further philosophical interest that existentialism and phenomenology retain. If Sartre has received the designation "the last philosopher," it is partly because later intellectual movements on the Continent which may have been comparably influential have not been so explicitly philosophical. The most influential versions of structuralism have been anthropological (Lévi-Strauss), literary (Barthes), and psychoanalytic (Lacan). There is as yet very little indication that poststructuralism will compose as coherent a philosophical movement as I shall claim existentialism does.

Becoming an Individual

The crucial difficulty in putting forward this claim I have so far skirted. Before going further I should admit that existentialism may seem a singularly inappropriate candidate for analysis as a philosophical movement. For if each existentialist starts out as a philosopher by exercising his own initiative as an individual, is there not a risk that particular differences among them as individuals will masquerade as general philosophical differences and reinforce the usual tendency of philosophers to be at cross-purposes, thus making it more difficult to keep existential philosophers corralled in a single philosophical movement? They would in fact seem to be violating the distinction between the philosophical and the autobiographical, which almost any philosopher would insist on drawing and which Hegel draws with reference to Kierkegaard's prototype: "With Socrates it is not so much a matter of philosophy as of the life of an individual."[28] It is a distinction which Kierkegaard would seem to violate expressly, since the initial and persistent behest in his philosophy is "to become an individual."[29]

Another version of our difficulty can be stated in Kierkegaard's own terms. He not only endorses Socratic self-knowledge but also observed the historically obvious—that "a multitude of schools" derived from Socrates, so that their "attempts . . . to trace their origins back" to him were inevitably "discordant."[30] This acknowledgment goes along with his own indifference to founding a philosophical movement. He may have been scornful of Hegel, but he was even more scornful of Hegelianism, as a philosophical movement perpetuated by other philosophers each of whom continued constructing or reconstructing a philosophy that was not his own.

Similarly, Sartre pays his philosophical respects to Descartes as an individual but is so contemptuous of the incoherence and inconsequentiality of Cartesianism as to reopen the question of whether a philosophical movement can be distinguished as philosophical from an intellectual vogue:

> The absolute is Descartes, the man who eludes us because he is dead, who lived in his own time, who thought from day to day with the means that were on hand, who developed his doctrine in terms of a certain stage reached by the sciences, who knew Gassendi, Caterus, and Mersenne, who loved in his youth a girl who was cross-eyed, who went to war, got a servant pregnant, who attacked not the principle of authority in general but specifically the authority of Aristotle ... ; what is merely relative is Cartesianism, that philosophy which is all over the place, which keeps going from one century to another and where anyone finds what he puts there.[31]

But this suggests that there is still something to be said on behalf of selecting existentialism as a specimen of a philosophical movement: if the legitimacy of a philosophical movement is particularly subject to challenge by the philosophical individualism of an existentialist, existentialism may be a philosophical movement particularly worth examining as a test case for the general concept of a philosophical movement itself.

Although accentuated by the individualism of the existentialist, the issue of the difference between an individual philosophy and a philosophical movement turns up with any philosophical movement. Few philosophers focus less than Marx on the individual's experience as such, since the individual's "nature" in Marx's philosophy "dissolves into the *ensemble* of his social relations."[32] Yet Marx's famous denial, "I am not a Marxist," may suggest his own resistance to being dissolved into the *ensemble* of his relations with other philosophers in order to compose a philosophical movement. His denial indeed illustrates a recurrent predicament faced by an individual who starts a philosophical movement, whether or not he intends to do so. But in the case of Marxism, Hegelianism, Cartesianism, Neo-Kantianism, Neo-Thomism, etc., the texts of the founder can be supposed to exercise some inhibitory control over the vagabondage of his successors. Or at least we can check back to these texts and make some effort to examine the credentials of those who claim to be successors and to assess the coherence of the movement they constitute. It then deserves the label "philosophical movement" to the extent that it can be regarded as a legitimate development of the founder's philosophy and not just a tearing loose of ideas from this original complex. But the pretensions of such a movement to be philosophical are less interesting than in the case of existentialism. Here we are confronted with a paradox. On one hand we have seen that an existentialist philosophy would seem to render the very notion of a philosophical movement problematic, insofar as each existentialist starts out as an individual with the impetus of his own personal experience. On the other, none of the existentialists has in fact bequeathed his personal name to a movement, as have such relatively impersonal philosophers as Aristotle, Descartes, Hegel, Marx, Kant, Thomas Aquinas. We are not dealing here with Kierkegaardianism, Heideggerianism, Sartrianism, or Merleau-Pontianism. Existentialism is instead an impersonal label suggesting a transpersonal movement—like rationalism, empiricism, idealism, realism, pragmatism, and analytic philosophy. The impersonality of the label would seem to imply that existentialism is not merely a matter of compiling the evidence of an individual's personal experience.

Becoming a Philosopher

Existentialism is in fact an attempt to have it both ways. On one hand a "characteristic" of "existence" which Heidegger stresses is "its being mine," so that it must be "addressed by using a personal pronoun." On the other, "existence" (*Dasein*) itself remains neuter.[33] And in describing the "vocation" of the philosopher, Heidegger insists that it is not a matter of "the psychology of the creative personality." It "concerns only the structure of movement that belongs to the work itself, as it works itself out in him" ("zum Werk selbst gehörige Bewegungsgestalt des in ihm Erwirkten".[34] Whatever may be a suitable interpretation of this pronouncement in terms of Heidegger's own philosophy, the concern he would enforce suggests that we may be able to discern in existentialism some structure that ensures its coherence as a philosophical movement. As I remarked earlier when I drew the analogy of artistic style, we refer to a philosophy as found in either a specific work by a philosopher or a succession of his works. If it is not merely the philosopher's "creative personality" that is finding expression, if a philosophy is being "worked out" or "taking effect" or "becoming actual" in him, then there may be a comparable prospect of a philosophy being "worked out" and "becoming actual" in the works of a succession of existentialist philosophers.

English fails to preserve the word play of Heidegger's German original, but we shall see that "actuality" is one of the traditional implications of "existence" and that "existential" can refer to the process by which something is brought or comes into existence. One juncture at which this reference occurs in Kierkegaard is the process by which one becomes a philosopher. This is the juncture that interests us most, especially in its relation to "becoming an individual." And Kierkegaard explicitly reached it when he took up the problem of becoming a philosopher in an auto-biographical work which he probably started in 1842 and to which he gave the pseudonymous title *Johannes Climacus*. Here he takes the prob-lem up first while sneering at Hegel's philosophy as having ended up as a philosophical movement, with others "lending a hand in putting the coping stone to the system," in order to bring it to a conclusion. This Johannes Climacus refuses to do himself. Instead, he poses the dia-lectically opposed problem of starting out on his own initiative:

> Whether he would ever become a philosopher he did not know. . . .
> With quiet solemnity he decided he would start. He recalled Dion's
> enthusiasm when he embarked with but a few men to start the war with
> Dionysius: "It is enough for me that I have taken part in this war,
> even if I should die the moment I reach land."[35]

The tyrant Dionysius in this parable is Hegel. In order to attack Hegel's philosophy as a system, it is enough to raise the problem of starting out (in fact, Kierkegaard never finished *Johannes Climacus*), for starting out is not even a problem for Hegel. By virtue of the fact that thinking becomes intrinsically systematic for him when it becomes philosophical, there could be no moment when it could start outside the system.

Perhaps it would be helpful if I dealt in a slightly more technical man-ner with the way Hegel eliminates the problem of starting point. I am not trying to do justice to Hegel, for Kierkegaard himself does not. My own concern is not with Hegel but with the difference between the dialectical and the phenomenological treatment of the problem of starting point, and though Hegel's method is dialectical, it is a dialectic in which the problem is eliminated. Yet some minimal understanding of the way he eliminates the problem will enable us to understand a little better what is at stake in Kierkegaard's retrieval of it. Hegel dismisses "the starting point as such" as "something subjective" (i.e., as reflecting the contingent, idiosyncratic experience of a particular individual). Hegel temporarily retains the term "the principle of a philosophy" which "also has reference to a starting point," but in an "objective" sense, since it has to do with "the nature of the content," with "what is the truth," and so reaches a level of generality which a "subjective" starting point lacks. Examples of an "objective" starting point is Thales' claim that every-thing is water, Anaxagoras's claim that everything is mind, Leibniz's claim that all things are monads.

But even in its "objective" version, the problem of starting point can be eliminated from Hegel's system, and with it (Hegel adds) his own discussion of the problem. He argues that philosophy should not start with a principle that refers to "a particular determinate content" (whether it be water, mind, or monads, etc.); its starting point should instead be "absolute"—that is, it should "start from thought as such" and explicate whatever is indispensable to carrying out the thought process. In other words, it should abstract from any "particular determinate content." It then is strictly speaking not a starting point at all. In his *Logic* Hegel accordingly "starts" with Being as entirely "in-determinate," so that to start with it is to start in some sense with Nothing. In starting out this way, philosophy is not presupposing any "particular determinate content."[36] It is presuppositionless.

To abstract from any "particular determinate content" left Johannes Climacus feeling "as he did in childhood when he played the game of blindman's buff." He disposes of Hegel's "objective" starting point as well as his "absolute" starting point, since it is the starting point by which an individual who had not been a philosopher before could start to become a philosopher.[37] But his philosophy will then differ from Hegel's where reference to the individual's own experience must be transcended as "subjective."

THE TWO LEVELS

Now that we have watched Kierkegaard attempt to reinstate this reference, we are better able to assess the *Constant Reference to Socrates* in the dissertation on *The Concept of Irony*. This reference is justified historically by Socrates having been "the first to introduce irony,"[38] but Kierkegaard also finds "sanction" for it in a passage from Hegel which I have already cited and which Kierkegaard cites over and over again, "With Socrates the question is not so much a matter of philosophy as of the life of the individual."[39] Kierkegaard adds, "I shall venture to see in this pronouncement a sanction for the procedure I shall follow throughout my whole undertaking [forsøg]."[40] The undertaking he is thinking of is his dissertation. But the pronouncement could be regarded as a sanction for the procedure he follows throughout his whole undertaking as a philosopher, if we suspect him of a certain irony. He will retain between philosophy and life a distinction of level in a sense which has still to be pinned down but which is already illustrated by the distinction between "The concept of irony" and its treatment "with constant reference to Socrates." In another sense, as the dissertation also illustrates, he will cross this distinction and treat as a matter of philosophy the life of the individual. Not this life as it usually is lived (a "jumbled heap," in Keats's appraisal) but as exhibiting the kind of philosophical consistency which makes possible constancy of reference to the life of an individual in treating a concept.

Kierkegaard's earliest preoccupation with philosophical reference to the life of the individual took mainly the traditional and rather static neoclassical form of typological personification.[41] Thus he identified Faust as "personified doubt,"[42] the Wandering Jew as despair; Don Juan as desire. Consistency, and not just personal idiosyncrasy, is at stake in the behest "to become an individual." In the dissertation we shall watch Kierkegaard take becoming into account and advance beyond static personification. Socrates does not just personify irony but is carefully fitted to "the development of the concept,"[43] in order to exhibit dialectically the dynamic relation irony introduces between philosophy and the life of the individual.

Without blurring the distinction between these two levels, Kierkegaard would bring them into relation and argue that the life of an individual can be a matter of philosophy. This is the point of his famous disparagement of Hegel as "someone who constructs a splendid castle [his philosophical system] and lives in a shack near by."[44] It was his own life as an individual that Hegel left outside his philosophy—the badly constructed life of a professor.

Kierkegaard starts out in the dissertation itself by elaborating ironically on the problem of relating the two levels which Hegel failed to relate and which are implicit in Kierkegaard's own double title. Both levels are personified:

> If there is something for which modern philosophical endeavor should be commended, with its magnificent progress, its grand appearance, it is certainly for the strength of genius with which it grasps and holds fast to the phenomenon. Now if it is proper for the latter, which as such is always *fœmini generis*, to surrender itself, because of its feminine nature, to the stronger, then one may in fairness demand of the philosophical knight the courteous demeanor, the deep enthusiasm, instead of which one too often hears the jangling of spurs and the voice of the master. The observer should be an eroticist: no feature, no moment should be a matter of indifference for him; on the other hand, he should also feel his own preponderance, but only use it to assist the phenomenon to its full revelation. Even though the observer brings the concept with him, for this very reason it is appropriate that the phenomenon remain inviolate and that the concept be seen coming into existence through the phenomenon.[45]

This deference accorded the phenomenon becomes in the following paragraph a reference to Socrates, as the starting point for the development of the concept:

> Before proceeding to the development of the concept irony, it will accordingly be necessary for me to secure a dependable and authentic apprehension of the historical-actual, phenomenological existence of Socrates. . . . This is absolutely necessary because it is in Socrates that the concept of irony has its inception in the world. *Concepts, like individuals,* have their histories.[46]

Later in the dissertation it becomes even more evident that the initial emphasis on keeping "the phenomenon inviolate," on allowing the concept "to be seen coming into existence through the phenomenal," on Socrates as the starting point for this development, is a shift of emphasis in opposition to Hegel, whose genius had not been strong enough to grasp and hold fast the phenomenon.[47]

However, the two levels cannot easily be kept distinct. Both "concept" and "constant" are probably ironical. Irony cannot satisfy the requirements of a concept in Hegel, since as defined by Kierkegaard it involves contradictions which cannot be removed. The most relevant contradiction now is between the conceptual and the phenomenal (in the simplest instance of verbal irony, I do not mean what I say or say what I mean),[48] so that reference to the phenomenal is necessary for the definition. But the reference to the phenomenal (Socrates) cannot remain phenomenal, since irony is a disavowal of the phenomenal (for example, Socrates *says* that he is ignorant but that his interlocutor knows) in favor of the conceptual (what is *meant* is that his interlocutor does not know that he is ignorant, whereas Socrates does).[49] Such ironical complications are additional indications that one level cannot be treated without taking the other into account.

DECIDING WITHIN ONESELF

Kierkegaard is still manipulating the two levels when he announces ironically that with respect to the "interpretation of Socrates," he will "start and end with Hegel" but then comments that "what is strange about Hegel's representation is that it ends as it starts with Socrates' person."[50] Kierkegaard is going along with Hegel in starting with Socrates' person but is rebuking him for stopping short of recognizing the criticism, personified by Socrates, of Hegel's conception of philosophy.

With respect to starting with Socrates' person, Kierkegaard found additional justification in Hegel:

> The subject is the determining, the deciding principle [*das Bestimmende, das Entscheidende*]. . . . The issue of deciding within oneself starts its development with Socrates. . . . With Socrates the deciding mind [*Geist*] is located in the subjective consciousness of man. . . . In that the person, the individual, comes to make the decision, we are brought back to Socrates *as a person*, as subject, and what follows is an analysis of his personal relations.[51]

"Person," "subject," and "personal relations" retain in Kierkegaard philosophical implications which are transcended in Hegel. Specifically, "the issue of deciding within oneself," which only "starts its development with Socrates" in Hegel, undergoes development beyond Socrates until it is transcended in Hegel's social ethics. It is this development that is undercut by Kierkegaard's returning to a Socratic starting point. Thus "deciding within oneself" remains crucial in Kierkegaard's individualistic ethics. There in fact the Socratic "Know yourself" can only be implemented with the further injunction, "Separate yourself from the Other,"[52] in order to "become an individual." Prior to Socrates this separation had not been carried out, which was why the "self did not exist" and so was not yet available to be known. With Hegel, however, knowledge has pushed on to a juncture at which this separation is transcended.

The separation is the negative "liberating function" of irony, which can accordingly be identified as "the absolute starting point for personal life."[53] Kierkegaard is ironically misusing Hegel's terminology: "an absolute starting point" in Hegel can only be a starting point for philosophy, which starts out by eliminating the problem of starting point; "an absolute starting point for personal life" would be an unphilosophical contortion.

BLUNT OPPOSITIONS

A distinction of level (or levels) does, however, survive in Kierkegaard. On one hand there is his decision to start to become a philosopher, and he gets beyond the merely personal here by telling us a story about it and his opposition toward Hegel in *Johannes Climacus*. On the other, when he salvages this pseudonym from the unfinished work, he assigns the character a higher-level methodological task: "The dialectic of the starting point must be made clear."[54] It is made clear by opposing Hegel.

Before we can reach this higher level in *Concluding Unscientific Postscript*, we have to gain some agility in dealing with the relation between levels, as they are illustrated by Kierkegaard's attempts to get started as a philosopher, for Climacus means "climber," and dialectic is visualized by Kierkegaard as skill in climbing.[55]

The dissertation, with its familiar figures of Socrates and Plato, provides us with an opportunity to deal in a preliminary way with the dialectical relation of opposition. When Kierkegaard makes "the life of the individual" a "matter of philosophy," he distinguishes carefully the philosophy of a Socrates or a Kierkegaard from that of a Plato or a Hegel. Thus he ironically attacks Hegel's attempt "to vindicate a positivity [i.e., an objective content] for his philosophy."[56] Positivity Kierkegaard himself reserves for Plato. Hegel did distinguish Socrates' role from Plato's: "Socrates taught his associates to know that they knew nothing. ... It may in fact be said that Socrates knew nothing, for he did not reach the scientific construction of a systematic philosophy."[57] Yet Hegel nonetheless traced a certain continuity of development between Socrates and Plato: "The aim of Socrates' philosophy was that it should have a universal significance."[58] But in Kierkegaard "irony requires blunt oppositions."[59] Any continuity Hegel would endorse Kierkegaard disrupts with a blunt opposition between "negativity" and "positivity."

This bluntness Kierkegaard would also associate with the distinction between a subjective and an objective dialectic which Hegel draws: irony "is in Socrates' case a subjective form of dialectic, and is a way of conducting oneself with one's associates. Dialectic [in the proper sense] involves the reasons for things [*Gründe der Sache*]. Irony is a particular mode of conduct between one person and another person."[60] The bluntness of Kierkegaard's dialectic, its bipersonal character, as well as his use of the Hegelian distinctions between negative and positive, subjective and objective, are all illustrated by the way Kierkegaard rescues Socrates from Plato's interpretation in the *Symposium*, where Kierkegaard again discerns his two levels, since the dialogue "renders love visible in the person of Socrates." Kierkegaard's first step is to utilize Plato's interpretation in the ironical way he utilizes Hegel's interpretation—as a sanction for his own interpretation. Love in Plato is "love of the beautiful," and it "displays itself *not* as the love of this or that [e.g., of the "actual" or "phenomenal" beauty of particular Athenian youths]." But in Plato this negative moment is transcended when love reaches the philosophical level and finds in "ideal" or "essential" beauty positive recompense for its abnegation at the level of particular experiences. In Kierkegaard, however, Socratic love suffers the ironical predicament of remaining "merely a relation to something which is not given." Accordingly, Kierkegaard's Socrates remains suspended between the level of "actual" or "phenomenal" particulars, which he (like Plato's Socrates) can transcend, and that of the "ideal" or the "essential," which he (unlike Plato's Socrates) cannot reach.[61] To import as Kierkegaard does, additional Hegelian jargon, "irony is infinite absolute negativity. It is negativity because it only negates; it is infinite because it negates not just this or that phenomenon; and it is absolute because it negates by virtue of a higher which *is not*."[62] Thus irony will subvert Plato's and Hegel's philosophy, where the higher *is*.

This ironically blunt opposition between Socrates' "negativity" and Plato's "positivity" is a relation of mutual exclusion. One of the notable ironists of our own century, Max Beerbohm, has pointed out that Socratic irony is not a game that two can play. The excluded participant in the game that Kierkegaard is playing is Hegel, who by and large Kierkegaard equates with Plato as interpreted by Hegel. Kierkegaard is playing this game by subverting the role Hegel's Plato had assigned Socrates. In Kierkegaard's own idiom, Socrates is the "starting point" for philosophy in that he "launched the ship of speculation" when he used the statements of his interlocutors ironically in order to demonstrate their ignorance of what they thought they knew. But he did not "himself go on board" by engaging in speculation.[63] Nevertheless, he was in effect taken on board when Plato transformed him into a proponent of what Plato thought he knew and systematized as his positive philosophy.

Since Kierkegaard's Socrates did not arrive at a positive philosophy, Kierkegaard can only try "to get hold of Socrates *via negationis*"—that is, by the "negative procedure" which Socrates himself employed ironically,[64] extending it to negate ironically the positive content that Plato and Hegel attributed to Socrates but in fact supplied from their own positive philosophies.

A HEGELIAN FOOL

It might be interesting to continue with Kierkegaard's dissertation, especially since it would make a chronologically attractive starting point for an interpretation of existentialism. It was only after World War II that existentialism attained its worldwide vogue. Marxism was then the most influential competing movement in Europe, and existentialists frequently converted to Marxism or borrowed from it. The effort to decide if they can then still be regarded as existentialists has been perhaps the most frequent fashion in which the issue has been raised as to the coherence of contemporary existentialism as a philosophical movement. Under these circumstances, it would be worth recalling that Marx published his dissertation the same year that Kierkegaard published his—in 1841, ten years after Hegel's death.

However, a dissertation is not often the place where a philosophy is "worked out" and "becomes actual," in the further existential sense of embodying an individual's initiative. It is designed to satisfy the requirements imposed by professors, although it may also be designed to out-maneuver their supervision—as in fact Kierkegaard's seems to have been. His dissertation may have been more specifically designed to express contempt for the Hegelianism of certain of his professors.[65] Yet he later became contemptuous of himself too for having failed, at least at one point in the dissertation, to emancipate himself from Hegelianism. "Oh, what a Hegelian fool I was," he exclaims.[66] (Marx had similar misgivings regarding his own early writings.) Kierkegaard's interpreters often debate whether they should interpret as itself ironical his pronouncement in the dissertation, "I shall start out with Hegel, and I shall end up with Hegel."[67] If this is to be taken at its face value, Kierkegaard had not yet quite emancipated himself from Hegelianism and reached his own starting point as a philosopher.

DOUBT

Yet the dissertation remains helpful in interpreting another effort by Kierkegaard to get started as a philosopher. His avowed "plan" in *Johannes Climacus* was to attack modern philosophy with "melancholy irony." The "melancholy irony" was in part his own sense of frustration at the lack of assistance modern philosophy provides in starting out. In retrospect we can see that Kierkegaard's maneuver in returning to a Socratic starting point was itself a way of negating the "modern philosophical endeavor . . . with its magnificent progress," which he had ironically commended at the start of *The Concept of Irony*.[68] Here again two levels are involved. In the dissertation irony, as the subjectively oriented "starting point for personal life," was apposed to doubt, as the objectively oriented starting point for modern philosophical speculation.[69] In *Johannes Climacus* Kierkegaard identifies this starting point with Descartes, who becomes a stand-in for Hegel in much the fashion in which Plato became a stand-in for Hegel in the dissertation. This casting too Kierkegaard finds sanctioned by Hegel, who had himself stressed that the "subjective" problem of starting point took on new significance when attention turned to "the cognitive process," as a result of Descartes's procedure of doubting everything—a new significance that was only fully manifest in Hegel's own philosophy. Although his doubt provided Descartes with knowledge of his own existence as a subject, this starting point, Hegel explained, is not "subjective" in the philosophically irrelevant sense that it is a matter of "what each individual happens to find"

when he starts thinking—"some contingent idea which can be differently
constituted in different subjects." It is, rather, that "the cognitive process"
has come to be "conceived as an essential moment of objective truth," so
that a question of general principle is being raised by Descartes's doubting
everything. Descartes was attempting to eliminate all prejudgments
(*préjugés*) and in Hegel's view had thereby "started philosophy anew,"[70]
in a fashion that culminates in Hegel's own system, which is presuppositionless (as we have seen) by virtue of having eliminated any reference
to any "particular determinate content." Hegel accordingly translated
Descartes's starting point into his own terms: "That we must start from
thought as such Descartes expresses in the form that we must doubt
everything (*de omnibus dubitandum est*) and that this is an absolute
starting point."[71] Hence the subtitle of *Johannes Climacus* is the general
principle *De omnibus dubitandum est,* which Kierkegaard is attacking.[72]

Hegel conceives this universal doubt as vindicating the "autonomy" of
philosophical knowledge, which finally gains with Descartes "its own
native ground."[73] This is a common enough metaphor. But when Kierkegaard employs it in his dissertation on irony, it is just possible that he
may have been transferring it from Descartes to Socrates, in order to suggest that it applies properly only to the autonomous individual Socrates
became through knowing himself rather than to an ostensibly autonomous system of absolute knowledge. At any rate, Johannes Climacus's
metaphor regarding the start of his attack on Hegel, "even if I should die
the moment I reach land," probably does recall the famous metaphor
with which Hegel in his history of philosophy hailed Descartes as recognizing philosophy's autonomy: "Here, we can say, we are at home, and
like the sailor after a long voyage on a stormy sea we can now shout
'land.' "[74]

THE FALSE START

Climacus challenges this proclamation: "Can it not be imagined that
modern philosophy might come to realize that it has made a false start,
which viewed as a starting point, would prove to be no starting point at
all?"[75] Of course Hegel had presented his "absolute" starting point as no
starting point at all, because doubting all things abstracted from any
"particular determinate content," but Kierkegaard pulls off a dialectical
reversal. He is not just proposing a return to the Socratic starting point;
he is restoring a "subjective" starting point by demonstrating that Hegel's
"absolute" one is no starting point at all, but in a different sense from
Hegel's:

> The starting point must be a breaking off . . . and therefore it pre-
> supposes a whole line of thought in order to make a start; for if some-

thing [i.e., any "particular determinate content"] is not presupposed, the ["subjective"] act whereby I abstract from everything [i.e., all "determinate content"] is presupposed. . . . I cannot get around to making a start, since I am using all my powers in order to abstract from everything.[76]

In effect, then, Hegel had "never started" as a philosopher in spite of his boast (in a later parody of Kierkegaard's entitled "The Dialectic of Starting Out") that he had "written twenty-one volumes."[77] Hegel's antagonist in this parody is Socrates, who is still for Kierkegaard (as in the dissertation on irony) the spokesman on behalf of the individual's "subjective" starting point.

With the restoration of this "subjective" starting point, the "particular determinate content" of "the life of an individual" enters philosophy.[78] And there is a concomitant change in procedure. *Johannes Climacus* is the rejection of the abstract logic of pure thought in favor of a "storytelling method" (*fortællingens form*). Thus it has a further subtitle—*A Story*—which brings out Kierkegaard's opposition to the procedural principle that has presided over the development of modern philosophy—*De omnibus dubitandum est*. The story told is of the experiences of the young Climacus when he attempted to start to become a philosopher and found himself struggling with the general principle *De omnibus dubitandum est*. And the story includes stories within it—for example, the parable of Dionysius, which I have cited. Kierkegaard never finished *Johannes Climacus*, and it cannot be regarded as his starting point. But he continued to reject abstract thought in favor of the "particular determinate content" of individuals' lives and to employ as appropriate to this content a "storytelling method" which he opposes to Hegel's "objective" or "scientific" dialectic. Kierkegaard will tell stories in what he calls his "esthetic" works, starting with *Either/Or* and concluding with *Concluding Unscientific Postscript*. But since Kierkegaard himself does not offer sustained reflection on this method until *Postscript*, I shall defer further consideration of its appropriateness. Some of the stories themselves should be examined first.

There will be other delays. *Either/Or* is not only explicitly designated by Kierkegaard as the starting point of his "authorship," as I have mentioned; it is also a starting point which is elevated to the level of a philosophical principle. *Either/Or* is an assertion of the principle of contradiction. After the difficulties Kierkegaard had experienced in getting started as a philosopher, we can expect that *Either/Or* should exhibit sensitivity to the issues of starting point. But it will be some time before we shall be able to investigate exactly how Kierkegaard does start out in *Either/Or* by applying the principle of contradiction. Since he is the founder of existentialism, his attempts to get started as a philosopher have facilitated a preliminary exploration of some of the issues posed by an "existential" starting point with respect to the relation between "the life of an individual" and "philosophy." But I am interpreting these issues as ones to be explored in the setting of existentialism as a philosophical movement. We cannot settle down to examine Kierkegaard's own philosophy without considering other existentialists. For we need to determine some overall traits of this movement if we are to be assured of its coherence and of its other credentials to be accepted as philosophical.

Notes

1. In a BBC Third Programme interview.

2. Charles Taylor, pp. 133–34 (italics in original). He is reviewing *La philosophie analytique*, a record of a conference held in "an attempt to make contact between two philosophical worlds that touch today at very few points, and which one can name for short Anglo-Saxon and Continental." But "the dialogue didn't come off." Since Oxford is no longer the center, I shall use the shorthand "Anglo-American philosophy," which embraces tendencies much more diffuse than those that prevailed fifteen years ago, when "Oxford philosophy" and "analytic philosophy" were virtually interchangeable labels.

3. E.g., by Bernard Pingaud, in *Arc* 30 (1966): 94.

4. The apocalypse is usually of rather short duration. Specific differences reemerge not only with respect to the sense in which philosophy has come or is coming to an end but also with respect to what exactly the general assumptions and homogeneous characteristics of philosophy have been; and these differences may be as considerable as some of the differences that once separated philosophers before philosophy came to an end.

5. XI^1 A 18. "The single individual" is too weak a translation for Kierkegaard's recurrent term *den enkelte*. "The solitary individual" might be better, for we shall see that Kierkegaard's philosophy is to a considerable extent a procedure for isolating the individual from others. But "solitary" fails to bring out the extent to which his conception of individuality has been influenced by (though it is not the same as) Hegel's *Einzelnheit (singularitas)*, which combines the preceding levels of universality and particularity. Neither "solitary" nor "singular" brings out the unity at stake in such a combination (see n. 29, this chapter). I shall retain the usual translation for *den enkelte*, "the individual," but the Hegelian (as well as the Danish) associations should be kept in mind, especially since an obvious link between Kierkegaard's and Sartre's individualism is Sartre's identification of Kierkegaard as "The Singular Universal" (see chap. 3, n. 90 below).

6. These citations from *Glimpses and Impressions of Kierkegaard* (pp. 94, 114–15) are excerpted by Croxall from contemporary accounts.

7. *Search for a Method*, p. 8.

8. "Existence as Understood by Kierkegaard and/or Sartre," p. 389.

9. "Existentialism," p. 147. MacIntyre is of course laboring under the burden of being encyclopedic.

10. Ayer, p. 202. He begins his exposition with the warning that "the Philosophy of Existentialism is hardly a body of systematic doctrine." The similarities of attitude which he proposes to bring out he characterizes as a "family resemblance." That the

32. *Theses on Feuerbach*, p. 198.

33. *Being and Time*, pp. 41, 42. The problem of translating *Dasein* will be dealt with in chap. 3.

34. *What Is a Thing?* p. 151.

35. *Climacus*, pp. 102, 116.

36. *Science of Logic*, pp. 67, 70, 74. I am quoting from "With What Must the Science Start." The "difficulty of finding a starting point" is raised in the first sentence of the first book of Hegel's *Logic*.

37. *Climacus*, pp. 183, 133.

38. Thesis 10, in *Irony*, p. 349.

39. Ibid., pp. 193, 243, 245, 247.

40. Ibid., p. 193.

41. For examples from this tradition, consult "typological" in the indices to my *Human Nature*.

42. See, e.g., *Papirer*, I A 72.

43. In making this advance Kierkegaard is clearly indebted to Hegel's dialectical treatment of such figures as Antigone, and I am deferring detailed examination of the differences here between Kierkegaard and Hegel until we reach Kierkegaard's Antigone in chap. 6.

44. *Papirer*, VII A 82. Having recognized this distinction of level, I shall take as Kierkegaard's starting point where he starts philosophically with reference to his life as an individual. But it would make no essential difference if we took instead where he deliberately started in life. For in his reflections on how he should start out (alluded to in my introduction, n. 19 above), he argued in effect that the issue is philosophical— "to find a truth which is true *for me*, to find *the idea for which I can live and die*"— though not philosophical in the Hegelian sense: "What would be the use of discovering so-called objective truth, of working through all the systems of philosophy and of being able . . . to show up the inconsistencies within each . . . ? I certainly do not deny that I still acknowledge an *imperative of understanding* . . . , *but it must be taken up into my life.*" Needless to say, there is no fixed and final starting point. In the same journal entry, he reports, "I stand once again at the point where I must start my life in a different way" (I A 75; italics in original). We shall watch him start out in different ways in successive philosophical writings (the dissertation, *Johannes Climacus, Either/Or*, and even within *Either/Or*), but these starting points are more easily located, and there is a sense in which *Either/Or* does represent his final starting point.

45. *Irony*, p. 47. The commendation is of course ironical, and the allusion to Hegel is particularly evident in the "grasps" (*griber*), since this is the Hegelian function of the concept (*Begriff*); but the erotic elaboration of the idiom is Kierkegaard's (see chap. 6, n. 83 below). Such elaborateness (including the use of Latin for "female in gender") is a characteristic opening flourish on Kierkegaard's part. Such flourishes indicate the importance he attaches to the fashion in which he starts out a work, and I have therefore cited the passage in full.

46. Ibid.; my italics. Here "phenomenological" refers merely to the actual existence of Socrates and presupposes Hegel's opposition of the phenomenal and the conceptual.

47. Hegel's failure (introduction, n. 18 above) was due to his having been "infatuated" with romantic irony as "the form of irony nearest him." Hence, as Kierkegaard goes on to complain, "the discussion of Socratic irony is very brief," and "the occasion is used to declaim against irony as a general principle," as if all irony were romantic irony (*Irony*, pp. 282–83). The charge of infatuation is ironical; Hegel was implacably hostile toward romantic irony, especially Schlegel's.

48. For an example of such verbal irony, see p. 241 below.

49. This example is simpler than Kierkegaard's. For Socrates' break with the phenomenal, see p. 43 below.

50. *Irony*, pp. 243, 245. Kierkegaard may be parodying the relation Hegel assumes between where his philosophy starts and where it ends. At the end of the *Logic*, Hegel

problem of providing an exposition should be framed between two extrem
apart as "a body of systematic doctrine" and a "family resemblance" sugg
little precise philosophical status attaches to the notion of a philosophical m
11. "Existentialism," p. 147.

12. Karl Jaspers might once have been in the running, but his influence
first to suffer eclipse. I would claim that the traits I shall single out would be
to the examination of most philosophers who are regarded as existential
philosopher who is sometimes so regarded, but in my view mistakenly, is I
The biological cast of his philosophy sets him apart, to mention only one diff

13. *Bulletin de la Société Française de Philosophie* (octobre-décembre 1937):

14. To the accusation of "humanism" Sartre in effect retorted in 1952,
emerged from a discussion with Heidegger and accused him of "mysticism"
de Beauvoir, *Force of Circumstances*, p. 289).

15. *Either/Or*, 1:31.

16. *Dialogue avec Heidegger*, 3:108–9.

17. *Prime of Life*, pp. 68, 112.

18. Spiegelberg, 1:463.

19. Ibid., p. 282.

20. Ibid., p. 89; *Ideas*, p. 20. Because these pronouncements are well known,
the usual translation "beginning" rather than substituting "starting point."

21. "Husserl has always regretted that a term which really reached the ess
philosophy was already taken by a positive science—the term 'archaeology' "
Fink, "Das Problem der Phänomenologie Edmund Husserls," p. 240).

22. This passage Husserl suppressed, possibly because he felt renewed confid
the new start he was about to make. It is found in *Husserliana*, 10:393.

23. *Ideas*, p. 21.

24. To avoid future terminological confusion, I should point out that the
of Hegel's *Phenomenology* is dialectical and should be distinguished sharply
interpretation from phenomenological method defined by reference to Husserl.
interpreters have tended to find what Derrida (following Hyppolite) describe
"profound convergence between the thoughts of Hegel and of Husserl" (*Origine
géométrie*, p. 58). At the same time, Derrida also applies the label "dialectical"
movement of temporalization in Husserl (p. 157). The issue is only partly terminol
and the question of whether it is philosophically worthwhile to draw my distinctic
have to wait upon the outcome of my interpretation. But I can plead now that H
himself was disdainful of both Hegel and dialectic.

25. *Perception*, p. viii.

26. For a brief but remarkable retrospective interpretation, see Derrida, *Marges
philosophie*, pp. 136–42.

27. *Papirer*, X3 A 239. See my introduction, n. 19 above.

28. *Irony*, p. 193. Kierkegaard oversimplifies what Hegel actually says; see H
History of Philosophy, 1:392. I shall not be concerned with the different ways th
tinction can be drawn between the philosophical and the autobiographical. In
Anglo-American tradition, to rely on the autobiographical is to commit the ge
fallacy—i.e., to suppose that the way something came about has anything to do
its logical or normative justification. But of course Hegel himself violates this ve
of the distinction.

29. See esp. *The Point of View for My Work as an Author* and the essays publi
along with it. We encounter a comparable problem in Heidegger, and in both cas
is partly a problem of translation. *Dasein* (for the moment we can translate it as
man being") is in Heidegger "the only [*einzig*] being which can be of itself as i
vidualized in individualization [*vereinzeltes in der Vereinzelung*]" (*Being and T
p. 188). The translation leaves out the criterion of unity, which in Heidegger a
Kierkegaard is one of consistency or constancy.

30. *Irony*, p. 222.

31. *Situations*, 2:15–16.

visualizes "the science ... as a circle, coiled into itself, its end being coiled back to the start" (p. 842). There is another parody of the relation between starting and ending in *Climacus*, pp. 131–32. In justifying such parodies, Kierkegaard proclaims, "Every development is . . . only complete with its own parody" (*Papirer*, I A 285). If this is a commentary on his relation to Hegel, it also echoes Hegel. But see chap. 6, n. 40 below.

51. *Irony*, p. 245 (Hegel, *History of Philosophy*, 1:420). "As a person" is italicized not in the German edition of Hegel's lectures but by Kierkegaard.

52. See introduction, nn. 17, 20 above.

53. *Irony*, pp. 85, 339.

54. *Postscript*, p. 101.

55. See p. 258 below.

56. *Irony*, p. 245. Kierkegaard has in mind Hegel's attribution to Socrates of the positive doctrine of the Idea of the Good.

57. Cited ibid., p. 199.

58. *History of Philosophy*, p. 392. Hegel only ensures this continuity by explaining that the "absolute demand, 'Know yourself,' does not mean . . . a self-knowledge of the particular capacities, character, drives, and weakness of the individual but a knowledge of the truth about man as this is . . . the essence of mind itself" (*Encyclopaedia*, pt. 3, par. 377). Thus the individual and the particularities that individuate him are left behind.

59. *Irony*, p. 124.

60. Cited ibid., p. 283. Kierkegaard's development of the distinction between his dialectic as subjective and Hegel's as objective will be analyzed in chaps. 6, 11, and 12.

61. Ibid., pp. 84, 82, 83. Thus "irony . . . negates the phenomenal, not in order to posit anything by means of this negation" (p. 235). For the suspension of Socrates, see p. 43 below. Kierkegaard's love suffered a comparable ironical suspension, and he used this metaphor with regard to breaking his engagement (see p. 412 below). Although he wrote the dissertation to secure a position that would enable him to marry Regina, his relation to her remained merely a relation to something which he felt could not be given. The dissertation was accepted on July 16, 1841; he returned the engagement ring on August 11 and defended the dissertation on September 29; and the engagement was finally broken on October 11.

62. Ibid., p. 278; my italics.

63. Ibid., p. 239.

64. Ibid., p. 222.

65. The reader who has been disconcerted by the ironical convolutions through which Kierkegaard puts Socrates may obtain some consolation from the complaints of professors who passed on Kierkegaard's dissertation (cited by Capel, ibid., pp. 10–11). But the reader should recognize that the convolutions are not just the "excrescences" which these professors would like to have cut out but are intrinsic to Kierkegaard's conception of his ironic Socratic role.

66. *Papirer*, X³ A 477. An introduction is not the place for the dispute as to whether, or to what extent, Kierkegaard was ever or was still a Hegelian when he wrote the dissertation. As my interpretation so far indicates, I am quite certain that the dissertation is not Hegelian, though the Hegelian jargon is thicker there than it usually is later. But from now on I shall take the precaution of using the dissertation only in conjunction with Kierkegaard's later, indisputably anti-Hegelian writings.

67. *Irony*, p. 243. Of course Kierkegaard may again be parodying Hegelian circularity; see n. 50, this chapter.

68. Hegel starts his *Logic* by stressing the modernity of the problem of starting point itself: "It is only in modern times that thinkers have become aware of the problem of finding a starting point" (p. 67).

69. *Irony*, p. 339. The opposition is set up in terms of the same distinction of level with which we have been concerned elsewhere in the dissertation: "In our time there

is much talk about the significance of doubt for philosophical knowledge; but doubt is for philosophy what irony is for personal life. As philosophers claim that no true philosophy is possible without doubt, so with equal justification one may claim that no authentic human life is possible without irony" (p. 338).

70. Since the scholarship of Gilson and others, it has become a philosophical commonplace to dismiss Descartes's claim of having "started out anew," for he is supposed to have failed to shed the prejudices his doubting process was designed to eliminate. But Descartes did confer new philosophical significance on the undertaking to start out anew in philosophy. Although the Husserl of the *Cartesian Meditations* will eventually be our most relevant example, there are many others. Derrida cites Condillac: "I start at the starting point. . . . This is why I start where one has never started before. . . . What is a genius? . . . He starts at the starting point and proceeds straight ahead" (*Essai sur l'origine des connaissances humaines*, ed. Derrida, pp. 16, 39). The citation is from Condillac's *La langue des calculs.* The mathematical model provides Condillac, as it provided Descartes, with confidence in the ease with which one can start out and proceed deductively "straight ahead." See p. 148 below.

71. *Logic*, pp. 7, 74–75; *History of Philosophy*, 3:224. In exploiting Hegel's sense of his relation to Descartes, Kierkegaard is again playing up the relation between starting out and ending up (see n. 50, this chapter); for Hegel not only claims philosophically that he is resolving with his "absolute starting point" the modern "problem of finding a starting point" but also claims historically that his philosophy is the culmination of the development which started with Descartes.

72. The double title not only conjoins this philosophical principle with a narrative of an individual's personal effort to start out as a philosopher but also sets the stage for the work as an attack on the leading ecclesiastical Hegelian in Denmark, Martensen. (For some of the textual evidence, see Croxall's comments in *Climacus*, pp. 47–48.) Martensen had presided over Kierkegaard's start in theology and philosophy, both as his tutor and as a lecturer at the university. When Martensen acquired a chair, he became at the personal level the object of Kierkegaard's attack on the Professor; when he became primate of the Danish church, he became at the personal level the object of Kierkegaard's *Attack on Christendom.* Two generations of Danish scholars have familiarized us with such contemporary intellectual figures in Denmark who should be taken into account in dealing even with Kierkegaard's interpretation of Hegel. But Niels Thulstrup's *Kierkegaards forhold til Hegel* has demonstrated that this relation usually survives intermediaries. In any case, this relation must remain central in an introduction, and I shall take Kierkegaard's contempt for the undertaking of Martensen and others to "go beyond" Hegel as warrant for my not doing so here.

73. *History of Philosophy*, 3:217.

74. Ibid. The "long voyage" is the long medieval period of philosophy's alienating subservience to theology, and it may have caught Kierkegaard's attention because his effort will be to emancipate theology from its subservience to philosophy in Hegel. See chap. 10 below.

75. *Climacus*, pp. 119–20.

76. *Papirer*, V A 70. Kierkegaard's reinstatement of "the act whereby I abstract from everything" assumes the relevance to "philosophy" of "the life of the individual," since it is the individual who must perform this act.

77. Ibid., VI A 145.

78. I reemphasize that there are two separate issues here. Hegel upheld Plato's objective dialectic over against Socrates' subjective dialectic: "Plato is termed the discoverer of dialectic, and rightly so, since the Platonic philosophy first gave dialectic . . . its objective form. Socrates . . . employs the dialectical in a predominantly subjective guise [*Gestalt*]—i.e., that of irony" (*Encyclopaedia*, pt. 1; par. 81). But at the same time Hegel interpreted the Socratic "Know yourself" as commitment not to any "particular determinate content" but to "the essence of mind itself" (see n. 58, this chapter).

2

The Wiggling Bottom

Walking forward is the image of existence.—Kierkegaard

SUBJECT MATTERS

A philosophical movement, when it is not simply the fanning out of the influence of its founder, might nonetheless retain some measure of coherence in either or both of two ways. Philosophers belonging to the movement might on one hand deal with roughly the same assortment of problems, range of experiences, or subject matter. Or, on the other, they might apply roughly the same method to whatever problems, etc., they encounter. I shall begin with the issue of subject matter. Even though it may be of minimal significance for the coherence of a movement, as compared with the coherence achieved by applying the same method, a subject matter is usually visualized in our Anglo-American philosophical tradition as more or less available at the start, while a method is usually visualized as to some extent adapted to the treatment of a subject matter. Let me cite from the methodological treatise which instituted the approach that still prevails fairly much in our tradition today. Mill's *Logic* was published in the same year (1843) as *Either/Or*. When Mill sorts out different methods in the *Logic*, his labels—"Chemical Method," "Geometrical Method," "Physical Method"—all indicate the subject matters to which each has proved appropriate.[1]

What then is the subject matter that existentialists treat? A. J. Ayer lines up some of their problems:

> Existentialists do discuss philosophical questions, such as solipsism, negation, the analysis of time, but in a very confused and uninstructive way. For the rest they describe certain psychological states, fascinating enough in some cases, but of a rather special character, and they make some general recommendations as to conduct.[2]

The miscellaneousness of this list suggests, perhaps deliberately, that the range of problems existentialists treat is not in fact sufficiently coherent to constitute a recognizable subject matter. But the list also reflects a conventional identification of "philosophical questions" with metaphysical or epistemological questions, and a conventional sorting out of questions belonging to psychology as a descriptive discipline from ethical questions which are normative.

Perhaps existentialism is not this conventional. But let us try to use Ayer's list. It is not obvious that there is anything distinctively "existential" about the questions of "negation" or "time," granted that Sartre has written a *Being and Nothingness* and Heidegger a *Being and Time*. Although "solipsism" heads Ayer's list, Heidegger brushes this question to one side; Sartre is the only prominent existentialist who discusses it with any thoroughness, and he seems to have inherited it from Husserl's phenomenology rather than from the existentialist tradition proper. In any case, we do not wish to become "confused and uninstructed," so let us move on to the other questions Ayer lists. These we cannot dodge. After all, there is a brand of ethics known as "existential" as well as a brand of psychology known as "existential." What is distinctively "existential" about the questions the existentialist assigns to these subject matters?

Let us begin with existential ethics. For I observed earlier that "recommendations as to conduct" are often implicit in the Anglo-American appraisal of certain acts as "existential." In fact Anglo-American philosophers have been responsive to the intellectual vogue of "existential" acts. When they pay attention to existentialism, many of them assume that it is primarily an ethical doctrine. If Iris Murdoch interprets existentialism as "a wild leap of the will," Olafson explicitly attaches it to the voluntaristic tradition in his *Ethical Interpretation of Existentialism*. This interpretation he justifies in his opening pronouncement: "Among contemporary philosophical movements, none has addressed itself more directly to ethical issues than has existentialism."[3] But this ethical interpretation does not seem quite so inevitable an interpretation of the leading Continental existentialists as of their American influence. Sartre has not yet written his ethics; Merleau-Ponty never wrote one; Heidegger has explicitly refused to do so. Kierkegaard did write on problems which he identified as "ethical," but he treated these problems in a series of works, starting with *Either/Or*, which he identified as "esthetic." One is tempted to correct Olafson's pronouncement to read, "Among contemporary philosophical movements that have addressed themselves to ethical issues, none has addressed itself more *indirectly* than existentialism." The existentialist seems reluctant to disentangle ethical questions from other matters with the confidence that has been characteristic of contemporary American ethical philosophers.

Why are Continental existentialists not so inclined as some of their Anglo-American interpreters to write works on existential ethics, existential esthetics, and existential psychology? The procrustean attempt an Ayer makes to lay down the subjects which existentialists treat is misconceived. An existentialist does not start out his treatment of a problem by allocating it to a single subject matter: psychology, ethics, esthetics, etc. Indeed the first approximation I would offer in the attempt to identify an "existential" problem, is that it is one which cannot be allocated for treatment to a subject matter.[4] Heidegger generalizes,

> In all my philosophical work I have not bothered with the traditional forms and classifications of the various philosophical disciplines. In remaining bound by them, one tragically fails to return to the inner problematic of philosophy itself.[5]

But how, it will then be asked, can a philosopher start out, except by delimiting a problem—that is, by drawing some distinctions around it that dispose of the irrelevant and bring the relevant into focus? Of course he cannot. But rather than employ distinctions that simply pinpoint a problem or segregate a subject matter, the existentialist determines relevance by reference to relations. How he determines the relative relevance of different relations is a question that will have to await our later interpretation of the dialectical method of existentialism. But a succinct example can be given now of Heidegger's insistence on the relational character of what he is analyzing—his reliance on hyphens. Thus an influential dimension of his treatment of "existence" (*Dasein*) is his analysis of "being-in-the-world."

In *Either/Or* Kierkegaard analyzes an array of relations which enter into the composition of the overall relation between the esthetic and the ethical. Earlier I anticipated that this overall relation, as evoked by the title, was one of contradiction. But we should not think of an existential contradiction as a blanket contradiction which would preclude any relation. In Kierkegaard's own phraseology, a "relation underlies the disrelation."[6]

The "relation" which "underlies the disrelation" (the contradiction) between the esthetic and the ethical is conceived by Kierkegaard not as fixed or static but as a relation between *Stages on Life's Way* (they are to be distinguished as "stages" and related as "on life's way"). This is the

title of a work in which Kierkegaard recapitulates his treatment in
Either/Or of the contradictory relaton between the esthetic and the
ethical stages and adds a religious stage. There are four differences between a stage and a subject matter which can be presented schematically
now, insofar as they effect the way a philosopher starts out. A schematic
comparison, if regrettable, is a necessary preliminary, for Anglo-American
philosophers are quite ready to accept something as abstract as distinctions of subject matter, but they are likely to be queasy about accepting
distinctions between stages as comparable.

1. As *Either/Or* illustrates, a stage assumes its significance in relation
to at least one other stage in the course of some overall development
(e.g., "life's way"). "In the course of" is to be taken in a strong sense:
the relation of contradiction between the esthetic and ethical stages only
develops at the ethical stage. A subject matter, in contrast, is subject to
an investigation in which one is able for the most part to keep it distinct
from other subject matters; otherwise it would not qualify as a subject
matter. It is an area which can be circumscribed sufficiently to enable
one to pin certain problems down, so that one can remain largely undis-
tracted by anything transpiring beyond its limits.

2. Because a stage is related to other stages in an overall development,
the treatment of a later stage develops out of and presupposes the preceding treatment of an earlier one. Thus one cannot understand what
transpires ethically at the later stage of Kierkegaard's *Or* (including the
contradiction that only develops when this stage is reached) unless one
has understood what has already transpired esthetically at the earlier stage
of *Either*. But when ethics is conceived as a subject matter (as when
Olafson visualizes the existentialists as addressing themselves directly
to ethical issues), it is assumed that its treatment is by and large feasible
without a prior treatment of esthetics.

3. A long-run stage (such as *Either*) is a process of development which
is itself composed of short-run stages or processes of development. A
subject matter, in contrast, is not only more or less supplied at the start,
but the set of problems composing it can also be taken as more or less
fixed. Of course a philosopher who is treating a subject matter can
decide that a certain problem is improperly formulated. When he then
reformulates it, the initial formulation is left behind. But when a philosopher is proceeding by stages, the relation between the reformulation
and the initial formulation will remain significant as a feature of the
development that has taken place. The concepts employed will participate in this reformulation. The most available example is the concept of
starting point, which will undergo reformulation during the development of my interpretation of existentialism and acquire different impli-

cations in each of the four parts. In the present part we are trying to start out with a problem or subject matter—existence, though we do not yet know what the term means; in part II we shall start out with existential method and try to discover what its dialectical character is. But even then we shall discover that further reformulations of the concept of starting point are needed.

4. The relation between short and long-run stages will be examined later. That this examination has to be postponed itself illustrates a difference between a stage and a subject matter which is so fundamental that the comparison I am undertaking tends to break down. If the term "subject matter" is to retain its usual meaning in the disciplines with which we are familiar, some distinction between subject matter and method must be maintained. But the method of treating the problems that develop during a stage is a matter of following out its development, so that it is not feasible to distinguish the problems themselves from the method for their treatment. Thus further examination of a stage has to be postponed unil its methodological function can be clarified.

LEVELS

For the present we can get by with the weaker concept of "level" and the anticipations it permits. Different stages occupy different levels, but the concept of stage adds to the concept of level the previously noted implication of a process of development which takes place during a stage and from one to another. And it is this implication which cannot be dealt with until we have dealt with existential method as a way of following out this development.

An illustration of a distinction of level already available is that between a starting point and a principle, though this illustration is still rather difficult to press, since both terms are vague in their application. As I indicated at the very outset and again later in Hegelian terms, a starting point is the particular experience (or the problem which it poses) that an individual brings to the fore in his philosophy. One can try to locate it by turning to his first philosophical work, as I did by considering Kierkegaard's experience of irony or of his relation to Socrates as an ironist, or by turning to the first work in which he feels he really gets started. This is *Either/Or* in Kierkegaard's case. But here we run into complications. Where does he start? The work is attributed, like *Johannes Climacus*, to a pseudonym; it has an intricate title page, a preface, then a scattering of aphorisms, before we reach an essay which is designated a first stage; and yet the whole of *Either* is in some sense a first stage in relation to *Or*. The explanation of these complications is that the esthetic experience with which Kierkegaard starts out in *Either* is not easily segregated, since he is not dealing with esthetics as a subject matter. It is instead caught up in various relations to other esthetic experiences whose relevance can only be controlled by employing certain methodological procedures. The only one we have been able to anticipate so far is the procedure of bringing out the contradictory character of the initial experience, thereby raising it to the level where the principle of contradiction applies to it.

Thus a principle is a starting point which is no longer merely a particular experience but can be credited with higher-level generality. Principles too are found at different levels. Irony, which we encountered in the dissertation, doubt, which we encountered in *Johannes Climacus*, are (at least in the retrospect provided by *Either/Or*) relatively lower-level principles, for they are themselves experiences of contradiction.[7]

What we are able to illustrate now are some of the broader issues over the relation between levels. When the particular experiences of an individual are discounted philosophically as merely of autobiographical interest, no "relation underlies the disrelation" which is introduced by the distinction between the experience the individual starts out with and philosophical principles. Thus no "relation" survives when Hegel dismisses a "subjective" starting point as referring to "some contingent idea which can be constituted differently in different subjects" or when he remarks that "with Socrates it is not so much a matter of philosophy as of the life of an individual." The subtitles Kierkegaard adds to his titles are one way he indicates that he is restoring the relation between the two levels: he treats *The Concept of Irony—with Constant Reference to Socrates*, the principle *De omnibus dubitandum est* with reference to the story he tells in *Johannes Climacus* about how he, under this pseudonym, started out to become a philosopher. He is reasserting over against Hegel the significance of the "subjective" starting point and criticizing him for constructing a philosophy which is a "splendid castle," while neglecting philosophically the "shack" he actually lives in.

There is another idiom with which Kierkegaard restores in opposition to Hegel the relation between the two levels:

> The person of a abstract thinker is irrelevant to his thought. An existing thinker . . . in presenting his thought . . . sketches himself.[8]

Our Anglo-American tradition is one of abstract thinkers in which the individual is discouraged from sketching himself in presenting his thought. We assume that a philosopher must be self-effacing, for what counts philosophically is not autobiography; it has nothing to do with him as an individual but is whatever "objective" justification can be offered for whatever position he puts forward.

There is one respect in which this relation between levels in existentialism arouses especially virulent skepticism on the part of Anglo-Americans who are alert to philosophical criteria. Existentialists, Ayer reports, "describe certain psychological states . . . of a rather special character." Philip Thody similarly cautions, "The main argument against existentialist philosophy is that it often rests on a highly specialized personal experience."[9] So far we have been concerned with the strain the individualism of the existentialist imposes on the coherence of existentialism as a philosophical movement. Ayer's "special" and Thody's "highly specialized" now add the imputation that "the psychological states," the "personal experiences in question," are so very particular to the individual that they cannot support any reliable generalization about human experience. Ayer and Thody are in effect denying that the thought of even an individual existentialist can qualify as a philosophy. If philosophy (at least in the more obvious scentific sense) started with Aristotle, it is a tradition in which there can be no knowledge of the particular individual; there can only be knowledge of what is general.[10] If the personal experience the existentialist proffers is merely particular to the individual, it cannot qualify as philosophical. When Ayer reports that existentialists describe "psychological states . . . of a rather special character," he is assuming that a criterion to be met by any philosophy is the attainment of a certain generality in the scope of what it treats. Thus, before we worry further about existentialism meeting the criterion of coherence, we have to test it against this criterion of generality, since some measure of generality must be attained before the criterion of coherence would become fully applicable.

GENERALITY

The issue of generality is raised again by Ayer when he reaches the climax of his appraisal of what he refers to with obvious disdain as "the existentialist technique." They "forsake analysis for the description of some psychological condition, preferably an abnormal one, *generalize* this psychological condition, sometimes even to the point of making it a logical necessity, and then transfer the whole concoction to the metaphysical plane, and treat the metaphysics as a background to some literary conclusion about the tragic stage of man."[11] This appraisal is emotive sputtering and would apply as convincingly or as unconvincingly, say, to Hamlet's "To be or not to be" speech. It illustrates how the Anglo-

American philosopher often clings to subject matters ("psychological," "logical," "metaphysical") and is insensitive to a dialectical development through stages or even to distinctions of level. In spite of all the animation with which Ayer offers us a step by sequence, there is no corresponding sequence in existentialism. Where exactly, for instance, does the "transfer" take place, and how is it distinguished from the previous operation of "making it a logical necessity"? What is the textual evidence that Sartre, Heidegger, or Kierkegaard arrives at "some literary conclusion about the tragic state of man"? Even Sartre's and Heidegger's references to the "tragic" are extremely rare; whereas Kierkegaard treats the "tragic" not surprizingly as an esthetic category, while his conclusions are religious. Why "*some* literary conclusion"? Is it impossible to specify? What in fact is a literary conclusion? Or is it just that whatever is literary does not matter philosophically, so that one can be offhand about it?

Thody too finds certain existential experiences abnormal or at least very highly specialized:

> If Kierkegaard had been brought up by a moderately reasonable father with intelligent ideas on religion, his whole attitude to God and to his own sense of sin would have been radically different, and his attitude towards life much less a philosophy of despair. If Sartre did not at one period of his life experience existence as physically nauseating, his early philosophy would likewise have been much closer to the conclusions of commonsense.[12]

But let us allow Thody to cite what he takes to be a concrete example of Sartre's experience of revulsion:

> Sartre writes: "The sight of a naked body, seen from behind, is not obscene. But certain involuntary wiggles of the bottom are obscene. [Thody interpolates Barnes's alternative translation, "waddlings of the rump," but it is doubtful if the change in translation improves matters.] This is because the legs alone are being deliberately moved by the walker, and the bottom looks like an isolated cushion which they are carrying, and whose movement is pure obedience to the laws of gravity. It cannot be justified by its situation, on the contrary it is entirely destructive of any situation, since it has the passivity of a thing and is carried like a thing by the legs. Immediately, it reveals itself as unjustifiable facticity, it is *de trop* like all contingent beings. It is isolated from the rest of the body whose present meaning lies in moving forward, it is naked even if veiled by some fabric, for it no longer participates in the transcended transcendence of the body in motion." The purely subjective and rather unpleasantly puritanical nature of this passage is obvious. For some people a wiggling bottom is a delightful and irreplaceable thing expressly created for the pleasure of man.[13]

At one level the sense of revulsion from a wiggling bottom does seem an experience which is "of a rather special character," so that it would hardly yield anything as general as philosophical implications were they not extracted by the rampantly technical superimposed jargon which would seem to belong to a higher, more speculative level in our experience. Now we see why the distinction of level in existentialism is so dismaying: a welter of personal experiences (of wiggling bottoms, of extravagently unreasonable fathers with stupid ideas on religion) may be all right in its place; philosophical technicalities may be all right in their place. But when we encounter the welter conjoined with the technicalities, we may feel affronted by "a riot of intellectual ugliness" (to borrow a comment from Stuart Hampshire) or a "carnival" of "fetishized interiority" (to borrow a comment that Iris Murdoch borrows herself from Lukács).[14]

PRINCIPLES

Beset by this contempt, we need to acclimatize ourselves to that use of the distinction of level whereby a "relation" between "specialized personal experience" and philosophical generality can underlie the "disrelation." Let me begin with a brief side excursion. We can perhaps become less uncomfortable with the relation itself if I show how it might be applicable to the English philosophical essay which is the most widely read and must accordingly have some congeniality for Anglo-American philosophical experience.

Mill starts out *On Liberty* by stating, "The subject of this essay . . . is the nature and limits of the power that can be legitimately exercised by society over the individual." The principle with which he eventually backs up this selection and which will guide him in arguing for the limits to be set up is "the principle of individuality." A principle acquires higher-level generality by becoming attached to some considerable range of our experience. Thus in *On Liberty* a typical formulation of the principle of individuality takes the individual as a starting point: "The initiation of *all* wise or noble things comes and must come from individuals, generally at first from some *one* individual."[15]

Principles are found at different levels of generality, and only those at the higher levels are sufficiently general in their scope to qualify as philosophical. We are not necessarily convinced that Mill has gained with the principle of individuality a sufficiently high level of generality to yield a significant treatment of the problem of liberty, much less of attendant political and social problems. The philosophical loftiness that Mill himself thinks he has gained with the erection of this principle is dramatized by his playing the "all" off against the "one." But this drama, we may suspect, was a feature of his own personal experience. By "all wise or noble things" he should, as his father's son, have meant whatever things can be vindicated by appealing to the principle of utility. This principle, like Mill's, dictates starting out with the individual; but it attains its general scope in a different way—by counting each individual as one in computing the pleasures and pains of all relevant individuals.[16] However, keeping accurate count becomes notoriously difficult when the principle of individuality intervenes and heightens the significance of differences between individuals and the unique relevance of certain individuals—most obviously of "*one* individual," Harriet Taylor, to whom *On Liberty* is dedicated as "the inspirer, and in part the author, of *all* that is best in my writings."[17]

To insinuate an inspiring reference to the mildly liberated Harriet Taylor and a depressing reference to Mill's authoritarian father is to suggest that Mill's application of the principle of individuality to "the struggle between liberty and authority" may be too permeated by the "rather special character" of Mill's own personal experience to qualify as a principle. But to dismantle it is not quite this easy; as a principle it upholds the general significance of experience (and concomitant behavior) which is in some sense idiosyncratic to some individual, so that Mill's own experience cannot be disqualified on this ground.[18] At the same time, such a principle can dislodge or detract from another principle (e.g., in Mill's case the principle of utility) as so abstract in its generality as to be out of touch with significant experience.

INDIVIDUALISM

Before returning to the distinction of levels in existentialism, I should mention a broader consideration that has prompted my recourse to Mill. However much existentialism may differ from his philosophy (and I am not being facetious about the difference in flavor between Mill's Victorian "wise and noble things" and what in Sartre is "carried like a thing by the legs"), *On Liberty* became a classic and existentialism a vogue; and both developments would seem to be associated with the injunction to become an individual and have experiences "of a rather special character," which is in our culture so liberatingly or oppressively close to each of us, regardless of what Ayer may think of the philosophical import of such experiences. We may grant that Mill's liberal conception of individuality reflects the rise of the bourgeoisie (which has been rising off and on ever since the later Middle Ages), while the existential conception may reflect its disintegration, as Sartre has conceded to Marxism.[19] This is a cultural area in which social history and social psychology have often gone to work without sufficient sorting out. Whatever social, economic, or other pressures may have produced the modern individual's sense of himself, some conception of the individual thus produced must be taken into account if our description is to be accurate and complete as to how these pressures have operated. And this conception itself became full-fledged only as a consequence of certain procedures which some of those pressed upon followed out in their thinking. These procedures then need to be examined in order to decide how the individual conceived his individuality.

The examination is all the more difficult and important because our own self-knowledge is at stake. Since the injunction to become an individual and have experiences "of a rather special character" is in our culture integral to our own thinking about ourselves, is not some discrimination between different conceptions of the individual then incumbent upon us? When Mill adopted the principle of individuality, he was at pains to distinguish his individualism from utilitarian individualism. And in dealing elsewhere with liberalism as an individualistic tradition, I have argued that the composition of Mill's individualism cannot be appreciated fully unless one discriminates (in addition to the "utilitarian" conception of the individual who must be counted as one) the "classical" or "typological" conception of the exemplary individual, the "romantic" conception of the individual who is developing into someone he is not yet, and the "historicist" conception of the representative individual who significantly sums up something about his particular time.[20]

Here I admit that I have "torn" each of these conceptions "loose" from "the complex of ideas" to which it "originally belonged." In my earlier interpretation these complexes were accorded detailed consideration. Now I am only trying to suggest how confusedly varied are our conceptions of the individual, so that even if I had not already furnished other reasons for paying attention to existentialism as a philosophical movement, it would still be worthwhile to learn what we can from the most recent philosophical movement that promotes individualism and, correlatively, experiences "of a rather special character."[21]

AUTOBIOGRAPHY

Principles may determine not only what is to count as significant experience but also how experience is to be significantly organized. If in his philosophy Mill had not adhered to the principle of individuality, if he had not concluded that "individuality is the same thing with development," he presumably would not have found it worth his while to write an *Autobiography* in which he is concerned to organize his experience in terms of his own development as an individual or, rather, into an individual. Indeed the relevance of Mill's philosophy to his *Autobiography* is illustrated by his suppression and reshuffling of chronological evidence of the actual facts of his life.[22]

The failure of readers to observe the distorting influence of Mill's philosophy on his *Autobiography* is partly due to the sharpness of the distinction which philosophers have conventionally drawn between the philosophical and the autobiographical. The issue is not whether or not a philosopher discusses his philosophy in his autobiography. Mill does so extensively; Sartre breaks off his autobiography before the period in which he began writing his philosophical works. Nor is the issue simply a matter of the philosophy influencing the autobiography. Of course, just as Mill's *Autobiography* illustrates his philosophical preoccupation with individuality and development, so Sartre's illustrates the preoccupation with starting out that is a trait of existentialism as a philosophy. On page 207 of the 213 pages of Sartre's autobiography, Sartre surveys the ground he has covered: "Voilà mon commencement." Conversely, there is nothing distinctively existential (as my comparison with Mill has shown) about a philosophy being influenced by the "special character" of an individual's personal experience. But from the conventional philosophical point of view, insofar as we feel warranted in interpreting a philosophy only autobiographically, we are implying that the philosophy does not warrant a philosophical interpretation.

Mill's application of his principle of individuality hardly disturbed, even in his own view, the conventional disjunction between philosophy and autobiography.[23] Existentialism is more disturbing. It complicates the relation between these different levels at which experience can be organized. Reconsider, as an example, the philosophical significance Sartre attaches to the special character of Descartes's personal experience:

> The absolute is Descartes, the man who eludes us because he is dead, who lived in his own time, who thought from day to day with the means that were on hand, who developed his doctrine in terms of a certain stage reached by the sciences, who knew Gassendi, Caterus, and Mersenne, who loved in his youth a girl who was cross-eyed, who went to war, got a servant pregnant . . . ; what is merely relative is Cartesianism . . . which keeps going from one century to another.[24]

An entering wedge for this interpretation may have been provided by the Descartes of the quasi-autobiographical *Discourse on Method* as distinguished from the Descartes of the *Metaphysical Meditations*, who predominates in the philosophical tradition, although the differences between these two works probably has less to do with any sense of individuality that can safely be attributed to Descartes himself than with the different audiences for which these two works were written—laymen with "common sense" (according to the preamble to the *Discourse*) and "those most learned and most illustrious men" the "reverend doctors of the Sorbonne," to whom the *Metaphysical Meditations* are dedicated in the hope (according to an influential interpretation) that this metaphysics would help him sneak his physics past them. But even the *Discourse* does not deign to mention the cross-eyed girl or the pregnant servant. Unlike Sartre, Descartes did not appreciate their philosophical relevance; such chitchat is left to Baillet's biography.

PERSONAL EXPERIENCE

Sartre's unconventional interpretation of Descartes permits certain preliminary points to be made regarding existentialism. I have indicated on one hand that an existential philosophy is a relational analysis and that among the relevant relations are those between levels. Thus relativity to the individual's personal experience can be incorporated as a feature of this kind of analysis, but without necessarily deflecting the philosopher from tracing other relations and reaching a higher level of generality. On the other hand, this relativity to the individual is in some fashion privileged (hence Sartre's peremptory "The absolute is Descartes"), as compared with what is conventionally regarded by Anglo-American philosophers as philosophically privileged—for example, the reconstruction of Descartes's arguments in a generally cogent form, whatever Descartes as a particular individual may have had specifically in mind in putting them forward.

We are getting at what is distinctive about existentialism as a philosophy: the relation between the particular personal experience of an individual and philosophical generality is brought within the compass of philosophy itself. Although (as we have seen) "an existing thinker . . . in presenting his thought . . . sketches himself," as opposed to "an abstract thinker," whose "person . . . is irrelevant to his thought," the "existential thinker" also "must be imagined as essentially thinking." This unconventional conjunction of what is particular to an individual and what is essential is illustrated by Heidegger. His "Hölderlin and the Essence of Poetry" is avowedly an attempt "to read off from the work of a single poet the general essence of poetry."[25] What literary critic (and critics are ordinarily much less timid than philosophers) would force so brutal a conjunction? But Heidegger forces it even on philosophy when he describes "the double character of metaphysical questioning." On one hand "any metaphysical question always embraces the whole problematic of metaphysics." On the other, "any metaphysical question can only be put in such a way that the questioner as such along with the question is put in question."[26] What rash hurdling of distinctions is this that takes us all the way from "the whole problematic of metaphysics" to the questioning of the questioner?

Less extravagant in its sweep is Simone de Beauvoir's report of how Sartre started out to become an existentialist, but it does further illustrate this "double character" of existentialism. Raymond Aron returned in 1933 from a year spent in Germany and explained over drinks what was going on there philosophically:

> Aron pointed to his glass. "Look, pal, . . . you can talk about this cocktail, and it's philosophy." Sartre turned almost pale with emotion. For years this had been his fervent wish: to speak of things, as he came into contact with them, and that this would be philosophy.[27]

The reader may not have turned almost pale with emotion at this report. The episode hardly recommends itself as philosophical profundity. But what it does draw to our attention is Sartre's double aspiration even before he became officially an existentialist: to come to grips with his own actual experience and for this coming to grips to be philosophy.

What de Beauvoir goes on to emphasize—Sartre's preoccupation with "the presence of the world"—may seem to sharpen up the contrast with the comment, "I do not think that the world . . . would ever have suggested to me any philosophical problems," with which G. E. Moore admits his dependence on what "other philosophers have said." Yet the reference to "things" and to the "world" suggests that Sartre fully knew what he had been "waiting for" (in Merleau-Ponty's phrase) only when he encountered Husserl's analysis of "consciousness of something" and Heidegger's analysis of "being-in-the-world."

In brief, existentialism is not what it may have seemed earlier—just a historical reaction to the professionalization of philosophy. Nor is it, as a result of this reaction, just personal experience masquerading as philosophy. Whatever else it may be, existentialism is an attempt to bridge that gap, whose widening I traced earlier, between the impetus of an individual's personal experience and the requirements of philosophy. But the attempt is itself made within philosophy. As I also noted earlier, "existential" is, or was, a technical term. Even when Sartre offered a popular exposition of existentialism, he still cautioned that existentialism "is intended for technical philosophers."[28]

PHILOSOPHICAL EXPERIENCE

I have been arguing that the gap between the personal experiences a particular individual starts out with and technical philosophy is itself a cultural fact: most personal experiences are experienced most of the time by most people without reference to philosophy. But another cultural fact noted at the outset is the vogue of such erstwhile technical terms as "existential," "alienation," and "authentic." Indeed a banal feature of many personal experiences is that they pose larger issues which slip away from us, even while we are having the experience; we just go on to other experiences, so that we may be left feeling we have not really had the experience. If we feel that this is because we are accepting some version, prefabricated by others, of what these larger issues are, we may be left with a sense of "alienation." Our experience is not "authentic"—not "our own." Such larger issues are vaguely philosophical.

In existentialism the gap (as well as the perhaps concomitant sense of "alienation," of "inauthenticity") becomes itself a philosophical experience—that is, an experience which is allowed to pose problems internal to philosophy. While a distinction of level is acknowledged between personal experiences and philosophy, an attempt is made to maintain a relation between these levels. Such an attempt must not be disdained as mere philosophical uncertainty or awkwardness. Even in Kierkegaard's *Johannes Climacus*, where he is still uncertain and awkward, he is certain of one thing—that the problem of disentangling himself from Hegelianism can only be formulated by distinguishing levels.

It is true that we do not necessarily identify larger issues as philosophical. Sometimes our competence is doubtful, and we feel that the larger issues are matters for scientific expertise. But more often most of us associate larger issues with literature and art as well as with philosophy. Thus matters here are not simply reducible to the relation between two levels; there are other procedures besides philosophy and autobiography for articulating and organizing experience. It was through reading poetry that Mill became aware at one level of himself as an individual and at a higher level that his philosophical principles were no longer strictly utilitarian.[29] For the present I would only take advantage of an analogy which the relevance of poetry in Kierkegaard encourages me to adopt and which will help me deal with the relation between autobiography and philosophy, inasmuch as a certain level of generality is attained in poetry as compared with the particularity of the individual's personal experiences. "Modern philosophy," Kierkegaard complains in his autobiographical *Johannes Climacus*, "proceeds as if it were enclosed within the system in the same sense as if a historical individual were so poetical that his every word, his every gesture, were pure poetry, so that he would therefore require no transformation to go on to the stage but could go straight there from the street, just as he is and without the slightest embarrassment."[30]

None of our existentialists pretends that the individual can go into philosophy straight from the street, as if his personal experiences were pure philosophy. But drawing the distinction does not mean that philosophy, any more than poetry, is irrelevant to life. Once again it should be stressed that "a relation underlies the disrelation" endorsed by the distinction. A certain transformation is indeed requisite as one moves from one level to another, and there are differences too in the transformation, depending on whether one moves to the level of poetry or to the level of philosophy.

What was in *Johannes Climacus* "still by no means clear" to Kierkegaard (and, insofar as he is not being ironical, may help to explain his failure to finish the work) was how he was to think of such a combination (of the level at which the "historical individual" has his personal experiences with the level of philosophy"). For he reasoned,

> if modern philosophy was like this [an all-inclusive system], the philosopher must be conscious of himself, conscious then of his significance as a moment in [the development of] modern philosophy; then modern philosophy must in turn be conscious of itself as a moment in [the development of] previous philosophy; and this philosophy in turn must be conscious of itself as a moment in the historical evolution of the eternal philosophy. The consciousness of the philosopher must therefore embrace the most vertiginous oppositions within it: on one hand his own personality and his little emendation; on the other, all the philosophy of the world as the evolution of the eternal philosophy.[31]

Johannes Climacus concedes that "it was a long time before he could manage to think this immense thought. He was like someone rolling a heavy load up a mountain and being often overcome, so that his foot slipped and his load went rolling down." Finally "he fainted," and "when he came to himself, he scarcely dared turn his attention to the same thought. It seemed to him that it was meant only to drive a man mad, at any rate unless he had stronger nerves than he had." Although "the individual's knowledge was forever a knowledge of himself merely as a moment in a whole, . . . it was not clear to him how a moment could know that it was merely a moment. The individual would have to be omniscient . . . , and then the world would be finished."[32] The fainting and the coming to oneself are ironical metaphors, but the latter is a regular formula for the reflexive movement which Kierkegaard undertakes in opposition to the omniscience of absolute knowledge. I shall examine this movement later when I consider existential dialectic.

The fact that existentialism requires the individual to come to himself, instead of requiring him to be omniscient or the world to be finished, is one reason why the existentialist resorts to less comprehensively enclosing ways of organizing experience than a philosophical system. I have mentioned that Mill gained his sense of individuality partly from reading poetry.[33] But the impact poetry had on his philosophy seems not to have affected his methodology, which remained modeled on scientific procedures. But Kierkegaard adopts "a storytelling method" in *Johannes Climacus* and in his esthetic works, where he tells over and over again in various versions the story of his "unhappy love." Sartre tells stories, too; I shall be examining later the story he tells in *Being and Nothingness* of the woman about to be seduced. Heidegger carries on the "dialogue of the poet and thinker," in which a particular poet, Hölderlin, assumes an almost unique role.[34] Indeed what is characteristic of existentialism is not only the extent to which the existentialist has resorted to esthetic works and procedures but also the fact that this is not just a matter of some impact made on his experience from outside his philosophy but is intimately related to it. When Merleau-Ponty examines the particular perceptions of Cézanne as a painter in his *Phenomenology of Perception*, he is dealing not specifically with painting (as one might in esthetics) but with the general character of the act of perception. When Kierkegaard starts out by dealing with the "esthetic," he is not just dealing with esthetics but is recognizing that "one must first and foremost take care to find a man where he is and start there," and men in general remain stuck at the "esthetic" stage on life's way.[35]

This existentialist resort to esthetic works and procedures is not necessarily to be interpreted as the debasement of philosophy. Sartre's *Nausea* has been interpreted as an attempt to make "metaphysics descend to the cafés."[36] But the movement between levels can equally be interpreted as proceeding in the opposite direction. Sartre explains:

> I would never have dreamed of expressing my ideas except in some beautiful form—I mean in a work of art, novel, or short story. But I realized that this was impossible. There are matters which are too technical and require a terminology that is purely philosophical. Thus I recognized that I had to duplicate [*doubler*], so to speak, each novel with a philosophical essay.[37]

Since this new respect in which existentialism exhibits a "double character" may seem incongruous with philosophy proper as it is usually conceived, I shall postpone its further consideration until later.

ADJUSTMENT

If I have anticipated the existentialist reliance on esthetic genres, it is
in order to take advantage again of the comparison which I obtained
earlier from Kierkegaard's analogy between pure philosophy and "pure
poetry." I want to suggest that between philosophy and the personal
experiences of an individual's life there is no fixed adjustment of level
which can be maintained in order to eliminate impurities from philosophy, any more than there is any fixed adjustment of level which can be
maintained between poetry (or literature or art) and life in order to
eliminate impurities from the genre. A French philosopher once found
it necessary to propose two contrasting approaches in esthetics—*Art Remote from Life* and *Art Close to Life,* but even this distinction is not
sufficiently flexible.[38] There is likewise no predeterminable remoteness or
proximity that will guarantee a mutually significant relation between
philosophy and life.

The lack of flexibility I am taking exception to is exhibited by Thody's
comment on existentialism, "One of the disadvantages of using literature
to illustrate philosophy is that the highly personal note which literature
invariably contains draws attention to the highly personal origin of the
philosophy."[39] But does literature in fact "invariably" contain a "highly
personal note?" (The very crudity of the metaphor "contains" here indicates insensitivity to the relation between literature and personal experience.) A considerable range of variation with respect to the closeness (or
remoteness) of the literary work to (or from) the personal experience of
the writer has to be tolerated or our appreciation of the variousness of
literature as well as of personal experiences will become impoverished. A
comparable range of variation might be tolerated in philosophy. Consider
the more or less analogous relation between philosophy and scientific
experience: one cannot reject out of hand a philosophy which is a
philosophy of science by appealing to some fixed norm as to how close
it should get to the actual formulations scientists employ in carrying out
their experiments.

Sartre's explanation as to why he found it necessary "to duplicate . . .
each novel with a philosophical essay," would suggest that it is not simply
the function of his literary works simply to illustrate his philosophy.
There is a distinction of level here which should be respected in order
to allow the two genres to assume relatively distinguishable functions.

While I shall respect such distinctions, I do not intend to keep my own interpretation of existentialism positioned at any predetermined level—whether personal experiences reported by existentialists, their revision in esthetic genres, or their further revision in technical philosophies. I cannot any longer shelter behind the simple conjunction of the wiggling bottom with technical philosophical jargon. The resort to esthetic genres as well adds up to the disturbing effect of pastiche; but this is an effect which is characteristic of existentialism itself from the start. As an illustration I shall eventually deal with Kierkegaard's *Either/Or*, which puts together aphorisms, music criticism, the sketch of a tragedy, a diary, etc.

It is the way these genres are put together which I interpret as Kierkegaard's philosophy at its esthetic stage. There is an implicit ambiguity in the description "philosophical" when it is applied to existentialism. But we should not be disconcerted. The ambiguity is a familiar feature of philosophies which are dialectical. Dialectic in Plato's *Republic* is in one sense the highest science, which is only reached at the top level of the divided line, but it is also the philosophical procedure by which one climbs out of the cave and eventually reaches this height. Philosophy in Hegel is both the highest science and the science which allocates other versions of human experience (e.g., art and religion) to their lower levels as stages on the way to itself as this highest science. "Existence" carries a comparable double reference in Kierkegaard: "Existence itself combines thinking with existing."[40] Thus his philosophy of existence is the dialectic of this combination and of such subordinate combinations as the literary genres in *Either*. I shall bring out their philosophical design in chapters 6 and 11.

EVERYDAY EXPERIENCE

For the present I would claim only that interpreting existentialism as a movement should enable us to exhibit a range of variation in the levels relied upon, in order to cope with the gap which we have watched open between the particular experiences an individual starts with and technical philosophy. The gap itself, I have said, is a cultural fact, but it reopens at different junctures in different existentialists. And examining the range of variation with respect to its location should be some assurance of attaining a measure of generality in the treatment of this gap. Indeed we are not up against anything as simple as only one gap any more than we are up against only one distinction of two levels.

Kierkegaard's interpreters are themselves regularly interpreted as divided between those who focus autobiographically on his crucial personal experiences (notably breaking his engagement with Regina and the personal attack on him by the journal *Corsair*) and those who focus on his philosophy as such. There are changes in fashion from one focus to the other. My own interpretation is an attempt to be "bifocal" (a term which I shall explicitly introduce later), for I am claiming that, whenever either approach is adopted to the exclusion of the other, Kierkegaard's philosophy loses its characteristic "double" focus. The dialectic of its combination of thinking with existence is hamstrung. This is what happens, for example, when Lowrie justifies writing biographies of Kierkegaard "because his works were so largely biographical" and concludes, "No interpretation of them can be intelligible which is not biographical."[41]

The problem of level is renewed when Heidegger is accused of having extrapolated from Kierkegaard's experiences, refashioning what was intimately personal for Kierkegaard into the abstrusely technical philosophy of *Being and Time*. Thus in a chapter on "Heidegger and Kierkegaard" in his *Etudes kierkegaardiennes* (1938), which was the first widely influential interpretation of existentialism in France, Jean Wahl exclaims over the philosophical "repercussion of the secret experiences of a solitary individual who was not primarily a philosopher [Kierkegaard]," points up "the danger" of philosophical "attempts [such as Heidegger's] to translate into concepts the results of these experiences," and suggests that " 'existential concepts' perhaps cannot be separated from the experiences themselves from which they emerged. Once separate, they risk losing some of their authenticity."[42] Observe that where Thody is worried about philosophy being contaminated by personal experiences, Wahl is worried about philosophy draining personal experiences of their authentic meaning.

Kierkegaard's experience with Regina is too complicated to deal with yet. A more accessible example of the problem of level is provided by Kierkegaard's attack on journalism, which we saw at the outset betrayed his fear of and contempt for the popularizer. But it was also a counterattack on the *Corsair*, and what was a bitterly personal experience in Kierkegaard's case seems to have been absorbed at a much higher level in Heidegger's more general and ostensibly morally neutral analysis of "everydayness" as a temporal dimension of human existence. Yet two levels (if not the same two) had clearly been distinguished here by Kierkegaard himself: just as the existential thinker both "sketches himself" when he thinks and nonetheless is "essentially thinking," so Kierkegaard is not merely attacking the journalist for having "his own [particular] assortment of opinions" but also for impressing "upon us with all his power that it is necessary [as a matter of general principle] for everybody to have an opinion."[43]

Of course Kierkegaard had "opinions," and the perversity of his denial reemphasizes that he is raising an issue of philosophical principle: "To have an opinion is both too much and too little for my uses. To have an opinion presupposes a sense of ease and security in life, such as is implied in having a wife and children."[44] We shall see later that "having a wife and children" carries in turn quite general philosophical implications.

In *Being and Nothingness* Sartre can be visualized as having dragged Heidegger's analysis in *Being and Time* down from the high level of generality Heidegger had reached by extrapolating from Kierkegaard's personal experiences. I have cited Sartre's example of the "obscene." There are no references to sex in Heidegger, and Sartre has rebuked him for overlooking so fundamental and everyday a dimension of human existence; Sartre makes up for this oversight with a lengthy analysis of the caress, etc.[45]

The insistence behind my exposition of existentialism is that the line of demarcation between philosophy and the array of one's particular personal experiences must be drawn somewhere, if only for clarity's sake, but once the relevance of one to the other is acknowledged, it is not easy to stabilize and keep the line fixed. The interest of dealing with existentialism as a movement is that we shall be exposing ourselves to shifts of level which may illuminate this difficulty.

TRANSCENDENTAL EXPERIENCE

Let me offer what is philosophically perhaps the most striking exhibition of a shift of level. This is the influence on contemporary existentialism of the transcendental philosophy which Husserl himself opposes to existentialism. Husserl assures his philosophy this status by the "phenomenological" or "transcendental" reduction. This is not the place to examine this procedure for its own sake, but it is the way in which Husserl "brackets" or "sets to one side" contingent experiences in order to reach the transcendental, a priori level, where the necessary structure of experience as such can be analyzed. But in Sartre's philosophy the transcendental reduction, Sartre himself explains, is "no longer an intellectual method, a technical procedure; it is an anxiety which imposes itself on us and which we cannot avoid, at one and the same time a pure event which is transcendental in origin and an ever possible contingency of our everyday life." As an illustration Sartre cites an example from the psychiatrist Janet:

A young bride was in terror, when her husband left her alone, of sitting at the window and summoning passersby like a prostitute. Nothing in her education, past, or character could serve as an explanation for such a fear. It seems to me [Sartre] that some inconsequential circumstance (reading, conversation, etc.) had determined in her what might be called "a vertigo of possibility."[46]

In short, it is possible for her (in Husserl's terminology) to "bracket" or "set to one side" her role as a young bride.

Again note that the distinction of level survives, but with a shift in its location. In fact this shift ties in with the previously noted shift from Kierkegaard to Heidegger: Sartre's ungainly transposition of Husserl's "transcendental reduction" into an "ever possible contingency of our everyday life" has undoubtedly been facilitated by the influence on Sartre, in interpreting Husserl, of Heidegger's analysis of "everydayness" and of the way it can be subverted by the experience of anxiety which is "transcendental in origin" in Heidegger himself. What I previously noted was that Heidegger's analysis of the general character of "everydayness" seems to have been influenced by the particular character of Kierkegaard's counterattack on the *Corsair*. Heidegger himself explicitly acknowledges his debt to Kierkegaard's treatment of anxiety.[47] This succession illustrates not only the shifts of level that take place with successive existentialists but also how dependent each has remained, in spite of these shifts, on some previous existentialist; and thus it suggests another advantage (besides those previously adduced) of trying to interpret existentialism as a philosophical movement rather than a miscellany of individual philosophies.

The relevance of a distinction of level to Sartre's existentialist effort to do justice to the experience of an individual is especially evident in the setup of his existential psychoanalysis: "Each 'historical' fact will be considered at once as a [particular] *factor* in the psychic evolution [of the subject] and as a *symbol* of that evolution [as a whole]. . . . Its influence depends entirely on the way in which the individual takes it."[48]

An illustration of this distinction of level is "the vertiginous word"— " 'You're a thief' "—which was not just a particular historical "factor" in Genet's psychological evolution into a saint but becomes a "mythical moment," inasmuch as one way in which Genet "takes it" is by continuing to "relive" the episode when he was (in Husserl's terminology) "endowed" with this "meaning."[49] The "shame" is not just prompted by the particular identity ("thief") conferred on him but is more fundamentally the shame of being identified as an object as such by another subject and thus still represents a transcendental dimension.[50]

VULGARIZATION

The reliving may itself be another instance in which "an intellectual method, a technical procedure" is transposed into an everyday experience. The application of Husserl's phenomenological method depended on "reactivating," as the starting point of an analysis, the original experience one has had (e.g., of perception). Of course, just as Husserl wanted his phenomenology rescued from the influence of Heidegger, so proponents of Husserl and/or Heidegger want either or both of their philosophies rescued from their influence on existentialism. One can be expected to appreciate the superior technical subtlety of Husserl and/or Heidegger and from this perspective to interpret existentialists as irredeemable vulgarizers.[51] But Husserl and Heidegger do operate under certain constraints which may not be entirely fortunate. One cannot blame Husserl for leaving to epigoni to work out the esthetic, ethical, and political implications of his philosophy. One can hardly blame Heidegger for dismissing, not without some contempt, the prospect of his ever writing an ethics. But one must remain aghast not only at his having become a member of the Nazi party but also at his later attitude toward his membership—an attitude which has been aptly described as *mollement évasive*.[52] His membership has sometimes been condoned as the naiveté of a profound philosopher confronted with passing events. But the evasiveness or naiveté may illustrate disabilities from which his philosophy suffers. This is not the place to decide what philosophical depths have been plumbed when *Ereignis* is no longer a mere "event" but becomes the crucial term in Heidegger's philosophy or when "history" (*Geschichte*) is "certainly not the merely contemporary, which never happens [*geschieht*] but only 'passes.' "[53] But if Sartre and Merleau-Ponty have taken at times most debatable political positions toward passing events, at least these positions were sufficiently articulated to be debatable.

EXISTENTIAL EXPERIENCE

In making so much of the relation in existentialism between personal experience and technical philosophy, I may well seem to have skirted a prior implausibility. Why should not existentialism have remained a relatively untechnical affair—some sort of philosophy of life that has to do with a convenient design for the cozy "shack" one actually lives in rather than with the pretentious "castle" the professional philosopher may construct? Why should not existentialism be a do-it-yourself kit?

Why should it be as technically difficult as much of traditional philosophy, which we have seen that it is from the jargon Sartre deploys in
dealing with so unprepossessing an experience as that of a wiggling
bottom? Thody's explanation seems inadequate. Even a most unpleasant
puritan would hardly find it necessary to be so cumbersome: "unjustifiable facticity" as well as "transcended transcendence." What is similarly
disconcerting about the terror of the young bride, as it is diagnosed by
Sartre, is less that it is an experience "of a rather special character" than
that it is an instance of a "transcendental reduction."

Since existentialism is obviously too technical to be merely a philosophy
of life, let us take a further step in trying to determine its character by
comparing it with a sometimes rather technical rendering of experience—
empiricism. Why does an existentialist have to appeal to "existence"?
Why can he not, like the empiricist, appeal simply to "experience"?
After all, I have myself have so far been relying on this term.

Indeed existentialism is sometimes interpreted as a might-have-been
empiricism. MacIntyre observes that, "in countries where empiricism has
a long history, existentialism does not seem to flourish."[54] He is thinking
of England and the United States. The immunity of Anglo-American
philosophers to existentialism prompts his suggestion that existentialism
is a kind of Continental surrogate for Anglo-American empiricism. Existentialists are, he explains, "disappointed rationalists"; they are struggling against rationalism as their own dominant Continental tradition.
He is implying that their disappointment might not have taken the form
of existentialism if it could have been assuaged by having an empirical
tradition on hand as an alternative to rationalism. We shall soon see that
the existentialist comes up against more dislocating experiences than
disappointment.

What is already apparent is that "existence" is a more technical philosophical term than "experience." All of us have had some sense experiences, so that an introduction to traditional empiricism can begin quite
smoothly with some elucidatory references to these experiences. But
"existence"? It may be something we are much taken up with, but to
find out what it means we have to turn more promptly to philosophy
than we do for "experience."

ACTUAL EXPERIENCE

In fact the term "existence" is so obscure that the *Yale French Studies*
(a major importer of French influences into this country) translated
"existence" as "essence" in the final clinching sentence of an essay by

Sartre.[55] This may illustrate what I noted earlier—that American intellectuals like to have a technical term to play around with but are not always fussy as to which one and do not always bother to respect its implications. At any rate, no one involved was sufficiently responsive to the technical implications of the term "existence" to notice that Sartre himself, consistent with traditional philosophical usage, treats "existence" (the fact that something actually is) as the opposite of "essence" (what it is, whether or not it actually is). In medieval scholasticism *existentia* was closely associated with *actualitas.*

This particular medieval usage is more or less discernible in Mailer's commendation of the liberation of Columbia buildings as "existential" because "these kids went out and did something they had never done before, and they did not know how it was going to turn out." More than the buildings were being liberated; like the young bride for Sartre, the students were liberating themselves from what they had done before in their lives (which was no longer "actual") and what might happen as a consequence (and so was not yet "actual"). To this extent, to commend some performance as "existential" is to appeal to what is "actual." This appeal is found in Kierkegaard, though in contemporary existentialism it is reinforced by the more technical phenomenological appeal to actual experience as "immediately given." But Mailer's usage is not dialectical; in existentialism the "actual" is handled in terms of its relation to its opposite, the "possible." The young bride contemplating prostitution was experiencing a "vertigo of possibility."

Congruent with this use of "existential" to refer to the actual is the individualism of existentialism that I have been emphasizing, for the individual is after all the only agency capable of having actual experiences. This emphasis is also derivable from the tradition, as Kierkegaard explains when he points out; "Existence corresponds to the individual—this was already Aristotle's doctrine of the individual; however, the individual remains outside and is not subsumed in the concept."[56] In Aristotle, on one hand it is the individual who "actually" exists; on the other, there is (as I have noted before) no knowledge of this individual as a particular individual but only of the general—that is, of the universal or the essence, which does not "actually" exist for Aristotle. In Hegel this opposition is ostensibly overcome, but at the expense of the "actually" existing individual who is, as Kierkegaard has put it, "subsumed in the concept." "Subsumed" introduces into the Aristotelian formulation the Hegelian movement of *Aufhebung,* which I shall examine shortly. It is a movement by which an opposition is transcended by reaching a higher level, so that it can be said that Kierkegaard (with Aristotle's help) is restoring the opposition between the two levels which we distinguished earlier.

EXISTENTIAL MOVEMENT

Our comparison with the tradition can be enlarged, for there is no longer any reason to restrict the comparison to the experience of empiricism, now that the qualification "actual" has been added. Consider other descriptive labels for philosophical movements: "voluntarism," "intellectualism," "realism," "idealism," "pragmatism," "analytic philosophy," etc. Is there any difference detectable in the label "existentialism"? Our answer can be guided by the procedure which contemporary existentialists themselves have adopted (and which I shall examine later)—the revival of dead metaphors. To this end Heidegger often exploits (as do Sartre and Merleau-Ponty, following Heidegger) the etymology of the term "existence."

This etymology, in contrast to the other labels, incorporates a reference to a movement. (Thus Merleau-Ponty can allude to "the momentum of existence.")[57] When we saw earlier that an existentialist philosophy traces a "development" by which something "becomes actual" (e.g., an individual or a philosopher) we were recognizing existentialism's commitment to movement as a subject matter. Not surprisingly, the significant movement for existentialism is human. In Kierkegaard's metaphor of *Stages on Life's Way,* "existence is apprehended as a movement of going along a way." Kierkegaard can be more specific: "Walking forward is the image of existence."[58]

When we later see that existential method (in its involvement with movement as a subject matter) is also conceived as a movement, the fuller significance of movement for existentialism will emerge, though the precise character of the movement will have to wait upon a still later analysis of the stages involved in it. But for the present we can chalk up another argument for interpreting existentialism as a specimen of a philosophical movement: by virtue of the philosophical significance existentialism accords movement, it lends itself to interpretation at a higher level as a philosophical movement.

The existential subject matter (if that term can be risked) which Heidegger analyzes is generally the way man "goes about" (*umgeht*) the "world about" (*Umwelt*) him. Heidegger's method of treating this subject matter is at the same time conceived as a specific way of "going about" this "world." Heidegger breaks up the German term for movement, *Be-weg-ung,* so that it comes to mean "going along a way [Weg]."[59] As I have already noted, he finds too that *Erfahrung* ("experience") is associated etymologically with *fahren* ("to journey").[60] But Heidegger thinks in Greek as well as in German. *Odos* in Greek means "way" or "journey [along a way]"; and the compound *methodos* means "following up [along a way]," a "pursuit," an "inquiry," and finally a "method of inquiry."

Thus there is a certain general "structure of movement that belongs to the work [of the existentialist], as it works itself out [or "becomes actual"] in him"—if I may adopt Heidegger's appraisal for my own purposes.[61] This general structure is found in Sartre too: he takes over Heidegger's *Umwelt*—"the world of our desires, our needs, our acts" which is "furrowed by narrow and difficult roads," and he employs the notion of "hodological space."[62] When in the longest of his works, his three volumes on Flaubert, Sartre attempts to understand the "experience [which] has sought its expression a hundred times" in Flaubert's writings, one kind of evidence he considers reliable is proposed by Flaubert's edict "There is no better proof of the limited character of human life than movement [*déplacement*]." Sartre explains that "a journey [*déplacement*] stimulates Flaubert to actualize his life as a whole." The climax of Sartre's analysis is a "ride" Flaubert took wherein he "saw the image of his life." Similarly, the selection from *Madame Bovary* to which Sartre has devoted the most attention in the three volumes is her seduction during the ride in the horse cab.[63]

Not only does existence in an existentialist analysis refer to a movement, but almost any stretch of such an analysis also "follows up" some more specific movement. If "journies" and "rides" are prominent, there is also much "sliding" (*glissement*) and "gliding" (*vol à voile*) in Sartre. Heidegger goes in for "flight," and Sartre retains this movement. In Kierkegaard, as well as in Heidegger and Sartre, the "fall" of man has obviously more than merely biblical significance. There are various forms of "turning" in Heidegger, culminating in "whirling" (*Wirbel*), which is perhaps reproduced in Sartre by "merry-go-rounds" (*carrousels*) and "whirligigs" (*tourniquets*).[64]

Some of these specific movements will be examined later. But process philosophies are a dime a dozen and include the philosophy of Hegel, who is, after all, the preferred antagonist of existentialists. Development in a process philosophy can take the form of an "actualization" (the bringing into existence) of a possibility (an idea or an ideal) which did not previously exist. And this implication (we have noted) is sometimes relevant to existentialist usage: the young bride in Sartre entertains the possibility of becoming a prostitute. But Aristotle and the tradition had already treated movement as the actualization of a possibility or potentiality.[65]

EKSTASIS

To get deeper than the notion of actualization, in order to discover what is distinctive about the existential "structure of movement," we need to probe further the dead metaphor embedded in the etymology of "existence," as Heidegger does in order to distinguish his usage from the traditional use of *existentia* as more or less a synonym for *actualitas*. The Greek noun *ekstasis* comes from a verb which in its passive form means "to be dislocated" or "displaced." (Compare the Latin derivative *ex-sistere*, which can carry the weaker meaning of "emerge" or "become actual," with which we have gotten by so far.) The Greek noun itself means "dislocation," "displacement," "removed from its proper place." Our English term "ecstasy" derives from a late usage which is found in the New Testament and refers to "being moved outside oneself" (e.g., of one's body in a "trance").

Of course, broadly speaking any movement involves "dislocation" or "displacement." Usually in a process philosophy, continuity of movement or development in the long run prevails over discontinuities. To the extent that dislocation in a stricter sense is characteristic of an existential philosophy, discontinuity prevails. The contrast we can be more precise about later, when we compare Hegel's philosophy, in which continuity of development does prevail in the long run, with Kierkegaard's, in which this continuity is disrupted.[66]

For the present let us restrict our attention to differences in etymology. Hegel explains that the derivation from the Latin *existere* "suggests the fact of having proceeded from the ground."[67] The existentialist in effect disrupts this process when he defines existence as contingent—that is, as without ground or reason.[68] The reduplicative *sistere* reacquires its vigor, and the *ex* is no longer an easygoing "from," so that *ex-sistere* gains the stronger etymological meaning "to stand forth outside of itself."[69]

This metaphor of spatial dislocation can be read into Kierkegaard's free translation from Aristotle: "The individual remains outside and is not subsumed in the concept." "Subsumed" introduces into the Aristotelian formulation the Hegelian movement of *Aufhebung,* which we shall see Kierkegaard subvert; "remains outside" acquires a correspondingly active, dynamic, dislocating sense entirely absent from Aristotle. In short, we have two existential movements: put in "Aristotelian" terms, the movement by which the possible becomes actual and the subversive movement by which it is recognized that the first movement, inasmuch as it is a matter for the particular individual to decide, will disrupt any effort to bring it within the scope of a general philosophical concept.

OUTSIDE

When it comes to specifying the character of the dislocation and where "outside" is, existentialists differ. In Heidegger "ex-sistence" involves standing outside itself "within the truth of Being."[70] Sartre and Merleau-

Ponty both often use *ekstasis* in what they take to be Heidegger's technical sense, but they in fact elide its implications with the meanings of other terms which in Heidegger convey distinct meanings. Consider the following pileup of terminology in Sartre: "The nihilation by which we achieve a withdrawal in relation to the situation is the same as the *ekstasis* by which we project ourselves toward a modification of this situation." Sartre's term *projet* translates Heidegger's *Entwurf*, which refers to the specific movement of dislocation involved in being "thrown forward" toward the future, which is the primary temporal *ekstasis* in *Being and Time*. Sartre's "nihilation" also derives ultimately from (a vaguely Hegelian misunderstanding of) Heidegger. But one prompter fashion in which Sartre gets from Heidegger's ontology in *Being and Time* to his own *Being and Nothingness* is by manipulating the *ex*: "It is characteristic of Heidegger's philosophy to employ in describing existence positive terms, all of which conceal implicit negations. Existence is 'outside of itself, in the world'; it is 'a being of distances.' . . . What all this amounts to is that existence 'is not' in itself."[71]

The phenomenological concept of "meaning" comes to the fore in Merleau-Ponty, but his existentialism too derives from Heidegger, though with a considerable assist from Sartre: "Underneath all the senses of the word meaning, we retrieve the same fundamental notion of a being oriented or polarized toward that which it is not, the subject as *ek-stasis* . . . in a relation of active transcendence between the subject and the world."[72] The term "transcendence" is Heidegger's, and it is employed by Sartre as well as Merleau-Ponty to render the force of the *ex*—that is, of the movement by which for both of them existence is "outside of itself, in the world" as "a being of distances." Hence "transcendence" is blurred not just with "project" but even with "existence" itself.[73]

At the same time, all these terms are equated by Sartre with our freedom. Thus when he deals in *Huis clos* (*No Exit*) with our enclosure in our "habits and customs," this disavowal of our freedom can take the form of another manipulation of the *ex*—of a disavowal that there is an outside:

> And outside? Outside? Outside, on the other side of these walls? There is a passageway. And at the end of this passageway? There are other rooms and other passageways and staircases. And then? That is all there is.[74]

The other configurations, "in the world" and "distance," will be examined in chapter 3, as Heidegger's contribution to existentialism, and the significance of the manipulation of prefixes will be examined in chapter 4.

Heidegger uses "ekstatic" as a technical term, but because of its misleading associations in English, I shall use instead the term *ex-sistential* when I wish to bring out the dislocated or dislocating character of existence. But a feature of Sartre's tendency to vulgarize (whether or not it is inspired by Heidegger's "everydayness") is to take Heidegger's spatial metaphors in a literal, everyday sense. Thus he attaches *ex-sistential* significance to "ecstasy" in the usual English sense of a trancelike state that takes us "outside" of ourselves. The vision in *Nausea* of "existence" is itself described as "ecstasy." In this vision "things" are dislocated when they become detached from their "meaning," their "relations," their "explanations," so that their "contingency" is felt. Their "existence" no longer proceeds, as in Hegel, from a ground; in Sartre's own terminology, they have no "reason" to be and are *de trop*.[75] "Ecstasy" is similarly used of a trancelike state in *Saint Genet*, where the crucial episode in Genet's life is in question, and Sartre offers several analyses of Flaubert's trances.[76]

DISCONTINUITY

This is enough terminology. Its implications are best pinned down for the time being with a few examples of discontinuity. Sartre's style in *Nausea* provides a readily accessible illustration of disrupted continuity. In the second paragraph "a word is left out," another "crossed out (possibly 'force' or 'forge'). . . ." The reader is expected to conclude that the writer would have been guilty of forcing matters or of forgery if he had supplied his experience with a continuity which his experience in fact lacked. It does not proceed from a ground. The diary form of *Nausea* is itself a way of exhibiting discontinuities, explicitly so when an entry begins by disavowing the previous entry: "How could I have written that pompous, absurd sentence yesterday . . . ?"[77] The ultimate discontinuity is the discrepancy between the novel the diarist plans to write at the end of the novel and the novel as we have it, which is itself only the diary.

Other examples of discontinuity we have already encountered. "Walking forward" can be generalized by Kierkegaard as "the image of existence," because life itself "must be lived forward." But he visualizes this forward movement as the disruption of the "backward" movement of reflection, whereby one reaches some understanding of his life.[78] There is a similar disruption of continuity in Sartre's very different example of the "vertigo of possibility" that reflection can induce. A young bride's envisaging the possibility of becoming a prostitute would hardly have been regarded in 1939 (when Sartre diagnosed the episode as a process of development; too much discontinuity would have been felt to intervene between the two roles, so that we have, instead, an illustration of what Kierkegaard calls "blunt oppositions." Similarly, the to-and-fro movement of the wiggling bottom exhibits a movement which is *ex-sistential* in its structure inasmuch as the movement of one wiggle in one direction is the dislocation of the preceding wiggle in another direction. During the ride in which Flaubert "saw the image of his life," he suffered some sort of blackout or epileptic seizure and fell. Sartre characterizes the episode as an "explosion" (*éclatement*).[79] I am suggesting that it is Sartre's *ex-sistentialism* which has induced him to attribute more significance to this dislocation than previous interpreters or apparently Flaubert himself.

Even Mailer's "existential" act can perhaps again be accommodated: "Those kids went out and did something that they had never done before." Thus on one hand the action they performed was discontinuous with what they had done in the past. They also "did not know how it was going to turn out." Thus on the other hand the future consequences of the action might well turn out to be discontinuous with what they thought they were doing when they performed the action. But ordinarily when we act, we take more or less for granted certain continuities that govern our course of action: out of habit, because of our characters, we continue to act more or less the way we have acted in the past; we do not usually do something we have "never done before," and we usually act with some conviction as to how our action is likely to turn out in the future. As a final example of the distinctively dislocated "structure of movement" delineated by an *ex-sistential* course of action, recall the discontinuities played up by Iris Murdoch's definition of existentialism as "freedom . . . 'to fly in the face of the facts,' escaping from science by a wild leap of the will." Instead of facing up to the facts, as we conventionally try to do when we act, we are flying in the face of the facts; instead of respectfully acknowledging the place of science in our lives, we are escaping from science; instead of keeping our moral feet on the ground, we are making a wild leap of the will.

EMOTION

I originally took up these examples of existential action in an effort to get at the subject matter of an existential ethics. Another subject matter which was then contemplated was existential psychology. Sartre's *Sketch of a Theory of the Emotions* is the only completed portion of a comprehensive work he once planned in psychology. Although the *Sketch* is usually classified as phenomenological, along with Sartre's other pre-World War II writings, his singling out this portion of psychological subject matter can be accounted for as *ex-sistential*.[80] "E-motion" is etymologically close to *ekstasis*. It was once applied, in a now obsolete sense, to a "physical moving out," a "transference from one place to another," and its application to being psychologically moved "outside" oneself may be regarded as metaphorical. We are now recognizing that an *ex-sistential* experience is distinctively dislocated or dislocating. The distinction is implicit in the emotions Sartre selects for treatment. The more delicate (*émotions fins*) he neglects in favor of the dislocating ones, in which one does indeed feel "moved outside" of oneself—for example, fear, anger, and other violent emotions.[81]

Two profoundly dislocating emotions are favored in existentialism: anxiety (or dread) and despair. These are the only two emotions to which Kierkegaard has devoted separate works. Let us take despair as an example, because we have seen that Kierkegaard's focus on this emotion has disconcerted Thody. The psychological dislocation despair entails is brought out when Kierkegaard generalizes in the fashion that Thody finds so unwarranted:

> Perhaps there lives not one single individual who after all is not to some extent in despair, in whose inmost depths there does not dwell a disquietude, a disturbance, a discord.[82]

But despair is not just an inescapable ingredient (according to this citation) in the way one lives one's life; despair receives the biblical identification *The Sickness unto Death*. Thus a reference to the dislocation that threatens life itself is introduced. Death plays a comparable if more intricate role in Heidegger's treatment of anxiety.

Consider too the way Sartre handles a life in his existential psychoanalyses. His starting point is *ex-sistential*, in that he seizes upon some dislocation. In the case of Baudelaire, it is "the first shock" (his mother's remarriage) by which he was "split apart" (*s'était fêlé*).[83] The title of the first chapter of Sartre's analysis of Genet, like the title of Kierkegaard's treatment of despair, carries a metaphorical reference to the dislocation of his life itself, "The Melodious Child That Died in Me Long before I Was Severed by the Ax." Sartre's analysis starts out identifying the severing of this first death: "Genet is a passéist"—that is, someone who is dislocated because he lives in the past of a childhood memory. Sartre admits,

> This "rupture" [*coupure*] is not easily located—it shifts around. . . . But this does not matter. . . . His life is divided into two heterogeneous parts.[84]

The actual location does not matter, because what does, *ex-sistentially* speaking, is the fact of dislocation itself. Simularly, Sartre's analysis of Flaubert is an analysis of the dislocations in his life whereby he eventually became committed to the novelist's life of the imagination, in order to "dislocate" (*dé-situer*) himself and ultimately to "disassociate himself from himself" (*se désolidariser de soi*). Although he regularly engaged in "dislocating performances" (*pratiques de dé-situation*),[85] his life, like Baudelaire's, is more fundamentally dislocated by an "irreversible event which cut his life in two."

Flaubert's most significant attempt to "dislocate himself" is by committing himself to the novelist's life of the imagination. This attempt requires for its analysis its distinction from an ordinary life. Now of course anyone lives to some extent an imaginary life (or even relives the remembered life of childhood). That Sartre's analysis is intended to reach a higher level of philosophical generality than the particular experiences of Flaubert is suggested by his regarding his analysis as a "sequel" to his general phenomenological analysis of the imagination, in which he first established a distinction of level between ordinary life and the life of the imagination.[86]

Role Playing

A work of Kierkegaard's provides an easier example of how an existential dislocation can be combined with a distinction of level to reach higher generality. It happens to be an "esthetic" work which is not fitted to his sequence of stages and so can be considered separately, even though we have not yet examined his methodologically crucial notion of stages. This work has a double title: *The Crisis and A Crisis in the Life of an Actress*. Kierkegaard is not entirely explicit about the implications of the doubling. But since the work is not too much more than a jeu d'esprit, we can be satisfied with an approximate interpretation. On one hand there is *The Crisis*, the *general* sense of dislocation, which anyone has to go through when he recognizes (in Sartre's phrase) that his life is cut "in two" and yet at no neatly locatable juncture, because (to return to what I take may be Kierkegaard's implication) one is either too young or too old for the role one has to play. On the other hand (and here there is no uncertainty as to the interpretation) Kierkegaard is referring to a crisis in the life of an individual actress who when she was sixteen played the *specific* role of Juliet. He is offering an appreciation of her performance now that she is taking the role on again nineteen years later. A girl of sixteen may be able to play the role of Juliet during the first part of the play, but she cannot imagine, or summon the dramatic power to render, the intense emotions of Juliet further on in the play. This only an older woman can do, but then she is no longer the youngster Juliet is supposed to be in the play. An actress is either too young or too old for the role.

At both levels something else transpires which has already been singled
out as characteristic of an *ex-sistential* experience—a dislocating development. The actress is transformed during the passage of the years; Juliet
is transformed during the play. But there is also, as it were, the vertical
transformation of the actress, who is either too young or too old, into
Juliet.[87] Kierkegaard's preoccupation with this process of transformation
was betrayed earlier by his reference to the dislocating "transformation"
which the individual must undertake if he is to "go on to the stage . . .
from the street," as compared with the transformation an individual
would have to undertake to become purely philosophical. The comparison, like the movement from the lower level (*A Crisis*) to the higher level
(*The Crisis*), is only feasible insofar as there is some significant relation
between acting a particular role on the stage and acting a general role
in life.[88] In fact (to anticipate a conclusion which Kierkegaard's comparisons encourage but which will be justified only in the sequel), should we
obstinately want to force a subject matter on existentialism, role playing
would be as plausible a candidate as any other, along with the concomitant problem of self-identity. The problem of becoming an individual
or a philosopher could be rephrased in these terms, which at least have
the merit of suggesting a subject matter which cannot be held fixed but
is transformed at a succession of levels, as illustrated by the following
process of reflection on the part of the heroine of an existential novel:

> But then, this also, this cynical distaste for her own role, was delib-
> erately put on, and this contempt for that distaste which she was about
> to contrive, was it not also play acting, and this doubting of that
> contempt . . . ?[89]

Here the transformation clearly involves successive dislocations: at the
first level she is acting an undefined role; at the second she is repudiating
this role with "cynical distaste"; at the third she is repudiating this
"distaste" as itself a "deliberately" adopted role; at the fourth, she is
repudiating "contempt for that distaste" as also roleplaying; at the fifth,
she is beginning to suspect her "doubting of that contempt."
     It is true that her reflection does not reach a philosophical level and
that the succession of levels is confined within the scope of her own
experience as an individual. But the passage is cited by Merleau-Ponty
in *The Phenomenology of Perception* in order to make a general philosophical point. Indeed, whenever we do reach the philosophical level we
are not even there spared dislocation. Heidegger generalizes, "Philosophy
involves a continuous dislocation of standing place and shifting of level
[*Verrückung des Standortes und der Ebenen*]."[90]

Loci

At whatever level of experience *ex-sistentialism* takes a stand, the experience is found significant in that the relations composing it are dislocating or dislocated. My examples have suggested that the relevant relations can differ from one existentialist to another. Although I have not paused to take note of the differences, I am not pretending that the primary locus of the dislocation is the same with each existentialist, any more than is the level at which it takes place. A philosophical movement, like an artistic style, allows room for a certain range of options. In Kierkegaard (if we overlook for philosophical purposes the individual's dislocated relation to God) the primary locus is in the role the individual plays in relation to himself,[91] as illustrated by Kierkegaard's analysis of the emotion of despair. The precariousness of this relation is further illustrated by his analysis of the emotion of anxiety by reference to the "fall" of man.[92] The individual's relation to himself remains precarious in later existentialists, but this relation is not necessarily the primary locus of the threatening dislocation. In Sartre the primary locus of dislocation is in the role the individual plays in relation to the Other. I become conscious of myself in Sartre as the self which the Other is conscious of; or (to retain Sartre's as well as Kierkegaard's biblical metaphor) "my original fall is the existence of the Other" in whose presence I become conscious of having an "outside." The significant moment in the individual's falling outside himself is the e-motion of shame which was felt when Adam and Eve "knew that they were naked."[93] In Merleau-Ponty the presence of the Other is less dislocating than in Sartre. For the primary locus of the dislocation is the body itself and the role it plays in relation to the individual: "Existence is actualized [*se réalise*] in the body," which is "a constant principle of distraction and bewilderment."[94] If we wish to include Heidegger in our list of existentialists, then we have to recognize that, in spite of the attention that we are paying to spatial relations, what are eventually crucial to the "movement" he analyzes as "falling" are temporal relations. The future, past, and present are the three *"ekstases* of temporality," which, he explains, is itself "the *ekstatikon* in the strict sense, . . . the primary 'outside of itself.' "[95] But these specific differences in the primary locus do not alter the fact that the general "structure of movement" characteristic of an existential experience is dislocated or dislocating. I apologize for having employed so clumsy a spatial metaphor. My only extenuation is that it is jargon worthy of an existentialist. In fact it has been employed by an existentialist, as we shall see in the next chapter.

Notes

1. For Mill's use of these distinctions, see my *Human Nature*, 1:14.
2. Ayer, p. 218.
3. *Principles and Persons*, p. xi.
4. This is one reason existentialists seem so untidy. Problems overlap (or, if you prefer, are shuffled together) which are segregated in more piecemeal Anglo-American philosophy.
5. *Revue philosophique de Louvain* 67 (1969): 532.
6. *Postscript*, p. 477. In the Marxist dialectic a "relation" similarly "underlies the disrelation." E.g., "The antithesis between *propertylessness* and *property* . . . still remains indifferent, not grasped as a dynamic connection in its internal relation as contradiction, so long as it is not understood as the antithesis of *labor* and *capital*" (*Writings of the Young Marx*, p. 301; italics in original).
7. See *Irony*, pp. 264–65, for contradictions that verbal irony involves. For an example from *Either* of the contradictory evidence that prompts doubt, see p. 544 below.
8. *Postscript*, p. 319.
9. Ayer, p. 218; Thody, p. 17.
10. *Papirer*, X^2 A 328. This is the doctrine of the *Categories*, but Kierkegaard may have picked it up from some secondary source.
11. Ayer, p. 214; italics mine.
12. Thody, p. 17.
13. Ibid., p. 257.
14. In a BBC Third Programme interview; *Sartre: Romantic Rationalist*, p. 67.
15. *On Liberty*, pp. 3, 68, 81; italics mine. "Originality" (p. 78) is an alternative term to "individuality" and brings out the initiative required of the individual. From the "principle of individuality" is derived the "principle of individual liberty" (e.g., p. 116), which is most clearly formulated on p. 13. For some of Mill's characteristic applications of the principle of individuality, see my *Human Nature*, 2:293, 299, 326, 330, 340, 422.
16. *Human Nature*, 2:243.
17. *On Liberty*, p. 1; italics mine. For the methodological implications of her inspiration, see my *Human Nature*, 2:325–30.
18. Idiosyncratic behavior is significant, if only because it is idiosyncratic: "In this age, the mere example of nonconformity, the mere refusal to bend the knee to custom, is itself a service. Precisely because the tyranny of opinion is such as to make eccentricity a reproach, it is desirable . . . that people should be eccentric" (*On Liberty*, p. 81).
19. *Search for a Method*, pp. 17–18. Sartre is thinking primarily of Jaspers's version of existentialism, but he does not entirely spare his own version.
20. For the classical conception and Socrates' role as its vehicle, see my *Human Nature*, 2:3–24. Its relevance to Mill's individualism (ibid., pp. 364–65) I would reemphasize inasmuch as Socrates (a very different Socrates) is also the vehicle for Kierkegaard's individualism. For Mill's romantic conception of his development into an individual, see pp. 380–82, 387–88; for his historicist conception, see pp. 366–70, 401–3, 42; for his conflation of these various conceptions, see esp. pp. 412–15.
21. These comparisons with my *Human Nature* have not been intended to suggest that the present work is strictly a sequel. It is a different kind of analysis, adapted to different materials. In *Human Nature* I dealt with the development of individualism as a tradition—i.e., with the constraints that were embodied in the conceptions of the role of the individual that were "handed down," so that even individualistic behavior remained in some measure traditional. The changes that did take place in these conceptions I correlated with changes with respect to the subject matter (or subject matters) taken to be relevant to the political role of the individual. Nevertheless, the present work is a sequel in more than the broad sense that I continue to be concerned with

individuation. I have also carried over as an attendant problem the relation between autobiography and philosophy—the problem which was posed with reference to Mill in the concluding chapter of *Human Nature*. Mill's equation of "individuality" with "development" has been noted by previous interpreters—e.g., by Iris Mueller: "The standard by which he tried to justify personal freedom itself was its tendency to foster self-development. It was this process of growth, undefined and obscure in his writings, that Mill came to view as the absolute good and the absolute end of life" (cited in *Human Nature*, 2:447, n. 138). I tried to show that in the *Autobiography*, which reports Mill's own self-development, this process is not entirely undefined and obscure; indeed "development" through "stages" provides Mill's life with its structure. This structure I show Mill derived from Continental philosophy, and to the extent that it does become undefined and obscure in his own writings, it is because it is downgraded in Mill's own philosophy. I am now examining the philosophical significance of this structure insofar as it bears on the problem of starting point in an existential dialectic. I might add that what Mill and Kierkegaard further share in common as postromantics is the significance we would accord to the conjunction in their lives of a relation to an authoritarian father and a relation to a married muse. I shall consider this conjunction in Kierkegaard's case in chap. 15.

22. *On Liberty*, p. 77; *Human Nature*, 2:370–75.

23. For the place I assign the *Autobiography* in relation to Mill's philosophy, see *Human Nature*, 2:376–80, 432.

24. For the full quotation, see p. 36 above. Contrast Hegel's interpretation of Descartes as relative—i.e., as the starting point of a development culminating in the absolute knowledge Hegel's philosophy embodies. Sartre's interpretation of Descartes himself as "the absolute" likewise involves at the philosophical level an interpretation of Descartes's *cogito* as a starting point (*Being and Nothingness*, p. 120), but as the consciousness of a particular individual as distinguished from other individuals. Thus the absolute is the consciousness of any individual. If Descartes is singled out, it is because Sartre takes Descartes's consulting his consciousness to be self-conscious, phenomenological justification for individualism.

25. *Existence and Being*, p. 294.

26. Ibid., pp. 355–56.

27. *Prime of Life*, p. 112.

28. *Existentialism Is a Humanism*, excerpted in *Existentialism and Human Emotions*, p. 12.

29. *Human Nature*, 2:378–85.

30. *Climacus*, pp. 124–25. The metaphor of being "enclosed within the system" will be examined in chap. 11, as well as the concomitant criterion whereby the "system" can be regarded as "finished."

31. Ibid., p. 125.

32. Ibid., pp. 124–25.

33. *Human Nature*, 2:386–87.

34. *Existence and Being*, p. 392.

35. This is the reformulation of the problem of starting point which I shall undertake in chap. 7.

36. Poulet, *Le point de départ*, p. 226.

37. Contat, 1:57.

38. The philosopher is Charles Lalo (*L'art loin de la vie*, p. 10).

39. Thody, p. 19.

40. *Postscript*, p. 274.

41. Lowrie, *Kierkegaard*, 1:lx.

42. P. 467. How influential Wahl's interpretation was is suggested by Sartre's citation of this chapter, rather than either Heidegger or Kierkegaard, when he deals with the existentially crucial phenomenon of anxiety (*Sartre*, p. 116).

43. *Papirer*, XI² A 58. For Heidegger's analysis of "everydayness," see chap. 8 below.

44. *Philosophical Fragments*, p. 6.

45. For the rebuke, see *Sartre*, p. 211; for the caress, pp. 215–23. The most sustained illustration of this dragging down is *L'idiot de la famille*, where Sartre borrows general philosophical terminology from Heidegger (e.g., "being-toward-death") as well as from his own earlier philosophical writings (e.g., the feeling of being "contingent" [*de trop*]) and employs it as if it had particular reference to Flaubert. See also n. 74, this chapter.

46. *Transcendence of the Ego*, p. 100. Vertigo is associated with anxiety and awareness of possibility in Kierkegaard (see *Concept of Dread*, p. 55). The distinction between transcendental experience and everyday experience should not be confused with the traditional distinction between the transcendental and the empirical, for Husserl's contribution to existentialism here is that the transcendental dimension comes within the scope of our experience.

47. *Being and Time*, p. 190, n. 4.

48. *Sartre*, p. 297; italics in original. Consistent with this individualism, Sartre rejects Freud's "universal symbolism," explaining, "It is not conceivable that there can exist elementary symbolic relations (e.g., the feces = gold, or a pincushion = the breast) which preserve a constant meaning in all cases" (p. 301).

49. *Saint Genet*, pp. 17, 1–2.

50. *Sartre*, p. 207; *Saint Genet*, p. 18.

51. The issue of what might be called "vulgarization" I brought up at the outset with respect to existentialism as a popular vogue. But vulgarization is a persistent feature not only of the history of thought (e.g., take Nietzsche's appraisal that "Christianity is Platonism for the people," cited in Heidegger's *Introduction to Metaphysics*, p. 11) but also of the history of philosophy itself, though it is rarely examined as an explicitly philosophical problem. Insofar as "existence" is associated with actualization (as we shall shortly see that it is in Kierkegaard and Sartre) there is a built-in predisposition toward vulgarization in the sense illustrated by Sartre's comments on Russian Marxism: Marxism "became a dogma, precisely to the extent that it enabled these mystified peasants to jettison all dogma. It became vulgarized, as it made them more sophisticated. It was alienated in them, as it set them free. It was fossilized, as they transcended and recreated it in each systematic deciphering of their experience. When it became incarnated, its fundamental character as the 'actualization of philosophy' helped to give it a new preponderance in everyone's eyes, as the constancy renewed, lived actuality of the Soviet masses" ("Socialism in One Country," p. 153). Here Sartre uses the term "actualization" as Marxist, but his usage is one juncture at which his existentialism and his Marxism overlap. The process of vulgarization need not go the length of a popular vogue, for it is an important phase in the development of philosophy itself. In *Human Nature* I interpreted Polybius's cyclical philosophy of history as a vulgarization of Plato's philosophy of history and Cicero's political philosophy in his *Republic* and *Laws* as a vulgarization of Plato's political philosophy in his *Republic* and *Laws*. Alongside Sartre's claim on behalf of Russian Marxism (as opposed, presumably, to more sophisticated Western versions) can be set Cicero's claim on behalf of the actual Roman republic (as opposed to Plato's more sophisticated version of an ideal state in his *Republic*): "What argument of theirs [philosophers] is so well formulated as to be compared with a state with a legal system and traditions?" (cited in *Human Nature*, 1:206). Cicero's pushing his own claim to be actually the ideal statesman may be more awkward, but it is similar to Kierkegaard's use of Socrates as a vehicle for his critique of Plato (Hegel), in that Cicero pits the Socrates who "brought philosophy down from the heavens into the cities and homes of men" (cited ibid., 1:290) against the transcendental aspiration of Plato. In spite of their awkwardness, Polybius's and Cicero's vulgarizing reconstructions were, I argue, of more influence on the development of modern political philosophy up until the nineteenth century than the original Platonic works, just as Roman and Hellenistic statues which were copies or derivative were more influential in the development of art than the classical Greek originals that did survive. See the analogies I draw to Renaissance and neoclassical art as *ars post artem* (ibid., 1:129, 133–34).

52. Maurice de Gandillac, "Entretien avec Martin Heidegger," p. 716. The full sentence is the conclusion of the interview and reads, "Whatever his genius, how can one fail to measure the contrast between the requirements of his philosophy [e.g., "resoluteness"] and the flabbily evasive attitude of the 'man in situation'?" I would suggest that Gandillac may be crediting Heidegger's doctrines of "resoluteness" and "situation" with a specificity of historical reference which would be more justified in the case of Sartre than of Heidegger, who was usually more cryptic, even during his Nazi period. Nevertheless the description *mollement évasive* retains its aptness, even when one takes into account Heidegger's posthumous apologia in *Der Spiegel*. The interview took place on September 23, 1966, and was published May 30, 1976. A translation is available in *Philosophy Today* (Winter 1976). Not only is Heidegger here still *mollement évasive* with respect to the sharper issues, but his insistence on posthumous publication, which removed him from the hurly-burly of any ensuing debate, was *mollement évasive*—not to mention his parting thought, "Only a God Can Save Us," though it may have been an editor's decision to erect this into a title. For a general discussion of Heidegger's "politics," see Karsten Harries, "Heidegger as a Political Thinker," in *Heidegger and Modern Philosophy*, ed. Murray.

53. *Introduction to Metaphysics*, p. 36. For *Ereignis*, see chap. 3, n. 118 below.

54. "Existentialism," p. 147.

55. *Yale French Studies* 16 (Winter 1955–56): 44.

56. *Papirer*, X² A 328.

57. *Perception*, p. 137.

58. *Postscript*, p. 402.

59. *Hegel's Concept of Experience*, p. 167. Heidegger further explains, "Consciousness makes its own way [*Weg*]. The being of consciousness resides in its being in movement, its going its way [*sich be-wegt*]." There is similar word play in the preface Heidegger adds to *Being and Time*: "The path [*Weg*] it [*Being and Time*] has taken remains necessary even today, if our existence is to be moved [*bewegt*] by the question of being."

60. To etymologize is itself to appeal to a development.

61. See p. 37 above.

62. *Emotions*, p. 57. Sartre ties Lewin's psychological concept of "hodological" in with Heidegger's ontological conception of the *Umwelt*. The metaphor appears in the title of Sartre's sequence of novels, *Roads to Freedom*.

63. *L'idiot*, 2:1870, 1823.

64. See chaps. 4, 8 below. The present compilation of dynamic, developmental route metaphors is relatively random. Need I remind the reader that we are at a preliminary stage of our analysis? Methodological implications are being deferred, as are the differences between existentialists which would account for the metaphors each prefers.

65. Kierkegaard acknowledges a debt to Aristotle's conception of the "transition from possibility [to actuality] as a movement" (*Papirer*, IV B 117, p. 290). The implication Kierkegaard is pursuing is the following: "In coming into existence the possible becomes actual. . . . Everything which can come into existence shows in this very way it is not necessary" (ibid., V B 15). As in the case of his conception of the individual, Kierkegaard is pitting as Aristotelian his own conception of a "transition" which is a "contingent" movement against the Hegelian conception of "transition" as a "necessary" movement. Although Kierkegaard equates "existence" with "actuality" (e.g., *Postscript*, p. 111), Heidegger undercuts etymologically the traditional meanings of crucial philosophical terminology. See his "Letter on 'Humanism'" (p. 378), where he is attacking Sartre for making this traditional equation. It is only Lowrie's ignorance of the philosophical tradition which leads him to suspect a "monstrous hoax" (p. 22 above) in Sartre's use of Kierkegaard's term "existence." Ayer is debonair and neglects Heidegger's attack: "I shall begin with the elementary question: Why is the movement to which these writers loosely belong called Existentialism? Because they are thought to maintain that existence is prior to essence" (p. 203). But the only one of the existential-

ists he examines who ever maintained this is Sartre, who has disavowed the popular lecture in which he put matters this baldly. Ayer is presumably covering himself with the phrase "thought to maintain." But it is what the existentialists themselves maintain that should count. When Ayer goes on to the question, "What does it mean to say that existence is prior to essence?" (p. 203), he finds his answer by citing not any existentialist but Quine, though I cannot recall his ever citing Heidegger or Sartre in expounding Quine.

66. I intend the prefix "dis" to suggest the discontinuities that the dislocation can involve. In Latin *dis* "indicates separation, dispersal, movement in the opposite direction, and thus contradiction and negation" (Ernout and Meillet, *Dictionnaire étymologique de la langue latine*).

67. *Encyclopaedia*, pt. 1; par. 123, *Zusatz*).

68. In Heidegger's interpretation the philosophical tradition has been committed to the principle "Nothing is without reason"—i.e., to the explanatory procedure of tracking anything back to whatever the reason for it is—ultimately the first cause or God. When we are deprived of the necessity which this reason or ground yields—and of our confidence in scientific and theological procedure—we are confronted not just with contingency but with the problem of finding a starting point. A good illustration of the difference in level (or depth) between Sartre and Heidegger is the fashion in which Sartre takes contingency (and the rejection of the concept of reason or ground) so largely for granted, whereas Heidegger is engaged in an unremitting probe of the tradition (see esp. *Der Satz vom Grund*, where the principle *Nichts ist ohne Grund* takes on deeper implications; but see also *On the Essence of Reasons* and chap. 4, n. 11 below).

69. Heidegger may have selected this metaphor of "outside" because it is already employed by Hegel with reference to the "finite" as determined by what is "outside" of it.

70. "Letter on Humanism," p. 203.

71. *Being and Nothingness*, p. 52.

72. *Perception*, p. 430.

73. "The project as transcendence . . . is existence itself" (*L'idiot*, 2:1813). Thus this existential terminology and the dislocated structure it presupposes have survived Sartre's ostensible conversion to Marxism and his adoption of Marxist terminology: "The continual production of oneself by work and *praxis* is our distinctive structure. . . . Our needs, like our passions or the most abstract of our thoughts, participate in this structure. They are always *outside of themselves toward*. This is what we call existence" (*Search for a Method*, p. 151; italics in original). For the sequel see chap. 3, n. 50 below.

74. *No Exit*, p. 6. See Contat, 1:99. Matters are complicated in two ways. Sartre also employs the metaphor of "outside" with reference to our alienation by the Other (see p. 87 below)—e.g., as members of the bus queue (*Critique of Dialectical Reason*, p. 256). He employs it too with reference to a particular individual at some stage of his life (see n. 45, this chapter). Thus the young Flaubert is "enclosed in himself and exiled outside of his being" and has "the feeling of being himself outside himself" (*L'idiot*, 1:155, 156). As this passage and *Huis clos* illustrate, "enclosure" is another spatial metaphor recurrent in existentialism. "The Wall" was the first short story Sartre published as an adult, and his last play, *Les séquestrés d'Altona* (the theme of enclosure disappears from the English title, *The Condemned of Altona*), he regards as a more complex version of *Huis clos* (Contat, 1:357). See also the metaphors with which he envisages a novelist treating a particular hero: "The man is locked up *inside*; he does not cease to be bound by all these walls which enclose him or to *know* that he is immured. All of these walls make a *single prison*, and this prison is *a single life, a single act*" (*Search for a Method*, p. 110; italics in original). When I have explored the dialectical relation between "the inward and the outward" (or "the internal and the external") in Kierkegaard, I shall deal with his handling of the metaphors of enclosure (p. 428 below), imprisonment (p. 458), and being locked up (p. 484).

75. *Sartre*, pp. 64, 59, 61, 64.

76. *Saint Genet*, p. 17.

77. *Nausea*, p. 56. Sartre has commented on this discontinuous style in his review of Camus's *Outsider*: "*The Outsider* is . . . a novel of discrepancy, divorce and disorientation. Hence its skillful construction. . . . Each sentence is a present moment, but not an indecisive one that spreads like a stain to the following. . . . It is separated by a void. . . . It was in order to emphasize the isolation of each sentence unit that M. Camus chose . . . the present perfect tense. The simple past is the tense of continuity: *Il se promena longtemps.* But with the present perfect, *Il s'est promené longtemps,* . . . the verb is split and broken in two" (*Literary and Philosophical Essays*, pp. 33, 38, 39). This stylistic example is worth considering, because Sartre's one and only debt to American philosophy is to "the American neo-realists . . . when they deny the existence of any but external relations between phenomena" (p. 37). They would have been surprised to learn that this denial is a key to Camus's philosophy of the absurd and to Sartre's own experience of contingency during his nauseous ecstasy.

78. For the full quotation, see p. 166 below. Kierkegaard's reliance on such dialectical oppositions as that found here between "forward" and "backward" suggests a sense in which an individual has to be in two places at once. Hence a meaning of "existing" that Kierkegaard stresses is the "striving" required in order to cope with these oppositions. See chap. 7 below.

79. *L'idiot*, 2:1823, 1467.

80. Similarly, Sartre has selected for his most sustained psychoanalysis Flaubert, who could write of himself, "There is nothing I want so much as to be moved [*ému*]" (cited by Sartre, ibid., 1:525).

81. *Emotions*, pp. 81–82.

82. *Sickness unto Death*, p. 32.

83. *Baudelaire*, p. 19. Sartre similarly refers to the "split" (*fêlure*), Flaubert's own term; see *L'idiot*, 3:161). The idiom of "split" is employed by Kierkegaard too. See p. 246 below.

84. *Saint Genet*, p. 1. Sartre finds a "connection between death and metamorphosis" (p. 2), and (as the table of contents makes clear) his psychoanalysis of Genet is organized in terms of the succession of metamorphoses Genet went through. The term "metamorphosis" itself is borrowed from Kafka (p. 2) but suggests that the transformations in an *ex-sistential* dialectic, because of its discontinuity, are more drastic than can be conveyed by the term "development," which I have employed so far. "Transformation" is apparently used interchangeably with "conversion" (see Sartre's table of contents again), and in chap. 9 I shall consider existential "conversion" as a dialectical disruption of continuity.

85. *L'idiot*, 2:1186, 1787, 1558–63, 1834. Thus Flaubert himself can claim, "I have had two quite distinct existences" (p. 1799). Later we shall see how such doubling lends itself to a dialectical analysis. Sartre also refers to his own life as "divided in two by the war" (*Life/Situations*, p. 48).

86. *Between Existentialism and Marxism*, p. 46; *Sartre*, p. 90.

87. Sartre is similarly preoccupied with the relation between these levels. Thus the problem of the Other, which he confronted in writing *Huis clos* (originally published under the title *Les autres*), was not just the fact of everyday life that "hell is other people" but the problem of the other actor: "I had three friends and I wanted them to act in a play, . . . without any one of them having any special advantage—that is, I wanted them to be onstage together the whole time—because I said to myself, 'If one of them goes off he'll think the others are getting a better role' " (Contat, 1:98–99). The relation between levels is complicated, and becomes dialectically significant, by virtue of the further fact that we can playact not only on the stage but also in life. This ambiguity is presented in the plays *Dirty Hands* and *Kean*. And *Either/Or* can be interpreted as dealing with the relation between acting as an esthetic gesture and as moral action.

88. It should not be supposed that this dropping to the lower level is just an easy way to illustrate more general problems. The existentialist tries to come to grips with what is particular to the individual, and it is here that he runs into his most serious difficulties. Kierkegaard points out, "It is more difficult to describe a particular actor than it is to write a whole esthetics, more difficult to describe one single performance of his than to describe the particular actor. . . . The more one dares use the method of general survey [Kierkegaard's conception of the Hegelian method], the easier it is, for when the volume of material is so great, one still seems to be saying something with these completely abstract observations which everyone knows by heart. The more concrete the task is, the more difficult. God knows how long philosophers will continue to grow fat on the illusion . . . that surveys are the most difficult" (*Papirer*, VI A 133). I trust my present work cannot qualify as a general survey; at least I try to anchor my generalizations to particular performances of individual existentialists.

89. Cited in *Perception*, p. 384.

90. *What Is a Thing?* pp. 1–2. See chap. 4, n. 92 below.

91. The notion of self is subject to the relational analysis which I outlined in chap. 1: "The self is a relation which relates itself to itself" (*Sickness*, p. 24), and despair as a "sickness in the self" (p. 25) is analyzable as "the disrelation in a relation which relates itself to itself" (p. 21).

92. This analysis in *The Concept of Dread* is dialectically the sequel to the analysis of despair in *Sickness*.

93. *Sartre*, pp. 201, 205. Flaubert's "fall" took place in the presence of a menacing sibling (*L'idiot*, 2:1828–31). The reaction of "obscene" to the wiggling bottom, which I shall continue to make much of, of course presumes the presence of the Other. The primacy of this locus is illustrated by the way *L'idiot* starts out: "When the little Gustave Flaubert, astray, still brutish, emerged from infancy, techniques were awaiting him. And roles." This locus is also established with respect to Genet's starting out: "This innocence comes to him from others—everything comes to us from others, even innocence" (*Saint Genet*, p. 6).

94. *Perception*, pp. 353, 166, 27.

95. *Being and Time*, p. 329; see also p. 365.

3

The Dislocated World

Existential philosophy is . . . the expression of a dislocated world.
—Merleau-Ponty

THE POSTWAR PERIOD

When Ayer drew up his list of what existentialists treat, he overlooked political and social problems. Taking these problems into account will complete my canvass of existential subject matter. It is true that the social analysis Sartre offers in the *Critique of Dialectical Reason* and the kind of social history he offers in the third volume on Flaubert he himself regards as Marxist. These works would take us well beyond his starting point as an existentialist. Yet we cannot entirely disregard the tendency of contemporary existentialism to assimilate or to become assimilated by Marxism. If Husserl's antagonism poses the issue of the coherence of contemporary existentialism insofar as it has become phenomenological, a similar issue is posed by the antagonism of the conventional Marxist toward contemporary existentialism insofar as it has become Marxist. But as I indicated earlier, before the criterion of coherence can become fully applicable, the prior question must be posed as to whether existentialism achieves that generality of scope which an intellectual performance must exhibit to pass muster as a philosophy. And this prior question is posed by the familiar argument of Marxist critics, among others, that existentialism is merely a by-product of the experiences of a period in social history which was of "a rather special character." As my requoting of Ayer suggests, this sociological argument runs roughly parallel to the psychological argument that existentialism is the by-product (to requote Thody, too) of "highly specialized personal experiences" which Sartre, for example, suffered "at one period of his life." The parallel prepares us to deal with the assignment of existentialism to a "special" period of social history.

In 1843, we recall, Kierkegaard published *Either/Or*, which he wished to have regarded as the starting point of his "war" against Hegelianism.

But it was only a century later, after World War II, that existentialism finally achieved a large Anglo-American audience. It was in a French version that it became a widely recognized movement, most prominently represented philosophically by Sartre's *Being and Nothingness*, which was published in 1943.

After World War II a respected French academic philosopher, Gaston Berger, was imported from France to provide Americans with an assessment of this new philosophical movement. He reminded his American audience of what France had "in the last thirty years experienced—war, victory, defeat, occupation, and revolution." Berger utilized this historical background in denying that existentialism is a philosophy. "Existentialism" he protested, "is not the philosophy of the post-war years." It merely "gives expression to preexisting feelings," and "its strength comes from its lack of originality." Existentialists merely "follow a trend," and "Sartre is a kind of newspaperman of genius."[1] The implication Berger was pursuing is the one I have anticipated: existentialism need not be explained as a philosophy, for if it can be explained away as the expression of a quite special period in social and political history, it falls short of that generality of scope which is one of the criteria to be met by a philosophy.

LOCAL PERSPECTIVES

This *post hoc propter hoc* argument acquired more detail when it was elaborated by Marxists who were competing after the war with the existentialists for an intellectual following. Our present purposes can be satisfied with a crude paraphrase of the Marxist argument: during World War I the German bourgeoisie suffered the dislocations of defeat and inflation which undermined the value of property; the result was that a member of this class himself suffered a diminished sense of his own value, of his own reality. He felt threatened with being left with nothing; hence Heidegger's existentialism, with its despairing preoccupation with nothingness. During World War II the French bourgeoisie in turn suffered the dislocation of defeat and inflation and felt similarly threatened; hence Sartre's *Being and Nothingness*. Doubtless this sociohistorical depreciation of existentialism could be extended back to take care of Kierkegaard, who was born in 1813, a year (as he tells us himself) when "so many another bad note was put into circulation."[2] He is alluding to the inflation that followed the disastrous defeat of Denmark by Britain during the Napoleonic war.

This explaining away of existentialism by reference to "postwar" periods may dispose of Kierkegaard, Heidegger, and Sartre. But where does it lead us? If after the Napoleonic war we get Danish existentialism; after World War I German existentialism; after World War II French existentialism; then we may be led to the conclusion that after World War III extentialism could turn out to be American. It could be the philosophy of our future, and this prospect may lend a certain socio-historical relevance to an introduction to existentialism, especially since we are living at a time when it is uncertain when this future may begin, though there is evidence (some of which was presented earlier) that the term "existential," along with inflation, has already made considerable headway in America.

Be all this as it may, existentialists themselves do not necessarily deny the philosophical significance of the special sociohistorical circumstances that have been alleged to explain their philosophy away. Merleau-Ponty repudiates the argument that philosophy is a "lofty point of view that transcends with its scope all local perspectives." It does not "keep the world crouching at its feet."[3] When in *Humanism and Terror* he encounters the kind of argument with which Berger depreciates existentialism, Merleau-Ponty quietly turns it around into an argument on behalf of existentialism:

> One is not an "existentialist" for no reason at all, and there is as much "existentialism"—in the sense of paradox, division, anxiety, and decision—in the *Report of the Court Proceedings at Moscow* as in the works of Heidegger. Existential philosophy is said to be the expression of a dislocated world [*monde disloqué*]. Of course. This is what constitutes its truth.[4]

I have already noted the dislocation "anxiety" entails, and dislocation could probably also be discerned as a feature of "paradox," of "division," of "de-cision." Now, however, the dislocation is to be taken as socio-historical.[5] It is here that existentialism is likely to face the challenge that it is the expression of experiences of a period of "a rather special character," especially when the "dislocated world" is so specifically dated by reference to the Moscow trials. Why, in any case, should such general philosophical significance be attached to dislocation?

THE DISCOVERY OF THE WORLD

That the challenge can be raised with Sartre too is suggested by the general significance he, like Merleau-Ponty, would accord the dislocations of relatively recent social history:

> The whole bloody history of this half century was necessary to locate us in a society that was disrupted [*déchiré*]. It was the war which ex-

ploded the antiquated context of our thought. The war, the occupation, the resistance, and the years that followed the war. We were discovering the world.[6]

There is some evidence that this discovery was philosophical, at least in
the textual sense that it betrays a debt to Heidegger's *Being and Time*.

Admittedly, philosophers cannot patent their discoveries, especially in
the case of something as extensive as the discovery of the world. And of
course this is an old philosophical idiom. (One version we have already
come across was applied by Hegel to Descartes's discovering the new
world of the autonomous subject and of autonomous philosophy.) But it
is improbable that it would have been the world that Sartre was discovering (instead of just "a society that was disrupted") were it not for Heidegger's philosophical analysis of the world and of the way its disruption
contributes to its discovery. Similarly, when Merleau-Ponty acknowledges
that "existential philosophy" is "the expression of a dislocated world"
and adds that "this is what constitutes its truth," he may wish to draw
our attention to the Moscow trials rather than to "the works of Heidegger,"
but it is improbable that it would have been the world which was dislocated, or at any rate that its dislocation would have been credited with
its truth-bestowing function, were it not for "the works of Heidegger."

The world Heidegger discovered in these works (in particular in *Being
and Time*) could inspire Sartre and Merleau-Ponty because it was neither
the scientific world of mathematical physics, which usually had been the
world for philosophy since Descartes's *Le monde*, nor the environment of
Darwinian biology but was in a sense a social world—the world of "everyday" life. This "everydayness" I have already anticipated as having perhaps encouraged Sartre's vulgarization of Husserl's transcendental analysis,
but perhaps it may also have encouraged Sartre's and Merleau-Ponty's
vulgarization of Heidegger's own analysis of the world. The "everyday"
character of Heidegger's world will be considered later.[7] What now requires consideration is the way it becomes dislocated.

THE COVER-UP

Dislocation is indispensable to the discovery of the world in Heidegger's philosophy, because this discovery is a dis-covery—a dislocating uncovering. "At the start and for the most part" (*zunächst und zumeist*) the
"world about us" (*Umwelt*) is "covered up" (*verdeckt*) in its structure.
One usually is "pre-occupied" with whatever one happens to be about:
the latch is being used "in order to" (*um-zu*) open the door "in order to"
enter the house; the hammer is being used "in order to" pound the nail
"in order to" put up the etching "in order to" impress my expected

guest with my consummate taste. One goes places and does things. But as one "goes about" (*umgeht*), involved in such "transactions" (*Umgang*), one becomes "scattered" (*zerstreut*) about the *Umwelt* and "distracted." Implicitly one knows what one is about, but such knowledge (*Umsicht*) is not knowledge of how the relations composing the world "hang together" as its *Zusammenhang*—that is (to employ Sartre's phrase), as the "context of our thought." One's "preoccupation" (*Besorgen*), with where one is going and what one is doing tends to "cover up" (*verdecken*) this general structure.[8]

How then is the world dis-covered (*ent-deckt*)? When some piece of equipment from this context cannot be used in the usual way (e.g., the handle of the hammer breaks, or the nail that is needed is wanting), the reference (*Verweisung*) which is implicit in the "in order to" (e.g., of the nail) is "disrupted" (*gestört*), and the other referential relations themselves emerge between the different pieces of equipment (hammer, nail, etching), each of which has its place assigned by my "pre-occupation." The order of the ordinary having been dislocated in one of its sectors, I discover its topography as the "context" of the transactions in which I have been engaged.

The way this "context" is then seen to "hang together" in its "structure" is set forth by the nursery rhyme:

> For want of a nail, the shoe was lost,
> For want of a shoe, the horse was lost,
> For want of a horse, the rider was lost,
> For want of a rider, the battle was lost,
> For want of a battle, the kingdom was lost,
> And all for the want of a horseshoe nail.

In short, the world has been there all along, but it is discovered as a "context" only when a "break" (*Bruch*) occurs, dislocating its structure.[9]

The context discovered in the nursery rhyme is not simply the structure of a feudal kingdom which we have forgotten all about because its technology is primitive. During World War II the rhyme was framed and hung on the wall of the Anglo-American Services of Supply headquarters in London. Nor does the rhyme merely betray military and technological preoccupations. Another version of the rhyme was duly entered in *Poor Richard's Almanack* by Benjamin Franklin, a significant embodiment of the preoccupations of *The Protestant Ethic and The Spirit of Capitalism*, according to Max Weber, who himself significantly embodied preoccupation with the social world on the part of a new sector of the academic world—that assigned to the social historian. One ordinarily confronts only whatever one is occupied with (a nail to be pounded), without confronting one's pre-occupations which compose a network of referential relations. These preoccupations themselves are jumbled together, but in a fashion (we shall see later) which permits their analysis as a social world.

In Sartre's version of his generation's discovery of a social world, it took "the war" to "explode" the "antiquated context" of the thinking of his generation: they finally recognized the "context" and saw that it was "antiquated." The dislocations of the "occupation, the resistance, and the years that followed the war" functioned in the same way; in fact "the whole bloody history of this half century was necessary to locate us in a society that was disrupted."

Aufhebung

Before I can continue with Sartre's or Merleau-Ponty's sociohistorical version of Heidegger's *Umwelt*, I must try to give some impression of the distinction Heidegger uncovers between this *Umwelt* and the world of scientific investigation. For the traditional effort in modern philosophy—whether it is Descartes's philosophy or Hume's or Kant's or Hegel's—is to render philosophy scientific. And the result of this effort, according to Heidegger, is another way in which the *Umwelt* has been covered up. I shall take matters step by step by tracing the recovery of first its spatial character and then its temporal and historical character.

In Hegel the effort to render philosophy scientific takes the form of the movement of *Aufhebung*. In English *Aufhebung* is often condemned to such opaque translations as "subsumption" or "sublation." It has, as Hegel comments, "a double meaning." The movement of *Aufhebung* is, on one level, a "removal" in the negative sense of "eliminating," "canceling out" something; but the movement is also a "removal," a "taking up" to a higher level where something is "preserved."[10] (The German *bewahren*, unlike the translation "preserve," indicates that truth [*Wahrheit*] is at stake in this restoration of continuity.) Now this movement of *Aufhebung* is exemplified by Hegel's *Science of Logic*, in which he explains that it is a movement whereby whatever is "preserved" as "true" is "withdrawn from an existence that is exposed to external influences."[11]

This withdrawal is assumed by existentialists not to have begun with Hegel but to have been characteristic of the development of the entire intervening philosophical tradition, though Descartes's contribution is regarded as the most decisive. If Hegel's *Aufhebung* is the culminating illustration of this process, it is largely because *Aufhebung* was the movement which was crucial to Hegel's interpretation of the way philosophy itself (as well as other areas of human experience) had developed during its history to its culmination in his own scientific philosophy. Hegel thereby provided existentialists (as we have already observed to some extent in Kierkegaard's case) with a perspective that embraced the history of philosophy as a single tradition, so that they have obtained a certain sense of scope with respect to what they are breaking away from in becoming existentialists.

Here we have a partial answer to the persistent question why existentialism should be so technical: existentialism does not start out as a spontaneous, straightforward response on the part of the existentialist as an individual to his own existence—that is, as we are by now aware, to his "actual" personal experiences as "dislocating." It acquires what was earlier described as its "double character," since the existentialist can only gain philosophical access to his own response to his own existence by subverting the dominant tendency of the philosophical tradition to abstract from existence. This subversive operation is a higher-level form of dislocation that *ex-sistentialism* enforces. To carry it out, the existentialist has to turn back to the tradition, dis-cover and question its presuppositions and procedures; and in the process existentialism becomes as technical as the tradition itself.

This subversive operation cannot be considered as such until we have taken existential method into account.[12] But now that we have recognized a certain rationale for the technicalities of existentialism, we are perhaps ready to seek understanding of several of the broader technical terms which are associated with existence as a subject matter. For the present we can neglect the imprint of existential method which the terms bear. Heidegger's discovery of the *Umwelt* is a sufficient model.[13] But we must refocus the present discussion on the individual.

<h2>SUBSTANCE</h2>

In the preceding chapter we have seen that contemporary existentialists took over from Heidegger the dislocated structure of *ex-sistence*. It is this "structure of movement" (in Heidegger's phrase) which has lent existential subject matter a measure of coherence. Attention to the dislocation implicit in the *ex* of existence also enabled us to revise the more superficial conception of existentialism as simply an appeal to "actual" experience. We can now revise the conception of existentialism as an appeal to the experience of the individual who "actually" exists. Of course the philosophical tradition has acknowledged (at least since Aristotle) the "actual" existence of the individual—but, the existentialist protests, as a "substance." Heidegger cites from Descartes the definition of a substance as something which "needs nothing to exist [*nulla re indiget ad existendum*] besides itself."[14] But Heidegger complains that Descartes presupposed this definition, as an inheritance from the scholastic tradition which went back to Aristotle, without examining its implications.

This traditional definition Heidegger subverts by redefining "the substance of man" as "existence." The two technical terms can be brought into conjunction, since their roots carry comparable spatial implications. Here we must turn from the *ex* to the *sistere in ex-sistere*, which is merely the reduplicated form of *stare* ("stand"). On one hand "*substance*" indicates that what is so characterized "underlies" and stays itself essentially unchanged, whatever changes take place in relation to it, and thus retains the identity that renders it an individual. It then is, according to Heidegger, "*selbständig*"; it "stands by itself," is "self-supporting," and "the substantiality of such a substance" is its "remaining static" (*ständigen Verbleib*).[15] What is so characterized has acquired the abstract fixity, independence, and objectivity of a thing—the characteristics which were required when the nature of things became the privileged subject matter of philosophy as oriented toward and by scientific investigation.

BEING-IN-THE-WORLD

These traditional spatial implications cannot survive the dislocation which is introduced when Heidegger redefines "the substance of man" as "existence." Man is no longer *selbständig* when he is visualized as "exsisting": he "stands forth outside himself" in relation to the things he is "going about" in the *Umwelt*, and his being is "displaced" by virtue of his "pre-occupations which assign these things to their places in this world. The hammer, the nail, the etching, all assume their "significance" by virtue of my consummate taste; yet I am then "referentially dependent"[16] on the hammer, the nail, the etching—and on the prevailing canons of taste, if my own is to be rated consummate. Thus the subversion of the spatial implications of *sub-stance* by those of *ex-sistence* is the transformation of a subject matter, which (it was traditionally assumed) could be abstracted, held fixed and separate during the progress of its scientific investigation, into the dynamic relational context that compose the *Umwelt* that one is "going about" in Heidegger.

The traditional "self-supportingness" of substance is also subverted in Sartre's nauseous vision of the world, but by mocking the supine tiredness of existence, and (at a higher level, I would guess) of the tradition itself:

> All things, gently, tenderly, were letting themselves exist like weary women giving way to laughter, saying, "It's good to laugh," in a damp voice; they were sprawling in front of each other, abjectly confessing their existence. . . .

Softnesses, weaknesses, yes. The trees were floating. Gushing toward the sky? Rather, collapsing. At any moment I expected to see the tree trunks shrivel up, like weary penises. They didn't want to exist, only they could not help themselves. . . . Weary and old, they kept on existing, reluctantly, simply because they were too weak to die.[17]

The vulgarized Heideggerianism of this vision of existence is more readily appreciated if we take into account how Sartre translates *Geworfenheit* ("thrown-ness") in expounding his famous paradox: "We are condemned to be free, . . . thrown into freedom, or as Heidegger says, 'délaissés' [left behind, abandoned]."[18] In Sartre our *délaissement* becomes our passivity, and this is the theme that he elaborates on in the first line: "All things . . . were letting themselves exist like weary women giving way to laughter" ("se laissaient aller à l'existence comme ces femmes lasses qui s'abandonnent au rire"). Sartre prefers the reflexive *se laissaient* and *s'abandonnent* as providing scope for our freedom.[19]

Aside from his debt to Heidegger, there are also direct reminiscences elsewhere in Sartre of Descartes's traditional definition of substance as "something which needs nothing to exist besides itself." For one way in which "nothingness" enters Sartre's analysis in *Being and Nothingness* is as something a human being feels he "lacks" in order to be himself. In his later supposedly Marxist *Critique of Dialectical Reason*, he borrows from Hegel and Engels, and Heidegger's *Umwelt* becomes an environment: what a human being "lacks" becomes more fundamentally what he "needs" for survival.[20] His is an "existence" which (as Hegel put it before existentialism was ever heard of) "is exposed to external influences."

SPATIAL REPRESENTATION

A terminological complication here can no longer be overlooked. There are two terms in Hegel and Heidegger for "existence." In addition to *Existenz*, whose etymology has already been examined, there is the synonym *Dasein*, which Hegel employs in the passage I have cited and translated "existence." Hegel explains that *Dasein* when "etymologically construed means 'being in a certain place.' "[21] But he adds that "spatial representation [*Raumvorstellung*] is irrelevant here," and etymology can accordingly be overlooked. Thus the usual translation for *Dasein* in Hegel is "determinate being." However, in translating Heidegger etymology cannot be overlooked, for "*Dasein* takes up space, and this is to be understood literally."[22] Heidegger accordingly reasserts the relevance of spatial representation, and the usual translation for *Dasein* in Heidegger is *being-there*.[23] Heidegger also reasserts the relevance of spatial representation when he redefines "the *substance* of man" as "*existence*" (*Existenz*).

We have watched him pit against the traditional spatial implications of "substance" the dislocating spatial implications of *ex-sistence*. This reassertion of the relevance of spatial representation provides a certain justification for my previous reliance on the makeshift etymological metaphor of "dislocation."

Kierkegaard too found spatial representation relevant. In *Johannes Climacus* he recalls learning Latin grammar. But the grammar took on larger implications:

> When it was explained to Johannes Climacus that, for example, the accusative implies extension in time and space, that it is not the preposition but the relation which governs the case, then it all expanded for him. The preposition vanished; extension in time and space became a huge, empty image for his intuition. His *imagination* was set in *motion*. . . . What had hitherto entertained him on his walks was filled space. He could not get it sufficiently tightly around himself. . . . But now instead of the filled space his imagination took in empty space.[24]

At the time this may have been, he admits, "an almost vegetative tendency to drowse in imagination," but it acquired a more mobile reference during the period when he got started as a philosopher by launching his attack on Hegel. He then adopted the heading "Philosophica" for a series of entries in his *Journal*, and under this heading the subheading "Problemata" for the problems which perplexed him the most. He picks out "movement" as "perhaps one of the most difficult problems in all philosophy." He remarks that Hegel "is essentially occupied with movement . . . in logic" but has not in fact "ever accounted for movement."[25]

Not even as individualistic a philosopher as an existentialist works out his problems as single-handedly, as Kierkegaard likes to boast. He soon found an ally in Trendelenburg. "There is no philosopher," he recalls, "from whom I have benefited as from Trendelenburg."[26] What attracted Kierkegaard in particular was Trendelenburg's taking movement as his first principle. "Not," Trendelenburg stresses, the abstract "movement of pure thought," which was the movement ostensibly exhibited by the development of Hegel's system, but "spatial movement [*räumliche Bewegung*] . . . without which pure thought could not move from its place." This "secret presupposition" with which Hegel's ostensibly "presuppositionless philosophy" in fact started Trendelenburg ferrets out. Thus where Hegel "tries to presuppose nothing except pure thought which possesses no external intuition, no image [*Bild*] but simply itself," in fact, Trendelenburg continues,

Movement reflecting the images in the space of the imagination lends thought the logical structure which it could never have produced from itself. By means of this alien but hidden service, the productions of pure thought receive a sensuous freshness without which they would have been less than fleeting shadows.[27]

This "service" has to be kept "hidden" by Hegel, inasmuch as this spatial movement is impure: we shall soon see that such imaginative representation is (in Hegel's own terms) the exposure of thought to "external influences." And it is precisely this impurity which the development of the Hegelian dialectic is supposed to have "eliminated" with its movement of *Aufhebung*, as soon as the "scientific" sphere of "thought" and the *Logic* is reached.

SPATIAL MOVEMENT

There is a difference between spatial movement in Trendelenburg and in existentialism. In Trendelenburg it is "a geometrical movement which designs structures in the space of the imagination" ("in dem Raume der Vorstellung die Gestalten entwirft").[28] In existentialism the movement is not "geometrical." While acknowledging his debt to him, Kierkegaard yet protests, "Trendelenburg recurs far too much to examples drawn from mathematics and the natural sciences."[29] As examples to be cited will illustrate, spatial movement in existentialism is not to be envisaged in the mathematical terms of Newtonian physics, where, as Heidegger remarks,

no movement or direction of movement is preferred to another. Every place is equivalent to every other. No point of time is superior to any other. Every force is only its consequences in motion—that is, is determined only by the magnitude of change of place in the unit of time. Every occurrence must be interpreted in terms of this blueprint of nature.[30]

Existentialists are notorious for going outside the sphere of scientific thought and indulging in imaginative representation. It is usually supposed that this is a question of existentialism as a philosophy having been contaminated by literature, since existentialists characteristically resort to esthetic genres as well as to philosophical works. But their reliance in their philosophical works on imaginative representation is a philosophical refusal to withdraw in their thinking from the "external influences" to which it is thereby "exposed." Existential thought is *ex-sistential* in that its movement (in Trendelenburg's phraseology) "designs structures in the space of the imagination."

THE SPACE OF THE IMAGINATION

Before examining some more specific *ex-sistential* structures as examples, we should take into consideration their general construction. This can be more readily understood if we first examine Hegel's analysis of *Vorstellung*, which I have been translating as "imaginative representation."[31]

The psychological operation which precedes *Vorstellung*, broadly conceived, and which it presupposes is *Anschauung*, "sense impression" or "sense perception." At the level of mere "sense impression," we are "outside of ourselves in the medium of space and time, which are the two forms of externality [*Aussereinander*]." Our "mind is immersed in the external material, is one with it, and has no other content besides that of the perceived object."[32] This is the level where it is almost entirely "exposed to external influences."

The next level is "recollection," which is the lowest level of "imaginative representation" broadly conceived. Hegel is fond of playing with the etymological meaning of recollection [*Er-innerung*] as "inwardizing" or "internalizing." Thus he explains that "mind posits the sense impression as its own, pervades it, makes it into something inward, recollects, and inwardizes itself in it." Once this "internalization" is achieved, the mind no longer needs to receive an external impression, since it can now externalize within itself as an "imaginative representation" the external impression it has previously internalized.[33]

Vorstellung is not only the "imaginative representation" of something in the setting of its spatial (and temporal) relations but also itself a spatial metaphor, and Hegel himself exploits its etymological meaning of "placing" something "before" the mind.[34] In performing this operation, *Vorstellung* is conscious of the internalized impression as an image of whatever it was that the image represents. However, this "synthesis" of "impression" and "image" is not consummated and remains unstable: the impression is no longer simply a mere "this," which is spatiotemporally a mere "here" and a mere "now," for the image under which it is subsumed is universal, but it is not completely subsumed. The applicability of the spatial metaphor *Vor-stellung* to the operation betrays the duality that still has to be overcome. It is not overcome by the "imagination," strictly conceived as the "reproductive representation" (*Einbildungskraft*), which as voluntary is distinguished from representation at the lower level of "recollection" where the representation is "unconsciously preserved." Nor is it overcome at the higher level of "productive" or "creative" or "poetic imagination" (*Phantasie*), for even its productions are still dependent on materials that were originally derived from the data of "sense impression."

To this extent the mind is still "exposed to external influences," for "the general representation is the internal side; the pictorial image [*Bild*] . . . is the external side," and "these two mutually opposed determinations still fall apart."[35]

HOVERING

This duality of *internal* and *external* is only finally overcome in Hegel at the level of "thought" (*Denken*), where the movement of *Aufhebung* at last transcends "imaginative representation." "Thought" reaches its own climax in conceptual knowledge. But we do not need to climb to this level, since Kierkegaard refuses to go along with the *Aufhebung* with which Hegel transcends the imaginative level:

> Imagination . . . is not a faculty on the same level with the others but . . . the faculty *instar omnium* [i.e., the faculty that operates on behalf of all the others]. What feeling, knowledge, or will a man has depends in the last resort upon what imagination he has—that is, upon how these things are reflected.[36]

To elude the Hegelian movement of transcendence here, Kierkegaard goes on to appeal to Fichte, who "quite rightly assumed, even in relation to knowledge, that imagination is the origin of the categories." It is characteristic of Kierkegaard to rely on traditional philosophers for epistemological doctrines.[37] I have cited Hegel on the relation to knowledge of the imagination, not only because Kierkegaard usually relies on him for terminology but also in order to bring out, more fully than I could in Kierkegaard's own terms, the epistemologically ambiguous juncture at which we remain in Kierkegaard: the "image" is not completely subsumed and the mind is still "exposed to external influences."

This epistemological ambiguity helps explain why Kierkegaard in the dissertation endorses Aristophanes' interpretation of Socrates, as opposed to Xenophon's and Plato's: "Aristophanes' imaginative representation of Socrates has come closest to the truth."[38] The comparison is dialectical. Xenophon in his interpretation is faulted for "dragging Socrates down" to the level of the "phenomenal" and the "external," just as Plato is faulted for the opposite—"lifting Socrates up into the superterrestial regions of the Idea. But irony is the point which lies in between." In lieu of an *Aufhebung* which would transcend the opposition between Xenophone and Plato, Aristophanes

> has assigned Socrates a place in the Thinkery in a suspended basket. . . . It is this hovering which is most significant: it is the attempted ascension into heaven, . . . rising up to the whole region of the ideal. . . .

The ironist is indeed lighter than the world, but he still belongs to the world.[39]

Socrates is hung up between the "phenomenal" or the "external," which he discredits with his irony, and the "ideal" or the "essential," which he cannot reach, as Plato and Hegel pretend.[40] Kierkegaard is disputing their pretensions with Socrates' dislocation, as represented by Aristophanes.

At the same time that he is endorsing poetic, imaginative representation, he is denying the philosopher's conceptual grasp of essences, with which Plato populated the realm of the ideal.[41] Indeed these erstwhile essences dissolve (in Kierkegaard's interpretation of Aristophanes' play) into clouds, which "hover" like Socrates. They are nebulous—"without inner coherence."[42]

UNSELBSTÄNDIGKEIT

We can better appreciate Kierkegaard's endorsement of Aristophanes and "imaginative representation" if we recognize that images of "hovering" and "suspension" are prominent not only in Kierkegaard's treatment of Socratic irony but also in his treatment of the imagination itself.[43] We shall discover in *Either* that the seducer's mere "perception" of beauty is esthetically insufficient: "I could become embittered at the thought I have lost sight of her, and yet in a certain way it gives me pleasure. The *image* I now have of her *hovers* indefinitely between her actual and her ideal form."[44]

Let me acknowledge some risk that opposing "hovering" to the philosophical movement of Hegel's *Aufhebung* may seem possibly effective as imagery but of no great philosophical consequence. However, we have arrived here in Kierkegaard's first philosophical work at the edge of the dislocations which are so flagrant in existentialism. "Floating" (*flottement*) is a recurrent image for the experience of nauseous "ecstasy" in Sartre. The experience (or the description, if that was all Sartre was "waiting for")[45] doubtless derives from the experience of being "in suspense" from anxiety in Heidegger.[46] I do not allege any similarly direct influence by Kierkegaard on Sartre, but comparison is still possible. In Sartre as in Kierkegaard there is an ideal Platonic realm of being which is out of human reach and which has its own intrinsic justification: "In another world, circles, musical themes, keep their lines which are pure and rigid. But existence is a sagging" (*fléchissement*), since it is "contingent"—lacks this justification. "The world of explanations and reasons is not the world of existence. A circle is . . . clearly explained by the rotation of the segment of a straight line around one of its extremities. But a circle does not exist."[47]

When existence is recognized to be contingent (or put more concretely, *de trop*), "one is disconcerted [*ça vous tourne le coeur*], and everything starts floating,"[48] including (it might be observed, by way of comparison with the "clouds" in Kierkegaard's interpretation) "little patches of foggy warmth" which "float in the cold air."[49] This nauseous experience of "revulsion" (*écoeurement*) is the dislocating experience of loss of stability, of *Unselbstständigkeit*, in Sartre,[50] just as irony is in Kierkegaard. The experience of "revulsion" acquires social impact when it is turned by Sartre against those who find a sense of justification (*l'esprit de sérieux*) in their established roles,[51] just as irony is turned in Kierkegaard against Xenophon's interpretation of Socrates as a pillar of the Athenian establishment.

HUMAN SPACE

"Imaginative representation" is "spatial representation" for Hegel, and the spatial dislocations which we have been considering I have placed against the background of Hegel's discounting "spatial representation" as "irrelevant" to "existence" (*Dasein*) in the *Logic*. I have indicated that, even when Trendelenburg protests its relevance there, like Hegel he still has in mind the physical space of external nature. The structures, however, which are designed in the space of the imagination belong to "human space" or (more technically) to "hodological space" or (as Sartre also puts it) to "the symbolic arrangement of space."[52]

Contrast with the "blueprint of nature" that physics provides the map of the social terrain where the seducer is maneuvering in Kierkegaard's *Either*:

> When a small number of people come into frequent contact with each other in the same room, a sort of easy arrangement develops in which each has his own place, his location. Thus is formed a picture or image [*billede*, like its German cognate, can have either meaning], which one can reproduce for oneself—a map of the terrain. . . . Usually the aunt who has previously been sitting on the sofa *moves* to the little worktable, which place Cordelia [the prospective seducee] in turn leaves. She *moves* over to the tea table in front of the sofa. Edward [the suitor whose place in Cordelia's life will eventually be usurped by the seducer] follows her. I follow the aunt. . . . I usually sit with my back toward the tea table and the infatuated conversation of Edward and Cordelia.[53]

But this movement, in a literal external sense, of each of them into his usual social place is a development which is metaphorically dislocated by the place the seducer occupies (or perhaps, rather, imagines he occupies) in the internal space of Cordelia's imagination: "It is readily apparent that Cordelia feels that I am constantly, if invisibly, present between her and Edward." External and internal (in Hegel's terminology) "fall apart."

Once we have recognized the discrepancy between the physical locations of the participants in the "Diary" and their dislocation in the psychological space of Cordelia's imagination, it is perhaps easier to manage the test case with which Thody confounded us as implausibly idiosyncratic on Sartre's part. I have commented that the wiggling bottom is a to-and-fro movement which exhibits an *ex-sistential* structure inasmuch as the movement of one wiggle is the dislocation of the direction in which the movement of another wiggle was proceeding. Although these physical movements are mechanical ("pure obedience to the law of gravity"), they would not occur were it not for the voluntary movement of the walker; and without this conjunction the dislocated psychological movement on the part of the observer would not occur—his dis-gusted reaction. In Kierkegaard's phrase, a "relation underlies the disrelation" between these different kinds of movement—between the involuntary and mechanical physical movements of the wiggles and the voluntary physical movement of walking and between this conjunction and the involuntary psychological movement of disgust. One would not react this way to the deformation of a "cushion,"[54] to which Sartre likens the bottom as an inert object, unless one were in a remarkably anthropomorphic frame of mind.

A similar design can be discerned in the case of Madame Bovary's seduction by the clerk during the ride in the horse cab: "Their fuck, viewed from outside [the cab, as it is viewed in the novel] is assimilated to the *fureur de la locomotion* which took possession of an inert object [the cab]," as the instruction repeatedly issues from within it, "Drive on." The impact of forcing on the reader this point of view from outside resides in his being induced to extend, the *fureur de la locomotion*, the *rage de la motricité*, which the mechanical movements of this inert object embody, so that he ascribes them to the movements with which he imagines the seducer is meanwhile entering Madame Bovary's body.[55]

AUSLEGUNG

If these examples still seem (in Ayer's phrase) "of a rather special character," consider the general significance Heidegger attaches not only to the interpretation of our existence in spatial terms but also to the spatial interpretation he offers of the procedure of interpretation itself.

Here methodological considerations inevitably encroach, but perhaps it is well to be reminded of the difficulty of severing subject matter from method. Heidegger emphasizes that the German word for "interpretation," *Aus-legung*, means etymologically "laying out," a notion I have already adopted for certain spatial arrangements in "The Diary of the Seducer."

Let me now turn to a familiar example, where what Heidegger is "laying out" is the "lay out" of Plato's cave.[56] In his interpretations of past philosophers, Heidegger often prefers the writings of pre-Socratics which have come down to us only as fragments dislocated from their original settings. But Plato's cave is a locus classicus which was not a dislocated fragment until Heidegger wrenched it from its setting in the *Republic*, so that it is no longer interpretable (as in the *Republic* itself) by reference to the preceding mathematical analogy of the "divided line" and no longer prepares the way for the education that follows in the mathematical sciences. It is not just the *Republic* that is being subverted here but the entire tradition stemming from Plato in which the thinker is debarred from the precincts of philosophy until he has qualified in mathematics. What Heidegger has segregated for interpretation must have enticed him not only because it is offered by Plato himself as an "image" (and an image indeed of man's dislocation to a place underneath the earth) but also because the spatial layout of the cave is first carefully designed by Plato and then carefully interpreted by Plato as a spatial layout—not to mention that the prisoners in the cave are themselves engaged in interpreting or, rather, misinterpreting its layout. Plato's interpretation in turn becomes in Heidegger a misinterpretation. Thus the prisoners' interpretation, Plato's interpretation, Heidegger's interpretation, are all the "laying out" of the layout of a spatial structure. Just as the interpretations pile up at a succession of levels, so the layout of the structure of the cave is a succession of levels.

All that can be taken into account here is the way Heidegger's interpretation dislocates Plato's interpretation by accentuating the *ex-sistential* distinction of level between inside and outside the cave. Heidegger is not always so straightforward in his admission of a discrepancy between his interpretation and what was at stake for the author undergoing his interpretation:

> The presentation of the "image" and Plato's own interpretation take the cave under the earth and its outside almost for granted. . . . The power of the illustration does not emerge from the image of the enclosure by a vault under the earth and of confinement within this enclosure; it does not even emerge from the view of openness outside of the cave.[57]

Ausrichtung

The cave in effect provides Heidegger with an "image" of the "way" in which one "goes about" the *Umwelt*, as this movement had been traced in *Being and Time*. Thus accentuating the spatial distinction between inside and outside is merely preliminary to the hodological movement through space as this movement is structured by the cave:

> The authentic meaning is not yet grasped [in terms of a static spatial distinction], for the image is a report of a movement of going forward and not just a description of the places where men stay and find themselves located inside and outside the cave.[58]

In fact Heidegger gains additional space for this forward movement by transferring the adjective which in Plato describes the mouth of the cave as "wide," so that it instead increases the length of the "passageway" (*eisodos*) between the outside and the inside of the cave.

"Going about" the *Umwelt* itself is a "laying out." A human being who *ex-sists* (whose structure is his dislocation "outside" himself "in-the-world") is involved in "structuring" (*Ausrichtung*) this world in relation to himself.[59] Examples are General MacArthur's departing from Corregidor, announcing, "I shall return," or the story (cited by Sartre) that Pershing's deputy arrived in Paris during World War I and announced, "Lafayette, we are here."[60] Less elaborate examples are feeling "low," feeling "near" someone far away (as distance is usually measured), feeling "in the depths," pulling off some "low-down" trick. To detract from the significance of such examples by construing them as simply metaphorical is to succumb to the usual distortion of our experience that takes the neutralized, measurable, objective space of physics as what space really is and our feelings about it as subjective. In interpreting Hölderlin's nature poetry, Heidegger pauses to protest; "How much longer are we going to suppose that there was first of all a portion of nature which is objective, a landscape which is objective, and then with the help of 'poetic experiences' this landscape became colored with myth?"[61]

Entfernung

There is another and complementary dimension to the fashion in which our experience is laid out. Since being-there is *ex-sistentially* dislocated by standing outside itself at a distance from itself, it finds itself engaged in a "de-distancing" (*Ent-fernung*) of this "distance" (*Entfernung*).[62] Obvious examples of *Ent-fernung* are climbing Everest, breaking speed records, telephoning, television, sexual intercourse—if Heidegger had stooped to this level in his philosophy.[63]

Sartre quotes Heidegger's characterization of *Dasein* as "outside of itself in the world" and as "a being of distances" (*être des lointains*). He agrees with Heidegger that " 'human being' is *ent-fernend*."[64] Let me offer an example (taken out of its setting, to which I shall later restore it) of what the *ex-sistentialist* phenomenon of dis-stance means in Sartre: "Distance, after all, was created by man and has meaning only in human space; it separated Hero from Leander and Marathon from Athens, but not one pebble from another." The mention of pebbles may seem to exclude any reference to physical space, but of course the Hellespont was a certain physical distance, and there was a certain physical distance between Marathon and Athens; however, measurement would be an abstraction, for the distance takes on its meaning as distance only by virtue of Hero's desire for Leander and the runner's desire to get the news of the victory back to Athens.

Sartre continues his appraisal of distance with an appeal to his personal experience as an individual:

> I first understood what it was one evening in April 1941. I had spent two months in a prison camp—one might as well say in a sardine can; I had experienced absolute proximity. The boundary of my living space was my skin. Day and night I felt the warmth of a shoulder or a thigh against my body. But it didn't bother me, as the others were still me. On my first night of freedom, a stranger in my native city, not having reached my friends of former days, I pushed open the door of a cafe. Suddenly I experienced a feeling of fear—or something close to fear. . . . I was lost; the scattered drinkers seemed more distant than the stars. Each of them was entitled to a huge hunk of bench, to a whole marble table, while I, to touch them, would have had to cross the "gleaming parquet floor" that separated us. . . . I had rejoined bourgeois society, where I would have to learn once again "to keep my distance."[65]

ABSTÄNDIGKEIT

I shall explain "the gleaming parquet floor" in a moment. But first let me interrupt Sartre to note that "human distance" can have the social character which the metaphor of "keeping one's distance" implies and as such is not a measurable physical distance. (How close does one get before intruding on someone else's privacy?) But of course the interplay between the physical and the psychological, which we have already noted, often includes the factor of distance, as in Elaine May's line "There was proximity but no relating."

In Heidegger's analysis of "being with others" the social character of distance is brought out by the spatial metaphor of *Abständigkeit. Abstand* means "distance" and *Abständigkeit* has been translated "distantiality,"[66] but since Heidegger is undercutting our scientific preoccupation with quantitative measurement, it is likely that he is exploiting the qualitative implications of the adjective *abständig*, which means "spoiled (e.g., by having been kept "standing" around too long), "dried up," "stale," "tasteless," "musty," "flat." Even in English a social relation like marriage can go "sour."

Let me now restore Sartre's comment to its setting. He is engaged in an appraisal of painting as exhibiting the structure of space—what Heidegger (when engaged in a similar appraisal) calls the "interplay" (*Ineinanderspiel*) between *Art and Space*.[67] Sartre is commenting on a quotation from a letter of Giacometti's to Matisse:

> Some naked women seen at the Sphinx with myself seated at the back of the room. The distance separating us (the gleaming parquet floor seemed untraversable in spite of my desire to cross it) made as much of an impression on me as the women themselves.

Having explained the allusion to the floor, we can complete Sartre's commentary:

> For Giacometti distance is not voluntary isolation or even a movement of drawing back. It is a requirement, a ceremony, a sense of difficulty, the product . . . of powers of attraction and forces of repulsion. If he was unable to cross those few feet of floor separating him from the naked women, it was because shyness or poverty riveted him to his chair. But if he felt so strongly that the distance could not be traversed, it was because he so yearned to touch that luxurious flesh.[68]

Sartre frequently deals with the dislocations effected by such opposing forces.

LINES OF FORCE

Earlier we recognized the existentialist commitment in general to movement as a subject matter. In dealing with what he calls "the symbolic arrangement of space" (which is Sartre's version of Heidegger's *Ausrichtung*), Sartre stresses that the spatial relations in question are not static but "lines of force." On a Masson drawing he reports,

> The female sex organ . . . does not evoke either fecundity or lust—at least not at the start. It represents the discord, the gaping, the explosive dislocation of a body. . . . His model's legs spread apart suggest the action of two forces brought to bear at the same juncture, each

pulling it in a direction opposed to the other, so that the organ is the rupture of the flesh this tension fissures.[69]

This kind of design is frequent in Sartre. In a Masson "imagery is at the service of movement," and the movement is dislocating: "Everywhere expectations are contradicted, disappointed, and sensations are deliberately transmuted—this sex organ explodes, that head breaks out in flowers, that female body frays into fog, the fog bleeds."[70] A scholar who has surveyed Sartre's esthetic appraisals comments on how Sartre's taste remains the same whatever artist he is appraising.[71] Thus it is not just the particular artist's imagination which is relevant, and Sartre finds essentially the same dislocated structure in Lapoujade's objective—"to maintain the rhythm of explosive space, to exploit in depth the strange and terrifying disintegration of being and its whirling movement."[72]

This kind of design extends in existentialism from physical to psychological movements, as we saw earlier was the case with e-motions. Far-fetched as it may seem, the "relation" which we shall recognize "underlies the disrelation" between the esthetic and the ethical stages in *Either/Or* can be visualized in much the same fashion as the legs of Masson's model which "suggest the action of two forces brought to bear at the same juncture, each pulling it in a direction opposed to the other." In *Either/Or* "the same juncture" is the esthetic way of life, which is defined first esthetically in *Either*, only to have the definition contradicted by the ethical redefinition of *Or*, so that the reader is dislocated by being pulled apart in two opposing directions.[73] Such dislocations are the dynamics of *ex-sistential* thought.

BACKWARD AND FORWARD

Another opposition which can be extended from physical to psychological movements is between backward and forward. Recall that the "obscene" is defined by Sartre with an example in which the movements of a wiggling bottom are "seen from behind" and opposed to the "forward movement" of the legs. We have noted that Kierkegaard admits that "life must be understood backward" (i.e., by re-flecting upon it) but insists that it "must be lived forward."

The problem of movement as posed in terms of this dislocation between backward and forward is developed in Kierkegaard's *Repetition*:

When the Eleatics denied movement, Diogenes contradicted them by actually carrying out a movement, for without saying a word, he went a few steps [*gange*] forward and backward.[74]

Kierkegaard undoubtedly culled this anecdote from Hegel's *History of Philosophy*. Hegel himself rather contemptuously dismisses the refutation:

> When principles are at issue the only refutation which is valid relies on principles. One is not to be satisfied with sense certainty; one must understand.[75]

Kierkegaard is interpreting Hegel's own system itself as Eleatic and is drawing attention to "actual" movement, as Diogenes had. But Kierkegaard is not attempting to resolve the problem of movement by reinstating an appeal to "sense certainty" with respect to a physical movement. It is "imaginative representation" that enjoys the prerogative in Kierkegaard as over against both sense certainty and the understanding, with which the mind withdraws itself in Hegel from its exposure to "external influences." Diogenes' movement backward becomes in Kierkegaard an image for the psychological movement of "recollection" with which one reflects upon one's life and comes to some understanding of it in retrospect, and Diogenes' movement forward becomes an image for the opposing movement of "repetition."

Thus the existential problem of an "actual movement" is not to be resolved, as Hegel supposed, by understanding. There is, accordingly, a slight but perhaps significant change of phrase in Kierkegaard's version of the anecdote. Where Hegel stressed that Diogenes is refuting the Eleatics "by an action" (*durch die Tat*), Kierkegaard is emphasizing that it is by "actually [*virkelig*] carrying out a movement." The point is not only that the abstract movement of reflection in Hegel does not qualify as an actual movement for Kierkegaard but also that existential movement itself is an actualization of a possibility and as such is an image for the dislocating transition that has to be made from understanding some possibility by reflecting on it to its becoming "actual" in one's own life as one lives forward.

Kierkegaard's insistence on the dislocating character of this transition from a backward to a forward movement helps dispose of efforts to assimilate existentialism to empiricism or an existential experience to an empirical one. Kierkegaard's "Life must be understood backward . . . but must be lived forward" happens to have been the first existential formula to catch the attention of an empiricist. It was cited by William James, whose commitment to scientific prediction, as a way of understanding forward, enabled him to smooth over the dislocation.[76] In fact scientific understanding is usually interpreted as normally developing in the relatively continuous fashion which Lord Snow has described as "cumulative, incorporative, collective." This prospect of maintaining or restoring the continuity of experience is generalized in empiricism.

Discrepancy

By now it must be evident that my characterization of existential experience as a dislocated "structure of movement" does not turn just on the etymology of the single term "existence" or the comparable implication that I read earlier into the term "e-motion."[77] Terms and phrases that we have encountered since (like "discord," "gaping," "explosive," "rupture," "fissures," "breaks out," "frays," "the rhythm of explosive space," "the strange and terrifying disintegration of being") also design dislocated "structures in the space of the imagination." Perhaps they can hardly count as technical. But *décalage* ("discrepancy") is a technical term which is frequently employed by Merleau-Ponty as well as Sartre.[78] *Décalage* means more specifically "displacement of an object" or "lag" or "want of synchronism." A similar term which almost has to be regarded as technical because it is Merleau-Ponty's own coinage, as far as contemporary philosophical usage is concerned, is *déhiscence*, which derives from the Latin *dehisco*, meaning to "divide," "split open," "gap." (An example in which it is accompanied by the metaphor of "explosion" is Merleau-Ponty's characterization of "the explosion or *déhiscence* of the present toward a future" as "the archetype of the relation of self to self.")[79] A term Merleau-Ponty uses more frequently than Sartre is *écart*, which means "discrepancy," "deviation," "swerve," "stepping aside," as when a horse shies.[80] These terms for dislocation can be employed at different levels. Thus Merleau-Ponty once retorted, when confronted with a defender of the scientific character of philosophy, that philosophy as he conceived it "measures the *écart* between our experience and that of science."[81] This is, of course, the *écart* which Heidegger had discerned between the *Umwelt* of "everyday" experience with its "existential spatiality" and the "objective" scientific world which had been the world for philosophers since Descartes.

The Philosophy of Our Time

Having dealt with the dislocated structure of "existential spatiality" at various junctures, we can finally return to Sartre's report, "We were discovering the world." It will be remembered that the world discovered was "a society which was disrupted" but that I postponed dealing with the report in its own terms, because the discovery was modeled on the discovery in Heidegger of the *Umwelt*, whose structure was exposed only when it became a "dislocated world"—to borrow the phrase Merleau-Ponty extends to the social world.

Sartre recalls his discovery of the world in an essay originally entitled "Existentialism and Marxism," in which he identifies Marxism as "the philosophy of our time."[82] What then happens to the influence of Heidegger or to existentialism? Ostensibly it is assigned by Sartre a subordinate place which it is to occupy only temporarily in relation to Marxism. But as a matter of fact neither Sartre's interpretation of Marxist philosophy nor his preoccupation with "our time" is Marxist. Both, we shall see, are existential.

Sartre criticizes as "positivistic" what I shall label "conventional Marxism."[83] But since there is nothing distinctively existential about such criticism of the "scientific" pretensions of Marxism, it need not detain us. What is more striking is the way in which the dislocations and discontinuities distinctive of existentialism are attributed by Sartre to Marx himself:

> When Marx reproaches Hegel for having stood the dialectic on its head, he is not just opposing a materialism to an idealism . . . ; he wants to reintroduce . . . the delay, discrepancy [*décalage*], distortion that are constant characteristics of our undertakings; in short, the permanent possibility of disorder which reveals the constant danger of humanity's annihilating itself.[84]

"Reintroduce" is a curious way of referring to what had not previously been a feature of the dialectic, but it can perhaps be explained by recognizing that "delay, discrepancy, distortion" had previously been "constant characteristics" dislocating our "undertakings" in Sartre's existentialism before he became a Marxist. In other words, when Sartre does become a Marxist, he offers an existentialized version in lieu of conventional Marxism. From his existential point of view, conventional Marxism has become "paralyzed," and its development has been "halted." Existentialism is assigned the temporary function of imparting its sensitivity to dislocation to Marxism, so that Marxist analysis will get moving again, renew its development, and catch up with the disruptions that are taking place in contemporary society.[85]

Sartre's Marx is already *ex-sistential* in his thinking, dwelling more definitely than Marx himself on "the permanent possibility of disorder." Sartre's interpretation also sharpens the discontinuity between Hegel and Marx: Hegel's dialectic, according to Sartre, "belongs necessarily to times past" when "each thing always has its place; whereas Marx has enabled us to recover the real time of the dialectic"—its operation in the present, when (we have to add to complete the contrast) everything is dislocated and out of place.[86] Quite aside from the "permanent possibility of disorder," the dislocations multiply in Sartre. To cite only one example,

Sartre observes a "discrepancy [*décalage*] . . . often separating Flaubert from his contemporaries" and comments that such discrepancies may reflect "the *rupture* between the generations which Marxists systematically neglect."[87]

THE SINGULARIZED UNIVERSAL

As this comment on Flaubert suggests, one reason why dislocations multiply in existentialism, as compared with conventional Marxism, is that the existentialist attempts to bring a social analysis within the reach of an individual's own experience. But this way of putting the matter is too succinct and risks blurring the distinction of level that survives the conjunction of the personal dimension with some higher level of generality—here the sociohistorical dimension. At one level there is the movement by which the individual himself can come to have experiences which are distinctively personal—the movement which Sartre in his volumes on Flaubert describes as *le mouvement récupérateur et personalisant*.[88] But the individual is not simply a particular individual; we have seen that he is identifiable as a "singularized universal." At the higher level the sociohistorical dimension of his experience is reached.

This double character of existentialism is sufficient to distinguish existentialism broadly from Marxism. In other words, the obvious difference between Sartre's sociohistorical analysis, predominant in the third of his volumes on Flaubert, and Marx's is that the former's analysis is tied in with his psychoanalysis, which predominates in the preceding two volumes, of the dislocating personal experiences of Flaubert. Marx writes on *Political Economy* or on *Capital*, not about an individual. When the conventional Marxist traces the necessary course of social history, he eliminates the personal dimension as merely contingent, in the fashion illustrated by the following pronouncement which Sartre cites from Engels:

> That such a man, precisely that particular individual, emerges at this particular time and in this particular country is naturally a matter of pure chance. If Napoleon had not turned up, someone else would have taken his place.[89]

We have recognized with Kierkegaard that philosophy has been since Aristotle's metaphysics a tradition in which there can be no knowledge of the particular individual. And it is not just in the Marxist version of social history that the individual loses out as merely contingent. In Hegel's social history, the individual enjoys only brief "paragraph importance," as Kierkegaard complains.[90] In retrieving Socrates Kierkegaard is rehabilitating what Hegel had discounted as "not so much a matter of philosophy as of the life of the individual." In fact many social historians, even when they are neither Marxists nor Hegelians, assume without hesitation that to consolidate their subject matter is to abstract from the "special character" of the experience of particular individuals.

CRISSCROSSING

Merleau-Ponty instead adopts a shifting focus:

> When history poses a question, when the anxieties and resentments that have piled up finally take on a form in human space that can be identified, we imagine that after that nothing could ever be the same as before. . . . But instead the question wears itself out, and an unquestioned state of affairs supervenes, the way an emotion one day ceases, undermined by having lasted too long. This country, bled by war or revolution, suddenly it is there, intact and whole.[91]

The shifting of focus involves "crisscrossing":[92] Merleau-Ponty cuts across distinctions of level we would conventionally respect; he draws our attention to the distinctions by his violations. On one hand he cuts across the distinction between the conceptual operation of posing a question and the way emotions take imaginative shape in "human space." On the other, he has begun with "history"—a broad, high-level social perspective. But history loses some of its lofty impersonality when it is assigned the role (usually reserved for individuals) of posing a question. This ellipsis might remain a permissible personification at the higher level of conceptual operations did Merleau-Ponty not drop abruptly to a lower level by dragging in an analogy to a personal emotion. (The emotions initially enter as plural—"anxieties and resentments"—but the analogy is reinforced by the artifice of isolating "an emotion" to match "a question." Here too conventional presuppositions are violated: it seems implausible that anything as complicated as history could pose anything as simple as a single question or that anything as complicated as the psyche could ever indulge in a single emotion.) However, Merleau-Ponty does not remain personal; he reverts to the larger configurations of history, and without making any attempt to ease the incongruity of the change of scale. He repeats the crisscrossing violation when the social phenomenon that is "intact and whole" (so that there would seem nothing about it which requires anything besides social commentary) is brusquely shown to comprise particular individuals, who are then saddled with a responsibility which would not conventionally be theirs:

This country, bled by war or revolution, suddenly it is there, intact and whole. Those who died are implicated in this appeasement, for it was only by living on that they would have been able to create anew that want, that need of themselves, which is obliterated.[93]

Superimposed upon the sudden dislocations of history itself, which he has previously indicated "exposes its truth only during brief moments of disarray,"[94] is Merleau-Ponty's own sudden crisscrossing from the fate of a historical question to that of a personal emotion, to the fate of an entire country, to the fate of particular individuals. In this way he is not only attentive to dislocations but also, at a higher level, dislocates the conventional tendency of historians to abstract large-scale social dislocations from the tiny psychological and moral dislocations that disturb the lives of mere individuals.

PERSONAL RELATIONS

Admittedly historians often attempt to compensate for these abstractions and to retrieve the personally significant, even though their attempts may not be as deliberately dislocating as Merleau-Ponty's. More important philosophically is the fact that the crisscrossing in Merleau-Ponty reaches the level not only of social generality but also of ideas. Philosophers, I commented earlier, traditionally think of the process by which ideas acquire their general justification as inevitably a process by which they become disentangled from the lives of their particular proponents. Yet Merleau-Ponty leaves them entangled: "Our relations to ideas are inevitably and justifiably our relations with other persons."[95] There is no allusion to Hegel here, but it is worth recalling that the distinction Hegel applies to Socrates between "philosophy" and "the life of the individual" orients his treatment of Socrates away from philosophy, not only toward his character as an individual but also toward his relations with other individuals. "In that the person, the individual, comes to make the decision, we are brought back to Socrates as a person, as a subject, and what follows is an analysis of his personal relations."[96]

Personal reference is a familiar feature of existentialism, but what has not received much attention is the philosophical significance of what Hegel takes for granted here as without philosophical significance—"personal relations." Existentialist concentration on relations which are at once relations to ideas and to persons, and on the dislocations of these relations—this concentration receives its most notorious illustration from the way Kierkegaard's relations to Hegel and Christianity became entangled with breaking off his engagement to Regina and the "earthquake" which took place in relation to his father. Such bipersonal relations we shall see are quite characteristic of existentialism. But these relations are complicated in Kierkegaard's case by the intrusion of Socrates—"the man," Kierkegaard admits, "to whom I have been inexplicably related from my earliest youth."[97] He was also the man whose significance Hegel had largely reduced to his "person" and to his "personal relations," so that he too became involved in Kierkegaard's general effort to rehabilitate philosophically personal relations. Additional complications are introduced by Kierkegaard's relations to his pseudonyms. Relations of such complexity I must postpone.[98]

The philosophical significance of Sartre's personal relation to Simone de Beauvoir is more obvious, in that he assigns her to the lower level of the two levels which existentialism, in opposition to traditional philosophy attempts to embrace:

> It is out of one's experiences that one writes. The other intervenes, when two have these experiences together. Without Simone de Beauvoir, . . . I would certainly speak of my experiences with fewer details, with fewer particular references. Something that I am reproached for (wrongly, in my judgment—I think it one of my virtues) is to attach too much importance in a philosophical work to particular examples. To describe a mode of behavior, an action, an individual's life, as an example of a philosophical theory. They say, "He bogs down in the incidental, the anecdotal; he does not ascend to the general." Well, that, it is a certain relation with Simone de Beauvoir.[99]

De Beauvoir herself is the first to admit little claim to a role in relation to Sartre at the higher level which is traditionally significant in philosophy. Thus more relevant to our purpose is the crisscrossing of the bipersonal relation between Sartre and Merleau-Ponty with the relations between their ideas. Where members of a philosophical movement are personally related, some delineation of their relation is appropriate to an introduction, if the movement in question is existentialism.

Let me accordingly continue with Merleau-Ponty's assessment of such relations themselves, before turning to Sartre's assessment of his particular relation to Merleau-Ponty. At the time Merleau-Ponty made his assertion that "our relations to ideas are inevitably and justifiably our relations with other persons," he was struggling with his own relation to Marxist ideas, including Communist policies; and his personal relations were dislocated by this struggle, including eventually his relation to Sartre.[100] He was also alert, as an existentialist, to the way Marxism neglects personal implications in favor of identifying its own implications with the course of social history. Yet in making his assertion Merleau-Ponty is referring specifically to the dislocating personal experience of Marxists who have broken with the Communist party. The point of his reference is how ungeneralizably and incommunicably personal their experience is, so he interpolates an analogy to the dislocation of an intimate personal relation:

> They left a party which is . . . the locus of all their hopes and the guarantor of man's destiny. The rupture with the party is complete, like one's rupture with a person. . . . It does not leave intact the memory of what has gone before. . . . A man who has left the woman he has lived with remains incredulous if she becomes precious to someone else: he knew her better than anyone, living with her day after day, and this image that someone else has of her, which is so different, can only be illusory.[101]

THE PORTRAIT

After Merleau-Ponty's death, Sartre composed a "portrait" in which the relational character of an existential analysis is illustrated by the fact that he is less concerned with Merleau-Ponty as a person separate from himself than with their relation: "It is the man I would restore: not as he was for himself but as he lived in my life, as I lived in his life."[102] This portrait could in fact be an illustration of Merleau-Ponty's own assertion that I have cited, for Sartre sketches the crisscrossing relations between their respective ideas and their personal relations to each other. Or, to be more precise, Sartre sketches the dislocations of all these relations. It was Merleau-Ponty's recognition of the dislocating course of history which, Sartre reports, "jolted me" (*me fit sauter le pas*). (Remember that Merleau-Ponty recognized that history "exposes its truth only during brief moments of disarray.") Sartre continues, "In *Humanism and Terror* I discovered method and subject matter, and it gave me the shove needed to wrench me out of my political inertia [*m'arracher à l'immobilisme*]."[103] Just as Sartre as an existentialist later envisages getting Marxism moving again, in response to the movement of history, so he envisages Merleau-Ponty's response to the movement of history as having gotten him moving. Sartre then became converted to fellow-traveling, as Merleau-Ponty had been earlier.

The next jolt, however, was Merleau-Ponty's deconversion, after the Communist invasion of South Korea, and his lapse into what Sartre considered political inertia. Sartre generalizes with regard to the dislocating course of history:

> In fact it was the fault of history that the thread was broken: history uses up the men she employs; she rides them to death like horses. She picks her actors, transforms them to the marrow by the role she

imposes, and then, with the least change [in her course], she casts
them aside and takes on other brand-new actors, whom she throws
into the fray without any training.

After these dislocations, what Merleau-Ponty and Sartre still shared were
dislocating "feelings of disgust," but they parted company politically with
respect to what they were disgusted with: "At the same moment one
[Merleau-Ponty] discovered the horror of Stalinism, the other [Sartre]
the horror of his own bourgeois class." Thus discontinuity, which characterized the course of history for them both, intruded on their personal
relationship: "The discontinuity [déphasement] between our lives was
such that each always took the initiative at the wrong time."[104]

THAT PARTICULAR INDIVIDUAL

The same dislocated relation held between the respective developments
of their philosophical ideas:

> Each of us understood the other's work as a startling deviation from
> his own work—the alien, sometimes hostile, work that the other was
> carrying out. Husserl became at one and the same time the distance
> between us and the basis of our friendship.

But when the rupture in their relation finally came, it was at once more
personal and more ideological:

> Beneath our intellectual divergencies, so calmly accepted when
> Husserl was the only issue, we discovered to our stupefaction conflicts
> deriving on one hand from our different childhoods and the basic
> rhythm of our organisms and on the other from . . . a crazy activism
> on the part of one of us [Sartre] which concealed his disarray [ses
> déroutes] and, on the part of the other, a relentless apathy.

Grant the ferocious discontinuities of social history—with individuals shot
from under her like horses. Grant too the part played by these discontinuities with regard to the personal relation between Sartre and Merleau-
Ponty, so that Sartre can generalize,

> This is how men live in our time, what kind of friends they are—
> wretched friends. True enough.[105]

In the conventional Marxist treatment, "that such a man, precisely that
particular individual, emerges at this particular time is naturally a matter of pure chance."[106] But the rehabilitation of the particular individual
in existentialism is associated with what I have described as its "double
character." Thus Sartre finishes the portrait by reverting from his generalization at the higher level regarding "how men live in our time" to

the personal dimension, so that we are left with a double truth: "But it is also true that it was we, the two of us, who were such wretched friends." To this extent their dislocated personal relation survives the sociohistorical dislocations as "a wound," Sartre concludes, which "remains for me still inflamed."[107] I have been citing from a collection of Sartre's essays entitled *Portraits*. Most of the essays concern individuals to whom Sartre feels personally related. By now it should be clear that his adoption of this genre is not philosophically accidental.

TEMPORALITY

Another difference between an existential and a Marxist analysis is that the existentialist deals not only with the sociohistorical but also with temporality, which is a feature of the individual's experience. So far I have neglected temporality in favor of spatiality. Up until the juncture at which Marxism was reached as the "philosophy of our time," I followed a sequence which Heidegger justified in *Being and Time*: "Spatiality of the kind which belongs to being-there—and on the ground of which existence always defines its 'location'—is grounded in the structure of being-in-the-world."[108] This is why he started with this structure, as I have in this chapter, and then went on to deal with "spatiality."

Nevertheless, as I have anticipated, Heidegger later stresses that "temporality" is "the *ekstatikon* in the strict sense, . . . the primary 'outside of itself.' "[109] In the long run the primacy of temporal over spatial relations in existentialism cannot be gainsaid, especially since Heidegger criticizes the philosophical tradition—as well as ordinary usage—for distorting temporal relations by conceiving them in spatial terms. This is why Heidegger does not start out with an analysis of temporal relations. For were it not for the fact that "existence [*Dasein*] takes up space," temporal relations would not be misconceived in spatial terms.[110] The spatial structure of our experience is nearer and more accessible to us than the temporal. In fact the language we use to delineate temporal relations is usually drawn from spatial relations—not only such terms as "existence" and its affiliates which I have examined but also our casual references, for example, to an event as "nearer" in time.

Thus when Kierkegaard picked "walking forward" as an "image of existence" (and of the way it must be "lived forward," even though it can only be "understood backward"), it was partly because he needed an image of the way we move through space to bring home to us the way we move from the past into the future. Merleau-Ponty likewise imagined the relation of the present to the future as a dislocated movement—an "explosion" or *déhiscence*.[111] Similarly, Sartre first analyzed a disgusted reaction to a wiggling bottom in terms of its dislocated spatial relations, before he half translated this analysis into terms of temporal relations:

> The bottom looks like an isolated cushion which they [the legs] are carrying, and whose movement is pure obedience to the laws of gravity. . . . It is isolated from the rest of the body whose present meaning lies in moving forward. . . . Its swaying movement, instead of being interpreted starting out from what is to come [à-venir], is interpreted and recognized as a physical fact, starting out from the past.

Sartre's hyphenation of à-venir implies that French has derived its term for the future [avenir] by visualizing our relation to it as spatial—as if it were "coming" toward us. His use of this derivation is prompted by Heidegger's use of a similar derivation for Zu-kunft.[112] Sartre and Heidegger are suggesting that language itself embodies that feature of our experience whereby we find we translate our effort to get our temporal bearings, or to decide our place in history, into terms of spatial location.

BEING AND TIME

Even when we consult a watch to find out the time, the answer is reformulated in terms of the spatial relations between the hour and minute hands. The answer we obtain is not, however, the final answer to the problem of location, as Merleau-Ponty explains in commenting on a citation from Claudel:

> "From time to time, a man lifts his head, and sniffs, listens, hesitates, recognizes his location: he takes note, sighs, and, drawing his watch from his side pocket, looks at the time. Where am I? And what time is it? Such is the inexhaustible question we ask of the world." Inexhaustible because the time and place change continually, but more than that, because the question that arises here is not at bottom a question of knowing in what spatial location, taken as given, at what hour of time taken as given, we are—but above all, what is this indestructible relation between us and hours and places, this perpetual taking of our bearings through things . . . through which above all it is necessary that I be at a time, at a place, whatever they may be.[113]

Here we can trace the emergence of the ontological question. The empirical questions "Where am I?" and "What time is it?" involve us in more than an empirical relation. To translate the "indestructible relation" into Heidegger's terminology (to which Merleau-Ponty is clearly alluding), the "ekstatic" structure of our being-there is at stake. Our locatedness is not "a fixed stage with a permanently raised curtain" but a movement (in Claudel's phrasing) "from time to time."

When Heidegger characterizes his "preliminary aim" in *Being and Time* as "the interpretation of time as the possible horizon for any general understanding of being,"[114] one reason he adopts the spatial metaphor is that the horizon moves as I move. Another is the necessity that "I be at a time, at a place," whatever may be the particular time or place: a horizon is not something that I can go "beyond" in the way the meta-physical tradition attempted, when its definitions located man hierarchically by going beyond the "animal" to the "rational," the "finite" to the "infinite," and reaching a Being which is purely rational, infinite, and eternal. This metaphysical tradition started out with Aristotle's proposition at the beginning of his *Metaphysics*, "All men by nature desire to know,"[115] for this desire could only be satisfied by knowledge of the universal, of the necessary and the eternal—what "cannot be otherwise." As was noted earlier, knowledge cannot then be of the particular individual, who is merely contingent, temporary, and always becoming otherwise—for example, in the role that he plays. Knowledge can only be concerned (as Aristotle's proposition itself illustrates) with what is common to "all men." Existentialism has in effect further emended Aristotle's proposition so that the desire to know becomes the desire to know the time. The emendation brings with it a corresponding adjustment in the criterion for knowledge—the adjustment implicit in Merleau-Ponty's reply to the dismissal of existentialism as a product of the dislocations of our time: "Of course. This is what constitutes its truth."[116]

OUR TIME

It is at this juncture that history tends to impinge on the existential formulation of the problem of time. One of the characteristics of our time is that the problem of time is no longer a metaphysical one in the traditional sense. The problem of time is a problem of our time. In other words, among the dislocations of our time that find expression in existentialism is our awareness of time, which is not only the traditional awareness that clocks, calendars, or even "a journalist of genius"[117] do not provide a final reply to the question "What time is it?" but also our awareness of having been finally deprived in our time of any final reply:

> The ancients read in the heavens the hour to wage the battle. We no longer believe that it is written anywhere. But . . . what takes place would not be entirely real for us if we did not know at what time. The hour is no longer destined ahead of time for the event, but, whatever it be, the event appropriates it to itself.[118]

Deprived of providential schedules, we turn to existentialism to salvage not only the particular individual whom Engels dismissed as contingent

but also the contingent itself. History "exposes its truth" when the contingency of its events is felt; and its "brief moments of disarray" become
even more dislocatingly eventful, inasmuch as they are no longer fitted to
an eternal destiny or even to the Marxist version of a providential
schedule.[119] The Aristotelian formula requires further revision: all men
in our time desire to know the time. It is no longer a question of what
"all men" are "by nature."

We began this chapter by watching the existential sense of dislocation
move from one country to another, from the period after one war to that
after another. But we now see that existentialism has reached an even
higher level of generality where our relation to the eternal is disturbed.
Existentialism has to do not just with the defeat of a country or the
decimation of a social class and the liquidation of its assets but with the
loss of a transcendent reference point—the loss which it was once fashionable to call "the death of God." Reformulated in these terms, existentialism can be interpreted as if it were an answer to a question once put by
André Malraux: "What is one to do with his soul, now that God is
dead?" A soul is something (to fill out the existential implications of
Malraux's question) with which one was equipped for the purpose of
reaching out "beyond" to God, and so it is dislocating to be saddled with
it when God is no longer available. As Sartre has indicated with regard
to Flaubert's experience, "the death of God is not *un déficit localisable*"—
that is, the amount that is missing cannot be located at a single juncture
by an accounting that adds and subtracts more carefully. The location of
the deficit cannot even be restricted to the souls of atheists. "God is dead,"
according to Sartre, "even in the soul of the believer."[120] Here again
existentialism gains some of its generality by virtue of the scope of the
tradition it is breaking away from.

THE CONTEMPORARY

Traditionally the temporal, when pitted against the eternal, could be
relegated to the temporary. But nowadays nothing is more demanding
than the contemporary. When Sartre argues, "We Write for Our Own
Time" ("Ecrire pour son époque"), he is arguing that the time is a "new
absolute." As such it displaces the Absolute Spirit which was for Hegel
involved with the outcome of the whole of history. Sartre's concept of a
time can be compared with, and may derive in part from, Heidegger's
concept of world, which is also historical in structure.

Sartre is in effect endorsing the "local perspectives" which Merleau-
Ponty insisted philosophy cannot transcend. Sartre explains that to appreciate anything written—including presumably his own philosophy—it has

to be eaten on the spot, "when it has just been picked"—like bananas.[121] If existentialism can receive the temporal demarcation "postwar," it is partly because of its preoccupation with what traditional philosophy would have dismissed as temporary; if it has enjoyed a contemporary vogue, it is partly because of its preoccupation with the contemporary. When Sartre receives the designation *'contemporain capital'* (i.e., the most contemporary of our contemporaries), when he is credited with "having the style of the age," so that to understand him "is to understand something important about the present time"—these are credentials he has earned with a philosophy which does not view the world as philosophy traditionally did, *sub specie aeternitatis*, but *sub specie temporalitatis*.[122]

How many plays in the past have ended, as Sartre's last tragedy ends, with the protagonist's speech on the place of our time in history?

> Centuries of the future, here is my century, solitary and deformed. . . . I have taken this century upon my shoulders and have said, "I will answer for it. This day and forever." What do you say?[123]

The curtain falls. There is finally no reply. We are left with the contemporary—with our deformed century. Who else would accept it? But it is absolutely what we are. On one hand we are conscious, as no past century has been, of how "local" our perspective is as to our own location in history: we know that "we shall be judged" and judged differently from the way in which we judge ourselves. But on the other hand we also know that we do not know what this different judgment will be and that no Last Judgment—Christian, Hegelian, or Marxist—can be anticipated that would assign our century its indisputable place in history. (It is not, in Merleau-Ponty's phrase, "destined ahead of time.") This dislocating ambiguity heightens the other dislocations of the tragedy. As Sartre himself has explained, the protagonist and his audience are left "unreconciled," with the "contradictions" of our time "unresolved."[124]

What has been dealt with so far as dislocations characteristic of the subject matter of existentialism are, methodologically speaking, "contradictions." (An excuse for having deferred the introduction of this term is that Anglo-American philosophers often get hot under the collar when confronted by Continental manipulation of contradictions.) That fundamental contradictions remain "unresolved" is a distinctive trait of existential method, as opposed to many other dialectical methods. Contrast, for example, the ending of Sartre's tragedy and his explanation of it with Hegel's claim in his *Esthetics* that a tragedy's "true development consists in the transcending [*Aufhebung*] of contradictions as *contradictions*," so that the audience, though "shaken by the fate of the heroes," are "reconciled to what is really at issue."[125] The dislocation then is merely transitional in the progress of the Absolute Spirit; neither the heroes nor the audience are absolutely what they are in their own time.

We are reminded that the starting point of existentialism as a philosophical movement is Kierkegaard's raising contradiction in *Either/Or* to the level of a principle, which contradicts the conciliatory principle of "both/and" whereby Hegelianism develops into a system by resolving contradictions. But dialecticians generally make some use of contradictions: Plato, Cicero, Augustine, Abelard, Aquinas, as well as Hegel and Marx. If we are to appreciate the distinctive way contradiction is applied as a methodological principle in existentialism, there are other traits of an existential dialectic which will first have to be taken into account in the next chapter, for they will modify the application of this principle.

Notes

1. *Existentialism*, pp. 172–73. Berger was a phenomenologist of sorts, whose best-known work was *The Cogito in Husserl's Philosophy*, so his contempt for existentialism may be taken to illustrate the seeming incompatibility between the two movements which was acknowledged in chap. 1.

2. Cited by Rohde, *Søren Kierkegaard: et geni i en købstad*, p. 7. My parody of vulgar Marxism is not meant to suggest that a sociohistorical interpretation of existentialism is necessarily invalid. I myself offered a crude *post hoc, propter hoc* explanation of American existentialism in my introduction, but I was only trying to get it out of our way as philosophically trivial.

3. *Signs*, p. 22.

4. *Humanism and Terror*, p. 187.

5. The distinction between this approach to existentialism and that adopted in the preceding chapter is a version of the distinction that I drew between a sociohistorical approach, which is the traditional Continental treatment of political problems, and a psychological and moral theory of human nature, which is the traditional British treatment (see my *Human Nature*, 1:68–75). I mention this distinction to help explain why existentialism has tended to become in our Anglo-American tradition existential psychology and existential ethics and why Ayer overlooks the existential treatment of political and social problems. He has been philosophically conditioned to annex political problems to psychological or moral problems and not to think of sociology or history as philosophically relevant disciplines. Thus Ayer reduces Sartre's politics to his doctrine of commitment, with only the following comment added: "His reason for allying himself with the Communists, to the extent of saying in *La* [*sic*] *critique de la raison dialectique* that Marxism is the only serious philosophy for our times, is basically that history is on the side of the working class, which means presumably that this class is going to come to power anyway (but what sort of reason is this for supporting it?) and that the Communist Party objectively represents the working class, no matter what policy it actually pursues. This is Hegel taking his revenge on Kierkegaard" (pp. 217–18). Quite aside from the ignorance of Hegel and Kierkegaard and their relation betrayed by this remark, how can one account for his summarizing the *Critique* with a banal anti-Communist argument that suggests he has never read the *Critique*, which in fact does not deal at all with history as such? See, e.g., the following: "We must give notice that the investigation we are undertaking . . . does not attempt to

discover the movement of history" (*Critique*, p. 39). The analysis of this movement Sartre deferred to a second volume which he never completed and does not intend to publish. Ayer may have glanced at *Search for a Method*.

6. *Search for a Method*, pp. 20–21. In a footnote on Georges Bataille's use of *déchirure*, Sartre asks, "Has Jaspers had any influence on him?" and comments, "Bataille does not cite Jaspers, but he seems to have read him" (*Situations*, 1:144). The term is so common that one can hardly argue that Sartre has been influenced here by Jaspers, but he not only read but proofread him (see chap. 9, n. 65 below), and he does discuss Jaspers in *Search for a Method*. In any case my general argument is that metaphors of disruption are the stock in trade of the existentialist.

7. See chap. 8 below for the "everydayness" of this world which has perhaps encouraged the vulgarization of Heidegger's analysis by his successors. We have seen that Sartre takes *ex-sistence* to refer to man's being dislocated "outside" himself "in-the-world." In now expounding Heidegger's analysis I am of course not denying that Sartre eventually blends this portion of Heidegger's philosophy with "Marxism as 'a philosophy which had become the world'" (*Search for a Method*, p. 20). See also chap. 2, n. 51 above, on the vulgarization entailed in the "actualization of philosophy."

8. *Being and Time*, pp. 63–69, 56–57, 36.

9. Ibid., pp. 74–76.

10. *Logic*, p. 104. When a loose translation of *aufheben* is feasible, I shall usually employ "transcend," since this is the positive moment the existentialist would subvert, and to avoid confusion I shall no longer employ this term in the sense that derives from Heidegger.

11. *Logic*, p. 107.

12. See chap. 9 below.

13. The model is retained by both Sartre and Merleau-Ponty, but there are differences, even though for both Heidegger's world eventually becomes a social world conceived in more or less Marxist terms. Since I shall be dealing later mainly with Sartre, I might warn that terms closely associated with "world" in Merleau-Ponty are "field" and "landscape." "The world," he explains, is the "field of my experience" (*Perception*, p. 406). This usage is consistent with his focus on perception and hence on "The Phenomenal Field" (the title of the chapter in which he makes his transition from his review of "Traditional Prejudices" to his own phenomenological analysis). The term "field" is significantly ambiguous because it can acquire more concrete reference to a landscape one perceives (see n. 113, this chapter), which is also a genre of painting (see p. 526 below).

14. *Being and Time*, p. 92.

15. Ibid., pp. 117, 303, 92. The relevance of this terminology for existential individualism is more obvious if one recalls that *Selbstand* was used in the sixteenth century to translate *persona*.

16. *Being and Time*, p. 84.

17. *Sartre*, pp. 61, 66.

18. *Being and Nothingness*, p. 623. Heidegger would not employ the adjective in the plural as referring to us as individual human beings.

19. Thus Sartre goes on to argue, "This abandonment has no other origin than the very existence of our freedom" (ibid.).

20. Ibid., pp. 134–46; *Critique*, pp. 79–83.

21. *Being and Time*, p. 368. Heidegger himself notes that the two terms have traditionally been used "interchangeably" ("The Way Back to the Ground of Metaphysics," in Barrett, 3:133). In fact it was in order to translate the Latin *existentia* that *Dasein* entered philosophical German in the seventeenth century. Hegel took advantage of the availability of the two terms and reserves "existence" for what proceeds from a ground (see chap. 2, n. 68 above). I did not initially bother to distinguish the two terms, for the earliest French interpreters of Heidegger (e.g., Gurvitch, Lévinas) often translated *Dasein* as "existence," and Sartre and Merleau-Ponty themselves often

blend their implications. Thus in the vision of *Nausea* "to exist is simply *to be there*" (*Sartre*, p. 64; italics in original), and in explaining existentialism Sartre defines "an existence" as "a certain effective presence [i.e., *Dasein*] in the world [i.e., as being-in-the-world]" (Contat, 2:157). Sartre sometimes keeps the German *Dasein* or employs the etymological translation, *être-là*, but he ordinarily follows Corbin, who did the first influential translations of Heidegger into French (1938), and renders *Dasein* as *la réalité humaine*. This "monstrous translation," Derrida explains, "prevailed by the authority of Sartre" and betrays his humanizing of Heidegger's existential analytic (*Marges*, p. 136; see p. 23 above). I prefer to characterize Sartre as vulgarizing Heidegger's existential analytic, because of the other distinctions he is collapsing in implementing this translation. Be suspicious of a philosopher who adds up another philosopher's distinctions and concludes, "What all this amounts to is . . . " (see p. 81 above). When Sartre does discriminate, it is by developing in effect a dialectical opposition between terms which refer to the dimension of our passivity, of our being "thrown" (the most prominent of these is "facticity," which is equated in Sartre with "contingency") and the terms which refer to the active way man "makes himself" (*se fait*) or "throws himself forward." The latter we encountered earlier: "project," "transcendence" (recall how Merleau-Ponty referred to our "transcendence" as "active"), and "existence" itself. *Being-there* is assigned a passive reference by Sartre (e.g., "the simple fact of *being-there*, as pure receptivity"; *L'idiot*, 1:54; italics in original) and becomes equivalent to "facticity." I am citing *L'idiot* where the discrimination is clearest because Sartre is analyzing what he describes as Flaubert's "active passivity" (1:52).

22. *Being and Time*, p. 368. Heidegger is expressing his distrust of spatial metaphors insofar as their use can be taken to imply a distinction between the metaphorical and the literal.

23. When I occasionally use the traditional translation "existence," I shall add *Dasein* in parentheses. Otherwise I shall use the translation "*being-there*." The spatial implications of the German are often paraphrased by French existentialists. Thus in discussing "Husserl et la notion de nature," Merleau-Ponty allows Heidegger's term to intrude in the guise of "a localized being" ("Husserl et la notion de Nature," p. 263). Merleau-Ponty frequently employs the concept of "subject," which is entirely alien to Heidegger, but then adds a qualifying paraphrase incorporating what he takes to be Heidegger's adjustment in the meaning of the concept. Citing *Being and Time*, p. 366, he explains that "the subject is a being-in the-world" (*Perception*, p. 430). Similarly, he refers to "a subject modified by locality and himself situated in the space in which he unfolds the spectacle of a point of view" (*Themes from the Lectures*, p. 8).

24. *Climacus*, p. 106; italics mine.

25. *Papirer*, IV C 97, A 54.

26. Ibid., VIII[1] A 18.

27. "The Logical Question in Hegel's System," *Journal of Speculative Philosophy* 5 (1871): 358. As stated so far, the question of movement is from Kierkegaard's point of view essentially the same as the question of whether a "transition" (in existence) is logically necessary or contingent (see chap. 2, n. 65 above).

28. Trendelenburg, p. 359.

29. *Papirer*, V C 12.

30. "The Age of the World Picture," p. 19. The different character of existential movement in *Being and Time* is illustrated by the bestowal of a ring: "When a ring gets 'handed over' and 'worn' . . . , it does not suffer in its being a simple change of location" (p. 389).

31. This translation, like *Vorstellung*, can refer both to the psychological process of representing something and to its outcome. (I also need a translation which will later enable me to bring out the etymological overlap with *Darstellung*, which I shall translate simply as "representation.") In chap. 14 we shall see that history is a matter for

"imaginative representation" in Hegel and that this raises issues for Kierkegaard regarding the status of what he calls his "storytelling method" as well as of the biblical narrative. But the issues raised cannot be restricted to the differences between their psychological and historical dialectics. In my sequel issues between a dialectical and a phenomenological method and the various blends can be brought out as differences between the resulting analyses of imagination. Husserl emphasizes "The Privileged Position [*Vorzugsstellung*] of Free Imagination [*Phantasie*]" in the application of his phenomenological method *(Ideas,* p. 181). Sartre cites Husserl's emphasis but objects both to features of Husserl's phenomenological analysis of the imagination itself and to his failure to provide a complete analysis *(Imagination,* p. 128), which is what Sartre proceeds to attempt in *L'imaginaire.* Heidegger's attack on *Vorstellung* broadly conceived is pivotal to his "destruction" (see p. 386 below) not only of the metaphysical tradition but also of its esthetics with its representational theory of art.

32. *Encyclopaedia,* pt. 3, par. 450, *Zusatz.*

33. Ibid., pars. 445, 450, *Zusatz.*

34. Heidegger attacks the concept of *Vorstellung* in the process of undercutting the distinction between a "subject" who "places" something as an "object" before his mind. But he is not simply attacking "imaginative representation" but the more fundamental concept of "representation" (see translator's note to "The Age of the World Picture," p. 120). Consideration of his attack is best deferred until we can take into account the phenomenological way Husserl draws the subject/object distinction, as opposed to the way it is drawn dialectically.

35. *Encyclopaedia,* pt. 3, pars. 454; 455, 456, *Zusatz.*

36. *Sickness,* p. 46. Reflection here retains the character of a mirror image—i.e., it is intrinsically incapable of transcending duality. For Kierkegaard's reliance on this analogy, see p. 160 below. This meaning that Kierkegaard assigns to the term "reflection" is frequently found in Hegel. See, e.g., the following: "Reflection is the activity which establishes the antitheses and goes from one to the other without, however, being able to effect their combination [*Verbindung*] and bring to pass their pervasive unity" *(Philosophy of Religion,* 1:204–5). But Kierkegaard extends this conception of reflection to include the movement of speculative thinking which in Hegel transcends reflection and does grasp the pervasive unity.

37. Kierkegaard is satisfied to borrow terminology, since aside from retrieving the subject/object, internal/external distinctions, he is not really concerned with epistemological issues, as I shall try to explain in my postscript. His casualness is illustrated by his employment of the term *Phantasie* when he appeals to Fichte, although Fichte himself employed the term *Einbildungskraft.* I shall accordingly translate both the Danish cognates as "imagination." Kierkegaard also uses rather indiscriminately the Danish cognates for *Vorstellung* and *Einbildungskraft.* Sometimes his choice seems to be dictated by etymology—i.e., by whether he wishes to take advantage of the metaphor of "placing before" the mind or prefers the range of meanings of *billede (Bild)*—"image," "picture," "metaphor."

38. *Irony,* p. 348. The Latin original reads, "Aristophanes in Socrate depingendo proxime ad verum accessit." What I am trying to bring out is the notion of imaginative truth which is at stake in this thesis.

39. Ibid., pp. 158, 180. "Lifting . . . up," the "ascension," and "rising up" (see p. 77 above, where *gaaer op* was translated "subsumed") all allude to Hegel's *Aufhebung.* I shall deal in chap. 13 with Hegel's analogous theological references to Christ's ascension, transfiguration, and resurrection.

40. I do not claim that the quoted terms are equivalent in Hegel himself. But it is characteristic of the vulgarizer (whether he is Cicero or Polybius quarrying Plato [see chap. 2, n. 51 above], Sartre or Merleau-Ponty quarrying Heidegger [see n. 21, this chapter], or Kierkegaard quarrying Hegel [see n. 37, this chapter]) to take over from the predecessor more terminology than he in fact needs to carry out his own analysis,

which is less complicated at the traditional philosophical level. The complications emerge instead in relating philosophy to life or existence (see chap. 2, n. 88 above), and these complications (we are beginning to see) are best dealt with imaginatively.

41. Matters are complicated here by Plato's reliance on imagery, which is much more frequent than Hegel's. So far I have treated Kierkegaard as identifying Plato with Hegel, just as in opposing Hegel he identifies himself with Socrates. But there is a wobble in this dialectic. Kierkegaard has to admit that "Plato's element is not thought [Hegel's element] but imaginative representation" (*Irony*, p. 134) and that "the dialectical movement is never fully fulfilled" in Plato as it is in Hegel (p. 136). For "fullness" as a Hegelian criterion, see pp. 482–83 below.

42. *Irony*, pp. 167, 166. The clouds as the chorus also represent society and more specifically the dissolution of the established social norms to which Xenophon's Socrates remains dedicated, as "an apostle of finitude, an officious advertiser, propagandizing for mediocrity" (p. 157).

43. For other instances of the image "hovering" in *Irony*, see pp. 54, 85, 151, 180, 184, 240, 279; for "suspension," see pp. 412, 470 below.

44. *Either*, p. 330; my italics. Socrates as ironist is identified as a seducer (*Irony*, pp. 84–88, 213–16), and irony is identified as seductive in a sense which will be explored in chap. 7.

45. See p. 33 above.

46. "On the Essence of Truth," p. 106.

47. *Sartre*, pp. 61, 62. The novel that the protagonist of *Nausea* anticipates writing the reader "would have to be able to suspect . . . behind the pages, something which did not exist, which would be above existence. It would have to be beautiful and hard as steel" (ibid., p. 72). Just as "hard as steel" is a concretization of the theme of rigidity, so "sagging" is a concretization of the theme of passivity (see n. 21, this chapter; for concretization, see chap. 4, n. 47 below). Sartre's romantic Platonism is Baudelairean. See, e.g., *L'irrémédiable*: "Une Idée, une Forme, un Etre / Parti de l'azur et tombé / Dans un Styx bourbeux et plombé / Où nul oeil du Ciel ne pénètre." For Bouville as "un Styx bourbeux," see chap. 9, n. 54.

48. *Sartre*, pp. 61–62.

49. Ibid., pp. 64, 61.

50. Insofar as it is relevant to existential individualism, Heidegger's argument that "the *substance* of man" is "*existence*" is a recognition of the "possible *Unselbständigkeit* of the self" (*Being and Time*, p. 117), which is closely related to its "inauthenticity" (p. 128). The structure of movement involved is characterized by Heidegger as "inconclusive falling" (p. 322), and it will be examined in chap. 8. For Sartre's comparable character-ization of the self as a "composite" which is "ambiguous, contradictory, and unstable," see chap. 5, no. 61 below. This unstable structure survives Sartre's ostensible conversion to Marxism. He explains that by "what we call existence [see chap. 2, n. 73 above] . . . we do not mean a stable substance which remains in itself but a continual disequi-librium, an entire wrenching away from itself" (*Search for a Method*, p. 151).

51. See the disposal by Sartre's protagonist of the founding fathers of Bouville who are portrayed in the museum, where their roles have been transfigured by art: "Fare-well, beautiful lilies, elegant in your painted little sanctuaries, farewell, . . . our pride and reason for existing, farewell, you filthy bastards" (*Nausea*, p. 94). For *l'esprit de sérieux*, see *Sartre*, pp. 124–29.

52. See p. 205 below.

53. *Either*, p. 330; my italics.

54. See p. 60 above.

55. *L'idiot*, 1:1277–78. "The jolting of the cab" is "the projection into the practico-inert of the spasmodic movements of copulation" (p. 1286). The "practico-inert" is (roughly) the material realm as it has been articulated and shaped by practical activities. It is the materialist analogue of the earlier Sartre's phenomenological and Gestaltist conception of "hodological space."

56. I dwell on the "layout" of Plato's cave for two reasons: first, in order not to not give the impression that such "interpretation" is restricted to a text; second, to indicate that "interpretation" as "laying out" is always spatial, in that what is interpreted is thereby recognized to occupy a "place" which is specific to it. Thus "poetry, like the thinking of the philosopher [which in Hegel transcends spatial "determinants"], has always so much world space to spare [*soviel Weltraum ausgespart*] that in it each thing—a tree, a mountain, a house, the cry of a bird—loses all indifference and commonplaceness" (*Introduction to Metaphysics*, p. 22).

57. "Plato's Doctrine of Truth," p. 183. There is no explicit reference in Plato to the vault [*Gewölbe*] of the cave. I suspect Heidegger wants a feature of the "layout" comparable to his own "horizon" (*Being and Time*, p. 1).

58. "Plato's Doctrine of Truth," p. 177.

59. *Being and Time*, pp. 108–10. This reflexive relation is developed in Sartre, who brings "the world" within the compass of what he describes as "the circuit of selfhood" (*Sartre*, pp. 178–81).

60. *Sartre*, p. 273.

61. *Existence and Being*, p. 275.

62. In ordinary German *Entfernung* means "removal to a distance" or "at a remote distance," but Heidegger detaches the prefix and gives it independent force, so that he can take the term to mean "de-distancing." Perhaps one point of the word play is that *being-there* would remove in its "goings about" a distance that cannot ultimately be circumvented, inasmuch as the *being* that is *there* is itself spatial. Put in the very different terms of Sartre's "circuit of selfhood," the "world appears as the pure distance between the self and the self" (*Being and Nothingness*, p. 336).

63. See p. 73 above.

64. *Being and Nothingness*, pp. 52, 55. See chap. 2, n. 74 above.

65. *Essays in Aesthetics*, p. 47.

66. *Being and Time*, 126–27.

67. *Die Kunst und der Raum*, p. 5.

68. *Essays in Aesthetics*, pp. 46, 48.

69. *Situations*, 4:399. See also the expulsion promoted by the "lunging in two opposing directions" (n. 77, this chapter).

70. *Situations*, 4:403.

71. Bauer, pp. 142, 152–53, 156.

72. *Essays in Aesthetics*, pp. 70–71.

73. See chap. 10 below.

74. P. 3.

75. *History of Philosophy*, 1:267–68.

76. *Essays in Radical Empiricism*, p. 238.

77. I have also drawn attention to Sartre's predilection for the more dislocating emotions (p. 84 above). The part we have seen "revulsion" play in Sartre himself prepares us for the frequency with which the dislocating emotion he finds significant in Flaubert's case is dis-gust (e.g., 2:1473). Despair is the next most frequent. The only emotion more frequent than disgust is discomfort (*malaise*), which rather regularly provides Sartre with a starting point for his dialectical analysis. Thus by the time "Flaubert was six, a fundamental fixation was a certain 'difficulty in being,' which translates as a psychosomatic *malaise*" (*L'idiot*, 1:57). For other striking examples of *malaise*, see 1:48, 180; 2:1467, 1507, 1723, 1682. It becomes clear in the third volume of *L'idiot* that this *malaise* is not just psychoanalytic but sociohistorical in its scope. But let us take a case where Sartre begins with the sociohistorical background and where his analysis is less convoluted: Tintoretto poses for Sartre the problem of discovering "if his time recognized itself in him without *malaise*" (*Situations*, p. 16; the published translation misses the force of *malaise*). We can then turn from his "time" to the painter as an individual: "Tintoretto was born in a city in upheaval [*ville bouleversée*]; he has breathed the Venetian *malaise*, it gnaws away at him, it is *all* that he knows how to

paint" (p. 46; my italics). We are now ready to consider the way he paints, for as observed in Contat (1:488), Sartre's appraisal of the painting he analyzes, "Saint George and the Dragon," is an attempt "to find corroboration . . . for the socioexistential analysis." Thus the e-motional *malaise* of the "city in upheaval" is conveyed by the *décalages* ("cracks" in the translation, *Between Existentialism and Marxism*, p. 183) of the painting. The first instance adduced is the "passive abandonment of a body [the princess] to the disorders of fear" (p. 181). This Heideggerian predicament (see p. 103 above) is imparted by the painter's treatment of her cloak: "A lunging in two opposing directions expels the knight and propels toward us a display of the blindest of passions—fear. . . . In this painting . . . the only fine plumage [i.e., the cloak] is that of fright; only it is allowed to be pink. Why? Does he want to demoralize us? Yes, in a certain fashion" (p. 180). In chap. 9 I shall deal with Sartre's own attempt to demoralize us.

78. *L'idiot*, 1:27, 72, 128; 2:1450.
79. *Perception*, p. 426.
80. Sartre comments on Merleau-Ponty's terminology: *"Ecart, déviation, dérive*—words he repeated a hundred times" (*Situations*, p. 170).
81. *Primacy of Perception*, p. 29.
82. *Search for a Method*, p. 30.
83. This label enables me to beg questions which are not directly relevant here; what Sartre himself has in mind by and large is Engels's interpretation consolidated by certain French Stalinist intellectuals. But some of the traits that Sartre criticizes are prominent in his general critique of the "conventional" (see chap. 8 below).
84. *Situations*, 7:57–58. The proletariat itself is characterized as a class undergoing "uninterrupted upheaval" (p. 19).
85. On one hand "a living philosophy" is "one with the movement of society"; on the other, "if this movement on the part of philosophy no longer exists, . . . either philosophy is dead or it is 'in crisis.'" Sartre opts for the second alternative: "The 'philosophical crisis' is the particular expression of a social crisis, and the immobility of philosophy is conditioned by the contradictions which split [*déchirent*] society." (*Search for a Method*, p. 7).
86. *Situations*, 7:56.
87. *Search for a Method*, p. 137; italics in original.
88. *L'idiot*, 2:1690.
89. *Search for a Method*, p. 56.
90. *Postscript*, p. 250. See also *Either*, p. 220. This complaint is developed at length by Sartre as integral to existentialism: "Predicted by the system [as the moment of the "unhappy consciousness"], he discredits the system entirely by not appearing . . . as a moment to be transcended or at the juncture which the master has designated for him" ("The Singular Universal," in *Between Existentialism and Marxism*, p. 144).
91. *Signs*, pp. 3–4.
92. The expression is Kierkegaard's (see p. 540 below).
93. *Signs*, p. 4.
94. Ibid., p. 3.
95. *Humanism and Terror*, p. 170.
96. See p. 42 above.
97. *Papirer*, X5 A 104.
98. See my postscript (pt. V).
99. *Nouvelle observateur*, vol. 7 (February 1977).
100. Sartre mentions in particular the rupture between Merleau-Ponty and Camus, and his own effort to reconcile them: "What perverse temperament prompted me to become the mediator between two friends, both of whom, a little later, would reproach me for my friendship with the Communists, and who are now both dead, unreconciled" (*Situations*, p. 175).
101. *Humanism and Terror*, pp. 160–61.

102. *Situations*, p. 209. The *ex-sistentialist* focus on dislocated relations is illustrated by the attention Sartre pays to the rupture between Merleau-Ponty and Camus and then to the rupture between both of them and himself. The focus is established at the very start of the memorial essay on Merleau-Ponty: "How many are the friends I have lost who are still alive. No one was at fault. They were. I was" (ibid., p. 156).

103. Ibid., p. 174. Translators are often disconcerted by *ex-sistential* dislocations, and *me fit sauter le pas* is unforgivably weakened to "caused me to make an important decision," while *m'arracher* is weakened to "release me."

104. Ibid., pp. 194, 198, 225. Aside from the initiative which "each . . . took," they were both, Sartre adds, "carrying out the 'work of rupture' in the sense in which Freud has demonstrated that mourning is work."

105. Ibid., pp. 159, 204–5.

106. I am requoting Sartre's citation from Engels.

107. *Situations*, pp. 225–26. These personal portraits are opposed dialectically to "Official Portraits" (Contat, 2:64–66), such as those his protagonist contemplates during his visit to the museum at Bouville (see chap. 00 below). But (in Kierkegaard's phrase) a "relation . . . underlies the disrelation"—Sartre's preoccupation with "Faces" (Contat, 2:67–71), which takes a particularly personal form in his conduct of his sexual affairs (see *Life/Situations*, p. 65).

108. *Being and Time*, p. 132.

109. See p. 87 above.

110. *Being and Time*, esp. pp. 417–18.

111. See p. 117 above.

112. *Being and Time*, p. 325.

113. *Visible and Invisible*, p. 121. A pocket watch also turns up in Heidegger (*Being and Time*, p. 416). In Merleau-Ponty even a view of a landscape can suffer change over time: "It is pointless my telling myself, as I contemplate those russet mountainsides [of Mt. Hymettus], that the Greeks saw them too" (*Perception*, p. 406).

114. *Being and Time*, p. 1.

115. *Metaphysics* 980a; *Nichomachean Ethics* 1139b.

116. See p. 97 above.

117. See p. 96 above.

118. *Visible and Invisible*, p. 104. "The event appropriates it to itself" probably reflects Heidegger's manipulation of *Ereignis*, whose ordinary meaning is "event." One affiliation Heidegger discovers is *Auge*, which Merleau-Ponty could associate with visibility. (He has also written on "Eye and Mind.") Another is *eigen* ("own"), which suggests appropriation—a theme which Heidegger does not emphasize (at any rate, not in the sense of property [*Eigentum*]), but which Hegel does (see p. 263 below), as do Kierkegaard and Sartre, as well as Merleau-Ponty.

119. "The contingency of the human event is now no longer a defect in the logic of history; it becomes its condition. Without contingency there is only a phantom of history. If it is known where history is inevitably headed, each successive event by itself has no importance or meaning, the future ripens whatever happens, nothing is really at stake in the present since, whatever it is, it is headed toward the same future" (*Praise of Philosophy*, p. 52).

120. *L'idiot*, 1:245; *Saint Genet*, p. 497.

121. Contat, 2:174, 176. Sartre does allow a little respite: "It is said the runner from Marathon was dead an hour before he got to Athens. He was dead and he was still running; he was running dead; he announced the Greek victory dead. It's a fine myth; it shows that for a little while longer the dead continue to act, as if they were living. A little while—one year, ten years, maybe even fifty, but in any case a *finite* period— and then they're buried a second time" (ibid., p. 178). It is ironical that Sartre has not himself been allowed this respite but in France at least has suffered so complete an eclipse, while still alive, before his burial the first time, that he can volunteer the information (in English) that he is "a has been" (*Life/Situations*, p. 22).

122. These are opening phrases in Murdoch's *Sartre: Romantic Rationalist.* Sartre's own conception of his contemporaneity seems to be comparable to his conception of Tintoretto's relation to *his* time: Sartre would have his time recognize itself in him with *malaise* (cf. n. 77, this chapter).

123. *Sartre,* 484–85.

124. *Sartre on Theater,* pp. 277, 271; see also pp. 300, 261.

125. Hegel, *Aesthetics,* 2:1215.

Part II

Dialectic

Expositions of dialectic are as misguided as the procedure of attempting to explain the flowing of a spring at its source by starting out from the stagnant waters that have accumulated from its overflow.
—Heidegger

4

The Unsteady Vision

We see the world unsteadily and flickeringly in accordance with our moods.—Heidegger

METHOD

At the beginning of part I reasons were lined up why an introduction to existentialism should at the same time provide a suitable introduction to the problem of interpreting a philosophical movement. I even suggested that this interpretation might provide a suitable introduction to philosophy itself, since there is a sense in which any individual starts out as a philosopher in some relation to a philosophical movement as well as to his own experience. Indeed existentialism affords the further advantage as an introduction that it is a philosophical movement in which the relation to one's personal experience as an individual is deliberately maintained.

I shall consider in this chapter respects in which the existentialist handling of this and other relations is dialectical. But let me first claim that existentialism should provide a suitable introduction to the workings of a dialectic generally. Such an introduction is badly needed today. Other conceptions of philosophical method have enjoyed frequent sifting and appraisal. Questions of methodology in the physical and social sciences have been a large part of the careers of several generations of Anglo-American philosophers. But no one has taken very much trouble to sort out and illustrate in detail the general traits of a dialectical method, though there are of course notable accounts of the specific methods of individual dialecticians—Plato, Aquinas, Hegel, Marx, as well as particular existentialists.

Of course the fact that an introduction is badly needed suggests that an acceptable introduction is not entirely likely. It is not only that less significant attention has been paid to dialectic but also that Anglo-American criteria for appraising methodological procedures derive so exclusively from logic and the philosophy of science, and criteria so derived do not fit when a procedure is dialectical. The specifics of John Stuart Mill's own logic and philosophy of science may have been long since outmoded in our tradition, but no methodological conviction has been renewed so regularly by Anglo-American philosophers as his reaction to Hegel's dialectic:

> I found by actual experience of Hegel that conversancy with him tends to deprave one's intellect. The attempt to unwind an apparently infinite series of self contradictions not disguised but openly faced & coined into . . . [illegible word] science by being stamped with a set of big abstract terms, really if persisted in impairs the acquired delicacy of perception of false reasoning & false thinking which has been gained by years of careful mental discipline with terms of real meaning. For some time after I had finished the book all such words as *reflexion*, *development*, *evolution*, etc., gave me a sort of sickening feeling which I have not yet entirely got rid of.[1]

Such nausea is perhaps the only form of existential experience that Anglo-American philosophers have not yet entirely got rid of.

Existential dialectic may not seem less sickening than other versions. But Hegel's dialectic is too difficult; the interpreter has to intervene so extensively and overlay the original text with so many elucidations that the reader is inclined to wonder if he is still making contact with Hegel himself. Plato's dialogues may seem easier, but the reader is likely to run afoul of the frequent presumption today that insofar as Plato's dialectic is plausible he is engaged in analytic philosophy at an "adolescent" phase of its development.[2] Why expose oneself unnecessarily to the naïveté of adolescence?

Although I am recommending existentialism as an introduction to a dialectical method, there is a complication which should not be forgotten, granted that it takes us beyond introductory considerations. I mentioned at the outset the widespread suspicion that it was the adoption of the phenomenological method which has lent contemporary existentialism a coherence it would not otherwise have attained. In fact the interpretation of contemporary existentialism has been caught up in debates over the criteria and merits of phenomenological method, as opposed to a more precise "logical" or "scientific" method. But these debates have themselves lacked precision to the extent that they fail to allow for the differences between a dialectical and a phenomenological method.[3] I have accordingly undertaken to set forth in this introduction the distinctive traits of an existential method insofar as it is dialectical, as a necessary preliminary for probing in the sequel the general differences between a phenomenological and a dialectical method and the specifically different blends of the two methods which are characteristic of different existentialists.

LOCATION

One trait of existential dialectic we have already encountered: its application attains generality of scope. But this can hardly be considered a distinctive trait, since it is characteristic of most philosophical methods.

Hitherto I have been trying to interpret the scope attained simply by reference to subject matter: a dislocated structure is generally characteristic of an existential experience. But this evidence for generality remained incomplete, inasmuch as it did not include the methodological evidence of the attempt to locate which is dialectically implicit in the experience of dislocation—that is, implicit as the "opposite," the "contradiction," of the experience, in that we would not have this experience of dislocation if we were not making the attempt to locate. This attempt takes various other forms, which are not overtly existential. Recall the attempt of an antiexistentialist philosopher like Ayer to allocate existential problems for treatment to such subject matters as metaphysics, ethics, psychology; or the attempt by Gaston Berger to allocate existentialism itself to a particular time in social history, or the vogue of the term "existential" which was illustrated by the examples which had been compiled by an intellectual historian, not to expound existentialism itself but in order to give us an entertaining feel for the contemporary.[4] All these attempts could be construed in an existential dialectic as attempts to locate an experience or congeries of experiences.

We have heard Merleau-Ponty argue that the attempt to determine our place in history has itself become a pronounced trait of our place in history. Historians and journalists are perpetually taking our bearings. They are not only sensitive to historical changes as such, but they also look for those changes in our intellectual criteria, in our moral commitments, in our emotional susceptibilities, that would make us more sensitive to our location. There is no other quotation of the very quotable Virginia Woolf so frequently cited as her pronouncement, "Around 1910 people began to feel sorry for Clytemnestra."[5]

Whatever the particular guise which may be taken by this attempt to locate, the attempt itself is too general an undertaking to be allocated to any subject matter or time, though its general character may have emerged more definitely during our time. Sartre's "generation" may have had to live through "the bloody history" of "a society that was disrupted," and this may have been the experience of a particular period in history, but what the experience triggered was the more general attempt to "locate" (*situer*) oneself.[6]

When an existentialist refuses to allocate an existential experience to a particular subject matter for treatment, he is refusing to relinquish gen-

erality. A positive form taken by this refusal is the adoption by existentialists of an ontological language (and most obviously the term "existence"
itself), so it may be worth noting that the most primitive existential use
(in the standard linguistic meaning of "existential") of the term "being"
is the "locative sense." In English we still announce that something "is"
by employing the locative expression "there is," in French by employing
il y a. The *Oxford English Dictionary* explains that "to be" in its primitive sense meant "to occupy a place." This primitive sense becomes
existentially relevant when Merleau-Ponty defines a man as the "located
being" (*être localisé*).[7] Presumably he intends this definition as equivalent
to Heidegger's *being-there*. But it is not just a question of *being-there* as
a subject matter undergoing definition; Heidegger's analysis of *being-
there* also carries methodological implications in that *being-there* is
the being who "defines its own 'location.' "[8] Existentialism is an acknowledgment that man is perpetually attempting to determine his own location, as when he defines himself with Aristotle as "rational" (as opposed
to other animals) or with Descartes as a "thinking thing" (as opposed to
extended things) or, in the Christian philosophical tradition, which culminates in Hegel, according to Heidegger, as "finite" (as opposed to
"infinite"). By including such traditional generalizations as particular
instances of the attempt by *being-there* to define its own location,
existentialism is demonstrating its own more general scope.

DEFINITION

As these examples remind us, the existential attempt to locate is a
more concrete version of the traditional philosophical procedure of
definition. In fact in many traditional dialectics, as in existentialism, the
process of definition exceeds in its generality the usual scope accorded a
definition. If Plato's *Republic* takes in a remarkable range of topics in
order to define justice, so too does *Das Kapital* in defining capital. Kierkegaard's entire dissertation is spent defining irony, his *Concept of Anxiety*
defines anxiety, *Sickness unto Death* defines despair, and *Either/Or* defines the poet, as the paradigm for the esthetic stage of life's way. The conflation of existentialism with phenomenology will be facilitated inasmuch
as phenomenological method involves an "eidetic analysis" which can be
construed as a process of definition.[9] Sartre's *Being and Nothingness* he
characterizes as an "eidetic analysis of self-deception." In his earlier so-
called phenomenological writings, Sartre defines the self (*The Transcendence of the Ego*), the imagination (*L'imaginaire*), the emotions (*Theory*

of the Emotions). Merleau-Ponty's major work, *The Phenomenology of Perception*, defines the act of perception.

In considering this **first** procedure and other traits of an existential dialectic, I shall continue with miscellaneous examples from various existentialists. Later it will be easier to show how these traits consort if I focus on one philosopher at a time. In this chapter I shall eventually pay most attention to Heidegger, since his *Being and Time* played so pivotal a role in the emergence of existentialism as a contemporary philosophical movement and in its conflation with the phenomenological movement. I shall then go on in the next chapter to Sartre and in the remaining chapter on method to Kierkegaard.

I shall take up the traits of an existential dialectic in a sequence in which later traits can to a certain extent be presented as specifications of earlier traits. Thus the **second** trait to be considered specifies how generality of scope is attained by the process of definition. The process is a **relational analysis**—an analysis that travels along a network of relations. For the moment consider only larger-scale relations: Heidegger's *Being and Time* defines being in its relation to time. Sartre's *Being and Nothingness* defines nothingness in its relation to being. Sartre's *L'imaginaire* defines the act of imagination in relation to the act of perception: when one performs an act of perception, one is conscious of what one is conscious of as *being* there; when one performs an act of imagination, one is conscious of what one is conscious of as *not* being there.[10] *Either/Or* defines the poet in terms of the relation between the esthetic definition of himself the poet gives in *Either* and an ethical redefinition given in *Or*.

The relational criterion that controls an existential analysis as a process of definition is explicit. Kierkegaard sets up as "the requirement of existence—to put things together,"[11] and it is this requirement which is in effect being restated when he insists that the individual must put together the double movement whereby, if life can only be "understood backward," it must also be "lived forward." But it is in Heidegger's *Being and Time* that the criterion of "letting something be seen in its togetherness with something else" is most fully worked out.[12] The relational structure Heidegger analyzes in *Being and Time* "cannot be broken up into subject matters which can be pieced together" but is "primarily and continually a whole," though "this does not prevent it from having several dimensions," each of which can be "made to stand out in relief." Heidegger's effort, he explains, "is to place the analysis of single dimensions from the start . . . within the framework . . . of a view of the structural whole and to guard against any coming apart and splitting up of the unitary phenomenon."[13]

Transition

The fact that an existential method is an analysis of relations does not lend itself to elucidation as a single trait; different traits of an existential dialectic can be specified with respect to the relation or "dimension" that is "made to stand out in relief."[14] But more fundamental than any specific relation or "dimension" is the *relation between subject matter and method*. If Heidegger's resort to hyphenation (e.g., our "being-in-the-world" which we are "going about") seems merely intended to bring out the relational character of the *subject matter* undergoing analysis, recall the relational character of Heidegger's *method* of analysis which this subject matter requires and which is conveyed by the fact that it is a *methodos*—"a going after . . . along a way."[15] That method is also a "going" indicates that it cannot be severed from the subject matter of which it is a portion any more than portions of the subject matter can be severed from each other to become such particular subject matters as psychology and ethics.

This fundamental relation between subject matter and method can be taken up as a third trait of existential dialectic. Let me begin by renewing my earlier contrast between existentialism and traditional empiricism, in which the methods endorsed for the social sciences are (if we can rely on John Stuart Mill and most of his successors) "the methods of Physical Science, duly extended and generalized,"[16] and thus can be both abstracted from their original subject matter and applied to another to which their formulation originally bore no relation. This third trait, like the first two, existential dialectic shares with many other dialectical methods. Thus Hegel denies that subject matter and method are merely "externally related" to each other: "The form is the immanent becoming of the concrete content," and "the content is in itself transition [*Übergehen*] into form."[17]

This transitional relation is easing our own transition from existential subject matter ("content"), which we were investigating in part I to existential method ("form"). For advantage can be taken of the extent to which this previous investigation was in effect a preliminary illustration of the application of the method of existentialism. Thus some earlier examples can be refurbished.

The "transition" from subject matter to method in Heidegger can be traced in his own terms. *Being-there* is not only the subject matter already examined—a "determinate," "definite," or "located" being; it is also methodologically a "defining," "determining," or "locating" being. For as we have seen, "being-there defines [or "determines"—*bestimmt* can be translated either way] its own location."[18] This **third** trait of existential dialectic, whereby method is related to subject matter, can be more specifically characterized as the **reflexivity** of its method of definition. It commits Heidegger to "letting being-there interpret itself."[19] The method he is employing is not borrowed from elsewhere and imposed upon the subject matter (in the fashion propounded in my citation from Mill); its application is a "listening in" to what is already "going on" with being-there. The method's reflexive involvement with this subject matter of what is already "going on" is a "going along with it and after it" (*Mit- und Nachgehen*).[20]

DEVELOPMENT

Nachgehen may recall *methodos*, which we have seen meant in Greek a "going after" or "pursuit," while *odos* itself meant "way" or "journey along a way." Since the subject matter is in movement, as we have also already seen, the method involved with it must keep up with its movement. This **dynamic** or **developmental** character of the method is a **fourth** trait of existential dialectic. This is why I often employ the term "trait" rather than "characteristic" of dialectical "procedures." "Trait" (like "procedure") is a very dead metaphor but can perhaps be revived by recalling its derivation from *trahere*, which means "to draw along," "draw away," or "draw out."[21]

This dynamic character of the method requires us to rectify too literal a notion of starting point. The starting point is not comparable to a mathematical point but is the initiation of a development, of a process of transformation. This process is relational in character: it is not a succession of points; it is "movement along a way" (*Be-weg-ung*).[22] There is accordingly a problem of determining the relation between where one starts and the ensuing development. I shall take up this problem later in connection with Kierkegaard's dialectic.[23]

In Heidegger *being-there* is "stretched out" en route [*unterwegs*].[24] In other words its "thereness" is not a static location and is not subject to a fixed definition. When *being-there* "de-fines" its being reflexively as "definite being," it is by locating itself within "limits" ("fines") that set it "off" ("de") as "there." We usually think of "limits" as settled. But we have noted that Heidegger identifies his "preliminary aim" in *Being and Time* as "the interpretation of time as the possible horizon for any general understanding of being." "Horizon" derives from the Greek *horismos*, which can mean "definition," though we recognize that Heidegger uses the spatial metaphor to bring out not only the all encompassing but also the dynamic character of the process of definition. A "horizon" moves as we move along the way.

But a qualification must be added. We usually think of "limits" (e.g., a "horizon") as externally related to what they surround, whereas in the case of *being-there* they are relations which are internally pervasive. Their pervasive as well as dynamic character is brought out by Heidegger's warning that they do not constitute a "rigid framework within which the possible modes in which *being-there* conducts itself [or "relates itself"— the German speaks of the *Verhaltungen des Daseins*] . . . take their course without touching the framework itself."[25]

The metaphor of going along a way already carried in Kierkegaard the implication of reflexive involvement in a movement. Kierkegaard plays the metaphor off against the literal meaning. He explains that the physical moves of a traveler along a route can easily be mapped, since "he changes his situation without changing himself." Thus he can report, "I left Peking and arrived at Canton on the fourteenth and stayed there." But "the various stages [on life's way] are not like towns on a route of travel."[26] For a change from one stage to another involves reflexively a change in the traveler himself. This reflexivity implies in turn that there is no preexisting way; there is only the way each individual makes for himself. In the south German dialectic which Heidegger sometimes exploits, *bewegen* can be used transitively—for example, to refer to the way one makes for oneself through the deep snow. In Sartre "each man must find his own way."[27]

In both cases the procedure itself is reflexive and permits the personal reference that has been treated so far as a feature of existential subject matter: "Personality," Kierkegaard explains, "is not a collection of doctrines, nor is it immediately accessible; personality is bent in on itself, something closed, a shrine, a place of mystery." The reflexive structure of *being-there* also has a personal dimension; its being "is in each instance mine," so that "a personal pronoun must always be used in addressing it."[28]

DIRECTION

Although the metaphor of following a way is traditional in philosophy, a traditional presumption has been that the route to be followed not only can be laid down in advance but is also straight. Descartes's procedure is reflective, but it is not bent, as in Kierkegaard. It is a "straight route" (*le droit chemin*) that Descartes proposes with the rule of method that he models on a geometrical deduction: "To think in sequence, starting with matters which are simplest and easiest to understand and reaching step by step more complex knowledge."[29] The criteria controlling Descartes's procedure here are the mathematical ones of "clarity and distinctness," but when Heidegger starts out his treatment of the problem of being, though he acknowledges that the problem is "obscure," it is also *richtunglos* ("directionless").[30] The problem does not come with any built-in indication as to the direction in which we should proceed in dealing with it, such as the mathematical model provided Descartes, so that he could equip himself in advance with *Rules for the Direction of the Mind.*

This use of the "straight route" metaphor is not restricted to the rationalist as opposed to the empiricist tradition. Bacon's "new method" is designed to preclude "wandering" in one's investigations.[31] He explains that a "method rightly ordered leads by an unbroken route through the woods of experience to the open grounds of axioms."[32] The existentialist is less straightforward. His route is not a street, which etymologically should be straight, but a path which turns. It is a field path or wood road.[33]

The difficulty we have in finding our direction is posed by our dislocation. There is a difference between launching a scientific investigation and the start of philosophical inquiry: in the former case "there is always an immediate transition and approach [*Übergang* and *Eingang*], starting out from common representations, beliefs and thoughts. . . . The level of investigation selected will not be left behind when the investigation becomes more complicated and difficult. In contrast, philosophy involves a continuous dislocation of starting place and shifting of level." The contrast can be broadened to include Descartes's "scientific" philosophy, since he sought as his starting point a *fundamentum inconcussum* (an unshakable foundation), as Heidegger observes.[34]

Just as the relational character of existential dialectic is signalized by Heidegger's employment of hyphens, so changes in the direction in which he is proceeding are signalized by his changing prefixes. Our relevant example is the problem of "starting point" (*Aus-gang*). Initially the only problem of starting point, as we assumed in part I, would seem to be the problem of "going up to," of gaining "access to" (*Zu-gang*) the subject matter. But it then develops that this "access" is "obstructed" (*verdeckt*). Other features of the obstruction will be considered later, but we have already had one illustration; our usually being "scattered about" by our pre-occupations tends to preclude our dis-covery (*Ent-deckung*) of the relational structure of the world. Since we have no direct "access" to this structure, the meth-odological problem is, rather, a matter of "getting through" (*Durch-gang*) the obstruction. And this will be a reflexive problem of "going back" (*Rück-gang*) through the obstruction in order to uncover its structure.[35]

We have seen that the structure of our having been "scattered about" may become uncovered when "breaks" occur—the want of a nail, the breaking of a hammer, the failure of an expected guest to show up. But analysis does not usually wait upon the occurrence of an actual break. Verbal signs can be employed, as in *Being and Time*, to pick out the relations that are to "stand out in relief." But Heidegger's elucidation of this signifying procedure is itself based on an analysis of how we usually "go about" the world. The example in this analysis of a sign suggests how methodologically crucial changes in direction are. The example is a directional signal. He observes how "automobiles" are sometimes fitted up with an adjustable red arrow whose positions indicate the direction [*Weg*] the vehicle will take, for instance, at a crossroads [*Wegkreuzung*]." This signal, like the nail or hammer, is a "tool," a piece of "equipment," but it is adjustable; like the vehicle, it is a mobile piece of equipment. But unlike the vehicle, it is a piece of equipment for "signifying" or "indicating" (the German is *Zeigen*)—that is, for picking out and making explicit the shifting referential relations that compose a portion of the world about us. Note that this example does not suggest that a sign assigns a meaning ostensively. The signal instead articulates relevant relations, so that it solicits a relational analysis of how one indicates how one is "going about." We are presented not just with a crossroad, where the possibility has to be envisaged of one vehicle moving in a different direction from other vehicles, but with movements which are controlled by interrelated regulations. For traffic has its rules of *meth-odos*—rules for proceeding along a way—and Heidegger stresses the "interrelation" too between "vehicles" (*Verkehrsmitteln*) and "traffic regulations" (*Verkehrsregelungen*).[36] But *Verkehr* incorporates a root meaning "to turn" (*kehren*), and what Heidegger is focusing on in this relational nexus is a signal designed to indicate a change in direction. Merleau-Ponty similarly likes to play with the double meaning of *sens* in French: "meaning" and "direction."[37]

As I have anticipated, this analysis of the sign is basic to the elucidation of Heidegger's own meth-odological procedure. He has adopted the title *Signposts* (*Wegmarken*) for a collection of his essays. A signpost is valid only for a certain stretch of the way, when the way is not straight. The traveler himself can see no further, as Heidegger has admitted in his retrospective appraisal of *Being and Time*. He was following

> a way which was leading he knew not where. Only the immediate prospect was known. . . . The field of vision often shifted.[38]

Such shifts entail changes in the direction in which the later successive essays as "signposts" point.

Insofar as proceeding in a certain direction for a stretch of the way retains a methodological justification, it constitutes a *stage* in the development of an existential analysis. Proceeding by stages is a trait whose further treatment I am deferring until the chapter on Kierkegaard's dialectic. But successive stages are, broadly speaking, **changes in direction,** and such changes can be distinguished as a **fifth** trait of an existential dialectic.

THE REVERSAL

A specific change in direction which will come up for further illustration is that which is crucial to an existential dialectic—the **reversal.** This **sixth** trait too I shall deal with in more detail later, for it can also be construed as a dynamic and developmental specification of the principle of contradiction.

But one version of an existential reversal can be outlined now. This is a reversal of traditional philosophical procedure. One form in which Hegel (as we know, the favorite antagonist of the existentialist) presented his philosophy was as the outcome of the progressive evolution of the history of philosophy. An opposing form is Heidegger's presentation of his philosophy as a "going back" through this evolution in order to uncover the structure of the obstruction to philosophy which philosophy itself has become. I stress this *Rückgang* for two reasons. On one hand it is implicit in the way Heidegger starts out in *Being and Time*, when he claims that the problem of being has become "forgotten," so that his entire treatment is a "re-collection" (*Wieder-holung*)[39] and as such involves a reversal of direction. On the other hand all the traits of the existential dialectic which I have listed thus far, including the reversal, were already traits of traditional dialectic—and in particular Hegel's dialectic. What then is distinctively existential about an existential dialectic? A reversal in the more specific sense of the refusal, which was partly examined in part I, to abstract from spatial and temporal as well as personal relations. When Hegel starts out in his *Logic* with "being" as "the most abstract," "indeterminate," or "indefinite" of the categories,[40] he is abstracting from the determinacy of existence (*Da-sein*), which is a category that he defers to the next stage in his dialectic. There it is defined as "determinate being" (*bestimmtes Sein*), on the basis of the argument that "spatial representation is irrelevant here," though he admits that *Dasein* means etymologically "being in a certain place."[41]

We have seen that with this argument Hegel is discounting "imaginative representation" (*Vorstellung*), whereby something is located, "placed before," the mind in its spatial relations. Thus Heidegger is reversing the sequence of Hegel's treatment by starting out his own treatment of the problem of being (*Sein*) with being-there (*Dasein*).[42] (Reversal in sequence is the most obvious form of reversal in direction when method is itself represented imaginatively as proceeding along a way.) At the same time, Heidegger's redefinition of *Dasein* itself reverses Hegel's procedure of abstracting from etymology and from spatial relations. *Being-there* in Heidegger accordingly "takes up space," and its being-in-the-world is the assignment of a directional structure (*Ausrichtung*) to this world. It is this directional structure which is respected by the sequence Heidegger is following by starting out his own treatment of *being-there* with the direction it takes when it "goes about" the world or, rather, with its being "scattered" in different directions by its "goings about."[43]

The traditional procedure of abstraction has left its mark on the evolution of language as well as of philosophy. Having explained that "to be" in its primitive sense meant "to occupy a place," the *Oxford English Dictionary* adds that the sense now prevailing was "derived by abstracting from the notion of particular place" so as to arrive at an abstract notion of "existence" as meaning "to be somewhere, no matter where." The process of abstraction, I would add, was probably in some measure the progressive accomplishment of the philosophical tradition. In ordinary Greek it was still "necessary," as Plato explains, "for everything which is to be somewhere, in some place."[44] The philosophical tradition may have been encouraged to carry out this process of abstraction by the fact that it was (as Heidegger puts it) an "onto-theological" tradition—that is, a tradition in which the problem of being was the problem of a supreme being, for the Christian God did not occupy a place and could not be approached by traversing "intervals of place."[45]

EFFACEMENT

The spatial metaphors examined in the preceding chapter are to be visualized as an attempted reversal of the movement of meta-physical abstraction with which the philosophical tradition effaced such imagery. This was a traditional procedure long before it was codified by Hegel as the *Aufhebung* of "canceling out" and "transcending" the spatial relations of *Vorstellungen*. The traditional procedure is itself accorded a metaphorical rendering by a French philosopher who has been influenced by Heidegger but who has also sought out the help of a novelist:

> Metaphysicians, when they construct a language, resemble knife grinders who, instead of grinding knives and scissors, would grind medals and coins, in order to efface . . . the effigy. When they have reached the point where one can no longer see on their coins either Victoria, or William, or the French Republic, they claim; "These coins have nothing English, nor German, nor French about them; we have withdrawn them from time and space; they are worth no longer

five francs but a value beyond price, and their currency is extended indefinitely."[46]

Heidegger is concerned with "effacement" (*Verwischung*) primarily as a process in which "being" has become, in Nietzsche's phrase, "the last hazy streak of an evaporating reality" which (Heidegger goes on to embroider metaphorically on the phrase), "if we grasp it, dissolves like a tatter of cloud in the sunlight." Heidegger traces the process of abstraction and effacement as delineated by "the rigid forms" of grammar in which "language has been caught fast, as in a steel net." The philosophical tradition took over from grammar for conceptualization the substantive *Sein* ("being"), which derives from the infinitive *sein* ("to be"). An "in-finitive" is an "un-limited," "in-determinate," or "in-definite" form of a verb; its "meaning is cut off and abstracted from all determinate or definite relations"—not only the personal relations which we earlier saw are so prominent in existentialism (e.g., "I am," "you have been," "we were") but also the temporal relations which are likewise exhibited by the conjugation of the verb (*Zeitwort*—"time word" in German). The meanings at stake in both instances were not originally abstract grammatical relations (the rigid "steel net") but could be represented spatially as "changes of the same word in accordance with definite directions of meaning."[47]

SITUATION

The reversal of the traditional procedure of abstraction can be illustrated by all the traits of an existential dialectic that have already been examined. Existential reliance on such spatial metaphors as "location" renders more concrete the procedure of *de-finition* (our first trait). But we can also observe that the notion of location undergoes in turn that crystallization of meaning which is found in the most prevalent of existentialism's spatial metaphors—"situation."[48] We do not ordinarily speak of the "situation" a physical thing is in; we ordinarily reserve "situation" for a location which has some concrete significance in "human space." *Situations* has become a general title for the ten-volume collection of Sartre's essays, including the volume *Portraits* which I cited in the preceding chapter. Even his longer—his very long—works he refuses to regard as anything but *livres de circonstances*.

Although the stress on location and situation is common to existentialists, there are still more concrete differences which I have already acknowledged as differences of loci but which do not concern us in this volume. These are differences in the *relations* (our second trait) which are (in Heidegger's phrase) "made to stand out in relief." Kierkegaard analyzes primarily psychological relations that compose the structure of the self; in "Division One" of *Being and Time*) Heidegger analyzes the cosmological relations that compose being-in-the-world. In Merleau-Ponty our relation to our bodies is primary, since "the body is our general medium for having a world", and "we must know at every moment of our life where our body is, without having to look for it as we look for an object moved from its place during our absence." For the body is "the place of appropriation" where "we take on [*assumons*] space." But in Sartre it is primarily in the setting of my relation to the Other that "I have a body" and "occupy a place."[49] The relational concepts of location and situation acquire further concreteness with other spatial metaphors. Merleau-Ponty, for example, not only prefers the metaphors of "field" and "landscape"[50] (just as Heidegger prefers the metaphor of "horizon"), but he also seeks the even more concrete spatial implications exemplified by a football field:

> For the player in action the football field is not an "object." It is pervaded by lines of force (the "yard" lines; those which demarcate the "penalty area") and articulated in sectors (e.g., the "openings" between members of the other team) which call for a certain line of action and which initiate and guide the action as if the player were unaware of it. . . . The player becomes one with the field and feels the direction of the "goal," for example, just as immediately as the vertical and the horizontal planes of his own body.[51]

Our ordinary reservation of the term "situation" for a location which has some concrete significance in "human space" cannot be fully explained without taking into account the term's *reflexive* reference—our third trait, which we characterized in Heidegger's terminology as the procedure by which *being-there* "defines its location." I have already examined the reflexive relation between method and subject matter implicit in Heidegger's method as a method of interpretation which can be construed more concretely as a method of "laying out" (*Auslegung*) and which is applied to the subject matter of Plato's cave as a layout which had already undergone "interpretation" by its occupants as well as by Plato. Any existential "situation" is a layout inasmuch as it has already undergone "interpretation" by the being who "defines its location."[52]

Sartre accentuates this character of my situation by adding a further reflexive twist to what is already the reflexive outcome of Kafka's story:

> A merchant comes to plead his case at the castle where a terrifying guard bars the entrance. The merchant does not dare to go further; he waits and dies still waiting. At the hour of his death he asks the guard,

"How does it happen that I was the only one waiting?" And the guardian replies, "This gate was made only for you." This is precisely the case with the subject, if we may add that *each man makes for himself his own gate.*"53

THE BRIDGE

Heidegger's method, as we have already seen, is a "going along a way" (the metaphor is a more concrete version of its *dynamic* character—our fourth trait) and determines the relevant *change in direction* (our fifth trait) to be taken. Changes in direction as one moves along this way are also embodied in concrete spatial imagery. Heidegger's *Signposts* "mark the way" he has himself followed. Thus his very concrete example of a sign, the directional signal on an automobile, takes on general significance:

> Giving way, as taking a direction, belongs essentially to the being-in-the-world of *being-there*. *Being-there* is always somehow directed [*ausgerichtet*] and on its way. . . . The sign is addressed to a being-in-the-world which is concretely "spatial."54

Another example of the concretely spatial character of this being-in-the-world and of the way it "interprets" itself in Heidegger's thought is provided by his later essay "Building Dwelling Thinking." Here Heidegger is letting each of these three procedures (to borrow the methodological behest of *Being and Time*) "be seen in its togetherness" with each of the others. But "Thinking" is not so much a portion of the subject matter he is treating as it is exemplified by his treatment of the other two procedures. We can gain some appreciation of this reflexive relation if we consider one of his comments on "Dwelling" insofar as it is related in turn to the most prominent example he offers of something built:

> The relationship between man and space is nothing other than dwelling when it is thought of essentially. When we think . . . about [*nachdenken*] the relation between location and space, but also about the relationship between man and space, a light falls on the essence of things that are locations and which we call dwellings.
>
> The bridge is a thing of this kind. . . . The bridge provides a spatial and directional structure to the locale [*die Stätte in Räume einrichtet*]. . . . The construction of such things is building.
>
> The bridge does not just bring together banks which are already there objectively. The banks emerge [*hervortreten*] as banks only with the bridge's going over the stream. The bridge lets them lie over against each other. . . . Along with the banks, the bridge brings to the stream the expanse of landscape lying back behind the stream on either side. It brings stream and bank and land into the reciprocal

nearness of neighborhood. The bridge brings together the earth as land-scape around the stream.[55]

Here we discern the procedures not only of *Ausrichtung* but also of *Entfernung* (de-distancing) which were described in *Being and Time*.

But since both were described there as procedures of *being-there*, or (to retain the terminology of the present essay) since the "relation between man and space" is being thought about, the structure of thinking is at the same time being exhibited. To put the matter crudely (as I have to, since I am abstracting the example from its relational setting), the func-tion of the bridge is relational—to "locate," to "bring together," to "bring near"; and these are also concrete ways of describing the relational func-tion of thinking. Subject matter and method are being brought together as they were when the interpretation of the layout of the cave was itself interpreted as a "laying out." Not that the bridge or bridge building should become a symbol of the relational way one should think. Heideg-ger warns us against this traditional, abstract interpretation of symbols as meta-physical meta-phors:

> Bringing together . . . by an ancient word of our language is called "thing" [*Ding*]. The bridge is a thing. . . . To be sure, people think of the bridge as primarily and really merely a bridge; after that, and occasionally, it might possibly express much else besides; and as such an expression it would then become a symbol. . . . But the bridge, if it is a genuine bridge, is never first of all a mere bridge [i.e., something merely objective] and then afterward a symbol [i.e., something merely subjective].

The bridge should instead be thought of relationally in terms of the way *being-there* defines its thereness—its "location" and "the relation between location and space."[56]

There would be a risk of the process of definition becoming abstract and generating symbols if "thinking" were treated independently of "building" and "dwelling" instead of in relation to them. Hence such cryptic comments as this: "That thinking itself belongs together with dwelling in the same sense as building, though in a different fashion, may perhaps be attested by the way of thought sought in this essay."[57] In other words, "thinking" is reflexively involved in the fashion in which "building" and "dwelling" are thought of.

Now that we have been alerted by Heidegger's warning against the abstractness of a symbol, some of the concretely meth-odological features of the bridge can be noticed:

> The bridge . . . at the same time allots [*gewährt*—the German suggests that truth is at stake] their way to mortals, so that they may journey

from the land on one side to the land on the other. Bridges escort [*geleiten*] in many ways. The city bridge pursues its way [*führt*] from the precincts of the castle to the cathedral square; the river bridge near the country town brings wagons and teams of horses to the surrounding villages. . . . The highway bridge is tied into the network of long-distance traffic. . . . Always but in different fashions the bridge escorts the lingering and hastening ways of men to and fro, so that they may reach other banks and in the end, as mortals, arrive on the other side.[58]

Heidegger paid comparable attention to a passageway when he laid out the layout of Plato's cave,[59] only this attention was more evident because less attention was paid by Plato himself. In the *Republic* (at least as it is traditionally interpreted) the philosopher passes out of the cave and eventually leaves physical imagery behind (including presumably the "image" of the cave itself) in favor of purely intellectual operations. The philosopher's motive for returning then to the cave is political, not epistemological, but since Heidegger segregates the image of the cave from the rest of the *Republic*, Plato's political motive disappears, and the return to the cave becomes a *reversal* which illustrates the fashion in which Heidegger thinks in opposition to the philosophical tradition as a Platonic tradition of transcendence and abstraction.[60] For Heidegger it is no longer feasible to abstract philosophical thought from what traditionally has been a transient and ultimately dispensable aid to thought— its embodiment in such spatial imagery as a cave or a bridge.

DISLOCATION

I have been tracing as existential the reversal of the direction in which philosophy has traditionally abstracted from spatial relations and movements. What still has to be brought out is the dislocating character of this reversal as distinctively *ex-sistential*. Earlier we discovered the dislocated structure of an *ex-sistential* subject matter. Now we must reconsider its dislocation from a methodological point of view.

Let me begin by acknowledging that, just as the existential process of "location" resembles the traditional process of "definition," aside from the existential refusal to abstract the *definiendum* (traditionally the "essence") from the spatial, temporal, and personal relations of "existence," so the reversal is a process of "dislocation" which resembles (as I mentioned before) the traditional dialectical process of contradiction, aside from this refusal. We have watched the refusal take the form of this metaphor of "dislocation" as well as of other spatial metaphors. Now we should recognize not only that "existence" (to remain with our crucial example) is revived as a metaphor when its spatial reference to "disloca-

tion" is recovered but also that any live metaphor is itself *ex-sistential* to
the extent that it is (as the dictionary explains) "the replacement of the
more usual word or phrase by another." This replacement is itself a dislocation of ordinary usage; the existential replacement with metaphors of
the usually more literal terms of the philosophical tradition is a dislocation of philosophical usage. Their replacement with metaphors which
are distinctively spatial takes on methodological significance in the program proposed by Merleau-Ponty: "Replace the notions of concept, idea,
mind, representation, by the notions of dimensions, articulations, levels,
hinges, pivots, configurations."[61] In other words the traditionally abstract,
static, meta-physical terminology that has largely effaced physical references from its meta-phors for the operations of thought should be replaced
by hardware which is more "flexible, pliant, supple, nimble"[62] in its metaphorical reference to spatial relations and movements.

So drastic a reversal may be too programmatic. This is not an issue to
be decided here, since the decision would take us beyond an introduction
and demand, in Heidegger's case, an interpretation of how destructive
is the "destruction" of the philosophical tradition which he undertakes.[63]
But a dialectical reversal cannot be a simply unidirectional change such
as Merleau-Ponty apparently intends. Existentialists seem not to have
been in fact quite this drastic. If they had been, existentialism would
not display that version of its "double character" whereby traditional
abstract concepts (such as "contingency" or "meaning" or "truth") are
imposed on or found immersed in concrete experiences (such as those of
wiggling bottoms, directional signals, and bridges).

To bring out the dynamics of these and other conjunctions, I employ
the metaphor **interplay** to describe a **seventh** trait of an existential dialectic. It is the *developmental* form taken by what was frequently observed earlier with reference to subject matter—that a "relation underlies
the disrelation." This trait must be insisted upon, or the rest of my list
will degenerate into a cutting and drying of the traits in question, which
would be incompatible with the fluid relational analysis I am attempt
to delineate. One form of interplay, "crisscrossing," we encountered
earlier.[64] The metaphor itself can be obtained from Heidegger. The
"world," whose relational structure we have partly explored in *Being
and Time*, he defines in a later work as "the appropriating mirror play
[*ereignende Spiegel-Spiel*] of the simple being folded into unity [*Einfalt*]
of earth and sky, gods and mortals."[65] For the purpose of dealing with
existentialism as a movement, we can get by with less complicated "mirror

play" than this, and I shall shortly produce a quite adequate mirror from Kierkegaard. The four members participating in Heidegger's "mirror play" are specific to his thought and do not concern us here, except for the fact that the "play" is visualized as taking place between them, so that Heidegger locates this place as "the in-between" (*das Zwischen*).[66]

Congruent with this location, the metaphor of "moving along a way" can be revised (with perhaps an allusion to Parmenides) to become the more complicated proceeding—"*inter vias*, between separate ways."[67] Interplay then becomes a dynamic rendering of what happens at a "crossroads," at a "bridge" where ways intersect, between passing out of the cave and returning to it. With these spatial metaphors Heidegger is in effect discarding the notion of "level" (*niveau*) upon which he relied in *Being and Time* and the likewise too abstract, too static, and too grammatical hyphens upon which he also relied to bring out the relational character of whatever he was analyzing.

Indeed we can no longer be satisfied with our earlier handling of the relation between levels, whether between "philosophy" and "the life of an individual" or between literature (or art) and this life, for interplay must be recognized as interfering with the traditional unidirectional upward movement of *Aufhebung*. An existentialism cannot be regarded as a philosophy of life—a philosophy which simply generalizes from the particular experiences of living—when a reversal or inversion of this relation is carried through with Sartre's comment that "it was Kierkegaard's accomplishment to formulate the problem [what *Sartre* construes as the crucial philosophical problem] *in terms of his own life* [*par sa vie même*]."[68]

I have already anticipated the constraints of consistency and constancy with which philosophical irony found its formulation in terms of Socrates' own life, according to Kierkegaard. A comparable inversion can take place in the relation which is commonly assumed between life and art— two levels we have seen to be relevant also in existentialism. A reviewer of *Nausea* appraised it as "a novel in search of a life."[69] The inversion received its justification from Sartre's treatment of the jazz lyric whose composition supplied a paradigm for the composition of the novel: "It is the worn-out body of this Jew with coal black brows that it ["Some of These Days"] has chosen in order to be born."[70]

Detailed examination of such interplay between levels must wait until it can be interpreted as involving the application of the principle of contradiction. For the present our attention to interplay is limited to those cases in which it involves a *reversal* in the direction in which philosophy has taken in "effacing" the concreteness of experience. "Defining power" (*Bestimmungskraft*) can be "recovered only if we reverse the process of expanding and emptying concepts" which has characterized, according to Heidegger, the development of the philosophical tradition.[71]

To bring back the vulgar but accessible example Sartre provides: in the instance of the wiggling bottom, interplay takes place not only between successive wiggles but also between them and the traditionally abstract concept of "contingency."[72] A similar reversal with respect to the traditional emptying of concepts of their concrete meaning is carried through by Kierkegaard, but he smuggles in these concepts with more respect for the surface of experience, however needed they may be to following out its philosophical implications. Reconsider an example where the philosophical implications may have seemed minimal. We recall how the participants in "The Diary of the Seducer" change places in their spatial relations to each other and how their movements into their later locations is hinged to the contradiction between the seducer's visible physical location, his back "toward the tea table and the infatuated conversation of Edward and Cordelia," and the place he imagines he occupies in the space of Cordelia's imagination, "constantly, if invisibly, present *between* her and Edward."[73] Here there is no very obvious involvement of traditional concepts in the interplay. Nevertheless, the Hegelian distinction between the stage of immediacy and the stage of reflection is pivotal here, and I shall explore Kierkegaard's handling of this distinction later, when the notion of "stages" has been worked out.

For the present we need only remember that reflection is imaginative for Kierkegaard.[74] Thus the reflective process that culminates in "The Diary of the Seducer" starts out with his reflecting on her image as it is reflected in a mirror:

> A mirror hangs on the opposite wall; she does not reflect on it, but the mirror reflects her. . . . Unhappy mirror, which can indeed grasp her image, but not her; unhappy mirror, which cannot hide her image in secret . . . but must on the contrary betray it to others, as now to me. What anguish if men were like that! And are there not many men like that, who own nothing except in the moment when they show it to others, who grasp only the surface, not the essence, who lose everything if this shows itself, just as this mirror would lose her image, were she by a single breath to betray her heart to it. And if a man were not able to keep an image as his own in recollection, even at the moment when he is present. . . .[75]

"Grasp" (*gribe*) alludes to the way reflection grasps with a con-cept (*Begriff*) in Hegel. The distinction between "surface" and "essence" is the Hegelian distinction between the phenomenal and the essential with which we are familiar from Kierkegaard's ironist, who (for example) neither says what he means nor means what he says.[76] Such double entendre promotes second thoughts—reflection. For the interlocutor is not allowed to take anything phenomenal at its face value. He is impelled to undertake the "internalizing" movement of "recollection." But the interplay between "external" and "internal" is renewed at the level of *Vor-stellung*. Thus in the next sentence of the diary the "distance" required for "the outward sight of beauty" is opposed to having beauty "*before* the eyes of his soul . . . when he cannot see the object itself because it is too near, when lips are closed on lips."[77]

Kierkegaard is not simply playing off reflection in the metaphorical spiritual sense against reflection in the "immediate" physical sense of the mirror. Interplay is introduced with the ambiguity signalized by each successive "if." When the shift takes place from "What anguish if men were like that!" (i.e., as spiritually unreflecting as a mirror when it reflects physically) to "And are not many men like that?" we are left without any firm distinction between men and mirrors. (The implication is that "many men" remain at the level of immediacy.) The interplay is enhanced by subordinate interplay between "lose" and "keep" as one's "own" as well as between "breath" (to which the loss is due) and "spirit."

THE INTERESTING

The accumulated interplay is diverted in a new direction with the *reversal* by which the seducer proclaims his own sophisticated reflectiveness (in contrast to "many men"), which he pretends enables him to cut across the distinction between reflection and immediacy and recollect "even in the moment when he is present." Not that the seducer will display such dexterity initially. His "mirror play" is the starting point in a dialectical development in which interplay is achieved by his recollecting her when she is absent:

> How beautiful it is to be in love [level of immediacy], how interesting to be conscious of being in love [level of reflection]. Lo, that is the difference. I could be bitter at the thought that . . . I have lost sight of her, and yet in a certain sense it pleases me. The image I now have of her hovers indeterminately between her *actual* and her *ideal* form.[78]

Kierkegaard often plays with the etymology of "interesting" and its cognates. In *Johannes Climacus* "consciousness is relation and brings with it interest, a duality which is fully expressed with the pregnant double meaning by the word *interesse*."[79]

But let us turn our attention now to the Hegelian implications of the "interest" the seducer eventually takes in the spaciousness of Cordelia's imagination. Once he has brought her from the stage of immediacy (dramatized by her not reflecting on her "immediate" reflection in the mirror) to such a pitch of reflection that she becomes an unusually "interesting" prospect for seduction, what is pivotal to his "interest" is the Hegelian movement of *Aufhebung* whereby the limitations of the "finite" can be transcended by reflection reaching for the "infinite." Yet interplay is retained by opposing Cordelia's "infinite audacity of far horizons" to the earthbound vision of a previous undertaking:

> What a different image appears to me when I think of my little Emily, and yet again, how appropriate was the situation. I cannot imagine her or, rather, recall her except in her little room adjacent to the garden. The door stood open, a little garden limited the view, forcing the eye to halt there. . . . Emily was not as significant as Cordelia. Her situation was designed for her. One's vision was held to the earth. . . . It remained in the little foreground. . . . Cordelia's situation must have no foreground, but only the infinite audacity of far horizons.

The seducer is in fact anticipating the different layout he finally arranges as a setting for Cordelia's seduction:

> Nothing is forgotten which could have any significance for her. . . . The situation is everything she might wish for. If she sits in the middle of the room, she can look out in both directions with nothing to obstruct the view; on both sides it stretches away to an infinite horizon. . . . If she comes near a row of windows on one side, there, far on the horizon, is a forest curving like a wreath [the noun *krands* means "wreath," but the corresponding verb means "surround"], limiting and enclosing. What does love love? An enclosure; was not paradise itself an enclosed place? . . .
>
> One turns to the other side, where the sea spreads out before the sight with nothing to limit it, filled with thoughts which nothing holds back. What does love love? Infinitude. What does love fear? Limitation.[80]

The interplay which was introduced by the opposition between the earthbound vision of his "little Emily" and Cordelia's "infinite audacity of far horizons" has been further articulated by providing for Cordelia's seduction a room with two views from the windows—on one side "far on the horizon . . . a forest curving like a wreath" (its distance being an expansion of the limitations of "little Emily" which are themselves played up by her "little garden") and on the other side the open sea "with nothing to limit it." Not only is there interplay here between the limitations of the "finite" and transcending these limitations toward the "infinite" (as in the philosophical tradition and especially in Hegel), but concrete spatial metaphors for rendering these limitations and their transcendence are being played off against the abstractness of the traditional concepts.

Another kind of interplay is between the different meanings of an expression. A "scientific" expression, according to Sartre, is "univocal," whereas a literary style is "above all a way of expressing three or four things at once. There is the simple statement with its immediate meaning, and then underneath it, at the same time, different meanings arranged in depth. If one is not capable of getting out of language this plurality of meanings, it's not worth the trouble writing." During one phase of his attempt to become a Marxist, Sartre pulled philosophy away from literature toward science by announcing that "in philosophy each statement should have only one meaning," and he therefore regretted the climactic statement in *Being and Nothingness*, "L'homme est une passion inutile," since both "passion" and "useless" are ambiguous.[81] But he admits that if philosophy would "renew" (as I am arguing it does in existentialism) "its technical terminology," it must pile up meanings "at various levels."[82] A prime example of this (as we shall see in Kierkegaard as well as in Sartre) are the meanings of "passion."[83]

Heidegger's defense of a range of meanings is not restricted to literature:

> This multiplicity of possible interpretations does not discredit the strictness [*die Strenge*] of the thought content. For all true thought remains open to more than one interpretation—and this by reason of its essential character. Nor is this multiplicity of possible interpretations merely the residue of a not yet achieved formal-logical univocity which we properly should strive for but do not attain. Rather, multiplicity of meanings is the medium in which all thought must move in order to be strict. To employ an image: to a fish, the depth and expanse of its waters, the currents and quiet pools, warm and cold layers, are the medium of its multiple mobility [*Beweglichkeit*]. If the fish is deprived of the fullness of its medium, if it is dragged onto the dry sand, then it can only wriggle, twitch, and die. Therefore we must always seek out thinking, and its burden of thought, in the medium of its multiple meanings, else everything will remain closed off from us.[84]

Such interplay is exhibited in Heidegger himself. The title of the work from which I am quoting, *Was heisst Denken*? can mean "What is it that is called thinking?" or "What is it that calls us to think?" or "What is it that thought calls us to?" Similarly, *Grundfrage der Metaphysik* (the title of the first chapter of his *Introduction to Metaphysics*) can mean either "the fundamental question of metaphysics," "the metaphysical question concerning the ground," or "the question of the ground of metaphysics."[85]

THE JOLT

Reversal and interplay are procedures carried out in existentialism by employing not only metaphors which are spatial but also those which embody distinctively dislocating spatial movements. Heidegger is entirely aware of the "violence" of his method of interpreting other philosophers.[86] We have watched his interpretation of Plato's cave dislocate its original layout: with Heidegger's lengthening of the passageway, his accentuation of the distinction between inside and outside the cave, men are located more dislocatingly under the earth than they are in Plato. But just as Heidegger attributes some features of his interpretation of the cave to Plato himself (e.g., the length of the passageway), so he attributes something of his own "violence" to Plato. Spatial metaphors may be employed by Plato (in a passage Kierkegaard pounced on when he found it in Plutarch) to characterize an intellectual operation dialectically "as a motion and movement of the mind,"[87] but Heidegger interprets the intellectual operation which Plato himself carried out in treating the problem of being as Plato's having "wrenched" (abgerungen) with the "most strenuous effort of thought. . . ."[88] Sartre is perhaps indebted to Heidegger's interpretation when he generalizes and characterizes the operation of reflection as such as a "wrenching away" (arrachement).[89] Correspondingly more strenuous wrenching seems to be required on Heidegger's part, if he is to "recollect" a problem which since Plato has been "forgotten," having been "covered over" by the philosophical tradition.

Even Heidegger's procedure for extracting the implication of dislocation from the term "existence" involves a dislocation of the term's traditional meaning. I am thinking of the famous definition with which Heidegger has equipped existentialism: "The 'essence' of existence [Dasein] lies in existence [Existenz]."[90] He is obviously undercutting the traditional distinction between essence and existence as one between what something is as a matter of its definition and the fact that it actually is, which is traditionally irrelevant to its definition. The scare quotes around essence warns us that its traditional meaning is being dislocated. But we are more intimately concerned with the meaning of "existence" as it illustrates Heidegger's procedure of definition. Here Heidegger is dislocating the philosophical tradition of definition by contradicting the traditional requirement that a definition be informative. He deliberately adopts a definition which instead appears redundant: "The 'essence' of existence lies in existence." The frustrated traditional requirement can only be satisfied perversely by prying the traditional meaning of the *definiens* and the *definiendum* apart and reverting to the etymologies of *Da-sein* and ex-sistence. The definition can then be paraphrased: "The essence of 'being located there' lies in 'being dislocated outside itself.' "

We have seen that philosophy itself is defined by Heidegger as something "dislocated" (*verrückt*—the physical movement here is already in ordinary German a spatial metaphor for an intellectual performance which is "deranged"). Starting out philosophically requires, Heidegger claims, a break with scientific and commonsense procedures, and this break is a *Verrückung* ("dislocation" or "derangement") of the movement of thought. Earlier I noted Kierkegaard's protest, against Hegel, that "the starting point must be a breaking off." This is a movement which Kierkegaard describes as a "leap."[91] If the starting point for an existentialist is less a point than a movement, the movement is not simply a movement but a disruptive movement. The "dislocation" (*Verrückung*) in question can only be achieved with a "start" (*Ruck*)," which implies a "movement" that is "sudden," involving a "jolt."[92]

REPETITION

When Heidegger defines philosophy as starting out with a "dislocation" (*Verrückung*), the root permits the further implication of a jolt "backward." Thus the movement of philosophy, at least as it starts out, is not visualized as the progressive forward movement which is characteristic of Hegel's dialectic but as a "going backward" (*Rückgang*) or a "step backward" (*Schritt zurück*), and this is the route by which we have seen Heidegger approaches the philosophical tradition.[93]

Heidegger is probably indebted to Kierkegaard when he starts out *Being and Time* by presenting its *Rückgang* as the "re-petition" (*Wiederholung*)—the "bringing back again" of the problem which Plato and Aristotle had "wrenched away . . . from the phenomena." But because he presents his problem as long since "forgotten," I assume that he is also alluding to the Platonic doctrine whereby the fundamental intellectual operation is "re-collection." (The allusion seems more likely inasmuch as Kierkegaard had defined "repetition" as comparable to Platonic "recollection" but "carried forward" instead of "backward.")[94] However, when Heidegger employs a traditional conception, one must recognize that he is also dislocating it. In fact he dislocates the traditional conception of tradition itself, by playing with the etymology of "tra-dition":

> When tradition . . . becomes dominant, it does so in such a way that what it "hands over" is made so little accessible, at the outset and for the most part, that it rather becomes covered over [*verdeckt*]. . . . Tradi-

tion blocks our access [*verlegt den Zugang*] to the original "sources" from which the categories and concepts handed over to us have been in part genuinely derived. Indeed it makes us forget that they have had such an origin. It makes us suppose that there is no need even to understand such a going back [*Rückgang*] in its necessity.[95]

We assume that tradition is what we can remember; with Heidegger it is a forgetting. If we are persuaded to agree, we are likely to assume that forgetting is acquiescence. But Heidegger defines it more vigorously as a dislocation backward: "The *ekstasis* of being carried away [the German reads *die Ekstase (Entrückung)*], of forgetting, has the character of backing away [*Ausrückung*] . . . before what has been that is most one's own."

Kierkegaard had manipulated the forward/backward distinction in defining the concept of "repetition," which Heidegger has probably adapted from Kierkegaard. Now that the notions of *reversal* and *interplay* have been elaborated, we might reconsider the dislocation this distinction involves for Kierkegaard:

> Philosophy [as exemplified by Hegel] is perfectly right in saying that life must be understood backward. But then one forgets the other clause—that it must be lived forward.[96]

Not only is the movement of philosophy to be dislocatingly reversed in order to cope with the opposed movement of life, but there is also a secondary dislocation introduced (and hence the subordinate interplay), for when philosophy says that "life must be understood backward," it is propounding, according to Kierkegaard, the doctrine that understanding is (etymologically) "re-collection," but in fact the philosopher "forgets."

RECAPITULATION

It is perhaps unfortunate to translate Heidegger's term for "recollection" (*Wiederholung*) as "repetition," even though Kierkegaard's definition of "repetition" as "recollection forward" probably influenced Heidegger, who does visualize the procedure in question not just as a reversal (*Rückgang*) but also as initiating in some fashion an advance—even a new start. "Repetition" suggests to us instead a mechanical performance without methodological significance. The procedure in certain versions at least might better be labeled with the more technical term **recapitulation,** which can be distinguished as an **eighth** trait of an existential dialectic.

In the broad sense indicated at the start of *Being and Time*, the work as a whole is a recapitulation, but just as the term "reversal" is employed more restrictedly by Heidegger of a later dialectical stage (a stage which

I have not tried to reach), so also is the term *Wiederholung*. When he has ostensibly completed his "existential analytic," he goes on to undertake a "recapitulation in a more originative fashion [*ursprünglicher*] of the existential analytic." He is not implying, he hastens to explain, what *Wiederholung* can imply (or "recapitulation" as well as "repetition" can imply in English), that he is "to proceed again through [*wiederdurchlaufen*] the analysis just completed in an external and schematic fashion and in the same sequence of presentation." Rather, "recapitulation" here implies a specific procedure for satisfying the methodological behest of a relational analysis—by "making clearer the interrelation [*Zusammenhang*] between earlier phases." But it is not just a matter of added clarity in formulation; Heidegger is careful to remind us that the fundamental interrelation is between method and subject matter: "But beyond . . . exigencies of method the phenomenon itself compels us to articulate our analysis in a different fashion when we recapitulate it."[97] This reformulation will constitute the advance—the new start—I have mentioned.

Later we shall see that *Either/Or* is recapitulated in *Stages on Life's Way* and that this recapitulation constitutes an advance beyond *Either/Or*. The first stage of *Stages* is an esthetic stage which recapitulates *Either*, and most specifically its climax, "The Diary of the Seducer." We are presumably reminded of how 'the diary' started out by the epigraph which is displayed for this first stage and which is a more reflexive version of the mirror analogy: "Such works are mirrors: when a monkey peers into them, no apostle can be seen looking out."[98] The monkey qualifies as an erotic animal, and the seducer of 'the diary' puts in an appearance at this stage, clearly further advanced in his career of seduction. The allusion to an apostle, albeit negative, is an anticipation of the religious stage, which was lacking in *Either/Or* but is added in *Stages*. Associated with this addition is a dialectical advance in reflexivity (Kierkegaard himself will call it "inwardness").[99] This is probably emphasized by the fact that in the first scene of "The Diary" the seducer is looking at another person, Cordelia, who is not looking at herself. Of course we are no longer at the same level as in "The Diary." The reference of the epigraph is a higher-level reference to the work itself, and the person who is looking at himself is the reader of the work, for we have reached a stage in the development of "inwardness" when the problem of communication comes to the fore. This is evident in *Stages* itself, but it will become even more evident when *Stages* is followed by the *Concluding Unscientific Postscript*, which will deal explicitly with this problem.[100]

A shorter-run, less complicated example of recapitulation is the fashion in which the "limitations" of the "little garden" of "little Emily" are carried over at a higher level in the seducer's relation to Cordelia, where the "little garden" is replaced from one point of view with "a forest curving like a wreath" which is "far on the horizon," even though they are transcended from another point of view by the open sea "with nothing to limit it."

I am stressing recapitulation as a trait of a dialectical method because it is my own procedure.[101] My interpretation assigns different philosophies to the same movement of thought by "making clearer the interrelation" between their problems and procedures. In the shorter run my present interpretation of the procedures composing existential method is a recapitulation of my earlier interpretation of the problems composing existential subject matter, granted that there is a certain undialectical cumbersomeness in this recapitulation, since it has been forced on me by the tendency to separate method from subject matter in our own philosophical tradition. In the longer run that embraces the sequel to this volume, I shall be recapitulating my present interpretation of existentialism as dialectical from the vantage point of the distinction between a dialectical and a phenomenological method.

It seemed sensible in this introductory volume to approach existentialism in terms of the dialectical traits of their method, for different philosophers, insofar as their method is dialectical, lend themselves to correlation by a dialectical interpretation which a recapitulation can fit over their philosophies. Although a philosophical interpretation of different philosophies need not be dialectical, it cannot be purely phenomenological. As I mentioned earlier, Husserl makes a direct appeal to experience and is largely indifferent to other philosophies, except to the extent that they betray a philosophical "yearning" which remained "secret" from their authors but which his phenomenological philosophy fulfills with its fresh start from experience.[102] It is true that Husserl, confronted by a French audience, cast his philosophy once in the form of *Cartesian Meditations*. He seems later to have regretted this format, but one reason he could accept Descartes as a predecessor was that the latter had started out by deliberately discarding other philosophers' opinions, and in a manner which Husserl takes as a faltering premonition of his own method of phenomenological reduction. In contrast, each existentialist makes extensive use of predecessors in developing his own philosophy, so that the interpreter is encouraged to attempt in turn a recapitulation "making clearer the interrelation."

MOOD

I was attempting a recapitulation of the traits of existential method which had previously emerged when I undertook to bring out the sense in which it is a reversal of the traditionally abstract procedure of philosophy. But a recapitulation proceeds more smoothly when it is restricted to a single philosopher. Let us then advance to the next trait of existential method by attempting another recapitulation in which we stay with a stretch of Heidegger's relational analysis long enough to let each of the successive traits "be seen in its togetherness" with the others.

Winding up the chapter in this fashion will also provide a transition to other existentialists. It is commonly assumed that the most influential stretch of Heidegger's analysis is his treatment of anxiety. Sartre explicitly acknowledges his debt here to Heidegger as well as to Kierkegaard, and Kierkegaard's treatment had already influenced Heidegger's, so that anxiety has seemed what existentialists most obviously share in common. But it is not prominent in Merleau-Ponty. And there are other complications. Sartre, for example, is indebted to Heidegger's treatment of anxiety in his own treatment of nausea as well as anxiety. We can postpone these complications by recognizing that Heidegger's treatment of anxiety, Sartre's treatment of both nausea and anxiety, and even Merleau-Ponty's treatment of perception all presuppose Heidegger's analysis of "Being-There as State of Mind."[103] It could even be claimed that this portion of Heidegger's analysis has become the starting point (in a sense which will emerge from his analysis itself) for contemporary existentialism. In any case it is fundamental to his treatment of other topics besides anxiety (e.g., "everydayness") which have also been influential.

"State of mind" is Macquarrie and Robinson's translation of Heidegger's *Befindlichkeit*.[104] But "state" is too static; by now we are well aware that the existentialist latches onto a movement with his method. And "mind" is too mentalistic, as we shall soon see. What Heidegger is taking into account are experiences, he explains, "of the most familiar and everyday sort." Some of the evidence is ordinary usage: *Wie befinden Sie sich?* The German means literally, "How do you find yourself?" (In English we say, "How are you?") Some of the usual replies (e.g., "I'm feeling low," "depressed," "elated," "on the top of the world"; "I'm getting nowhere fast," "losing my grip"; "I've dropped out") illustrate "the spatiality of being-there." But they further illustrate that this spatiality has an **affective** dimension, which now emerges as the **ninth** trait of an existential dialectic. This dimension is sacrificed when "the spatiality of being-there" becomes the abstract space of mathematical physics.[105] Its affective characteristics then become secondary or even tertiary qualities.

That we are dealing with the affective fashion in which *being-there* defines or locates itself is indicated by the fact that the experience which Heidegger is taking into account is *die Stimmung*, which usually means "mood" or "feeling." That we are also dealing with a process of *definition* or *location* (the first trait of an existential dialectic) is confirmed by the fact that *Stimmung* is associated for Heidegger with *bestimmen* ("define," "determine"). We have already seen that *being-there*, which is for Hegel a "definite" or "determinate" being in a sense that abstracts from spatial relations, is more concretely for Heidegger a "definite" or "determinate" or "located" being in that he does not abstract from these relations. Now we recognize that among the relations that render his definition of *being-there*—and the process of definition itself—more concrete are affective relations which he refuses to abstract from spatial relations.

The *relational* character (our second trait) of this definitory experience is in turn more concretely illustrated by Heidegger's offering *Gestimmtsein* as an approximate equivalent to *Stimmung*: the "mood" one is in is a matter of being "in tune with" or "attuned to" (e.g., one is in the mood for love), so that to find oneself there is to find oneself defined or located by the affective reference conveyed by this "with" or "to" or "for."

But at the same time one finds *oneself* affected. A "feeling" or "mood" is not just a portion of Heidegger's subject matter which has been patiently waiting for the arrival of his treatment on the scene. Rather, it asserts its own methodological significance as definitional. *Stimme* means "voice," and this concrete idiom is consonant with Heidegger's metaphor for his *reflexive* procedure (our third trait); he characterizes it as a "listening in," while *being-there* "defines its location."

We are already aware that at this juncture where *being-there* "defines its location" the philosophical tradition intervenes with its own impeding definitions. There seems to be an allusion to the tradition in that *Befindlichkeit* has the same root as *Empfindung* ("sensation," "perception," "feeling"), where traditional philosophy often starts out with a "finding." (Hegel, for example, indulges in punning interplay between *finden* and *Empfindung*.)[106] Here our earlier comparison with traditional empiricism can be renewed. The appeal to experience in this tradition has usually been on the assumption that it is possible to "find" something initially "given" which is passively received by the mind (e.g., a sense datum), so that the mind does not impose its own characteristics at the moment of reception and can thus be relied on to record accurately what is given simply as it is given. Since it is also sometimes assumed that what is initially given is given separately from its relation to anything else, it becomes a stable foundation, a building block, to which other building blocks can be added, whether the process of building up our experience from this foundation is conceived logically as inductive or psychologically as the association of ideas. Conversely, the process of verifying what experience amounts to requires an analysis which scrupulously breaks down what has been built up into its originally separate data.

In contrast, Heidegger's analysis is not only relational but also *dynamic* and *developmental* (our fourth trait). He challenges the prospect of starting out with something stable and simply given: "Is there given ultimately a seeking without presupposition, a seeking complemented by a pure finding?" ("Gibt es am Ende ein Suchen ohne jene Vorwegnahme, ein Suchen, dem ein Reines Finden zugehört?")[107] The "pre" of the English translation "presupposition" does bring out one meaning of the *vor*, but "pre-supposition" is static and eliminates the anticipatory "forward movement along a way" of the German *Vor-weg-nahme*, whereby one's seeking trespasses on what one is finding. "Pre-supposition" also fails to preserve the dynamic, developmental fashion in which one starts out in Heidegger.

In other words, if we cannot guard (as Husserl, among other philosophers, would have us) against assertions which go beyond what is really given at the moment, then method cannot be assigned the initial function of isolating something given but acquires the very different function it has in Heidegger of following out an anticipatory forward movement that gives us some sense of *direction* (our fifth trait) as to what one is about (what one is in the "mood" for) as one "goes about" the world.

Heidegger's "listening in" involves at its higher level the change in direction which has been distinguished as the *reversal* (our sixth trait). This trait has already been illustrated by all the other traits of existential method as well as by the *ex-sistentialist* resort to metaphors which are distinctively spatial and distinctively dislocating. Thus we watched Heidegger subvert the application to *being-there* of the traditional interpretation of "being" as primarily "sub-stance"—that is, as something that can be given because it maintains its fundamental "stability" (*Selbständigkeit*) and identity. *Selbständigkeit*, we remember, carries the implication of something "standing on its own feet" and remaining independent of changes over time. This traditional interpretation of being Heidegger dislocated by defining "man's 'substance' " as "existence," which (crudely put) implies that man "stands outside himself" instead of on his own feet.

But this dislocation is apparently insufficient, for the root "stand" survives the change of prefix from "sub" to "ex." Hence the dislocation of *being-there* is now characterized, for the purpose of the analysis of *Befindlichkeit* as "falling" (*Verfallen*), which is taken as the "fundamental mode [*Grundart*] of being of the there." The replacement of "standing" by "falling" is probably reinforced by "*Grundart*," for *Grund* ("foundation," "ground") would seem to refer to the implication of sub-stance whereby it is available to "stand under" and lend "support." The sense of dislocation is still further reinforced by the suggestion added by the *ver* of *Verfallen* that the "falling" is into "decay" or "ruin," whereas a

Grund should provide a "foundation" which is stable. If I stress these features of Heidegger's reversal, it is not only to bring out the dynamic character of "falling" but also because this spatial metaphor for dislocation has too often been neglected as merely a theological inheritance from the myth of man's fall in Genesis. But this myth carries the presumption that man's fallen condition can be appraised by reference to his previous pristine status, but this reference is itself subverted by a further dislocation whereby *"being-there* is something from which *being-there* has already fallen away."[108]

AFFECTIVITY

We now realize in retrospect why the existential process of definition cannot be assimilated to the traditional procedure of defining what something is, for this procedure assumes that what this thing is remains essentially the same insofar as it can be defined. But according to Heidegger, when anything is so defined, a previous step has already been taken. One no longer finds oneself going one's way about the world; one has halted and adopted a "theoretical point of view" which has "already dimmed the world down to the uniformity of what is simply given objectively." This shift to a theoretical point of view does not mean that the affective dimension of *Befindlichkeit* loses its "determining" character. Even "purest *theoria* has not left behind all moods." A sustained attitude of objectivity is also a matter of being "attuned" in a certain fashion. However, as long as one is going about the world, one "sees it unsteadily and flickeringly," and thus it is "never the same from day to day."[109]

A certain *interplay* (our seventh trait) accordingly prevails. One mood can be dislocated by its opposite, so Heidegger begins this analysis with "both the undisturbed equanimity and the inhibited ill-humor of our everyday preoccupation. . . ." But what he then focuses on are not these opposites themselves but the dislocating movement of interplay between them—"the way we slide [*übergleiten*] from the former to the latter and back again or slide off [*ausgleiten*] into bad moods." The change in prefixes indicates the change in direction involved in such interplay.

Heidegger is not claiming with this analysis that an unsteady vision is one's usual starting point for having an experience. If this were the case, his analysis would not be needed. Usually one does not "give in" to one's moods, so they are not "given." Usually one does not allow oneself "to be brought before what they disclose." One "goes about" his business, largely overlooking the temporal structure of experience and its personal structure—its reflexive reference to "the being" which "for each of us is mine." What we overlook is what has been examined as existential subject matter in part I. It is being in a mood for, which yields some initial, if transient, sense of location and direction, of *being-there*, of subject matter. Something "matters," is "going on," even if one does not "go along with it and after it" by applying existential *meth-odos*.[110] But if this method is applied, if a question is posed existentially, its reference to what "matters" to the questioner is not to "what he is" as a substance but to "how he is" or where he "finds himself," and this reference is also brought into question. Thus "the questioner as such is involved in [*gestellt*—"located by," "put in his place by"] the question" and thereby dislocated from his previous place.[111] Where he previously was is a topic we shall not be able to broach until part III, when we shall see that it is necessary for Heidegger to recapitulate (our eighth trait) the present analysis from the different perspective of "everyday" experience.

The moodiness of *Befindlichkeit* has now been "brought into relief" as a ninth trait of existential dialectic—its *affective* character. Its methodological significance emerges from Heidegger's claim that "ontologically mood is a primary kind of being for *being-there* in which *being-there* is disclosed to itself prior to all cognition." What he is denying with this claim is the primacy accorded to scientific knowledge in the philosophical tradition which has been by and large an epistemological one, explaining how we know what we know if what we know is already available to us in the sciences. An experience qualifies as cognitively significant in this tradition, according to Heidegger, only when a process of abstraction has eliminated, along with the "forward movement" of the experience, its unsteady affective dimension of "how one feels." The privileged form of knowledge will be knowledge dimmed down to complete uniformity:

> Mathematical knowledge is regarded . . . as the one manner of apprehending beings which can always give assurance that this being has been securely grasped. Such beings are those which always are what they are. That which remains stable [*ständige*] really is.[112]

Heidegger's denial of the primacy of such knowledge constitutes a rejection, for example, of any attempt to treat negation as fundamentally expressible by a symbol in mathematical logic: "More fundamental [*abgründiger*] . . . is the harshness of opposition and the sullenness of loathing. More responsible the pain of refusal and the mercilessness of forbidding. More burdensome the bitterness of renunciation."[113]

NAUSEA

As the title *Being and Nothingness* has already suggested, negation becomes even more prominent in Sartre. He would follow Heidegger in dismissing logical judgments as having "a purely abstract meaning." Indeed no portion of Heidegger has influenced Sartre in such discernible detail as the brief analysis of *Befindlichkeit*. Sartre is clearly drawing on Heidegger's conception of *Befindlichkeit* when he refers to our "fundamental and hidden affectivity which is our own way of living our anchorage," even though he continues with a Marxist definition of this location when he identifies "our anchorage" as "in a particular milieu which is defined within our class by the antagonisms fomented by the division of labor."[114] That "affectivity" is "fundamental" in Sartre is suggested by his favorite metaphor for the movement of consciousness, *glissement* ("gliding" or "sliding"), which reproduces Heidegger's *gleiten*.[115] But "affectivity" is no more just a portion of Sartre's subject matter than *Befindlichkeit* is just a portion of Heidegger's subject matter. It has methodological implications: Sartre, like Heidegger, denies "the primacy of knowledge" and prefers to analyze affective dialectic—the "logic of the passions."[116]

In Sartre's own dialectic nausea is a crucial affective moment, for it is the revelation of existence, which "ordinarily is hidden."[117] But Sartre arrives at his description of this revelation in *Being and Nothingness* by exploiting phraseology from the *definitional* maneuver with which Heidegger's analysis of moodiness achieved general scope. The *interplay* between moods, the way they "deteriorate and change over," Heidegger took as evidence that "in every case *being-there* is always attuned by some mood [*gestimmt ist*]." A final twist rendered the analysis comprehensive by bringing within its scope the apparent opposite of mood—"the indifferent and pallid, indeterminate lack of mood [*ebenmässig und fahle Ungestimmtheit*] which is often persistent and wherein being-there becomes satiated with itself."[118] Thus Sartre, without acknowledgment to Heidegger, describes nausea as the way one feels when one feels "no specific satisfaction or dissatisfaction." The description elaborates on Heidegger's *Ungestimmtheit*. Nausea is, Sartre adds, "an insipid [*fade*] taste . . . which stays with me in my efforts to get away from it."[119] *Fade* translates Heidegger's *fahle*, and the next phrase spells out Heidegger's "persistent" (*anhaltende*).

As Sartre has indicated, although "affectivity" is "fundamental," it usually remains "hidden." For any "specific satisfaction or dissatisfaction" gains its specificity, prominence, and stability from the object to which it refers. Nausea can perform the opposing reflexive function of disclosing what is usually "hidden" by such references; they are dislocated, so that one "finds" oneself. The disclosure takes the queasy form of feeling that one is "superfluous" (*de trop*)—a term which translates Heidegger's *überdrüssig*[120] as well as providing a concrete rendering for "contingent." There is no reason to doubt Simone de Beauvoir's report of Sartre's experiences of dislocation—of his experiments with mescaline and of how he took a look at a tree.[121] But he also obviously read Heidegger before he discovered what was "in question" in his bout of nausea.[122]

EXPOSITION

The time has come to make the transition from Heidegger to Sartre, for it is difficult to pin down the dialectical traits of a vision as unsteady as Heidegger's. We have to keep in mind his own warning:

> Ex-positions [*Erörterungen*] of dialectic are as misguided as the procedure [*Verfahren*] of attempting to explain the flowing of a spring at its source by starting out from the stagnant waters that have accumulated from its overflow.[123]

Although this warning should perhaps have discouraged the exposition I have attempted of the traits of Heidegger's dialectic, it can itself be expounded, with some belaboring, as illustrating these traits. *Erörterung* would usually be translated "discussion"; my translation hazards "exposition" because Heidegger often stresses the spatial root *Ort* ("place"), so that *Er-örterung* probably conveys metaphorically the implication of a process of *de-finition* that is a matter of *locating* (the first trait of an existential dialectic).[124] The *relational* character (the second trait) is probably suggested by the way "flowing" is conjoined with "overflow." The *reflexive* character (the third trait) Heidegger often delineates as an effort to return to "the source." The *dynamic* and *developmental* character (the fourth trait) is conveyed not only by the metaphor of "flowing" but also by the root *fahren* ("to go," "to journey") of *Verfahren*. This recurrent metaphor for method in Heidegger is picked up in the next sentence: "The source may still be a long way off, but we must attempt to point in its direction. . . ." The prefix *ver* implies that the "procedure" of "ex-position" is "mis-guided"—that one is going in the "wrong" *direction* (the fifth trait) so that the return to "the source" becomes explicitly a *reversal* (the sixth trait). This reversal is promoted by the *interplay* (the seventh trait) between "the flowing of a spring at its source" and the "stagnant" version an "ex-position" affords, and further recapitulative (the eighth trait) interplay may be introduced by the final opposition between *erklären*, which means "ex-plain," "make clear," and the ordinary implication in German that *Abwasser* ("overflow") is "waste water" which could carry the suggestion of "murkiness," even if we do not go so far as to adopt the suggestion of pollution, supplied by the published English translation.[125] Whatever the exact interplay here, it has some *affective* tinge (the ninth trait).

Since Heidegger's own attempted clarification of dialectic remains merely an attempt "to point," the exposition may be easier if we turn now to Sartre. As the example of nausea has already illustrated, when compared with its prototype in Heidegger, an "indefiniteness of mood" (*Ungestimmtheit*), Sartre can identify more definitely than Heidegger what is "in question." Here he betrays a double debt to Husserl. At one level he is indebted to Husserl's analysis of consciousness as "intentional" consciousness of something. Consciousness in Husserl does not simply "point" in a certain direction; "directedness upon" (the in-tentionality built into consciousness) is an "aiming at" something which is thereby definitely identified. It is consciousness of something as a "tree," a "triangle," "anger," etc.[126] At a higher level Sartre is indebted to Husserl's analysis as eidetic—that is, as a method of defining the "essential" structure of such acts of consciousness as intentional acts by analyzing examples of these acts.

Since the rationale for an eidetic analysis of examples derives from Husserl, I postpone until the sequel considering it as well as any examination of the intentional structure of consciousness. But one result of Sartre's adoption of this procedure is that separable examples acquire a methodological importance which they could not acquire in Heidegger's denser relational analysis but which is too often attributed to Sartre's unphilosophical taste for literature. These examples will facilitate the task of introduction. In particular they will introduce us at last to the principle of contradiction, for Sartre conflates Husserl's eidetic analysis with a dialectical analysis that is based on this principle.

Notes

1. Mill, *Collected Works*, 16:1324: italics in original.
2. Ryle, "Plato's *Parmenides*," 44. Having conceded the risk of anachronism, Ryle goes on to warn that "the opposite policy of trying to chart the drift of some adolescent theory [Plato's] without reference to the progress of any more adult theories is subject not to the risk but to the certainty of failure." I take note of Ryle's "certainty" for the contrast afforded when its analogy to human growth is compared with the return of Kierkegaard to Socrates and of Heidegger to the Pre-Socratics. Recall the satire of the notion of progress with which Kierkegaard starts his philosophical career in the first paragraph of *Irony* (p. 40 above.)
3. An example of the way differences have multiplied (however they should be described methodologically) is what began as the debate over *Verstehen* ("understanding"), which has usually been handled as if it were simply a confrontation between the claims on behalf of a scientific method (such as Mill makes when he argues that "the backward state of the Moral Sciences can only be remedied by applying to them the methods of Physical Science" [see p. 146 above]) and some operation of the "under-

standing" identified as specifically appropriate to the *Geisteswissenschaften* (a phrase originally used to translate Mill's "Moral Sciences"). The method of *Verstehen* was developed for this purpose by Dilthey but became associated with the application of the different method which Heidegger employed in *Being and Time* and which he characterized as "phenomenological." Meanwhile *Verstehen* had also become a password for sociological and anthropological investigations that take as their starting point the experience of the participant or native informant. Matters have been further complicated with the development out of Heidegger of a "hermeneutical method" of understanding, which is blended by Gadamer with certain features of Hegel's dialectical method. A somewhat comparable blend, with perhaps more of a debt to Husserl, is found in Paul Ricoeur. The procedures of Derrida and his entourage represent quite a different development, but it is still comparable with respect to much of its philosophical inheritance (except for the prominence of Nietzsche, in part as interpreted by Heidegger). Multiplying these references sheds little light on contemporary Continental philosophy, but they may suggest that just as scientific method can be conceived very variously by different philosophers of science, so the method often opposed to it can hardly be supposed to be entirely homogeneous.

4. See pp. 53, 96, 7, 10 above.

5. The preoccupation of our time with its demarcation is so taken for granted that it may be worthwhile to spell out some possible variations on Woolf's pronouncement. From the time Aeschylus wrote his trilogy there was no comparably drastic revision in reaction to it: Agamemnon, who gave his name to the first play, and his son Orestes, who gave his name to the entire trilogy, remained the pivotal figures; the adulterous wife was a subordinate or at least a sordid character—up until 1910. Since that time, so much demarcation has gone on, and into ever thinner slices (as was illustrated by the attempt to compile instances of "existential" as a vogue word of the 1960s), that 1910 now seems very long ago. If we were to update to the post–World War II period, we could assess the change in sensibility indicated by Sartre's first play, *The Flies*, which reworked materials from the *Oresteia*, and we would conclude that we were not supposed to feel sorry for anyone; such emotional weakness is to be cauterized by existentialist despair, which promotes a more austere sense of responsibility.

6. See p. 97 above. Although we shall soon see that this reflective attempt is crucial, existentialists employ other locational metaphors. Thus when Merleau-Ponty takes up the problem which we are on the edge of here, he asks, "This immanent meaning of events which are social—where should we, as a matter of fact, place it? It is not or not always in men, in consciousness; but outside of them there are only blind events, ever since we have renounced putting absolute knowledge on the other side of things. *Where* then was the historical process?" (*Praise of Philosophy*, p. 53; italics in original). The allusion to "absolute knowledge" suggests how the problem of the status of events arises with the renunciation of the Hegelian perspective. See chap. 3, n. 119 above and p. 506 below.

7. See p. 144 above.

8. See p. 125 above.

9. "Merleau-Ponty," in *Situations*, p. 171. Sartre may employ Husserl's terminology here because he is thinking of Husserl as "at one and the same time the distance between us and the basis of our friendship" (see p. 124 above).

10. *L'imaginaire*, pp. 32–33. Inasmuch as Merleau-Ponty's analysis is less disrupted by dislocations (less "exclusively antithetical," he would say) than Sartre's, it seems a more obvious illustration of the relational character of an existentialist analysis (see chap. 5, n. 18 below).

11. *Postscript*, p. 473. This "requirement" follows from the dislocated character of the movement of *ex-sistence*, which implies that it is two places at once. The requirement is already found in Hegel, who takes the term etymologically as referring to a state of "having proceeded from" (*Hervorgegangensein*) a "ground." Thus one confronts a world where existents are "related reciprocally as ground and consequence," so that

a relational analysis is required in order to "follow out these relations in all directions" (*Encyclopaedia*, pt. 1, par. 123, *Zusatz*). The comparison with Hegel is complicated by Kierkegaard's tendency to succumb to the traditional identification of "existence" with "actuality" (see chap. 2, n. 65 above), but to the extent that Kierkegaard is still influenced by Hegel's usage, "actuality" still poses, as it did for Hegel, the problem of the relation between "internal and external" (*Encyclopaedia*, pt. 1, par. 142). See chap. 6, n. 17 below.

12. *Being and Time*, p. 33.

13. Ibid., p. 131. Heidegger refuses to treat even a thing as something significantly isolatable: "Only what conjoins [*gering*] out of world becomes a thing." This is the conclusion of "The Thing" (*Poetry, Language, Thought*, p. 182). The joining together involved is played up (p. 180) with the notion of *Gering*. See Hofstadter's prefatory comments (p. xxii).

14. The German *abzuheben* may entail a contrast with Hegel's procedure, since the reconciliation sought by his *Aufhebung* would blur a relation from Heidegger's viewpoint.

15. As a rather lame reminder of this etymology, I shall overwork the expression "procedure" as if it were not a dead metaphor.

16. See my *Human Nature*, 1:12.

17. *Phenomenology*, pp. 34–35. This relation between form and content, like other relations in existentialism, is subject to dislocation, though a "relation" still "underlies the disrelation." I shall examine in detail later Kierkegaard's dislocation of this relation as instanced by what is usually regarded as Hegel's classicism. A simpler example is the discrepancy Sartre exhibits between the aristocratic and beautiful literary form Genet adopts and the vulgarity of the content conveyed. When the French slang expression is employed, which would be translated "We're making the pages," it ordinarily means "We're making the beds." But Genet "takes the word 'page' in the noble sense of young aristocrat ... and the word 'make' in the erotic vulgar sense" when he expatiates, " 'They meant they were going to make the bed, but a kind of luminous idea transformed me there, with my legs spread apart, into a husky guard or palace groom who makes a palace page' " (*Saint Genet*, p. 290). But a "relation" still "underlies," and when Sartre beseeches the reader "To Use Genet Properly," he warns us against divorcing form from content: "Don't take refuge in estheticism; he'll dislodge you. I have seen people who can read without flinching the coarsest passages: 'These two gentlemen sleep together? Then eat their excrement? And after that, one goes off to denounce the other [to the police]? What difference does that make! It's *so* well written.' Such people stop at Genet's phraseology.... But form and content cannot be separated: it is *this* content which requires *this* form" (ibid., p. 585; italics in original).

18. The German *Bestimmung* (and its Danish cognate) can be translated "definition" or "determination" (in the sense of the Latin *determinatio*, "specification"), or "destination," or "vocation." It is the crucial term in German for conveying the definitional character of a dialectic as proceeding from indeterminacy (see p. 47 above) toward determinacy and concreteness. The "transition" in Hegel of "the content into form" is definitional in this broad sense. The process of definition is often linked with the problem of starting point, as in the following passage: "Principle derives from *principium*, starting point [*Anfang*]. The concept corresponds to what the Greeks call *archē*: that whereby something of itself is determined [*bestimmt*] to be what it is as it is. Principle —that is the ground" (*Nietzsche*, 1:40). But the process of "definition" or "determination" also expands in a dialectic to become demarcation by stages (see chap. 10, n. 7 below).

19. *Being and Time*, p. 140. *Being-there* may be defined by Hegel as "definite" or "determinate being" (see p. 103 above), but Hegel's *being-there* is not implicated in a definitional procedure; it is not reflexively determining itself. From now on I shall take terminological advantage of the distinction whereby *Reflexion* may, but does not necessarily, refer in Hegel to "reflection" as a psychological operation. In Heidegger *being-*

there "interprets itself," but this reflexive "layout" is an ontological, not a psychological structure, though it can be exhibited by "reflection" (see chap. 6, n. 114 below). I shall restrict "reflective" to the psychological operation. But there are important differences between the dialectical and the phenomenological conception of this operation—differences which must await the sequel for discrimination. Examples of reflexive structure are prominent in other existentialists. We have already encountered Sartre's "circuit of selfhood" (chap 3, n. 59) and his announcement that "God is dead even in the soul of the believer" (p. 128 above). For Kierkegaard, see pp. 246, 276 below.

20. *Being and Time*, pp. 139, 185. This reflexive effort to determine one's own location can be compared with Merleau-Ponty's identification of "dialectical thought" as conceiving "its own starting point as a problem" and as becoming the reflective "consciousness of its own dependence on an unreflective life which is its initial situation" (*Themes*, p. 55; *Perception*, p. xv).

21. This derivation is utilized by Joan Stambaugh in her translation of Heidegger's *Identity and Difference*.

22. See p. 78 above. We have already observed Kierkegaard's preoccupation with "becoming"—an "individual," a "philosopher." Remember too that in Heidegger "experience" is a journey (see p. 31 above). Or, as he also puts it, "Experience means . . . *eundo assequi*—in going, on the way, to attain something, to reach it through going along the way" (*On the Way to Language*, p. 66).

23. See chap. 6.

24. *Being and Time*, pp. 373–75, 409–10. The characterization "on the way" applies at both the level of our "going about" the world, which we would be tempted to distinguish as Heidegger's subject matter, and at the higher meth-odological level. Thus his list of modes of "going about" the world reaches its climax with *bestimmen*: "having to do with something, undertaking, accomplishing, exploring, questioning, considering, discussing, *defining*" (ibid, pp. 56–57; my italics). At the end of *Being and Time*, we find that in this work itself we are still "on the way."

25. Ibid., p. 176.

26. For the full quotation, see p. 522 below.

27. *On the Way to Language*, p. 92; cf. pp. 21, 129. *Sartre*, p. 240.

28. *Papirer*, XI¹ A 237; *Being and Time*, pp. 41, 43; italics in original.

29. *Discourse on Method*, pt. 2.

30. *Being and Time*, p. 4. The problem of direction is a recurring *meth-odological* problem; see, e.g., pp. 61, 131, 185, 245, 253, 256. The translators sometimes bring out the more sweeping character of the problem by the translation "orientation," and I shall often follow their precedent.

31. "Wandering" is a recurrent metaphor in Bacon for error. Heidegger considers that "wandering" is unavoidable. (p. 308 below).

32. *Novum Organum*.

33. Heidegger's *Der Feldweg* has been translated under the title *The Pathway*. For his *Holzwege*, see p. 400 below.

34. "What Is a Thing?" pp. 1–2; *Being and Time*, p. 24.

35. *Being and Time*, pp. 36, 37, 57, 389–90. The *Rückgang* will be considered in chap. 9.

36. Ibid., p. 78. Otto Pöggler dismisses this example as if it were merely a matter of Heidegger's "obvious astonishment at a new gadget" ("Heidegger Heute," p. 42). But I have tried to bring out its significance for Heidegger's *Way of Thought* (*Denkweg*), which is the title of Pöggler's exposition of Heidegger.

37. In the chapter on "Temporality" in *Perception*, Merleau-Ponty cites as an epigraph not only Heidegger's "The meaning of being-there is temporality" but also Claudel's "Time is the *sens* of life, as in the phrase the *direction* of the flow of water, the *meaning* of a sentence, the *feel* of a fabric, the *sense* of smell" (p. 410; my italics). The last two implications of *sens* Merleau-Ponty would associate with his own focus on perception.

38. Richardson, *From Phenomenology to Thought*, p. x.

39. *Being and Time*, p. 2.

40. Heidegger alludes to Hegel's treatment (ibid., p. 3). It is possible that his criticism here too was influenced by Kierkegaard (see p. 116 above).

41. See p. 103 above. We have recognized that with this argument Hegel is discounting "imaginative representation" (*Vor-stellung*), whereby something is "placed before" the mind in its spatial relations.

42. Heidegger's initial reversal is also *reflexive* in the direction taken: "To work out the question of being adequately, we must make a being, the questioner, transparent in his own being. . . . This being which each of us is himself and which includes questioning as one of the possibilities of its being [see n. 24, this chapter] we shall denote by the term 'being-there.' To put our question explicitly and transparently, we must first of all give a proper explication of a being [being-there] with respect to its being" (*Being and Time*, p. 7). The criterion of "transparency" (*Durchsichtigkeit*) is associated with the *meth-odological* problem of *Durchgang*—of "getting through" the obstruction which the traditional philosophical treatment of being largely is.

43. Another criterion which controls Heidegger's reversal in direction is movement toward "definiteness" or "determinacy" or concreteness (see n. 18, this chapter). At the start *being-there* "understands itself as being-in-the-world, but without adequate ontological *Bestimmtheit* ["definiteness" or "determinacy"]" (*Being and Time*, p. 313). *Being and Time* itself is the process of "definition" whereby "temporal definiteness" (p. 49) is sought in treating the question of being. The "reversal" or "turn" (*Kehre*) that is attempted in Heidegger's later works has its own specific character. Yet insofar as he was unable in the projected sequel to *Being and Time* to carry through this reversal "with the aid of the language of metaphysics" (Barrett, 3:202), we can discern a continued struggle to reverse the abstract direction which the metaphysical tradition had taken. In "The Thing" (1950) Heidegger no longer asks a metaphysical question, as he still did in his lectures, "The Fundamental Questions of Metaphysics" (1935–36), which were published under the title "What Is a Thing?" that implies the question of "essence" is being raised. And instead of setting up such quasi-metaphysical categories as *Ausrichtung* and *Entfernung* to challenge Descartes's "extension," his analysis in "The Thing" proceeds much more concretely. See, e.g., its opening paragraph, where television is mentioned.

44. *Timaeus* 52B.

45. "Approach to God is not by intervals of place" (Augustine, *De trinitate*, in *Patrologia Latina*, 7.6.12).

46. Derrida, *Marges*, p. 250. The novelist is Anatole France. We also find in Heidegger an analogy between linguistic expressions and "the many worn-out coins that we pass unexamined from hand to hand in an everyday life that has grown flat" (*Introduction to Metaphysics*, p. 84). Note the interplay with "flat." Heidegger may have taken the metaphor over from Nietzsche.

47. *Introduction to Metaphysics*, pp. 29, 33, 43–47, 55–61. In France the broad reversal I have been discussing received its first formulation in a book by Jean Wahl, *Toward the Concrete*. Wahl was an influential academic expositor of Hegel, Kierkegaard, Husserl, and Heidegger. In reviewing his intellectual development, Sartre cites Wahl's title but recalls his sense of protest: "But we were disappointed by this 'toward.' The total concrete was that we wanted to start out from" (*Search for a Method*, p. 19; the English translation here is incorrect). Sartre's protest seems to have been inspired by Heidegger's approach or at least became reformulated in its terms: "The concrete is man within the world in that specific union of man with the world which Heidegger, for example, calls 'being-in-the-world' " (*Sartre*, p. 110).

48. *Being and Time*, p. 299; *Sartre*, pp. 273–77.

49. *Perception*, pp. 146, 123, 154; *Sartre*, p. 196.

50. See chap. 3, n. 13 above.

51. *Structure of Behavior*, p. 168. The metaphor of goal-directedness is probably implicit in Husserl's description of consciousness as in-tentional, but the goal is the object

toward which consciousness is directed. Merleau-Ponty is carrying out a dialectical revision of Husserl's teleology, inasmuch as consciousness becomes embodied in a course of action, which is inserted into a relational setting which is "not an 'object.'" See Sartre's comparable revision: "Consciousness is an abstraction.... The concrete is man within the world" (see n. 47, this chapter). For the further concreteness which is achieved when the temporal as well as the spatial dimension is introduced, see chap. 3, n. 113 above.

52. See pp. 125, 144 above.

53. *Sartre*, p. 276; italics in original. For the role "waiting" plays in Sartre, see chap. 7, n. 66 below.

54. *Being and Time*, p. 79.

55. *Poetry, Language, Thought*, pp. 158–59, 152.

56. Ibid., p. 153, 155. For Heidegger's distrust of symbolism, see p. 112 above.

57. *Poetry, Language, Thought*, p. 160.

58. Ibid., pp. 152, 153. Consider the structure of Heidegger's dialogue with Nietzsche: "Only a dialogue can respond ... to Nietzsche's thinking which is a transition [*Übergang*]—a dialogue whose own way is preparing a transition. In such a transition, Nietzsche's thought as a whole must of course take its place on the one side which the transition leaves behind to move to the other.... The superman [*Übermensch*] goes beyond [*geht über*] man as he is, the last man. Man, unless he stops with the kind of man as he is, is a passage across [*Übergang*]; he is a bridge.... We are intent on the passage across. From this point of view we ask what he goes away from, and where he goes who goes across. Thus we are asking about the bridge for the passage across" *(What Is Called Thinking?* pp. 51, 60, 86).

59. The structural similarities should also be noted between the bridge as an intersection and the crossroads of *Being and Time*, although Heidegger's focus there on the directional signal indicated that he still remained within the environs of the intentional analysis which Husserl had launched in the first logical investigation, where he dealt with how a "sign" can be the "expression" of a "meaning." The similarities among the three examples are due to specific characteristics of Heidegger's relational analysis, which the examples embody so concretely that Heidegger would object to my characterization of them as examples which embody.

60. Heidegger's attempt (abetted by Nietzsche) to regard the entire philosophical tradition as Platonic commits him to a traditional interpretation of Plato as sharply distinguishing between the sensory image and the intelligible (see n. 63).

61. *Visible and Invisible*, p. 224.

62. I am borrowing from Heidegger's exegesis of *ring* and *gering*, which are old German, as *"schmiegsam, schmiebar, fugsam"* ("The Thing," in *Poetry, Language, Thought*, p. 180), for these criteria seem to be implicit in the more concrete thinking of his later writings, where he abandons even the label "philosophy" in favor of "thinking."

63. "Destruction" I have so far treated by reference to the negative moment in Hegel's *Aufhebung* (see p. 100 above), but Heidegger probably derives the metaphor more directly from "destruction of the world," which was one idiom, among others, that Husserl used of his transcendental reduction. A casualty is the conception of symbol or metaphor itself: "the metaphorical only occurs within metaphysics" (*Satz vom Grund*, p. 89; see Derrida's remarkable commentary in his discussion of metaphor [*Marges*, p. 270]). In undercutting such distinctions as those between physical and metaphysical, sensory and spiritual (e.g., *Introduction to Metaphysics*, pp. 89–90; *On the Way to Language*, pp. 14, 178), Heidegger is also undercutting the distinction between the literal and the metaphorical. We then face the further issue as to whether language itself can survive the destruction. In the present volume I shall continue to rely on the literal/metaphorical distinction even in dealing with Heidegger, for it is indispensable in interpreting existentialism.

64. See p. 120 above.

65. *Poetry, Language, Thought*, p. 179. The metaphor itself may be Heidegger's, but the dynamics are ancient. Consider the following fragment from Heraclitus, which I

cite from Heidegger's version: "Opposites move back and forth, the one to the other; from out of themselves they gather themselves together" (*Introduction to Metaphysics*, p. 111).

66. See, e.g., *Poetry, Language, Thought*, p. 204.

67. *What Is Called Thinking?* pp. 45–46.

68. *Between Existentialism and Marxism*, p. 149; italics in original.

69. Armand Robin, cited by Contat, 1:55.

70. *Nausea*, p. 235.

71. *Poetry, Language, Thought*, p. 27.

72. Sartre himself was well acquainted with the traditional concept. He wrote on it when he finally passed his *agrégation* in 1929. He had in fact become preoccupied with contingency even before he ever read Heidegger. In 1931 he began a "factum on contingency" (*Prime of Life*, p. 89), but Simone de Beauvoir complained that it was "a long and abstract meditation." In the successive rewritings Sartre resolved the problem of achieving the literary concreteness which de Beauvoir refers to as "fictional depth" (p. 90).

73. See p. 109 above; my italics.

74. See p. 107 above.

75. *Either*, p. 311. The metaphor of possession—of making something one's "own" through "internalization"—is also a feature of Hegel's epistemology (see p. 000 below).

76. See p. 241 below.

77. *Either*, p. 311; italics mine.

78. Ibid., p. 330; italics mine. Pleasure is an esthetic criterion, but it can be either immediate or reflective. In chap. 7 we shall discover that interplay is characteristic of the "Diary" author as "a reflective seducer" (as opposed to the "immediate" seducer, Don Juan) and that what is seductive ultimately is the interplay introduced by the process of reflection itself. The moment of transition from the "actual" toward the "ideal" when Socrates is "hovering" corresponds to the transition here from sight to imagination—the transition which I have brought out by the comparison with Hegel (see p. 106 above).

79. Pp. 151–52. The Latin *interesse* meant "to be between," though it came to mean (in the third person impersonal) "it is of interest."

80. *Either*, pp. 385–86, 436–37.

81. P. 352.

82. *Situations*, 10:137–39.

83. See p. 255 below.

84. *What Is Called Thinking?* p. 71.

85. These crude paraphrases obliterate the subtler resonances of *heissen*. Heidegger provides a precedent for Derrida allowing the proliferation of meanings to get apparently out of hand and become *dissémination*, which itself has multiple meanings. But in Heidegger unity is still a criterion (e.g., with the *Einfalt*), and the different "ways of asking the question [about thinking] are not just superficially strung together. They are all interrelated. What is disturbing about the question, therefore, lies less in the multiplicity of its possible meanings than in the single meaning toward which all four ways are pointing" (ibid., p. 114).

86. *Being and Time*, p. 183; *Introduction to Metaphysics*, pp. 147–48.

87. *Postscript*, p. 100. It is curious that Kierkegaard did not track this passage in "Isis and Osiris" (Plutarch's *Moralia* 375D) back to its source in Plato (*Cratylus* 397D). His failure to do so is a good illustration of how modern classical culture has traditionally been Hellenistic and Roman, rather than in direct contact with classical Greece (see chap. 2, n. 50 above).

88. *Being and Time*, p. 2. This interpretation may elaborate on Plato's own reference, which Heidegger quotes, to the "battle of the giants" between philosophers. Heidegger associates Aristotle with Plato in this wrenching.

89. E.g., *Sartre*, p. 115.

90. *Being and Time*, p. 42.

91. *Postscript*, esp. pp. 90–97; see p. 401 below. Heidegger frequently uses the same metaphor, and he brings out the *reflexive* character of the movement: "The leap [*Sprung*] of thought does not leave behind it that from which it takes its leap [*abspringt*] but appropriates [*eignet*] it in a more original [*ursprünglichere*] fashion" (*Satz vom Grund*, p. 107).

92. The prototype for this dislocation is the first philosopher, Thales, who fell into a well (*What Is a Thing?* p. 2).

93. Similarly, for Sartre reflection is the backward movement of a *recul* (*Sartre*, p. 114) as well as the violent movement of a "wrenching away."

94. See p. 115 above. Kierkegaard himself had identified "repetition" as "a decisive expression for what 'recollection' was for the Greeks." It is "recollection forward" (*Repetition*, pp. 3–4). Whether or not there is a debt to Kierkegaard, the reflexive movement of a *Wiederholung* seems to be opposed by Heidegger, as Kierkegaard opposes it), to the progressive movement of the Hegelian *Aufhebung*.

95. *Being and Time*, p. 21.

96. *Papirer*, IV A 164.

97. *Being and Time*, p. 33. Recapitulation is a procedure which was adopted in the seminar on Heidegger which is summarized in *On Time and Being*: "The Reversal" . . . was read as a conclusion. This was done in order that what was discussed during the seminar might be heard again, so to speak, from another perspective (as it were) and in a more unified way" (p. 54).

98. *Stages*, p. 26. The epigraph is taken from Lichtenberg, but my interpretation is of the implications it acquires in *Stages* itself.

99. "What was misleading about *Either/Or* is that it was rounded out to a conclusion ethically. . . . In *Stages* . . . the religious . . . is assigned its place. The esthetic and the ethical stages are again brought forward [as in *Either/Or*] in a certain sense as recapitulation, but then again as something new. It would indeed be poor testimony to existential inwardness if every such stage were not capable of a renewal" (*Postscript*, pp. 261–62).

100. The first stage of *Stages* is subtitled "A Recollection" (*erindring*), which marks not only the passage of time that has taken place since the stretch of life covered in *Either* but also the advance in "inwardness," inasmuch as *erindring* brings with it Hegel's etymologizing of recollection as internalization. There is also a shift to the higher level—the shift which is completed with the treatment of the problem of communication in *Postscript*. There recollection is "repetition" no longer at the level of life (as it was in the work with that title which came between *Either/Or* and *Stages* [see p. 115 above] but at the level of the work itself: "Had the author of the *Stages* consulted me, I should on esthetic grounds have advised him against recalling a preceding work. . . . A repetition relative to things that require good fortune [for chance as an esthetic category, see p. 254 below] is . . . always risky. . . . The merely interested [merely esthetic] reader is repelled by the fact that it is the same, for he requires external changes in names, decorations, cloths, hair style, etc. The attentive reader [i.e., the reader who can get behind the external; see p. 241 below] is rendered more strict in his requirements, because there is nothing seductive, nothing distracting, . . . no information about the external appearance of known characters. . . . I have risked repeating . . . only by use of considerable abbreviation and with important changes in the starting point" (*Postscript*, pp. 253–54). One of these is the shift of level which I have noted is completed in *Postscript* and which we see in the citation involves relinquishing, at the level of the work itself, the undertaking to seduce. For seduction as distraction, see chap. 7; for the repulsion of the reader, chap. 10 below. In *Postscript* the epigraph is interpreted as applicable to the "merely interested reader" (p. 254).

101. In Heidegger's usage, which I shall follow, "recapitulation" includes the advance. Kierkegaard, like Hegel, reserves the term instead for the reformulation that leads up to this advance. Like most other dialectical as well as rhetorical procedures,

"recapitulation" is an ancient device. The recapitulation of the *Republic* in the *Timaeus* has long fretted scholars (see my *Human Nature*, chap. 4, n. 6).

102. *Ideas*, p. 166.

103. This is the title of sec. 29 of *Being and Time*. My exegesis is restricted to p. 134, unless otherwise indicated.

104. *Befinden* and its cognates have a wide range of meaning that Heidegger would take advantage of. *Befinden* can mean "find," "think," "feel"; *sich befinden*, "to be found in or at some place," "to be," even "to exist"; *es befindet sich*, "It is the case," "This is how it is." Such English translations as "predisposition" are too precise and too psychological. Sartre's translation seems to be the "inexpressible affective quality of experience" (*L'idiot*, 3:1853), though he makes no explicit reference to Heidegger. Sartre also sometimes retains the German *Befindlichkeit* (e.g., *Being and Nothingness*, p. 330).

105. See p. 105 above.

106. See, e.g., Hegel's *Encyclopaedia*, pt. 3, pars. 446, 448.

107. *Existence and Being*, p. 362. The presupposition is an ingredient in the preoccupation, which was analyzed above (p. 98).

108. *Being and Time*, pp. 180, 176.

109. Ibid., p. 138.

110. Ibid., pp. 134–35, 42, 43, 137.

111. *Existence and Being*, p. 355.

112. *Being and Time*, pp. 95–96. Heidegger is referring to mathematical knowledge as its privileged character was established by Descartes.

113. *Existence and Being*, p. 373. "Fundamental" displays a treacherous ambiguity permitting *interplay* here, since *Abgrund* means "abyss."

114. *L'idiot*, 3:18. "Anchorage" itself seems to have been originally Merleau-Ponty's metaphor for rendering *Befindlichkeit*.

115. This metaphor is so frequent in Sartre that one cannot dismiss it as inoffensively nontechnical. It describes the movement of consciousness not only as affective (this is betrayed by the derivation of the metaphor itself from Heidegger's "moodiness") but also as intentional. Thus, when Sartre announces that "consciousness is a slippery slope [*pente glissante*]" (*Sartre*, p. 353), he is explaining that consciousness cannot hold itself back from its intentional thrust as Husserl's "consciousness of something." See chap. 5, n. 44 below.

116. *Sartre*, p. 102: *Anti-Semite and Jew*, p. 10. The discovery of his own existence by the protagonist in *Nausea* is clearly a parody of Descartes. (When exalted, he is "a fellow in the style of Descartes," p. 56). One significant difference is that he discovers his existence not as thought but as feeling—"*ce sentiment d'exister*" (p. 99).

117. *Nausea*, p. 127.

118. Recall that Kierkegaard similarly argued for the universality of the mood of despair, by treating not being in despair as a form of despair. See p. 84 above.

119. *Being and Nothingness*, p. 444. *Fade* is one of Sartre's favorite phenomenological characterizations of existence as contingent: e.g., *fade contingence* (*L'idiot*, 2:12), *la contingence nauséabonde du vécu* which is associated with the *âcre fadeur de l'existence* (ibid., p. 2066). See also Franz's curtain speech on the contingency of our time (*Sartre*, p. 484).

120. *Sartre*, pp. 61–62. For differences between the nausea of the novel and nausea as defined in *Being and Nothingness*, see p. 193 below; for the dislocating character of the experience, chap. 9, n. 51 below.

121. *Prime of Life*, pp. 89, 216.

122. Perhaps misled by Corbin's translation, Sartre reports Heidegger's "definition" of *Dasein*, "that it is a being such that in its being, its being is in question" (*Sartre*, p. 108). The second "its" is a misinterpretation of Heidegger and is in effect a point of entry for Sartre's "humanism" (see chap. 3, n. 21 above). The two passages in Heidegger from which Sartre has extracted the definition refer to *Dasein* as a "being" (*Seiendes*)

for which "in its Being [*Sein*] itself Being is going on [i.e., is at stake]" (*Being and Time*, p. 42). The translation *en question* for *es geht* is a point of entry for Sartre's psychologism—i.e., for interpreting *Dasein* as consciousness. Indeed Sartre seems to have interpreted the *en question* in the light of Heidegger's own account elsewhere of "questioning" (*Being and Time*, p. 5) and to have taken advantage of the *reflexive* character of the relation of *Dasein* to *Sein* in developing his own psychological account of questioning as a *reflective* operation of consciousness (*Sartre*, pp. 110–15). *Es geht* ties in instead with the "goings about" which are analyzed in *Being and Time* and are not restricted to the operations of consciousness.

123. *Hegel's Concept of Experience*, p. 117. Although Heidegger is expounding *Hegel's Concept of Experience*, he comes close here to suggesting that his own method is dialectical, if only in that it is so fluid as to elude exposition. One can appreciate Heidegger's elusiveness, but it seems unfortunate that some of his disciples sometimes have remained so mesmerized by it that they are reluctant to recognize that he follows discernible procedures that can be compared (even though they are not identical) with the procedures of other philosophers. Indeed one of his procedures, as the present instance illustrates, is dialogue or confrontation with other philosophers, and this procedure is traditionally dialectical. The other philosophers whose procedures I am comparing are less elusive. But the reader should be warned that the traits I am extracting as dialectical from this comparison are not offered as such by the philosophers themselves. In fact Sartre regards Merleau-Ponty as undialectical or as dialectical only in a quixotic sense: "He jumps from one point of view to another, denying, affirming, changing more to less and less to more. Everything is contradictory and also true" (*Situations*, p. 212). And Merleau-Ponty in turn regards Sartre as undialectical: "In Sartre there can be no dialectic between the being which is wholly positive and nothingness which 'is not.' . . . The negative is equivocal in principle" (*Themes from the Lectures*, p. 59; see chap. 5, nn. 3, 18 below). Confusion is compounded by the fact that Sartre and Merleau-Ponty are each measuring the other's performance against dialectical materialism rather than any analysis of an existential dialectic. But their mutual recriminations do involve genuine differences which will be considered in the sequel.

124. *On the Way to Language*, p. 159.

125. Kenley Dove translates "sewer."

126. For a brief account of intentionality, see *Sartre*, pp. 10–11.

5

The Principle of Contradiction

Existence first starts out with contradiction—Kierkegaard

Being and Nothingness

Reliance on contradiction is the most familiar trait of dialectic, whether it be sophistic or Socratic, Abelard's *Sic et non,* Aquinas's *sed contra,* Kant's antinomies, or Marx's class struggle. "Dialectical" is often used simply to designate this reliance. The principle of contradiction is explicit in the title *Either/Or* with which Kierkegaard starts the series of works which compose his "authorship"; he also comments in his journal that "existence first starts out with contradiction."[1] The principle is implicit in Sartre's title *Being and Nothingness,* the work most closely associated with the vogue of existentialism after World War II.

But the specific ways in which a contradiction is relied on to advance an analysis depend on the other dialectical traits which I have been sorting out. A dialectical analysis would never reach a *definition* (its first trait) unless it can be assumed (in Kierkegaard's phrase) that a "relation . . . always underlies a disrelation [*misforholdet*]" represented by the contradiction. A blanket contradiction (e.g., a round square) gets us nowhere. Hegel carefully distinguishes the disrelations of difference, diversity, opposition, and contradiction. But these distinctions belong to one stage in his *Logic,* "The Doctrine of Essence," so their implications could only be determined in the setting of the relational analysis undertaken at this stage in its relation to the relational analysis of the *Logic* as a whole. Furthermore, the existentialist is almost inevitably less careful, since he is following out an "affective dialectic" which remains immersed in concrete experiences. Thus I shall often employ as rough equivalents for "contradiction," where this may suggest too formal a polarization, the vaguer term "opposition" or the weaker "contrast." But my effort is not to do justice to the technicality a dialectical method may be capable of attaining but to take advantage of existentialist immersion in concrete experiences in order to provide an easier introduction to this method. The understanding of the dialectical method that is gained will become more precise when the comparison with the phenomenological method is carried out in the sequel.

But at least we can anticipate that the "relation", like the "disrelation" it "underlies," differs in different dialectical analyses. Although Sartre's method of definition, like Heidegger's, is a *relational* analysis (our second trait), the fundamental ontological relation and thus all derivative relations are differently conceived. Sartre's title *Being and Nothingness* is doubtless modeled on Heidegger's *Being and Time*, but being in Heidegger is brought into relation to time as its "horizon," and what exactly this relation is Heidegger has prolonged difficulty in establishing. Indeed he rejects the criterion of exactitude. Thus the most difficult term in his title is the "and", whereas the relation proposed by Sartre's title is specifiable as a relation of contradiction. Implicit in Heidegger's "and" is his procedure of "letting something be seen in its togetherness with something else." He is in some sense trying to undercut the traditional opposition between being as eternal and time. Although Sartre's "and" indicates that his analysis is *relational* too, he regularly lets something be seen in its opposition to something else. Heidegger's unsteady vision of the world becomes in Sartre a vision in which "nothingness makes the world iridescent, casting a shimmer over things."[2] This "shimmer" is composed of dislocations which are more rapid and sharper than those we encountered in Heidegger, for they are successive acts of consciousness conceived both *phenomenologically*, as articulative acts whereby I am "conscious of something," and *dialectically*, as applying the principle of contradiction to the process of articulation. Thus Husserl's "consciousness of something" becomes consciousness of this thing (being) as not (nothingness) that thing. In other words, consciousness is discriminatory, and the act of discrimination is a negation. his *omnis determinatio est negatio* Sartre takes over from the Hegelian dialectic.[3]

BEING FOR THE OTHER

The precise adjustments that enable Sartre to combine debts to Husserl, Heidegger, and Hegel do not concern us in this volume. But I am trying to complete my explanation at the end of the last chapter as to why Sartre is able to introduce distinctions which are sharper than Heidegger's and hence more easily discerned, so that they will facilitate our grasping more definitely the traits of an existential dialectic. Certain broader adjustments do, however, need to be acknowledged. If I began with Heidegger in spite of the difficulty of his analysis, it was partly by way of recognizing his pivotal role in the development of contemporary existentialism. There was another reason, too. Sartre's avowed starting point in *Being and Nothingness* is phenomenological and betrays more of a debt to Husserl's analysis of consciousness than to Heidegger's analysis of existence as *being-there*. In fact Sartre complains,

> Heidegger starts his existential analytic without going through the *cogito* [the act of consciousness]. But since *Dasein* has originally been deprived of the dimension of consciousness, it can never regain that dimension. . . . One must start out with the *cogito*.[4]

If matters were this simple, Sartre could not have earned a place in this volume. By the time he makes this pronouncement regarding the appropriate starting point, he has long since conflated consciousness in Husserl with *Dasein* [existence] in Heidegger, so that his own analysis of consciousness is not Husserl's but is irreparably modified by Heidegger's existential analytic.[5]

Sartre's treatment of consciousness as nauseous has already provided us with evidence of Heidegger's influence. This example and the others with which I shall now illustrate the dialectical character of Sartre's method may take us beyond his phenomenological starting point in *Being and Nothingness*. But our concern is with his existential individualism. And it is primarily in the presence of the Other that I am located ("occupy a place") in Sartre and am dislocated—"My original fall is the existence of the Other." In fact the most prominent form of "affectivity" in *Being and Nothingness* is no longer nausea but the at least equally dislocating emotion of *honte* ("humiliation" or "shame"), which is felt when I become conscious of myself in the presence of the Other as "having my being *outside*."[6] It could be argued that Sartre reaches his own starting point as an *ex-sistentialist* in *Being and Nothingness* only when he arrives at this analysis of "being for the Other." Up to this point his analysis is largely derived from Husserl, Heidegger, and Hegel; and only here does his analysis prepare the way for his own characteristic undertaking—the existential psychoanalysis of the individual's relation to the Other in *Saint Genet* and the three volumes on Flaubert.

The humiliation of "having my being outside" in the object that I am for the Other, but cannot be for myself, is most dislocating if the Other takes me by surprise—for example, when I am suddenly caught peeping through a keyhole and identified as a "peeping Tom." Humiliation is similarly felt by Jean Genet when he is *"caught in the act"* and identified as a "thief."[7] But the adjustment in the dialectic after *Nausea* should not be exaggerated. Humiliation in the presence of the Other was felt in *Nausea* too: the diarist became dislocatingly conscious of his own "sagging" and "contingent" existence in the presence of the work of art, which is upheld by its own intrinsic necessity, as an object which "has taken us by surprise while we were living our sloppy, easygoing lives," and the work of art is "a witness without pity."[8] Nor is the adjustment in the *Critique* a drastic departure: "My having my being outside" is now my having my being involved in some "shaped" or "worked matter"; the "art" is now some mode of production, but the "work" is now the work of others, or of myself as Other.[9]

At the point where the Other explicitly intervenes in *Being and Nothingness*, not only is the analysis readied for Sartre's existential psychoanalysis, but it also becomes more fully dialectical:

> Everything which holds for me in my relations with the Other holds for him as well. While I attempt to free myself from the ascendancy of the Other, the Other is trying to free himself from mine. . . . It is a question not of unilateral relations with an object-in-itself but of reciprocal and moving relations.[10]

Insofar as Sartre's method derives from Husserl, his analysis is structured (to borrow his own term) by the "unilateral" reference (the "directedness upon" of intentionality) which is built into consciousness as "consciousness of something." But the "reciprocal" relations which emerge with the intervention of the Other Sartre would respect by rendering his analysis *bilateral*. This new term I shall explain further when I have explored other methodologically relevant relations.

THE STRUCTURE OF MOVEMENT

In Sartre's *relational* analysis, as in Heidegger's, method is intimately related to subject matter and cannot be separated from it. An existential subject matter is something which "matters" to its investigator, and the method of analysis he applies to it makes explicit his *reflexive* involvement (our third trait) with it. Where Heidegger explained, "The questioner as such is put in his place by the question," Sartre explains, "The truth of a dialectical movement can only be demonstrated . . . if one is drawn into the movement."[11]

The movement itself requires an analysis which is *dynamic* and *developmental* (our fourth trait), and it has already been illustrated by the "moving relations" between myself and the Other. As a more specific illustration, let us reconsider the example which was presented earlier to exhibit the *ex-sistential* character of Sartre's subject matter. Reconsidering the wiggling bottom from a methodological point of view might be worthwhile, for originally it seemed to be Sartre at his most preposterous.

Since this example is employed by Sartre in *defining* "the obscene," it illustrates the first trait of a dialectical method. It also illustrates the *relational* character (the second trait) of a dialectical definition: what is being defined is the dislocated psychological movement of revulsion on the part of consciousness of the subject from what he is conscious of—the dislocated physical movement of the object. Since the subject is visualized as himself defining the "obscene" by his reaction, the third trait is illustrated too—the *reflexive* character of an existential dialectic.[12]

When Thody was contemptuous of this example, he was overlooking the unsteadiness of the observer's vision. We are confronted with a relation between *movements* (our fourth trait), with respect not only to the object but also to the consciousness of the subject. For the reaction "obscene" to occur, the subject must "not be in a state of sexual desire."[13] The qualification suggests that Sartre is not always "unpleasantly puritanical"; when he is in the right mood, he might be quite prepared to acknowledge what Thody regards as "a delightful and irreplaceable thing." Only a relatively brief acknowledgment, inasmuch as an existential dialectic is dislocated by changes in *direction* (our fifth trait), so that nothing is any more likely to stay irreplaceable than delightful. There is a contradictory swaying to and fro not only on the part of the object but also between the possible reactions on the part of the subject—between desire and revulsion. In short, Sartre's dialectical method of definition is *definitio a contrario*, whether we take it at its highest level of *Being and Nothingness* or at the rather low level we are considering here. One can be "moved" psychologically "outside" of oneself in either of two opposed *directions*, granted that the movement of disgust is obviously the more *ex-sistential*; it is a *reversal* (the sixth trait), disrupting what would usually be taken to be the normal movement of attraction, and thus is the more dislocating of the two opposed reactions.

That we are dealing with "a structure of movement" of some significance for Sartre can be reemphasized if we recall other examples which we dealt with before. Giacometti was pulled psychologically in opposite *directions* when "he felt so strongly that the distance [represented by "the gleaming parquet floor"] could not be traversed" but "yearned to touch that luxurious flesh." The female sex organ in the Masson drawing was interpreted by Sartre as "the explosive dislocation of a body"—the "juncture" at which "the action of two forces" were "brought to bear" with "each pulling . . . in a direction opposed to the other, so that the organ is the rupture of the flesh this tension fissures."[14] These and other examples of dislocated structures, which were considered simply as characteristic specimens of existential subject matter, can now be seen to betray characteristics that derive inseparably from the application of dialectical method.

UNSTEADINESS

Lest there be lingering doubts about the wiggling bottom, we can confirm its dialectical significance by reference to Kierkegaard, who provides an example of unsteady walking. It is true that there are differences between this example and Sartre's example of the wiggling bottom: Kierkegaard employs his in defining the comic. Yet there is perhaps an overlap with Sartre's example since Sartre admits his debt to Bergson's *On Laughter*,[15] and the admission suggests an awareness that a certain comic flourish may attach to what Thody takes so seriously. Admittedly Kierkegaard has no interest in the obscene. The only flesh in Kierkegaard is his biblical description of his own affliction as "a thorn in the flesh," and the remarkable variety of the scholarly speculations as to where this thorn was inserted suggests how little real flesh clings to the metaphor. Even the seducer of "The Diary of the Seducer" is not properly incarnated but puts on "a parastatic [i.e., a phantom] body."[16] But these differences need not detain us now. We are only interested in the unsteadiness as dialectical.

Instead of the opposition found in Sartre between the involuntary movements of the bottom and the purposive movement of walking, Kierkegaard makes his walker half drunk while keeping a sober eye on him as an observer. Instead of the secondary dialectic found in Sartre between the involuntary movements of the bottom in opposite directions, Kierkegaard reinforces his basic opposition with a secondary dialectic, introducing an extra observer who is extra purposeful and so imposes an extra reflexive effort on the part of the half drunk to appear sober:

> A man who is drunk can make so comic an impression because he expresses a contradiction in his movements. The eye [of an observer] expects steadiness [*ligelighed*] in walking; and the more there still remains some sort of reason to expect it, the more the contradiction is comical. Now if, for example, a purposeful type comes by and the drunk, feeling that he is being observed, pulls himself together and attempts to walk steadily, then the comical becomes more obvious, because the contradiction is more obvious. He succeeds for a couple of steps, until the spirit of contradiction runs away from him. If he succeeds entirely while going past the purposeful man, the initial contradiction becomes another contradiction: that we know him to be drunk and yet this is not apparent. In the first case we laugh at him

when he sways [*svingler*], because the eye demands steadiness of him;
in the second case, we laugh at him because he holds himself steady,
while our knowledge that he is drunk leads us to expect to see him
sway.[17]

Kierkegaard himself was afflicted with an unsteady gait, so this comedy
may have carried a reflexive reference for him.

INTERPLAY

This dialectical reversal which supervenes with the secondary dialectic
involves *interplay* (the seventh trait of an existential dialectic). I apply
this label because the movements in question are interrelated, even
though they are opposed. Some of the comedy of the unsteadiness in the
example of unsteady walking is in fact associated with the shift in the
locus of the contradiction. But there the interplay is relatively loose, since
it depends on the introduction of a second observer.

Return to the example of the "obscene" where we have only one observer. Here the interplay is full-fledged, requiring for its delineation
both a distinction between subject and object and a distinction of level.
To draw these distinctions new terminology is needed. Heidegger tried
to undercut the distinction between subject and object with *being-there*
as being-in-the-world. But in Sartre's example (as in Kierkegaard's) the
interplay is *bilateral*: the "obscene" is a dislocated psychological movement of disgust on the part of a *subject* reacting to the dislocated physical movements of the wiggling bottom as an *object*.[18] The interplay is
also *bifocal*: the wiggles are related to the voluntary movement of walking
(since they would not occur without this movement), but they are at the
same time opposed to it as movements which are involuntary and
mechanical—or, as Sartre puts it grandiloquently, "pure obedience to the
laws of gravity." Thus the interplay between the successive wiggles is
physically determined by (and so can mimic and reinforce in *the space
of the imagination* the effect of) the interplay operating between these
mechanical movements and the voluntary movement of walking. This
interplay is associated with the dialectical doubling with which Sartre describes the wiggling bottom as naked with a nakedness that is "obscene"
and reaches the contradiction that it would be (obscenely) naked "even if
veiled by some fabric."

In resorting to the terms *bilateral* and *bifocal*, I am recognizing that
only one opposition can readily be developed at a time in a dialectic, so
that other oppositions are likely to remain secondary. We have of course
encountered distinctions of level before, and the most important has been

the distinction between the universal scope which is traditional with philosophy and the particular experiences of the individual which come to the fore in existentialism. *Bifocal* seems a suitable metaphor for this distinction, though I am extending it to any conjunction of levels.

REVULSION

So far we have been focusing on the object, the wiggling bottom. Let us now reconsider this dialectic as *bilateral* and move over to the subject and also up to a higher level, considering it as *bifocal*. Only with these moves can we cope with the difference between two notable experiences of revulsion in Sartre. In *Being and Nothingness* "the obscene" is *reflexively* a subjective experience of revulsion which belongs to one stage in the revelation of the body of the Other. (Another stage I shall take into account shortly.) But in *Nausea* the experience of revulsion is a cosmic vision, even though when this novel is mentioned in *Being and Nothingness* nausea is accorded a much more limited assignment—it merely "reveals my own body to my consciousness."[19] It does seem a long way from the revelation of a body to the revelation of the world.

We can find clues, however, in the revelation of the body as obscene, with its metaphorical extension of the meanings of "naked" and its dialectical opposite, "the fabric" by which nakedness can be "veiled." The effective veil that is envisaged for the naked body is also metaphorical—the graceful movements of a dancer. These, Sartre explains, "enclose the body with an invisible garment." For the dancer moves with her whole body, in contrast to the ordinary walker, whose functional movement is more or less restricted to the legs. But "obscene" is a reaction to the dysfunctional, dislocated movements of the bottom which are assigned by Sartre "to the genus *disgracieux*" ("awkward") as opposed to the "graceful."[20]

Once we have taken into account the metaphorical fashion in which Sartre dresses up his interpretation of "the sight of a naked body from behind," we are better able to appreciate the vision in *Nausea*:

> Existence had suddenly been revealed [*dévoilée*]. It had lost the harmless look of an abstract category. . . . The diversity of things, their individuality, was only an appearance, a veneer. This veneer had melted, leaving lumps which were monstrous and soft [*masses monstrueuses et molles*], in disarray—naked with a frightful and obscene nakedness.[21]

This shift from an "abstract category" to the concrete is integral to the dislocating unveiling of existence and thus, I have argued, to existentialism itself.[22] The vehicle is a series of metaphors, comparable to but more vivid than the dialectic of "fabric" or "garment" and "nakedness" which we have met in *Being and Nothingness*. To the abstract phenomenological term "appearance" is succeeded by the concrete reference to "veneer" *(vernis)*. The "melting" of this "veneer" may restore concrete metaphorical meaning to *Auflösung*, which had referred more abstractly in Hegel to the "dissolution" (in the sense of "resolution") of a contradiction.[23]

Perhaps *vernis* itself should be translated as "varnish" rather than "veneer," since it is probably should be associated with the "dark brown" of the dignifying *vernis* on the portraits of the founding fathers of Bouville: "Under the artist's brush," the diarist explains, "there had been removed from their faces the mysterious weakness of human faces." Confronting these portraits, the diarist had another revelation, which had occurred with a previous encounter with an official portrait: "When one confronts a face glowing with righteousness, after a moment the glow fades, and only an ashy residue remains."[24] What takes place with the unveiling of existence in the public garden is a comparable "reduction."[25]

LUMPS

The indeterminacy of what is revealed when the varnish melts is also no longer an abstract category but metaphorical: *"masses monstrueuses et molles,* in disarray—naked with a frightful and obscene nakedness." The "obscene nakedness" is Sartre's own contribution. But the *ecstase horrible* betrays here a double debt to Heidegger. On one hand (i.e., with respect to the subjective pole of the dialectic Sartre would distinguish) the "frightening" *(effrayant)* nakedness reminds us that according to Heidegger, one usually confuses anxiety with fear as modes of *Befindlichkeit.*[26] From the start of *Nausea* the diarist's problem is that "it is certain that I was afraid or had some feeling of that kind. If I had only known what I was afraid of, I would have made progress."[27] As with anxiety in *Being and Time*, one cannot know: a "what," an object, cannot be identified. "The threat," Heidegger warns, "is indeterminate."[28]

On the other hand (i.e., with respect to the opposing pole) objects generally can no longer be identified. Sartre is presupposing Husserl's intentional analysis of consciousness as "consciousness of something"—that is, as performing a "meaning-endowing" act which identifies something as what it is. But he has also been influenced by Heidegger's undercutting of Husserl's analysis with his own functionalist analysis of the "everyday" identifying operation, which one performs "at the outset and for the most part," as determining what something is "for."[29]

The original motive for keeping the diary, which in some unexplained contingent fashion has become *Nausea*, was "to see clearly" and "above all to classify."[30] But classification is an effort at categorization and identification, which is frustrated by the *ecstase horrible*. The frustration acquires concrete rendering with the metaphor for the unidentifiable and unclassifiable—for "qualities," the diarist complains, that "elude me, slip through my fingers." The metaphor is *louche*, which literally means "squinting" but takes on the extended meanings of "suspicious looking" and "equivocal."[31] The metaphor may retain for Sartre a literal reflexive reference to his own squint,[32] just as Kierkegaard's dialectical elaboration on unsteadiness may retain for him a reference to his own gait. However, *louche* also conveys philosophical implications, which are probably inherited from Heidegger's *Unselbständigkeit*[33] but which in Sartre subvert Husserl's "consciousness of something" as an act of steady, univocal identification. Identification and classification became impossible for the diarist once he "felt the arbitrariness of relations; they no longer bit into things."[34] Ordinarily we identify things by reference to their functions, and we have watched Heidegger follow out references to what they are used "for" until their relational context is disclosed. It is these relations which are dissolved by anxiety in *Being and Time*.[35]

To return to our favorite example, legs are to walk with. When a determinate identifying reference cannot be followed out, a *reflexive*, *affective* reaction supervenes; we feel that we are dealing with something which is not quite a thing but, rather, an ill-defined lump that just happens to be—with something "contingent," "superfluous," "in the way," "unjustifiable," "obscene." "In the final analysis the awkward is the unjustifiable."[36] The wiggles of the walker's bottom seem functionless and superfluous movements in contrast to the movements of his legs; and they seem the movements of lumps of superfluous flesh. They are not endowable with meaning; the bottom is "naked" of "the fabric" of meaning that intentional action can confer.

THE DREAM

When existence is "unveiled" as "naked" a second time, the vision is still *bifocal* but is refocused on other lumps:

> I was watching the shoulders and neck of the woman. Existence which was naked. That couple—it suddenly horrified me—that couple were still existing somewhere in Bouville; somewhere—in the midst of what smells? —That soft [*douce*] bosom . . . and the woman still feeling it exist under her blouse, thinking, "My titties, my lovely fruits," smiling mysteriously, attentive to her swelling breasts tickling her, and then I shouted and found myself with my eyes wide open.

Had I dreamed this enormous presence? It was there, deposited in the garden, tumbling down in the trees, all soft [*molle*], sticking to everything, thick, a jelly. I found it so stupid, so out of place; I hated this ignoble marmalade. . . . It spread everywhere, filling everything with its gelatinous slither. . . . I was no longer in Bouville, I was nowhere, I was floating. I was not surprised. I knew it was the World, the naked World suddenly revealing itself.[37]

The couple in question the diarist had watched eating at a restaurant the previous Sunday, and he had recognized that her seduction was proceeding normally.[38]

The suspicion, "Had I dreamed this enormous presence?" marks the shift back to a more cosmic vision, but ambiguous, metaphorical interpretation survives. The "jelly" and "marmalade" of the second paragraph presumably continue the theme of "fruits" from the first, although now the "fruits" are squashed.[39] "What smells" in the first paragraph probably anticipates (among other body odors) the viscous seminal dream of the second. The sexual significance of lumps and their relative indeterminacy is emphasized in *Being and Nothingness* in connection with the *bifocal* character which is attributed to desire itself, which "while aiming at the body [of the Other] as a whole reaches it primarily through lumps of flesh which are least differentiated, largely nerveless, hardly capable of spontaneous movement, through breasts, buttocks, thighs, stomach: they compose an image of pure facticity."[40]

The dream phase of the nauseous experience with lumps in the public garden we have been prepared for by an earlier dream in *Nausea*. The present dream is a Heideggerian vision of the world; the earlier involved "something" the diarist was "conscious of" in Husserl's fashion. I should explain that the diarist rather regularly slept with the woman who ran the café, for it relieved him of what he will later diagnose as his nausea. But on the last occasion, he was disgusted by her smell, went asleep while playing "distractedly with her cunt, . . . suddenly saw a small garden with low, broad trees on which huge leaves were hanging covered with hairs. . . . The Velleda of the public garden pointed a finger at her cunt. 'This garden smells of vomit,' I shouted. 'I didn't want to wake you up,' she said, 'but the sheet got folded under my bottom.'" This conflation of Husserl with Heidegger leaves us with two public gardens: the first "something" he was "conscious of" in his earlier dream, and its public character is stressed by the comment "She had to have a man a day and has many others besides me;"[41] the second "the naked World suddenly revealing itself" in his later dream or trance. The conflation might alternatively be regarded as *bifocal*: the original focus becomes wide-angle.

METAPHOR

Existentialist reliance on metaphors (and on the extended significance which metaphors foment) is a matter of some complaint on the part of less literary and more straitlaced Anglo-American philosophers. I have redescribed the transpositions and extensions as illustrating the bifocal way an existential dialectic attains general scope, and I have shown that they are sometimes in Sartre's case the way he conflates Husserl's "something" we are "conscious of"—a cunt, a bottom, a breast—with some sense [*Befindlichkeit*] of "being-in-the-world" in Heidegger.[42] Just as we must watch for the *interplay* at one level and avoid interpreting the *bilateral* dialectic unilaterally (as Thody does, when he interprets Sartre's reaction to the wiggling bottom as "purely subjective"), so we should alert ourselves to the *interplay* between levels.[43]

Sartre's playing up of the concretely literal component of his crucial metaphors accommodates a distinction of level which holds between Husserl's and Heidegger's analyses. Take, for example, a metaphor he shares with Heidegger. "Play," which has inspired my term *interplay*, we would certainly not want to construe as a literal reference in Heidegger, but in Sartre it gains its metaphorical extension while retaining its literal reference. Sartre is speaking metaphorically when he offers the definition "As soon as a man apprehends himself as free and wishes to use his freedom, . . . then his activity is play." Play in this extended sense is closely associated with Sartre's *reflexive* individualism: "Play, like Kierkegaard's irony, emancipates subjectivity. What indeed is play, if not an activity of which man is the initial starting point, for which man himself determines the principles, and which can have no other consequences than those which follow from these principles?" But in the ensuing demonstration, "play" is equated with sport, taken quite literally. And the privileged form of "play" (given the self-determination that Sartre reads into the movement of consciousness as "intentional") is *glissement* in the literal sense that it is the activity of which the skier is exhilaratingly conscious, inasmuch as it embodies a movement analogous to that of consciousness itself.[44]

RUMINATION

Interplay is of course not limited to the relation between levels which is introduced by metaphors, though these are usually prominent vehicles for interplay.[45] Let us consider the relation of contradiction, for it is important to recognize that in a dialectic this is not a relation between fixed opposites. Characteristically for Sartre it is a "contradiction that is turn-ing" (*contradiction tournante*). A humble example is the common plea with which one deceives oneself, "I know that, of course, but even so. . . ."[46] As construed by Sartre, the first clause carries an objective refer-ence to the public world; the second clause, to "the subjective world." Here the turn is a single turn in the *reflexive* direction. But the turning can continue and generate extremely twisted structures whose *interplay* can only be readily followed out insofar as the turning psychological move-ments are metaphorically traceable in *the space of the imagination*, by reference to comparable physical movements. Thus Sartre frequently traces "merry-go-rounds" (*carrousels*) and "whirligigs" (*tourniquets*).[47] When he has traced a circuitous stretch of Flaubert's "rumination," he offers a justification which illustrates the complexity of the *interplay* in question.

> That is the complete whirligig. . . . If I have indicated in detail all the moments of the merry-go-round, it is in order to bring out clearly how we experience [*vivons*] our convictions: we recognize in Gustave "what you all are, a certain man who lives, sleeps, eats, entirely shut up in himself; wherever he travels, the same ruins of hopes shat-tered as such as soon as they have been lifted up, the same dust of things that are crushed, the same paths traversed a thousand times"; and it is one of these circular paths, traversed a thousand times and leading back each time—at least in appearance—to the starting point, that I have wanted to describe: the internal movement of Flaubert, passing and repassing in the same places without interruption. . . . The circular structure of the "rumination" is perfectly clear, landmarks which are fixed, interpretations which are contradictory and pass one into the other without ever passing over toward a synthesis. Of the fixed marks here I recognize two: God exists, I cannot believe; an exit is never found from this illogical and profound reflection: I cannot believe in God in whom I believe. The interpretations turn, come into opposition to each other, and often interpenetrate: although contradictory, none is essentially distinct from the others, since all are attempts to take into account a lack of logic that is rigid and yet experienced.[48]

Flaubert's "rumination" provides a certain analogue to *recapitulation* which I distinguished (as an eighth trait) from a *reversal* in the strict sense. Here we need the further distinction that has just been drawn: Flaubert's "rumination" is almost mechanical in its rigidity and "lack of logic." It is neurotically repetitive: "one of those circular paths, tra-versed a thousand times and leading back each time . . . to the starting point."

RECAPITULATION

Recapitulation does have its logic: it leads a dialectical development back to a starting point in order to achieve a reformulation that permits a new start. Let me offer as an example Sartre's reutilization of the experience of the "obscene," even though it may not have been deliberately intended as a recapitulation and may border on "rumination." The example overlaps the one we have just examined of the experience of nausea,[49] but there we are dealing with two separate works, *Nausea* and *Being and Nothingness*, and now we are dealing with two stages of the dialectic in *Being and Nothingness* itself. Since Sartre's analysis is at once *bilateral* and *bifocal*, one fashion in which it can be said to develop is by introducing a *bilateral* distinction when a new level or stage is reached. At the level or stage of the analysis where the example of the wiggling bottom was employed to define the "obscene," the observer was reacting relatively passively. At a later and higher level or stage, he becomes an active participant as a sadist, for Sartre's definition of the "obscene" is only one stage in a longer-run dialectical development in which "sadism" is defined:

> The sadist manipulates the Other's body, leans on the Other's shoulders so as to bend him toward the ground and make his haunches stand out . . . in order to make the Other's flesh appear . . . in an obscene expanding passivity.[50]

"Obscene," I have pointed out, was originally the observer's relatively passive reaction to the mechanical, involuntary, passive movements of the walker's fleshy bottom as opposed to his voluntary and active movement of walking. This opposition is carried over, when "sadism" is defined, in a fashion which imposes *recapitulation*, in that the example of "sadism" can only be understood fully if one takes a look back at the example of the "obscene" and reconsiders the example of "sadism" as a reformulation.

Recapitulation is one way the methodological requirement of a *relational* analysis is met—the requirement (in Kierkegaard's phrase) "to put things together" or (in Heidegger) "to let something be seen in its togetherness with something else."[51] At the new level in Sartre the movements of the flesh still "appear . . . obscene" to the observing sadist, but the relation of opposition has been tightened up (as it often is when things are "put together" in a *recapitulation*), in that these movements are not just involuntary but against the victim's will. The opposition between the sadist and his victim is itself opposed to the previous opposition: the other subject is no longer being observed "from behind" by the first subject, who quite possibly may have been indifferent to being observed as he walked forward. (His attitude in fact remained indeterminate.) The voluntary action is now reassigned to the first subject, who earlier remained a merely passive observer but who is now actively seeking to make the victim "appear . . . obscene."

WEIGHT

If we did not recognize the methodological exigencies of *recapitulation*, we would be at a loss to account for the specific details of this example of "sadism" and might conclude that Sartre's selection is "purely subjective." After all, the repertoire of the sadist is not easily exhausted. Why should he be visualized as making his victim's haunches "stand out," by leaning on his shoulders so as to bend him toward the ground? In our answer we must not forget what Heidegger characterizes as "existential spatiality" or contemporary existentialists as "human space." Whatever else distinctively *ex-sistential* examples exemplify, they also often exemplify spatial relations. The sadist is designing in *the space of his imagination* relations which exemplify literally the metaphorical relations supervening between him and his victim at the psychological level, just as the environmental arrangements the seducer designed for Cordelia's seduction were appropriate to the spaciousness of her imagination, as opposed to the "limitations" of what "little Emily" was metaphorically capable of at the psychological level,[52] or just as the *glissement* of the skier embodied for him the metaphorical *glissement* of his consciousness.

In fact the *interplay* between metaphorical and literal should be recognized in order to overcome the danger of taking the spatial metaphor of levels itself too literally. A complete and fixed separation between levels which would preclude *interplay*. I have pointed out that after *Being and Time* Heidegger drops the notion of level (*niveau*) and in his later writings stresses instead the metaphor "in between" (*das Zwischen*)."[53] Sartre retains the notion of levels but insists that "they still condition each other reciprocally" when he locates certain of Flaubert's attitudes "at different levels."[54]

Though we can hardly avoid distinguishing the literal and physical from the metaphorical and psychological, we can avoid flatness. The meta-phorical must not be interpreted as if it occurred at one level of a dialectical movement; it is a movement of trans-position from one level or focus to another. This movement, moreover, can proceed in either direction, for the shifting focus of the *interplay* defeats any effort to interpret "human space" or *the space of the imagination* as simply a metaphor which is derived from physical space to describe an experience that can be distinguished as psychological. Indeed it is in order to resist any such elevating procedure of *Aufhebung* that Sartre's metaphors tend to be weighted more toward the physical than conventional metaphors.

In dealing with this tendency of his metaphors, I have so far mainly probed Sartre's sexual imagery, for it is more familiar to us. But it is less fundamental in Sartre himself than imagery deriving from *ex-sistential* spatial relations. And just as the social world was "disrupted" in Sartre in a fashion that could be fully understood only when the dislocation of Heidegger's *Umwelt* is taken into account as background, so too Sartre's "world of [sexual] desire" is "a destructured world . . . in which things jut out like fragments of pure matter, like brute qualities."[55]

Return to the example of "sadism." When the sadist makes the Other's "flesh appear . . . in an obscene expanding passivity," what had been (in the example of the bottom) merely a wiggle of the flesh now expands, so that the haunches of his victim are seen to "stand out" (*resortir*),[56] and this dislocation might be taken as a literal physical exemplification of an ex-sistential structure. At any rate Sartre does stress its significance for *the space of the imagination*: "This disfigured and heaving body is the image of the freedom that is broken and enslaved."[57]

Here the "image" emerges with a metaphorical movement from the physical to the psychological level, but comparison with the earlier example provides us with an illustration of how the movement can also proceed in the opposite direction. In the original example of the "obscene" the physical movement of the bottom was perceived by the observer as "pure obedience to the laws of gravity [*pesanteur*—literally "weight"]."[58] Since "obedience" must, strictly speaking, be psychological and yielded voluntarily, mechanical "obedience" to a physical law on the part of a wiggle of the flesh is literally a contradiction in terms, so at this stage in the dialectic "obedience" is metaphorical, and its psychological or moral meaning intrudes a certain dislocation (or at least a wiggle) in ordinary usage, which is accentuated, if "pure" can be taken as a perverse denial that anything but "obedience" is in question. But "obedience" loses its inappropriateness or, rather, acquires psychological appropriateness in retrospect when the opposition between the voluntary and involuntary movements is relocated as a struggle in which one will is attempting to "bend" another. The original disconcerting use of "obedience" may thus have prepared for its use in what I am interpreting as a *recapitulation*. Moreover, the struggle between wills is now initiated with the weight which is imposed by the voluntary movement of the sadist who physically "leans on" (*pèse sur*) his victim's shoulders to "bend" him to the ground. The resulting involuntary movement on the part of the victim literally exemplifies the experience we describe metaphorically as "humiliation."

There is thus a literal vertical dislocation (being bent to the ground) as well as an implicit metaphorical dislocation (humiliation), combined with a *recapitulation* of the earlier literal horizontal dislocation (the flesh of the haunches is now forced to "stand out"), and the double dislocation constitutes the disfigurement which becomes an "image of the freedom that is broken." Of course what is finally at stake is not physical disfigurement but psychological enslavement. This is suggested not only by the fact that "broken" is followed by "enslaved" but also by the fact that all that is transacted physically is a leaning, a bending, and a standing out. No bones are actually "broken"; even though the preceding transactions render this prospect relevant, "broken" remains a metaphor, so that the final dislocation is psychological.

HUMILIATION

It is possible that the interpretation of the movement of Sartre's dialectic from the earlier to the present level can be carried a step further. In the original example of the obscene not only was the observer passive, but it could also be taken for granted that he was observing at the same (physical) level as the walker. The relation he was observing between the movements of the walker's bottom was established at this horizontal level, even though we introduced a metaphorical distinction of (psychological) level by recognizing that these movements were involuntary, whereas the movement of walking was voluntary. Now the dialectic has itself moved on to what we refer to metaphorically as a "higher" level, for the new example of "sadism" presupposes and recapitulates the previous example of the "obscene." But the new example also incorporates literally this difference of level, for whereas the observer observed "from behind," the sadist "leans" from above on his victim's "shoulders" in order to secure his victim's humiliation. At the same time the *interplay* between levels is assured by carrying over from the previous example both the psychological "obedience" and the physical "weight" which were brought together at the lower level.

Of course to describe this *recapitulation* as taking place at a "higher" level may be misleading, for we tend to think of a succession of levels as an upward ascent and to associate the movement onward and upward with human aspiration in the fashion proposed by Hegel's *Aufhebung*.[59] But Sartre's restructuring of the previous example, with the sadist now leaning upon his victim's shoulders and bending him to the ground in order to disfigure his body and humiliate him, is methodological progress with respect to letting "something be seen in its togetherness with something else," for the interrelatedness of the interrelations being analyzed is being tightened up. But the restructuring perhaps further embodies a repudiation of the presumption that such methodological progress entails the elevation implicit in Hegel's *Aufhebung*, as a procedure whereby the human mind eventually frees itself from imaginative or figurative representations (*Vorstellungen*) which are its exposure to "external influences." The victim's freedom is ostensibly "broken," but what happens meanwhile to our minds—to their freedom? Exposed to the "image" of a disfigured body, they too are humiliated, if we measure what has happened against the methodological norm of progressive elevation as demanded by the Hegelian *Aufhebung*.

My interpretation may seem to have gone too far in reading a *reversal* of the Hegelian perspective into this particular stretch of Sartre's dialectic. There is always some risk of short-circuiting a dialectic, unless "patience" is exercised until we have reached that stage in the dialectic where *recapitulation* is warranted. Let us accordingly go on to the climax of the analysis of sadism, which is provided by the castration of the "nigger" in Faulkner's *Light in August*. I include portions of Sartre's quotation and his ensuing generalization:

> "For a long moment he looked up at them with peaceful and unfathomable and unbearable eyes. Then his face, body, all *seemed to collapse*, to fall in upon itself, and from out the slashed garments about his hips and loins the pent black blood seemed to rush like released breath. It seemed to rush out of his pale body like the rush of sparks from a rising rocket . . . upon that black blast [translated as *explosion*] the man seemed to rise soaring into their memories forever and ever. They are not to lose it, in whatever peaceful valleys, beside whatever faces of whatever children, they will contemplate old disasters and newer hopes. *It will be there, musing, quiet, steadfast, not fading and not particularly threatful, but of itself alone serene, of itself alone triumphant. . . .*"
>
> Thus this explosion of the Other's look in the world of the sadist makes the meaning and aim of sadism collapse. The sadist discovers that it was *that freedom* there which he wanted to enslave, and at the same time he realizes the futility of his endeavors.[60]

The example is not simply the image of a climactic physical disfigurement. Metaphorical transpositions take place from the physical to the level of Sartre's psychological generalization from the example: the victim's body "seemed to collapse [*s'éffondre*]" in Faulkner, but in the reflexive dialectic which Sartre superimposes it is the aim of the sadist that collapses. The "explosion" of "black blood" in Faulkner becomes the "explosion of the Other's look" in Sartre, who takes this look as the reference of Faulkner's repeated "it." But Faulkner's reference is less sharp and not so abruptly dislocating.

This "collapse" of "the meaning and aim of sadism" could be taken as subverting the teleological movement of *Aufhebung* whose contradictory implications Hegel was fond of bringing out with the metaphor of "going to ground" (*gehen zu Grunde*), which implies that whatever is involved "founders" on a contradiction and yet thereby transcends its destruction as contingent and comes into its own at a higher level, as what it essentially is. But again I defer examination of the existential subversion of *Aufhebung* until we reach an instance when the reference to Hegel does not have to be dragged in but is explicit.

THE CONTRADICTORY COMPOSITE

Having followed out a stretch of Sartre's dialectic helps us assess its character. "Sadism" has been defined by reference to a structure whose dislocation is the result of factors which were only loosely interrelated in the original example of passive observation of the wiggling bottom of the walker but which are later pulled together by the sadist's actions:

"The object actualized for the sadist is ambiguous, contradictory, and unstable, since it is at once the strict effect of a technique relying on determinism [e.g., when the sadist leans on his victim's shoulders] and the manifestation of an unconditioned freedom." (Mere physical determinism cannot encroach on freedom, since the victim cannot acknowledge his humiliation by becoming—as we have seen a physical object can—"pure obedience to the law of gravity.") The *ex-sistential* object, which was examined in the second chapter as a subject matter and characterized as a dislocated structure, is now a *contradictory composite* which is characterizable more dynamically as the actualization of a structure which is *ambiguous, contradictory,* and *unstable.*[61] Actualization is the minimal and broadest implication of existence, as we recognized earlier, before we went on to recognize the further implication of dislocation.

This process of actualization is itself a dialectical *development*: the structure first displays its *ambiguity,* which then sharpens into a *contradiction,* which eventually renders the structure *unstable,* until its "collapse" finally supervenes.[62] The rudiments of this dialectical development were barely discernible in the original example, when the object was the wiggling bottom of the walker. But the contradiction fully emerges only when physical determinism exhibits its full ineffectiveness as a means of psychologically capturing the freedom of a victim. Then finally "the meaning and aim of sadism collapse."

This dialectical development could be pursued to its highest level where the relations between *Being and Nothingness* are actualized as "human reality" in successive *ambiguous, contradictory,* and *unstable* structures, until we reach the final collapse not just of the specific endeavor of the sadist but of human endeavor as such:

> The individual human reality is . . . a project to transform its subjectivity into an objectivized subject. . . . Thus the passion of man is the reverse of that of Christ, for man loses himself as man in order that God may be born. But the idea of God [as an objective subject] is contradictory, and we lose ourselves in vain. Man is a useless passion.[63]

In view of the length and complexity of this long-run reversal in *Being and Nothingness,* it has seemed more manageable in an introduction to track down a short-run dialectical development which is less comprehensive than human endeavor as such. Tracking down a long-run development is tedious, and I cannot offer more than one example. It seems best to wait until we return to Kierkegaard, where we can follow out the initial development in *Either,* for it is the first stretch not only of his own dialectic but also of the development of existentialism itself.

INTERIOR SPACE

For the present I am staying with Sartre. What may have seemed least plausible about the short-run development just traced was my interpretation of Sartre as manipulating at once the horizontal and vertical dimensions of the dialectic. Let me accordingly offer next an example in which their manipulation is an explicit feature of Sartre's own interpretation of Flaubert. What is in question is "the strict way his interior space is structured." This interpretation can serve as an example of what can take place existentially in *the space of the imagination,* for Sartre considers such structures "of very general significance." What is specific to Flaubert is only "the use he makes of them." To take the vertical dimension first, "the best known" of the relevant pronouncements by Flaubert is his "The ignoble is the high point of the low-down," if I may be allowed to bring out too starkly in my translation (as does Sartre in his interpretation) the spatial relations that are dislocated in "L'ignoble est le sublime d'en bas."[64] Here we get a reversal in the vertical dimension similar to the one I detected in Sartre's pitting of humiliation against the elevation implicit in *Aufhebung.*

The transition to the horizontal dimension can be made by recognizing once again that extension of meaning does not necessarily proceed in the more conventional direction of extrapolating from the literal or physical to arrive at a metaphor for a psychological performance; it can proceed in the opposite direction, so that a psychological performance receives physical exemplification. Thus Sartre cites Nietzsche, "who attached so much importance to verticality" but who also illustrates the type of those who "seek to bring into conformity with their internal space the structure of the objective space where they live." Sartre adds, "It was no accident if Nietzsche had, or thought he had, his fundamental illumination at Sils-Maria." He introduces the space of Nietzsche's imagination for the purpose of contrast with the importance Flaubert attached to the horizontal, as a matter of the objective space where he preferred to live as opposed to the verticality of his internal space:

> Flaubert spent almost his entire life at his worktable; he is, moreover, a man of the plain, a Norman whose actual journeys [déplacements] are almost always made at sea level, whether he goes up the Nile river or looks for the remains of Punic Carthage. Once during his life he spent some days for the sake of his health in the mountains at Kaltbod-Rigi. There he "dies of boredom." He coldly comments, "The landscape is very beautiful, of course, but I don't feel disposed to admire it." Nevertheless, this man of the lowlands, this recluse, spends his life, ascending and descending, flying up like an eagle only to fall, head foremost. . . . Humiliation casts him down, but (and he says so in all his letters) he bounces back with pride; or, rather, in pursuit of art, looking upward he falls into a well, like the astronomer in the story. His works and correspondence involve an incredible number of metaphors and images which aim at reducing his behavior, the behavior of others, or his relations with them . . . to positive or negative translations along the vertical dimension.[65]

As a more precise illustration of the way Flaubert's interior space is structured, Sartre detects a similar opposition in Flaubert's recollection of one of his moments of ecstasy: " 'Happy time of his youth when his heart was pure as the water of fonts and only reflected the arabesques of the stained glass with the tranquil elevation of celestial hopes.' " Here Sartre finds "the double movement which is so characteristic of Flaubert." While "the stained glass deigns to confide its image to the water of the fonts," there is "at the same time the suggestion of a reverse movement of hope, of 'tranquil elevation.' . . ." The contradiction is that

> the objects the image brings together to evoke movement in contrast refer to perfect immobility . . . This water, low and level, which the recipient must protect against the least vibration is Gustave lying on his back, the horizontal dimension . . . borne aloft by a timeless and vertical

ascension. In short, it is the very symbol of quietism. The reflection of the infinite in the finite, with the reverse and complementary ecstasy of the finite outside itself in the infinite.[66]

Finding the infinite reflected in the finite makes possible the reverse and complementary ecstasy which is in one sense the movement of *Aufhebung*. But bringing out the spatial meaning of ecstasy, as Sartre's "outside" does, introduces a slight dislocation which disturbs the spiritual tranquillity of Flaubert's elevation and discredits his quietism.

SOCIAL STRUCTURES

The examples which have so far illustrated traits of Sartre's existential dialectic may have been such "specialized" experiences as revulsion from a wiggling bottom, nausea, "sadism," Flaubert's "rumination." In chapter 3, after my original interpretation (in chapter 2) of the wiggling bottom as a portion of Sartre's subjectmatter, I followed the process of dislocation exemplified up to the level of existentialism's social analysis. We can sample this social analysis again, but now in order to continue illustrating Sartre's dialectical method. We shall find that social phenomena exhibit the same *ambiguous, contradictory, unstable* structures as our previous examples. The social analysis will also illustrate the differences between an existential and a Marxist dialectic that were examined before in a preliminary way as differences of subject matter.

Perhaps the most prominent of these differences is the reflexive effort of the existentialist to retain some reference to the "specialized" experiences of the particular individual even while generalizing with respect to social phenomena. The existentialist must accordingly manage the transition with some care. In the case of Flaubert, the transition was made by taking intervening phenomena into account—his family setting as well as generational differences. This transition can now be reexamined methodologically. Flaubert's family "testifies at once to the persistence of the past and to the difficult emergence of a new order," so it can be identified as an "unstable product." Its "disequilibrium" is generalized as "common to the epoch." Whatever level at which Sartre analyzes Flaubert's family, he discloses ambiguities, contradictions, instability: sociologically it is "halfway bourgeois" but still "halfway rural in its structures"; ideologically the father, a doctor, is committed to experimental science, but the mother is still prone to Catholic piety.[67]

If we move on to the longer-range social development, we find that, "since the middle of the last century [i.e., since Flaubert's period], there has existed a dislocation [*décalage*] in France between the social reality

and its political expression," for "two images of the country coexist without it being possible to impose either on the other; one is presented by
the outcome of elections; the other, more profound, only appears in lightening flashes, when spontaneous popular movements occur."[68] In other
words, what these lightening flashes reveal is that France is an *ambiguous,
contradictory,* and *unstable* structure. The conventional, more stable
image presented by the outcome of elections is contradicted and hence
cannot be reconciled with the other, "more profound" image of the
country.

This appraisal of France Americans may be all too ready to accept as
empirically convincing, so we need to find another example which will
bring home to us the peculiar exigencies of Sartre's dialectic. Perhaps
America will do. Furthermore, by using a single example, and one which
has the advantage of familiarity, we can at last pull together more tightly
the relations between various traits of the dialectic which we have so far
sorted out by using miscellaneous examples, for we have found that one
specific trait of dialectic itself is that it can move to higher levels by pulling together in a *recapitulation* relations which were more loosely analyzed at lower levels but which now can be shown to be related themselves.
The time has come for us to extend this treatment to the other specific
traits themselves in order to bring out their relevance to the relation of
contradiction.

If we go back to the postwar epoch when existentialism first came to
American attention, we meet Sartre himself arriving in the United States
on a journalistic assignment arranged by Camus. A French academic
philosopher could still concede that Sartre was a "journalist of genius"
when he denied that Sartre was a philosopher.[69] But we shall see that
Sartre's journalism manifests the same traits as his philosophical method,
and in a readily accessible fashion that is suitable for an introduction.
Thus when he characterizes his experience of America as an attempt to
determine "what America is," we recognize again that the first trait of the
dialectical method is *definition.* Sartre's *Critique of Dialectical Reason*
elaborates definitions of several social structures, but we can be satisfied
here with his simpler definition of the structure of American society.

How is something defined dialectically? "Yesterday," Sartre reports, "it
was Baltimore, today it is Knoxville, the day after tomorrow it will be
New Orleans, and after admiring the biggest factory or the biggest bridge
or the biggest dam in the world, we fly away with our heads full of figures
and statistics."[70] But the dialectical method does not proceed inductively
by accumulating objective facts or statistics in a scientific fashion. This
scientific procedure he identifies in the *Critique* as "analytic reasoning,"
to which he opposes his "dialectical reasoning."

Nor does Sartre substitute for objective facts more enticing, more literary, subjective impressions: "the electric blue of the oxyhydrogen blowpipe in the pale light of a shed."[71] The objective facts he has listed, and the subjective impressions, are alike random and unrelated; their range of implication is indefinite. The biggest dam? So what! The biggest bridge? So what! Electric blue, pale light? So what! A dialectical method cannot operate on isolated facts or impressions but only by correlating *relations*. This second trait, I have conceded, is a quite general characteristic of a dialectical method, as is also the significance attached to the relation between opposites or a contradiction. The most recent illustration is the way Sartre's method of "dialectical reasoning" is itself defined by its opposition to the scientific method of "analytic reasoning."

To return to our lower-level illustration, we find Sartre defining America by pouncing on "the two contradictory slogans that are current in Paris—'Americans are conformists' and 'Americans are individualists.'" These presuppositions he has brought with him from Paris. The third trait of a dialectic is that it is a *reflexive* analysis, and in this instance its function is to expose presuppositions in a fashion which can be described as constituting a "critique." The contradictory definitions of justice that Socrates started out with in the *Republic* were also current slogans in Athens. Whether in Athens or Paris, dialectic dislodges such presuppositions from the back of men's minds by forcing them into relation with each other and in this way displaying the contradiction between them.

SOCIAL TRANSFORMATION

Contradiction impels the *movement* of thought that is the fourth trait of an existential dialectic. In considering how Sartre handles the first slogan, shift back briefly from method to subject matter. Conformism itself is an attitude which is opposed to movement. It is solid, inert. A dialectical movement asserts its *dynamic* character by taking hold of what is to be defined and putting it into motion. At the beginning of the *Republic* old Cephalus exhibits his conformism by the slogans he offers in lieu of definitions of justice. But when Socrates defines justice, it is by tracing the process of *development* by which an unjust society might be transformed into its opposite, and the process involves reflexively a critical redefinition of the participants' presuppositions as to what justice is. Kierkegaard starts out in *Johannes Climacus* by attempting to define what it means for an individual to become a philosopher: examining the presuppositions one starts out with, as opposed to remaining preoccupied, as Hegelians had, with putting the finishing touches to a system.[72] Kierkegaard's works as a whole he himself lumps together as attempts to define what it means to "become a Christian";[73] becoming a Christian he treats as a process of transformation or conversion which dislocates our presuppositions, for a Christian is the opposite of what a Christian is conventionally supposed to be. Sartre's definition of America as conformist is similarly an attempt to trace the process by which an individual is transformed into a conforming American. In fact the original title of Sartre's report was "How a Good American Is Made."

Sartre starts out with a presupposition: "Like everybody else, I had heard of the famous American 'melting pot' that transforms, at different temperatures, Poles, Italians, and Finns into United States citizens. But I did not know what the term 'melting pot' actually meant." Why did he not know? Because his criteria for knowledge are existential. He finds out what the term *actually* means by being exposed personally to the *dislocating* experience of the melting pot as it actually operates:

> The day after my arrival I met a European who was in the process of being melted down. I was introduced, in the big lobby of the Plaza Hotel, to a dark man of rather medium height who, like everyone else here, talked with a somewhat nasal twang, without seeming to move his lips or cheeks, who laughed with his mouth but not with his eyes, and whose laughter came in sudden bursts, and who expressed himself in good French, with a heavy accent, though his speech was sprinkled with vulgar errors and Americanisms.
>
> When I congratulated him on his knowledge of our language, he replied with astonishment, "But I'm a Frenchman." He had been born in Paris, had been living in America for only fifteen years, and before the war had returned to France every six months. Nevertheless, America already possessed him halfway. . . . He felt obliged every now and then to throw me a roguish wink and exclaim, "Ah, New Orleans, pretty girls." But what he was really doing was conforming to the American image of the Frenchman rather than trying to be congenial to a countryman. "Pretty girls," he said with a laugh that was forced: I felt puritanism just around the corner, and a chill ran through me.
>
> I had the impression I was witnessing an Ovidian metamorphosis. The man's face was still too expressive. It had retained the rather irritating mimicry of intelligence which makes a French face recognizable anywhere. But he will soon be a tree or a rock. I speculated curiously as to the powerful forces that had to be brought into play in order to actualize these disintegrations and reintegrations so reliably and rapidly.[74]

We saw that Sartre started out with opposed presuppositions regarding Americans—as "conformists" and as "individualists." We now see that he

next defines the way conformity is secured by redefining the presupposition that America is a melting pot. His redefinition is dialectical: a Frenchman is transformed into his opposite—an American. This Franco-American
is an *ex-sistential* phenomenon: as a French expatriate he is "outside"
himself, dislocated from his proper place. The process of his transformation is a dislocating movement because it is composed of opposing movements—his disintegration as a Frenchman and his reintegration as an
American. In other words, existential definition is here for Sartre (as in
the previous examples of the "obscene" and "sadism") the exposure of a
structure which is *ambiguous, contradictory,* and *unstable.* The dialectically opposed movements composing the present structure are carefully
balanced: the Frenchman is visualized as having reached the "halfway"
point in the process of transformation, just as the Flaubert family was
still "halfway rural" but had become "halfway bourgeois." The climactic
opposition between French and American culture in 1945 was in the attitudes toward sex. (The only area where Sartre could have found Frenchmen and Americans so diametrically opposed today would have been in
their attitudes toward philosophy.) The American attitude toward sex is
in turn contradictory—that once prurient and puritanical. Observe too
how even Sartre's detailed touches are dislocating: the Franco-American
talked "without seeming to move his lips or cheeks"; he "laughed with
his mouth but not with his eyes" and "in sudden bursts."[75]

THE AFFECTIVE REACTION

"What America is" is defined in terms of the process of transformation
that makes a Frenchman over into an American, but a dialectical process
of definititon cannot be reduced to this sort of process of transformation.
The *definiendum* is only the objective pole of the dialectic, which sets up
a *bilateral* relation between a subjective pole and this objective pole. The
objective pole in an existential dialectic is frequently another subject who
then can function, as he does so prominently in Sartre, as the Other. Or
at least it is something closely associated with another subject (e.g., a
wiggling bottom). (In contrast, "consciousness of something" in Husserl's
phenomenology is usually consciousness simply of an object—a cube, a
tree, etc.) I therefore often employ with reference to an existential dialectic the description *bipersonal* in lieu of *bilateral.*

But why in the present episode has Sartre selected as this other subject
an ex-Frenchman instead of an ex-Italian or an ex-Pole? In terms of statistics, the number of Frenchmen that have been melted down into Americans is not comparably significant. The reason for the selection is, of
course, that Sartre himself is a Frenchman or, rather, a stand-in for his

French reader. And not only is this ex-Frenchman undergoing a dislocating transformation but the Frenchman Sartre's process of defining him
as well. Sartre's initial impression that he is talking to an American is
transformed into the realization that he is talking to a Frenchman who is
being transformed into an American. For the process of definition is designed less to delineate objectively the way the melting pot operates as a
process of transformation than to elicit a *reflexive* reaction to the process
—in fact an *affective* reaction, for the reaction is tinged with disgust. In
other words the subject is disconcerted, disoriented, dislocated, disgusted
by the discovery that the apparent American was once a Frenchman like
himself but is being melted down into a real American.[76]

We remember that Sartre began by admitting that he did not know
what the term "melting pot" actually meant until he met this man who
was in the actual process of being melted down. He only knows when he
finds himself affected by an emotional reaction.[77] We recognize again that
Sartre's reflexive emphasis is a denial of the primacy ordinarily accorded
to knowledge. Or, as he himself puts it when he prepares the way for his
report of the encounter at the Plaza,

> I distrust those perspectives which are already generalizations [such
> as, we may assume, the slogans "Americans are conformists" and "Amer-
> icans are individualists"]. Thus my decision is to present my own per-
> sonal impressions and interpretations, on my own responsibility. This
> America may be my dream. At any rate, I shall be honest with my
> dream: I shall set is forth just as it happened to me.

This *reflexive* criterion also applies to the other subject. Sartre initially
becomes conscious of someone who appears to him to be an American; but
this subjective appearance is contradicted by the claim "But I'm a Frenchman." This is not, however, what he really is objectively; it is only what
he still appears to himself to be. And Sartre's own feeling of disgust
reaches its climax when he discovers that the Frenchman is no longer a
Frenchman and not quite an American in the obvious sense but, instead,
is "conforming" (*obéit*) to the subjective requirements of "the American
image of a Frenchman."

Finally, since the entire dialectical process of definition turns reflexively
on the fact that Sartre and his reader are French, it cannot remain objectively and straightforwardly anti-American in what it is opposed to but is
complicated by the reflection that

> the man's face was still too expressive. It had retained the somewhat
> irritating mimicry of intelligence which makes a French face recogniz-
> able anywhere.

Thus if the Frenchman at the Plaza had been discounted reflexively as only a subjective appearance (not a real Frenchman but only "the American image of a Frenchman"), a real Frenchman enjoys no real superiority, since he is only apparently intelligent.

ACCELERATION

The *reflexive* character of an existential dialectic is one of the differences between an existential and a Marxist dialectic. It is the difference that was explored more casually with respect to subject matter as the reference to personal experience. *Reflexive* twists, often incorporating some affective reaction, or larger-scale *reflexive* maneuvers, are often designed to dislodge conventional, ostensibly objective presuppositions (e.g., with respect to what America is, to what the bourgeois class is, or to the way the world is), so the individual "finds himself there" (to vulgarize Heidegger's *Befindlichkeit*) by having to consult his own experience.

Closely associated with this *reflexive* character of an existentialist dialectic are other differences between it and a Marxist dialectic. Marx's *Kapital*, as a dialectical attempt to define what capital is, is broadly similar to Sartre's definition of the melting pot: it is an analysis of the contradictions operating in the process of transformation whereby a capitalistic society must disintegrate in order to be integrated into its opposite—a socialist society. A difference that I suggested earlier was that social processes in Sartre's existentialized Marxism are more dislocating than in conventional Marxism. Now a related factor has been uncovered. In the case of Sartre's encounter with the Franco-American, the movements of disintegration and reintegration are accelerated, as if they were taking place right there in front of Sartre in the lobby of the Plaza rather than proceeding at what wolud be the historical pace of a melting pot—the pace a Marxist analysis would respect. Their acceleration accentuates the sense of dislocation deriving from the transformation of Sartre's initial impression and thus seems to have more to do with the rapidity with which Sartre reacts reflexively to the Franco-American than with any actions on the part of the Franco-American as they might be appraised objectively.

Other examples can be cited in which scope is rapidly sought reflexively. When Sartre suggests the *reflexive* reference required to analyze anti-Semitism by quoting Richard Wright, "There is no black problem in the United States, only a white problem," it is clear from the brusque shift that Wright was addressing himself to white readers in the hope of eliciting their *reflexive* recognition of the truth of his pronouncement. When Sartre similarly defines the Jew as "a man whom other men consider a Jew,"[78] it is clear that he is peremptorily circumventing a considerable accumulation of specific sociohistorical evidence and addressing these other men directly in the hope of eliciting their *reflexive* recognition of the truth of his definition.

CONDENSATION

In considering the way social scope can be gained, we should notice that in an existential dialectic, the *reflexive* reference can take place not only at either pole, since the dialectic is *bilateral*, but also at different levels, since it is *bifocal*. One of the problems that dogged our steps at the beginning was how the existentialist, starting out with the idiosyncratic experiences of the particular individual, can yet manage to reach the higher level of social generalization. Here we need a more fully worked out analysis than the encounter at the Plaza.

The interpretation of Flaubert takes three volumes but, like the encounter at the Plaza, is a report of the experience of an individual caught up in a social transformation. France is being transformed into a bourgeois society. But instead of analyzing the social transformation as such, as Marx does when he sifts objective facts and figures, Sartre focuses on the experience of Flaubert. Maintaining this focus in a social analysis is justified by a process of condensation, of which the most obvious form is a variant of the dialectical procedure of *recapitulation*. The individual's experience acquires density by a tightening up of some of the relations that compose a social transformation; he is visualized as bringing within the *reflexive* scope of his own experience in a condensed version the larger social transformation. Thus there are respects in which Sartre finds Flaubert's existence "an excellent résumé of a century of vicissitudes in French society." Flaubert's "neurosis" (a term which is more often used for an analysis of the personal experience of an individual) Sartre identifies as "historical and social"—as "constituting an objective and dated fact where characteristics of a society, bourgeois France under Louis-Philippe, are gathered together [*se ramassent*]."[79]

A particular individual can lend himself to this recapitulative role because he is never simply a particular individual, but a contradictory dialectical composite—an *universel singulier* (a universal becoming individualized and an individual becoming universalized). This is why it is necessary for Sartre to offer an interpretation of Flaubert which is dialectical in that it proceeds "simultaneously from both ends,"[80] thereby bringing out the interplay between the two levels—the individual's own personal experience and the general character of the social process.

Sartre introduces the term "condensation" in a preface he wrote for

Promenade du dimanche (Sunday Walk). Like the Franco-American or Flaubert, this institution is a *contradictory composite*: "Loved, detested, looked forward to, always a disappointment, Sunday is a collective cere- mony." The walk itself is not simply a particular ceremony but the par- ticularization of a totality: "It is human life ... but this life itself gathered together [*ramassé*] in one of its particular moments, as the whole is wholly present in each of its parts." Life as "summed up in a walk" can take on significance for the reader, provided recapitulatory techniques (familiar to us from Sartre's handling of the Franco-American or Flaubert) are employed to assist the condensation:

> What is necessary to provide a glimpse of our life through one of its manifestations? Merely a little cleaning up—some acceleration and some foreshortening.
> This dismal family who goes up "their" street to the nearest movie and goes down again after the show: the entire world—our world—is reflected in their smallest gestures. . . .[81]

EXISTENTIAL EXPERIENCE

Sartre can deal succinctly with the Franco-American and with the "dismal family" because their conformism is the suppression of any sig- nificant reflexive reference. But he handles in elaborate detail particular experiences of Flaubert insofar as each of them carries implications for his experience as a whole, including its social dimension. A particular experi- ence with this scope Sartre identifies as "existential." It is distinguished as a summation from a mere "sum of experiences in the sense in which empiricism would understand this." For it is "at one and the same time singular and complete." It is an "episode which as lived through [by Flaubert] tells the whole story about himself."[82]

Although this characterization of an "existential experience" helps correct any impression that the *reflexive* reference is a movement in which the significance of an experience is contracted, it does not impose any departure from my previous terminology. Rather, it brings out the *recapitulation* which is involved and which is rendered feasible by the relational character of what is susceptible of an existential analysis in its opposition as "dialectical reasoning" to the "analytic reasoning" of empir- icism. The characterization is consistent, moveover, with the conception of an *ex-sistential* experience as dislocating. For the movement from a par- ticular experience to experience as a whole, whether carried out by the individual himself or by another interpreter, subverts the individual's

usual preoccupation with particular experience in favor of his relation to
his experience as a whole. This dislocating movement can be illustrated
by the way Sartre reinterprets particular imaginative experiences:

> It is not this or that image that is chosen but the imaginary state with
> all its implications. An escape is sought not just from features of reality
> (poverty, frustrated love, failure of our undertakings, etc.) but from
> the form itself of reality, its character of presence, the responsiveness
> it demands of us, the subordination of our actions to their object, the
> inexhaustibility of our perceptions, their independence, the very way
> our feelings have of developing.[83]

In other words, my particular choice of this or that, insofar as the choice
is significant, entails a *reflexive* choice of myself that carries some larger
implications for my life as a whole.

LITERATURE AND PSYCHOANALYSIS

Sartre explains that his intent in the three volumes on Flaubert is "to
display a method and a man." The man is displayed by reference to his
choice of himself. The method for fathoming this choice is dialectical and
is complicated by the succession of levels that have to be distinguished.
Whenever an "attempt is made 'to locate' an event, a social group or an
individual," any "single action," Sartre comments, "can be appraised at a
series of levels which are more and more concrete, so that it can find
expression in a series of quite diverse meanings." Two levels are crucial
inasmuch as Sartre combines psychoanalysis dialectically with Marxist
analysis. As he himself explains, "I employ the two methods conjointly."[84]
Neither of these levels is itself a single level, and Sartre complains that
"what psychoanalysts lack is opposition."[85] It is "opposition" which promotes interplay between levels and requires their distinction for the
analysis of the interplay. He admits that in psychoanalysis "there is
dialectical conflict among the id, the superego, and the ego." But to recognize the oppositions involved fully is to recognize that the psyche is a
contradictory composite, whereas psychoanalysts tend to reduce its "being"
to "passivity."[86] Even "the *work* of the ego" becomes, when it is visualized
as functioning merely as a defense mechanism, "a priori inertia."[87] Thus
the active dimension which Sartre insists upon is left out. I shall return
to it when I consider the *reflexive* dimension which he adds to the Marxist
conception of "work."

But first I must consider the *reflexive* dimension he adds to psychoanalysis, whereby he himself is "drawn into the movement." Sartre cannot
be left out of his psychoanalysis of Flaubert as if he were simply applying

a method of interpretation which is demanded by his subject matter. Even his selection of Flaubert for the most extended and ambitious of his writings he explains as due to Flaubert's being "the opposite of what I am." He generalizes, "There is a need to rub oneself against what contests you."[88] Such a need clearly applies the principle of contradiction, but its application is *reflexive*: "One has to put oneself at a level where one is oneself implicated, where the investigation contests the investigator."[89] But if (in Kierkegaard's terminology) the "disrelation" is to have any dialectical significance, the "relation" must survive. Thus "the real psychoanalyst is mad by vocation; his madness is his best instrument for penetrating the madness of others." Likewise "long married couples humiliate each other without interruption, for they are at one and the same time profoundly at one with each other and profoundly *compromising* for each other."[90] In Sartre's case the relation, the madness, and what is compromising is literature: while he opposes his own conception of literature to Flaubert's conception of literature as autonomous—as "art for art's sake," Flaubert still remains for him "the creator of the modern novel" and "at the crossroads of all our literary problems today" (where Sartre finds himself as a writer). Indeed even his interpretation of Flaubert is itself offered as a "novel" (*roman*).[91]

Sartre can be more specific about the reflexive relation: "Why shouldn't I try to explain the mixture of profound admiration and repulsion that Madame Bovary has inspired in me ever since my adolescence?" This formulation is personal, but the problem can be raised to the philosophical level: "I saw him in every way as the opposite of myself. I asked myself, 'How is such a man possible?'" The answer is the recognition that Flaubert is psychoanalytically a *contradictory composite*. Flaubert's edict "Madame Bovary is myself" Sartre interprets as a "logical scandal," by virtue of its dialectical violation of the principle of contradiction, for although the statement, as Sartre admits, has never surprised anyone, it confronts us with "a masculine woman and a femininized man." The literary form which Flaubert adopted in *Madame Bovary* is correspondingly a *contradictory composite*—"a lyrical and realistic work." Hence the analyst faces a further contradiction, "Who then can he be, must he be, in order to objectify himself in his work first as a mystical monk [in *The Temptation of Saint Anthony*] and then some years later as a resolute, 'rather masculine' woman?"[92]

The relation between the two works themselves seems contradictory: "The *Temptation* deals with the great metaphysical themes of the period (the destiny of man, life, death, God, religion, nothingness, etc.)," whereas "Madame Bovary" is "a work which is (to all appearances) dry and objective"; and yet Sartre asserts in effect the "relation" that "underlies the disrelation"—the two works are "fundamentally identical." Finally, we can return to the contradictions of Flaubert as the author of both: "Who then can he be, must he be, to express his reality in the form of a frenzied idealism and of a realism more malicious than detached?" I have said "finally," but perhaps a reminder is needed that what we would complacently refer to as Flaubert's bisexuality is not just a personal dialectic for Sartre. What is at stake must be lifted to a higher philosophical level: "The reply is independent of all biography, since the problem could be posed in Kantian terms: 'Under what conditions is the feminization of experience possible?' "[93]

<h2 align="center">LITERATURE AND SOCIETY</h2>

If I were to sort out all the respects in which Flaubert, as the subject of Sartre's psychoanalysis, lends himself to the further role of recapitulating or condensing the collective experience of his social class, I would be reviewing once more all the traits of an existential dialectic. I need reemphasize only the two important traits which have been prominent in the psychoanalysis: reliance on the principle of contradiction and its reflexive application. Thus the "vicissitudes" of the nineteenth century entail in Flaubert's case "a struggle . . . which opposed him to himself."[94]

The starting point of Sartre's interpretation of this struggle is an interpretation of Flaubert's childhood "relation to words."[95] Sartre announces, "Words are matter." But this starting point is hardly Marxist; language is not the starting point of Marx's dialectic any more than the interpretation of writers is central to it. Yet language is the first social institution, the first form of property relation, to undergo analysis in Sartre's *Critique*: "Every word . . . lives outside, as a public institution; and speaking consists not in inserting a vocable into a brain through an ear but in using sounds to direct the interlocutor's attention to this vocable as public external property."[96]

Here too we are aware of the reflexive dimension of Sartre's analysis: his own autobiographical account of how he himself became a writer is an account of his own childhood relation to *Words*. This relation of course develops when Flaubert and Sartre (or Baudelaire or Genet) become writers. And since Sartre repudiates Flaubert's conception of "art for art's sake" in favor of a conception of art for society's sake (to formulate his opposing conception quite crudely), their relation as writers to words is less fundamental than their social relation as writers to their audience—or, rather, the "disruption" of this relation. Flaubert's conception of art as autonomous betrays his reflexive experience as a writer who has "withdrawn [*replié*] into solitude" because there is for his period "between literature and society an abyss, an inert gap which cannot be crossed."[97] Here we have a dislocation so extreme that there can be virtually no interplay, no relation, between the writer and his audience. Under these social circumstances the artist is likely to conceive art as if it were for art's sake. This dislocation of the relation between the writer and his audience is still for Sartre as a writer the problem of modern literature. It is the problem of his own role as a writer.

SUBJECTIVE AND OBJECTIVE

Sartre's relation to Flaubert holds to a certain extent at the philosophical level, too. The last century, whose "vicissitudes" Flaubert condenses, was a period "when French society found itself compelled to absorb and digest—with great difficulty—the methods and results of experimental science."[98] If this struggle opposed Flaubert to himself, it was (as we earlier noted) because of the opposition Sartre finds between his father's commitment as a doctor to experimental science and his mother's piety. Sartre is engaged in a somewhat comparable struggle, to the extent that he opposes the reversion of conventional Marxism to the bourgeois methods of analysis which are mechanistic and seek an ostensibly objective justification in the procedures of experimental science. This reversion has been in Sartre's view the destruction of what survived in Marxism that was dialectical and its transformation into an analysis of the material conditions of the historical process.

In developing his own reflexive dialectical analysis in opposition to the "reversion," Sartre accuses his adversaries of "objectivism" which makes "subjectivity an absolute effect—that is, an effect which never transforms itself into a cause." What I have termed dialectical *interplay* is thereby eliminated. The individual becomes the predetermined product of social history, never the voluntary agent who can carry out the *reflexive* accomplishment of remaking himself by making history. Sartre criticizes Marx himself for writing, "The materialist conception of the world simply refers to the conception of nature as it is in itself, without an extraneous addition." A reference simply to objective nature is undialectical, and Sartre interprets Marx as "stripping himself of all subjectivity"[99] and adopting an ostensibly objective point of view. But the notion of an objective point of view conceals a contradiction which an existentialist dialectic discloses: a point of view is always that of a subject. Granted the sequence of levels Marx distinguished as constituting the objective hierarchy of social structures, this dialectical sequence does not determine by

itself the way in which it is experienced. What Marx allows for as the
reaction of the superstructures on the infrastructures from which they
derive Sartre would construe as a distinctively *reflexive* reaction.

Even when Sartre felt close to the Communist party politically, his
summons to collaboration included a reflexive twist: "One cannot struggle
against the working class without becoming an enemy of mankind and of
oneself."[100] Even when his existential analysis would seem to overlap the
Marxist analysis, the insertion of a *reflexive* movement alters the analysis. The "essential discovery of Marxism," Sartre suggests, "is that work,
as a historical reality and as the utilization of specific tools in an already
determined social and material situation, is the real foundation of the
organization of social relations."[101] But we must watch out for what happens to "work" and to "tools" in Sartre. "Work" comes to involve not
only the transformation of the external environment but also the reflexive transformation that attends self-choice: "Kierkegaardian existence is
the work of our inner life—resistances conquered and perpetually reborn,
efforts perpetually renewed, despairs surmounted, provisional setbacks
and precarious victories." Perhaps partly because Kierkegaard himself
stresses "inwardness" without employing the term "work," Sartre also
cites psychoanalysts who "consider certain evolutions of our inward life to
be the result of a work which it performs upon itself" and who thereby
recognize "one must 'work oneself over.' "[102] The addition of this *reflexive*
dimension to "work" in the Marxist sense indicates one way in which
Sartre combines psychoanalysis with Marxism.

There is another accretion. Sartre's conceptions of "work" and of
"tools" are Heideggerian as well as Marxist. It is difficult to tell which, as
when Sartre claims, "Work is itself a grasping [*saisie*] of the world and as
such varies in accordance with the tool that is used."[103] But sometimes he
in effect redefines Marx's definition in terms of Heidegger: "Work, as
man's reproduction of his life, can hold no meaning if its fundamental
structure is not to pro-ject."[104] When Heidegger's contribution is discernible, it often undergoes dialectical manipulation. In the first place, Sartre
supplements Heidegger's conception of "instrumentality" (*Zuhandenheit*
—the conception of something being used "in order to")[105] with its opposite, and for this purpose he borrows Bachelard's conception of a " 'coefficient of adversity' in objects"—that is, of something that resists being put to
use.[106] In the second place, Sartre introduces a *reflexive* dimension: "The
structure of the world implies that we can insert ourselves into the field
of instrumentality only by being ourselves an instrument, that we cannot
act without being *acted on*."[107]

This *reflexive* dimension becomes, methodologically at least, the primary dimension in Sartre.[108] Where the starting point for the Marxist

would be some technological development, the invention or utilization of some tool, Sartre starts out with the individual and his immediate experience, as constituted by the reflexive movement with which he makes himself his own tool. To spell this out, where the Marxist would start with the lever, the wheel, the stirrup, the pulley, the steam engine, Sartre would start with the moment when the individual leans on a lever, pushes a wheelbarrow, or pulls a rope over a pulley. He is using his own body as a (subjective) tool for using the (objective) tool. Thus his immediate experience is the *reflexive* experience of his own instrumentality, and the transformation of the structure of his experience has to be taken into account in dealing with his becoming a worker, or a different kind of worker from the type that prevailed at a previous stage of social history. In other words, technological development is more than man's transformation of his external environment; his *reflexive* self-transformation is involved. Thus when the tool that is introduced is the machine, we are dealing with a technological development which can be visualized by Sartre not as lying at the basis of the substructure and generating a sequence of effects which extend into the superstructure but as "interposed between men" as their dialectical antagonist—"the inhuman" which "disrupts [*déchire*] human relations."[109]

In its opposition to the human the machine not only disrupts human relations but also is interposed between the individual and himself, disrupting this *reflexive* relation. Thus "girls working in a factory are ruminating a vague dream," but they are "at the same time traversed by a rhythm external to them," so "it can be said that it is the semiautomatic machine which is dreaming through them." The rhythm of the machine was "so alien to a girl's vital personal rhythm that during the first few days it seemed more than she could endure." But "she wanted to adapt herself to it, she made an effort." So she "gave herself to the machine," which "takes possession of her work," until finally "she discovers herself *the object of the machine.*"[110]

A dislocating reversal has taken place: the machine is no longer her tool; she has become its tool. But the machine cannot qualify as a subject; we are left with the contradiction that she is no longer the subject of her own experiences. This contradiction is not fixed but ushers in further reflexive dialectic. She is forced "to live as her reality a destiny which is prefabricated."[111] Sartre explains how her destiny is worked out:

> In vain would she take refuge in her most intimate "privacy"; this attempt would betray her at once and would be transformed into what is simply a mode of subjective realization of objectivity. When semiautomatic machines were first introduced, investigations showed that woman workers who were trained to use them surrendered to sexual fantasies

as they worked; they recalled their bedrooms, their beds, the previous night—everything that specifically concerns a person in the isolation of the couple closeted with each other. But it was the machine in them which was dreaming of caresses: the kind of attention demanded by their work allowed them neither distraction (thinking of something else) nor total mental application (thinking would slow down their movement). The machine demands and creates in the worker an inverted semiautomatism which complements its operation—an explosive mixture of unconsciousness and vigilance. The mind is absorbed but not used. . . . It is accordingly appropriate to give way [*laisser aller*] to passivity.[112]

This analysis of her rumination Sartre suplements with a male/female dialectic: "In such a situation, the 'first sex,' the active sex, have less of a tendency to erotic reverie. If they were to think of 'taking' a woman, their work would be effected; conversely, their work absorbs their entire activity, renders them disinclined toward sexual behavior. The female worker thinks of sexual abandonment, because the machine requires her to live her conscious life in passivity, in order to preserve a supple, anticipatory vigilance without ever mobilizing herself for active thought."[113]

Appearance and Reality

We need not, however, bog down in the details of female rumination which are ferreted out by Sartre, or of Flaubert's rumination which demands many pages of analysis. In both cases the impetus, whatever the absorption in other matters, is an effort at self-definition or self-redefinition. And other, less complicated examples than these are available. The problem of Sartre's *Respectful Prostitute* is also a problem of definition, just like that of the Franco-American. It is (to employ Sartre's reflexive version of Husserl's intentional analysis) a problem of identification, of identifying with others and ultimately of the individual's own identity, which is reflexively involved in one's identification with others.[114] The protagonist of Sartre's *Respectful Prostitute* is, as a prostitute, a victim of her society, and so the audience is conscious of her as identifiable with the black who is to be lynched. At one moment she does identify with him. But at another this identification is dislocated, and she becomes "respectful," identifying with their common persecutors and conforming to the mores of the South. (Similarly, both Sartre's initial identification of the Franco-American as an American and any sense of identification Sartre might later have been expected to have with him as a fellow Frenchman, as well as the Franco-American's own sense of his identity as French, were dislocated, in order to play up his still to be consolidated identity as a conforming American.) In fact the prostitute's character is so dialectically *ambiguous, contradictory,* and *unstable* that, although Sartre at the end of original play had tilted her toward identification with the persecutors, he was able in the film version to tilt her in the opposite direction—toward identification with the black. This alternative ending was adopted in the Moscow production of the play because the Soviets, with their stiffer dialectic, could not accept the instability of an *ex-sistential* dialectic. Or, as Sartre explained it on their behalf, "they could not accept her having a glimmer of consciousness and then becoming completely duped."[115]

In either version the contradiction of the title holds: a prostitute is duped, temporarily at least, into respecting Southern gentlemen and their mores, in terms of which she is herself beneath respect. What is respected as the reality, by both her persecutors and herself, is an appearance, as it was in the case of the Franco-American who was respecting the American image of the Frenchman. The contradiction then is that the prostitute respects the Southern male image both of Southern ladies and of her own defilement. Sartre plays the moral metaphor of defilement off against the appearance of skins—white and black.

Interplay between image and reality undergoes further development in Sartre's existential psychoanalysis of the playwright Jean Genet, whose identity is also problematic. Sartre's title *Saint Genet,* like the title *The Respectful Prostitute,* embodies a destabilizing contradiction, for it confers sanctity on a criminal. The sanctity introduces a secondary dialectic with an additional contradiction: if Saint Genet was a saint, Jean Genet was a passive homosexual, and Sartre is equipping him for this female role with a pun on "saint"/*seins* ("breasts").[116]

Should anyone feel that the austerity of philosophy is being violated by a pun that does not even have Heidegger's usual excuse of etymology, we might remind him again that traditional dialectical oppositions are lingering here in the background—the distinction between image (or art) and reality is traditionally associated with the distinction between subjective appearances and objective reality. In a *reflexive* dialectic, moreover, subjective appearances retain a significance suggested by Sartre's frequent endorsement of Hegel's claim that "the appearance possesses a reality as appearance."[117]

Genet merely appears to be a woman; as a passive homosexual he plays the sexual role of a woman, but he is really a man. Thus Sartre's subtitle for *Saint Genet* reminds us that the real Saint Genet was a *Play Actor* as well as a *Martyr.* He was a play actor who attained sainthood through his conversion from a mock performance to real martyrdom:

> In the course of an entertainment given to Diocletian in Rome, [Genet] played the part of a candidate in a mocking representation of

Christian baptism. But the grace of God touched him, and when afterward he was presented to the emperor, he declared that he had suddenly been converted to Christ during the performance. He was therefore put to the torture; but he would not recant, and so his head was struck off.[118]

This real Saint Genet became the patron saint of play actors.

I have been identifying him as "the real Saint Genet," for his story did provide the subject for a seventeenth-century play, *Le véritable Saint Genet*, and it is also necessary to distinguish him from the playwright Jean Genet. But I suspect Sartre is himself assigning Jean Genet a mock performance which will allow for further manipulation of the dialectic of appearance and reality, in order to dislocate traditional prerogatives. Saint Genet never was real; his story is just a pious legend. Jean Genet, in contrast, may seem to be real, but in his plays and other imaginative writings he is seeking to attain the legendary identity of a saint.

A PASSION STORY

Furthermore, as a homosexual who plays the passive role of a female, he can be identified as a *martyr*, since his legend is a "passion story." There is an ambiguity and instability of meaning here too. Passivity, we have already seen, can disgust Sartre (whether the passive obedience of the wiggling bottom to the force of gravity, the Frenchman passively obedient to the pressure to conform, or the prostitute passively respecting her oppressors). But "passion" also has the traditional Christian sense of suffering accepted; the martyr attains sanctity by reenacting the passion of Christ, thereby identifying himself with Christ. He is then not just a passive "victim" (which is only a secondary sense of *martyrion*) but a "witness" (the primary sense), which is for Sartre the role of the writer.[119]

We must not conclude that Sartre is just juggling with the idiosyncrasies of Genet as an individual. His dialectic is *bifocal*; any man is a passion story. The conclusion of *Being and Nothingness*, as I have already anticipated, is that

> the passion of man is the reverse of that of Christ, for man loses himself as man in order that God may be born. . . . Man is a useless passion.

Having reached Sartre's conclusion, we can take the advice he gave us at the outset: "To understand better the present ambitions and function of existentialism we must return to Kierkegaard's time."[120] Sartre is thinking of the way Kierkegaard rehabilitates personal experience in opposition to Hegel's system. This rehabilitation we have already considered in Kierkegaard's earlier writings—before the opposition became explicitly an *Either/Or*.

In turning next to this work we can be more specific about what is relevant to Sartre. Kierkegaard cast his own personal experience in the form of what he called "A Passion Story" and played with the ambiguity of the title as referring at once to his unhappy love as an individual for Regina and to his "suffering" as of more general religious significance. Kierkegaard's title could be borrowed for Sartre's psychoanalyses of Flaubert as well as Genet. In both analyses Sartre capitalizes "Passion," thereby stressing the allusion to Christ and thus the *bifocal* character of his interpretation. He tells how even as a youngster Flaubert "attempted to live his condition as a Passion," and so is "very close to Christ, that other voluntary [*consentant*] victim of the will of another Father: he suffers for all."[121]

Flaubert's life as an individual acquires more general significance as that of "the romantic hero" who "considers his life as the Passion of Christ renewed: he is Jesus, returned to earth, condemned by the will of the Other (an Other who is himself and his father at one and the same time) to expiate a sin which he has not committed; he knows it, he knows in advance the stations of his way of the cross." Kierkegaard likewise traveled along the "Stages on Life's Way" which culminate in "A Passion Story."

Although Sartre's christology attains its full generality only when the conclusion of *Being and Nothingness* is taken into account, sociological conclusions tend to supersede or blend with ontological conclusions in his later writings. But even in the *Critique* the climax of the sociological analysis is "the group as *passion*."[122] Now that we have watched Sartre tie Flaubert's experience into social history, one of his conclusions here might accompany our return to Kierkegaard:

> Flaubert writes for a Western world which is Christian. And we are all Christians, even today; the most radical disbelief is still Christian atheism. In other words it retains, in spite of its destructive power, schemata which are controlling—very slightly for our thinking, more for our imagination, above all for our sensibility. And the origins of these schemata are to be sought in the centuries of Christianity of which we are the heirs, whether we like it or not.[123]

Whatever the merits of this generalization as social history, it does suggest the relevance Kierkegaard's version of these schemata might retain for contemporary existentialism. If Sartre is radical in his disbelief, yet he attaches crucial importance to the affective character of thought—to the "logic of the passions." And we have seen that the predominance "sensibility" thereby enjoys is in part a debt to Heidegger's *Befindlichkeit*.

Our interest, however, remains philosophical; it is interest in the dialectical character of Kierkegaard's version of Christian schemata. But the first requirement of Kierkegaard's dialectic is that we should start at the start. "A Passion Story" as a religious stage of life's way is deferred by Kierkegaard to the very end of *Stages*, which is itself the final work in his "authorship." In *Either/Or* we start out at the low level of the passions.

Notes

1. *Papirer*, IV A 57.
2. *Sartre*, p. 115.
3. *Being and Nothingness*, p. 47. In crucial instances of its employment by Merleau-Ponty, "and" carries still other implications. Thus "the comparisons between the invisible and the visible . . . [such as are implicit in his title] are not comparisons (Heidegger) [Merleau-Ponty is associating his interpretation with Heidegger partly to indicate his disagreement with Sartre, whose sharper articulation by negation he repudiates (see n. 18, this chapter); they mean that the visible is pregnant with the invisible. . . . Being is this strange encroachment [*empiétement*] whereby my visible, although it cannot be superimposed on that of the other, nonetheless opens out on it, and both open out upon the same sensible world" (*Visible and Invisible*, p. 216).
4. *Being and Nothingness*, pp. 119–20.
5. See chap. 4, n. 47 above.
6. See p. 87 above for the Other and p. 81 for "outside."
7. *Sartre*, pp. 188–89, 196–201, 379. The problem of identity the individual faces in existentialism is methodologically a problem of definition (see p. 144 above). It is not solved by my identification by the Other, inasmuch as it is "the Other's freedom" which "is revealed to me across the uneasy indeterminacy of the being which I am for him" (*Sartre*, p. 200). The problem of definition survives—indeed is accentuated by the malaise—and becomes a reflexive problem of self-definition—i.e., a problem for the exercise of my own freedom. The process of definition is dialectical in that its movement is from the indeterminate to the determinate (see chap. 4, n. 18 above). In chap. 10 I shall deal with this process in Kierkegaard's somewhat different terminology.
8. See p. 108 above; *Nausea*, pp. 175–76. It is the jazz lyric which is described as "a witness without pity" (see p. 525 below).
9. *Critique*, e.g., p. 255.
10. *Sartre*, p. 209. The shaping and producing, which will become literal in the *Critique*, are already present here in *Being and Nothingness* as metaphors: "I am possessed by the Other; the Other's look shapes [*façonne*] my body in its nakedness, makes it emerge, sculptures it, produces it as it *is*, sees it as I shall never see it" (*Sartre*, p. 209; italics in original). The experience here is still visual, but the shaping will become literal in *Being and Nothingness* itself with the ensuing discussion of the caress (see *Sartre*, p. 216). The sculpturing is not just embroidery on the shaping. Whether or not it is reminiscent here of the role of the work of art in *Nausea*, sculpture and statues play a distinctive role in Sartre (see p. 519 below).
11. See p. 66 above; *Situations*, 7:21.
12. Since this example is reportedly "of a rather special character" (see p. 53 above), it may be appropriate to offer another example which illustrates how (in Kierkegaard's

formula) the "relation" which "underlies the disrelation" is fundamentally a *reflexive* (and *affective*) one—when the disrelation takes the negative form that is fundamental in Sartre. To an "external negation," where the negation does not impinge on either object (e.g., "A cup is not an inkwell") Sartre opposes an "internal negation." When "with a certain melancholy" I announce, "I am not handsome," the implication is not only that I am denied a certain quality but also that I am qualified by the denial, for "this negative quality will explain my melancholy as well as my disappointments"— in not being successful with women (*Being and Nothingness*, p. 243).

13. *Sartre*, p. 225. The relational character of the dialectical process of definition is brought out by the "reciprocity . . . which is human truth—the object defining us to the very extent to which we define the object" (*L'idiot*, 3:12).

14. See chap. 3 for these examples.

15. *Sartre*, p. 223.

16. *Either*, p. 304.

17. *Postscript*, p. 461. This dialectic of swaying in the horizontal dimension can be compared with hovering in the vertical (see p. 107 above).

18. Like Heidegger, though less drastically, Merleau-Ponty tries to undercut the distinction between subject and object: "The relations between the subject and the world are not strictly bilateral" (*Perception*, p. ix). Indeed the year he published the *Phenomenology of Perception* he complained, "From my point of view *Being and Nothingness* remains *too exclusively antithetical.* . . . The antithesis of subject and object often takes on the guise of an alternation instead of being described as a vital living *interrelation*" (*Sense and Non-Sense*, p. 72; italics mine; see n. 3, this chapter). If it were "exclusively antithetical," there would be no underlying relation and hence no interplay. Here Merleau-Ponty disregards Sartre's doctrine of "internal negation" (see n. 12, this chapter). But interplay in Merleau-Ponty does take more closely inter-related forms than in Sartre. Hence his regular resort to the metaphor of "fabric" (*tissu*) for experience, as in the following definition: "Existence is not a set of facts . . . but the ambiguous setting of their intercommunication, the juncture at which their boundaries run into each other, or again their woven fabric" (*Perception*, p. 166; see also pp. x, xii). Other favorite metaphors are "net" (*filet*, pp. xv, 12), "to tie together" (*se nouer*, p. 173), and "knot" (*noeud*, p. 456).

19. *Being and Nothingness*, p. 445. Sartre may misremember the novel. At any rate the restriction to the body in *Being and Nothingness* seems to encroach in his later interpretation of the novel: "I was Roquentin; I used him to show, without complacency, the texture of my life. At the same time, I was myself, the elect, chronicler of hell, a glass and steel photomicroscope leaning over my own protoplasmic juices" (*Words*, pp. 251–52).

20. *Sartre*, p. 224.

21. Ibid., p. 60; *Nausea*, p. 127.

22. See p. 151 above.

23. I am not sure of the allusion to Hegel here, but evidence of it would be the nauseous character of Sartre's complaint against idealism as a philosophy where consciousness digests things. See p. 388 below.

24. *Nausea*, pp. 83, 89. The "weakness" of the flesh is "mysterious" inasmuch as there is no teleological, functional explanation for it (see n. 36, this chapter). The artist relieves the flesh of both its contingency and its mystery by the intrinsic necessity his work of art confers (see p. 189 above). For the dialectical opposition between "Faces" and "Official Portraits," see chap. 3, n. 107 above.

25. I employ Husserl's term "reduction," for if Sartre has not been influenced directly by Husserl here, he has been influenced by Heidegger's account of anxiety, which I shall argue in my phenomenological sequel is a version of the "reduction."

26. *Being and Time*, p. 189.

27. *Nausea*, p. 2.

28. *Being and Time*, p. 187.

29. See p. 98 above.

30. *Nausea*, p. 1. The effort at classification is recalled and discussed at the start of the nauseous vision (*Sartre*, p. 60; *Nausea*, p. 127).

31. *Sartre*, p. 63; *Nausea*, p. 130.

32. For Sartre's squint, see *Situations*, p. 90.

33. See p. 102 above.

34. *Sartre*, p. 61; *Nausea*, p. 128.

35. See p. 108 above. The comparable dissolution in *Being and Time* is also an exposure to indeterminacy: "That before which one is anxious is not a being within-the-world. Thus it is essentially incapable of having a relational involvement [see translator's note, p. 84]. . . . That before which one is anxious is entirely indeterminate" (p. 186).

36. *Sartre*, p. 224. Explanatory justification must be teleological, when one is dealing with a human being and is opposed by Sartre to the mechanical explanation which can of course be supplied for the wiggles. This opposition is a dialectical distortion of Husserl's distinction between the intentional relation of consciousness to whatever it is "consciousness of" and the causal, mechanical relations which phenomenology relegates to empirical science but which Sartre in effect retrieves as the opposing pole of his dialectic. What is necessary in the perspective of mechanics can be contingent in a teleological perspective and set aside by Sartre's dialectical version of Husserl's reduction (e.g., when the dancer lends an intrinsic teleological necessity to the movements of a body, some of which remain extraneous and mechanical with the ordinary walker). Thus in Sartre it is the work of art which survives the reduction: "There must be a scratch on the record there, for it makes a funny sound. And that's something which clutches the heart: the melody is absolutely untouched by this tiny coughing of the needle on the record" (ibid., p. 70; *Nausea*, pp. 175–76).

37. *Sartre*, p. 67; *Nausea*, p. 134.

38. *Nausea*, p. 111.

39. *Marmelade*, which Lloyd Alexander translates as "mess," can have the further connotation of something "squashed."

40. *Sartre*, p. 220. *In-tendere* in classical Latin can refer to stretching a bow in aiming it toward something, and Sartre follows Husserl in reading a target-aiming metaphor into the intentional consciousness of something, but in Sartre the teleology becomes literal. I have already noted that Sartre uses Heidegger's term "facticity" as if it were a synonym for "contingency" and could be assimilated to "passivity." But I also recognized (chap. 3, n. 21) that Sartre is not so undialectical as to treat existence only in terms of its passivity—its softness, meltingness, weakness. It is also experienced as dislocatingly active and aggressive. This version too is described with a movement from the abstract to the concrete: "Existence is not something which lets itself be thought about from a distance; it must invade you suddenly, master you, weigh heavily on your heart like a huge motionless beast" (*Sartre*, p. 65; *Nausea*, p. 132). This phase of the ecstatic vision is prepared for by the newspaper report of the rape and murder of a little girl (*Nausea*, pp. 100–101).

41. *Nausea*, pp. 6, 59.

42. I have an ulterior motive for stressing the distinction between literal and metaphorical as to some extent Sartre's way of accommodating the difference between the level of Husserl's analysis of "consciousness of something" and Heidegger's analysis of "being-in-the-world." Just as at the end of philosophy philosophers tend to become preoccupied with the homogeneous structure of the philosophical tradition (see p. 19 above), so they tend to become preoccupied with the homogeneous structure of metaphors throughout this tradition. Just as my long-run concern is with differences dividing our philosophers, so it is more specifically with differences in their construction of metaphors. Indeed I shall argue that any of their significant metaphors involves a process of transposition which illustrates in microcosm differences in the setup of their dialectics, which their philosophies as a whole also illustrate.

43. I am not suggesting that this interplay can be fully accounted for as a conflation of differences between Husserl and Heidegger. Perhaps no successful contemporary French writer is as disconcertingly a mixture of styles as Sartre; at the level of "consciousness of something" he is clearly influenced by the realism of certain American writers, whereas at the cosmic level there is often considerable debt to French surrealism, as the conflationary character itself of the earlier dream suggests, as well as the dreamlike character of the trance. Heideggerian anxiety is, in contrast, vigilance.

44. *Sartre*, pp. 310–11; see chap. 4, n. 102 above. The significance of *glissement* is brought out at the philosophical level when Sartre cites as a commentary on skiing, "Glissez, mortels, n'appuyez pas" ("Glide, moral men, don't bear down"; *Sartre*, p. 315; see my interpretation in the introduction, p. 32). The significance of *glissement* is dropped down to the level of "the life of an individual" by its citation at the end of Sartre's autobiography (*Words*, p. 255). The metaphor, and thus the concreteness Sartre sought, is eliminated by the translator in favor of rather abstract virtues: "Gently, mortals, be discreet." But Sartre has never particularly cherished gentleness, and certainly not discretion. Because translators so often assume that metaphors are commotion that hardly matters, I have gone into the dialectic of Sartre's metaphors. Sartre himself would not dismiss his metaphors as mere metaphors. Observe his phenomenological plea in another setting: "I beg you not to regard the following considerations as metaphors. I am simply stating what I see" (Contat, 2:68). Thus in the crucial case of nausea Sartre warns, "We must not take the term 'nausea' as a metaphor derived from physiological disgust" (*Being and Nothingness*, p. 445).

45. Since metaphors are stylistic devices, it should be observed that interplay is involved in Sartre's explanation of how "an author can achieve a style"—by trying "to write as a painter paints—i.e., by pursuing his undertaking on two levels at once without losing sight of either level or of the moving relation between them" (*L'idiot*, 2:1983).

46. Ibid., 1:427; see p. 303 below. Another example is the cliché "See Naples and die" (*L'idiot*, 1:927). Sartre points out that "two meanings interpenetrate each other: 'If one must die to see Naples, so be it,' and 'Better lose one's life after having seen it, lest one pollute one's eyes by allowing them to linger over ordinary sights' " (ibid.). In other more serious examples Sartre often inveighs against such interpenetration as a slackening of interplay, so that what transpires is no longer genuinely dialectical. From his point of view such slackness is (or became) characteristic of Merleau-Ponty: "One day Merleau-Ponty got in a bad temper about dialectic and abused it. . . . With him contradictory truths never enter into conflict; there is no risk of their blocking movement or provoking an explosion" (*Situations*, p. 212). Compare Merleau-Ponty's point of view toward Sartre (n. 18, this chapter).

47. In Genet's case Sartre visualizes their production as follows: "The two dialectics that control his inner life run counter to each other, they jam, and finally they get twisted and whirl about idly" (*Saint Genet*, p. 329; see p. 198 above). I have anticipated that Kierkegaard is similarly fascinated by "crisscrossing" (see p. 540 below).

48. *L'idiot*, 1:587–88.

49. This reliance on specific examples is not accidental; it is an intrinsic feature of the phenomenological procedure of "eidetic variation," which will be examined in the sequel. Its relevance here is the movement it involves in Sartre from abstract to concrete which I traced in chap. 4 as a reversal of the movement of the philosophical tradition (as interpreted by existentialism) and retraced in detail in this chapter with reference to the interplay metaphors promote. The similar significance of an "example" is suggested by Derrida's etymology "at play" for *Bei-spiel*, but he presumably takes "play" in a Nietzschian sense, not in the dialectical sense that his citation from Hegel might warrant (*Glas*, pp. 37–38).

50. *Sartre*, p. 226.

51. The notion of "recapitulation" is itself played with in one of Sartre's short stories ("*The Wall*" *and Other Stories*, p. 40).

52. See p. 162 above.

53. See p. 159 above.

54. *L'idiot*, 2:1666.

55. *Sartre*, p. 218. "Pure matter" here, as "brute" suggests, is a variation on Heidegger's "facticity."

56. Ibid., p. 226.

57. Ibid., p. 228.

58. For Sartre "inertia" is "the contrary of the living man" (*L'idiot*, 2:1953), and the interplay between the two is prominent in his *Critique*.

59. This movement of advance in Hegel is often associated with a recapitulation of what has gone before.

60. *Sartre*, p. 230; italics in original.

61. Ibid., p. 227. The phrase "contradictory composite" (*Transcendence of the Ego*, p. 84) is applied by Sartre to the *ex-sistential* "object" which is pivotal in his reflexive dialectic—the self one is "conscious of" as "something." He explains, "Myself-as-object is . . . a malaise, the experience of being wrenched away from the ekstatic unity of the subject" (*Being and Nothingness*, p. 367). "Transcendence" in Sartre's title is itself (as well as the "ego") a "contradictory composite," since the self or ego in question is not "transcendental" (i.e., does not transcend experience as does the ego in Kant) but is "transcendent" in that it does transcend the act of consciousness by which it is constituted, as does any object in Husserl.

62. From now on I shall employ *ambiguous, contradictory*, and *unstable* as a rough and ready formula for tracing the dialectical development of any significant *contradictory composite*.

63. *Sartre*, p. 352. "Passion" as well as "God" Sartre analyzes as a *contradictory composite*, inasmuch as he regards activity as required to sustain or even initiate the passion one undergoes. In his later writings he renders the contradiction explicit by employing the expression "passive activity" (e.g., *L'idiot*, 3:9).

64. *L'idiot*, 1:589.

65. Ibid., 1:590–91. Before Sartre ever employed this contrast in spatial terms between Nietzsche and Flaubert, Merleau-Ponty had defended his doctrine of "verticality" (*Visible and Invisible*, e.g., p. 234) by attacking Sartre as speaking "of a world that is not vertical but in itself—i.e., flat—and for a nothingness which is an abyss that is absolute. Ultimately for him there is no depth" (pp. 236–37). This is the criticism cited in n. 18, this chapter, of Sartre's handling of relations, but now translated into terms of spatial relations. I am not suggesting that Merleau-Ponty's criticism inspired Sartre's contrast. What is illustrated in both cases is existentialist dependence on spatial metaphors.

66. *L'idiot*, 1:510–11.

67. Ibid., vol. 1, chap. 7, "Les deux idéologies."

68. *Situations*, 8:208–9. For another illustration of Sartre's predilection for "lightning flashes," see p. 365 below.

69. See p. 96 above.

70. *Literary and Philosophical Essays*, p. 97.

71. Ibid.

72. See p. 38 above.

73. *Point of View*, p. 22.

74. *Literary and Philosophical Essays*, pp. 97–98. Sartre tends to equate Americanism with Puritanism. In denouncing, on behalf of the Russell Tribunal, American genocide in Vietnam, Sartre faced the question of whether its perpetrators "were clearly aware of their intent," and one portion of his reply was to refer to the "miracles that puritan self-deception [*mauvaise foi*] can pull off" (*Between Existentialism and Marxism*, p. 80).

75. Other articles in Sartre's series of reports from America are also organized in terms of dialectical contrasts: "Each Day a City Is Born; Each Day a Town Dies";

"For Us It's a Past; for Them It's a Future." Contat summarizes, "Sartre sees above all 'a contrast between wealth and parsimony, pleasures and profound melancholy, comfort and anxiety' " (Contat, 1:121, 119).

76. Disgust is a dislocating reaction of revulsion which frequently impels Sartre's dialectic and which we have seen Sartre can elicit, even to the extent of nausea. For the dialectic of repulsion in Kierkegaard, see p. 401 below.

77. This affective reaction not only ensures reflexive involvement but also is itself the "subject matter" that Sartre characteristically selects for treatment. Thus in analyzing Flaubert's writings Sartre assumes that Flaubert "does not think of coming to know himself by writing but to dream himself [*se rêver*]. Tout est là" (*L'idiot*, 1:948). He often finds a point of insertion for his analyses in some feeling of disgust, despair, or at least malaise on Flaubert's part. These three terms occur hundreds of times in *L'idiot*. More detailed examination of the affective character of existential "subject matter" will be undertaken in chap. 7.

78. *Anti-Semite and Jew*, p. 152; Contat, 1:145; see also *Anti-Semite and Jew*, p. 143.

79. *L'idiot*, 2:2135.

80. Ibid., 1:7–8.

81. *Promenade du dimanche*, p. 10. Sartre generously fails to note that the obvious inspiration for this play was the Sunday walk in *Nausea* (pp. 40–56). Condensation need not take this form of a social ritual. Indeed "the function of the theater is to present the individual in the form of a myth. A person must be found who embodies in a more or less condensed fashion the problems we face at a given moment" (Contat, 1:363). Though Sartre is speaking of the theater, his interpretations of Flaubert and Genet latch onto their efforts to become mythical, legendary figures. Like Kierkegaard (see chap. 1, n. 43 above), Sartre may be indebted to Hegel with respect to the scope of what can be conveyed in this fashion.

82. *L'idiot*, 1:481. Sartre compares such an experience with William James's conception of a religious experience. I would prefer the comparison with Kierkegaard, for whom what was for Regina hardly more than a brief episode in her own life told Kierkegaard the whole story about himself.

83. *Sartre*, p. 90. Kierkegaard's conception of self-choice will be examined in chap. 10.

84. Contat, 1:571. See also *Search for a Method*, p. 108; *Situations*, 10:100.

85. *Critique*, pp. 17–18. He complains in much the same fashion about Merleau-Ponty (see n. 46, this chapter).

86. *Critique*, p. 18. A more graphic description of the psyche as a contradictory composite Sartre borrows from Flaubert—*profondeurs terribles et ennuyeuses* ("terrifying and tedious depths," *Between Existentialism and Marxism*, p. 40). Sartre's attempt to incorporate psychoanalysis may have been inspired in part by Merleau-Ponty's criticism of his philosophy as lacking the dimension of depth (see n. 65, this chapter).

87. *Critique*, p. 18; italics in original.

88. Contat, 1:481. See also *Between Existentialism and Marxism*, p. 45: "Flaubert represents for me the exact opposite of my own conception of literature."

89. *L'idiot*, 2:1204. Contestation is an opposition which can be given a further reflexive twist. Thus in the heat of 1968 Sartre commented that Raymond Aron was "not fit to be a professor" because "he has never contested himself" (*Situations*, 8:188).

90. *L'idiot*, 1:8. Sartre links Baudelaire and Flaubert together as "the two men who foresaw and forged modern literature" (2:1621). Without worrying about the scope of Sartre's generalization, we can recognize that his selection of these two writers for psychoanalysis has not been just on psychoanalytic grounds. A distinction of level is relevant.

91. *Between Existentialism and Marxism*, p. 49.

92. Ibid., pp. 13, 45; *Search for a Method*, pp. 140–42. Again the contradiction carries over into the form of the work—*The Temptation of St. Anthony* is "a diarrhea of pearls" (*Search for a Method*, p. 141; the characterization is Bouilhet's).

93. *Search for a Method*, pp. 141–42.
94. *L'idiot*, 2:1199.
95. Ibid., 1:13.
96. *Critique*, pp. 98–99.
97. *L'idiot*, 3:196; see also 3:18.
98. Ibid., 2:1199.
99. *Situations*, 6:27; *Search for a Method*, p. 32. The second quotation is actually from Engels. This is a curious mistake on Sartre's part, since he is eager to saddle Engels with as much of the blame as possible for rendering Marxism undialectical.
100. *Situations*, pp. 6, 87.
101. *Critique*, p. 152.
102. *Search for a Method*; pp. 12–13. The particular rhythm Sartre attributes to "Kierkegaardian existence" would be better illustrated by his analysis of Flaubert's "rumination" than by any performance by Kierkegaard. In referring to psychoanalysts, Sartre is thinking primarily of Lagache, *Le travail du deuil* (*The Work of Mourning*), which would be an instance of actively sustained passivity (see n. 40, this chapter). Sartre also mentions "the work of rupture," a "dismal rumination" (*Situations*, p. 205, where Sartre refers directly to Freud), in which he and Merleau-Ponty became engaged in breaking off their relation (see p. 124 above).
103. *Situations*, 9:93. "Grasping" is suspiciously ambiguous but may betray the influence of the analysis of consciousness that Sartre derives from Husserl. Neither in Marx nor in Heidegger is there an explicit "grasping of the world" when a "tool" is "used." Though "work" in Heidegger does "carry with it that referential totality within which the tool is encountered" (*Being and Time*, p. 69–70), "work" is not taken in its subjective relation to the worker but is "that which is to be produced" (p. 69).
104. Sartre's hyphenation indicates that he is translating Heidegger's *Entwurf* (see chap. 3, n. 21 above).
105. For the juncture where *Zuhandenheit* fits into Heidegger's analysis, see p. 99 above. Sartre's own analysis here is a further specification in the analysis of the spatial structure of the world which was examined in chap. 3: "The space which is originally revealed to me is hodological space; it is furrowed with paths and highways; it is instrumental, and it is the *location* of tools" (*Being and Nothingness*, p. 424; italics in original).
106. "Bachelard properly reproaches phenomenology for not sufficiently taking into account what he calls the 'coefficient of adversity' in objects" (*Being and Nothingness*, p. 428). Heidegger does discriminate three ways in which the requirements of *Zuhandenheit* may not seem to be met empirically, but he does not indulge in any simple opposition. I am assuming that Sartre interprets the reproach as directed against Heidegger as well as Husserl, since Sartre is discussing "instrumentality." To the extent that it is directed against Husserl, it illustrates Sartre's conversion of Husserl's intentional analysis into a dialectical analysis. The outcome of Sartre's "ontological proof" (*Sartre*, pp. 107–9) is that the "something" which "consciousness" is "of" in Husserl (an "intentional object") becomes an actual external thing, and thus Husserl's phenomenology becomes a "phenomenological ontology." (The subtitle of Sartre's *Being and Nothingness* is *An Essay on Phenomenological Ontology* and presumably echoes Heidegger's ostensible declaration of loyalty to Husserl, "*Only as phenomenology is ontology possible*" [*Being and Time*, p. 35; italics in original], although Sartre's own argument is in effect that only as ontology is phenomenology possible.) Thus in Sartre the intentional relation between the subject (consciousness) and the object can become dialectical, for the object can be visualized as either conforming to or as resisting the intentions of the subject.
107. *Being and Nothingness*, p. 426. Here the introduction of a reflexive dimension brings with it Sartre's own active/passive distinction.
108. "The *methodological* principle which holds that certainty starts with reflection in no way contradicts the *anthropological* principle which defines the concrete person

by his materiality. . . . Reflection is a starting point only if it throws us back immediately among things and men, in the world" (*Search for a Method*, p. 32; italics in original). Observe that this reconciliation of phenomenological method with materialism is Sartre's usual dialectical combination of initiative with passivity but depends in fact on combining Husserl's starting point (the initiative accorded to reflection) with what Sartre takes to be Heidegger's starting point (our being thrown back into the world).

109. *Situations*, 7:27.

110. *Sartre*, pp. 462–63; *Critique*, p. 325); italics in original. Perhaps an apology is needed for the length of my quotations from the *Critique*. Let Sartre supply it: "Fundamentally the reason why each sentence is so long and so full of parentheses, quotes, expressions like 'insofar as,' etc., is that each sentence represents the unity of a dialectical movement" (Contat, 1:371). There is the same difficulty in quoting Kierkegaard and Hegel briefly.

111. *Critique*, p. 233; italics in original. Sartre can sometimes be understood more readily in German. Although he does relish the term "predestination," with its Calvinist associations, one should keep in mind that "destiny" comes within the range of meanings of *Bestimmung* (see chap. 4, n. 18 above). Sartre would sometimes seem to shift from one meaning to another: e.g., "the whole is entirely present in the part as its present meaning and as its destiny. In this case, it is opposed to itself as the part is opposed to the whole in its *determination* . . . and . . . each part is both the negation of the others and the whole, determining itself in its totalizing activity . . ." (*Critique*, p. 47; italics in original). In the case of the female worker the definitory process which *Bestimmung* involves is reversed: she does not determine the significance of the machine by her consciousness of it; the machine largely determines the significance of what she is conscious of, intruding even into the process of what should be her self-definition.

112. *Critique*, p. 233. To appreciate how much of the early Sartre survived his becoming aware of "the force of circumstances" (*Between Existentialism and Marxism*, p. 33) that converted him to Marxism, it may be worth recalling the nauseous vision in which (without any intervention by a machine) "all things . . . were letting themselves exist like weary women giving way to laughter, saying, 'It's good to laugh' in a damp voice" (see p. 102 above).

113. *Critique*, pp. 233–34.

114. Though familiar usage has encouraged its vulgarization, the terminology of identification and the problem of self-identity derive in Sartre from Husserl's intentional analysis of "consciousness of something" as a meaning-endowing act. I am in Husserl "conscious of something" as "a tree," "a cube." In Sartre I also become conscious of myself as something: I identify attributes with this self (e.g., "courage," "cowardice"), just as in Husserl I identify attributes ("greenness," "squareness") with a thing. While Sartre takes this model over from Husserl, it is never employed for the purpose of analyzing self-reference by Husserl himself; indeed Sartre himself argues that the model does not in fact hold (*Transcendence of the Ego*, pp. 72–75). The issues here I shall take up in my sequel on phenomenological method.

115. Contat, 1:40.

116. "Collisions of images" and other contradictions are generated by "the conflict between the female principle and the male imperative. . . . Each illusion discovers itself thwarted by the opposite illusion: though he may want to resume his female dreams, the male *character* in him no longer believes in them" (*Saint Genet*, p. 416; italics in original). We have already observed how dialectically enticing Sartre finds Flaubert's supposed bisexuality, as well as the sexist sharpness with which he opposes male and female as active and passive performances when he deals in the *Critique* with the female worker dreaming. Indeed another respect in which Genet is a *contradictory composite* is that "he *wants* and *does not want* to dream" (p. 355; italics in original). To take a broader, sociological view of his contradictory composition, Genet is "an

aberrant synthesis of two attitudes"—a product of both the naive substantialism of rural areas and the rationalism of cities," so that he belongs "to two groups at the same time" (pp. 61–62, where Sartre lists "two irreducible systems of values" or "categories which he [Genet] employs simultaneously in order to reflect upon the world").

117. E.g., *Search for a Method*, p. 9. This endorsement marks one juncture at which Sartre's phenomenological analysis of what "appears" to consciousness becomes conflated with a dialectical analysis. See chap. 1, n. 24 above.

118. Attwater, *Penguin Dictionary of Saints*, p. 146.

119. At the end of *Words*, the story of Sartre's own quest for salvation, this is the role that he salvages: "Culture doesn't save anything or anyone, it doesn't justify. But it's a product of man: he projects himself into it, he recognizes himself in it; that critical mirror alone offers him his image" (p. 254).

120. *Search for a Method*, p. 8. I shall not deal with Sartre's essay on Kierkegaard (*Between Existentialism and Marxism*, pp. 141–69) in this volume, because it represents in part phenomenological distortion of Kierkegaard's dialectic and can only be dealt with satisfactorily in my sequel, where I shall distinguish the phenomenological method from the dialectical method.

121. *L'idiot*, 2:1391–92.

122. *Critique*, p. 348.

123. *L'idiot*, 2:2124.

6

Stages

Whenever there is a dialectic, there is an eagerness which is so eager to enjoin the second point that in its eagerness it gets rid of the first point and therefore fundamentally makes the second point impossible.
—Kierkegaard

THE PASSIONS

At the outset of my attempt to interpret existentialism, I encountered Walter Lowrie's protest that assigning Kierkegaard and Sartre to the same philosophical movement was a "monstrous hoax," for "between these two men there is hardly enough likeness to make it easy to define the difference." I now want to show that Kierkegaard's method displays dialectical traits which are quite like those which have been displayed by Sartre as well as somewhat like those displayed by Heidegger, though I shall not merely list them again but try to employ them in a detailed analysis of the way Kierkegaard (and hence existentialism) got started.

In Sartre's case some of the traits he shares with Heidegger could be judged a matter of Heidegger's influence. But Kierkegaard cannot be said to have exercised any comparably direct influence on Sartre: in fact there is no textual evidence that he read Kierkegaard with any care until relatively late in his career.[1] Remember that I am in any case concerned not with influences as such but with the exigencies of the dialectical method as it is used by existentialists.

If tracking influences were my concern, we would have to recognize that what Sartre shares most obviously with Kierkegaard is a debt to Hegel's dialectic. The index to *Being and Nothingness* lists only five pages which refer explicitly to Kierkegaard, and the references are all made in passing, without elaboration. There are forty-six pages on which Sartre explicitly refers to Hegel, and some of these references are lengthy discussions. But one endorsement of Kierkegaard is highly pertinent to my interpretation: "Everywhere we ought to oppose to Hegel Kierkegaard, who represents the claims of the individual as such."[2] It is on these claims that I am focusing, since I am trying to determine the kind of individualism existentialism is.

It must be admitted that Sartre is rarely an accurate interpreter of other philosophers, but no one would dispute that Kierkegaard does represent the claims of the individual as such. Indeed we have seen that his dialectical method, in its ironical version at least, is an analysis of the process of "determination" by which one "becomes an individual"—that is, "defines" or individuates oneself.[3]

Further interpretation of Kierkegaard will advance my interpretation of dialectical method. In utilizing Sartre I took advantage of his extensive reliance on separate examples, which provided more easily isolated illustrations of the traits of this method than Heidegger's denser philosophy. But Sartre's reliance on examples is more obviously a feature of the phenomenological method of eidetic variation, which is not our present concern and does not illustrate as well as does Kierkegaard's more purely dialectical method the *developmental* character of a dialectic.[4]

We have recognized too that Sartre is more obviously indebted to Husserl than to Heidegger with respect to the fashion in which he starts out in *Being and Nothingness*.[5] The progress that will be possible in the present chapter will be the discovery of how a dialectical starting point is a point from which the a dialectical analysis is able to develop. I have long since anticipated that the work which Kierkegaard eventually arrived at as the starting point for this analysis is an exposition of the principle of contradiction which is evoked by the title *Either/Or*. One application of this principle is suggested by the epigraph on the title page, "Is reason alone baptized; are the passions the pagans of the soul?" Hegel's dialectic, characterized as rationalistic, is to be contradicted by an *affective* dialectic—what Sartre also calls "a logic of the passions."[6]

Furthermore, reason in Hegel was the pursuit of what he had characterized as "investigations toward unity,"[7] and these culminated in the final unity of his system. Kierkegaard's rejection of this outcome is implicit in his opposition of the passions to reason. As he indicates later in *Either/Or*, "life will soon teach one that there are many kinds of dialectic, that almost every passion has its own dialectic."[8] Kierkegaard is implementing this lesson in pluralism by investigating the "many kinds of dialectic" which are exhibited by different passions, but with a predilection for those which involve extreme psychological dislocation and suffering, as we earlier saw to be the case with the *Sickness unto Death* that despair is.

LEVELS

Another trait of an existential dialectic is that it is *bifocal*. This trait was illustrated earlier by two double titles of Kierkegaard's—*The Concept of Irony with Constant Reference to Socrates*, and *The Crisis and*

A Crisis in the Life of an Actress. In *Either/Or* we again encounter two levels: besides this title, which imposes a formal principle that is philosophical in the generality of its scope, there is a subtitle, which refers to a particular content—*A Fragment of Life*. This subtitle prepares us for Kierkegaard's appeal from Hegel's systematic philosophy to what "life will soon teach one"; the "passions" which will be most emphasized will mark dislocating moments when some individual comes up against contradictions which disrupt the continuity of his life, leaving it fragmentary.

It is not just a matter of discovering miscellaneous contradictions at the lower level indicated by the subtitle. *A Fragment of Life* as such would constitute a contradiction in terms for Hegel. A criterion to which he regularly repairs is the *Lebendigkeit* ("aliveness" or "vitality") which an organism manifests in its development: first the bud, then the blossom, then the fruit—to abbreviate a famous line.[9] These are distinct episodes; yet living through them is an organic development, and "life" is more than a merely metaphorical rendering of the way philosophy must develop into a system. Conversely, death is associated with episodes in which organic wholes suffer mutilation and connections are disrupted. In Kierkegaard too death is a metaphorical criterion associated with the process of fragmentation that he opposes to the process of development into a system.[10]

Besides the unity of a whole that is the outcome of a development which is organic, other criteria are met by Hegel's concept of system. Some of these criteria which are involved with the outcome itself (such as "finishing" and "completeness"). I am postponing until part III. For the present I am risking oversimplifying Hegel in order to deal with features of Kierkegaard's opposition to him which are initially prominent in *Either/ Or*. The methodological problem in Hegel is not merely a matter of correlating particular experiences; there are also, at levels above these, the partial perspectives, points of view or stages (e.g., ethical, esthetic, religious) which have been brought into play in achieving certain correlations, before philosophy arrives officially on the scene. These perspectives must be fitted together by philosophy if the fuller significance of particular experiences is to be grasped. In other words, Hegel does not attempt to compile raw experience in his philosophy. (Here the existentialists have followed in his wake.) Instead, he by and large takes over experiences at higher levels where they have already been interpreted and organized in social institutions, works of art, religious creeds and rituals, and the sciences; and he then reinterprets and reorganizes the relations between these perspectives or stages, so that they all contribute to the fitting together of his philosophical system, and experience itself thereby acquires its fullest significance.

Kierkegaard, in contrast, does not assume that all these perspectives will fit together. He pits his either/or (the contradiction between the ethical and the esthetic point of view) against the both/and of Hegel's reconciliation of these points of view. With respect to how experiences fail to fit together, he raises the further issue of the status of the particular, contingent experience of the individual. In Hegel not everything fits together, but what does not fit loses its significance. Thus particular contingencies have to be overlooked: the portrait painter (or photographer) first poses you and then leaves out the warts (or retouches the photograph) in order to bring out more fully what you are as "sweet sixteen" or as "a man of distinction," so that a certain level of significant generality is reached. I pick this example since we shall be dealing in *Either* with works of art, and Hegel is quite contemptuous of portraits as a genre, whereas we have seen that they become a metaphor for a literary genre that Sartre favors because of his individualism. We shall see that Kierkegaard too goes in for portraiture as a literary genre. Hegel, in contrast, entertains the prospect of a system as a matter of transcending the particular experiences of particular individuals, and one level where their coalescence into more stable, fuller significance can be grasped is as the institutionalized experience of the social community. Indeed in Hegel the true, the significant individual is in a sense the social community itself,[11] and one fashion in which the fragmentation will proceed in Kierkegaard is the fragmentation of this community into particular individuals. But if this were all that was at stake in existentialism, it would be a rather simpleminded individualism. What is also at stake are the repercussions this process of fragmentation has for the development of Kierkegaard's analysis at other levels. These repercussions I shall postpone until after I have traced in the present chapter Kierkegaard's retrieval of the individual. This retrieval has to do with the content of his dialectic. But to follow it out, we shall eventually have to take into account how Kierkegaard proceeds by stages.

THE PSEUDONYM

The first individual we meet in Kierkegaard's "authorship" is the pseudonymous Victor Eremita, to whom as editor *Either/Or* is attributed. Especially since the romantic movement, authors have donned masks. But the most obvious reason Kierkegaard adopts pseudonymity or "polynymity" as a device is that he is investigating the "many kinds of dialectic" which the passions will display from different points of view.

I have already mentioned some different perspectives that Hegel reconciles in his system. They are the points of view of a society or of a stage in social history. But when Kierkegaard multiples points of view, they are assigned to pseudonyms as individuals, and he leaves them unreconciled. Even the point of view of an individual pseudonym can be internally contradictory: the point of view of Victor Eremita is later identified as "sympathetic irony."[12] Thus the editor, as well as *Either/Or* itself, embodies the principle of contradiction; Eremita is a *contradictory composite,* if I may borrow Sartre's phrase, like the Franco-American, the Respectful Prostitute, and Saint (*seins*) Genet.

We are already acquainted with irony as the procedure which Kierkegaard examined in his dissertation and adopted in attacking Hegel in *Johannes Climacus.* Sympathy is the additional qualification which Eremita requires.[13] He must "participate" in the "passions" and the concomitant points of view of the characters he is to portray. Many of these characters turn out to be themselves authors, so Eremita's explanation is that "I sought guidance to the way from authors whose points of view I shared."[14] When we encounter these authors, we shall find that the most important are 'A,' the exponent of the esthetic point of view in *Either,* and 'B,' the exponent of the ethical point of view of *Or.* While sympathetic toward different points of view, Eremita must also maintain the aloofness his name suggests—the esthetic distance which only ironical detachment can provide—lest he become so blindly involved in the passions and views of the exponents that he is unable to trace the dialectical development which is going on.

DOUBT

This is how Eremita starts out in his preface to *Either/Or:* "Perhaps it has sometimes happened to you, Dear Reader, to doubt a little the correctness of the familiar philosophical proposition that the external is the internal, and the internal the external."[15] This doubt is a dialectical doubling of Hegel's Cartesian doubt, the starting point for modern philosophy which we have already seen Kierkegaard would outmaneuver, not only when he started instead with irony but also when he attacked the principle *de omnibus dubitandum* in *Johannes Climacus.* I characterize Kierkegaard's higher-level doubt as a "dialectical doubling." The Danish for "doubt," like the German *Zweifel,* is cognate with the term for "two" (*zwei*), and the point of view being developed in *Either/Or* is being set up, as in the dissertation and in *Johannes Climacus,* in opposition to the point of view of Cartesian doubt, which was taken up by Hegel (we recognized in *Johannes Climacus*) as the starting point for the development of modern philosophy, interpreted as reaching its completion in his own system. Cartesian doubt was to Hegel of more than merely historical significance, inasmuch as the procedure of "doubting everything" eliminates any presupposition and thereby any problem of starting point. But a pre-supposition that Hegel failed to eliminate, according to Eremita, is that the contradiction between the *internal* and *external* points of view can be overcome by the movement of *Aufhebung*.

I have characterized Eremita's doubt regarding the prospect of over-coming this contradiction as a dialectical doubling of Descartes's doubt, not just because it is a higher level doubt, but also because Eremita seems to be alluding to Hegel's term *Entzweiung* ("disruption") in order to sug-gest that he is preserving the contradiction between the "two" points of view—the *internal* and the *external*—and thereby disrupting Hegel's sys-tem. "The view [*betragtning*]," Kierkegaard argued, "which recognizes life's doubleness [*dupplicitæt*] (dualism) is higher and deeper than that which seeks unity."[16]

Eremita's doubt is an existential starting point both at the level of the philosophy it is fragmenting and at the level where "the life of an individual" is disintegrating. Philosophically, when Kierkegaard identi-fies existence with actuality, his contradiction between the *internal* and the *external* disrupts Hegel's system where actuality is "the unity, be-come immediate, of essence with existence, or of internal with external." With respect to "the life of the individual," despair (*fortvivlelse*/*Verzweif-lung*) is its disruption by this same contradiction, for the individual suffers this sickness unto death.[17]

Either is a long-run demonstration that the contradiction between the *internal* and the *external* cannot be overcome, and the demonstration gains impact slowly from successive encounters with the contradiction at successively higher levels, for Kierkegaard's long-run objective is to sub-vert Hegel's reconciliation of this contradiction at the highest level, the system as a whole. Hence it may make matters easier if we first consider illustrations of the contradiction, which are of a shorter run and yet bear on the long-run objective.

IRONY

Eremita's point of view has already provided one such illustration: his sympathy is externally oriented toward the "passions" of others which he is attempting to share; his irony is, in contrast, retention within him-self of their meaning. Consider the ironical component in his point of view by itself. This will enable us to take advantage of our previous deal-ing with Socratic irony. But let me begin with a somewhat less compli-cated specimen of what irony is. In the case of verbal irony, one does not say what one means or mean what one says; there is a discrepancy or contradiction between the *external* statement and the *inner* meaning. Put more dialectically (since a "relation underlies the disrelation"), a discrepancy develops between what seems at the start to be meant by what is said and the implications that eventually develop. But the effectiveness of the irony depends on the reader's initial acceptance of what is said at its face value, so that when he eventually does a double take, he will get the full impact of the dialectical *reversal,* as the discrepancy between what he has understood superficially and its eventual implications dawns on him.

The most obvious instances of verbal irony in *Either* will be Eremita's reliance on the jargon which Hegel employs in the development of his system but which Eremita often empties of its meaning. But these instances assume acquaintance with Hegel, so let us initially ease matters by stepping outside *Either* and examining a well-known form of verbal irony —understatement. Here is an instance from Swift: "Last week I saw a Woman *flay'd,* and you will hardly believe, how much it altered her Person for the worse."[18] What Swift means was that it was horrible, but this is not what he says. He conveys his meaning indirectly by an understatement whose overt traits have the shock value of sharp contrast with what he is implying. He is pretending to be callous about her suffering with his urbane "you will hardly believe"; he is depriving his statement of anything graphic with his evasive reference to "her Person" as "altered" and with his casual "for the worse," which is deferred to the end, where it maintains the balance of the sentence, leaving us initially with a sense of Swift's equanimity. Such irony is a rhetorical device, a means of communication, and we shall examine later the problem of communication with which Kierkegaard is coping when he is ironical about Hegel's system. But it is already evident from Swift's specimen that irony can be put at the service of individualism. The ironist witholds *reflexively* for himself the meaning a particular experience has for him, though he may do this (as we shall eventually see is the case with Kierkegaard) to induce his reader's *reflexive* reaction in turn. The reader must consult his own particular experience as an individual in order to get at the withheld meaning.

INTERNAL AND EXTERNAL

Now we can reconsider Socratic irony, which will help us understand the ironic fashion in which Kierkegaard manipulates the contradiction between the *external* and the *internal.* For his definitional procedure in the dissertation, as in *Either/Or,* is to confront these points of view as contradictory. But this confrontation is itself a third point of view. What we should watch for is how these points of view successively emerge.

When Xenophon got back from marching the 10,000 to the sea, he apparently did not find credible the *Apology* Plato had composed for Socrates, so he wrote another. Aristophanes had already given Socrates the treatment in the *Clouds* while Socrates was still alive.

Kierkegaard accepts Xenophon's point of view toward Socrates as providing a plausible description of the ironist's "hard exterior" (*haarde udvortes*)—his overt behavior: "With Xenophon one may readily accept that Socrates liked to go about and talk with every kind of man, because every external thing or event is an occasion for the ironist, who is always prepared for the conflict." Yet such a description of Socrates' overt behavior leaves him indistinguishable from a traveling salesman and does not account for the conflict he faced:

> Xenophon defends Socrates in a manner that makes him not only innocent but altogether harmless, so that one is profoundly puzzled as to what demon must have bewitched the Athenians to such an extent that they were able to see more in Socrates than in any other good-natured, garrulous, ridiculous character, who . . . opposes no one and who is so amiably disposed toward the whole world, if only it will listen to his chatter.

Xenophon has failed to recognize that the *external* is not the *internal*. This proposition, we have already seen, is implicit in the employment of irony, so Kierkegaard can conclude that, "with respect to irony, we find not the slightest trace of it in his [Xenophon's] Socrates."[19]

"In contrast, Plato and Aristophanes have made their way through the hard exterior." With Plato's Socrates we leave the actual, the phenomenal, the *external* behind and reach the level of the *internal* and the ideal. Thus when the question is raised in the *Republic*, "What is justice?" Plato's Socrates discovers that it cannot be defined in terms of any actual earthly state but only in terms of an ideal state—the heavenly state within, of which each of us can become a citizen regardless of our external citizenship.[20]

When the third point of view finally emerges in the dissertation, it is not (as it would usually be in Hegel) the reconciliation of the contradiction between two previously opposed points of view. If "Aristophanes' imaginative representation of Socrates has come closest to the truth," it is not because the contradiction has been resolved in Hegel's fashion; instead, it has been preserved. For Aristophanes, as I have already observed, *de-fines* or *locates* Socrates by keeping him "suspended" between earth and heaven, the actual and the ideal, the *external* and the *internal*. Such suspension is in fact consistent with the contradictory character of the poet's "imaginative representation" as visualized by Hegel himself. But in

Hegel's analysis of mental operations, the contradiction involved at this level between the *external* and the *internal* is overcome when the *Aufhebung* takes place that reaches the higher level of thought or reflection.

THE ESTHETIC

If imaginative representation comes closest to the truth, if it takes the poet to define the philosopher as ironist, then the next task is to define the poet. This approach to *Either/Or* would link it up with the dissertation. But Kierkegaard prefers to regard *Either/Or* as itself the starting point of his authorship." One justification already suggested for this preference is that here Kierkegaard reaches with his starting point the level of principle—the principle of contradiction. But since he is contradicting Hegel, another justification is that esthetics is in Hegel's system the first stage in the development of absolute spirit (the three stages are art, religion, philosophy), and it is at this first stage that the presupposition that the *internal* is the *external* gets its initial and most striking plausibility, as Hegel himself claims: "The most general thing that can be said . . . about the ideal of art comes to this—the true [the internal] which the artist would express has existence only as it unfolds into external reality [the work of art]."[21] Thus truth becomes during the esthetic stage in Hegel externally accessible to our perception (*aisthēsis*).

Later in his career Kierkegaard will argue that the predominant human point of view toward life is esthetic. In fact when he supersedes the multiple points of view of his pseudonymous "authorship" by addressing posterity in his own name in *The Point of View for My Work as an Author,* he acknowledges in an addendum, "Now [i.e., in 1847] one hardly hears the system any more mentioned," whereas "the pseudonyms in their time, when . . . all the talk was about system, always system, aimed a blow at the system with the category of 'the individual,' " This does not mean that *Either/Or* has become dated, for Kierkegaard can still defend having started out with the esthetic point of view. The procedural problem, he explains, is a problem of "determination"—"to bring a man to a definite position [*bestemt sted*]," and it is only by arriving at a position which is definite that one becomes an individual. (What this entails we shall begin examining in the next chapter.) But "one must first and foremost take care to find a man where he is and start there." By and large a man's point of view is confused and indefinite, yet remaining confused and indefinite is indulgence in "imaginary illusion" (*indbildning*). Since "imaginary illusion" is an esthetic phenomenon, Kierkegaard "must start out as an esthetic writer, and up to a point he must maintain this role."[22]

The character of this illusion turns on the confusion between the *in-*

ternal and the *external*, which we have already recognized *Either/Or* is designed to expose. This is the confusion which seemed to gain plausibility during the esthetic stage in Hegel, when truth becomes externally accessible to our perception. Eremita will expose this confusion psychologically by exhibiting the *ambiguous, contradictory,* and *unstable* relation between perception and imagination. I shall soon examine his procedure.

But it might be noted first that in *Point of View* Kierkegaard does consider the alternative approach to starting out esthetically:

> Denounce the magic spell of the esthetic. . . . Where does this get you? That inwardly with a secret passion men cherish the magic spell.[23]

Thus Kierkegaard visualizes himself as having had instead to "represent the esthetic with all its magic spell, captivate if possible the other man, present the esthetic with the sort of passion which exactly suits him. . . ."[24]

From this later point of view toward his work, Kierkegaard lines up the levels at their two starting points: "The movement described by the authorship is this: from the poet (from esthetics), from philosophy (from speculation) . . . , from the pseudonymous *Either/Or.* . . ." These two levels are related; we have seen that Kierkegaard's analysis is *bifocal,* and much of his dialectical skill is exercised in securing *interplay* between the levels. He assures us in *Point of View* that "the movement described . . . as away from the philosophical, the systematic . . . is essentially the same movement as from the poet."[25]

THE POET

Let us start "from the poet" and extrapolate later to "the philosophical." Contradiction between the *internal* and the *external* is exhibited in the first selection found in *Either:*

> What is a poet? An unhappy man who within harbors a deep anguish in his heart but whose lips are so fashioned that the moans and shrieks which pass out over them are transformed into beautiful music. His situation is like that of the unhappy victims whom the tyrant Phalaris imprisoned in a brazen bull and slowly tortured over a steady fire: their shrieks could not reach the tyrant's ears so as to terrify him; when they reached him, they sounded like sweet music. And men crowd around the poet and say to him, "Sing soon again," which is to say, "May new sufferings torment [*martyre*] your soul, and may your lips be fashioned as before, for the shrieks would only make us anxious, but the music is delightful." And the critics [*recensenterne*] come forward and

say, "Quite correct, as it should be according to the rules of esthetics."
Now it is to be understood that a critics resembles a poet to a hair, aside
from having no anguish in his heart, no music on his lips. I tell you I
would rather be a swineherd and be understood by the swine than a
poet and be misunderstood by men.[26]

In his journal Kierkegaard explains that this first selection poses the
"problem" (*opgave*) of *Either/Or* as a "whole."[27] It also illustrates traits
of an existential dialectic with which we are familiar in Heidegger and
Sartre. It is an attempt to define the poet, a short-run attempt as compared
with the long-run attempt in *Either/Or* as a whole. It is in fact the first
of a series of brief selections which are characterized in the preface as
"aphorisms." *Aphorizein* in Greek means "to separate off, mark off by
boundaries." Thus "a-phorism" has an etymology similar to that of "definition." But this short-run definition, like the long-run, is a *definitio a
contrario*: an existential repudiation of poetry which raises at once a
doubt about the validity of esthetic experience and about the feasibility
of communication. The repudiation may also be meant as a parody of the
fashion in which Hegel starts out his *Aesthetics,* by dealing with various
doubts as to its "value" (*Würdigkeit*) especially as a subject for critical
philosophical treatment.[28]

Kierkegaard may also have in mind a specific passage in the *Aesthetics*:
"Shrieks, whether of suffering or joy, are not music at all. Even in suffering, the sweet tone of lament must sound through the sufferings and trans-
figure them [i.e., an *Aufhebung* takes place], so that the trouble seems
worth suffering in order to understand such a lament. This is the sweet
melody, the song in *all* art." Thus the passage ends with Hegel reaching
for general scope (which may have attracted Kierkegaard's attention),
although earlier Hegel was merely protesting that "an outburst [*Aus-
bruch*] should not remain unrestrained, if the Ideal is not to be surrendered."[29] Kierkegaard may be suggesting that he is throwing off the re-
straint aphorisms as a literary form impose by classifying these aphorisms
as "outbursts" (*udbrud*).[30]

The content of each of these aphorisms, Eremita explains, is "an essential mood."[31] In the case of the first, the mood which is essential to being
a poet is suffering. That existentialism employs a method of definition
which is associated with the *affective* content of what is defined we have
known ever since we examined Heidegger's analysis of moodiness, in
which something as indefinite as a mood, or even as "a lack of mood,"
turned out to have its own definiteness. We also watched Sartre borrow
this "lack of mood." Finally, the epigraph has alerted us to the fact that
Either/Or would be a dialectic of the passions.

THE REFLEXIVE REACTION

Earlier I noted the *ex-sistential* function of the e-motions in Sartre. The contradiction between the *internal* and the *external*, which is exposed in the definition of the poet in the first aphorism, is later redescribed. In a *recapitulation* it is explained that the first aphorism "poses a *splid* ["rift" or "dislocation"] in existence."[32] What is dislocated ultimately is the relation between the poet as an individual and his audience: the poet's mood of suffering is arrayed in opposition to his audience's mood of enjoyment. (The contradiction between suffering and enjoyment will remain basic to the dialectic of the passions in *Either.*) But this *bilateral* relation is not evenly balanced: the poet is not just suffering internally, while his poetry, as the external expression of his suffering, is enjoyed by his audience; at a higher level he is also suffering internally from this discrepancy between the *internal* and the *external*. This contradiction is never reconciled by an *Aufhebung*; instead, it becomes the repudiation of his role as a poet along with his audience: "I would rather be a swineherd and be understood by the swine than a poet and be misunderstood by men." The final dislocation, discrepancy, contradiction is that the poet can only be defined, "what is a poet" can only be determined, by reference to the moment when he would no longer be a poet. But this reference is not merely negative. This repudiation of his audience is a *reflexive* resolution of the poet's identity crisis, though it is not a resolution in the Hegelian sense; as when Socrates was defined as an ironist, the contradiction is not reconciled but preserved.

The *reflexive* character of his resolution is generalized by the epigraph *Ad se ipsum* (To oneself"), which is prefixed to the aphorisms. Confronted by the misunderstanding of other men, the poet can address only himself, become his own audience. Such a resolution warrants attention to the autobiographical fact that most of the aphorisms are entries transcribed from the journal Kierkegaard kept in order (he explained in one of them) "to let my thoughts appear with the umbilical cord of their first mood."[33] In other words, he wanted to keep the *reflexive* reference to his immediate experience still attached, without having to face up to the prospect of eventually refurbishing these thoughts for publication.

Reflexive reference remains crucial to *Either/Or*. The last sentence of *Or* announces, "Only the truth which edifies is truth for you."[34] "Edifying" truth is to be taken here in its etymological sense: *Or* is a summons to "reconstruct" your life. You will recognize in *Or* that your life has become fragmented by having been lived from an esthetic point of view, so that you have lost your identity. At a higher level the summons is also a reassertion of Kierkegaard's opposition to Hegel, who was disdainful of edification and satisfied, we recall, to live in "a shack." In the long run this ethical reconstruction of your life is also to be opposed to the movement of *Aufhebung* with which reflection reconstructs experiences in Hegel at a higher level where philosophy transcends your particular life as an individual.

AUFHEBUNG

In defining the poet Eremita is starting the prolonged process of defining the esthetic point of view toward life. In *Either* he is defining the poet poetically; an aphorism is a distinctively poetic or esthetic form of definition, matching the content of what is to be defined. But as I have anticipated, the problem of the esthetic content is psychologically a problem of determining the relation between perception and imagination. Although the first aphorism defined the poet in terms of the contradiction between the *internal* and the *external*, this contradiction was represented externally as a *bilateral* relation between him and his audience. However, once the poet becomes his own audience, by virtue of the *reflexive* movement *ad se ipsum*, the contradiction becomes *bifocal* in a fashion which is a parody of the Hegelian *Aufhebung*, with which particularity is transcended:

> No one can take my stronghold by storm. From it I swoop down to the actual world [*virkeligheden*] grasp my loot; but I do not remain down there. My loot I bring back home. It is the picture [*billede*] I weave into the tapestries of my castle [*slot*]. There I live as one dead. There I immerse everything I have experienced in a baptism of forgetfulness unto an eternal recollection. Everything temporal and contingent is forgotten and canceled out. . . .[35]

Distinguishing the two levels or foci brings out a contradiction latent in the indefiniteness, the ambiguity, of the esthetic point of view itself. Traditionally "esthetic" referred etymologically to an actual "experience" (*aisthēsis*), in the rudimentary sense of an "awareness," a "sense perception." This reference remains a traditional justification for Kierkegaard's "esthetic" starting point. When we return later to the preface, we shall see that Eremita starts out with sensory experience, like Descartes and Hegel in the *Phenomenology*. But during the eighteenth century "esthetic" had come to refer philosophically to an artistically heightened "experience." What goes on between these two levels or foci in the aphorism I interpret as a parody of the movement of *Aufhebung* from the level of sense perception to the level of the imagination.

The distinction of level can be discerned in the ambiguity of the term *billede*. Like its German cognate, *Bild*, it can mean either an "image" *internal* to the mind or an *external* "picture," and it is the root of the

Danish *indbildning* (cognate with the German *Einbildung*), which, I
have noted, can refer not only to the "imagination" but also to the
"imagination" of something "illusory." In *Either/Or* it acquires a reference to the illusion that the contradiction between the *external* and the
internal can be overcome esthetically.

Kierkegaard is reinstating this contradiction. His philosophy is not
simply a philosophy of "inwardness," though it is too often interpreted as
if it were; the contradiction between the *internal* and the *external* retains
a double thrust, which is dramatized by the fact that what Eremita was
doubting in the first sentence of his preface is "that the external is the
internal, and the internal the external." Hence Kierkegaard regularly
resorts to spatial metaphors, granted that they have to be followed up by
some reassertion of the contradiction, unless the purposes of irony are
better served by leaving the contradiction implicit.

The first level in the aphorism I have cited is the moment of actual
experience—"perception" or "impression (*Anschauung*). It is the moment
in Hegel which was described earlier as the mind's being "exposed to external influences." To allow for the artist's initiative, as the existentialist
must ("I swoop down to the actual world"), we could characterize this
moment as the movement of the mind exposing itself to these influences.
But the artist does not remain at the level of actual experience. The second moment is the movement of "recollection" (*erindring/Erinnerung*)—
an "internalizing" movement. This movement has to be considered first
as the negative aspect of *Aufhebung*, when the "temporal and contingent"
character of an actual experience is "canceled out." (This is the character
which, I indicated earlier, the existentialist insists experience should retain.) The aphorism interpolates "forgotten" to play up the contradiction
with the process of "recollection." The artist forgets the actual (the
"temporal and contingent") experience, for it is no longer needed once
the mind has internalized it as an "image." The "eternal recollection" is
the positive aspect of *Aufhebung*. Whatever is "essential" to the experience is "preserved" as "true." When the process of preservation is esthetic
in the artistic sense, the experience which was previously internalized as
an "image" is now externalized in the "picture" the artist weaves into
the tapestries of his "castle," where it can be perceived. The contradiction
between the *internal* and the *external* has been overcome.

But there is still an implicit difference between Eremita's handling of
this relation and Hegel's. In Kierkegaard, as the rubric for all the
aphorisms indicates, the *orientation* is *ad se ipsum*, toward the poet's own
self, but the outcome of the dialectical movement in Hegel is a system
(including, at the lower level of his *Aesthetics*, a "system of the arts," as
we shall later see) which transcends such personal reference. Here Kierke-

gaard's metaphor of the "castle" (*slot*/*Schloss*) may be significant both in his own esthetic terms and in terms of his extension of the metaphor to Hegel's system. For Hegel, both in interpreting his philosophy as a system and in his *Aesthetics*, frequently plays with derivatives from the root *schliessen* ("to close," "conclude"), in order to bring out the autonomous, self-enclosing character of the system or the work of art. This character of a work of art is its apparent advantage in Hegel over an ethical action. Whatever autonomy is achieved by an ethical action depends on its fulfillment of an *internal* intention; an ethical action is not something *external* which can be hung on the wall of a castle or a museum.

DISCONTINUITY

This aphorism we have been examining is one which defines the aphoristical procedure itself. As I have noted, each aphorism "belongs to the moment of an essential mood." The aphoristic procedure (form) is to "separate off" from the rest of experience whatever experience (content) can be taken as "essential" to the "mood" of the "moment," so that it can be elevated to the realm of art where it becomes self-enclosed. Since the mood of each aphorism is essential and separable, successive aphorisms "often contradict each other."[36] This discontinuity of the aphorisms is itself "separated off" for comment is one of the aphorisms: "I seem destined [*bestemt*] to have to suffer every possible mood [*stemning*], to have to acquire experience in every direction."[37]

Eremita draws our particular attention in the preface to the contradictory relation between the *first* and the *last* aphorism: "As the one feels for the suffering that lies in being a poet, the other enjoys the satisfaction which lies in always having the laugh on one's side."[38] Kierkegaard is punning: "side" translates *side* and "last" translates *sidst*. His punning is designed to play up an ironical reference to Hegel's *Aufhebung* as overcoming "one-sidedness."[39] On one side (the first aphorism) there is suffering; on the other (the last aphorism) enjoyment. This relation between *first* and *last* is dialectically significant, for it often takes the entire course of a dialectical development to reach a point which is opposed to the point where one started out. When Kierkegaard reaches this point he is in effect breaking the circle in Hegel where "the essential requirement is that the whole of the science [of logic] be within itself a circle in which the first is also the last and the last is also the first," where "the science" is "a circle, coiled into itself, its end being coiled back to the start."[40] Kierkegaard is breaking out of the "enclosure," the "castle" which is Hegel's system.

Let me quote enough of the *last* aphorism to indicate the contradiction with the *first* and how Hegel's *Aufhebung* is parodied:

> Something wonderful has happened to me. I was caught up in ecstasy to the seventh heaven. There sat all the gods in assembly. By special grace I was granted the privilege of making a wish. . . . For a moment I was at a loss. Then I addressed myself to the gods as follows: . . . I choose this one thing, that I may always have the laugh on my side.[41]

The frustrating contradiction in the first aphorism was between the poet's own suffering and the enjoyment of his audience, from which he also suffered as a misunderstanding of his suffering. This contradiction is overcome by the satisfaction he now enjoys himself. He is still arrayed as an individual in opposition to other men, but he is no longer at the mercy of a tyrannical audience or reduced to the companionship of swine; he regains the initiative and now enjoys the divine superiority of laughter. But such an *Aufhebung* is not Hegelian: the orientation is still *reflexive*, *ad se ipsum*, "on my side." Personal reference has not been transcended.

LITERATURE

We are not quite ready to turn from the aphorisms to the longer essays which follow in *Either/Or*. When we do so we shall discover that Eremita is employing the "storytelling method" which Johannes Climacus assumed is required if a life is to be treated and which he had opposed to the philosophical method with which Hegel had constructed his system and overlooked his own life. This opposition poses one version of the persistent question that must be raised regarding existentialism. Sometimes a philosopher will jeopardize his reputation by supposing that philosophy has some relevance to life. But it is really intolerable for him to become literary. "Aphorisms" and "storytelling" are literary procedures. Are the dialectical traits we have been sorting out of merely literary import rather than genuinely philosophical?

Either/Or may be an exposition of the principle of contradiction. Sartre may define "the obscene" by pitting it against "the graceful" and the predetermined wiggle against the voluntary walking. Characters may be portrayed as contradictory composites: a Franco-American, a respectful prostitute. The criminal Genet may be a saint without breasts, Victor Eremita may exemplify "sympathetic irony," and his poet may suffer in his heart with music on his lips. Merleau-Ponty may likewise dramatize oppositions, as is evident even from his titles, *Humanism and Terror*, *Sense and Non-Sense*, *The Visible and the Invisible*. But instead of considering such manipulations of contradictions philosophical, should we not admit that it is a standard literary procedure—in fact almost anybody's game? Indeed some of my examples from the existentialists themselves were from their literary or journalistic writings.

Similar examples can be found in more strictly literary writers. The proclamation by Camus that he was not an existentialist was one of the few matters on which Sartre continued to agree with the former friend who had arranged for him to make his American trip. (Sartre thought too, I suspect, that Camus was not even a philosopher.) Yet some of Camus's devices seem close to those I have distinguished as characteristic of an existential dialectic. In *The Fall* Camus presents as the protagonist a Judge-Penitent. To be a judge is to function officially in a *bilateral* or *bipersonal* situation: a judge judges some other man. But a judge cannot ex officio also be a penitent, precisely because it is his function to judge objectively without reference to himself—to his subjective feelings. He must judge and perhaps condemn the other man, whereas a penitent is judging and condemning himself. In fact penitence is not the sort of thing that can be undertaken convincingly ex officio; its *reflexive* reference might distract one from performing any official function in relation to other men. Thus we have here a contradictory *definition* of someone's character or role, and the definition accentuates a *reflexive* reference.[42] In short we have a thinker who was avowedly not an existentialist but who also applies two procedures which have been singled out as distinctively existential.

Of course we might regard Camus as on the edge of existentialism, as we might Beckett, who can be as careful when he manipulates contradictions as Kierkegaard in handling a "disrelation" as the expression of a "relation":

> The Dives-Lazarus symbiosis, as intimate as that of fungoid and algoid in lichen. . . . Here scabs, lucre, etc., there torment, bosom, etc., both here and there *gulf*. The absurdity, here or there, of either without the other, the inaccessible other. In death they did not cease to be divided. Who predeceased? A painful period for both.

But we would not want to identify Beckett as a philosopher.

Interplay between levels is another existential procedure which I have emphasized. But again, what procedure is more trite in literature? In a novel of Iris Murdoch's a character responds to the behest, "C'est impossible de trop plier les genoux, impossible, impossible." Interpreting the refrain as "the voice of some teacher . . . from convent days, from earliest childhood," she is tempted to kneel in prayer. But when she receives the instruction later in the novel and asks,

Who had said those beautiful words to her and what did they mean?
Then suddenly she remembered. It had been her skiing instructor at
Davos. . . . So that was all that it was, another senseless fragment of
ownerless memory drifting about like a dead leaf.

Perhaps not entirely "senseless," not just "drifting" or quite "dead." In a
moment she will herself be "dead," "senseless" and no longer remembering. But in the mean time *interplay* of some sort has taken place between
levels: between prayer as a spiritual activity and skiing as one of the most
physical, between the "beautiful" and the "senseless," and possibly with
the ambiguity of "senseless."[43]

CONTINUITY

How then is existentialism still to be distinguished from other intellectual performances which also apply the procedures that have been
singled out? The most obvious distinction is that existential reliance on
these procedures is not sporadic but continuously maintained until that
generality of scope is achieved which has traditionally been regarded as a
differentiating trait of a philosophy. But so far what I have stressed is the
discontinuity of an existential dialectic—the fact that its contradictions are
more disruptive than those featured by Hegel or Marx. The most recent
example has been the discontinuity of the contradictory aphorisms with
which Kierkegaard's "authorship" started out.

In his preface Eremita stressed the discontinuity of his aphorisms by
explaining that he happened to find the papers which compose *Either/Or*
in the drawer of a desk he bought and that the papers he classified as
"aphorisms" were on "slips of paper" which "lay loose in their hiding
place."[44] This explanation doubtless encouraged the critical suspicion,
as Kierkegaard reports it, that he had in *Either/Or* unloaded "a collection
of loose papers I had lying in my desk." But the suspicion infuriated him:
"As a matter of fact it was the reverse." And he insisted that *Either/Or*
"has a plan from the first word to the last." Kierkegaard could not have
been entirely taken by surprise by the criticism. Eremita in his preface ad-
vises *Either/Or* to "elude if possible the attention of critics,"[45] and his
contempt for them finds advance expression too in the first aphorism,
where we are told how they are able to supply the rules of esthetics for
writing poetry, notwithstanding the contradiction that they cannot
actually write it themselves.

What particularly annoyed Kierkegaard was the inability of Heiberg,
Denmark's leading critic and a Hegelian to boot, to fathom the rules of
dialectic which had been applied in the esthetics of *Either*. Heiberg could
not discern any continuity, for he complained in his review;

One stumbles upon many piquant reflections; some of them perhaps are even profound; one doesn't know for certain, for when one believes one has seen a point one is again disoriented.[46]

As a Hegelian Heiberg did not recognize that Eremita's dialectic was individualistic and designed to disorient and dislocate the reader, in order to induce him to take the initiative and discover the "plan" that still holds in spite of the discontinuities introduced by successive contradictions.

Eremita does provide some help. For his failure to rearrange the loose slips of paper, he offers an extenuation of which we have not yet taken full advantage:

> I have left the ordering of the single aphorisms to chance. That the separate expressions often contradict one another seemed quite in order, since each one of them belongs to the moment of an essential mood. I did not think it worth the trouble to adopt an order that would make these contradictions less striking. I followed chance.

There is *interplay* here between discontinuity, as the disorder that chance promotes, and order. That the successive aphorisms contradict each other is not itself contradictory but "quite in order,"[47] for it accentuates the "separateness" which the aphoristic form must impose on a "mood" if it is to bring out what is "essential" to it.

Moreover, when the critics generalized from the admitted looseness of the slips of paper on which the aphorisms were written, they were overlooking the distinctions Eremita drew between the aphorisms and the other papers and between the papers, including the aphorisms, which he assigned to A as the exponent in *Either* of the esthetic point of view, and those he assigned to B as the exponent in *Or* of the ethical point of view. He may have left the ordering of the aphorisms to chance, but he did sort out the other papers:

> I tried to arrange in order the papers as well as I could. In the case of those written by B this was rather easy. Each of his letters presupposes the one preceding.

This continuity conforms to their internal content: a defense of marriage as a continuously maintained relation between one individual and another, whereby the ethical individual "takes time into his service" and forces an order, a continuity, on the course of his life by his own choice.[48] For "character is essentially continuity." When the esthete chooses, he "chooses only for the moment and accordingly can choose something else for the next moment," but ethical choice is "the ethical victory of continuity."[49]

There is also a relation between form and content in the case of the papers of A. As opposed to B, the poet or esthete portrayed in these papers indulges in chance, momentary experiences.[50] Thus the disorder, the discontinuity, in the sequence of his aphorisms is a matter of "chance"; yet it is "quite in order" with respect to the content (as we have already seen with respect to the form) because living by chance is a requirement of the esthetic life. The lack of continuity has been illustrated by one of the aphorisms already cited. Let me cite another: "My foot slips [*glider*]. My life is still a poetic existence."[51] *Glide* is the Danish cognate of the German *gleiten*, which in Heidegger characterizes the unsteady, uncontrolled movement of dislocation that takes us from one mood to another. Such *glissement* in Sartre's *affective* but more emotional dialectic tends to become characteristic of the movement of consciousness in general.[52] What the aphorisms indicate is that living a poetic existence is a matter of "slipping" from moment to moment. "Suddenly," the aphorism goes on, "fate shows me how everything I do to oppose [this movement] remains a moment in such an existence." Thus even the higher-level effort, which we have examined, to capture in an aphorism the momentary mood as "essential" is still to live a slippery, chancy, discontinuous poetic existence.

The contrasting continuity of his life means that B has acquired an occupation and a personal identity, so that he is identifiable not only as B but also as "Judge William." But A can only be identified as A, inasmuch as the discontinuity of his life precludes acquiring any actual identity as an individual. Given this discontinuity of content, there is a corresponding editorial difficulty in putting his papers in order:

> Arranging the papers of A in order was not so easy. I have accordingly let chance determine the order—that is to say, I have left them in the order in which I found them.[53]

We must again recognize the relation between *external* form and *internal* content. If Eremita lets chance determine the external ordering of the papers that can be assigned to A, it is because A himself let chance determine what happened next in his life.

Eremita's comments as editor illustrate how he is appealing, in opposition to Hegel, from philosophy to life. The continuity imposed by Hegel's dialectic was "the patience of the concept"; the continuity that Judge William achieves as the ethical individual is that of a patiently maintained choice. And if the poet's life is in contrast (at least as so far interpreted by the aphorisms) a succession of discontinuous and contradictory moods, it is because, as the poet admits in one of the aphorisms;

> I lack the patience to live. I am not able to see the grass grow, but, since I cannot, I do not care to look at it at all.[54]

The organic continuity with which grass grows does not lend itself to the esthetic, aphoristic procedure of "separating out" successive, momentary, discontinuous experiences.

DEVELOPMENT

A dialectical method cannot function simply by separating, contradicting, and indulging in *interplay*. The *dynamic* process of *definition*, which I have illustrated from some of the aphorisms, must expand into a process of *development*. Even a contradiction, if it is to become philosophical, must be allowed to develop its implications, until it gains the scope which the length of Kierkegaard's *Either/Or* suggests is sought, not to mention the length of Sartre's *Being and Nothingness*. Thus the aphorisms are only the initial form taken by esthetic experience in *Either*. And though Eremita has not tried to arrange the aphorisms themselves in any order, he has located them in relation to the other papers he assigns to the esthetic stage: "I have placed them first because it seemed to me that they might best be regarded as provisional glimpses of what the longer essays develop more connectedly [*sammenhængende*]." Quite aside from the longer-run contrast between the discontinuity of the esthetic stage and the continuity of the ethical stage, there is an adjustment during the esthetic stage between the sharp discontinuity with which the poet seems "destined to have to suffer every possible mood" and "to acquire experience in every direction," so that his "foot slips," and the relative continuity of the more connected development exhibited by the longer essays. That this continuity can be only relative is indicated by Eremita's insistence in his preface that "a single coherent [*sammenhængende*] esthetic point of view toward life can hardly be carried out."[55] We shall in fact encounter the different points of view of different individuals in *Either*, although we shall encounter in *Or* only the single point of view which Judge William attempts to carry out coherently. The first of the longer essays is entitled "The Immediate Stages of the Erotic." Now a stage itself is a specific procedure for adjusting the relation between discontinuity and continuity. It is, as I indicated earlier, separated from another stage or stages within some overall continuous development. The separations are marked by the shifts in *direction* which are introduced with a different point of view or perspective. In Kierkegaard's "authorship" the most obvious continuity is his preoccupation with "passion," and the most obvious discontinuities are introduced by the shifts in the meaning of this term. While its eventual religious significance is hinted by the protesting epigraph of *Either*, "Is reason alone baptized?" the "passions" remain "pagan" during the esthetic stage. The boundary of the ethical stage is approached when the concept of *pathos* is adopted from Hegel as referring to an ethically justified passion (e.g., Antigone's passion to bury her brother).[56] When the religious stage is reached, passion explicitly takes on the ordinary Greek meaning of *pathos* (or the Latin *passio*)—suffering, as instanced by the passion of Christ, the paradigm of suffering for martyrs like Kierkegaard, or Flaubert and Genet as they are interpreted by Sartre.[57]

In my concluding chapter the issue of adjustment between discontinuity and continuity will be brought into final focus by concentrating on Kierkegaard's opposition to Hegel, since complete generality of scope is precisely what the latter attempted to attain with his system of philosophy, whereas what Kierkegaard is offering is fragmentary and incomplete. I am deferring the question of the system as such, since its construction is a long-term undertaking for Hegel, and Kierkegaard cannot undertake its fragmentation all at once. But both Hegel's and Kierkegaard's undertakings are carried out by stages, and in the present chapter I shall try to discover the difference between them with respect to this apparently common procedure.

We can only determine what transpires during a stage in Kierkegaard by a commentary that follows out its development. But before we do so, let me offer some briefer and simpler literary examples, granted that they do not attain the scope which Hegel and Kierkegaard attain by stages.

The first example I used before to exhibit the dislocating character of *ex-sistentialist* reflection:

> But then, this also, this cynical distaste for her own role, was deliberately put on? And this contempt for that distaste which she was about to contrive, was it not also play acting? And this doubting of that contempt . . . ?[58]

The development here is continuous in that she is reflecting on her role playing, but it is discontinuous in that at each stage she tends to discard the role she is playing or about to play.

A standard literary procedure, which we shall soon watch Kierkegaard employ with reference to Don Juan and Antigone, is to offer different versions of the same story; and when the different versions are arranged in some significant sequence, the procedure can be regarded as approximating the use of stages. Consider Kafka's "Four Legends concerning Prometheus:"

> According to the first, he was clamped to a rock in the Caucasus for betraying the secrets of the gods to men, and the gods sent eagles to feed on his liver, which was perpetually renewed.

According to the second, Prometheus, goaded by the pain of the tearing beaks, pressed himself deeper and deeper into the rock until he became one with it.

According to the third, his treachery was forgotten in the course of thousands of years, the gods forgotten, the eagles, he himself forgotten.

According to the fourth, everyone became weary of the meaningless affair. The gods became weary, the eagles became weary, the wound closed wearily. There remained the inexplicable mass of rock.[59]

An overall continuity is assured by the fact that all four legends concern Prometheus. But my earlier distinction between a "stage" and a "subject matter" should be recalled, for we could not describe Prometheus as the subject matter of the legends, since a subject matter is somthing that can be held fixed; and while the first version summarizes the traditional legend about Prometheus, each of the succeeding versions is a revision which carries us a further stage away from the original legend. We need not concern ourselves with the exact implications of the details. But the process of revision itself is clearly designed to generate contradictions: the focus shifts from the excruciating suffering of Prometheus's soft liver until finally weariness leaves us with the hard, unfeeling rock; instead of his becoming "unbound" from the rock, as in the traditional legend, he becomes "one" with it; instead of becoming legendary, he becomes forgotten. The survival of these legends themselves then becomes as "inexplicable" itself as the "mass of rock."

Contradiction, or some other pairing procedure, often controls the employment of stages. Past and present are a favorite pair. Lillian Hellman explains in her autobiography, "I wanted to see what was there for me once, what is there for me now."[60] A double-entry method is likewise employed in the diary that composes the "passion story" of *Stages*: morning entries report the sufferer's state of mind "a year ago today," whereas the sleepless midnight entries report his present state of mind.

THE LADDER

The metaphors "level" and "stage" can often be applied to the same intellectual performance, but a rough distinction can be drawn: where the relation between levels involves *interplay* in the vertical dimension, a stage involves interconnected development, including *interplay*, in what Kierkegaard himself describes as the "longitudinal" dimension.[61] However, the contrast between vertical and horizontal should not be drawn too sharply. Examine Kierkegaard's pseudonym Johannes Climacus. He gave this name, we remember, to the unfinished work in which he had started out to become a philosopher. Later Kierkegaard retrieved Climacus as the pseudonymous author of his *Philosophical Fragments* and his *Concluding Unscientific Postscript*, the longest of his works. Johannes was a Byzantine monk who had earned the appellation "Climacus" ("he who climbs the ladder" [*klimax*]) by writing a mystical theology—*The Steps to Paradise (Scala Paradisi)*.[62] Now *klimax* refers etymologically to "something that leans" (*klinei*) and hence may reinforce the image of a slanted ascent which is incorporated in the metaphor of "steps." *Klimax* can also refer to the rhetorical figure of building up to a climax (*gradatio* in Latin), whereby the development of an argument gains momentum during the stages (*gradus*) of its elaboration.[63]

If the metaphor of "level" should sometimes be emended to "stage," it is because my earlier characterization of a dialectical analysis as a *relational* analysis involving *interplay* is too weak. "Stage" brings out the extent to which the interplay between levels expands into an interconnected sequential development. But "stage" should sometimes be emended to "sphere," in order to indicate that the interconnected development remains *interplay* while developing into "collateral" (i.e., secondary) dialectics between levels and so does not constitute a simply linear sequence.[64]

The sequence is, rather, a matter of "consequences." When I earlier described an existential dialectic as maintained until a certain generality of scope was attained, I was anticipating the kind of inference that is controlled by Kierkegaard's application of the criterion of *konsekvens*, usually translated as "consistency." Earlier we encountered the criterion of "constancy" applied by Kierkegaard to his "reference" to Socrates. Its application was feasible only because of Socrates' own "consistency."[65] In his case the criterion may have seemed simply ethical. Now we are ready to take into account its broader significance. Thus a better translation might be "implications," for "consistency" as well as "consequences" might suggest a sequence which is simply linear, whereas the root of "implications can suggest the "folding" or interweaving which permits the *interplay* between levels in existentialism. (In fact both Heidegger and Merleau-Ponty play with the metaphor of "fold" [*Falt/pli*].[66] Since Climacus proclaims that "consistency" is a *scala paradisi*, it is clear that the levels involved are stages, and that the "consistency" at stake must not be confused with the logical consistency of a formal deduction.

Beginning with my first comment in my introduction on the problem of starting point, I have regularly employed "implication" in what must have seemed merely its usual casual sense. But I was anticipating Kierkegaard's more technical usage, which should now (especially when taken in conjunction with his term "collateral") correct any surviving impression that dialectical *interplay* is composed of random motions. While

Kierkegaard is opposing Hegel's conception of dialectic as a logically necessary development that also holds at the level of existence, he describes his own dialectic as a "consistent development."[67] The "consistency" in question is achieved by a "development" in which the "implications" or "consequences" are followed out—for example, of adopting an esthetic point of view toward life. The implicit choice is contingent— up to you as an individual. But it carries a range of "implications"; from it a range of "consequences" follow, granted that their exact specification will vary from one individual to another. Here as elsewhere a distinction of level is to be respected, while acknowledging the interplay between levels. The individual is merely asked to recognize that "implications" do develop, "consequences" do follow, from his implicit choice, insofar as it can be characterized as the adoption of an esthetic point of view. Sartre's demonstration that his bourgeois intellectual reader is a "slimy rat" proceeds in much the same fashion,[68] without his pretending that your sliminess or rattiness is exactly the same as mine. His demonstration is generic, and he would only have us recognize the choice that is implicit in our accepting our class status.

At the same time there is always with dialectic the risk of unsteadiness in managing these implications. Consider the predicament which Climacus faces in his effort to be consistent:

> As long as he was laboring to climb up . . . he was afraid of losing the numerous implications which he had already formulated but which still had not become entirely clear to him and necessary. When we see someone carrying a large number of breakable articles stacked one upon the other, we are not surprised that he walks unsteadily and every moment tries to keep his balance. But if we do not see the stack, we smile, just as many people smiled at Johannes Climacus without suspecting that . . . his soul was uneasy [*ængstelig*] lest a single one of the implications should fall out and the whole stack fall apart.[69]

PATIENCE

Now it might seem appropriate to undertake a commentary on the way "implications" stack up in *Stages on Life's Way*, for there all three stages (esthetic, religious, ethical) are distinguished. But if the criterion of *konsekvens* demands that we follow out "implications," Climacus's uneasiness is a warning that one of them might fall out. Perhaps more than one. I have already admitted that a close commentary is needed to bring out the continuity of the development during a stage, and we could hardly expect to cover all three stages. Furthermore the sequential (or "consequential") relation between stages must also be respected. Thus Climacus further warns in *Postscript*;

> Whenever there is a dialectic, there is an eagerness which is so eager to enjoin the second point that in its eagerness it gets rid of the first point and therefore fundamentally makes the second point impossible.[70]

A dialectical development should not be short-circuited by skipping over whatever point is made at its first stage. This is why we cannot expect to make serious progress beyond the problem of starting point in this volume.

We cannot blithely anticipate the conclusion regarding Hegel's system which Climacus finally reaches in *Concluding Unscientific Postscript*, the last of the works composing Kierkegaard's "authorship." We cannot even skip *Either/Or* to reach the "second point" which will be made in *Stages*, where (Climacus explains in *Postscript*) "the esthetic and ethical stages are again brought forward as a recapitulation of *Either/Or* but then again as something new,"[71] without having taken fully into account "the first point" made regarding the relation between these stages in *Either/Or*. In fact our advance is held up in interpreting *Either/Or* itself, for Kierkegaard's warning would also keep us from skipping to the "second" and "new" point which will be made in *Or* regarding the relation between it as an ethical stage and *Either* as an esthetic stage. We must then first take into account "the first point" made in *Either* itself regarding the esthetic stage. This might seem to preclude examining the procedure of stages itself. But we shall see that there are stages within this first stage.

We have already met something approximating the procedure of stages in exploring the relation between Sartre's definition of the "obscene" and a portion of his definition of "sadism." We have observed that Heidegger employs essentially the same metaphor as *Stages on Life's Way*, when he conceives experience (*Erfahrung*) as "a journey along a way," and he, like Kierkegaard, curbs our eagerness, insisting that we linger for a while at some "halting place" (*Aufenhalt*), not for the purpose of resting but that we may be impelled to go on more energetically."[72] But I have also already conceded that stages do not constitute a procedure unique to an existential dialectic. Even Kierkegaard's warning against hurrying (and probably Heidegger's too) is an echo of Hegel's pronouncement:

> Impatience demands the impossible—to reach the goal without the means of getting there. Both the length of the way must be endured, for each phase is necessary, and we must linger at each phase.[73]

As I have already emphasized, we must eventually face the question of whether the procedure of stages has any distinctive function when it is employed in tracing the development of the individual in existentialism, as opposed to its application in Hegel to the development of the system.

IMMEDIATE EXPERIENCE

The present question, however, is what is happening to our notion of starting point. Ostensibly Eremita started out with "aphorisms," but the essay which follows these "aphorisms" is entitled "The Immediate Stages of the Erotic," and nothing in experience can precede immediate experience. There are in a sense two starting points in *Either*, even if we neglect the preface. The "aphorisms" have to do with immediate experience, but they do not constitute a stage. They are only (as we have seen Eremita explain in the preface) "provisional glimpses [*glimt*] of what the longer essays develop more connectedly [*sammenhængende*]." And it is the first of these longer essays which constitutes "The Immediate Stages" in *Either*. This first essay is on Mozart's *Don Giovanni*, and it starts out, "From the *moment* that Mozart's music first filled my soul with wonder. . . ."[74] This first phrase makes a transition from the "aphorisms," each of which defines the immediate experience of a momentary mood. Indeed we were given a provisional glimpse of Mozart's *Don Giovanni* in one of the moments captured by an aphorism:

> Two familiar strokes of the violin here at this *moment* in the middle of the street. . . . Now I hear nothing more. Just as they burst forth [*bryde ud*] from the . . . immortal overture, so here they emerge from the noise and confusion of the street. . . . The heavy wagons drown out the notes, which by snatches [*glimtvis*] sounded forth.[75]

Bryde ud suggests the momentariness of the experience which has been glimpsed by the aphorism. This momentariness is stressed in the preface by the classification of the aphorisms as "lyrical expressions" (more literally, "outbursts" [*udbrud*] [76] and by the application to them of the metaphor "lyrical," for we shall soon see the sense in which musical experience is regarded by Eremita as the distinctively momentary or "immediate" form of esthetic experience. What the provisional glimpse (or snatch) of music lacked in the aphorism—more connected development—will now be provided by an analysis of *Don Giovanni*. The relation between the aphorisms and music is indicated not only by their classification as "lyrical expressions" but also by the assimilation of poetry to "beautiful music" in the first aphorism and by the title "Diapsalmata" (i.e., "musical refrains") which is assigned the aphorisms as a whole. Thus the "rift in existence" posed in the first aphorism will be redescribed as a "monstrous dissonance."[77]

Implicit in their classification as "lyrical expressions" as well as in their alternative labels, "Diapsalmata" and "aphorisms," is an *ambiguity* which impels the dialectic on to the essay which follows on *Don Giovanni* and to the remaining essays which are on linguistic forms of art. In fact in the *Don Giovanni* essay itself the ambiguity develops into an explicit opposition between the musical form and any linguistic form. I shall consider this *ambiguity* as soon as I have completed working out the ambiguous relation between a provisional glimpse and the ensuing connected development.

CONNECTED DEVELOPMENT

We can on one hand catch a provisional glimpse of an immediate experience, and this glimpse is appropriate to the immediacy with which its content is given; on the other hand the immediate experience can also become the starting point of a stage. This ambiguity can be described in broad terms, for we are dealing with experience, which is something which we all have. But how we manage to "have" it is a function of the form we impose on it. The aphoristic form was dealt with in the aphorism on aphoristic procedure. There the movement of *Aufhebung* was traced from the level where the artist is exposed to an actual experience up to the level where he is back in his self-enclosed "stronghold" with the experience esthetically recomposed. But in an aphorism it is just a single "picture" (or "image") which the artist weaves into the tapestries of his palace.

We can make a transition from this as it were vertical dimension of an *Aufhebung* to the horizontal dimension by reexamining as temporal the relation between the external "impression" and its "internalization" in "imaginative representation." Hegel himself describes this dimension of an *Aufhebung*:

> When speaking of an impression that has been raised to an imaginative representation, language is quite justified when I say, "I *have* seen this." What is thereby expressed is no mere past but also in fact *presence*; here the past is purely *relative* and exists only in *comparison* of the *immediate* impression with what we now have in representation. But the word "have" employed in the perfect tense has quite peculiarly the meaning of presence; what I have seen is something . . . I still have. . . . In this use of the word "have" can be seen a general sign of the inwardness of the modern mind, which reflects not merely that the past in its immediacy has passed away but also that in mind the past is still preserved.[78]

The aphoristic form of *definition* is an attempt to capture "an essential mood" by "separating" it "off" from any other experience, so that I "have" it and do not just "slide" on to another experience. With an aphorism, as we have seen, the process of appropriation reaches the level where (in Hegel's terms) "the imaginative representation is the property of the mind [*die Intelligenz*], though it is one-sidedly subjective in that the right of property is still conditioned by contrast with immediacy."[79] In other words, "the right" lacks at this level the objective justification which will eventually be established in Hegel at the higher level of thought, so that Kierkegaard's dialectic remains subjective. This may be a reason why Eremita employed the "loot" metaphor for the experience of appropriation in both the aphorism defining the aphoristical procedure and for Don Giovanni's seduction. If the primary meaning of *aphorizein* is "to mark off by boundaries," "to define," its reflexive meaning (of which Kierkegaard would have been aware) is "to mark off for oneself," "appropriate." Presumably the occupant of the castle is a robber baron. Long before Kierkegaard became preoccupied with Don Giovanni, he had expressed surprise that "no one has ever . . . treated the Idea of a master robber." The idea survives as a metaphor. Thus the esthete will be denounced in *Or* for "living by robbery" since he "sneaks up" on his victim and "steals" her "happiest moment." His defense would be the definitional, appropriative function of imaginative reflection—"that those involved lose nothing by this, that they perhaps often do not themselves know what is their most beautiful moment."[80]

CONNECTION

Exactly what takes place in this process of appropriating an experience will be examined more carefully when its phenomenological analysis is contrasted in the sequel with its dialectical analysis, but for the present we are only examining an *ambiguity* which lends itself to a dialectical analysis. Just as a dialectical analysis (at least if it is existential) exposes contradictions, so it can itself be characterized at a higher level by its contradictory procedures: it involves "separating off" an experience from other experiences, but it also involves articulating the connections with other experiences as these connections develop out of the experience.

In other words, there is something *ambiguous* about the attempt to capture an experience in its immediacy so that one can claim to "have" it. The *instability* of the *contradiction* that then develops from this ambiguity impels us to go beyond the immediate experience as a starting point to a stage. The merely negative character of an im-mediate experience is then recognized in retrospect: it is an indefinite, indeterminate experience, and it cannot be defined adequately by "separating" it "off" aphoristically. We must follow out its "implications" as Kierkegaard's criterion of *konsekvens* requires. We do not "have" an experience until we have defined it, determined its meaning (as an experience of anger, love, poverty, guilt, etc.); and we can only determine its meaning by articulating its *relations* connecting it with other experiences. Simply to separate it off and disconnect it from other experiences is not to capture but to abstract from it—from relations which are intrinsic to its being the experience that it is.

There is nothing abstruse about this dialectical development. It can be read into T. S. Eliot's lines:

> We had the experience but missed the meaning
> To recover the meaning is to restore the experience in a
>   different form.[81]

The claim to have had an experience while missing its meaning is *ambiguous*, indeed *contradictory*, for we cannot even identify an experience unless we have at least a provisional glimpse of what it means. Yet the contradiction is not arbitrary but characteristic of how we go about trying to have an experience we feel we have not really "had." On one hand we do try to capture an experience in its immediacy; on the other we also recognize that the immediate experience yields only a glimpse, not the full meaning. Yet if we are then prompted to recover the meaning that is missing, we run afoul of another contradiction: the meaning is not recovered in its original elusive form but has undergone restoration in an effort to stabilize its meaning.

We have in effect proceeded in our interpretation of Eliot, as we did in interpreting Eremita's aphorism, from the "esthetic" in the rudimentary sense of a momentary experience to the "esthetic" in the heightened sense of its artistic recomposition. But we must now make the transition from the single "picture" of the aphorism to the stage, by recognizing the lengthier development that recomposition can involve.

Recomposition takes various forms more developed than the aphorisms. The first aphorism raised the question "What is the poet?" and the poetic answers provided by the aphorisms turn out to be lyric poetry. In the first aphorism poetry was defined by reference to the poet's suffering, and this provisional glimpse will be developed "more connectedly" in a triad of longer essays which begins with "The Ancient Tragic" and which will follow "The Immediate Stages of the Erotic." The next triad will shift from the tragic to its opposite, comedy, and will be a more connected development of the laughter of the last aphorism.

THE IMMEDIATE STAGE

We can consider the first longer essay itself, now that it and the other essays have been located in relation to the aphorisms. Its title page betrays the *bifocal* character of Kierkegaard's dialectic. "The Immediate Stages of the Erotic" assigns the essay its general location in relation to the later essays, which we shall see belong to the mediated or reflective stages of the erotic. The subtitle "The Musical Erotic" assigns "The Immediate Stages of the Erotic" to a particular art. In fact the essay itself is an argument for this assignment.

With its transition beyond the momentary experience of hearing Mozart, which was captured in the aphorism. "The Immediate Stages" develops into an examination of a first connection:

> From the moment that Mozart's music first filled my soul with wonder . . . , I have found it a loving and refreshing occupation to reflect on how the happy Greek view of the world, which calls it a *kosmos*, because it appears to be a harmonious [literally, a "well-ordered" (*velordnet*)] whole, a tasteful and transparent embellishment of the spirit, which acts in and becomes actual through it—how this happy view is repeated in a higher ordering, in the ideal world; how there is here a controlling wisdom, exercised principally in connecting together what belongs together: Axel with Valborg, Homer with the Trojan War, Raphael with Catholicism, Mozart with *Don Giovanni*.[82]

The "moment" when the writer first heard Mozart has become the starting point of a dialectical development—a process of reflection which links his mood of "wonder" at Mozart to "the happy Greek view of the world," for "wonder" had been the starting point of philosophical reflection (and "wisdom") for Plato and Aristotle, who arrived at this view of the world as a *kosmos*—a "whole" which is "well ordered" or "harmonious." It is living in a world so viewed which constituted the happiness of the Greeks, as Hegel claimed; they did not suffer from the dislocating "rift," the contradiction, which separates the *internal* from the *external* in the first aphorism.

At the same time the problem of "order" is being reformulated: a "whole" which is "well ordered" involves connections, whereas each of the successive aphorisms "separates" a "mood" in which the poet successively moves off in a different "direction." Thus when Eremita in the preface struggles with the editorial problem of "ordering" the papers of A, he gave up, finally deciding to leave them in the order he found them, and he did so "without being able to decide whether this order had any chronological significance or ideal meaning." We encountered the distinction between these two levels, the actual and the ideal, in the aphorism about the aphoristical procedure, which served to illustrate the dialectically tempting *ambiguity* of the term "esthetic." But the distinction was limited to the moment of actual experience and to the single "picture" recomposed. Now the dialectically tempting *ambiguity* is the term "classic." The two levels are again distinguished by referring not only to the single chronological "moment" when the interpreter first heard Mozart but also by the ensuing development of his reflection, first on the experience of "order" which was the actual experience of "classical" Greece, but then on the experience of "a higher ordering of the ideal world," the experience which is expressed in any "classic," whatever its actual chronological period, by virtue of its having transcended the limitations of this period. In a similar way the artist in the aphorism transcended the external "temporal and contingent" limitations of an actual experience and preserved its ideal meaning with an *Aufhebung*.

FORM AND CONTENT

Furthermore, the experience of "order" that a classic yields transcends the editorial problem, which was played up in the preface, of a merely sequential "order." With the normative stipulation "well ordered," the required "consequential" development becomes ideal. What is so ordered are the interconnections which compose a "whole" and render the development coherent. This order is not just a question of the composition of the opera. Its composition, like anything else analyzed in an existential dialectic, must be taken in its reflexive relation to the individual. Here he is the composer, as he was the poet in the first aphorism. Thus the primary interconnection is "Axel with Valborg, Homer with the Trojan War, Raphael with Catholicism, Mozart with *Don Giovanni*." It is the composer who imposes in turn the interconnection between his (external) form and the (internal) content or, rather, allows the form to develop from the content so that distinguishing what he imposes from what is elicited from him is impossible. In this impossibility his happiness as a composer is found:

> The happiness that belongs to every classic and makes it classic and immortal is the absolute interrelational [*sammenhold*] of the two forces of form and content. Their interrelation is so absolute that a later reflective age will hardly be able to separate them even for reflection, so intimate [*inderlig*] is their union, without running the risk of promoting a misunderstanding.[83]

The risk of misunderstanding, we see, is a recurrent problem in *Either*. But the risk is defined in this present essay in a way opposite to the way it was defined in the first aphorism. There the *external* was not the *internal*: the audience heard only the "beautiful music" and failed to understand the "suffering" in the poet's heart, so that he suffered also from being misunderstood. Now the failure would be to intrude any distinction between *external* form and *internal* content and thereby disrupt their continuity. Just as the unhappiness of the poet could be rendered by the spatial metaphor of "the rift in a poetic existence," so we are now faced with the opposite mood of happiness which received its first rendering from the classical view of the world as a *kosmos* but becomes in any classic "the union of those things that belong connected together," which is "a sacred joy to see."[84]

The opera *Don Giovanni* will not be merely the expression of the happy union which Mozart has imposed on his content (or, rather, has allowed to develop from the content); drawn into this union is the happiness of Don Giovanni himself, united in love with his woman of the moment, and the happiness of the audience who are no longer repudiated as they were in the first aphorism. They are in love with Mozart and understand him. Thus "The Immediate Stages" ends with a flow of continuity:

> I shall again rejoice over Mozart's happiness, a happiness which is in truth enviable, both in itself and because it makes it all of those happy who only moderately understand his happiness. . . . How much more, then, those who have fully understood him, how much more must they not feel themselves happy with the happy.[85]

MISUNDERSTANDING

The prospect of not fully understanding Mozart's happiness, the "risk" that reflection may promote "a misunderstanding," is signalized by the fact that the first sentence and the last, which are those that I have cited from the essay, are taken, respectively, from "A Meaningless Introduction" and "A Meaningless Postlude." In the process of "reflection" which started in the first sentence, the lover of Mozart is a writer who is relying on language as an instrument for conveying the meaning of the music. But he cannot finally rely on language. His final behest is, "Hear Don Giovanni; that is to say, if you cannot get an imaginative representation of him by hearing him, then you never can. . . . Hear, hear, hear Mozart's Don Giovanni."[86]

The trouble with linguistic expression is further illustrated by considering Molière's poetic interpretation of Don Juan "In Relation to the Musical Interpretation." Just as the relation between experiences was handled by the "aphorisms" as a problem of "separating off" "an essential mood," so the relation between the musical and the poetic interpretation of Don Juan is similarly handled as a problem of *de-finition*—that is, of *locating* the "boundaries"[87] which "separate" the realm of music "off" from the realm of language. The aphorisms were the shortest-run formulation of this methodological problem; the present formulation is sustained by the connections which can be followed out; but the problem itself is the long-run methodological problem of *Either/Or* as a definitional dispute over the boundary separating the ethical from the esthetic.

At the present stage, the line of demarcation is the fact "language involves reflection." When we hear the (external) sound of a word (or see the word on the page), reflection must intervene to interpret its (inner) meaning. But this intervention is disruptive. However prompt a reflex the "internalizing" process of "recollecting" the meaning may have become, the contradiction between the external and the internal is surmounted by discarding the physical sound while separating and preserving its meaning. This "internalizing" process is the movement of the Hegelian *Aufhebung* from a lower (external) to a higher (internal) level: "The physical experience [*sandselighed*] is as medium expressed to the level of a mere instrument and constantly negated." But in the case of music the moment of the physical sound itself is its meaning, which is given immediately without the intervention of reflection: "Music always expresses the immediate in its immediacy," whereas "reflection destroys the immediate, and hence it is impossible to express the musical in language."[88] The continuity of sound (external) and meaning (internal) is disrupted.

THE MUSICAL EROTIC

In the case of a literary form, in its opposition to the musical form, this *Aufhebung* introduces the same ambiguity into esthetics that was exposed in the aphorism on aphoristic procedure: at the level of immediate perception, a sound is heard, a letter is seen; but when the auditor or reader reaches the higher level of reflection, he discards the perception in favor of the meaning imaginatively represented. The corresponding risk to the musical which the reflective misunderstanding involves will become clearer if we consider the content to be expressed. When we do so, we shall rediscover what we initially found with respect to the "well-ordered" form that is so intimately united with this content. The "moment" when the writer first heard Mozart's *Don Giovanni* was not just a chronological *starting point* of merely autobiographical significance: "Erotic experience is apprehended in *Don Giovanni* as a *principle,* and it had never before in the world been so apprehended." It is a "principle, a power, a system."[89]

The "immediate" had already been a starting point and principle for Hegel. As content it had been, as it also is for Kierkegaard, "indefinite" and "indeterminate" (*ubestimmelig*). Hegel would have agreed too that "language cannot apprehend it." When Don Giovanni is interpreted in music, according to Kierkegaard, the auditor is not presented with a determinate content. Don Giovanni is "immediate life."[90] One is presented with "the power of nature . . . which as little tires of seducing . . . as the wind is tired of blowing, the sea of billowing, or a waterfall of tumbling downward." This "force in Don Giovanni, this omnipotence, this animation, only music can express," because it is itself immediately enjoyed by him. It is "the exuberant joy of life" and can only be immediately enjoyed as music: "The essence of Don Giovanni is music. He reveals himself to us in music, he expands in a world of sound."[91]

There is no pause to reflect beforehand: "The musical Don Giovanni's seduction is a handspring, a matter for a moment, swifter done than said," and "he requires no preparation, no plan, no time." There is no pause to reflect on what comes afterward: "When he is in love with one, he does not think of the next one." His love "exists only in the moment," just as "music exists only in the moment of its performance" and so is able to express his love. Thus "speech, dialogue, are not for Don Giovanni, for then he would be at once a reflective individual. . . . He hurries in a perpetual vanishing, precisely like music." With Don Giovanni, "to see her and to love her were one and the same."[92] Reflection does not intervene to extract the meaning of what he sees or of their union, any more than it should when the "lover of Mozart" hears the opera and shares the happiness of this union in its immediate union with the musical form.

FRAGMENTATION

The complete title of the next essay is

The Reflection of the Ancient Tragic
in the Modern
An Experiment [*Forsøg*] in Fragmentary Striving
Delivered before the Symparenkromenoi[93]

This title lines up several dislocating shifts to the opposite from the first essay, "The Immediate Stages," where happiness was wholeness. There is a shift in content: happy love is displaced by the tragic suffering of Antigone in her unhappy love for her fiancé, though a "relation" still "underlies the disrelation," since we are still concerned with love—with the development of the erotic. Concomitant with the shift in content, there is a disruption of the "harmonious whole" where Mozart was happy with his subject matter and the audience of Mozart lovers was (in the concluding phrase of the essay) "happy with the happy"—that is, with Mozart, who was happy with Don Giovanni, who was happy with the woman of the moment.

The subtitle indicates that the shift to the opposite brings us into line with the main thrust of *Either/Or*, with its subtitle *A Fragment of Life*. That the lives we shall now encounter are fragmentary is anticipated by the dislocation of the audience. Instead of sharing in "the exuberant joy of life" which Mozart expressed in *Don Giovanni*, they suffer from having been "buried alive." The Mozart lovers were so absorbed in being happy with the happy that it was not necessary to be more specific as to who they were, but Eremita's coinage "Symparenkromenoi" means "association of those who have been buried alive," and we shall learn more about them. Their not having lived out their lives is one level in the process of fragmentation which will extend to Hegel's system, in which "the truth is the whole" and a model for the interconnectedness of wholes was found in the way an organism develops continuously during its life.

Let me place their treatment of the "tragic" dialectically. Eventually the *ambiguity* of "passion" will help to impel us beyond the esthetic stage to the ethical and religious stages. But we are now remaining within the esthetic stage, where the primary content is the passion of love: happy in the first essay, it will turn out unhappy in the present one. With respect to form, the "esthetic" itself was found to be implicitly ambiguous in the aphorism on aphoristic procedure; in the first essay our esthetic scope narrowed to that classical harmony of (external) form with (internal) content) which Hegel not only considered characteristically esthetic (speaking ideally) but also characteristic (speaking chronologically) of ancient Greek art. In dealing with this *ambiguity* Eremita has already upstaged Hegel by finding this immediate harmony in the modern classic *Don Giovanni* instead of an ancient classic.[94] In the present essay the process of fragmentation will dispose of classical harmony, but while working out the relation of the modern to the ancient, which was left unsettled in the first essay. Indeed it is with respect to this relation that the "tragic" will be found ambiguous.

The essay starts out by exposing this *ambiguity* as a problem of adjustment between the continuity that connects and the discontinuity that separates. This adjustment is the recurrent problem we encounter with the dialectical method. It was involved in the transition to the more connected development of the essays from the aphorisms. It has been involved in the notion of a stage, which each of these essays represents, since a stage is a continuous development (internally) as well as a break (externally) with a preceding stage. A different adjustment (with the accent on continuity) is involved in the movement of *Aufhebung* in Hegel, and in the development of his system as an outcome of this recurrent movement, from the adjustment (with the accent on discontinuity) involved in Kierkegaard's subversion of this movement and fragmentation of this system.[95] There is a reference to the Hegelian adjustment in the way the essay on "The Tragic" starts out:

> Should anyone want to say that the tragic always remains the tragic, I should in a way have no objection to make, insofar as every historical development remains *continuously* within the sphere of the concept. . . . On the other hand . . . there is an essential difference between ancient tragedy and modern tragedy. If . . . one were to emphasize this difference absolutely, the procedure would be no less absurd than that of the man who denied any essential difference, since he would forget that the foothold necessary for him was the tragic itself and that this again he was so far from being able to *separate* that it really *connected* the ancient and modern. And it must be regarded as a warning against every such prejudiced attempt to *separate* them that estheticians still *continually* turn back to the established Aristotelian definitions [*bestemmelser*] and requirements with respect to the tragical, as being exhaustive of the concept.
>
> This may seem reassuring to him who desires no such separation, least of all a break [*brud*].[96]

We shall in fact be deprived of this reassurance and confronted with a break. As I have anticipated, an adjustment will be carried out in the relation between continuity and discontinuity which will be a readjustment in the relation that prevailed in Hegel. For unlike Hegel, Kierkegaard is not pursuing "investigations toward unity."

FOOTHOLD

Eremita has started out his analysis of "the tragic" by playing ironically with the scope of what Hegel tried to take within the unifying "grasp" of the "con-cept" (*begreb/Begriff*) of tragedy. One feature of the byplay here is Eremita's alternative metaphor of securing a "foothold." Since what is to be defined is in movement, undergoing development from the ancient stage to the modern, there is a danger of the dialectician's foot slipping. And this is peculiarly an esthetic predicament, as we have already seen.

We are already familiar with the metaphor of "con-cept" from *The Concept of Irony*, where the problem of starting out was represented as the problem of the "strength" with which "modern philosophical striving. . . . grasps and holds fast [*griber og fastholder*] the phenomenon." But the further byplay introduced by Eremita's metaphor will become clearer

in the opening scene in "The Diary of the Seducer," the climactic essay in
Either. The seducer is watching Cordelia descend from her carriage:

> Let this dainty little foot . . . venture forth [*forsøge sig*] into the
> world, trust that it will find a foothold [*fodfæste*]. . . . I have already
> seen the little foot, and . . . therefrom I have learned from Cuvier to
> proceed with certainty to conclusions. . . . Now how firmly [*fast*] stands
> this little foot.[97]

This episode is not just foot fetishism. The dialectical problem of starting
point is cast in the form of the problem of securing a foothold, and this
metaphor is probably being pitted against the Hegelian metaphor of
"grasping" in order to bring out the readjustment with which Kierkegaard
as an existentialist pins the dialectic down at a lower level than Hegel.
The development, for which this foothold is secured, is anticipated by
the allusion to Cuvier's procedure, and it is initiated as soon as Cordelia
enters a shop and the seducer reflects on her reflection in a mirror.[98]

REFLECTION AND ACTION

Eremita's treatment of the tragic also develops as a "modern" process of
reflection on "The Ancient Tragic." The "estheticians" who "still continually turn back to the established Aristotelian definitions" are Hegelians. And Eremita's first move against them in this process of reflection
is the same transposition which was carried through with the relation between the two ambiguous senses of "esthetic" and that between the two
ambiguous senses of "classic." Eremita likewise transposes the reflective
relation between ancient and modern tragedy into a parody of Hegelian
Aufhebung:

> The principal content of this little investigation is not so much the
> relation between ancient and modern tragedy as an attempt to show
> how what is characteristic of ancient tragedy is taken up [*optage*] within
> the modern, so that the truly tragic may emerge.[99]

What is characteristic of ancient tragedy will be "canceled out" or "destroyed" (the negative movement of *Aufhebung*) and yet will be "taken
up" by reflection and "preserved" (the positive movement of *Aufhebung*)
in the modern. The emergence from this dialectical movement of "the
truly tragic" indicates that truth is at stake with respect to what is "preserved," as implied by the Hegelian term for "preservation"—*Aufbewahrung*.

At this juncture Eremita takes a step beyond parody in his attack on
Hegel. The movement of arriving at modern tragedy by reflecting on

ancient tragedy will turn out in fact not to be the movement of *Aufhebung*, which Eremita's use of Hegel's term ostensibly implies, but its subversion. Watch what transpires. Eremita quotes Aristotle's account of the subordination of characters to action in tragedy, again introducing Hegel's term: "Individuals do not act in order to exhibit character, but the characters are taken up [*optage*] for the sake of the action."[100] To spell out this Hegelian *Aufhebung* that is being attributed to Aristotle, character in ancient tragedy is "negated" or "canceled out" as such, but in order that it may be "taken up" into the action and "preserved" or "verified" by it. But this *Aufhebung* is subverted in Eremita's interpretation of modern tragedy by a *reversal*, which could be brought out by suggesting that the individual is visualized as acting in order to be "true" to his character.

But the reversal is dialectical; it does not leave the meanings of the *relata* intact any more than the relation between them.[101] Thus the meaning of "action" is transformed by the intervention of reflection: "In ancient tragedy the action . . . is as much event as it is an action."[102] In other words, the modern distinction which reflection introduces between the *internal* and the *external* does not apply, nor does the distinction between the *subjective* and the *objective*. Thus the *reversal* Eremita would carry out in the meaning of "action" is not simply the replacement of the ancient *objective* concept by a modern *subjective* concept, though in opposing what he regards as the objective orientation of Hegel's dialectic he will sometimes rely on this simplification. It is, rather, the replacement of the ancient concept in which the distinction between *objective* and *subjective*, between "event" and "action," cannot be introduced "without running the risk . . . of a misunderstanding." For the ancient concept is of something which is indistinguishably as much something done to one as something one does oneself.[103]

In ancient tragedy the "destruction" (*undergang*, which is the Danish translation of the term *Untergang* that Hegel employs for the negative moment in the dialectic) is not, as with the modern tragic hero, "merely a consequence of his own deeds"; and his "action itself has a relative admixture of suffering (passion, *passio*)."[104] In modern tragedy the individual reflects on his action and comes to recognize his own agency.

OBJECTIVE AND SUBJECTIVE

The differences between modern and ancient tragedy are differences between the reflective stage in a dialectical development and the immediate stage that is being reflected upon. Perhaps I should stress again that the concept of immediacy itself is relative to the stage where it is applied (i.e., its meaning depends on the *relations* which have not yet been articulated at that stage but will be articulated at the next stage) and has accordingly undergone development since "The Immediate Stages of the Erotic," where immediacy could only be expressed in a musical form.[105] We have seen that the most prominent relations which have not yet been articulated at the stage of ancient tragedy are between *external* and *internal* or between *objective* and *subjective*. The actions of the ancient Antigone are still locked into "an objective dialectic" which "locates the individual in connection [*forbindelse*] with family and race," so that

> what affords the tragic interest is that Oedipus's sorrowful fate reechoes in the brother's unhappy death, in the collision of the sister [Antigone] with a simple human prohibition [Creon's prohibition against burying her brother]—aftereffects [*efterveerne*], so to speak, of the tragic fate of Oedipus, ramifying in every branch of his family. This is a totality. . . . It is not an individual who is destroyed [*gaaer under* doubtless reproduces Hegel's use of *Untergang* for the negative moment] but a small world. . . . Antigone's sorrowful fate is an echo [*efterklang*] of her father's. . . . In the necessity of fate there is also, as it were, a higher burden which envelops not only the life of Oedipus but also his entire family.[106]

In contrast, the "subjective dialectic" of the modern reflective reinterpretation of the ancient *Antigone* is the severing of the objective relations which determined her role: "The modern tragic hero, conscious of himself as a subject, is fully reflective, and this reflection has . . . reflected him out of every immediate relation to state, race, and destiny. . . ." Thus reflection "negates the connection and lifts the individual out of the continuity [*sammenhængt*]." Hence "the point of departure is the individual, not the family."[107]

Because the modern dialectic is *subjective*, as opposed to an *objective* dialectic, it lends itself to transposition into a dialectic of the passions. At the immediate stage illustrated by the ancient Antigone, the Hegelian assumption can be made that it is "as a bride" that "woman achieves her destiny [*bestemmelse*]." The internal (what a woman implicitly is, what she is meant to be) is actualized externally, objectified, by her marriage. But with the intervention of reflection, the modern Antigone becomes instead "a bride of sorrow" who "devotes her life to sorrowing over her father's fate, over her own." As she reflects upon it, her own destiny is her becoming wedded not externally to an *objective* bridegroom but internally to her own *subjective* mood of sorrow. Thus the intervention of reflection is the fragmentation of the life of the modern tragic hero: "Reflection has not only reflected him out of every immediate relation to state, race, and destiny but has often even reflected him out of his own past life."[108] This reflexive twist is the final severing; his life becomes, as the subtitle of *Either/Or* warned, *A Fragment of Life*.

LITERAL AND METAPHORICAL

The continuity of the ancient Antigone's life was, it is true, also disrupted when, instead of fulfilling her destiny objectively by marrying her fiancé and living out her life, she was buried alive. But at least she was buried alive in a literal and objective sense. Here we reach the juncture where we can look back and recognize the dialectical advance over the first essay, in which the distinction between the immediate and reflective was a distinction between the musical erotic and an interpretation of the musical erotic in the reflective medium of language. The distinction was reinforced by the fact that a feature of this reflective interpretation was a contrast between the erotic content as expressed in Mozart's music and in the reflective medium of language in Molière's *Don Juan*. In the present essay we have moved on with tragedy entirely into the sphere of language. What is now in question is the opposition not only between two stages in the development of tragedy, which renders the concept of the "tragic" ambiguous, but also between two ways in which language can be employed and which renders it *ambiguous*—with an immediate reference or an extended, metaphorical reference. Reflection's intervention transforms the (inner) meaning of Antigone's expressions, even though they remain (externally) the same as those in the "outburst" by her ancient prototype, which itself played up an ambiguity:

> I go to the heaped up rock of a tomb that is strange.
> How wretched I am
> To dwell
> Neither with the living nor the dead.

Eremita's comment on this ambiguity introduces further ambiguities:

> Our modern Antigone can say this about her whole life. The difference is striking. There is a factual truth in [the ancient] Antigone's expression [*udsagn*] which lessens the suffering. If our Antigone were to say the same thing, it would be unreal [*uegentligt*], but this unreality is the real suffering. The Greeks do not express themselves metaphorically [*uegentligt*], because the reflection which is involved in metaphorical expression was not the way they lived. So when Philoctetes complains that he lives isolated and left behind on a desert island, his expression corresponds to an external [*udvortes*] truth; when, in contrast, our Antigone suffers in her isolation, it is after all only in a metaphorical sense that she is alone, but just because of this her suffering is real suffering.[109]

Here the English translator must be "uneasy lest a single one of the implications fall out and the whole stack fall apart," as has indeed happened in the last sentence, where the interplay between "metaphorical" and "real" has had to be sacrificed.

But to track down the implications we need to allow for the shift from the ancient immediate stage to the modern reflective stage: reflection extrapolates from a particular episode in the life of the ancient Antigone to "the whole life" of the modern Antigone. Such extrapolation, we recognized in Sartre, can constitute an "existential experience," which is not (he explained) a mere empirical "sum of experiences" but a "summing up" (*résumé*) of one's "life as a whole"; it is an "episode" which as lived through "tells the whole story."[110] The present extrapolation is not only an enlargement to a "whole life" but also a subtraction from the ancient *Antigone* which was as a classic "a well-ordered whole" (even though she herself was buried before she lived out her whole life), so that its fragmentation serves to delineate the fragmentariness of the modern Antigone's life.

The scope of a "whole life" is gained by rendering the ancient Antigone's expressions "metaphorical." It is here that we reach at a higher level the *ambiguity* which betrays a discrepancy between (external) expression and (inner) meaning that corresponds to the lower-level discrepancy in the preceding essay between the immediate physical sound of a linguistic expression and the meaning abstracted by reflection. The modern Antigone might "say the same thing" (outwardly) as the ancient Antigone did in her "outburst," but it would not mean (inwardly) the same thing. This discrepancy or contradiction between *external* and *internal* undergoes further development with respect to what the author himself has to say about what it would mean for the modern Antigone to say the same thing. For his expressions about her expressions, like her expressions themselves, are *ambiguous* and bring out further *interplay* between the *modus loquendi* (the mode of speaking) and the *modus vivendi* (the mode of living).[111] Unfortunately it is impossible in an English translation to retain the same expressions as the different *ambiguities* develop into *contradictions*. On one hand *uegentligt* refers (with respect to the *modus vivendi*) to the "unreality" of what the modern Antigone suffers, as contrasted with the immediate physical reality of what the ancient Antigone suffered when she was buried alive. The modern Antigone's suffering has become "unreal" inasmuch as her reflecting upon it has disconnected it from any immediate reference to the real external world, but at this higher level where she has been lifted "out of the continuity" it is "this unreality" which is "her real [*egentligt*] suffering." On the other hand *uegenligt* refers in the *modus loquendi* to the "nonliteral," "metaphorical" meaning acquired by the expressions "bride," "burial," "tomb," "alive," "die," which had "literal" (*egentligt*) reference to the real external world when originally employed by the ancient Antigone but have now become metaphorical.[112] The "bride" of sorrow has become so "wedded" to her sorrow by her reflection that her reflection can be said to have "buried" or "entombed" her, for she is no longer "alive"—that is, capable of entering into organic connection with her fiancé.

SORROW AND ANXIETY

Needless to say, my translation is still at fault if it seems to suggest that Kierkegaard would accept unilateral external reference as a criterion of "reality." This would confer an unwarranted privilege on the ancient Antigone as compared with the modern. Since we are ultimately concerned not just with Kierkegaard but with existentialism, the dialectical character of the referential relations can be brought out by anticipating the later, very different existentialist use of the German cognate of the Danish *egentlig—eigentlich*, which is ordinarily translated "authentic" and taken to characterize an experience as one's "own" (eigen) as opposed to an "experience" which is "inauthentic" or "alienated"—that is, imposed on one by "others." One has lost the initiative.

I am reformulating here the problem of an "existential experience." Inasmuch as an existential dialectic is an analysis of relations in which some relation is exposed as relevant by a dislocation, the qualification "existential" is not redundant but points up some *reflexive* way in which I am related to the experience. A moment ago the relation was between what remained a particular episode in the life of the ancient Antigone and its metaphorical extension to the "whole life" of the modern Antigone. This extension is one fashion in which a particular episode can be claimed as my "own." But the extension is only feasible if my effort to "have" the experience as my "own" takes other forms. Strictly speaking, it is questionable if the ancient Antigone (as interpreted by Eremita) "has" her experience as her "own," since the meaning of what is happening to her is exhausted by its immediate, objective reference to her being buried alive. Fate is in control. In order for one to regain the initiative and "have" an experience, reflection must intervene. In Hegel's phraseology "the impression," which is the moment when one's mind is "exposed to external influences," must be "internalized" by "recollection" and "raised to an imaginative representation." Thus the experience becomes an experience that one "has," though at the risk of the *ambiguity* which we have seen is characteristically "esthetic." At the higher level or later stage of *imaginative representation* (which we recognize involves "meta-phorical" extension of language), the original experience we started out with and its inner meaning that is now reached are likely to "fall apart."

The risk becomes clearer when Eremita explains how the appropriate movement of reflection is propelled by anxiety. Or, rather, he brusquely asserts, "Reflection is anxiety." The evidence may be partly etymological: "reflection" implies a "bending back" upon the experience one would "have," and *angst* (cf. "angle," "anchor," etc.) also implies something "bent."[113] In any case Kierkegaard does identify anxiety as "the exploratory movement which is constantly in contact and by means of its probing explores sorrow, as it *goes round about* the sorrow." "Sorrow" (*sorg*), the mood of the ancient Antigone, carries an immediate or objective reference, which has justified Kierkegaard's characterization of her "fate," objectively determined though it is, as "sorrowful." But anxiety is a different phenomenon: "That anxiety is a determination of reflection is shown by linguistic usage, for I always refer to 'being anxious about something' and thereby separate the anxiety [as the subjective experience] from that about which I am anxious [the object], and I can never use anxiety with an objective reference; whereas, in contrast, when I say 'my sorrow,' it can just as well refer to what I sorrow over as to my sorrow over it." In the sorrow the distinction between *subjective* and *objective*, *internal* and *external*, is not yet explicit. In contrast, the *reflexive* force of saying "my anxiety" incorporates my subjective effort to "have" the experience as my own: "Anxiety is the instrument by which the subject appropriates sorrow and assimilates it."[114]

This process must not be thought of as just a transient episode. Anxiety's probing, exploratory movement of appropriation "is not swift like an arrow; it is successive; it is not over all at once but is constantly continuing." Thus anxiety can propel the dialectic through successive stages, including those to which Eremita will assign other, more reflective "brides."

Metaphors such as "bride of grief" develop with the shift of level that takes place with the process of reflective appropriation:

> As a passionate, erotic glance desires its object [at the lower level of immediacy], so anxiety looks upon sorrow to desire it [i.e., to appropriate it at the higher *reflexive* level where the experience of the subject becomes the object which replaces the original object of the experience]. As the quiet, incorruptible glance of love is preoccupied with the loved object [at the lower level], so anxiety occupies itself with sorrow [at the higher level]. Sorrow then becomes "reflective grief."[115]

COMMUNICATION

With this shift the discrepancy between the *subjective* and the *objective*, the *internal* and the *external*, takes a further form. Remember that the "subjective dialectic" that supervenes in *Either* "lifts the individual out of the continuity" and separates him from others. Thus the possibility of the modern Antigone saying "the same thing" as the ancient Antigone had said in her "outburst" has been left a hypothetical reflection ("If our Antigone were to say the same thing"). As a matter of fact, she does not say anything:

> When Epaminondas was wounded in the battle of Mantinea, he left the arrow sticking in the wound until he heard that the battle was won, because he knew that he would die when it was drawn out. Thus does our Antigone bear her secret in her heart like an arrow which life unrelentingly has driven in deeper without depriving her of life, for as long as it remains in her heart she can live, but in the moment it is drawn out, she must die.[116]

Here we may go behind the scenes, as one reader was intended to do—Kierkegaard's ex-fiancée Regina. The figure of a modern Antigone Regina was expected to identify with Kierkegaard, for in the symparenkromenous reconstruction of the ancient drama the tragic "interest" was refocused "on his [the fiancé of Antigone—that is, Regina] being able to wrest her [his] secret from her [him]."[117]

In negotiating the sex change the reader is assisted by the *reflexive* shift that is carried out from Antigone as the character being reflected upon to the personality of the author who is reflecting upon her and thereby producing the modern reconstruction. His drama is not a classic ("a well-ordered whole") like the original but is inconclusive: the arrow of suffering is not drawn out of the modern Antigone's heart but merely penetrates more deeply, and yet she does not really die in the literal sense. Thus his drama must have been the product of a process of reflection which was inconclusive. The author's life must have been interrupted by this process of reflection (as has been the life of his heroine), so that we are confronted with a "posthumous" essay and must reflect (as Regina was invited to reflect) about its "symparenkromenous" author:

> A fully completed work has no relation to the poetic personality; with posthumous papers, one constantly feels, because of their being broken off, . . . prompting to poeticize about the personality. Posthumous papers are like a ruin, and what haunted place could be more appropriate for the buried?[118]

But simply to respond to this prompting by pressing the autobiographical implications is to implement an undialectical version of existential reflexivity. Existentialism is never simply the effort at self-expression which has often earned it the label of belated "romanticism." An existential dialectic is *bifocal*. We must not overlook Kierkegaard's paradox which I interpreted as philosophically crucial: "An existential thinker must be represented as essentially thinking," even though "in presenting his thought he sketches himself."[119]

In working out this distinction of level, Kierkegaard is indebted to the philosophical significance Hegel had attributed to particular figures, and especially to Antigone. But it is only when the Hegelian movement of *Aufhebung* transcending the particular individual has been subverted that a modern Antigone can acquire implications for Kierkegaard's "own" experience of unhappy love. Anyone who is essentially thinking reaches a stage in appropriating his own experience when his reflection buries him alive and he becomes one of the Symparenkromenoi.[120] But Kierkegaard is also sketching his own inability, as a result of such entombment by reflection, to respond to Regina objectively: he is unable to respond either by marrying her (*modus vivendi*) or even by communicating literally (*modus loquendi*) his reasons for breaking off their engagement. His secrecy itself is *bifocal*: it is not only the outcome of his entombment by reflection; it also involves a particular secret regarding his father and his father's relation to his mother—the secret which is comparable to Antigone's regarding Oedipus. His motivation for metaphorical communication, in the guise of a reconstruction of the ancient *Antigone* which does not literally reveal his secret, is further developed by his deriving the metaphor "bride of grief" from the metaphor "bride of God," for this unclassical metaphor not only foreshadows his religious destiny (*modus vivendi*) but also introduces the theme of taking the veil in communicating with Regina.[121]

Because Kierkegaard is not only "sketching himself" as a particular individual whose particular secret separates him from Regina but is also thinking of the general requirement of appropriating experience through reflection in order to become a particular, separate individual, he draws a distinction in his preface between a possible "feminine reader" (i.e., Regina) and the "individual reader." Such a reader "would be disposed to separate himself as an 'Eremita,' since serious reflection always renders one isolated." Kierkegaard adds, "Perhaps there would come a next moment when he would call himself "Victor," however he may be inclined to understand this victory more particularly."[122] Whatever the "victory" may be in the long run, the first step toward it is to separate oneself by appropriating one's own experience. This is why there will be different particular understandings of this victory by different individuals.

THE APHORISTICAL

The status of the reader as a separate individual must await later treatment of the problem of communication as the problem of the relation between author and reader. But we have now reached a juncture where the interpretation of the procedure of stages can be wrapped up. It has been sufficiently illustrated by our comparison of "The Immediate Stages of the Erotic" with the succeeding immediate and reflective stages in the development of tragedy as well as with the preceding aphorisms which did not compose a stage. The repetition of the phrase "in her heart" with regard to the modern Antigone's suffering reminds us of the identical metaphor which was employed concerning the internal suffering of the poet in the first aphorism. "The Reflection of the Ancient Tragic" is linked even more definitely to the aphorisms, inasmuch as it is credited (along with the two following essays which also concern the tragic suffering of unhappy love) to the Symparenkromenoi, "whose activities . . . are essays devoted to the aphoristical and the contingent, . . . who do not merely think and speak aphoristically but live aphoristically, . . . who live *aphorismenoi* and *segregati*, like aphorisms in life, without community of men."[123] They are lifted "out of the continuity" of life with others. Here the expression "aphorism" is undergoing a metaphorical transposition of meaning which is comparable to the metaphorical transposition which we have watched the expression "metaphorical" (*uegentligt*) itself undergo as a characterization of a *modus loquendi* so that it comes to characterize a *modus vivendi* ("the unreality" of being "buried alive" by reflection). The *interplay* between the two modes is brought out by the contrast between the moderns and "the Greeks" who "do not *express* themselves metaphorically, because the reflection which is involved in metaphorical expressions was not the way they *lived*." [124] Since the ancient hero still "rests in the objective determinants [*bestemmelser*] of state, family, and fate," the movement of reflection required for the formation of a metaphorical expression does not get under way with him.

This movement does get under way when the expression "devoted to the aphoristical" is applied to the triad of essays on tragic suffering. Some of the so-called aphorisms at the start of *Either* might be construed as literally "aphoristical" in external form in the conventional sense of "short, concise pronouncements." But none of the triad of essays is short and concise. (Together they take up seventy-four pages in the Danish.)

So striking a contradiction between the requisite external literary form of an "aphorism" in its literal sense and the actual external literary form of these essays triggers our reflection; we are induced to go beyond the form of an aphorism as a *modus loquendi* and to interpret "devoted to the aphoristical" as a metaphorical reference to the content of a *modus vivendi*. The characterization then applies reflexively to the way reflection "separates" the individual "off" from his own external life by "burying" him "alive." The metaphorical meaning is reinforced by the use of the Latin *segregati* as a synonym for *aphorismenoi*, and the interplay between formal procedure and content is enhanced. Anyone who adopts the formal procedure of "defining" himself by "setting himself apart" from other men with respect to the content of his experience is to this extent an individual, as we learned from *The Concept of Irony*.

Ever since Plato the two dialectically crucial operations have been to "separate" and to "connect." These two operations were pitted against each other in the opening paragraph of this essay on the tragical. Just as "separation" can be transposed from its reference to the dialectical *modus loquendi* to the contradictory *modus vivendi* (burial alive) of Antigone and the Symparenkromenoi, so can its opposite "connection." Thus it referred in the opening paragraph to what "connected [as opposed to separated] the ancient and modern tragical," but it comes to refer to a *modus vivendi*—"the [objective] dialectic which locates the individual in connection with family and race" as opposed to a "subjective dialectic" which "negates the connection and lifts the individual out of the continuity." Similarly, the "determinants" which in the opening paragraph referred to the Aristotelian "definitions" or "specifications" to be satisfied by a tragedy have come to refer to the "objective determinants" of the life of the tragic hero, and in the singular to the "destiny" of a woman, whether "objective," if she connects with a husband, or "subjective, "if this connection is broken off in favor of her attachment as an individual to her own passion.

The "aphoristical" procedure by which one "becomes an individual" in Kierkegaard is intended to be opposed to Hegel's procedure by which the individual is to transcend his separateness. "The Ancient Tragic" is the first of three essays on unhappy love. These essays can be regarded as "aphoristical" in the further metaphorical sense that they de-fine by "separating off" from each other the three successive stages they represent in the process of reflection by which the individual "separates" himself "off" from others. The three stages require three separate essays, in contrast to the three stages of "The Immediate Stages of the Erotic," where reflection had not yet intervened to disrupt the continuity and harmony of happy love. The "lover of Mozart" himself pointed this out:

When . . . I . . . use the term "stage," it must not be thought that each stage exists independently, the one external to the other. . . . The different stages taken together compose the immediate stage. The other stages have no separate existence. The third stage [*Don Giovanni*] . . . is really the whole stage.[125]

The separation of the three stages in the three symparenkromenous essays emerges from the sustained reflection which began with the modern Antigone sharply separating herself from the ancient Antigone in the first of these essays.

THE SYSTEM

Their separateness indicates that the "investigations" on which Eremita has embarked are proceeding in the opposite direction to those which Hegel had undertaken as "investigations toward unity." Indeed if the "separation" of stages marks the disruption of the continuity which is regained at higher levels in Hegel, until finally a unified system is achieved, then stages becomes a rather different procedure in Kierkegaard from what it was in Hegel. Kierkegaard's warning to respect patiently the successiveness of stages echoes, as I admitted earlier, Hegel's warning. Indeed the spatial and temporal metaphor of stages itself Kierkegaard took over from Hegel. But examine Hegel's warning more carefully:

> Impatience demands the impossible—to reach the goal without the means of getting there. Both the length of the way must be endured, for each phase is necessary; and we must linger at each phase, for each is itself a complete individual structure [*Gestalt*] and is considered absolutely only in so far as its definite character [*Bestimmtheit*] is considered as something whole . . . or only insofar as it is considered with reference to the specific contribution of its definite character to the whole.[126]

In contrast, the spokesman for the Symparenkromenoi explains, "It is contrary to our association to produce coherent works [*sammenhængende arbeider*] or greater wholes,"[127] and we have seen that "The Reflection of the Ancient Tragic" itself is subtitled "Experiment in Fragmentary Striving." Thus a stage is not (in Hegel's phrase) "considered with reference to the specific contribution of its definite character to the whole." There is no ultimate whole, as in Hegel, to which the previous stages are subordinated and make their contribution. Their increasing "separateness" contributes instead to the disruption of the Hegelian system as a coherent whole. Thus proceeding by stages retains a significance for Kierkegaard that it could not retain for Hegel. Not only are they ultimately superseded in the system, but the spatial and temporal representation that is implicit in the metaphor of stages also becomes "irrelevant" there,[128] when the contradiction between the *external* and the *internal* is overcome by the movement of *Aufhebung*. Indeed Hegel gave different expositions of his system, but he never composed a work on stages, as Kierkegaard does in *Stages on Life's Way*, which is, strictly speaking, the final work in his "authorship" and as such covers all the stages.

In Hegel, moreover, the subordination of stages to the whole is conveyed with an emphasis on its organic unity:

> These forms are not merely differentiated; they also displace each other as being incompatible with each other. But their fluid nature makes them at the same time moments of an organic unity, where they not merely do not conflict with one another, but one is as necessary as the other; and this mutual necessity [of all moments] alone constitutes the life of the whole.[129]

In Kierkegaard, however, "life" does not attach to the whole in its organic unity, since reflection interrupts to separate the individual's life into stages; life is only the "way" along which the individual proceeds from one stage to another. The procedure itself is not a fluid movement but is disrupted by sharper discontinuities than in Hegel.

The process of disruption will be carried further with other "brides of grief" in the next essay, for they will carry the process of reflection itself even further than the modern Antigone. The only continuity that will survive for them is a "little ligament or two" which is still "whole and uninjured and is a constant cause of continued suffering."[130] Kierkegaard is stretching Hegel's organic analogy: disruption of the organism would constitute suffering in Hegel, but even the minimal organic continuity that will survive disruption in the case of the brides only accentuates their suffering in Kierkegaard.

Two issues still remain with respect to Kierkegaard's opposing his disruptive dialectic as an either/or to Hegel's more continuous and eventually systematic dialectic. My exposition so far of the significance that stages retain in Kierkegaard but cannot ultimately in Hegel sets up a dialectical opposition in Kierkegaard between stages and system. But this opposition remains insufficiently worked out until I deal later with Kierkegaard's attack on Hegel's system itself. I also have not yet dealt with the opposition between the way the two dialectics themselves develop. In Hegel "one [stage] is as necessary as the other," but in Kierkegaard there is no necessity that the individual should proceed from one stage to another. It remains instead a matter for the individual's own choice, even though his choice will have implications which it is the function of reflection to trace.

We shall see in chapter 10 how this problem of choice is brought into focus by Kierkegaard's dismantling of Hegel's system. I shall then examine the methodological commitment which Kierkegaard taunts Hegel for making—"All will be clear in the end"—that is, when the system is "finished." This commitment is the ultimate application of the principle of *Aufhebung*. Kierkegaard would oppose to Hegel's "end" not only the problem of starting point (and of recognizing the presuppositions we start out with) but also an alternative methodological commitment, that "each stage" must "be made clear by itself."[131] But to determine more precisely the need for this clarity, we must next reappraise the problem of starting point.

Notes

1. Sartre has admitted that he is not a "very methodical" reader (*Life/Situations*, p. 127), and there is abundant evidence to bear him out. At the time he wrote *Being and Nothingness*, his understanding of Kierkegaard seems to have been largely derived from Wahl's *Etudes kierkegaardiennes* (1938). See chap. 2, n. 42 above.

2. *Being and Nothingness*, p. 324.

3. See chap. 4, n. 18.

4. While Sartre's treatment of "sadism" clearly depended on his prior treatment of "the obscene," the example of the sadist leaning on his victim's shoulders, etc., is not so clearly a development of the earlier example of the wiggling bottom, and we could not be certain in chap. 5 that Sartre was recapitulating rather than merely ruminating.

5. See p. 188 above.

6. Kierkegaard may be opposing the *Aufhebung* with which the opposition between feeling and thought is overcome, when Hegel attacks those who would "separate feeling and thought so far as to make them opposites and so hostile that religious feeling is assumed to be contaminated, perverted, and even destroyed by thought" (*Encyclopaedia*, pt. 1, par. 2). See chap. 10 below for Kierkegaard's conviction that Hegel had destroyed religion by thought. At the present esthetic stage of the dialectic, the epigraph might just as well refer to "the passionless calm of a knowledge which is in the medium of pure thought alone"—the final phrase of Hegel's preface to the second edition of the *Logic* with which he characterizes its content.

7. *Papirer*, IV A 192.

8. *Either*, p. 157. The preceding sentence indicates that Hegel is being opposed: "Dialectic is generally thought of as quite abstract. . . ."

9. *Phenomenology*, p. 2.

10. Suffering, like its affiliate "passion," is dialectical and transpires at different levels or stages. Thus despair is suffering a process of disintegration (see, e.g., *Sickness unto Death*, p. 26) that proceeds by stages. Ultimately "the opposition it suffers" became for Kierkegaard a "differentiating characteristic of the true" (*Papirer*, IX A 304).

11. For Hegel on portraits, see *Aesthetics*, 1:155. See also *Philosophy of History*, p. 14.

12. *Postscript*, p. 264. Some expositors carefully avoid attributing to Kierkegaard the points of view of his pseudonyms. I shall not always be so fastidious, especially when general implications or contrasts with other philosophers seem present. The polyglot character of Kierkegaard's authorship I shall postpone explaining because Kierkegaard himself postponed it. But for the purpose of a very broad comparison with our later

philosophers, the use of pseudonyms can be regarded as a form of role playing, which we have already seen is a crucial phenomenon for the existentialist.

13. Irony need not be sympathetic. See p. 372 below.

14. *Either*, p. 3. It is worth drawing attention to the fact that the indispensable existential metaphor of "way" (omitted in the English translation) puts in an appearance in the first paragraph of *Either/Or*, since it is the first of the esthetic works and the last is, strictly speaking, *Stages on Life's Way*, which Kierkegaard will interpret as a "recapitulation" of *Either/Or*. We shall also see that the relation between last and first is dialectically significant for demarcating a development and that recapitulation is a procedure for bringing out its significance.

15. *Either*, p. 3. The implications of movement and direction would be clearer if the Danish were translated by the English cognates "inward" and "outward," which I shall sometimes employ.

16. *Papirer*, IV B 10, 2; IV A 192.

17. *Encyclopaedia*, pt. 1, par. 142. The esthetic stage is for Kierkegaard, as for Hegel, the "immediate" stage, but in Kierkegaard as in Hegel immediacy comes to grief with the emergence of a contradiction. And in Kierkegaard the esthetic stage is recognized in retrospect to be "despair" and "therefore not existence" (*Postscript*, p. 226)—i.e., not the "unity," the actualization, of the internal in the external that "existence" is in Hegel. It may seem that from Hegel's perspective Kierkegaard should be conceived as relapsing from reason's grasp of "pervasive unity," for Hegel would have us grasp the pervasive unity behind the contradictory accomplishments of the movement of *Aufhebung* by recognizing "the speculative spirit of our language surmounting the mere either/or of understanding" (*Encyclopaedia*, pt. 1, par. 96). But my argument is that the contradiction between the external and the internal that we encounter in Kierkegaard himself takes place at the level of the imagination as conceived by Hegel (see p. 000 above) rather than at the level of the understanding, although Kierkegaard does conceive Hegel himself as failing to surmount the level of understanding (see chap. 3, n. 36 above). I shall renew the argument in chap. 15.

18. *A Tale of a Tub*. I take as an example discrepancy between what is outwardly said and what is inwardly meant, because the contradiction that will eventually emerge in Kierkegaard is between the Christianity that survives as Hegelian verbiage and Christianity's intrinsic meaning.

19. *Irony*, pp. 51, 158, 53, 63.

20. I am offering a more familiar illustration than Kierkegaard's. His individualism leaves him largely indifferent to Plato's politics. Thus he fully exploits the *Apology* while neglecting the *Crito*. Similarly, he exploits the *Symposium*, where Alcibiades opposes to Socrates' "external" appearance what he found "within" him (*Irony*, p. 87) and neglects in *Irony* the *Phaedrus*, which winds up with prayer for harmony between the inner and the outer man. See my *Human Nature*, 1:260–61, for the dialectical opposition in the *Republic* between the internal and the external and 1:308, 311–18 for the way this opposition (crystallized in the formula *ab exterioribus ad interiora, ab inferioribus ad superiora*) carried over in later thought.

21. *Aesthetics*, 1:153.

22. *Point of View*, pp. 131, 27, 38. See also chap. 4, n. 18 above.

23. *Point of View*, p. 29. I cannot overindulge the privilege Kierkegaard accorded posterity when he provided it with *Point of View*, and I cannot reconstruct now what he refers to there as "the dialectical character of my position" (p. 7). For he makes clear in the introduction that he has been held back from presenting this point of view, because "the authorship was not yet available in so complete a form that the understanding of it could be anything but misunderstanding" (p. 5). Thus *Point of View* presupposes acquaintance with the "authorship." In fact the immediate occasion for its composition, he explains, was that "I am about to encounter for the second time in the literary field my first production, *Either/Or*" (p. 5). To be confronted with a

"second edition" is for the dialectician an invitation for a recapitulation, and I have only cited *Point of View* for the revision this involves in his handling of the problem of starting point.

24. Ibid., p. 29. Kierkegaard seems to be recognizing here that the problem of starting point is that of starting out with a *captatio benevolentiae*—i.e., an effort to capture the sympathy of one's audience and conciliate its goodwill (see *Either*, p. 155). This is a traditional rhetorical requirement for one's prefatory remarks, and Kierkegaard is very much aware of the tradition, although he will also sometimes defy it dialectically by repelling instead of conciliating his reader (see chap. 10, n. 9 below). *Point of View* may be prefatory by virtue of the appearance of the first esthetic work a "second time," but it is also in effect a second postscript (a postscript for posterity) to be compared with the *Concluding Unscientific Postscript* which followed *Stages* (see n. 14, this chapter) and brought the esthetic works to a conclusion (see my preface above). It is not possible here to deal with Kierkegaard's debt to the rhetorical tradition, especially since I concentrated in *Human Nature* on those moments when *conciliatio* contributed to the development of the political concept of consensus (see *Human Nature*, chap. 12, n. 93; chap. 14, n. 127), and Kierkegaard is indifferent to the political, as I have already indicated.

25. *Point of View*, pp. 146, 134. The characterization of the two movements as "essentially the same" presupposes Kierkegaard's eventual characterization of Hegel's system as "esthetic" (see chap. 10 below). But this characterization is not a simple reduction that would eliminate interplay between levels, and I shall continue to interpret Kierkegaard's dialectic as bifocal, inasmuch as it is always possible for the dialectician "at one and the same time to start out at two points" (*Point of View*, p. 84).

26. *Either*, p. 19.

27. *Papirer*, IV A 216.

28. *Aesthetics*, 1:3–12.

29. Ibid., p. 159; italics mine.

30. *Either*, p. 7. See n. 76, this chapter.

31. *Either*, p. 8.

32. *Postscript*, p. 226. In his journal Kierkegaard describes this dislocation as "a total rift with actuality" (*Papirer*, IV A 216). In chap. 2 I discussed the metaphor of dislocation in general. This particular metaphor is found in Hegel and in Sartre (e.g., his treatment of Flaubert's "soul" as a *"fêlure* in his body," *L'idiot*, 1:255), and Heidegger plays with the metaphor of "rift" (*Riss*) as an *Aufriss* (a "design" or "outline sketch": *Poetry, Language, Thought*, p. 63; "The Age of the World Picture," p. 118).

33. *Papirer*, II A 118.

34. *Or*, p. 356. In the journal Kierkegaard indicates that this "first" aphorism "finds its resolution [*løsung*]" in this "last word" (*Papirer*, IV A 216). For the relation between first and last, see nn. 14, 40, this chapter.

35. *Either*, p. 41. "Grasp" (*gribe*) suggests the *Aufhebung* which takes place in Hegel at the "conceptual" level, but the entire operation in the aphorism is pictorial or imaginative.

36. *Either*, p. 8.

37. Ibid., p. 31. Other aphorisms also stress this discontinuity—e.g., ". . . if I cannot spin, I can at least cut the thread" (ibid.). Aphorisms were of course employed by the romantics as a genre that embodied discontinuity. Friedrich Schlegel used the term pretty much interchangeably with "fragment," which he defined as "like a small work of art completely separated from the surrounding world and complete in itself . . . " (*Kritische Schriften*, p. 47), and he explained that "everything that he loved and thought of with love was isolated and disconnected. In his imagination his whole existence was a pile of unrelated fragments" (*Lucinde*, p. 78). Since I am mainly concerned (as was Kierkegaard himself) with his relation to Hegel, I shall not be able to do justice to Kierkegaard's debts to Schlegel and other German romantics.

But it may be worth noting that he regards the romantic genre of aphorism as merely esthetic, whereas its ultimate attraction for him is its dialectical foreshadowing of the religious "separation" of the individual from others (see n. 123, this chapter).

38. *Either*, p. 8.

39. For an example of this standard Hegelian usage, see p. 423 below.

40. *Logic*, p 71; see also chap 1, n. 50 above. Since there is no circle in Kierkegaard, one might characterize the relation between last and first as a version of recapitulation controlled by the principle of contradiction.

41. *Either*, pp. 41–42. Kierkegaard may again have in mind the passage in Hegel's *Aesthetics* where he deals with outbursts of suffering or joy, for Hegel refers there to "the inextinguishable laughter of the gods in Homer" (*Aesthetics*, 1:159; see n. 86, this chapter.

42. I am not risking an interpretation of *The Fall* but only of a Judge-Penitent—a role which Sartre has himself taken note of (*L'idiot*, 1:245). Sartre would insist of course on the reflexive reference: Flaubert "judges himself when he judges others, as we all do" (ibid., 3:15).

43. *An Accidental Man*, p. 361.

44. *Either*, p. 8.

45. *Papirer*, IV A 214; *Either*, p. 14.

46. Cited by the editor (*Or*, p. xvii).

47. *Either*, p. 8. Neither this pun nor the general emphasis on order in this paragraph comes across in the English translation. *I sin orden*, "quite in order," has been translated "natural," and *anordningen* in the preceding sentence has become "arrangement."

48. *Either*, p. 7; *Postscript*, p. 227.

49. *Papirer*, X^1 A 436; *Or*, p. 171; *Postscript*, p. 227.

50. Though "choice" in *Or* is opposed to "chance" in *Either*, they assume mutual significance in opposition to Hegel's conception of dialectic as a necessary development. We are of course already aware of the existential importance of "chance" or "contingency," which would be a more literal, if less esthetic, translation of Kierkegaard's *tilfælde*. The movements of the wiggling bottom were delineated by Sartre as "contingent," inasmuch as they had no intrinsic organization of their own but betrayed the disorganization of the *disgracieux*, which Sartre opposed to the way the "graceful" movements of a dancer were intrinsically organized. Granted that the examples are rather different (as is the relation between the esthetic and the ethical in Sartre), the ethical life of *Or* is intrinsically organized by the reflexive self-choice of the individual, as we shall see in chap. 10.

51. *Either*, p. 35.

52. See p. 174 above. But there is also a privileged moment in this movement, when one becomes conscious of one's "thrownness" or "abandonment" (Heidegger's *Geworfenheit*) in the world as one's fundamental dislocation which one is tempted to associate with not having asked to be born (see *Being and Nothingness*, p. 710). Sartre illustrates this association when he expounds Flaubert's affective reaction (Heidegger's *Befindlichkeit*) to his generation: "Certainly he feels it, this chance [of his birth]; it is the facticity, it is the singular taste of the lived insofar as, in its irreducible originality, it . . . expresses the uncontrolled violence of a copulation—the abandonment of the married couple to the foul kitchen of nature" (*L'idiot*, 1:214). But we enter here in Sartre a different dialectic: what Flaubert "detests" is "not so much that brief folly" (his parents' copulation) as his father's "premeditation"—the fact that he was chosen to be.

53. *Either*, pp. 7–8.

54. Ibid., pp. 24–25; see also *Or*, p. 11.

55. *Either*, pp. 8, 13.

56. Ibid., p. 145. For Hegel's adoption of the term *pathos*, see p. 446 below.

57. Suffering is the starting point of the "authorship." In the first aphorism it was already linked to martyrdom, which in turn is ambiguous. The ostensible reference was to the "sufferings" which "torment" (*martyre*) the soul of the poet, but the original

meaning of the verb was "to bear witness," though it had come in ecclesiastical Greek and Latin to mean to bear witness by one's sufferings and death to Christ's sufferings and death. For the way Kierkegaard expected to be misunderstood by professors, see my introduction; and for the way he felt linked to Christ since Christ was also "misunderstood," see chap. 15, n. 6 below. These links are a good illustration of the "crisscrossing" which tantalizes Kierkegaard as a dialectician. I am tracing them as they hold with respect to content, but it should be recognized too that Kierkegaard employs a "pathetic dialectic"—what I have called an "affective dialectic."

58. See p. 86 above.

59. *Parables*, p. 69. I have left off Kafka's last two sentences, which complicate matters.

60. *Pentimento*, p. 1.

61. See Malantschuk, p. 130.

62. *Johannes Climacus*, p. 104. *Scala* in Latin can mean "ladder" or "steps" or "staircase." The Platonic metaphor of "ladder" is employed by Hegel himself (e.g., *Phenomenology*, p. 14), and Kierkegaard's earliest use of the appellation "Johannes Climacus" is to characterize Hegel (*Papirer*, II A 335). Thus it is again evident that reliance on stages will not by itself be sufficient to differentiate Kierkegaard's dialectic from Hegel's.

63. Although *Either* ends in a seduction, I doubt if Kierkegaard's terminology is sufficiently medical to carry a reference to a sexual climax.

64. See references in Malantschuk's index to "collateral" and "spheres."

65. Kierkegaard likes to cite Socrates' claim that he "always says the same things about the same things" (see, e.g., *Postscript*, pp. 253–54).

66. See, e.g., p. 158 above; *Visible and Invisible*, p. 264.

67. *Papirer*, I C 85.

68. See e.g., *Situations*, 6:88.

69. *Johannes Climacus*, p. 104.

70. *Papirer*, X1 A 181. The procedure can be formulated succinctly as "first the first and then the next" (VIII1 A 49) and can be contrasted with the dialectic of "first" and "last."

71. *Postscript*, p. 262; see also chap. 7, n. 12 below. Climacus's further explanation helps to clarify the procedure of recapitulation: "I have risked repetition [which here takes place at a higher level than in the intervening work with the title *Repetition*] only with significant abbreviation and significant alterations in the point of departure" (p. 254). Since a dialectic is a relational analysis, one of the significant alterations is that in "A Passion Story" (or "A Story of Suffering") "suffering is differently related to the religious than to the ethical or the esthetic" (p. 256).

72. *Being and Time*, p. 303.

73. *Phenomenology*, p. 17.

74. *Either*, p. 45; italics mine.

75. Ibid., pp. 29–30. This was a provisional glimpse of what is later distinguished as the musical form of the erotic. We were given another provisional glimpse in the aphorism where the artist started out by grasping "his loot" and then wove it into the tapestries of his castle. In retrospect this will turn out to be the way the seducer handles the erotic content of his experience, but at Don Giovanni's stage the two operations are inseparable: Don Giovanni "at once beautifies and conquers his loot" (p. 98). The maximum separation will be reached at the stage of the reflective seducer who completes the operation of beautification by composing the "Diary."

76. *Either*, p. 7. In so classifying the aphorisms Eremita would seem to be stressing their association with music. (Hegel used "the laughter chorus of von Weber's *Der Freischütz*" as an example when he protested that "an outburst . . . should not remain unrestrained.") Kierkegaard is stressing not only their passionate vehemence (see n. 41, this chapter) but also the discontinuity between them, for we shall later watch him pun with *brud* ("break") (n. 108, this chapter).

77. *Papirer*, IV A 216.

78. *Encyclopaedia*, pt. 3, par. 450; italics in original. The preceding operation of *Aufhebung* alluded to in the first sentence is the operation of recollection which we examined earlier: "Mind posits the sense impression as its own, pervades it, makes it into something inward, recollects and inwardizes itself in it, becomes present to itself in it."

79. Ibid., par. 451.

80. *Papirer*, I A 11–18; *Or*, p. 10. Sartre will also generalize the idea of stealing well beyond the scope of Genet's accomplishment, so that it applies to items not usually thought of as transportable—to language as well as to experience.

81. "Dry Salvages," in *Four Quartets*.

82. *Either*, p. 45. I employ the singular, "The Immediate Stage," because it will turn out that "The Immediate Stages of the Erotic" do not in fact constitute separate, independent stages but a single stage.

83. *Either*, p. 47. "The erotic," which is the passionate "content" of *Either*, cannot be segregated as a content any more than *pathos* (more broadly speaking) can be segregated from the "pathetic dialectic" it requires (see n. 57, this chapter). Indeed the relation between content and form is itself comparable to an erotic relation. It will be recalled that *The Concept of Irony* started out with elaborate erotic play on the relation between "the concept," which the "observer" as "an eroticist" brings to bear, and "the phenomenon . . . which as such is always feminine in gender" (p. 40 above). But since the observer was relying on language, the erotic relation was less "intimate" than the "union" that we shall see holds in the case of the musical form. A contradiction emerged between the observer (the "knight" who "should feel his own [masculine] preponderance"—i.e., he is to impose the concept) and the requirement "that the phenomenon remain inviolate" (i.e., remain virginally what it is). Eremita is an observer (*Either*, p. 3) as well as an ironist, just as Socrates was a seducer (*Irony*, p. 213). The comparison suggests that all experience is erotic to the extent that the appropriate metaphorical illustration of the intimacy of "having" it is some relation between male and female.

84. *Either*, pp. 45–46.

85. Ibid., p. 134. The affinity between the interpreter's relation to Mozart and the relation of the young girl of the moment to Don Giovanni is suggested early in the essay: "I am like a young girl in love with Mozart" (p. 46). It is reemphasized later (e.g., p. 127). Youthfulness implies immediacy, as it still does in the only actual citation from the libretto of *Don Giovanni*, the epigraph for "The Diary of the Seducer"—"His dominant passion was for the young girl starting out [*la giovin principiante*]" (p. 298).

86. *Either*, p. 102. This is a final behest before Eremita turns to Molière's linguistic interpretation of the same content. We shall learn that understanding Don Giovanni can only be musical and cannot be mediated by language. But we are already prepared for this implication by the last of the "Diapsalmata," where communication which was denied the poet with men in the first aphorism became possible with the immortal gods —i.e., at the level where "everything temporal and contingent is forgotten and cancelled out." It did not take linguistic form but was instead immediate—a chorus of laughter. When the poet picked for his wish the last laugh, "not one of the gods said a word; on the contrary, they all gave way to laughter. Thereupon I concluded that my prayer was fulfilled and found that the gods knew how to express themselves with taste" (p. 42). Laughter as an immediate mode of expression is the tasteful mode at this stage, and "I concluded" indicates that this last of the "Diapsalmata" brings to a conclusion what for the time being we assume is the first stage in a dialectical development. If there is a reference to "the inextinguishable laughter of the gods in Homer, which springs from their blessed repose [*Ruhe*]" (see n. 41, this chapter), Kierkegaard could have regarded this episode as a pause, before starting the dialectical development of the immediate stage in the strict sense.

87. *Either*, p. 64.

88. Ibid., pp. 65, 68, 69.

89. Ibid., p. 59. Kierkegaard is probably assuming familiarity with Hegel's bifocal concept of "powers." These are at once "the universal, eternal powers of spiritual existence" which are quasi divine, but "they may not appear in their universality as such" but as "autonomous individuals," for they are "powers of the human heart, which man, because he is human, must recognize, accept their force, and provide them with actualization" (*Aesthetics*, 1:220, 223). Since Hegel's analysis is dialectical (and hence relational), these "powers" are envisaged as "the eternal religious and ethical relations"—e.g., "family" and "state." We shall see what happens to these two powers in Kierkegaard as opposed to Hegel. "Love" is included in Hegel's list of powers, but he could not have anticipated that Kierkegaard would identify a spiritual power with a "force of nature" (p. 95). But the relation does remain in Kierkegaard dialectically ambiguous in that the erotic desire which is in question emerges as a "principle"—i.e., a starting point which is philosophically established by the principle of contradiction, when erotic desire emerges as excluded by the contradictory Christian principle of spirituality (p. 62).

90. *Either*, pp. 69, 124. Don Giovanni as "a force of nature" is not a determinate content and thus not an autonomous individual, as is Hegel's Antigone as the "actualization" of family relations or Kierkegaard's Socrates as the "actualization" of irony. Yet the dialectic is still bifocal, and like the ironist (when he was imaginatively represented by Aristophanes), he is caught up in ambiguous interplay: "Don Giovanni constantly hovers between being an idea—i.e., force, life—and being an individual. But this hovering is a musical trembling" (p. 91). Thus the level of interplay is not that which will be reached later when imaginative representation becomes poetic. Eremita accordingly refuses to try to transpose the overture into "diffuse and meaningless metaphorical language [*billedsprog*]," explaining, "I am not friendly toward metaphors [*billeder*]" (pp. 127–28). Metaphorical transposition of meaning would be inconsistent with the immediacy with which the sound should be understood. Needless to add, Eremita is being ironical and does not respect his own inhibition. As the present passage indicates, *billede* has a wider range of meaning than I acknowledged earlier: "image," "picture," "portrait," "reflection," "metaphor." Most of the time I shall display the dialectic of the internal/external by translating it as "image" or "picture," but when I wish to bring out the dialectic of transposition and resulting interplay, I shall translate it as "metaphor." See n. 112, this chapter.

91. *Either*, pp. 91, 100, 133–34. Kierkegaard's references to "immediacy," "life," the "force of nature," indicate that this first essay probably should be interpreted as starting out at the level where Hegel started out in his *Aesthetics*—with a discussion of "The Beauty of Nature," whose first section is on "The Idea of Life."

92. *Either*, pp. 67, 93, 100–101, 107. The "music" (p. 70) and the erotic "passion" (pp. 55, 97) it expresses are both characterized as "impatient." Thus a contrast is prepared for between the way Don Giovanni "hurries in a perpetual vanishing, precisely like music" and the "patience" required for an ethical relation as well as for the dialectical development that must be gone through to reach the ethical stage.

93. Ibid., p. 135.

94. Eremita is concerned to give a dialectical version of the history of individual development, not (like Hegel) a dialectical version of the cultural history of the development of society. When Hegel treated the classical, he started with ancient art. Kierkegaard undertakes other correlative adjustments in Hegel's "system of the arts," and these will be examined in chaps. 11 and 12.

95. To characterize the adjustment as a shift to discontinuity is to attempt a more dialectical rendering of what was initially isolated in chap. 2 as the moment of *existential* dislocation. There I cited Sartre's interpretation of some visual artists. Now we could consider the way the metaphor of dislocation is developed when he interprets Braque and Juan Gris: "These solids are surrounded by lines so thick and somber, so profoundly centered on themselves, that the eye is perpetually shifting from continuity

to discontinuity in an attempt to fuse the various patches of the same violet, but each time stumbling against the impenetrability of the mandolin and the water jug" (*Situations*, 1:274).

96. *Either*, p. 137; italics mine. The assumption of course is that continuity is "reassuring" and a "break" disturbing.

97. Ibid., p. 310. There is a similar formulation of the problem of starting point in the essay on *Don Giovanni*: "I came to my thought and begged it yet once more to set itself in motion, to venture the utmost. I knew very well that it was in vain. . . . It constantly sought a foothold but could not find it (pp. 56–57). The seducer in the "Diary," who is also conducting an experiment (*forsøg*), initially "can hardly find a foothold (pp. 319–20). The metaphor may derive from a story Kierkegaard cites from Hegel. An Indian virgin chooses a husband. Confronted by five candidates, she "observes that four of them do not stand firmly [*fest*] on their feet and suspects correctly that they are gods." Since she wants "a real man, she chooses the fifth" (*Irony*, p. 22; *Philosophy of History*, p. 151). Kierkegaard may have felt that the story not only lent itself to his methodological lowering of the level of the dialectic and grounding it but was also relevant to its erotic content, for Hegel locates India as "a Land of Desire" and further explains that "at this point of history where we have now arrived [the Oriental stage], the form of spirit is not advanced beyond immediacy" (*Philosophy of History*, pp. 142, 169).

98. See p. 160 above.

99. *Either*, p. 138.

100. Ibid., pp. 140–41.

101. A recapitulation illustrates this transformation (see n. 71, this chapter). A more detailed illustration will be provided in chap. 11, where the character of the different arts is transformed when the relation that holds between them in Hegel's "system of the arts" is transformed by Kierkegaard.

102. *Either*, p. 141.

103. I am reapplying the phrase which was employed before with respect to the "risk" posed to understanding immediate experience when reflection intrudes with its articulations: in the case of Don Giovanni event and action (what is done through his desire and what he does to his "loot") could not be distinguished.

104. *Either*, p. 141.

105. Although we cannot distinguish in Don Giovanni's case event from action, what he does is not "what we in a stricter sense call an action," for "a deed undertaken with consciousness of its purpose cannot find its expression in music" (p. 119). Antigone's deed is undertaken with consciousness of its purpose, but she remains at the stage of immediacy in the sense that she does not define the purpose with reflexive reference to herself (i.e., existentially); it is defined for her by her relations to her "family" (see n. 90, this chapter).

106. *Either*, p. 154. The reechoing may remind us that comparison with the musical is still relevant, since we are still at the stage of immediacy, just as the "ramifying" may remind us that we are still at the stage of the "natural" and "organic" social unit—the family. A further reminder is the lack of explicit reference to Creon, who is the spokesman in Hegel for the authority of the state as opposed to the family.

107. Ibid., pp. 141, 157–58.

108. Ibid., pp. 141, 155, 156. Kierkegaard likes to play on the dislocation *et brud*—a "breach" or "break" involved in becoming a bride (*en brud*): "In order to become a bride you must make a break with the world and everything and yourself." Thus the term can be applied metaphorically to the "believer" who is wedded to Christ as "the bridegroom" (*Papirer*, XI[1] A 283). It is possible that Kierkegaard has the metaphorical extension in mind here in *Either*: when the "bride" is "wedded" to her "sorrow," she effects a "break" with the (external) world (and ultimately a reflexive "break" with herself—her past life). The later widening of the resulting "breach" between the internal

and the external will be traced in chap. 11. This is a feature of the dialectical development in *Either* which is latent in its starting point with the first aphorism, where a "rift with actuality" is already effected (see n. 32, this chapter).

109. *Either*, pp. 156–57. There was a provisional glimpse of the paradoxical metaphor of burial alive in the aphorism on aphoristical procedure. There the artist lived off his recollections in his castle "as one dead." The Christian theme of being dead to this world, including one's own past, is of course foreshadowed.

110. See p. 215 above.

111. Such interplay is of course not restricted to existentialists. In his analysis of *akrasia*, Donald Davidson quotes an interpretation of how the way Francesca tells her story reveals her weakness of character: "Dante so manages the description, he so heightens the excuse that the excuse reveals itself as precisely the sin, . . . the persistent parleying with the occasion of sin, the sweet prolonged laziness of love" (in Charles Williams, ed., *The Figure of Beatrice*, p. 118). My own initial example of interplay between the *modus loquendi* and the *modus vivendi* was the manipulation, cited in my preface, of prefaces as still another conventional arrangement of the way we come together. In *Either* itself only when an explicitly literary genre is reached with "The Ancient Tragic" does the interplay becomes explicit: Antigone's life "now becomes . . . passionate . . . within herself, . . . and her dialogue [*replik*] becomes pathetic" (p. 161; see n. 57, this chapter). One reason I risk dignifying with a technical distinction the way existentialists use language is that they are usually supposed to be careless in this matter, because they are preoccupied instead with some way of life. But Kierkegaard argues, "If it were the case that philosophers were [otherwise] presuppositionless, language and its entire significance and relation to philosophical speculation would still have to be taken into account, for here philosophical speculation does in fact have a medium which it has not supplied itself." This anti-Hegelian argument leads into a dialectical analysis of language: "Language is partly an original given and partly something freely developing." Acknowledgment of "an original given" prompts distrust of artificial languages: "We do sometimes encounter the mistaken disposition not to accept language as the freely appropriated given but, rather, to supply it onself. . . . Perhaps the story of the Babylonian confusion of tongues may be so explained, as an arbitrary attempt to construct an artificially formed common language" (*Papirer*, III A 11). Such distrust backs up Kierkegaard's attachment to his native language (introduction, n. 26 above).

112. A metaphor is an admission that "the whole idea cannot rest and be comprehended in the expression" (*Papirer*, I A 214), so that it is an instance where the "original given" must undergo dialectical development. Indeed the metaphorical *modus loquendi* (form) takes on its entire appropriateness to the *modus vivendi* (content) only when the religious stage of Kierkegaard's overall dialectical development is reached: "Does not . . . 'We see now as in a glass darkly' imply a recognition of the necessity of allegory for our present condition?" (I A 214).

113. See p. 148 above for the reflexive structure of "personality" as "bent in on itself" (*ind i sig selv bøiet*).

114. *Either*, pp. 152–53. In a more complicated fashion, anxiety in Heidegger also displays a reflexive structure (*Being and Time*, pp. 186–88), which distinguishes it from fear (instead of sorrow, as here in Kierkegaard) and ensures authenticity of experience.

115. *Either*, pp. 152, 156.

116. Ibid., p. 162.

117. For the most generally accepted interpretation of the secret Kierkegaard could not tell Regina, see chap. 15, n. 31 below. Apart from family reasons, Kierkegaard may have been ready to identify himself with Antigone because of his identification of himself with Socrates, whose "fate" Hegel has treated as "tragic" and had quoted with reference to it in Antigone's lines, which Kierkegaard would have found congenial, "If this seems best to the gods, suffering [*pathontes*] we shall recognize our guilt" (*History of Philosophy*, 1:446, 441).

118. *Either,* p. 155. Kierkegaard's coinage "Symparenkromenoi" is bad Greek. I am not making matters too much worse when I derive the English adjective "symparenkromenous" to facilitate reference to the essays assigned to them.

119. See p. 58 above.

120. Although commentators more intimate than I am with Kierkegaard's secrets have never proposed the hypothesis, it does seem possible that Kierkegaard's representation of himself as an Antigone is less an admission of latent homosexuality than dialectical. He is concerned not just with himself but also with Regina's ability to reflect, appropriate her own experience with him, and identify herself. With sympathetic irony he is offering her philosophical significance comparable to the philosophical significance Hegel had conferred on Antigone. His manipulation of the metaphor "burial alive" would then be requital for her assurance that his breaking their engagement would be "the death of her (*Papirer,* X5 A 149, alluded to in *Either,* p. 179). Later he does become preoccupied in his journal with the fact that she does not literally die but instead becomes engaged and eventually married. By then he recognizes that she was incapable of reflection, as we shall see in *Stages,* and had left him in full possession of the metaphor: "When I left her, I chose death" (*Papirer,* VIII A 100).

121. *Either,* p. 155. Eremita is contrasting the external "destiny" which "a woman achieves" when she becomes "a bride" with the "inward" destiny of "a bride of God." In the next essay the bride "does not enter a cloister but puts on the veil of sorrow which conceals her from every alien glance" (p. 181).

122. Ibid., p. 14; *Papirer,* IV B 59.

123. *Either,* p. 218. Although the etymological meaning of *aphorizein* is "to mark off by boundaries" and "define," Eremita is also thinking of the New Testament sense, in which this procedure is applied to individuals who are "set apart" and "separated" from others. For this religious sense, see *Papirer,* II A 396.

124. My italics.

125. *Either,* pp. 73; see also p. 83.

126. *Phenomenology,* p 17.

127. *Either,* p. 149.

128. See p. 103 above.

129. *Phenomenology,* p. 2. Stage is the spatial metaphor par excellence, if it derives from the Greek *stadion,* from which the Latin *spatium* also derives (see Heidegger, *Poetry, Language, Thought,* p. 155). Thus when the whole of the system supervenes in Hegel, he is abstracting from spatial relations as ultimately irrelevant (see p. 505 below).

130. *Either,* p. 178.

131. *Postscript,* p. 239.

Part III

Starting

In man there is always this impulse, which is both easygoing and anxious for reassurance, to secure something that is entirely firm and such as would exclude dialectic.—Kierkegaard

7

Seduction

One must first and foremost take care to find a man where he is and start there.—Kierkegaard

A DEFINITE POSITION

One difficulty in appreciating Kierkegaard's "aphoristical" procedure is that it is pitted against Hegel's "investigations toward unity." The ambition of more recent philosophers has usually taken other, less extravagant forms; they have not often been as committed as Hegel to completing a system. Thus so disruptive a procedure as Kierkegaard's is likely to seem *ad hominem* today, rather than of general philosophical significance. So before pursuing further the implications of his attack on Hegel's system, let me restate in more general terms the problem of starting point which is at stake. The restatement will enable me to take into account our contemporary existentialists who are not as enmeshed with Hegel as is Kierkegaard.

Traditionally a distinction has been drawn between where one starts out as a matter of autobiographical fact and the principle which when reached provides a properly philosophical starting point. In spite of having only one term to employ, *archē*, Aristotle distinguished between the "starting point" which is "more intelligible relative to us" (in the sequence in which we find things out—the order of discovery) and the "starting point" (our "principle") which is "more intelligible in itself" (as satisfying the requirements of scientific demonstration).[1] We saw Hegel draw a similar distinction between a subjective "starting point" and the objectivity of a philosophical "principle" where truth is at stake.[2] But relativity to the individual cannot be abstracted from and left behind in the *reflexive* dialectic of existentialism. The methodological issue for existentialism, as we have begun to see in Kierkegaard, is in effect the breaking up of Aristotle's "us" into separate individuals, for each of whom (to introduce the slogan with which Hegel's version of the distinction is undercut by Kierkegaard) "Truth is subjectivity."[3]

297

Kierkegaard may not draw the traditional version of the distinction, for the methodological issue in existentialism is no longer a matter of finding things out (as in the scientific tradition of philosophy that Aristotle launches) but the *reflexive* issue of where one finds oneself. However, Kierkegaard does not discard the distinction. When the question of starting point was first broached in part I, as if it were simply the question of the problem or subject matter we start out with, we were abstracting from the question of the method with which we start out. We then went on to this question in part II. But it is as implausible to assume that the application of a method simply generates problems as to assume that a problem or subject matter simply dictates the method by which they should be treated. Nor is the issue of starting point reducible to some tactful arrangement negotiated between a problem and a method. At least it cannot be so reduced in an existential philosophy in which a problem is accorded some existential status before it is taken over by philosophy. Hence Kierkegaard's behest: "One must first and foremost take care to find a man where he is and start there." Since what Kierkegaard then attempts is to "bring a man to a definite position [*bestemt sted*],"[4] we can infer that a man's "position" would remain indefinite—in fact not qualify as a "position" at all—until he applies the existential method of *definition*. Until then he would not find himself anywhere. In short, he would not find himself.

DEFINITION

Although there are obvious differences, we could compare Heidegger's byplay with *Bestimmung* in his analysis of *Befindlichkeit*—of how *being-there* "finds" itself "there." As indicated before, Kierkegaard's dialectic (like Hegel's in the *Logic*, Heidegger's in *Being and Time*, Sartre's in *Being and Nothingness*), is definitional in that it moves from the indefinite or indeterminate to the definite or determinate. We have seen in *Either* that this movement is by stages and that their function is to locate. Thus Don Giovanni as an "indeterminate content" is located as belonging to the first stage—the erotic stage which finds expression in music. Defining by locating is the procedure the Judge will follow in *Or* in dealing with the esthete of *Either*: "I shall sketch several of the stages of the esthetic life in order that we may work up to the point where you properly belong."[5] A similar procedure is applied by Sartre to Genet and Flaubert.

But Kierkegaard's procedure is most easily brought out by a comparison with Platonic dialogues, since Kierkegaard takes Socrates as a model. Socrates retains a roughly identical role whatever the adaptation of the particular Socratic dialogue to the interlocutor who usually gives his name to the dialogue by virtue of the relevance of his character to whatever is to be defined. But Kierkegaard adopts different pseudonyms, plays different roles, precisely because self-identity, self-definition, is the existential problem.

The indefinite or indeterminate is not simply an epistemological liability; it has an *affective* character, as we recognized from Heidegger's analysis of *Befindlichkeit*. In Kierkegaard a man would prefer to keep his position indefinite by indulging the "imaginary illusion (*indbildning*) that it is "a definite position."[6] Kierkegaard accordingly argues that when he starts out with esthetic experience, he is finding a man where a man usually is.

The argument seems less novel when we recall a somewhat parallel argument: starting out with what is "more intelligible relative to us" was traditionally a matter of starting out with particular sense perceptions; when we eventually arrive at what is "more intelligible in itself" (e.g., the universal), we recognize that our sense perceptions were indeterminate, indefinite, confused—indeed that we may have been deceived by them. As I have indicated before (and shall continue to stress, for it is pivotal to the *change in direction*, in orientation, that takes place philosophically with existentialism), the version of this skeptical argument which was posed by Descartes and Hegel at the level of *aisthēsis* as sense perception Kierkegaard has transposed to the higher level of the "esthetic," where it is the imagination which confuses us. At the lower level the mind was "exposed to external influences"; at the higher level what the mind was exposed to is internalized.[7] It is no longer a question of deception with respect to external things, as in traditional skepticism, but is ultimately self-deception—a question not of their identification but of my identity.[8]

SELF-DECEPTION

Here we reach the *reflexive* juncture which is privileged in existentialism. The reflexive justification for Kierkegaard's starting out esthetically as where men are is an adage he is fond of citing—*Mundus vult decipi; decipiatur ergo*.[9] Kierkegaard explains this dialectical procedure of counterdeception:

> From the point of view of my whole activity as an author . . . , the esthetic production is a deception [*bedrag*], and herein is the deeper significance of pseudonymity. . . . One must not let oneself be deceived by the word "deception." One can deceive a person for the truth's sake, and (to recall old Socrates) one can deceive a person into the truth. Indeed it is only by this means—by deceiving him—that one can bring into

the truth one who is in an illusion. Whoever repudiates this opinion betrays the fact that he is not much of a dialectician, and dialectic is precisely what is needed for such an operation. ... What, then, does it mean "to deceive"? ... It means that one ... starts by accepting the other man's illusion as the real thing. ... One starts as follows: "Let us talk about esthetics."[10]

Hence Kierkegaard has started with *Either.*

In interpreting *Either* I have paid attention to the "aphoristical" application of the principle of contradiction which renders Kierkegaard's method a method of de-finition, of allocation, which locates positions by drawing "boundaries" and "separating" stages. This method is designed to cope with the confusion that maintaining one's self-deception entails:

> In our own age everything is mixed up together. ... Philosophy has answered every question; but no adequate consideration has been given the question concerning what sphere it is within which each question finds its answer. This creates ... confusion in the world of the spirit.[11]

The "world of the spirit" has its obvious sense, but there is probably also a more technical reference, which I have mentioned before, to the realm of absolute spirit in Hegel that comprises the stages of art, religion, and philosophy, for it is Hegel's esthetic confusion of religion and philosophy (i.e., the confusion of all three spheres which Hegel thought he was distinguishing) that is the ultimate focus of Kierkegaard's attack.

When the different spheres or stages are "separated" and held apart by Kierkegaard (in a fashion which I shall examine later), each becomes confined within its own "boundaries" and becomes a "definite position." The point of proceeding patiently by stages is that "each stage must be made clear by itself"—that is, must undergo development by itself, until the prevailing confusion with the succeeding stage or stages is clarified.[12] Thus the esthetic stage undergoes development in *Either* until it finally becomes definable as a separate stage from the retrospective point of view of its contradiction by the ethical stage.

JUXTAPOSITION

Since the ethical and religious stages, which are separated by Kierkegaard from the esthetic stage, are not found in our contemporary existentialists, let me resume my effort to characterize in more general terms this process of clarifying de-finition, insofar as it bears on the problem of starting point. The general separative function in this process of the principle of contradiction is to clarify one's thinking, according to another adage of

Kierkegaard's—*opposita juxta se posita, magis illucescunt.*[13] This principle
applies at various levels, including its own formulation: the starting point
which would require a juxtaposition of opposites must itself be the opposite of the lucidity which is sought; it must be some confusion. That
some confusion is our starting point may seem merely a philosophical
banality. But there are confusions and confusions, as I have just illustrated by the distinction between confused sense perceptions and "imaginary illusion." Furthermore, a confusion that is to be elucidated by
applying the principle of contradiction, and the other dialectical procedures which have been sorted out in part II as existential, is not just any
old confusion but one which the process of elucidation will expose as having had certain traits.[14]

Just as we recapitulated in part II from the different angle of existential
method the traits of an existential subject matter, which were examined
in part I, so we must now recapitulate these traits as they emerge during
the process of elucidating initial confusion. With the familiarity gained
from the previous recapitulations we need not again consider our different
existentialists in different chapters.[15] Considering them together will help
us visualize the philosophical movement as relatively homogeneous.

The confusion from which we start is not a simple confusion, a simple
indefiniteness. We have some suspicion that we are confused, that matters
are ambiguous. (Sartre will refer to our *malaise*.) Otherwise we could not
entertain the prospect of clarifying our confusion. But our effort to cope
with the confusion in fact tends to take another form, as Kierkegaard explains: "In man there is always this impulse, which is both easygoing and
anxious for reassurance, to secure something that is entirely firm and such
as would exclude dialectic."[16] To require for its *definition* a "jolt"—the
application of so disruptive a principle as the dialectical principle of contradiction"—the confusion from which we start must be recalcitrant, and
not simply some sort of painlessly rectifiable cognitive deception that the
traditional examples from sense perception suggest.[17] Just as our suspicion
that we are confused takes the largely *affective* form of a *malaise*, so the
profoundly affective character of the confusion itself is brought out by
Kierkegaard's definition.[18] It is an impulse which is (in Sartre's formula) a
contradictory composite. Anxiety we have seen propels reflection and so is
opposed to and destabilizes our easygoingness. But the reassurance that we
are anxious for would restore stability to our experience. The juxtaposition of these opposites is involved in other existentialist elucidations of
our initial confusion. Thus in Sartre "anxiety is opposed to the spirit of
self-importance [*l'esprit de sérieux*], which rests on the reassuring substan-
tification of values as things," including the value I attach to being
myself.[19]

FUSION

Some of the other traits of the process by which confusion is overcome can be illustrated by a short-run example of a dialectical development—Sartre's encounter with the Franco-American. Recall how the effectiveness of the process of defining what America is depended on Sartre's displaying to his French reader how confused he initially was on meeting someone who appeared to be an American. His confusion was elucidated when the opposites were separated out in his mind: the Frenchman the Franco-American once had been from the American he was becoming. The moment when the process of elucidation became effective was Sartre's *affective* reaction of revulsion. The *reflexive* character of this reaction did not mean that Sartre's confusion was only *subjective*. If it had been, the process of elucidation would not have been effective; some measure of *objective* justification is needed if Sartre's reaction is to be imparted to his readers. In other words, the dialectic was *bilateral* or *bipersonal* inasmuch as the man confronting Sartre was also confused. He too entered the dialectic *reflexively*—confused with respect to what he himself was. Sartre's own confusion was elucidated by separating what the man thought he still was, a Frenchman, from what he really was—someone who was only conforming to the American's image of a Frenchman as a connoisseur of "pretty girls." Even this image was in turn on *affective* confusion, since it was a projection of the chilly puritanism of Americans who view their Latin opposites as hot-blooded.

Here we begin to reach a higher level which adds further scope to the process of elucidation. At the level of Sartre's personal experience, all that transpired at the Plaza was that he was temporarily confused and recovered from his confusion when he discovered that the man to whom he had been introduced was confused as to what he was, as to his identity. But the process of definition was *bifocal*; there was a higher-level confusion as well. Sartre was not just sorting out a particular individual's confusion; he was elucidating "what America is" as a "melting pot." The *interplay* with this higher level of social con-fusion is more obvious in French, since a term that Sartre used for "melting" is *fusion*: the Franco-American was *en voie de fusion*—"in the process of being melted down—of losing his identity and becoming relatively indeterminate.

Since the dialectic was *bilateral* at this higher level too, American confusion was matched by French confusion regarding America, just as at the lower level the Franco-American's confusion about himself was matched by Sartre's confusion about him. The meeting at the Plaza was only one stage in the dialectic: it was the elucidation of the French slogan "Americans are conformists." But there was another slogan, "Americans are individualists." When the two have been juxtaposed by Sartre and their implications drawn out, the general confusion in French minds will have been elucidated.

AFFECTIVE LOGIC

Sartre's undertaking as an existential psychoanalyst and social historian is to disentangle confusions which he conceives as *reflexive* performances. He goes further than he could in his rapid journalistic discovery of America and tries to explain the "affective logic" which animates one's *reflexive* effort to confuse oneself. He would explore, as he puts it in the case of the anti-Semite, "why one should choose to reason falsely."[20] Other examples will help to illustrate the character of some of the confusions he starts out with, even though we cannot take the time to follow out his elucidations themselves. In the course of his analysis of Flaubert, he deals with "conceptions" which "coexist in an indistinctness intentionally maintained," with a "short-circuiting of meanings," with "thoughts which interpenetrate each other flabbily [*mollement*] without any synthesis being carried out," with "two contrasting ideologies which, instead of repelling each other, interpenetrate," with "two forms of stupidity which reciprocally envelop each other." In all of these instances there is a "refusal of self-recognition,"[21] except insofar as there is some feeling of *malaise*, some sense of *ambiguity*, of discrepancy, which is (as a *reflexive* analysis requires) the juncture where the individual could, but usually does not, initiate an analysis in which he separates and juxtaposes the factors composing his confusion.

The confusion is not something that has taken place once and for all but something dynamic which he is generating, however repetitively, with "conjuring tricks" (*tours de passe passe*). He becomes entangled in "vicious circles in which he turns continually on himself, without any possibility of halting the movement."[22] The process can be analyzed briefly in the case of the illustration, which was cited earlier, of the *contradiction tournante*:

> "I know very well, but even so." Reality repudiates [*inflige un démenti à*] a belief which is itself based on some desire. The subject rejects the experience and denies the reality (Freud's *Verleugnung*). But the reality that has been denied survives and remains ineffaceable: it is disqualified rather than eliminated, and the subject cannot preserve the original desire except at the price of a radical transformation.

The entangling confusions produced by such processes of transformation are tracked down indefatigably by Sartre. And his analysis can be extended from the consciousness of the individual to class consciousness. Thus he refers to the *malaise* of members of a social group who "see them-

selves or rather catch a glimpse of themselves [*se voient, ou plutôt . . .
s'entrevoient*] as confused silhouettes, knots of contradictions."[23]

BEWILDERMENT

Since these complicated performances of consciousness in Sartre could
not be examined without attention to their phenomenological as well as
their dialectic character, let us return briefly to Kierkegaard for his characterization of the confusion he finds at the start. When Kierkegaard
launched his first attack on Hegel in *Johannes Climacus*, he expressed his
conviction "that philosophy has never been so perverted [*forskruet*], so
confused as now."[24] In a later entry in his journal he is more specific about
the "confusion" (*vorvirring*). It is "fraudulent" (*uredelig*). Kierkegaard
goes on to explain that he means not "deliberate deception" but "self-
deception." The "self-deceived individual" is "bewildered" (*vilderede*).[25]
The translation "bewildered" shares the root *vild/wild* and can still carry
the implication in Danish of "astray" in such constructions as *lede vild*
("lead astray"), which we shall soon come across. Even in English "to be-
wilder" once could mean "to lead one astray," "to lose in pathless places,"
"to confound for want of a plain road."

Because this kind of confusion is our actual starting point, I must revise
my earlier treatment of the existential metaphor of following a path—the
metaphor which was most strikingly illustrated by Kierkegaard's title
Stages on Life's Way. So far I have only refined on the earlier treatment by
recognizing that the confusion with which one starts out can be elucidated
only by separating stages on the way. But I must now go behind this procedure, for one does not at the start find oneself with a way along which
one can proceed. The indeterminacy of where one is can only be suggested
by recognizing that one is lost in a pathless place; one is confounded for
want of a plain road.

An appraisal of this predicament can be extracted from the methodological metaphors Heidegger derives from spatial movement. The word
with which *Being and Time* starts out is "clear." This might seem flaunted
irony in so obscure a work, were not the obscurity so promptly conceded,
granted that the concession comes in the form of a quotation from Plato.
The first word in the Greek is *dēlon* ("clear"), but by the end of the quotation a *reversal* has taken place, and we are confronted with a confusion:
"It is clear that you have long been confident of what you really meant
when you employ the expression 'being,' but we who used to think we
understood it have now become confused [*ēporekamen*]."[26] In spite of my
previous misgivings, it is safe to infer from this sentence that an existen-

tial philosophy does start out with a problem, but in the concrete Greek sense of an *aporia*.

Before we explore the implications of this term, we should remember that by the end of this first section of *Being and Time*, Heidegger further concedes that the problem of being which has been raised is not merely "obscure" but also "without direction" (*rictunglos*)."[27] Obscurity is a traditional characterization of the confusion that puts philosophers to work, and we have seen that they traditionally seek clarity in as straightforward a fashion as possible.[28] But Heidegger does not even know in what *direction* to proceed. Here again we need to go behind our earlier analysis, where we dealt merely with changes in direction.

APORIA

One fashion in which Heidegger himself goes behind is by getting back to the etymologies of traditional philosophical terms. The traditional meaning of *aporia* is "problem" or "difficulty." Aristotle started out his treatment of different subject matters by sorting out the relevant "problems," and he thereby instituted a philosophical method that became traditional—the "aporetic" method. But Heidegger excavates the etymology. The *a* of *a-poria* is privative. *Poros* referred originally to a "ford" or "ferry" as a means of passing over a river. It acquired the extended meaning of "passageway," "passage through," or "opening"; and we have already seen that the metaphor of "passageway" itself is a crucial methodological metaphor for Heidegger when he interprets Plato's cave and the bridge. *Poros* derives from *peirein*, which means "to pierce" or "penetrate." (Think of other English descendants besides "pierce"—"porous" and "pores.") Thus the adjective *a-poros* means "without passage," "providing no way in, out, or through," and more abstractly, "impractical," or "difficult."

Heidegger is not so humdrum as to rely on dictionary definitions, as I have. He relies, rather, on poetic usage. In analyzing the structure of human existence as *being-there*, Heidegger interprets the chorus of Sophocles on how "strange" (*unheimlich*) man is as a wanderer who "sets sail on the frothing waters. . . ." In his interpretation Heidegger pays considerable attention to the line which begins, *pantoporos aporos ep' ouden erchetai*, which he translates, "Everywhere journeying on his way [*Überall hinausfahrend unterwegs*], inexperienced and without any way out [*erfahrungslos ohne Ausweg*], he comes to nothing." Heidegger comments,

> The essential words are *pantoporos aporos*. The word *poros* means "passage through [*Durchgang durch*] . . . , passage toward [*Übergang zu*],

path." Everywhere man makes himself a path . . . and . . . is flung out of all paths. . . . On all ways without a way out [*auf allen Wegen Ausweglose*], he is cast out of all relation to the familiar [*heimlich*].

Sophocles may not still "see life steadily and see it whole," as he did in the nineteenth century for Matthew Arnold, but Heidegger's interpretation (like his interpretation of Plato's cave) introduces surprisingly violent dislocations, beginning with *unheimlich* (literally, "not at home," which could admittedly be predicated of a "wanderer") but proceeding with the succession of contradictions which oppose *aporos* to *pantoporos*, "flung out of all paths" to "makes himself a path, without a way out" to "on all ways."[29] Here an *aporia*, as I anticipated, is no ordinary confusion; it displays traits that yield to a dialectical analysis.

VERLEGENHEIT

Having dealt with the Greek sense in which a "problem" is encountered by Heidegger, we need to take the German sense into account. For German, like Greek, is a philosophically significant language for Heidegger. That he is thinking in both languages is betrayed by the fact that his translation of the first sentence in *Being and Time* is not literal. Here we need concentrate on the German translation of *aporia*: "It is clear [*offenbar*] that you have long been confident of what you really meant when you employ the expression 'being,' but we who used to think we understood it have now become confused [*in Verlegenheit gekommen*]."[30]

Verlegenheit, which is Heidegger's German for *aporia*, can conventionally mean "difficulty," and like *aporia* it also can carry a reflexive implication that one is "perplexed" as to how to cope with this "difficulty" and in this sense is "confused" as to what to do. So far abstract identity of meaning is preserved, but there is a concrete difference in the spatial metaphor. The etymology of *Verlegenheit* suggests how Heidegger copes with the "difficulty." His method, we are already aware, can assume the guise of a method of interpretation (*Auslegung*).[31] But it does so because it is a method of dealing with *Verlegenheit*. Interpretation is a matter of "laying out" what has been "laid out wrongly" (*verlegt*). Heidegger in *Being and Time* is undertaking to "interpret" a "misinterpretation."

The changes in *direction* which were described earlier can now be redescribed with some attention to the methodological predicament of *Verlegenheit*. The "difficulty" of "starting out" (*Ausgang*) seemed to be only a matter of gaining "access" (*Zugang*) to what we would deal with, but it developed that "access" was "obstructed" (*verlegt* takes on almost this meaning of *verdeckt* when a path is being followed), so that Heidegger can present his existential analysis not just as a "laying out" but also as a "laying open" (*Freilegung*).³² With Heidegger's translation of *poros* as *Durchgang durch*, there is a double emphasis on the "difficulty" of "getting through" the "obstruction." When the *Durchgang* turns out to be a "going back" (*Rückgang*) through the "obstruction," the difficulty is seen to be a matter of our finding out how we have become "confused" or (to repeat the German translation of Plato) have in *Verlegenheit gekommen*.

In the setting of *Being and Time* this initial sentence from Plato takes on larger implications. The "misinterpretation" becomes identifiable as the philosophical tradition itself, which "blocks the access to the original sources [e.g., Plato] of what the tradition has 'given over' to us." Or, to shift to the visual metaphor which has dominated the tradition itself, the criterion of clarification that must be adopted in dealing with the intervening tradition is not the traditional one of trying to see "clearly" whatever is "given" (and so first of all trying to see it "distinctly") but *Durchsichtigkeit*.³³ We must try to "see through" what has become "confused" by traditional "misinterpretation."

In *Being and Time* Heidegger planned to "go back" and "through" the traditional treatment of the problem of the meaning of being to its original Greek sources. We have watched Heidegger also trace the traditional grammatical treatment of the meaning of being as a process of effacement (*Verwischung*) in which the determinate temporal and personal relations involved in the conjugation of the verb "to be" are abstracted from. But concomitant with this process is the process of confusion (*Vermischung*) whereby the more concrete etymological meanings have become conflated in the modern conjugations. The Sanskrit root of "am" originally meant what "lives," while "be" and "been" derive from an Indo-European root from which the Greeks had obtained one word which meant to "go forth" (*aufgehen*), "unfold," and another word which would add the implication of "into the light"; while a root of "was" meant "to dwell" (cf. the Greek *'estia* [hearth of a dwelling], the Latin vestal virgins who tended the fire on the hearth, and the English "vestibule," deriving from the Latin). But these "determinate" or "definite" meanings no longer make themselves felt in the confused mixture.³⁴

VERSTELLUNG

The confusion that prevails at the start of *Being and Time* is conveyed by other metaphors which I sampled earlier. What he would deal with, Heidegger warns, has become "so inaccessible, at the start and for the most part, that it . . . has become covered over [*verdeckt*]." To this extent the methodological effort of *Being and Time* becomes dis-covery—a dislocating uncovering, as was observed when we tracked Sartre's metaphor "we were discovering the world" to Heidegger. We then followed out Heidegger's explanation in *Being and Time* of how the world has become "covered up": one's "goings about" (*Umgang*) doing this thing and that have involved one's becoming "scattered" (*zerstreut*) about the world, and one's knowing what one is about (*Umsicht*) has at the same time involved becoming "distracted" (another implication of *zerstreut*).[35]

But now we are able to recognize that the methodological "difficulty" is more serious. What is "covered up" may show itself only "disguised" or "distorted" (*verstellt*).[36] An "obstruction" which merely "covered over" or "blocked" our access might be moved out of the way. But a "distortion" has itself a structure which has to be "interpreted," "laid out," "seen through."

There are other intellectual undertakings besides existentialism that struggle with our distorted experience. There is not only the Freudian analysis of repression and the operations of the censor but also the Marxist analysis of false consciousness. But in these analyses the source of the distortion is more specifically localizable, so that its rectification is facilitated. Furthermore, the patient can ally himself with the analyst and endorse the latter's identification of the traumatic episode that has distorted his experience or his interpretation of his experience. A member of the bourgeoisie can ally himself with the proletariat, and his decision will be vindicated when the proletariat has fulfilled its prospective historical role. The more general, more philosophical scope of the "difficulty" in existentialism is indicated by Merleau-Ponty's brusque declaration:

> These truths are not hidden merely like a physical reality which we have not been able to discover, not like something which we will one day be able to see confronting us or which others, better situated, could already see, provided that the screen that conceals it is lifted. Here, on the contrary, there is no vision without the screen.[37]

Heidegger analyzes this predicament in the more *dynamic* fashion with which we are familiar from the "goings about" of *Being and Time* and from the "wandering" in the chorus he cites from Sophocles:

> Man is turned toward what is going on that is most accessible [*nächsten gangbarkeit*]. . . . Man's being driven about from one accessible going on to another . . . is erring [*irren* means "err," "wander," "lose one's way," "go astray"]. . . . The error which he goes through is not just something that runs along beside him like a ditch, something he off and on falls into. No, error belongs to the inner structure of being-there. . . . Error is the realm of interplay [*Spielraum*] for that turning [*Wende*] with which . . . *eksistence* maneuvers and keeps on forgetting and mistaking itself [*wendig sich stets neu vergisst und vermisst*].[38]

GOING ASTRAY

The compounding of confusion this turning comprises will be traced in the next chapter, insofar as it is analyzed in *Being and Time*. For the present we can deal with "error" as the somewhat less complicated matter of "wandering," "losing one's way," and "going astray," for we have already come across these metaphors in Kierkegaard. They are recurrent in existentialism, though of course not unique to existentialism or even to philosophy. Like "way" and "finding" oneself, they are prevalent religious metaphors.[39] What is probably more characteristic of existentialism is the contradictory fashion in which the metaphor of "losing one's way" and its associates are employed in conjunction with the metaphor of "self-entanglement." The Danish *uredelig*, which I translated as "fraudulent," has acquired this moral implication, but it refers etymologically to something which is "tangled up." Kierkegaard's "self-deceived" and "bewildered" individual is so "entangled" that he cannot "give an account" (*rede*) of his "fraudulence." Our translation "bewildered" does share the root *vild/wild* with the Danish *vildrede*, as I noted, but it fails to preserve the etymological meaning of "entanglement."

Through contradictory in spatial terms, the metaphors of "losing one's way," etc., and of "self-entanglement" can be put together because the confusion they delineate is a matter of lacking a sense of *direction*. These metaphors undergo considerable development in existentialism, often in the setting of an episode of seduction—of being "led astray." (The Danish *forførelse*, like the German *Verführung*, embodies almost the same metaphor as the Latin etymology of the English expression.) Seduction is the predominant theme of the esthetic stage on life's way in *Either*, where the climax is reached with "The Diary of the Seducer." As an illustration of the existential methodological problem, consider the seducer's reflexive predicament as it is envisaged by the editor in his preface to the "Diary." The illustration piles up the metaphors we have been examining:

> But how, I wonder, does he view himself? As he has led others astray [*vild*], so he ends, I think, by going astray himself. The others he led astray not outwardly but in their inward selves. There is something revolting when someone directs [*fører*] a wanderer, perplexed [*raadvild*] about his way to the wrong path, and then leaves him alone in his error [*vildfarelse*]; but what is that compared with making him go astray in himself? The strayed wanderer always has the consolation that the scene is continually changing before him, and with every change there is born the hope of finding a way out. He who goes astray in himself has not so great a range for his movements; he soon discovers that he is going about in a circle from which he cannot get out. I think this will happen to the seducer afterward, to a still more fright-

ful extent. I can think of nothing more torturing than an intriguing mind which has lost its way and now turns its whole acumen against itself, when conscience awakens and compels him to disentangle [*rede*] himself from this entangling confusion [*vilderede*]. It is in vain that he has many ways out of his burrow; at the moment that his anxious soul believes it already sees daylight breaking through, it turns out to be a new way in, and like a hunted animal [*vildt*] pursued by despair, he continually seeks a way out and finds only a way in, through which he goes back into himself.[40]

The reflexivity of the initial question, "But how . . . does he view himself?" is stressed by the qualifications "I wonder" and "I think," with which the editor as an outside observer admits that he can only speculate about what is going on within the consciousness of the seducer. At the same time, the distinction between the wanderer's "being led astray" in the literal physical sense and sexual "seduction" (which is a physical affair but already has etymologically a metaphorical connotation) is a point of entry for the *interplay* which is introduced with the contradiction that was the starting point of *Either/Or*. The application of this contradiction to the seducer is prepared for by its application to those whom the seducer had (the editor explains) "led astray not outwardly but in their inward selves." (In a moment we shall take a further look at the predicament of the seduced.) The contradiction is reinforced with the byplay that derives from the reflexivity of reflection, when the seducer "discovers that he is going about in a circle from which he cannot get out." (Later we shall see that turning in Heidegger too culminates in a circular movement.) Inasmuch as the seducer is reflecting, he "goes back into himself," even though he is reflecting about how he might "get out" of himself. Ultimately this contradictory predicament is Hegelian, for Kierkegaard is parodying what he denounces as "the confusion of thinking by self-reflection."[41]

THE INTERESTING

In reaching the climax of *Either* I have skipped over the intervening stages in the development of the theme of seduction, by taking advantage of the recapitulative relation between *last* and *first*. We are familiar with the first essay on *Don Giovanni*, and the relation between the "Diary," as the last stage, and the first essay is suggested by the rubric for the "Diary" which is taken from the opera. The suggestion is underscored in Eremita's preface:

The idea of the seducer is foreshadowed in the essay on the Immediate Erotic as well as in the Shadowgraphs—i.e., the idea that the analogue to Don Giovanni must be a reflective seducer who comes under the category of the interesting, where the question is not how many he seduces, but how he does it.[42]

This distinction between the immediate level of actual experience and the reflective level was glimpsed in the aphorism on aphoristical procedure:

> From it [my stronghold] I swoop down to the actual world to grasp my loot; but I do not remain down there. My loot I bring back home. It is the picture [*billede*] I weave into the tapestries of my castle.[43]

The *interplay* between levels is elaborately developed in the "Diary" where "the category of the interesting" takes over as referring to what transpires "between" the levels. Once the seducer has not only caught sight of his prospective victim but has also carried out the "internalizing" process of recollection, which enables him to represent her imaginatively, he exclaims,

> How beautiful it is to be in love, how interesting to know that one is in love. That is the distinction. . . . The image [*billede*] I now have of her hovers indeterminately between her actual and her ideal form.[44]

The shift to the *interplay* manifest in this hovering is associated with the shift in the "Diary" from what I earlier contrasted as the horizontal dimension of the dialectic (the dimension populated, for example, by the "many" Don Giovanni had seduced—1,003 in Spain alone) to the vertical dimension where interest is heightened by "how he does it," not just to her but also to his own consciousness of what he is doing to her (or has done to her)—keeping the "Diary" in which he recollects ("internalizes") what he has done. This upward climb is characteristic of the "Diary" itself: "As it progresses," the editor points out, "it becomes more and more sparing of dates, . . . as if the story, . . . although historically *actual*, comes nearer to having *ideal* significance, so that definite references to time become a matter of indifference."[45]

This process of esthetic idealization as carried out in the "Diary" itself has to be distinguished from the original process of esthetic idealization during the seduction. The editor explains;

> The poetic . . . he [the poet as seducer] brought with him and enjoyed in the poetry of the actual situation. He withdrew this again in the form of poetic reflection. This afforded him a second enjoyment. . . . In the first instance he enjoyed the esthetic personally, in the second instance he enjoyed his own esthetic personality. . . . In the first instance he constantly needed actuality as occasion, as factor [*moment*]; in the second instance, actuality was submerged in the

poetic. The fruit of the first stage is thus the mood from which the "Diary" emerges as the fruit of the second stage. . . . Thus the poetic was constantly present in the ambiguity of his life.[46]

At both levels the seducer was leading himself away from himself or (put in terms of the opposing idiom of self-entanglement) was unable to "get out" of himself. When he ostensibly did enter "the actual situation," his enjoyment depended largely on "the poetic . . . he brought with him," and so he in fact went "back into himself," and he went still further "back into himself" when "actuality" was "submerged" in the poetic "internalizing" recollections of the "Diary."

RECOLLECTION

The self-deception involved can be more readily appreciated if we take the "Shadowgraphs" into account as an intervening stage, which Eremita has drawn to our attention, in the development of the theme of seduction. At this stage the emphasis still falls on the "others" who are being "led astray," although already the *reflexive* shift is taking place, since they are being led astray (as it is phrased in the preface to the "Diary") "not outwardly but in their inward selves." "Shadowgraphs" is the essay which follows "The Ancient Tragic," and it presents a triad of "brides of grief"—seduced and abandoned women who abandon themselves in turn to the process of "internalizing" recollection, so that in each case a transition takes place from being deceived and "led astray" outwardly by her seducer to being self-deceived and "led astray" inwardly from herself by herself. This "subjective dialectic" is a further stage in the development of reflection beyond that of the first "bride of grief," Antigone, in whose "unhappy love" there was not yet any question of deception.

With respect to the first member of the triad, Marie Beaumarchais, it is explained that, "when unhappy love has its ground in a deception," the suffering is "due to its inability to find its object." Of course if the deception is demonstrated," the object is found, identified, and the suffering is no longer an attempt to establish what he actually was by a process of "internalizing" reflection. Reference to the object provides an exit from reflection; the suffering becomes "immediate"—that is, a direct response to what he actually was.

Nevertheless, "to establish certainty for the fact that a deception is actually a deception is always very difficult," so reflection is likely to continue. Then "the question whether or not he [the seducer] actually was a deceiver is . . . the unrest which gives perpetual movement to her grief." For whatever *objective* evidence there originally was cannot survive the *subjective* process of her reflection upon it:

If someone owned a letter which he knew, or believed, contained information bearing upon what he must regard as his life's salvation, but the writing was delicate and faint, almost illegible—then would he read it with restless anxiety and with all possible passion, in one moment getting one meaning, in the next another, depending on his belief that, having made out one word definitely, he could interpret the rest thereby; but he would never arrive at anything except the same uncertainty with which he began. He would stare more and more anxiously, but the more he stared, the less he would see. His eyes would sometimes fill with tears; but the more often this happened, the less he would see. In time, the writing would become fainter and more blurred, until at last the paper itself would crumble away, and nothing would be left to him except his tear-dimmed eyes.[47]

In short, the *objective* evidence disintegrates, and only the *subjective* evidence remains of his own feelings as an individual.

REFLECTION

Marie cannot "find" the "object" of her unhappy love, for his having deceived her would have been incompatible with his having loved her. And she is unable by reflection to resolve the contradiction:

"No, he was no deceiver. . . .
"Yes, he was a deceiver. . . .
"A deceiver he was not, even if I never understood him."[48]

The next seducee, Donna Elvira, represents a further, more *subjective* stage in this process of reflection. She cannot "find her own way . . . to herself." Unlike Marie, she had already renounced the external world by withdrawing into a cloister before she ever met Don Giovanni, so she was already at a further remove from anything *objective*. It can no longer be a question in her case of clinging to any *objective* evidence such as a letter. She is too confused to know what the relevant evidence would be:

If I were to imagine someone on a ship in distress, unconcerned for his life, remaining on board because there was something he wanted to save and yet could not save, because he was perplexed [*raadvild*] about what he should save, then would I have an image [*billede*] of Elvira; she is in distress at sea, her destruction impends; but this does not concern her, she is not aware of it, she is perplexed about what she should save.[49]

Finally we are presented with Margaret, the victim of Faust—a reflective seducer, as opposed to Don Giovanni, so that she represents a still further, even more *subjective* stage in the process of reflection, since she is so confused in herself with him:

"Can I remember him? Can my recollection [my internalization] summon him forth, now that he has vanished, I who am myself only a recollection [internalization] of him?"

The author of the "Diary" will likewise be a reflective seducer, but the seduction will be a dialectical advance beyond the seduction of Margaret. To seduce [*forføre*] Margaret, Faust "does not lead [*føre*] her up into the higher regions of the spirit, for it is from these he flees; he desires her physically."[50] He is trying to regain immediacy through her.

In contrast, the author of the "Diary" arranges an *Aufhebung* for his victim; what she ostensibly reaches through the development of her own process of reflection are these higher regions. And her seducer's own enjoyment will finally be less a matter of the physical seduction than of his own reflective idealization culminating in its recollection and in the production of the "Diary." Thus when the seducer recollects the rendezvous when the seduction will take place, he exults, "Everything is symbolic [*billede*]: I myself am a myth about myself." The final thrust here is *reflexive*. The editor's reference to the seducer's "infinite self-reflection" credits to him the reflective competence reserved for absolute spirit in Hegel, and the moment of seduction symbolizes the final moment of synthesis of subject and object in Hegel's dialectic.[51] I shall return later to some of the implications of this parody.

RENDEZVOUS

Sartre's analysis of the confusion of self-deception takes up one early chapter in *Being and Nothingness*. Yet it takes on a larger significance from Sartre's characterization of the whole work as "an eidetic of self-deception [*mauvaise foi*]." Self-deception is the crucial *reflexive* moment in Sartre insofar as his method is an existential dialectic. And this moment remains crucial even when his dialectic becomes quasi-Marxist, since it enables him to denounce the bias by which his own bourgeois class deceives itself.

In the chapter on self-deception, the episode analyzed in most detail is a seduction. Thus this theme is not restricted to Kierkegaard and cannot be explained away as something he inherited from romanticism. How does it earn its existential significance in Sartre? Before answering this question, let me allude briefly to the first example with which Sartre illustrates the character of self-deception. This is the case of women who claim that "disillusionment [*déception*] with their marriage has made them frigid," even though they do in fact "have orgasms during sexual intercourse." These "objective signs of enjoyment" can be observed by their husbands, but "when questioned by the psychiatrist the wives will fiercely deny them."[52]

The setup of this example displays traits of an existential dialectic with which we are familiar. Sartre has begun with a *bilateral* relation which is dislocated—the "disillusionment" which arrays the wives in opposition to their husbands. But whenever we have watched a *bilateral* relation develop in *Either*, it has been followed up with a *reflexive* shift—for example, the shift implicit in the transition "As he has led others astray, so he ends up . . . by going astray himself." Similarly Sartre's focus promptly shifts from the *objective* relation between wives and husbands (and from what is objectively observable with respect to this relation—the actual occurrence of orgasms) to the wives' *subjective* relation to themselves: "They succeed in concealing from themselves [*se masquer*]" the objective fact that these orgasms occur, even though "they cannot fail to recognize their enjoyment at the moment it is experienced." What is crucial for Sartre is not the effort the woman then makes to convince her husband or the psychiatrist but the *reflexive* effort to convince herself: "If the frigid woman thus distracts her consciousness from the enjoyment which she experiences, it is by no means cynically and in full concurrence with herself; it is in order to demonstrate to herself [*se prouver*] that she is frigid." This phraseology should not mislead us; here as elsewhere in existentialism knowledge has lost its primacy. And my translating *mauvaise foi* as "self-deception" in order to bring out its *reflexive* orientation should not let us forget that we are dealing with an act of "faith."[53] Conviction is sought by an *affective* reaction to the experience in question. A "logic of the passions" is being displayed.[54]

I shall soon return to this affective dialectic. But the *reflexive* shift from *objective* to *subjective* is a general tendency of Sartre's analysis, as it is of Kierkegaard's, and it will emerge more clearly if we examine other portions of his analysis, beginning with the dialectical foreplay with which the episode of seduction is presented. The woman in question is introduced as having "surrendered at the first rendezvous" (*s'est rendue au premier rendez-vous*). On one hand we have a *rendezvous* which is *objective*; on the other we have a *reflexive* sexual surrender (*s'est rendue*).[55] At the same time the fact that it is their "first" rendezvous is played off against the finality of such a "surrender."

That the notion of rendezvous itself is not entirely casual but a philosophical stratagem in a *bilateral* dialectic is suggested by a succession of previous examples that can be taken to represent earlier stages on the way to this example. In the first of these, I have a rendezvous with Peter at a café. I arrive late, and the question then is, "Will he have waited for me?" I look around the café and reach the conclusion "Peter is

not there." The next example is a *reflexive* revision of the first. Instead
of one individual expecting to meet some other individual, it is now a
matter of what I expect of myself: "I wait for myself in the future when
I make a rendezvous with myself on the other side of this hour, this day,
this month." Or, to be more specific, it is some possibility which I am
reflectively aware of as "a possibility for me," which is "waiting for me
over there in the future." I then become dialectically aware of the opposing possibility—"of not finding myself at that rendezvous or of even no
longer wanting to be there."[56]

The existential implications of rendezvous in Sartre can be more
fully brought out if we suspect some reminiscences of what I have taken
as the starting point of Heidegger's existential dialectic insofar as it entails
that "affective finding of oneself [*Befindlichkeit*]" which in Heidegger is
a dimension of existence as *being-there*. With the first rendezvous in
Sartre, when I looked around the café and reached the conclusion "Peter
is not there," Heidegger's *being-there* was undergoing a readjustment in
order to extract from it a dialectic of being and not-being.[57]

DISTRACTION

Another apparent debt to Heidegger for an affective version of the
opposition between being (there) and not-being (there) is the concept of
distraction, which Sartre illustrates with the case of the ostensibly "frigid
woman" who "distracts her consciousness from the enjoyment she experi-
encse." Distraction seems to be Sartre's translation of Heidegger's *Zerstreuung*. This translation is better adapted to the bilateral dislocations of
Sartre's dialectic of being and not-being, object and subject, than the alternative translation "scattering" which I preferred for Heidegger himself
as more compatible with the plurality of reference points on which we
rely as we turn from one thing to another in "going about" his *Umwelt*.[58]

Consider more details of the example of wifely self-deception: "To
distract themselves in advance from the enjoyment which they dread . . .
many of the wives during intercourse turn [*détournent*] their thoughts to
their everyday activities; they figure out their household accounts." In
Being and Time, "distraction" is linked with two other subordinate ways
in which being-there is being-in-the-world:' "never staying with" (*Aufen-
haltlosigkeit*) and "not lingering with" (*Unverweilen*). These two phenomena could have been interpreted by Sartre as coming close to
constituting a mode of not being-there, for the "in" of being-in-the-world
is initially analyzed by Heidegger as deriving from "to stay with" (*sich
aufhalten*), and one of the modes of being-in-the-world he analyzes as "to

linger with" (*verweilen bei*). Thus there may be a further reminiscence of Heidegger when Sartre identifies his phenomenon:

> What we are dealing with is a phenomenon of self-deception, since the efforts taken in order not to stay with the pleasure imply recognizing that it is experienced. These efforts imply it *in order to deny it.*[59]

It seems plausible to suppose that Heidegger has drawn Sartre's attention to the phenomenon of "not staying with" and that Sartre has fitted the phenomenon to the dialectic of being and not-being which is latent in the "efforts" which "imply it *in order to deny it.*

"Distraction" is also involved in the self-deception of the woman "who surrendered at the first rendezvous." Having already traced the reflexive revision of the earlier rendezvous with Peter, we can follow more readily the reflexive fashion in which she surrenders. Although Sartre begins by setting up an objective *bilateral* relation between the woman and her prospective seducer (as he began with the objective *bilateral* relation between the husbands and their ostensibly frigid wives), the seducer's intentions do not undergo dialectical development (any more than the husbands' did), for the focus again promptly shifts to the woman's relation to herself:

> She knows very well the intentions which the man who is talking to her cherishes regarding her. She knows too that it will be necessary sooner or later for her to make up her mind. But she does not want to feel the urgency.[60]

As in our previous example, it is not knowledge that is primarily at stake (she already has the knowledge) What is primarily at stake is a reaction which is *reflexive* and *affective.* But the reaction is a complex performance. Wanting to feel something is cumbersome enough; not wanting to feel something requires even more juggling, especially in the case of the wives and of this woman, since it is a not wanting to feel something which is felt. To describe the performance as "juggling" is not to suggest that Sartre is staging examples which are too theatrical; such performances are a staple of ordinary living.

The complexity of the present example represents an advance in reflexivity over the preceding example of the ostensibly frigid wives, for the something she does not want to feel is "urgency," which is not as *objective* as the physiological occurrence of an orgasm, so that almost the whole dexterity of her *affective* logic has to be *reflexive.*[61] The *affective* performance will in fact prove to be the kind which we have observed existential dialectical favors—*ambiguous, contradictory, unstable*— and in marked contrast to the cognitive evidence available to her, which is un-ambiguous and consistent and remains fixed from the outset, when already "she knows very well. . . ."

THE INITIAL MOVE

Her distraction can be interpreted methodologically as a small-scale illustration of the discontinuity which has already been encountered in *Either*—for example, when the seducer follows out only the short-run implications of leading others astray and refuses to anticipate the longer-run *reflexive* implication that he is leading himself astray. On one hand the woman in Sartre "attaches herself to what is respectful and sincere in the attitude of her companion"; on the other she refuses to discern in his attitude opposing characteristics which are perhaps not yet entirely manifest:

> She does not construe his behavior as an attempt to carry through what is called "the initial move"—that is, she does not want to recognize the possibilities of temporal development which his conduct offers and restricts his conduct to what it is at present.

The "initial move" is always in a dialectic a starting point which entails possibilities of *development* and which may offer some provisional glimpse of these possibilities. To the extent that she refuses to acknowledge this glimpse, her conduct can be condemned as undialectical—as a failure to elucidate what is going on by juxtaposing the relevant opposites. But of course one's conduct can never be entirely undialectical, or dialectic would not have anything to take hold of that it could elucidate. She is in fact nurturing ambiguous *interplay*, for she does "not know quite what she wants." Or, rather, she contradictorily wants it both ways:

> She is profoundly aware of the desire she excites, but this desire crude and naked would humiliate and horrify her. Yet she would find no charm in respect which was merely respect. What is needed to satisfy her is a feeling which is addressed wholly to her as a *person*. . . . But at the same time this feeling must be wholly desire—addressed to her body as an object.

In short, she wants a feeling which is an *ambiguous composite*, without being forced to recognize its *contradictoriness*. It is this confusion itself which she cherishes:

> She refuses to apprehend the desire for what it is. . . . She recognizes it only to the extent that it transcends itself toward admiration, esteem, respect, and that it is wholly absorbed in the more refined forms which

it produces, to the extent of no longer retaining any prominence except as a sort of warmth and density.[62]

This dialectical *interplay* constitutes "the disturbing and unstable harmony" which is "the attraction of the occasion."

An action on the seducer's part threatens to expose the contradiction, but it is countered by a maneuver on her part:

> Suppose he takes her hand. This action of her companion risks changing the situation by calling for an immediate decision. . . . Her aim is to postpone the moment of decision as long as possible. We know what happens next; the young woman leaves her hand there, but she *does not notice* that she is leaving it.

The dialectic is *bilateral*. But just as Kierkegaard's seducer was going astray himself, even though he seemingly was only leading others astray, so she is distracting herself while seemingly engaged in distracting him:

> She does not notice because it happens that she is at this moment wholly spiritual. She draws her companion up to the most elevated regions of sentimental speculation; she speaks of life, and of her life, she presents herself as she essentially is—a personality, a consciousness.

Her dexterity is ultimately *reflexive*. Her self-deception violates the dialectical requirements of a *developmental* and *relational* analysis by detaching herself in her own mind not only from her prospective physical relation to him but also from her own relation to her body:

> Meanwhile the divorce between body and soul is carried out; the hand rests inert between the warm hands of her companion, neither giving its consent nor offering resistance—a thing.
> While feeling profoundly the presence of her own body—to the extent perhaps of being excited, she . . . contemplates it from above as a passive object.[63]

She is being seduced, and not just in the physical sense which by itself is so dialectically uninteresting that Sartre never bothers to report its occurrence.[64] What concerns him is the movement of distraction with which she "leads" herself "away" psychologically from the se-duction that is happening to her physically. But the "divorce" between the psychological and the physical is not in fact complete; the disrelation presupposes a relation. The physical passivity of her hand embodies the psychological passivity of her not wanting to feel the urgency. The episode thus illustrates the effort (in Kierkegaard's terminology) to "exclude dialectic" by not allowing whatever experience is in question to become sufficiently defined, so that its *reflexive* relation to oneself must be acknowledged by either (to regain Sartre's terminology) giving one's "consent" to what is already being done or offering "resistance."

Once one recognizes that one is *reflexively* "drawn into the movement" by an existential dialectic,[65] one should recognize next that lucidity with respect to the movement can be obtained by discerning contradictions or (in Kierkegaard's formula) juxtaposing opposites. In the present case this criterion is not being met: the "warmth and density" of becoming a desired body is confused with the "admiration and esteem" she would like to command as a person. But knowledge is not primary in existentialism. An existential dialectic further imposes on us a sense of urgency, which is opposed to passivity just as lucidity is opposed to confusion. Her passivity is not merely the inertia of a physical object, an inanimate body: "It is a matter of postponing the moment of decision as long as possible."

The counteracting sense of urgency is built into the idiom of rendezvous. In its original objective form, the question was, "Will Peter have waited for me?" In its *reflexive* revision, I asked, "Will I wait for myself in the future, where I have a rendezvous with some possibility for myself?"[66] Even though she knows she will be there, the woman about to be seduced refuses to anticipate this prospective rendezvous as something determinate, as something which will define their relation—a definite position.[67]

PASSIVITY

The setup of this example, like that of the examples of seduction in Kierkegaard, carries implications well beyond the range of what is conventionally regarded as sexual behavior. These implications are worth canvassing, especially since sexual seduction has lost for us the intrinsic drama it enjoyed in Kierkegaard's time or even when Sartre wrote *Being and Nothingness.* The revulsion and contempt that Sartre displays, and would have us feel, concerning the ambiguous and passive conduct of the woman who still thinks of herself as a "person" even though she is merely conforming to the ritual of seduction is not very different from the revulsion and contempt he would have us feel concerning the Franco-American who thought of himself as still really a Frenchman, even though he was only conforming to the American's image of a Frenchman. The similar setup of the two episodes is more obvious with the transition from the conclusion, which I cited from the episode at the Plaza, to the next paragraph, where we find the melting pot is no longer irresistible:

He will soon be a tree or a rock. I speculated curiously as to the powerful forces that had to be brought into play in order to actualize these disintegrations and reintegrations so reliably and rapidly.

But these forces are mild and persuasive. You have only to walk about in the streets, enter a shop, or turn on a radio, to encounter them and feel their effect upon you, like a warm breath.[68]

The passivity with which the Franco-American is succumbing to the melting pot becomes ambiguous as soon as the "powerful forces" lose their metallurgical, biological ("tree"), or geological ("rock") irresistibility. The "forces" instead become merely "mild" and "persuasive." The relentless process of the melting pot has abated into the process of persuasion with which we are familiar as an "affective logic." Thus the process of transformation, as well as the Franco-American who is involved in it, becomes an *ambiguous, contradictory*, and *unstable* composite of the predetermined and the voluntary, like the wiggling bottom of the walker. The ambiguity leaves room for attributing some measure of responsibility to anyone who succumbs to the process, so that Sartre can elicit an additional feeling of revulsion from conformism. I have translated as "mild" the term *doux*. But the French term has an ambiguous range of meaning which is much favored by Sartre: *doux* can also mean "soft" (this meaning is initially elicited by the contrast with the hardness of the "rock") and "sweet."[69] Both "soft" and "sweet" can take on insidiously nauseous implications in Sartre, which are helped along here by the comparison with "breath" that initially seemed only to suggest that the pressure to conform is spiritual rather than irresistibly "powerful." But the persuasion of others is not likely to be relished when it is a matter of our being breathed on, and the warmth of the breath adds to the sense of their proximity and its unpleasantness.

LASSITUDE

In his polemical political writings Sartre regularly stimulates a sense of revulsion from the passivity of the individual who fails to acknowledge his *reflexive* relation to his experience and the existential imperative to make it his own experience; the individual instead succumbs to the "lassitude" which Sartre diagnoses as the "common malady" of our epoch. We remain "inert," neither giving our "consent" nor offering "resistance." Confronted with our inertia, Sartre would impart a sense of urgency: he would summon us from our effort to postpone as long as possible the moment of decision; he would have us recognize the "movement" into which we are being "drawn" and the contradictions which impel this movement but which we have allowed to become blurred into ambiguities; we are to emancipate ourselves from our confusion by taking sides—the opposite side, where the underprivileged are—in the class struggle which pits us against them. The answer to Gaston Berger's accusation that Sartre is a journalist rather than a philosopher is that Sartre's philosophy is implicated in the sense of urgency with which he resorts to journalism.

The example of the Franco-American or of the woman is of a particular individual. But the dialectic is *bifocal,* for Sartre induces us to climb from this lower level to the level of the social phenomenon exemplified. The climb can be justified by the process of "condensation" which was examined earlier. Thus the sense of revulsion from the Franco-American is to be extended to all forms of hyphenation which emerge when an individual is transformed into a conformist by a melting pot or other social pressures, as in such cases as the Respectful Prostitute. Even Merleau-Ponty, in Sartre's memorial essay, provides a particular exemplification of the "lassitude" that is the "common malady" of our time.[70]

There is, of course, nothing distinctively existential about the procedure of generalizing from an individual example to some social phenomenon. What is more distinctive is that the individual is never left behind, inasmuch as his moral responsibility for what is transpiring is not attenuated as soon as we recognize that we are in fact dealing with a social phenomenon, a "common malady," even though attenuation is a conventional commitment of such social generalizations. In existentialism individual moral responsiveness and responsibility survive the generalization intact or accentuated by virtue of the *reflexive* and *affective* character of the dialectic, which is designed to elicit the individual's response to his responsibility.[71] Hence Sartre focuses on the Franco-American's American image of himself as a Frenchman, and on what is going through the mind of the woman about to be seduced, as if not much more of what was going on mattered.

At the same time, the social dimension remains oppressively relevant in existentialism, since it is conformity that the individual is required to revolt against if he is to overcome his confusion and passivity and become an individual. The social dimension is not explored in either of these examples. In the case of the woman about to be seduced, we are not told the whole story, only about how things got under way—"the initial move." Prophecy was superfluous, "foreshortening" was feasible, because the episode is so conventional a social ritual—"we know what happens next." This does not mean that the story can be dismissed as inconsequential. The conventional makes up so large a part of the fabric of experience. In explaining the "rigid structure of fiction which renders it prophetic," Sartre cites Flaubert's swift generalization from a particular case of seduction: "My wretched Bovary doubtless is suffering and weeping in twenty French villages at this very moment."[72]

Conflict

Sartre counts on our already knowing "what happens next" in the case of the woman about to be seduced. Our knowledge sharpens our sense of the ambiguity and passivity of her conduct, by playing up the contrast with her not quite knowing what she wants, just as her not quite knowing was played up by the initial contrast with her knowing very well what he wants and will get. Thus the focus has not been on the conventional social ritual of seduction but on the *reflexive* process of self-deception with which the woman as an individual is letting herself become caught up in this conventional social ritual. Now that this focus has been established, I must try to do justice at least to the ability of the existentialist to move to a higher level. I cannot do more, for to try to follow through an existential analysis at the social level itself would take us too far beyond its starting point, where the effort is made to "become an individual." Thus I cannot deal with Kierkegaard's analysis of *The Present Age*, Heidegger's analysis of technology, or Sartre's *Critique*. But since the last work has often been singled out as no longer existentialist, I might add to my previous inadequate anticipations some evidence that Sartre's social analysis exhibits a dialectic which is comparable to, if more complicated than, his psychoanalysis of the individual.

When a social dimension is added, the individual's situation still remains *reflexive:* "Our actions resemble us, for they betray our egoism and our stupidity. And they do not resemble us, for they are deviated by the force of circumstances, are falsified, and become unrecognizable."[73] If on one hand the resemblance were pursued, self-deception might still be disclosed as implicated in "our egoism and stupidity." But on the other hand the emphasis has shifted, and alien factors beyond our control are now taking into account as altering the impact of our actions virtually beyond our recognition. Yet what we are up against is further deception.

A *bipersonal* model for its analysis is provided by Sartre's introduction of a second individual who participates significantly in a course of action, unlike the husbands of the ostensibly frigid wives or the seducer of the second example of self-deception. I am a boxer and my antagonist makes a feint to my head; I cover, and this action enables him to hit me in the stomach. It is now a question not of self-deception but of my having been deceived by an antagonist, yet the outcome is still reflexive: I am deceived into performing an action that enables my antagonist to employ my own action against me. Each of us is "outwitting and mystifying the Other, seeking to disarm his freedom and to make it his unwitting accomplice, . . . in order to get an opportunity of treating his *as a thing*."[74]

This example becomes explicitly social when Sartre expands it into two opposing armies. Although Sartre repeatedly endorses the Marxist doctrine of class conflict, when he deals with conflict himself it is as "the only human practice which actualizes in urgency everyone's relation to his being as an object." This relation the woman about to be seduced disavowed. She did "not want to feel the urgency," and she was avoiding any conflict. In the present case the "urgency" is a demand that "consciousness must be as lucid as that of the enemy. For "one not only has to actualize one's own objectivity, starting out from a particular action by the enemy," but one also has to carry out a reassessment. Thus "it is known that he is going to advance to a particular place to attain a specific objective." But for us this objective can be assessed as a "trap," an ambush." But in making this assessment, we have to recognize that "the enemy has his own game to play; he foresees the trap, and we foresee his foresight."[75]

What I am citing from the *Critique* is merely a footnote referring to "classical warfare." Deception plays a more complicated role with class conflict, where the antagonists do not just confront each other as opposing armies but are in many ways enmeshed with each other. What Sartre envisages here is often closer to the case of the woman about to be seduced.[76] At one extreme, if "*praxis ceases to be aware* of its end, its means, of the means and end of its adversary, and of the means of opposing the hostile praxis, it simply becomes blind ... ; it is simply an unconscious accomplice of the *other action* which overwhelms, manipulates, and alienates it and turns it against its own agent as a hostile force."[77]

These complications I shall shirk, since I cannot take up Sartre's social analysis for its own sake. But having focused in this chapter on the reflexive process by which a woman entangled herself as an individual in the social convention of seduction, I shall allow the focus to shift in the next chapter to Sartre's handling of this social convention itself, in order to bring out once again the *bifocal* character of his analysis. For before we can consider in the following chapter how the individual can find his way back to himself, we need to consider the different levels involved in his being led astray.

Notes

1. *Physics* 184a16. This distinction is not drawn by Plato, but it is not my present concern to compare different versions of the dialectical method.
2. See chap. 1.
3. This principle is stated as the title of the chapter of *Postscript* to which the recapitulation of the esthetic works is an appendix. Having just carried out a fairly close textual analysis of how Kierkegaard starts out in *Either*, I feel freer now to cite his later interpretations of this starting point from *Postscript* and *Point of View*. Remember that *Postscript*, as "concluding" the "esthetic production," is in one sense the last

esthetic work and so is dialectically related to *Either/Or* as the first work (see chap. 10, n. 31 below), while one reason Kierkegaard offers for composing *Point of View* is that "I am about to encounter for the second time . . . my first production, *Either/Or*, in its second edition" (*Point of View*, p. 5).

4. *Point of View*, p. 27. Corresponding to Kierkegaard's conception of "a definite position" is Sartre's conception of "situation," though it derives from Heidegger. Note the reflexive character of a situation in Sartre: "When we speak of *situation* ... we are speaking of a 'position apprehended by the subject' " (*Sartre*, p. 273; italics in original). Cf. *Being and Time*, pp. 299–300.

5. *Or*, p. 182.

6. Lowrie translates both *sandesbedrag* and *indbildning* as "illusion," but the first term draws attention to the fact that we are deceived with respect to the truth and the second to the fact that the illusion involved is imaginary.

7. See p. 248 above.

8. The shift from identifying consciousness of something to the problem of identity is illustrated by consciousness of something as "slimy" (*visqueux*): while it trammels one's attempt to become conscious of what it is and thereby appropriate it, one is "sucked in" by it, so that one is appropriated onself (*Sartre*, pp. 340–41). The "slimy" is a contradictory composite, halfway between the inert and the fluid, and "the slimy rat" whom we encountered in the preceding chapter likewise does not lend himself to being identified, for he is "the guilty party who cannot be blamed for anything" (*Situations*, 6:88). Like the experience of the "slimy," the experience of the *louche* is bilateral, since in order to have an experience as one's own, one must be able to identify what it is an experience of, but the reflexive dimension of the *louche* is less developed, since it is a visual rather than a tactile experience (see n. 69, this chapter). *Nausea* starts out with a reflexive shift. The diarist recalls "something which disgusted me, but I no longer know whether it was the sea [the fluid] or the stone [the inert]." The stone in turn was a contradictory composite—"flat and dry on all of one side, damp and muddy on the other" (p. 2). This consciousness of something becomes consciousness of his locale, *Bouville* ("Mucktown") and at a still higher level of his "sloppy" life—"everyday drifting" (*laisser aller quotidien*, p. 175). Besides Sartre's debt here to Husserl's consciousness of something and to Heidegger's "everyday being-in-the-world" (for the distinction of level involved, see p. 74 above), there may be a debt to Hegel's *Aesthetics*. The diarist's disgust is such that although he "wanted to throw a stone into the sea," he "dropped it." Sartre may be recalling Hegel's interpretation of art as self-expression—of how "man ... as a free subject" attempts "to enjoy in the shape of things an external actualization of himself," how "a boy throws stones into the river and now marvels at the circles in the water as an effect from which he gains an intuition of something that is his own work" (*Aesthetics*, 1:31). At any rate, the diarist feels his inability to throw the stone as a constriction on his own freedom. This is presumably related both to his inability to complete the work he came initially to Bouville for and to the ambiguous status of the diary/novel itself as a work of art (see chap. 9, n. 54 below).

9. "The world [everyone] wants to be deceived; let them accordingly be deceived" (*Irony*, p. 271; *Point of View*, p. 45; etc.). The adage brings out the reflexive validation of Kierkegaard's method and the character of his version of the *captatio benevolentiae* (see chap. 6, n. 24 above).

10. *Point of View*, pp. 40–41. Cf. Sartre's rebuke, "Don't take refuge in estheticism" (chap. 4, n. 17 above) for the dislocation that should follow.

11. *Postscript*, p. 288; cf. *Either*, p. 147. The terms "our own age" (i.e., modernity) and "Christendom" are virtually interchangeable in Kierkegaard's appraisals. This can be explained by Hegel's philosophy of history, where his philosophy is the revelation of both the age and Christianity.

12. *Postscript*, p. 239. Kierkegaard is referring to *Either/Or* and explaining why he could not there get beyond the ethical stage and introduce the religious stage. Granted "the way along which it was necessary to move in order to approach Christianity, . . . it

was necessary too to handle firmly and definitely the prior stages" (p. 251). Each has to be handled in its own terms. Thus esthetic criteria apply to the treatment of the esthetic stage: "The comic ... is careful in relation to the immediate that it lays to one side. [The idiom presumably reflects the Hegelian dialectic of on one side/on the other side.] The scythe of the harvest hand is equipped with a cradle, some wooden rods that run parallel to the sharp blade; and while the scythe cuts the standing grain it succumbs almost voluptuously upon the supporting cradle, to be laid tastefully and beautifully [the three adverbs represent esthetic criteria] on the stubble. . . . The task of cutting is a celebration, . . . and though it is the sharp blade of the comical and its biting edge that make the immediate succumb, its succumbing is not unbeautiful, and even in its falling it is supported by the cutter" (p. 251). The comic stage in the development of *Either* will be considered in chap. 12.

13. "Clarification [or "lucidity"] is to be achieved by juxtaposing opposites" (*Irony*, p. 95). "Lucidity" is perhaps to be preferred as a translation, since it suggests the reflexive relevance of this application of the principle of contradiction.

14. The claim "That Christendom Is a Monstrous Deception" (*sandesbedrag*) (the title of the first subsection of "The Esthetic Production" in *Point of View*) is to the effect that a "fearful confusion of concepts ... has arisen with regard to what is Christian" (*Papirer*, X^2 A 455; see chap. 11, n. 16 below). Clarification of this "confusion" would be the dialectical demonstration that "Christianity ... has been made into the opposite of what it is to be a Christian" (X^1 A 308). Broadly put, the deception is the obscuring of the opposition between the prevailing indeterminate meaning of "Christian terminology" and the determinate meaning which was originally authorized by the New Testament and which Kierkegaard would regain. A more specific way of putting the opposition is that his "esthetic production" constitutes an ironical attack on the hypocrisy of Christendom (and thus justifies the preliminary attention I paid to *The Concept of Irony*.) Kierkegaard's deception then dialectically matches the deception opposed, for he explains "irony and hypocrisy as opposite forms, but both expressing the contradiction: the internal is not the external" (*Postscript*, p. 287). Hence verbal hypocrisy can be defined (as verbal irony was defined) as not saying what one means and not meaning what one says.

15. Even if we turned to Sartre's so-called Marxist social analysis, we would find that what renders a *Critique of Dialectical Reason* possible and necessary is comparable to the reflexive situation just explored with reference to Christendom in Kierkegaard. Marxist terminology has become indeterminate in its application—"simply ceremonial. . . . The analysis consists entirely in getting rid of the details, in forcing the significance of certain events, in perverting the facts or even in inventing some" (*Search for a Method*, p. 27). The resulting "divorce between *praxis* which is blind and unprincipled and thought which is paralyzed" is "the obscuring of the dialectic" and the "contradiction" that is "lived in discomfort [*malaise*] and sometimes in agony [*déchirement*]." But it is this contradiction which prompts each of us to a critique—"to re-examine his intellectual tools" (*Critique*, p. 50).

16. *Postscript*, p. 35.

17. For Heidegger's "jolt," see p. 165 above. The recalcitrance of the deceptive illusion in Kierkegaard is brought out by his metaphor for "the negativity" of his ironical method for removing it—"caustic fluid" (*Point of View*, p. 40).

18. Sartre's commentary on how imagery can contaminate our thinking provides a simple illustration of confusion, of its affective and reflexive character, and of how *malaise* can launch either a search for reassurance or a dialectical analysis: "The laws of development that are native to the image are often confused with the laws of the essence under consideration. . . . The dangers ... are illustrated by the following example: 'I wanted to convince *myself* of the idea that every oppressed individual or group derives from its oppression the strength needed to shake off its oppressors. But . . . I felt a certain uneasiness. I made a new effort of thought: now there emerged the image of a compressed spring. At the same time I felt in *my* muscles the latent force of the spring. It would expand the more violently, the more it had been compressed"

(*Sartre*, p. 87; my italics). Of course the affective logic that he selects for analysis differs from Kierkegaard's selection; there is no evidence that Kierkegaard ever felt anything in his muscles. But Sartre, as we saw in chap. 5, favors experiences which are at once physiological and psychological.

19. *Ibid.*, p. 129. Here the confusion has to be cleared up at several levels: at the highest level by the demonstration (undertaken in *The Transcendence of the Ego*) that there is no self transcending one's experiences; at a lower level that the characteristics which I attribute to myself are not comparable to those I attribute to a thing (e.g., I am not courageous or cowardly in the sense that ink is black, or square in the sense that the table is square); and at the sociological level that I am *n'importe qui* (Sartre's identification of himself at the end of his autobiography, *The Words*).

20. *Anti-Semite and Jew*, p. 18.

21. *L'idiot*, 1:315; 2:1976; 1:341, 523, 211. In each instance Flaubert is "persuading himself affectively . . . and by relying on images" (1:489). The motivation for indulging in affective logic can itself be a *malaise* (see chap. 3, n. 77) which is affective: Flaubert "never succeeds in convincing himself altogether that he really feels his passions [*ressent ses passions "pour de vrai"*]" (*L'idiot*, 1:900; emphasis in original). For the role imagery can play in affective logic, see the simpler example cited in n. 18, this chapter. The example is introduced with the following generalization: "Always ready to bog down [*s'enliser*] in the materiality of an image, thought escapes by flowing into another image, and from it to still another" (*Sartre*, p. 87). A philosopher committed to rendering thought dialectical (to reaching a definite position by juxtaposition) must distrust short-circuiting, interpenetration, reciprocal envelopment, fusion—such as takes place in the case of the "slimy," where the fluid is bogging down and becoming inert (see n. 8, this chapter).

22. *Saint Genet*, p. 333. Sartre calls these devices "whirligigs" (*tourniquets*).

23. *L'idiot*, 1:427, 3:238. The parenthetical reference to Freud is Sartre's.

24. *Johannes Climacus*, p. 102.

25. *Papirer*, VIII² 86.

26. *Being and Time*, p. 1.

27. See p. 149 above.

28. See pp. 50, 148 above.

29. *Introduction to Metaphysics*, pp. 123–37. Heidegger's interpretation follows the punctuation adopted by Hölderlin, who places a period after *erchetai*. He may be quarreling with the traditional interpretation as found in Hegel (*Philosophy of Nature*, par. 245). "The Voyage," "Homecoming" (*Heimkunft*), "The Wanderer" are titles as well as recurrent themes in Hölderlin's poetry and are fitted by Heidegger to the development of his own path metaphor, which I discussed in chap. 4.

30. *Being and Time*, p. 1.

31. See p. 111 above.

32. *Being and Time*, p. 15.

33. *Ibid.*, p. 5.

34. *Introduction to Metaphysics*, pp. 58–61.

35. *Being and Time*, pp. 36, 56; see also p. 99 above.

36. *Being and Time*, p. 35.

37. *Visible and Invisible*, p. 150. Merleau-Ponty would seem to have been influenced here by Heidegger's conception of truth (see, e.g., the quotation from Kant in *Being and Time*, p. 26) which is to be set in opposition to Hegel's conception whereby the truth is revealed "without veil" (*Logic*, p. 50).

38. "Essence of Truth," pp. 135–36.

39. Kierkegaard draws attention to the biblical sources: "The strayed sheep—a metaphor for the misery of going astray; the lost penny—a metaphor for the misery of getting lost in the world" (*Papirer*, VIII¹ A 625 [Luke 15:3–10]).

40. *Either*, p. 304.

41. *Papirer*, VIII² A 86.

42. *Either*, p. 9.

43. See p. 247 above.

44. See p. 161 above.

45. *Either*, pp. 306–7; italics in original.

46. Ibid., pp. 301–2.

47. Ibid., pp. 177, 188.

48. Ibid., pp. 184–86.

49. Ibid., pp. 199, 202.

50. Ibid., pp. 211, 209.

51. Ibid., pp. 439, 303. With regard to this extension of the metaphor of seduction, consider Kierkegaard's comparison of "an actual seducer" with a conceptual seducer: the first "infatuates a girl, heightens her desires, all right, but in the deepest sense he does not actually confuse her conceptions as does that other seducer" (*Papirer*, X² A 143).

52. *Sartre*, pp. 145–46. *Enjouir* can mean both "to enjoy" and "to have an orgasm," and Sartre's selection of this example is another illustration of his favoring experiences with a physiological component. That the first meaning implies a conscious performance facilitates his phenomenological attack here on the Freudian notion of an unconscious.

53. Ibid., pp. 162–63.

54. Sartre's next example of self-deception is also disparaging to the practitioner, and the reader is perhaps too likely to say, "It couldn't be me." Since both examples implement a criticism of Freud, we might pause to consider a more impressive example. The movie script on Freud which Sartre wrote for John Huston is a good illustration of Sartre's dialectical predilections. They led him to linger not on Freud's discovery of the Oedipus complex in which his patients were entangled (this discovery was only the dénouement) but on Freud's own confusion due to his hatred of his own father. Thus Freud was shown "not when his theories had made him famous but at the time . . . when he was utterly wrong; when his ideas had led him into hopeless error. At one point he seriously believed that what caused hysteria was fathers raping their daughters. . . . This, for me, is the most enthralling time in the life of a great discoverer— when he seems muddled and lost, but has the genius to collect himself and put everything in order. . . . To arrive at the right ideas, one must start by explaining the wrong ones, and that is a long process: hence the seven-hour scenario" (interview in the *Observer* [London], June 18, 1961; excerpts are found in Contat, 1:608–9). Partly because of its length, partly because he had other predilections, Huston rejected the script.

55. In French *rendez-vous* can refer to the "objective" place where one meets others. (thus there is a café in *Nausea* called "The Rendezvous of the Railroad Workers") as well as to the "subjective" commitment one makes to meet someone there.

56. *Sartre*, pp. 112, 124, 131.

57. "Not-being" is a more accurate translation of *néant* in Sartre's title than "nothingness."

58. When Sartre first introduces the concept of *distraction* with this illustration (*L'être et le néant*, p. 93), he italicizes it as if it were a technical term. That it is an import from Heidegger seems confirmed by the fact that its relation to *mauvaise foi* is never straightened out. Presumably the two terms are equivalent in Sartre, since *mauvaise foi* would always involve *distraction*, and no instances of *distraction* are provided where it does not involve *mauvaise foi*. I am guessing that Sartre's *mauvaise foi* is a reflexive, psychologized version of Heidegger's *Zerstreuung*, adapted to Sartre's dualism. Though there can be no question of Kierkegaard having influenced Sartre's usage here, he does frequently use the term "distraction" in much the same fashion as Kierkegaard (e.g., *Postscript*, pp. 106, 109, 203; the translators sometimes prefer the translation "absentmindedness").

59. *Sartre*, p. 146 (italics in original); *Being and Time*, pp. 172–73, 54, 61.

60. *Sartre*, pp. 146–47.

61. Compare the dialectical advance in reflexivity illustrated in *Either* by the successive "brides of grief."

62. *Sartre,* p. 147; italics in original.

63. Ibid., pp. 147–48; italics in original. Observe the importance for Sartre of the physical component in consciousness of one's self as something.

64. When I stress the extended range of the process of seduction, I am recognizing that in English (and the history of the French term is not very different) a primitive meaning is "to persuade (e.g., a vassal, servant, soldier) to desert his allegiance" and that a widened meaning is "to lead a person astray in conduct or belief," so that seduction can become a metaphor for alienation. It is true that the physical reference of the metaphor is more prominent in Sartre than in Kierkegaard (see nn. 18, 52, this chapter), but it is impossible for me to deal with the differences between the composition of their metaphors without dealing with the differences between their dialectics, which is an issue for the sequel. Heidegger employs terms referring to our being "led astray," including *Verführung* (*Being and Time,* pp. 115, 116, 125, 144, 302, etc.), though without a trace of sexual reference (see p. 73 above).

65. See p. 189 above.

66. A sense of urgency is associated with the recurrent situation of rendezvous in Sartre, but it is a result of the affective motivation that "in-tention," which in Husserl is target aiming in fundamentally a cognitive sense, acquires in Sartre as *attente* ("expectation") or even as *"ad-petitio"* (*Sartre,* p. 264). Hence his characteristic idiom of rendezvous: I enter the café "expecting" to see Peter and ask myself, "Will he have waited for me?" ("Aura-t-il m'attendu?") The reflexive version can be generalized: we have *"to wait for ourselves.* Our life is only a long waiting [*attente*]" (*Being and Nothingness,* p. 688; italics in original). The generalization takes in the past: "Human reality is condemned to make-itself-past and hence to wait forever for the confirmation which is expected from the future. Thus the past is indefinitely in suspense [*en sursis*] because human reality 'was' and 'will be' perpetually expecting" (ibid., p. 644).

67. Self-deception also took the form of "postponement" in the Kafka story of waiting (*Sartre,* p. 276), which I cited earlier, and a social dimension was added in the novel *Le sursis* ("postponement" or "stay of execution," but translated as *The Reprieve*), which dealt with the period of the Munich crisis. A note of urgency was again struck by what was to have been the sequel to *Le sursis, The Last Chance,* but this title was later reserved for the final but never published novel in Sartre's tetralogy.

68. *Literary and Philosophical Essays,* p. 9.

69. We have already encountered *doux* (and *mou,* which can also mean "soft") in *Nausea.* Sartre's preferred metaphors derive from touch and taste (and sometimes smell, which provide a physical component of immediate contact as a literalizing rendering of Husserl's phenomenological appeal to immediacy of experience. Here too Sartre's criteria of reflexivity and affectivity (as versions of Heidegger's *Befindlichkeit*) take hold: I cannot touch or taste something without being myself reflexively affected. These senses are also opposed to the traditional esthetic senses: "What is sensory in art has reference only to the two theoretical senses of sight and hearing, while smell, taste, and touch remain excluded from the enjoyment of art. For smell, taste, and touch have to do with matter as such and its immediately sensory qualities. . . . For this reason these senses cannot have to do with artistic objects, which are meant to maintain themselves in their real independence [*Selbständigkeit*] and permit no merely sensory relationship" (*Aesthetics,* 1:38–39). Husserl was satisfied with the theoretical relevance of the traditional visual metaphors, but sight Sartre rejects as a distant sense, by developing Heidegger's concept of the "at hand" (see the introduction to *Sartre,* pp. 17–18).

70. *Situations,* p. 188. Kierkegaard treats our time as not only "confused" but also "flabby" (*slap; Papirer,* XI¹ A 126) and "Christianity" as wanting "the opposite of what easygoingness . . . wants—it wants to arouse" (XI¹ A 458). The active/passive opposition which Sartre utilizes in pitting his "activism" against Merleau-Ponty's "lassitude" (p. 124 above) is implicit in the handling of his relation to Flaubert (p. 206 above), whose

"passivity" is perhaps the most general characteristic that Sartre finds Flaubert attributing to himself. Sartre's disgust with "passivity" (as illustrated by the seducee's hand becoming inert) was illustrated earlier by his designation as "obscene" not the naked because unclothed body but the naked because denuded body—i.e., the body which "adopts postures which entirely strip it of its acts and which reveal the inertia of its flesh" (*Sartre*, p. 225). He also dwells on "the obscene *surrender* of the corpses [dissected by the father of Flaubert] which reflected to Flaubert his own passivity" (*L'idiot*, 1:474; italics mine), for out of this reflexive situation develops the literary procedure with which Flaubert dissects his characters. A corpse which is "naked and dead" is "more than naked" because its inertness as a thing we still see as human. In the *Critique* Sartre describes the "antidialectic" which we must struggle against as a "dialectic of passivity" (p. 66). We have watched this struggle in the case of the woman tending the semiautomatic machine: she becomes the thing of the machine as her rhythm becomes reified.

71. That the individual is never left behind is not fundamentally a moral matter but is to be explained by Sartre's individualistic phenomenology of consciousness, which I am deferring until my sequel. For the present let me merely cite Sartre's own comments on his transition to the social experience of the Munich crisis: "During the deceptive calm of 1937–38, there were people who could still maintain the illusion of having their . . . impenetrable individual histories. That is why I chose an ordinary narrative form for *The Age of Reason* [the first novel of the tetralogy], showing the relations among a few individuals. But when September 1938 arrived [in *The Reprieve*, the second novel] . . . the individual, *without ceasing to be a monad*, feels that he is playing in a game that transcends him. He is still a point of view on the world, but he is surprised to find himself involved in a process of generalization [*en voie de généralisation*]. . . . He is a monad which has sprung a leak and which will go on leaking *without ever sinking*" (Contat, 1:113; italics mine).

72. *L'idiot*, 2:1503.

73. Ibid., 3:419.

74. *Search for a Method*, p. 159; *Critique*, p. 806 (italics in original).

75. *Critique*, p. 807.

76. Sartre admits that the example of boxing represents a simplification as compared with class conflict, since the individuals involved are "of the same profession, the same age, in a closed-off sector" (ibid., p. 806).

77. Ibid. Again Sartre's example is an admitted oversimplification: "The simplest example is that of a lost regiment, cut off from the main army, fearing the enemy everywhere, imagining that everything is possible, but lacking any means of anticipating an unpredictable action. Such a regiment is no longer a social group; it is a herd." Sartre is apparently willing to oversimplify, because he is making a transition at the end of the *Critique* from a structural analysis of social groups to social history, to which many of the complications of class conflict must be left. He never completed and published this historical sequel, but we know that the example of the boxer was to be revived. One respect in which the example would seem to remain relevant is that "*praxis*" having become "blind" is the historical situation in which we find ourselves. Indeed it is the reflexive situation which was the starting point of the *Critique* (see n. 15, this chapter).

8

Communion in the Commonplace

Being with one another is . . . an intent, ambiguous watching one another, a secret and mutual listening in.—Heidegger

TALKING

The focus on individual responsibility that has emerged may suggest that what is at stake in an existential dialectic is simply a *modus agendi*. This is the oversimplified interpretation of existentialism which has prevailed in America and Britain. I shall continue to argue that one factor this interpretation neglects is the existentialist preoccupation with the *modus loquendi*. The woman about to be seduced Sartre may condemn for her unexistential passivity, but consider the *ex-sistential* sense in which she was active. When her interlocutor took her hand she did not "notice," because she was at that moment "wholly spiritual." She was distracting herself by ostensibly distracting him; she was leading herself away from herself by "leading her interlocutor up to the most elevated regions of sentimental speculation." Sartre does not bother to report the actual conversation that achieves this se-ductive *Aufhebung*. It would have been merely a "ritual exchange of commonplaces," if I may anticipate his appraisal of another conversation which he cites as illustrating the social dimension which for Heidegger is constituted by "talking."

The social is introduced into Heidegger's analysis of being-there by raising the question "Who is there?" The answer is indefinite:

> The "Who" is not this one, not that one, not myself, not some people, and not the sum of them all. The "who" is the neuter, *the one [das Man]*.

We have previously watched Heidegger take "the *affective* finding of one-self there [*Befindlichkeit*]" as the starting point for his analysis of "The Existential Structure of the 'There.'" In retrospect, however, raising the question "Who is there?" prepares for a *recapitulative* revision of this analysis. As Heidegger puts it, "the horizon" which was his original "start-

331

ing point" has been "lost sight of" and must be "regained."[1] Being, we
recall, was to have been brought within "the horizon" of time, and "at the
start and for the most part" the relevant temporal "horizon" for being-
there is "everydayness"—the daily round in which one becomes involved as one "goes about" the world. Thus "The Everyday Being of the
'There'" is an advance in the analysis which now takes precedence as a
starting point over the previous analysis of "The Existential Structure
of the 'There.'"[2] It is an advance which illustrates the general advance
we have been making in now treating the issue of starting point over the
previous treatments in parts I and II.

Heidegger's revision of his original analysis of "The Existential Structure of the 'There'" is initiated by asking if *the one* "finds" itself in any
mode which is "intrinsic to it." The mode which Heidegger takes up first
as a "guiding thread" for his analysis is "talking" (*Gerede*). Finding oneself carries over the same implication as in the earlier analysis of *Befindlichkeit*: *the one* "defines" or "determines" (*bestimmt*) what anyone is in
the "mood" (*Stimmung*) for. Only now we recognize that this is largely
done conversationally. As illustrated by the distracting conversation of the
woman about to be seduced, talking is dislocating. The speaker is *ex-
sistentially* outside of himself in a manner which Heidegger delineates as
the "ex-pressiveness" (*Ausgesprochenheit*: etymologically, "out-spokenness") of "speech" (*Rede*) and as the "interpretedness of *being-there*" ("the
laid-outness of *being-there*," to retain the spatial metaphor of *Ausgelegen-
heit des Daseins*).[3] When Heidegger moves on to an analysis of *Gerede*, he
is analyzing everyday *Rede*.

A certain everyday "understanding has already been laid down [*hinter-
legt*] in the way things have been expressed."[4] In developing his own in-
terpretative procedure of "laying things out," Heidegger warned us that
it was needed because things had been "laid out wrongly" (*verlegt*)—that
is, "misinterpreted," "distorted."[5] The unreliability of the way *being-
there* has laid things out is now played up by denying the openness, the
accessibility, which the spatial metaphor of laid-outness seems to ensure:

> It is never the case that being-there is ever unaffected and unseduced
> [*unverführt*] by this interpretedness and is located confronting the open
> country of a "world" in itself, so that it just contemplates what it en-
> counters. The domination exercised by what has become the publicly
> obvious [*öffentlich*] interpretation has already been decisive for the pos-
> sibilities of being in the mood for—that is, for the fundamental mode
> in which being-there lets the world matter to it.

Thus we now recognize that the structure of the *there* which was disclosed in the previous analysis of being in the mood for is a structure

which "at the start and for the most part" is not "disclosed" or "opened out." One does not walk barefoot into reality. "At the start and for the most part" something goes wrong with our sense of *direction*: "Disclosing is per-verted into a closing off (*Das Erschliessen verkehrt zu einem Verschliessen*).[6]

OUTSPOKENNESS

The world has already been talked about when one finds oneself there. "What is communicated" when we talk is by and large not what we are talking about but our "common understanding of what is said." Talking is not just a tendency to verbalize—to interpret an experience one has already had by putting it into words; it is, rather, a tendency to experience only what has already been put into words and become the "common understanding." Such communication is largely the procedure of going "along a way in which words are repeated and passed on" (*auf dem Wege des Weiter- und Nachredens*).[7] We "get the message"; coming under the "jurisdiction" of *the one*, we do its "bidding."

Previously our "going about" the world was analyzed as the procedure of "going out [*Aufgehen*] into the world" in which we become "taken in."[8] I am reverting to this hodological analysis in order to take into account the *recapitulative* revision of the earlier analysis; it is undergoing reconstruction as a social analysis. To bring out the character of the reconstruction, let me embroider the conventional episode with which I earlier elaborated on Heidegger's example of doing something: I am occupied with pounding the nail and hanging the etching, because I am preoccupied with the prospect of impressing my expected guest that she has been selected with the same consummate taste as the etching, when this piece of equipment becomes our conversation piece. But in this mutual exhibition of taste, whose experience is being relied on as evidence? Not very definitely mine or hers, however insistent we may be, but largely the dictate of *the one*.

In this revised version, *ex-sistential* dislocation is succumbing not just to what one is doing "outside" oneself in the world but to what one is saying—to its "out-spokenness." It is a "going out into what has already been said" (*Aufgehen im Gesagten*).[9] We assume that we have had the experience because we have been equipped with the words for what we have had—some *dictum*. Experience becomes verbiage: "Things are so because one says so."[10] The tools which are one's pieces of equipment for going places and doing things are not merely hammers, nails, and etchings but also verbal expressions. Man is not the "rational" animal (of the traditional interpretation of *logistikon*); for everyday purposes he is the "talkative" animal.

Human verbosity by and large subsumes all forms of communication. "It spreads," Heidegger explains, "to what gets written." He is not thinking particularly of gossip columns. If he has been influenced by Kierkegaard's attack on journalism, he has also been influenced by Kierkegaard's attack on the Professor. Heidegger would include what is most pervasively characteristic about all verbal proceedings: the grove of academe, the bureaucracy, and such varied agencies of acculturation as social science research and philosophy. For we must keep in mind that the process whereby "disclosing is perverted into closing off" takes place not only at the level of ordinary experience but also at the higher level of experience which is a philosophical analysis of experience. Here too "it is never the case" that *being-there* is "unseduced" by the already interpreted character of experience, so that there is a threat that "our existential analytic will be led astray ... in a fashion which is grounded in the being of *being-there* itself."[11] Indeed this is why the existential analytic has now become a precautionary analysis of the grounds in question.

SEEING

If a tendency to verbalize is the first ground, the second is a tendency to visualize. We assume that having an experience is getting a good look at something. Heidegger is not thinking of pornography any more than he was thinking of gossip in his analysis of the first tendency. It is even clearer with this second tendency that the preeminent illustration is philosophy, which can be viewed as taking as its starting point (in Aristotle's phraseology) "the desire all men have to know" (*eidenai*: etymologically, "to see").[12] The "idea" or *eidos* (etymologically, "what is seen") had already been a cognitively privileged experience in Plato and still remains privileged in Husserl, who conferred the title *Ideas* on one version of his phenomenological program and picked the term *eidos* "as a term that had not been put to use" previously by the tradition. He thereby overlooked the fact that philosophy as an "idealistic" tradition was still in control of his usage and his program, which is implemented by his eidetic and transcendental reductions. Thus Husserl's recurrent methodological behest is the metaphor "look and see." When he proposes the method of transcendental reduction in his *Ideas*, he enjoins us to "set aside all previous habits of thought and see through ... the mental barriers which these habits have set along the horizon of our thinking." We must "learn to see what stands before our eyes."[13]

It apparently occurred to Heidegger that there was one traditional habit of thought Husserl was not seeing through—the "idealistic" tradition of visualizing thought as analogous to visual perception. Heidegger subverts this mental barrier, by opposing (as the "everyday" experience that prevails "at the start and for the most part") the location of something "at hand" to Husserl's visual experience, for something which is seen remains an ob-ject (*Gegenstand*) over against us at a distance, which encourages the procedure of abstraction that existentialism would reverse. We have already sampled Heidegger's resort to the more concrete experience of contact with the "at hand": we press the latch to open the door; we pick up the hammer and pound the nail. We "go on" in this fashion, and unless our progress is disrupted, we do not usually "take a step back" and have the experience of visualizing anything as an object confronting us. In fact, as Heidegger points out,

> the less we just gaze at the hammer thing, the more we take hold of it and use it, the more fundamental does our relation [*Verhältnis*] to it become, and the more it is discovered and encountered as that which it is, a piece of equipment. The hammering itself uncovers the specific manipulability [*Handlichkeit*] of the hammer.[14]

It is the concreteness of such contactual experiences that is abstracted from in the philosophical tradition by the "remarkable precedence accorded to seeing," on which Augustine comments,

> Seeing belongs properly to the eyes. But we even employ this word for the other senses when we apply them to knowing. For we do not say, "Hear how it glows" or "Smell how it glistens" or "Taste how it shines" or "Feel how it flashes"; but we say all these things are seen. . . . We not only say, "See how that shines," when the eyes alone can perceive it, but we even say, "See how that sounds," "See how that is scented," "See how hard that is." Thus the experience of the senses in general is designated lust of the eyes.[15]

This tendency to visualize on the part of *being-there* Heidegger brings within the horizon of time by identifying it with "curiosity" (*Neugier*: etymologically, "lust for the new"). This is a desire to have an experience, and we feel we have an experience when it is visualizable as well as verbalizable. But I am no more reflexively involved (in the fashion required by an existential dialectic) by my visualizations than by my verbalizations, since sight is a distance sense. When our *Umsicht* ("knowing" our way "about" the world as we turn from doing one thing to another) has been set loose, with nothing at hand with which we must occupy ourselves by approaching, . . . *being-there* "tends away from what is nearest at hand toward a distant and alien world."[16] Thus no experience takes place in Heidegger's hodological sense of *Erfahrung*, which involves me in making the "journey" necessary to traverse each step of the intervening "way."

An obvious example which was not available to Heidegger when he wrote *Being and Time* is tele-vision. The world is experienced as seen from a distance, though what is seen is only fully visualized when it is newsworthy and not just the same old thing.

TURNING

When appraised against Heidegger's requirement that an analysis be *relational* and experience an *Erfahrung*, "curiosity" has to be regarded as a "jumping" about "restlessly" in the fashion which Heidegger earlier designated *Zerstreuung* (being "scattered" about). Sight is not only a distance sense but also the most discriminating of the senses and thus tends to reinforce the extent to which we are "dispersed" about the world and "distracted" by whatever we are preoccupied with. When we dealt previously with *Zerstreuung* as a violation of the requirement of a *relational* analysis, we recognized how one's "going about" is one's turning from one thing to another. When one uses the hammer "in order to" pound the nail, "in order to" hang the etching, the "reference" implicit in each successive "in order to" embodies "the metaphor . . . of turning from . . . something toward something else." Such turning, we later learned, is not restricted to overt movements. Recall how "the manner in which mood discloses is one . . . in which we turn toward or away" (*an- und abkehren*) and is "at the start and for the most part . . . an evasive turning away."[17] Our articulation of the structure of the world is in a sense the totality of our turning toward or away from.

But since we first considered tools and moods, we have come to acknowledge articulations introduced by *the one:*

> It is never the case that being-there is ever unaffected and unseduced by . . . interpretedness. . . . The control exercised by what has become the publicly obvious interpretation has already been decisive for the possibilities of being in the mood for—that is, for the fundamental mode in which being-there lets the world matter to it.[18]

The per-version (*Verkehrung*) of our experience by the tendency to verbalize is illustrated by Heidegger's comparison of the manner in which language is used as "a means of public transportation" (*ein öffentliche Verkehrsmittel*) that "everyone rides in."[19] Heidegger's metaphor incorporates the root *kehren*, meaning "to turn." In the earlier hodological analysis, where we were going places and doing things, the turning was from each thing done to another, and the changes in the direction of movement were determined by the definite "references" which were implicit in each successive "in order to." Now *the one* is determining the direction: to use language is to be transported publicly along with every-one else. Thus the answer to the question "Who is there?" is not only that the "who" is indeterminate but also that the "there" is indeterminate. One is "everywhere and nowhere."[20] This use of language is, of course, its misuse—it's per-verted use; the etymological implication Heidegger would add with *ver* is that one is "turning" in the "wrong" direction. Language used as "a means of public transportation" is "worn out and used up" (*verbraucht und vernutzt*).[21] It no longer really trans-ports us as it did originally when its meta-phors were still alive, and Heidegger's etymologically revived metaphors embody the *reversal* required to regain some sense of *movement* and *direction*.

Even though the tendency either to verbalize or to visualize "pulls the other along with it," the pull is ultimately characterized by the primacy of the *modus loquendi*:

> Talking regulates even the fashion in which one may be curious. It says what one "must" have read and seen. In being everywhere and nowhere, curiosity is surrendered to talking.[22]

FALLING

The third mode in which the structure of our experience is perverted is ambiguity [*Zweideutigkeit*), and it is also social: "When in our every-day being-with-one-another we encounter the sort of thing which is ac-cessible to everyone and about which everyone can say everything,"[23] we no longer understand what we understand as opposed to what we do not understand.

At the same time we ostensibly come to some understanding with each other but in fact fall prey to what Sylvia Plath calls "the incalculable malice of the everyday." In Heidegger hidden calculation is taking place, and the two preceding tendencies—the verbal and the visual—make their respective contributions.

> Talking intervenes from the start. Everyone keeps his eye on the other . . . watching how he will conduct himself and what he will say in reply. Being with one another in *the one* is by no means an indiffer-ent side-by-sideness in which everything has been settled but, rather, an intent, ambiguous watching one another, a secret and mutual listening in.

The mutuality itself is ambiguous: "Under the mask of for one another is being played an against one another."[24]

If the mode of being in question were "an indifferent side-by-sideness in which everything has been settled," there would be no *relation* and no *movement*, and a dialectical analysis would not be applicable. But the exposure of the mutual "for one another" as an "against one another" is the exposure of an *interplay* whose ambiguous structure can only be analyzed dialectically.

The dialectic becomes *reflexive* when Heidegger goes on to tighten up his analysis by bringing out the "interconnection" among the three ways in which the structure of experience is perverted. In this "interconnection" is "disclosed a fundamental kind of being which belongs to everydayness"—the " 'falling' of being-there." Heidegger's initial version of "The Existential Structure of the 'There' " and the present version of the per-version of this structure that is "The Everyday Being of the 'There' " are opposed. But a relation underlies the disrelation. The present version is a *recapitulation* in that it is, like the initial version, an analysis of "the motion" of "falling" but also an advance beyond it—an advance which turns back on the initial version as a *reflexive* reinterpretation. "Falling" is now "the movement of being-there" in its "downward plunge . . . out of itself into itself." To trace this contradictory movement of "falling" is to recognize the "groundlessness" of our experience, as its grounds have just been analyzed by Heidegger.[25]

As this description indicates, Heidegger can only cope with the ambiguous fashion in which everyday experience is "laid out" by deploying contradictions which dislocate not only our ordinary use of language but also our usual visualizations, since both are involved in conveying our everyday experience. Thus the movement of "falling" itself is reintroduced as a brusque shift to the vertical from a movement which previously has usually been visualized as horizontal:

> Going out into [the world] has by and large the character of being lost in the public obviousness of *the one*. Being-there has at the start fallen away [*abgefallen*] from itself . . . and has fallen into the "world."[26]

There is further tampering with the everyday "spatiality of being-there" when this visualization in turn is revised, and the movement of "falling" becomes "tranquilizing" or "reassuring" (*Beruhigend*), for the German incorporates a root meaning "rest."[27] (This reassurance can be compared with the "reassurance" which is sought, according to Kierkegaard, in order to "exclude dialectic.") Dialectical contradictions continue to intrude with Heidegger's other versions of the dialectically fundamental metaphor of movement. The "restfulness" of the perverted "reassurance" is subverted next: "This tranquillity does not seduce one into standing still and stagnation but impels [*triebt*] one into unrestrained activity [*Betrieb*]," so that in fact the "tranquilization speeds up the falling."[28]

There are additional contradictions. As a movement "away from (*weg*) itself" on the part of *being-there*, falling is an "alienation" (*Entfremdung*), but at the same time it is to be visualized as a movement in the opposite direction: in becoming alien to itself, being-there is impelled toward self-dissection, so that it becomes "entangled in itself."[29]

WHIRLING

The contradiction between the *being-there* that has on one hand "lost itself and in falling lives away from itself" and on the other is "self-entangled" is quite similar in its *interplay* to Kierkegaard's assessment of the seducer's predicament: the seducer lost his way in the reflexive sense—so contradictory to visualize—that he had se-duced himself (led himself away from himself), but this performance was then revisualized as his having gone "astray in himself," so that he must disentangle himself from the confusion that he is himself. The similarly *reflexive* predicament of *being-there* is indicated by Heidegger's revision of Satan's traditionally seductive role in the fall of man as Tempter [*Versucher*]: "Falling being-in-the-world . . . is itself tempting [*versucherisch*]."[30]

This movement of falling must not be assumed to be constricted when *being-there* becomes "entangled in itself," so that movement finally might "somehow come to rest." Heidegger heads off any static implication by combining, in effect, the metaphor of entanglement with the metaphor of falling, thus arriving at the metaphor of "whirling" (*Wirbel*), which characterizes the dynamically confused structure of *being-there*.[31]

The unsteadiness of the unsteady vision which was a feature of the earlier analysis of "The Existential Structure of the 'There' " has become reanalyzed as the "whirling" of "The Everyday Being of the '*There*.' " This "whirling" is the final acceleration of the "turning" metaphors with which Heidegger has tried to keep up with the commotion of being-in-the-world and to subvert any visualization of it as "a rigid framework."[32] Its "structure of movement" is constituted, as we have seen, by our "turning toward or away from," in what we do and feel, as we become "scattered" about this world and "entangled" in ourselves. Now we can better appreciate the crucial character of Heidegger's example of how a sign confers significance. The directional signal used on an automobile approaching a crossroad belonged to a "whole equipmental context of vehicles and traffic regulations" (*Zeugzusammenhang von Verkehrsmitteln und Verkehrsregelungen*).[33] Heidegger's focus on this example illustrated with respect to our "goings about" how crucial "turning" (*kehren*) is. But now it can also be taken to suggest, with respect to his own methodological "going about" his analysis of our "goings about," how he has to develop successive versions of this analysis in order to subvert the sense of direction conveyed by ordinary language as "a means of public transportation" (*Verkehrsmittel*). We now are better able to appreciate too why Heidegger started out *Being and Time* by introducing, besides the traditional philosophical criterion of clarity, the additional criterion of *direction*. In the next chapter we shall explore the subversive character of Heidegger's *reversal*, which is the *direction* eventually taken by his existential analytic.

<h2 style="text-align:center">EVERYDAYNESS</h2>

First, however, we must take note of what Sartre derives from Heidegger's analysis of "talking," just as we took note earlier of what he derived from Heidegger's analysis of "distraction."[34] I shall continue to skirt the subtler differences between Sartre and Heidegger, but some of the more blatant can hardly be avoided. We have seen how Sartre's ostensibly frigid women, in order to "distract themselves" from the experience of orgasm, "turn their thoughts to their everyday activities; they figure out their household accounts." The distraction in question is a specific and a single shift from their consciousness of what is happening to them as subjects to something as dispassionately objective as adding and subtracting. There is the contrast already observed between this shift and the unremitting turning from one activity to another in Heidegger. But there is also a further contrast: "turning" was a feature in Heidegger of the ontological structure of *being-there* and as such was exhibited by, but was not specific to, any particular activity; it is brought down in Sartre to the level of a particular, everyday psychological activity.[35] A similar point could be made regarding what happens in Sartre to "everydayness" itself, which was in Heidegger another feature of the ontological structure of *being-there*.

A vulgarization of Heidegger which is even more striking, because Sartre is not explicitly expounding his own philosophy but Heidegger's, is the conversation Sartre cites from a novel by Nathalie Sarraute as an example of "talking [*parlerie*], of the 'one' [*le 'on'*], and of the realm of inauthenticity" in Heidegger. The conversation shows, according to Sartre, "how women pass their time communing in the commonplace." The example in fact provides us with a more specific and palpable version of Heidegger's everyday *being-there*. This is Sartre's quotation from the novel:

> The women were talking: "Between them were the most frightful scenes, arguments over nothing at all. I must say he's the one I feel

sorry for, even so. How much? Why, at least two million. And that's only what Aunt Josephine left. It can't be. What else? He won't marry her. What he needs is someone who'll make a home for him, even if he doesn't realize it himself. You're wrong, listen to me. What he needs is someone who'll make a home for him, a home, a home." People [*on*] have always said that. That they had always understood, and they knew it: feelings, love, life—this was their domain, *their very own.*[36]

THE COMMON PLACE

Sartre generalizes from this example by playing with a double meaning:

The commonplace obviously designates the most hackneyed thoughts, but this is because these thoughts have become the meeting place of the community.

To trace the way the process of communication constitutes the commonplace as a meeting place, Sartre employs the broad *bifocal* distinction between particular and general:

I discard my particularity in order to adhere to what is general, to become what is general. Not similar to everyone else, but precisely the incarnation of everyone else. By this totally social adhesion I identify myself with all the others in the indistinction of the universal. . . . This is reassuring for others as well as for myself, since I have taken refuge in this neutral common zone.[37]

If existentialism were merely a lament that we discard particularity in order to adhere to the general, it would itself be commonplace and hardly distinguishable from other individualisms like Mill's, aside perhaps from a certain overweighting with philosophical implications as a result of the tendency to equate the individual with the particular and the social with the general.

What is more distinctively existential are the oppositions which emerge from Sartre's dialectical manipulation of the *modus loquendi*: the dead metaphor "commonplace" is revived by taking its spatial meaning literally. At the same time, "common" is taken advantage of as implying "social," so that the meaning of "place" is extended to the place where individuals meet.[38] But whatever individuality each might bring with him is neutralized by visualizing their meeting in merely spatial terms. The "place" is not individuated any more than *the one* is. Thus individuation, "becoming an individual," accordingly involves both his *modus vivendi* (the "place" becoming his individual "situation") and his emancipation of himself from the commonplace as a *modus loquendi.*[39]

Sartre himself in effect engages in this process of emancipation. He comments that "commonplace" is a "fine word" which "has several meanings." That it "has several meanings," I would add, is one reason that it is "a fine word" for a dialectician; "commonplace" lends itself to dialectical manipulation that rescues it from its commonplace meaning. "Rendezvous" and "seduction" were similarly rescued by a manipulation that promoted an opposition between an *objective* spatial visualization and a *reflexive* reference to the individual subject. Like "commonplace," "rendezvous" implied a meeting place where the individual comes together with someone else. "Seduction" too implied a "coming together." (This idiom I introduced in my preface in order to anticipate in the most economical possible fashion the ambiguous interplay we are now exploring between the *modus vivendi* and the *modus loquendi*: one "comes together" in some "common place" by relying on such "conventions" as prefaces.) "Seduction" offered the extra dialectical fillip of implying that the "coming together" can involve the separation of the individual from himself. We have seen "rendezvous" employed reflexively by Sartre to refer to meeting myself, just as "seduction" has been employed in Kierkegaard with reference not only to leading others astray but also to going astray oneself.

Ultimately what is at stake in this manipulation is rescuing (to borrow Heidegger's analogy) dialectical thinking from stagnation and restoring its fluidity. Here my successive recapitulations may play their part.

TRANSFORMATION

Let us reconsider another illustration where Sartre rescues a commonplace conception of how men can meet in a common place. The "melting pot" metaphor is crucial to Sartre's definition of the process by which America secures social conformity: "Like everyone else, I had heard of the famous American 'melting pot' that transforms, at different temperatures, Poles, Italians, and Finns into United States citizens." In dealing with the outcome of a process of social transformation, a Marx would have provided us with facts and figures. Sartre provides us with a metaphor, for a metaphor is the outcome too of a process of transformation. "Melting pot" has been transformed from its literal application to the transformation of some metal from a rigid to a fluid state, so that it has come to apply to the transformation of aliens into "United States citizens." Of course this metaphor has long since become a commonplace, as Sartre reminds us when he reports, "Like everyone else, I had heard. . . ." A metaphor so dead is undialectical; it is the stagnant or rigid outcome of the process of transformation that produced it, but it has been detached from its relation to this process. Thus when we conventionally refer to America as a "melting pot" we do not usually think of the derivation of the metaphor from metallurgy. In its detachment and rigidity this outcome is a challenge to the dialectician. Sartre does not simply revive the metaphor by exposing us to his experience at the Plaza when he lived through the social process by which a Frenchman is transformed into an American. He also indulges in *interplay* between the *modus vivendi* and the *modus loquendi*. We can better appreciate the *interplay* if we separate the two processes of transformation. Just as Sartre puts the social process of producing an American into motion again by introducing the contradiction of the man protesting, "But I'm a Frenchman" when Sartre takes him for an American, so he puts the process of producing the metaphor into motion again by contradicting the metaphorical character of the dead metaphor: "Like everyone else, I had heard of the famous American 'melting pot' that transforms, at different temperatures, Poles, Italians, and Finns into United States citizens. But I did not know what the 'melting pot' actually meant."

Sartre's interlarding "at different temperatures" construes the metaphor literally, so that the reader is half prompted to ask, "How hot for a Pole? Hotter for an Italian? Must be very hot for a Finn?" This reversion to the literal meaning dislocates the metaphor that has become dead and commonplace, renewing our awareness of the process of transformation that has gone into the making of the metaphor, at the same time that our awareness is renewed of the process of transformation that goes into the making of a "good American." In other words, the dead metaphor, like the Franco-American himself, becomes an *ambiguous*, *contradictory*, and *unstable* composite; a dialectical development is under way.

To characterize the revival as simply a reversion to the literal meaning is inaccurate. Such a reversion would be too facile to be impelling. Just as "commonplace" never in fact referred to a common meeting place, so "melting pot" never in fact referred to the process Sartre is living through in the lobby of the Plaza. Just as Sartre, when he takes the metaphor literally, is reversing the sequence (from the literal to the metaphorical) by which it was produced, so he is reversing the sequence in the process of transformation that a melting pot involves. In a literal melting pot something metal which is rigid is melted into something fluid; in America as a metaphorical melting pot, someone whose native culture gave him definite shape becomes malleable. But the Franco-American is instead losing his French fluidity and becoming rigidly American. Recall how "like everyone else here," he "talked . . . without seeming to move his lips or cheeks"; how he "laughed with his mouth but not with eyes"; how his

laugh was "forced" when he insinuated "New Orleans, pretty girls," and
Sartre "felt puritanism just around the corner," and "a chill" ran through
him. We are to assume in contrast that the lips and cheeks of a real
Frenchman move when he speaks, that he laughs with his eyes as well
as with his mouth, and that he is equally flexible in his relations with
girls. But the Franco-American, Sartre anticipates, "will soon be a tree or
a rock." The reversal from the rigid-becoming-fluid to the fluid-becoming-
rigid not only plays up the rigidity of American conformity but also helps
to release the metaphorical commonplace, "melting pot," from its own
moribund rigidity.[40]

INTERPLAY

In lingering with a metaphor, I am insisting that existentialism is not
simply a philosophy of life, as is often assumed. The existentialist is not
solely concerned with the *modus vivendi*; he is also attentive to interplay
in the *modus loquendi*. "Commonplace" can be singled out as a "fine
word" in three dialectical respects which might well be overlooked could
they not also be detected in what Kierkegaard does with "aphorism."
(1) Sartre can extract from "commonplace" a spatial metaphor—as Kierkegaard can extract from "aphorism" the opposing spatial metaphor of
"separation." (2) Sartre can extrapolate from this spatial metaphor to
social relations in the *modus vivendi*—as Kierkegaard can with "aphorism"
when he characterizes the Symparenkromenoi as those who live *aphorismenoi*; (3) at the same time, "commonplace" can also reflexively characterize the *modus loquendi*, because it is a word which refers to other words—
again like "aphorism." "Commonplace" has the additional dialectical advantage of displaying the contradiction whereby it is itself a "fine word"
while the other words which it designates are commonplace.

But the more striking advantage is the *interplay* introduced by the
ex-sistential definition of "commonplace." A phrase so designated "is defined outside of us,"[41] so that we are dislocated when we resort to it.
Sharing it with others is our dislocation, since it is the "outside, . . . the
neutral terrain within ourselves which we want to be for others and
which others encourage us to be for ourselves."[42] Kierkegaard's "aphorism" is similarly *ex-sistentially* dislocating, inasmuch as it belongs to a
dialectic in which the individual separates himself not only from others
but also from his own past life.

CONFORMITY

We have had other illustrations of *interplay* between the *modus
loquendi* and the *modus vivendi*. The metaphor of temperature is sus-

tained in Sartre's interpretation of America as a melting pot, although this continuity undergoes disconcerting changes from the original intense heat of the melting pot (where the significance of temperature is played up by taking it literally) to the "chill" of puritanism, until finally "the effect" of the pressure to conform is felt "like a warm breath." Thus the metaphorical temperature of the process of transformation into conformity has been transformed, along with the metaphor "melting pot" itself, as well as the life-style of the ex-Frenchman.

Abrupt transformations are characteristic of an *ex-sistential* dialectic in which opposites are juxtaposed in order to impart lucidity and a sense of urgency. Conformity requires the opposite rendering. Instead of abruptness we have encountered the metaphor of "melting" (*fusion*), and the pressure to conform is finally identified as *doux*, which we have seen can mean "gentle" as well as "soft" and "sweet."[43] Conformist "communing in the commonplace" undergoes much the same softening up: it is characterized as a "continual flabby [*mou*] coming and going between the particular and the general." The flabbiness of this transformation is illustrated by the sentimental speculations of the woman about to be seduced—by the way she talked "of life, of her life." Such flabby confusion is "the squalid promiscuity of the everyday," which is so yieldingly soft that we seem unable to "withdraw ourselves" from it.[44]

Since it is to the softness of this confusion that existentialism opposes its urgent summons to individual lucidity and responsibility, it becomes more obvious than it was at the end of the preceding chapter that Sartre is not dealing with a moral phenomenon which could be segregated as the specific subject matter of an existential ethics. Our general use of language manifests this promiscuity. "A landscape," Sartre notes, may be alluded to as "a Corot;" and "a family intrigue" may be alluded to as "Balzacian."[45] (These allusions may be more palpable versions of the everyday tendencies in Heidegger to visualize and verbalize, although *Vermischung* and *Verwischung* in Heidegger are less squalidly everyday than the promiscuity in *Sartre*.) Such allusions dilute a particular experience into the indeterminate generality which is our culture. Thus with the allusion to "a Corot" the particular landscape in view loses its particularity, as does the individual style of "a Corot."

APPROPRIATION

Kierkegaard also struggles against the indeterminate generalities of our culture. But his preoccupation is with the dilution of the Christian experience. With respect to his basic metaphor "life's way," he concedes that "when life in the common understanding of it—the fact that one lives—is compared with a way, the metaphor [*billede*] expresses only the commonplace [*almindelige*], what all the living have in common through living—that they all travel on the same way." But this commonplace metaphor must undergo revision as soon as "the question becomes how someone is to walk, in order to walk the right way on the way of life." The overall argument Kierkegaard advances twists even biblical usage because it has become common usage: "*It is not the way which is narrow but the narrowness which is the way.*" Kierkegaard carries out the revision with the help of the story of the Good Samaritan: "There were five travelers who according to the evangelist went 'on the same way,' and yet each went *his own* way."[46]

Similarly in Sartre you find on one hand the Sunday Stroll, which "takes place every week in every town in this world" and which is "a collective ceremony" equatable with "human life"; but on the other hand in *Nausea* the afternoon that a "hundred thousand Bouvillois were going to live in common was not my afternoon—theirs." The diarist almost succumbs: "I asked myself, for a moment, if I was not going to love men. But after all, it was their Sunday and not mine." In contrast with the Sunday Stroll, "each individual must invent his own path."[47]

Consider Sartre's psychoanalysis of how Jean Genet becomes an individual by inventing his own path. It is a "vertiginous word" which determines Genet's destiny in life, but then Genet takes his destiny into his own hands, not simply by transforming himself through the succession of his metamorphoses but ultimately by transforming words. The recurrent link in the succession is the existential conception of appropriation. It takes the obvious form of crimes against property—of robbery. But since a *bilateral* dialectic which is existential is more fundamentally *bipersonal*, the more fundamental form of appropriation is a crime against persons—rape. If Genet's initial transformation by the "vertiginous word"—"thief" —is "a rape," his transformation in turn of words is also a rape, sometimes a double rape, since slang is the first rape: "The pimp rapes the proper word [with his pimp slang], and Genet will challenge this act . . . by raping the slang term in turn."[48] In other words, since his ultimate transformation is his becoming a writer, which entails symbolization, the analysis of his *modus vivendi* takes the form of an analysis of his *modus loquendi*, and in particular his regular transformation of literal references into metaphors. Thus his first transformation, his "metamorphosis" into "a thief," bears the rubric from Genet himself, "The Melodious Child Dead in Me Long before the Ax Chops Off my Head."[49] Precedence over the literal reference to capital punishment is taken by its metaphorical extension to this initial transformation which "tells the whole story" about himself.[50] This story pits his effort at appropriation against the social dimension of conformity: "To Genet, the truth, separated from certainty, will be the intimidating, ceremonial, official thought of adults, judges, cops, respectable people."[51]

Such intimidation is not allowed the last word in Sartre's "logic of the passions." A contradictory motivation lies behind the arranging of ceremonies, the enthronement of officialdom and communion in the commonplace generally. The motivation is (to recall Kierkegaard's phrase) an "impulse which is both easygoing and anxious for reassurance"; it is an "impulse . . . to secure something . . . that would exclude dialectic." When reassurance is sought by meeting with someone else in some common place, anxiety may betray itself "first of all" as "a sense of discomfort [*malaise*], if I suspect that you are not of one mind with the commonplace you are speaking." The tension then can build up into a sense of terror: "One is talking, something is about to explode." But "the threat" is usually "avoided," and "one goes back to exchanging commonplaces tranquilly again." Yet "sometimes they collapse, and a frightening protoplasmic nakedness emerges, and it seems to the participants that their contours are dissolving."[52]

To illustrate the character of communion in the commonplace and the dialectic it attempts to exclude, I shall take a conversation from Sartre's *Age of Reason* during which Daniel and Marcelle "come together." The conversation was for Daniel a "communion," but a "communion which was repellent and vertiginous."[53]

This composite is *ambiguous, contradictory,* and *unstable*: as opposed to "repellent," a turning movement which draws us in is delineated by "vertiginous." This movement is prominent in Sartre's description of anxiety. It is explained at the beginning of the conversation; "Daniel always felt a little anxiety when he found himself on the edge of prolonged intimate conversations which he had to throw himself into." The imagery is recurrent in Sartre. It was when "Genet became aware of his solitude and was seized with anxiety" that "a little hand moved forward" (to perform the theft) and "the vertiginous word" was uttered—"thief." The "vertigo" which Genet felt, "in a strict sense of the word," was also a matter of being on edge: "The attraction" is "something . . . calling to us from the bottom of the abyss," and "that something is ourself." The same reflexivity is featured in the general analysis of anxiety in *Being and Nothingness*: "Nothing prevents me from throwing myself into the abyss. . . . It is myself that I am looking for in its depths. . . . I am playing with my possibilities." I am "impersonating my possible fall."[54]

Our first bout with this "vertigo of possibility" was provided by Sartre's bride who was "in terror, when her husband left her alone, of sitting at the window and summoning passersby like a prostitute." Since then we have become more familiar with "turning" metaphors. But Sartre's example still illustrates how in his existentialism Husserl's transcendental reduction is "no longer an intellectual method, a technical procedure; it is an anxiety which imposes itself on us and which we cannot avoid, at one and the same time a pure event which is transcendental in origin and an ever possible contingency of our everyday life."[55] It was not feasible to examine the transcendental reduction in Husserl's own terms or the relation between it and the reductive experience of anxiety in Heidegger and in Sartre. But there is no existential experience which has incurred more disdain except perhaps nausea, which we have recognized is an analogous (indeed a derivative) experience in Sartre.

Since the communion with Marcelle will turn out to be anxiously and nauseously repellent and vertiginous, it might be well to pause and fortify ourselves with Thody's protest: "If Sartre . . . did not experience existence as physically nauseating, his philosophy would . . . have been closer to the conclusions of commonsense." There are philosophers too who prefer communion in the commonplace. In fact one sometimes wonders how they have spent their lives, those steady philosophers who brush off existential anxiety with a neat quip. But there are serious philosophical issues which I was avoiding when I employed Sartre's example to indicate the range of variation in the levels combined by different existentialists and to prepare us for his vulgarization of Heidegger. In spite of this variation, whatever the combination of levels that frame different existential analyses, some distinction of level must be maintained between everyday life and what transcends it if the philosophy is to be *ex-sistentialist*. Otherwise existentialism becomes just another philosophy of life. In short, the *ex-sistentialist* has to reject the position that "in the end the everyday in our only resort." Such a position of course "represents an end to philosophy."[56]

But it also represents an end to literature. To suggest that ex-sistentialist philosophy does not have a monopoly of vertiginous moments, let me cite only one literary example, picked deliberately from a philosopher not notably partial to philosophy. (Sibling jealousy is, I assume, the common explanation.) Compare with the "vertigo of possibility" of Sartre's bride the reflection of Henry James's Maggie:

> . . . if she were but different—oh, ever so different!—all this high decorum would hang by a hair. There reigned for her, absolutely, during these vertiginous moments, that fascination of the monstrous, that temptation of the horribly possible, which we so often trace by its

breaking out suddenly, lest it should go further, in unexplained retreats and reactions.[57]

SEDUCTION

If we return from James's "high decorum" to a more familiar *modus vivendi* in Sartre, we find that the onset of anxiety takes another form besides Daniel feeling anxious about the conversation which he is about to launch with Marcelle or the "sense of discomfort" which Sartre has noted can sometimes be felt during a communion in the commonplace. A higher-level form is when the *modus loquendi* is designed to be discomfiting to the reader, and this is evidently Sartre's ultimate intent in the conversation between Daniel and Marcelle. Attention is drawn to the *modus loquendi* by assimilating it to a seduction. A conversation in *Being and Nothingness* prepared us for a seduction, but we were not supplied with the conversation itself. The conversation between Daniel and Marcelle starts out with her comment, "You should be ashamed; you cannot keep from seducing people." But the comment is unobtrusive and innocuous, for she is alluding to Daniel's preliminary exchange of remarks with her mother, and these merely demonstrates how charming he is. The mother leaves, and by the end of the conversation with Marcelle Daniel's performance is becoming impetuous:

> In a moment she would be all open, defenseless and fulfilled; she would be telling him, "Do with me what you want, I'm in your hands." . . .
> He raised his head and saw her look. It was a heavy and spellbound look which went beyond sexual gratitude [*reconnaissance*], a look that belonged after the act of love.
> He shut his eyes: there was between them something stronger than love. She had opened up, he had entered into her, they were now one.[58]

"Do with me what you want," "I'm in your hands," "There was between them something stronger than love," and "They were now one" are certainly commonplaces. They might have illustrated the "ritual exchange of commonplaces" which Sartre identifies with "talking" in Heidegger and which was presumably involved in the conversation between the woman about to be seduced and her seducer. But the commonplaces Daniel predicts are not exchanged; they do not constitute a common "meeting place." The dialogue between Daniel and Marcelle is in fact largely subordinate to his own monologue.[59] He is not communing in the commonplace with her but reflexively with himself. In the women's talk which Sartre cited as illustrating "talking" in Heidegger, the communion was anonymous. In Sartre's own *bilateral* dialectic, the individual tends to retain some consciousness of himself even when he is entangled with the other in the social process of communion in the commonplace. The reader is aware of the *reflexive* fashion in which the conversation is set up between Daniel and Marcelle, just as he is in the instance of the woman about to be seduced. While we are supplied Daniel's interpretation of their conversation as her seduction, we are denied Marcelle's interpretation.

<h2>TRANSCENDENCE</h2>

This *reflexive* skewing of the conversation is reinforced by the fact that Marcelle is not a woman about to be seduced in the literal sense that Daniel's commonplaces imply. She will never actually tell him, "Do with me what you want, I'm in your hands." In fact these predictions of Daniel's promptly lose much of their plausibility, for there is marked discrepancy not only between their actual conversation and the commonplaces to which he resorts in interpreting its impact on her but even between his interpretation and its conceivable relevance to him. The *ambiguity* here requires further examination. I previously retained the published English translation of *un regard . . . qui débordait de reconnaissance sexuelle, un regard d'après l'amour*. The more obvious translation of the first phrase would be "a look . . . which was overflowing with sexual gratitude." Because it is located "after the act of love," because of the appropriateness as well of the metaphor of overflowing both to an orgasm and to gratitude, one would be inclined to take *débordait* as meaning "was overflowing." But the translator has probably been influenced by the fact that no actual lovemaking will take place between Daniel and Marcelle, since Daniel is a homosexual.[60] He has accordingly translated *débordait* as "went beyond." Thus Daniel is visualized as taking advantage of the ambiguity whereby "went beyond" can mean "transcended" to a higher level instead of simply referring to reaching the moment "after the act of love" on the same level. Doubtless it would also be appropriate for a look which "transcended sexual gratitude" to occur "after" sexual gratification.[61] In this case the ambiguity would not be noticeably dislocating. But since no "act of love" will take place, the commonplaces of triumphant seduction, which are integral to Daniel's interpretation of their communion, are extravagantly ambiguous. What they do necessarily "transcend" is their literal implications. They become metaphors which are *ambiguous, contradictory,* and *unstable,* since they do not retain their conventional literal support. Daniel and Marcelle cannot come together sexually, and the distance between them never seems greater to the reader than at the moment when Daniel finally communes with himself about their sexual communion: "They were now one."

COLLAPSE

Daniel may not be able to carry through literally the performance of a seducer, but Marcelle's prospective performance must also be taken into account, as it is visualized from Daniel's point of view. It should be explained that Marcelle is the mistress of Mathieu, who is ostensibly a friend of Daniel's. But Daniel in fact detests him, and his dealings with Marcelle are in some measure an effort to get at Mathieu, so that her relation to Mathieu is undoubtedly present in his mind when he is indulging in his ambiguous sexual commonplaces.[62] Marcelle's relation to Mathieu has taken a rather specific form: Mathieu has gotten her pregnant, has been scrounging for money for an abortion, and has approached Daniel. In the conversation with Marcelle Daniel is ostensibly concerned to communicate to her not only his readiness to help her out financially but also his solicitude that she should not be swayed by Mathieu but should make up her own mind as to what she really wants—to abort or keep the child.

The *ambiguity, contradictoriness,* and *instability* involved in not knowing what one wants have already been explored in the episode of the woman about to be seduced, and only brief snatches of the present dialogue need be cited:

> "Marcelle, it doesn't make any difference to you if the child is gotten rid of?"
> With a gesture of weariness [*geste las*], Marcelle replied, "What else would you want one to do?" . . .
> "Think it over," he repeated with pressure in his voice. "Are you really *certain*?"
> "I don't know," said Marcelle. . . .
> It was very difficult to get her to face up to things.[62]

Daniel is really trying to get her to face up not to things but to herself in such a fashion that she would feel herself exposed to him. It may be appropriate to cite Heidegger: "Under the mask of for one another is being played an against one another."

Daniel's first moment of triumph came when she "shuddered" on discovering that Mathieu had already told him about her pregnancy and the proposed abortion.[64] She pleaded with Daniel, "It's filthy business," and his exultation relished her humiliation as if it were physical:

At last! This is it: she is naked. No longer was it a matter of an archangel, nor of a youthful photo. She had lost her mask of laughing dignity. All that was left was a fat woman who was pregnant, who smelled of flesh.[65]

Such collapses are recurrent during the episode, especially when Daniel forces the issue of her role as a woman:

"Marcelle, are you really certain that you don't want the child?
There passed a rapid little disruption [*déroute*] through the body of Marcelle; one would say that it wanted to dismember her. And then this initial dislocation [*début de dislocation*] suddenly halted, and the body collapsed on the edge of the bed, motionless and heavy.[66]

Since we see everything from Daniel's point of view, these collapses are probably partly due to the failure of her body to sustain the sexual re-action to it that is ordinarily produced by looking a woman over.[67] But they are also moments when Daniel gains the upper hand by exposing her to the humiliation of not knowing what she wants as a woman. She is suffering a collapse of functional identity which can be compared with the collapse suffered by things in the vision of *Nausea*.[68] The exposure itself is all the more humiliating because he is getting her to communicate what is going through her mind while not communicating to her what is going through his mind.

COMMUNICATING

Daniel's demand is, "Ne vous fermez pas," which we could translate as "Open up [to me]" or, to retain the negative, "Do not shut yourself up [against me]."[69] The metaphorical meaning of *fermer* is "to freeze," "to become inscrutable." The primary reference of the metaphor of opening up (as opposed to shutting herself up) is to her communicating with him. And since Daniel assimilates the metaphor of opening up to a physical seduction, which he cannot implement literally, what takes its place as literally relevant is the prospect of allowing herself to be opened up in order to abort the child. This displacing of the more obvious literal relevance to opening up for sexual intercourse with the "filthy business" of opening up for an abortion continues the discrediting of the process of communicating that began with its assimilation to a process of seduc-tion by a man who is impotent with women.[70]

The *interplay* between the literal and the metaphorical gets an extra flourish when Daniel characterizes his own relation to Marcelle with a comparison which is literally justified by her condition: "Now there was a new relation between them, a bond that was unclean and flabby [*mou*], like an umbilical cord."[71]

We are reminded of Sartre's commentary on the process of communication—"a continual flabby coming and going between the particular and the general," by which human relations are established in their "promiscuity." Let us consider this "coming and going" as it is illustrated by this present episode. Daniel's assimilation of communication to seduction, to sexual intercourse, and to an abortion violates its general character, at least as communication is conventionally conceived, for its distinguishability from such performances is indispensable to its being carried on with conventional confidence. But here as elsewhere the dialectic is *bifocal*. If at the higher level of generality the conventional conception of communication is being violated, the violations display at a lower level the potential for moral violence that is characteristic of Daniel as a particular individual.[72] It is true that at this lower level Daniel is ostensibly characterizing Marcelle and his relation to her, but since what she says and does, and their relation, are defined entirely from Daniel's point of view, the process of definition becomes *reflexive* in the fashion which we have seen regularly transpires with an existential dialectic. In other words, Daniel's characterizations of her and of his relation to her become in effect a character sketch of himself.

At one moment this *reflexive* shift becomes explicit: his assignment to her of a defining characteristic actually shifts over into an effort to define his own attitude toward her. This shift takes place when her own attitude has temporarily stiffened. She is insisting that her perhaps not wanting to have the abortion is something she definitely does not want Mathieu to know:

> "I don't want him to know," said Marcelle stubbornly. "I don't want it."
>
> Daniel looked at her shoulders and neck hungrily. That stupid obstinacy annoyed him; he wanted to break it. He was possessed by a desire that was huge and awkward [*disgracié*]; to rape this consciousness, to sink with it into the depths of humility. But it wasn't sadism; it was more groping, and more humid, more fleshly. It was kindness.
>
> "He must be told, Marcelle. Marcelle, look at me." He took her by the shoulders. . . .[73]

"Stupid obstinacy" not only remains Marcelle's fixed attitude throughout this stretch of Daniel's communion with himself, but since it is a fixed attitude, our interest also, along with Daniel's, shunts to the succeeding transformations in his attitude toward her. Recall the similarly *reflexive* fashion in which the example of the woman about to be seduced was set

up: the seducer's attitude was held fixed so that we would concentrate on
the development of her attitude.

KINDNESS

Presumably Daniel is looking at her shoulders as that portion of anyone's anatomy which is felt most able to embody stubbornness. When
he finally takes her by the shoulders, we assume that one reason may be
to shake her out of her stubbornness.[74] If he is also looking at her neck,
is it because the flesh is bare there? For a moment we may accept the
impression that Daniel's looking "hungrily" is an ordinary male reaction
to exposed female flesh. But since Daniel is a homosexual, sexual hunger
seems out of place. This is only the first of a series of contradictions. Our
initial impression of sexual hunger is in fact disconfirmed when the
"desire that was huge and awkward" turns out not to be what would
conventionally be expected; the hunger is displaced by hostility.

The succeeding contradictions are relentless but unstable. However
hostile one's reaction may be, how does one manage to break an obstinacy?
Raping a consciousness is at least as difficult a feat: rape is an arrantly
physical act; its metaphorical extension to a consciousness is perhaps
eased by the fact that Daniel's potential for moral violence is such as to
warrant his violation of conventional linguistic usage. And if so contradictory a feat as raping a consciousness could be brought off, one's
machismo aspiration would conventionally be assumed to be exultant
domination, not the prospect of sinking with that consciousness into the
depths of humility. Conventionally, it would also be thought incompatible with this humility for Daniel to envisage "sadism" next as defining
the way he feels, just as sadism in turn will seem incompatible with
"kindness."

Our sense of this incompatibility is reinforced by the characteristics
"more groping, and more humid, more fleshly," that lead us on toward
the conclusion, "It was kindness." For these are not characteristics which
we would ordinarily think of as congruent with "kindness." Some sort
of category mistake seems to have been committed, for such ingredients
as sexual hunger, humility, fleshiness seem much too subjectively felt,
much too physically degrading, to have to do with a character trait so
oriented toward others and so benevolently moral as kindness.

Several times we have observed how psychological (or moral) and
physical dimensions of an experience can be played off against each
other. Thus in the case of the definition of the "obscene" as a species of
the "awkward," there was *interplay* between the voluntary movement of
walking and the physical wiggles of the bottom as well as a secondary

interplay in their to-and-fro movements. Unfortunately, recalling this definition may revive the skepticism it earlier roused. We are inclined to repeat the earlier question with respect to the present episode. Why should Daniel's communion with himself be regarded as illustrating anything more than his "highly specialized personal experience"? Once again we must take into account the distinction of levels which is a feature of an existential dialectic. At the lower level the idiosyncrasy of Daniel's deviancy has already been given full play. But his communion has also involved commonplaces: most obviously, "Do with me what you want," "I'm in your hands," "There was something between them stronger than love," and "They were now one." When we ran afoul of these commonplaces, their irrelevance did not seem just a matter of Daniel's deviancy. The reader tended to feel that their general commonplaceness and hence general irrelevance was being played up. A culminating moment in this higher-level dislocation is when Daniel reaches a definition, which finally satisfies him, of his *affective* reaction toward Marcelle: "It was kindness."

The definitiveness of this final definition is clearly felt to be dislocating, for it does not seem to go with what has just gone before—in particular with "sadism." This sense of contradiction triggers a *reversal* in *direction*: as soon as "kindness" becomes the definition of Daniel's feelings, it also becomes for the reader a *definiendum*, for its conventional moral implications are subverted if Daniel's previous attempt to define his feelings as "sadism" is to retain any relevance and if "kindness" itself is to subsume the characteristics, "more groping, and more humid, more fleshly," that have been offered as differentiating it from "sadism." In fact the contradictoriness of the cumulative definition is stressed rather than assuaged by Daniel's acknowledging merely a difference of degree, for we do not conventionally think of "kindness" as differing merely in degree from "sadism." But before we continue further with Daniel's feelings, the *reversal* as such deserves fuller examination. Here it is a subversive dialectical procedure, and we have already encountered it several times in this guise, but without according it sufficient examination. And yet it is one way in which the conclusiveness of a new starting point can be achieved.

Notes

1. *Being and Time*, pp. 127, 166–67.
2. The relation between these two successive starting points for Heidegger's analysis of *being-there* is played up by his breaking the chapter on "Being-in as Such" into these two parts, demarcated as "A" and "B."

3. *Being and Time*, p. 167.

4. Ibid., p. 168. The static implication of "already . . . laid down" is contradicted by the titles of this analysis, "The Falling of Being-There," and its concluding section, "Falling and Thrownness." We shall see that analysis in these strenuously dynamic terms is designed to subvert consolidated common usage. Heidegger warns us about the *modus loquendi* which he himself employs: "We lack not only most of the words but above all the 'grammar.' . . . The complexity [*Umständlichkeit*] with which our concepts are constructed and the harshness of our expression will be aggravated" (ibid., p. 39).

5. See p. 306 above.

6. *Being and Time*, pp. 169–70. Common usage fails us when we attempt to bring out the dialectic of this perversion or the broader opposition between the opening up in which Heidegger's interpretation participates as a *Freilegung* and the closing off which he associates with what is already "publicly open" or "obvious." But I shall deal later with a version of this open/shut rhythm in Sartre.

7. Ibid., p. 168.

8. Ibid., p. 54. Here at the start "being-in-the-world" was understood as meaning "being within [*bei*] the world in the sense of . . . *Aufgehens in der Welt*." This previous use of *Aufgehen* refers to our being "taken in by," becoming "absorbed in" (the Macquarrie/Robinson translation) the world and probably derives from Husserl, where this absorption poses the methodological problem that is resolved by the "transcendental reduction," which resists this tendency by "bracketing" the world with respect to its existence, thus leaving available for phenomenological analysis what is "immediately given" within the domain of consciousness itself.

9. Ibid., p. 224. Heidegger is retaining Husserl's term *Aufgehen*, which is congruent with his own idiom of our "going about," but the meth-odological character of the analysis is altered, for our problem is not our "going out into the world" (the problem the reduction was designed to cope with) but "going out into what has already been said," so that Husserl's confidence in the immediacy of what will be given to consciousness (once the reduction has been carried out) cannot be sustained. See also the priority Kierkegaard assigns to language (chap. 6, n. 111 above).

10. *Being and Time*, p. 168. At the same time "talking" is a failure to appropriate: "Talking is the possibility of understanding anything without previously making the thing one's own" (p. 169).

11. Ibid., 168–69. Kierkegaard's contempt for journalism I mentioned in my introduction, and I suggested in chap. 2 that it may have encouraged Heidegger's analysis of "everydayness" as the "horizon of time" which we now realize is "nearest" to us "at the start and for the most part." Associated with this contempt is Kierkegaard's disparagement of talk: "Temporality is procrastination, extension; it therefore is related essentially to *talk* [*snak*]. Eternity is sheer urgency [*hasten*], the intensive, [and it] is related essentially to *action, the transformation of character*. . . . From the perspective of the concept of eternity, the specific deficiency of action is that it is so short—there remains nothing at all to talk about, no procrastination. This is why temporality loves the poetic, for it is a lingering which does not become action—and scholarship, which helps in sneaking out of action" (*Papirer*, XI2 A 76; italics in original).

12. *Being and Time*, p. 171 (Aristotle *Metaphysics* 980a21).

13. *Ideas*, pp. 42, 39.

14. *Being and Time*, pp. 68–69.

15. Ibid., p. 171 (*Confessions* 10.35).

16. *Being and Time*, p. 172.

17. Ibid.; see also pp. 169–71 above.

18. There are similar attacks in Kierkegaard on the public: "Nothing, nothing, nothing, no crime is God so unconditionally against as everything that is public [*officielle*]." Contrast the function of the public in Hegel as suggested by the citation in my preface.

"Why? Because the public is the impersonal, and therefore the deepest insult to offer a personality" (*Papirer*, XI[1] A 97).

19. *Introduction to Metaphysics*, p. 42. *Verkehr* has a broad sense covering other kinds of intercourse.

20. *Being and Time*, pp. 170, 177. As we saw in chap. 7, where a man is at the start in Kierkegaard is also indeterminate.

21. *Introduction to Metaphysics*, p. 42.

22. *Being and Time*, p. 172.

23. Ibid., p. 173.

24. Ibid., pp. 174–75.

25. Ibid., p. 178, 170.

26. Ibid., p. 175. I regret the translation "public," for it suggests a distinction between public and private which cannot be drawn at this stage in Heidegger.

27. Ibid., p. 177. This reassurance can be compared with the "reassurance" which is sought, according to Kierkegaard, in order to "exclude dialectic" and with the similar function of *l'esprit de sérieux* in Sartre (p. 301 above).

28. *Being and Time*, pp. 177–78. For Heidegger's later but still relevant *Betrieb*, see "The Age of the World Picture," pp. 124, 138.

29. *Being and Time*, p. 178.

30. P. 177. This function is taken over by the "slimy" in Sartre: "The subject is suddenly *compromised*. . . . I want to let go of the slimy and it sticks to me, it sucks at me" (*Sartre*, p. 344; italics in original).

31. *Being and Time*, p. 178.

32. Ibid., p. 176. One might recall the threat to "a rigid framework" represented by Copernicus's discovery, for a pseudo etymology was concocted: "Behold the world, how it is whirld around! And for it is so whirld, is named so." Heidegger himself has other allusions in mind: perhaps the conjunction of the "whirl" of the atoms in the void, which constituted the structure of the world for Democritus, with the social whirl in which his fellow citizens were caught up when they came out of the theater mechanically chanting the chorus of a play by Euripides.

33. The original introduction of the directional signal indicating a turn (p. 150 above) seems to be meant as a revision of Husserl's conception of intentionality. In the first of his *Logical Investigations* Husserl analyzes the notion of sign, and Heidegger refers to this analysis (*Being and Time*, p. 77). All the "turning" that goes on in Heidegger can be interpreted as a challenge to the straightforward, on-target character of Husserl's intentionality as "directedness upon." This interpretation does not supersede my earlier comparison with Descartes's *droit chemin*, for Descartes is to a considerable extent a surrogate for Husserl in *Being and Time*.

34. When I stress how derivative is Sartre's terminology, I am urging that the title of his autobiography, *The Words*, be respected and interpreted in the light of the pedantry which he has satirized in the humanist of *Nausea*. A theme of *The Words* is that "it is in books that I have encountered the universe: assimilated, classified, labeled, thought through, yet still formidable [*redoutable*]" (p. 51). Sartre himself is referring to literary, not philosophical, influences.

35. See pp. 74 above. The problem of level is also illustrated by the Macquarrie/Robinson translations, "idle talk" for *Gerede* and "gossip" for *Nachrede*, both of which misleadingly trivialize Heidegger. But they would do quite nicely for the example of women's talk which we shall see Sartre provide in interpreting Heidegger. For an example of the commonplace in Heidegger, see my introduction, n. 7 above.

36. *Situations*, p. 138; italics mine. When the claim of authenticity is made ("their very own"), a dialectician is likely to detect inauthenticity. At the same time "authenticity, true relationship with others, with oneself, with death, is everywhere suggested but invisible" (p. 139). Taking women's talk as an example of inauthenticity does not mean that Sartre is a sexist in any simple sense. In fact he prefers the company of a woman, apparently because she is a contradictory composite—at once "a slave and an

accomplice," which sharpens her perceptions in somewhat the fashion that anti-Semitism has sharpened the Jew's (Contat, 1:466).

37. *Situations*, p. 137. Ultimately language itself is a common place for Sartre: "Every word is . . . external to each and to all—*outside* as a public institution [*institution commune*]; and speaking consists not in inserting a word into a brain through an ear but in using sounds to direct the interlocutor's attention to this word as public property which is external" (*Critique*, pp. 98–99).

38. The deadness of the metaphor may also be taken advantage of by way of suggesting the inertness of their encounter. In the more refined sociological analysis of the *Critique*, the common place becomes in effect "the practico-inert," which is taken to be "fundamental sociality" (p. 318). Here (p. 320) "the individual finds his reality in a material object" (e.g., a machine; see p. 221 above). In Sartre's dialectic of subject and the object, one is conscious of the opposition between inertia of a material object as subject to external forces and the free flowing of consciousness itself. (Recall that the wiggles of the bottom are felt to be "pure obedience to the law of gravity.") Language as a "public institution" can display this inertia and Sartre can speak of the "invasion of the mind by the weight of the commonplace" (*L'idiot*, 1:268).

39. In Sartre's phenomenological adaptation of Heidegger's term "situation" (*Being and Time*, p. 299) the individual's circumstances are treated as indistinguishable from the meaning his consciousness has conferred on them (*Sartre*, pp. 273–77; see chap. 7, n. 4 above).

40. That extrapolation from the *modus loquendi* to social relations is fundamental to many dialectics is suggested by the extension of the notion of contradiction to social relations in Hegel and Marx as well as Kierkegaard and Sartre. A not so well known example is the title Merleau-Ponty borrows from Hegel's description of the Roman state as *The Prose of the World*. Merleau-Ponty explains his own use of this title: "While elaborating what prose is as a category, my work will give it a sociological significance which will carry it beyond literature" (p. viii).

41. *L'idiot*, 1:623. See also Heidegger's implication that our everyday *modus loquendi* is "out-spokenness."

42. *Situations*, p. 137.

43. Sartre indulges in numerous variations on this theme of con-fusion. There is the locale of *Nausea*, Bouville, with its implication of being sucked into the muck (*bou*) of bourgeois provinciality (see chap. 7, n. 8 above). In dealing with the experience of childhood he is less harsh, but taste metaphors (see chap. 7, n. 69 above) suggest the inextricable immediacy of the confusion: in Genet's case he refers to "sweet confusion with the world" (p. 5), "sweet natural confusion" (p. 16), "the 'sweet confusion' of the immediate" (p. 22); in Flaubert's case, to "the sweet immediate confusion of intersubjective life" (*L'idiot*, 1:675).

44. *L'idiot*, 2:1181. Sartre's notion of "a banal affectivity which conceals for the moment from subjects the true complexion of their feelings" (ibid., 1:614) is a psychologistic version of Heidegger's "Everyday Being of the There," which we have seen is itself a revision of his original analysis of *Befindlichkeit*. Indeed Sartre goes on to refer to "the impersonal domain of the 'one' " (p. 616).

45. *Situations*, pp. 137–38.

46. Italics mine. I am now translating *billede* as "metaphor" instead of "image," because I am bringing out transformations of meaning. But it should still be recognized that throughout this chapter I have been dealing with spatial imagery.

47. See p. 215 above; *Nausea*, pp. 50, 53; *Sartre*, p. 240.

48. *Saint Genet*, pp. 17–18, 289.

49. Ibid., p. 1. Childhood then became for Genet a "lost paradise"—dialectically speaking, "the immediate" (p. 18)—and he died of "shame" (p. 20). Since Genet's real life crimes are not those for which capital punishment is meted out, the death can only be metaphorical. Further metaphorical transformation with attendant interplay is introduced by "the connection between death and metamorphosis," which

Sartre establishes with the following reversal from Genet: "My death is in danger of being the knowledge of my shame" (pp. 3, 4).

50. See p. 215 above.

51. *Saint Genet*, p. 36. Sartre is adapting Hegel's distinction between the subjective certainty of the individual and objective social truth. The sharpness of the separation in existentialism precludes Hegel's *Aufhebung* of the individual in the social. I shall examine this difference between existential and Hegelian dialectic in Kierkegaard's term in pt. IV.

52. *Situations*, pp. 139–40. See p. 193 above for an early encounter with nakedness emerging from the dissolution of identifiable shapes. But a reflexive shift has supervened so that now it is not things but persons which are becoming shapeless and losing their identity.

53. *The Age of Reason*, p. 198.

54. Ibid., p. 211; *Saint Genet*, pp. 17, 21; *Sartre*, p. 120. The imagery of "throwing myself into the abyss" and the weaker version of Daniel's throwing himself into a conversation derive much of their relevance from Sartre's vulgarization of Heidegger's *Entwurf* as *projet*.

55. See p. 73 above.

56. I am borrowing from Michael Murray's comment, "Rorty holds that in the end the everyday is our only resort, which represents an end to philosophy still more radical than Heidegger's (*Heidegger & Modern Philosophy*, p. xvii). Murray is commenting on Richard Rorty's essay, "Overcoming the Tradition: Heidegger and Dewey," which is included in this anthology. The position that the everyday is our last resort is often attributed to Wittgenstein, as opposed to Heidegger.

57. *The Golden Bowl*, p. 504. The "high decorum" in question does not elevate itself above what the existentialist would describe as "everydayness." James brings persons together with their things within this horizon, explaining how they " 'placed' themselves, however unwittingly, a high expression of the kind of human furniture required esthetically by such a scene" (p. 596; this scene is later but involves the same "high decorum"). James's staging makes clear that there is a sense in which Maggie's experience transcends the original scene (including the experience of the other participants), even though for her the vertiginous possibility itself "figured nothing nearer to experience than a wild eastern caravan, looming into view with crude colours in the sun, fierce pipes in the air, high spears against the sky, all a thrill, a natural joy to mingle with, but turning off short before it reached her and plunging into other defiles" (p. 507).

58. *Age*, pp. 198, 210–12.

59. This erection of a male perspective is not just a literary device. In spite of his fervent endorsement of feminism, woman is clearly for Sartre the Second Sex. In a flippant interchange with a Spanish interviewer, Sartre defined man as "an optical illusion" and woman as the "illusion of an illusion" (Contat, 1:474–75).

60. In my commentary I am trying to bring out the interplay between literal and metaphorical, for it does not survive the debilitating published English translation. Thus, instead of translating *séduire* as "seduce" in Marcelle's initial allusion to how Daniel has charmed her mother, the translator substitutes "fascinate," so that we are not alerted for the metaphorical elaboration seduction will undergo. And the elaboration itself disappears when *dans un moment elle serait toute ouverte, sans défense et comblée* is translated as "in one moment all she was and had would stand exposed," while the final clause is simply skipped over. The damage done becomes clearer when the sequel to the last sentence I cited is taken into account: " 'Daniel,' Marcelle repeated. Daniel opened his eyes. . . . He took her hand. . . . 'My archangel,' Marcelle said. . . ." Here "repeated" solicits our attention to the repetition of an opening. The rhythm of Daniel's shutting and opening his eyes has its own sentimentality, but it also yields a literal physical analogue of the interplay between her opening up and what we shall see he feels she is also doing—threatening to shut him out.

61. Marcelle has always thought of Daniel not as a homosexual who is not up to a woman but as a transcendent being—her "archangel." Daniel expands on his sense of this role—"guardian angel, angel of the hearth" (p. 196). The later moment when Daniel "shut his eyes," savoring the feeling that "there was something between them stronger than love," probably indicates some regaining of his spiritual strength, since the final word in the conversation is her acknowledgment, "my archangel." Sartre, I expect, gets a dialectical kick not only out of Marcelle's flagrant misinterpretation of Daniel's transcendent status as an archangel but also out of playing off what could be visualized spatially as the horizontal temporal dimension ("after") against the vertical dimension of transcendence. Recall his manipulation of these two dimensions against each other in his interpretation of Flaubert's "symbolic arrangement of space" (p. 206 above).

62. It is not possible to unravel here the intricacies of Daniel's relation to Marcelle in relation to his relation to Mathieu, whereby Daniel becomes a contradictory composite —an "archangel of hatred" (p. 196). But with respect to Daniel's affective reactions, the familiar interplay between hard and soft operates. Conventionally the interplay attaches to the masculine/feminine dialectic, (see chap. 5, n. 116 above), though in the background is the dialectic between the identifiable and what tends toward shapelessness (i.e., between Husserl's identifying "consciousness of something" and a mood (such as Heidegger's anxiety or Sartre's own nausea) whose object is not readily identifiable. More interplay is generated when the masculine/feminine line is crossed in the literal sense. Thus Daniel "felt himself empty and flabby [*mou*]" as opposed to Mathieu, who "was compact and dry as a bone," so that one could hate him. (Woman is "empty" because she is fundamentally a hole: "The obscenity of the female sex organ is that of everything which 'gapes open.' . . . She is 'in the form of a hole.' " And Sartre points out that "a good part of our [*sic*] life is passed in plugging up holes, in filling empty places" [*Sartre*, p. 350].) Given Marcelle's circumstances, the opposition Daniel feels is between his effeminacy and impotency with women and Mathieu's manifest virility. His attempt to get at Mathieu through Marcelle is not simple homosexuality but also an attempt to get at someone who can be hated because his hateful characteristic can be identified; whereas in contrast, "one could not hate Marcelle," whom he thinks of, especially now she is pregnant, as primarily flabby flesh. But he can recall how before she became pregnant, she could cross the line by announcing "in a brusque and masculine manner, 'When a woman is fucked up [in the metaphorical sense], she can always go and get herself pregnant.' " (Here again the published translation is at best rather flat: "When a woman is completely up against it, she can always get herself into the family way" [p. 195].)

63. The "gesture of weariness"—its feminine passivity (cf. the vision in *Nausea*, p. 000 above)—is possibly meant as an ironical contrast with the "brusque and masculine manner" of her earlier announcement. Her being "scattered in all directions" may be a psychologistic reminiscence of Heidegger's idiom of being "scattered about," as was the "distraction" of the ostensibly frigid wives (see chap. 7, n. 58 above). In both instances the ability to identify one's experiences and ultimately one's self is lost.

64. *Age*, p. 201. The shudder is omitted from the published translation. As noted before, translators are often disconcerted by *ex-sistential* dislocations and fail to respond. Another example from the present conversation is "her head was quivering" (p. 200) as a translation for *sa tête était agitée de secousses raides.*

65. This "mask" is of course not the ontological "mask" I have just recalled from Heidegger, for it is a mask that Daniel is conscious of. Or, rather, it is his consciousness of her which is itself bifocal. Even in the "youthful photo," which she had shown him earlier in the conversation, he sees the same "limp flesh that hung loosely [*flottait*] about her like a dress too large" (p. 199). The double vision here is associated for him with "the mask of her pregnancy [*grossesse*]." The probable relevance of the "youthful photo" to her later "mask of laughing dignity" is that he still detects in her "a childlike and defenseless *bonne foi*, which does not go with her face of a woman in trouble" (p.

199). It is this ambiguous, contradictory, and unstable composite which collapses when the "mask" is dropped. The collapse involves a shift from the evidence of the photo, which was not only distant in time, since it was taken when she was younger, but was also visual (sight, we remember is a distance sense), to the immediacy of a smell. Daniel accompanies her in this reduction: "No longer was it a matter of an archangel, nor of a youthful photo." His elevated status in her eyes as her "archangel" he also describes in terms of what he feels it symbolizes to her—"her purity" (p. 203), which is associated in turn with the "youthful photo."

66. *Age*, p. 203.

67. There is, however, a carefully maintained ambiguity with respect to Daniel's point of view, which is rendered impersonally. Thus when it is reported that "her head was shaken by stiff jolts," the explanation supplied is that "she was able only with difficulty to support the look of a man" (p. 199). Apparently he views her as responding to him on two levels—as an archangel (she misconstrues his homosexuality) and as a man (on a par with Mathieu). But while his own sense of identity is uncertain in her presence in these obvious ways, the uncertainty is ferociously complicated by his own sense of identification with her: "He would have liked *to be her*" (p. 207; italics in original). At this juncture she is identified as confronting him with the challenge, "What was she feeling inside her, this heavy female in disarray?"

68. Presumably because she feels she cannot contemplate the role of child bearing, her body has collapsed—lost its functional identity as a female body by becoming simply a body—with the heaviness of a thing. (Unfortunately the translator omits "heavy.") Recall the transformation of the hand of the woman about to be seduced which "rests inert between the warm hands of her companion—neither consenting nor resisting—a thing." This inertia too was a refusal for the time being to be conscious of the femaleness of her anatomy. Later in the conversation between Daniel and Marcelle it is reported, "She was going to slide, dragged down by her own weight, toward resignation, surrender [*abandon*]" (p. 210). Unfortunately this time the translator omits "weight." I have already stressed the importance of weight imagery in the space of Sartre's imagination as contrasted with Kierkegaard's. Women as more fleshly than men are more subject to the law of gravity in Sartre; in Kierkegaard they are very light.

69. *Age*, p. 203. Here again the translator dismantles the open/shut rhythm of the relation by translating *ne vous fermez pas* as "don't be so aloof." It would probably be far fetched to regard this rhythm as a psychologistic vulgarization of Heidegger's opening up/concealing. For there does not seem to be any evidence that Sartre has ever understood Heidegger's *a-lētheia*.

70. Ibid., p. 201. Besides the open/shut rhythm, there is interplay in the vertical dimension between his transcendent status as her "archangel" (i.e., "her purity," as he himself interprets what he is to her) and "the filthy business." She accordingly protests, "I had so much wanted to keep you out of it all," and her metaphor produces further interplay with his effort to open her up and enter in.

71. The flabbiness of the relation—indeed the fact that there is any relation—is immediately contradicted, for in the next sentence she has "pulled herself together and hardened herself" (ibid.), so that there is overlapping interplay between the open/shut and the soft/hard rhythm.

72. We have been climbing a succession of levels. Marcelle is felt to be "flabby" by Daniel; he feels himself to be "flabby" as opposed to Mathieu (n. 62); his relation to Marcelle is "flabby"; but everyday human relations are "flabby," according to Sartre. However, once we have followed him through his transpositions of the metaphor, we have to recognize that opposing metaphors of violence are also relevant not just to Daniel, who is "glad to find his hatred [for Mathieu] intact" (p. 200) and to get at Mathieu by getting "*inside* his woman" (p. 194; italics in original), but also of human relations generally, as is abundantly demonstrated in the *Critique*, where the common place turns out to be a "place of violence" (p. 318). The abortive, intimately violent character of human relations is suggested in *Being and Nothingness* by the metaphor

of an "internal hemorrhage" (*Sartre*, p. 194), which is employed with reference to one's relation to the Other, though the immediate justification for the metaphor would seem to be the way the Other drains away my vitality—the vitality of my own immediately given *Erlebnis* (ibid., pp. 192–94).

73. *Age*, p. 209. The term for "rape" is *violer*, which makes etymologically more obvious the relevance of other forms of violence.

74. Cf. the way the sadist "leans on the other's shoulders, so as to bend him to the earth" (p. 201 above). There too the physical act is relevant to what is sought psychologically and morally—humiliation.

9

The Reversal

The process of entanglement can be reversed only if "being-there" takes itself back to itself from its lostness in the one.—Heidegger

THE REDUCTION

A broad illustration of the reversal is Kierkegaard's "Life must be understood backward, but . . . it must be lived forward."[1] In dealing with the requirement of living forward, he employs the idiom of *repetition* [*gjentagelson*] to indicate the reflexive way the direction of the movement of the understanding must be reversed: one "takes oneself again" (*tager igjen*) when one turns around to move forward with one's life[2] Heidegger is probably indebted to Kierkegaard's idiom when he traces the "reversal" (*Rückgang*) by which "being-there takes itself back [*sich zurückholt*] to itself from its lostness in the one" and becomes "authentic" (*eigentlich*)— that is, a self that is its "own" (*eigen*).[3] Sartre's debt to Heidegger is evident when he entertains in *Being and Nothingness* the prospect of a "radical escape from self-deception" and announces "this recovery [*reprise* —literally, a "taking back"] we shall call authenticity." But Sartre adds that "its description has no place in *Being and Nothingness* itself."[4] The prospect is postponed for later treatment and relegated to the footnote which I am citing.

Aside from the belatedness of the reversal, there is another difficulty we face in treating it here. The philosophical character of the reversal in contemporary existentialism has been reinforced by the influence of the phenomenological procedure of "reduction." Husserl identified this procedure as "radical," and his influence has just been betrayed by Sartre's identification of the "escape from self-deception" as "radical."[5] Merleau-Ponty sometimes uses for the "reduction" the term *reprise*, which I have translated as "recovery" when it is used by Sartre. Matters are still further complicated by the fact that Husserl's reduction influenced Sartre and Merleau-Ponty to a considerable extent independently of Heidegger's influence on them, even though the influence of Husserl's reduction had

363

already shaped the reversal which takes place in Heidegger. Thus it is
next to impossible to deal with contemporary existential reversals without
taking Husserl's reduction into account. I cannot do this here, not just
because the reduction is a quite technical procedure but also because it
is not in Husserl the dialectical procedure which it becomes in Sartre and
Merleau-Ponty.[6] For we have not yet examined the differences between a
phenomenological and a dialectical method.

A more obvious difficulty is to distinguish an existential reversal from
certain more traditional forms of dialectical transformation. The self-
knowledge Socrates sought when (according to Kierkegaard) he "isolated
himself from every external relationship,"[7] in order to achieve "inwardness" dialectically, provides Kierkegaard with a model for his reversal. As
a formulation for his reduction, Husserl cites Augustine's refurbishing
of the Socratic operation:

> The Delphic motto, "Know thyself," has gained a new meaning. . . .
> I must lose the world by the reduction, in order to regain it by a uni-
> versal self-investigation. "Do not wish to go out," says Augustine: "Go
> back into yourself, for it is in the inner man that truth dwells."[8]

This *reflexive* operation was presented in Plato's "image" of the cave as
a "conversion"—a "turning around [*periagogē*] of the whole soul."[9] The
fact that Heidegger assumes that this "image" by itself, removed from its
relation to "the divided line" and to the rest of the *Republic*, constitutes
"Plato's Doctrine of Truth" and the fact that this "image" is the only
Platonic text to which Heidegger has devoted an entire essay combine to
suggest that a certain contraction has taken place in the traditional scope
of philosophy, so that its focus is almost entirely upon the problem of
changing *direction*. We have been prepared for this problem by Heidegger's elaborations on the metaphor of "turning" which were traced in the
preceding chapter.

Conversions are pivotal in Sartre too. In *Saint Genet*, which has sometimes been interpreted as tracing the process of "recovery" anticipated in
Being and Nothingness, Sartre lines up in a series of Genet's conversions.[10]
In *Being and Nothingness* itself, the structure which Sartre attributes to
a conversion displays his dialectical predilection for composites which are
ambiguous, *contradictory*, and *unstable*:

> These extraordinary and marvelous moments when the prior project
> collapses into the past in the light of a new project which emerges from
> its ruins, . . . in which humiliation, anxiety, joy, hope are delicately

blended, in which we let go in order to grasp and grasp in order to let go—these have often appeared to furnish the clearest and most moving image of our freedom.[11]

Sartre passes as a philosopher of freedom, but his is a philosophy in which (as we observed before) images are crucial and must be moving and in which (the eloquence of the present passage encourages us to add) the most moving image of freedom is a conversion.

Sartre adopts the traditional term to identify the dislocating and exhilarating moment when he himself became fully committed to fellow traveling:

> I had reached the breaking-off point [*pointe de rupture*]. . . . In ecclesiastical terms . . . it was a conversion.
> I wrote at top speed, rage in my heart, gaily, without tact: even with the best-prepared conversions, when they explode there is joy in the storm, and the night is black, except where the lightning strikes.[12]

A thunderstorm is not an unprecedented locale for a conversion. And Sartre's comment on the way he wrote can be matched by the comment which Kierkegaard derived from the circumstance of Luther's conversion:

> Note the strong pulse beat of personal appropriation in the entire trembling propulsive movement of his style, which is as it were driven from behind by the terrible thunderstorm that . . . created Luther.[13]

How then can an existentialist conversion be differentiated from a conventional conversion?

TRANSCENDENCE

A conversion as such is likely to be an extraordinary and marvelous moment. I have already drawn attention to a vertiginous moment in Henry James. With respect to what then transpires, one might well claim that "humiliation, anxiety, joy, hope are delicately blended" as (if I may brutally oversimplify) Maggie lets go (her father) in order to grasp (her husband) and grasps in order to let go. But there are differences. The pulse beat in an existential conversion is dialectical, for dialectic yields the traits needed to delineate it: a dialectic traces some process of *development* or transformation, and the transformation involves some change in *direction*. An existential dialectic further involves a distinction between subject and object. With many conversions (e.g., to Marxism) the objective dimension of what one is converted to looms large. But the *reflexive* dimension is more prominent in existentialism. As a student Sartre had read *Capital* and *The German Ideology,* and he explains, "I had

understood everything clearly, and I understood nothing at all. To understand is to transform oneself [*se changer*], to go beyond oneself."¹⁴ If
Sartre is echoing Marx's thesis on Feuerbach—"The philosophers have
only *interpreted* the world differently; the point is to change it."¹⁵—he is
introducing a *reflexive* dimension into the process of change. Referring in
effect to philosophy, when its method is phenomenological reflection,
Merleau-Ponty explains, "Reflection is really reflection only if . . . it knows
itself as reflection on prereflective experience, and thus as a transformation in the structure of our existence."¹⁶ Heidegger explains, referring to
his "On the Essence of Truth," in which this explanation is the last sentence, "The sequence of the questioning is intrinsically the way followed
by a thinking which, instead of furnishing representations and concepts,
experiences [*erfahrt*] and tests itself as a transformation of its relation to
Being."¹⁷ Although these three explanations of philosophical understanding, reflection, or thinking are different, each stresses the transformation
or conversion that takes place and its *reflexive* dimension.

Furthermore, the *reflexive* act of "personal appropriation" is so sweeping that "it tells the whole story" about oneself. This may be the case
with other conversions too, but an existential conversion would not gain
its full sweep if it did not involve a philosophical episode—a transcendental reduction which "brackets," "sets to one side," "puts out of action"
one's ordinary everyday experiences in favor of the "essential structure"
of one's experience.¹⁸ Let me briefly illustrate this dislocating, *ex-sistentialist* character of Sartre's conversion to Marxism. When at the age of
seventy he tries to tell the whole story, he discounts the fact that "I have
made during the course of my life for one reason or another a lot of mis-
takes, some small, some big." Then he adds, "But fundamentally each
time I made a mistake, it was because I was not radical enough." Thus
he can generalize, "It always comes down to my not having gone the
whole way in my radicalism."

Sartre is of course thinking in political terms. But it is difficult to specify
what under particular circumstances would be in fact the most radical
political thing to do. His effort to go the whole way in his radicalism
(*radicalité*—note the sweeping abstractness of the term), or his regret in
not having done so, can only be comprehended philosophically against
the background of what Husserl himself regarded as the "radical" character of his transcendental reduction.

To suggest this is not necessarily to disparage political radicalism or even
Sartre's radicalism, though my interpretation of transcendental experi-
ence in Sartre as a vulgarizing combination of Husserl's reduction and
Heidegger's anxiety may seem to imply such disparagement. It may be

that political radicalism is only a feasible position insofar as it is possible to "bracket," "set to one side," "put out of action" one's ordinary everyday experiences in favor of the "essential structure" of one's experience. All that I am recognizing now is the *bifocal* character of Sartre's reduction: it is "no longer an intellectual method, a technical procedure [as in Husserl]; it is an anxiety which imposes itself on us and which we cannot avoid [as in Heidegger], at one and the same time a pure event which is transcendental in origin and an ever possible contingency of our everyday life." The claim "at one and the same time" points up an existential trait —the conjunction of the transcendental and the everyday.

The Leap

Sartre's conversion to Marxist atheism may indeed seem objectively a very different performance from Kierkegaard's conversion to Christianity.[19] It is the reflexive and transcendental character of the conversion in both cases that makes the comparison feasible. The prominence of the reflexive dimension in Kierkegaard is suggested by his devotion of 22 pages of *Postscript* to book 1 ("The Objective Problem concerning the Truth of Christianity") and 484 pages to book 2 ("The Subjective Problem—the Relation of the Subject to the Truth of Christianity—the Problem of Becoming a Christian").

Sartre could have brought out the strenuously *reflexive* character of his conversion to atheism by borrowing Climacus's phrase from Kierkegaard: the individual must "turn against himself."[20] Admittedly conversion conventionally involves the turning of the individual against what he has been. But the discontinuity demanded by this reversal is more than usually dislocating in existentialism. Recall the sharpness of the contradictions with which Sartre plays up the emergence of the new project from the ruins of the collapse of the old: "humiliation, anxiety, joy, hope ... we let go in order to grasp and grasp in order to let go."[21] Consider the dislocation in Kierkegaard too. The metaphors of "climbing" a "ladder" and "steps" were all applied by Hegel, as they are by Climacus, to the relation between stages. But Climacus revises these spatial metaphors when he deals with the individual's becoming a Christian on reaching the religious stage. The individual's conversion requires a "leap."[22] The movement is still to a higher level, but where "climb" and "ladder" and "steps" imply some measure of continuity and support, a "leap" accentuates the discontinuity conversion requires: "The exister must have lost continuity with himself, must have become another...."[23] A conversion in Kierkegaard is not a question of reaching a conclusion from the point where one originally started out. The leap delineates so salient a discontinuity that the point reached by it qualifies as a new starting point and to this extent can come within the scope of this volume.

To suggest the dislocating abruptness of the movement toward a higher level which a leap is, Climacus denies the possibility of a running start:

> Everyone knows that the most difficult leap, even in the external realm, is when someone leaps into the air from a standing position and comes down again at the same place. The leap becomes easier, the more space intervenes between the initial position and the place to which the leap is made.[24]

Similar in its strenuousness to the difficulty encountered in becoming a Christian for Kierkegaard is the "cruel and long-range undertaking" of becoming an atheist for Sartre.[25]

There is another respect in which the two conversions are comparable. After his conversion Sartre could still fluctuate with regard to what precisely he was converted to (e.g., with regard to the exact distance between his commitments and the Communist party program), but his conversion was the moment he could no longer fluctuate with regard to what he was opposing:

> In the name of the principles which the bourgeoisie had inculcated in me, in the name of its humanism, ... in the name of liberty, equality, fraternity, I pledged the bourgeoisie a hatred which will end only with my death.[26]

In a similarly *reflexive* fashion, Kierkegaard launched in the name of Christianity an *Attack on Christendom*,[27] and what he would subvert by this attack is more obvious than the precise version of Christianity he is proposing Christians should be converted to.

To the traditional term "convert" Sartre in fact often prefers "traitor,"[28] which retains the preconversion perspective that is so recalcitrant that its subversion is a "cruel and long-range undertaking." Hence we can avoid the risk of going too far beyond the starting point which we are supposed to be examining in part III; we can linger with the moment when a conversion is still the subversion of communion in the commonplace, whatever the more specific coloration of this meeting place where "reassurance" is available, whether it is bourgeois society and culture in Sartre or established Christianity in Kierkegaard. At either juncture the subversive process is dialectical in the tensions it generates.

REVULSION

In sampling these tensions, we can further curb our impatience, as dialectic demands that we should, by concentrating on short-run reversals; for we can assume that a conversion, even when "long-range," would display much the same subversive character, and we have already familiarized ourselves with the relation between the short and the long run in Kierkegaard's dialectic.

Let us accordingly return to the short-run reversal which took place when Sartre met the Franco-American at the Plaza. The reversal there was a matter of Sartre's disentangling himself from confusions at several levels. He was confused when he took the particular individual he met to be a native American who had learned French. This confusion Sartre had to disentangle from the confusion of the individual himself who was *en voie de fusion* and not what he thought he still was, a Frenchman, but someone conforming to the American's image of a Frenchman. A more general, higher-level confusion was also involved. Sartre was generally confused as to what an American is, having arrived with French commonplaces in the back of his mind: "Americans are conformists"/"Americans are individualists." But to entice an existentialist a commonplace has to lend itself to a more *dynamic* rendering, and here Sartre was saddled with another commonplace—the conventional conception of the process of transformation by which American conformism is secured: "Like everyone else, I had heard of the famous American 'melting pot.'" (Thus French conversations had already taken place before he began the conversation with the individual whom he took to be an American.) On one hand we have the melting pot as a process of transformation which produces individuals whose behavior is conventionally American. On the other, this process of transformation is "famous" because it is conventionally considered an inspiring American tradition. The feeling of revulsion from the Franco-American as a particular individual that Sartre's report of the conversation at the Plaza induces is also a reversal which is designed to subvert this inspiration generally.

Reconsider too the impact of the reversal subverting the commonplace that Daniel reached for in his attempt to define his feelings toward Marcelle. Here Sartre was engaged in a double maneuver, as in the case of the commonplace "melting pot." The conventional requirement that one be "kind" and the conventionally inspirational quality of "kindness" are both to succumb, with a twinge at least of revulsion on our part, during the "communion which was repellent and vertiginous." These traits of the communion were traceable to Daniel's *ambiguous* sexual feelings towards Marcelle (and Mathieu) and to the *interplay* between his different feelings at different levels.[29] But the repellency of the communion also promotes a reversal: the homosexual confronted with a woman and her pregnancy was "turned back" on himself.[30] He was briefly compelled (if Heidegger's phrase is not too solemn) to "take [himself] back from [his] lostness in *the one*"—that is, to disentangle himself from two prominent conventions with respect to human relations—seduction and kindness.

RECOGNITION

Although belaboring the philosophical implications of an episode from a literary work may distress the literal-minded, it is obvious that Sartre is not entirely literal-minded himself in the way he set up this conversation; several levels of implication carry over from one to another. The more philosophical still await examination. They were less apparent in the account of "How a Good American Is Made." But *bonté* is ambiguous. I have translated it as "kindness," but it not only refers colloquially to this *affective* attitude it can also mean "goodness" and so can embrace the loftier abstractness that "the good" enjoys in philosophical arguments.[31] Sartre may perhaps be crediting Daniel with some measure of insight into the disputable nature of what conventionally passes for being "good" in these arguments, as well as into what conventionally passes as being "kind" in everyday life.

Be this as it may, what is evident is that Daniel would have Marcelle recognize his "kindness." Here another ambiguity is encountered which also involves a difference in level. The usual presumption, I observed earlier, would be that Marcelle's look (as interpreted by Daniel) *débordait de reconnaissance sexuelle* in the sense that it "overflowed with sexual gratitude." It was located as "a look which belonged after the act of love," and because of its location, as well as the appropriateness of the metaphor of overflowing both to the physical experience of an orgasm and to the moral experience of gratitude, we were inclined to take *reconnaissance* as meaning "gratitude," and this translation did suggest the *affective* reaction Daniel was soliciting from Marcelle by his "kindness."[32] But this implication was partly closed off, before it could fully develop, by Daniel's homosexuality, which deprived the sequence in which sexual seduction takes place of its literal relevance. There may have then been a certain shifting to the implication that the "look which belonged after the act of love" "transcended" anything sexual.

"Recognition" is the alternative possible meaning of *reconnaissance*. And it would superimpose cognitive implications on the affective reaction. Both are of course being discredited. Daniel wanted to feel that his seduction of Marcelle was the "opening up" to him not of her body exactly but her most intimate thoughts, so that the sequence he would associate with her seduction culminates not in sexual gratitude for sexual gratification duly administered but in some "recognition" of his kindness as opposed to the callousness of her lover Mathieu. We need hardly go outside the novel to suspect this implication. But Sartre is in fact preoccupied in his philosophical writings with the kind of recognition one individual attempts to obtain from another in order to shore up his own moral judgment of himself, in spite of the fact that their difficulty in communicating with each other is apparently so nearly insuperable as to render the attempt quite hopeless.[33] Thus it does not seem implausible to assume that Sartre is showing his own hand as a philosopher when he assigns Daniel a sexual deviancy which equips him with a certain leverage in the process of subversion.[34]

FAKING

The subversiveness of deviancy is confirmed by Sartre's generalization in *Saint Genet* regarding the homosexual *modus loquendi*. That Daniel is not a thief as well as a homosexual does not preclude the comparison, for a comparable reversal takes place. Thus Sartre notes

> the resemblance of the universe of theft to that of homosexuality: in both cases, inner reality becomes pure appearance without efficacy, and it is appearance in contrast which becomes reality. In this world which is faked [*truqué*], language is employed in reverse [*à rebours*]: designed to unite, it separates; to reveal, it conceals; to ensure agreement, it ensures disagreement; a complex of signs, which is supposed to be offered to be understood by people, makes one of the speakers an unconscious instrument of the other.[35]

Daniel's conversation with Marcelle can be compared specifically with the episode from which Sartre is generalizing:

> Genet enters a bookstore with a briefcase that is rigged [*truqué*] and pretends he wants to buy a rare book. While the bookseller goes to get the volume, Genet spots another on a table or a shelf and rapidly slips it into his briefcase. When he spoke to the bookseller, it was for the purpose of sharing with him an intention which did not exist: he was not engaged in *buying*. . . . He wished only to get a troublesome witness out of the way. Yet he *communicated* with his interlocutor; but it was a pseudo communication which destroyed any prospect of real communication. In short, like the surrealists who painted with the aim of destroying painting, but more effectively than they, he is employing language to destroy language. The bookseller actually believes he is

performing once again the act which he continually repeats during the day. . . . But he is not acting. . . . He is going to get for no purpose a book that no one wants to buy; his eagerness, his smile, which ordinarily aim at seducing customers, are mere pantomime, since there are no customers in the store, only a thief who cannot be seduced. And the result of this pantomime is a denial of the real world in favor of a universe of pure appearance. . . . He has become a fake bookseller, a true accomplice of a thief.[36]

PSEUDO COMMUNICATION

Much of Sartre's commentary is also applicable to Daniel's conversation with Marcelle. It too was "a pseudo communication which destroyed any prospect of real communication." The language Daniel used was designed to unite, reveal, ensure agreement but in effect separated, concealed, ensured disagreement. When Kierkegaard deals with the problem of communication, he too is very much aware of the risk of a pseudo communication: when there is no "common situation with the other," the "conversation is constantly prevented from becoming a conversation, though it appears . . . to be a conversation, perhaps even a cordial conversation.[37]

That Daniel is a homosexual but not a thief like Genet makes less difference than might be thought. The process of communication in his case has been assimilated to a sexual seduction which is faked and unconsummated; the process of communication in Genet's case has been associated with a faked and unconsummated commercial transaction, and Sartre has indicated that commercial transactions are seductive.

The resemblance is even closer. The succession of levels of implication in Genet's case, including the *modus loquendi*, are senses in which something is stolen, though what is significantly stolen is not external property but, by a *reflexive* shift, what is Genet's own:

> For Genet to speak is to steal words, and these retain, even in the depths of his own throat, the indelible trace of their true owners: swindled [*truqué*] even in his inner monologue, Genet is a robber who has been robbed; he steals language, and in return his thought is stolen from him.[38]

Daniel is conducting in his inner monologue a similarly *reflexive* struggle to keep his thought from being stolen from him—for example, by the conventional meanings of seduction and of kindness. The crucial resemblance between the two cases is Sartre's own overriding concern with the dialectically related acts of appropriation for oneself and communication with the Other.

Here Sartre draws a distinction in interpreting the slang of both thieves and homosexuals. Slang is "a language which is crooked or dislocated [*décalé*]," for the reference of "the slang word is not to the bare thing but to the thing with its conventional name," which is being displaced. Thus when an *enfant* is called a *chiard* ("shitter"), the reference is not simply to a child itself but to something already named an *enfant*. This conventional name

> goes directly to the essential characteristic of a child—to the fact that it does not speak. If man is defined as a rational or political animal, it is a fact of prime importance that he is unable at the beginning to use reason, because he does not possess speech, or to communicate with his fellowmen.

To coin slang terms, then, "terms of the common language are chosen which apply to lateral, secondary, or implicit properties of the object in question," and the "direct route is thus replaced by oblique routes."[39]

We are reminded of the obliquity of Daniel's sexual assault on Marcelle, when he entertained the prospect of raping her consciousness. Indeed Sartre identifies the passive homosexual's resort to slang as "symbolic rape," explaining that "the violence that Genet commits he imposes on the language of the respectable, on that language which is denied him."[40] Rape is ipso facto not a consummation which the participants share significantly in common, and in both Genet's case and Daniel's, whatever else is symbolic about the "rape," the breakdown of communication itself is also symbolized.

THE CONCEPT

The breakdown supervenes in a somewhat different way with Daniel and Marcelle, where there is dialectical *interplay*, not between two languages but between two conversations—Daniel's external dialogue with Marcelle and his internal monologue to himself. Marcelle does acknowledge Daniel's "kindness," and Daniel does not in his own mind actually coin another term (comparable to a slang term) to convey such implications of his own disabused concept of "kindness" as his desire to rape her consciousness. The breakdown of communication is not just a matter of concealing these implications from her. Their concealment also tends to deprive these implications of the objectivity to which they might pretend if he shared them with her. Instead, a reversal takes place: we are induced to turn back from the concept of "kindness" itself to the subjective process of its conception.

Even under the best of circumstances, which are conventionally assumed to be heterosexual, nothing is more difficult to define than particular feelings toward a particular individual at a particular time. We usually leave such subjective problems of definition to literature; we do not try to make philosophy out of them. But not all philosophical issues are thereby eliminated. Feeling can be either a *subjective* affair or an *objective* tactile affair, and this *ambiguity* lends itself to manipulation by the dialectical process of *definition*. I have admitted on one hand that subjective feelings are difficult to define. But on the other, there is in some sense no more definite or definitive way of convincing oneself of something's objectivity than by getting it within one's grasp and getting an actual grip on it, so that one really knows what it "feels" like and at the same time both possesses it and has the experience of it as one's "own." If this were not our feeling, the knowledge claim implicit in the term "concept" (or its German or Danish equivalent—*Begriff/begreb*) would not embody the metaphor of grasping with the hand.

Daniel reached his concept of "kindness" by a peculiar mixture of subjective feelings and tactile metaphors. The mixture merits further examination:

> Daniel looked at her shoulders and neck hungrily. That stupid obstinacy annoyed him; he wanted to break it. He was possessed by a desire that was huge and awkward; to rape this consciousness. . . .[41]

Daniel's realization that it was a desire he was possessed by presumably prompted his effort to pry himself loose from it by defining it. But for the purposes of definition "rape" seemed an irrelevant metaphor, quite aside from his not desiring literally to possess Marcelle. For "rape" is conventionally applied (like "break") to a consummated physical act and thus becomes inapplicable when it is pitted against something as intangible and out of reach as a "consciousness." Hence Daniel soon found that the motivation he was attempting to define was not something that could be consummated but something tentative—"more groping" (*tâtonnant*).

But there are probably other reasons why it is "more groping." Since it is impossible for Daniel to get at Marcelle objectively by some tactile sexual act, he is reduced instead to the *reflexive* performance of getting at this feeling of wanting to get at her. But since this feeling remains uncomfortably subjective, it can hardly be distinguished from the subjective process of defining it, for there is not really very much to get a grip on which is shaped in any other discernible way besides the effort to get a grip on it. The initially proposed consummated acts of breaking and raping are replaced by "groping," and lose their hard-edged violence, and go soft ("more humid, more fleshly"), until Daniel is engulfed in the revelation of his own "kindness."

This interpretation of his hungry look at her shoulders and neck is finally implemented by a physical gesture: "He took her by the shoulders, and his fingers submerged into warm butter." Taking her by the shoulders is rather a tame gesture, considering all the metaphorical seducing, breaking, raping that has been going on. It is nonetheless climactic, since it is at least literally physical. The gesture must have been specifically intended to break her stupid obstinacy about not wanting Mathieu to know. But after the meditation we have been through with Daniel we suspect it must also have been intended to get a grip on her feelings toward Mathieu and shake them, as well as a grip on his own feelings toward her. Instead of achieving a grip, "his fingers submerged into warm butter."[42] This eventuality we are partly prepared for by the qualities, "more groping and more humid, more fleshly," which he has been assigning himself under the eventual rubric "kindness." Yet Sartre is spreading the metaphors rather thick. Daniel's feeling obviously involves the melting not only of too solid flesh but also of too sullied flesh. The "warm butter" of Marcelle's flesh is becoming somewhat rancid.[43]

FLATULENCE

This is not the first time we have felt a sense of revulsion propel a short-term reversal in Sartre. We recall the *affective* reaction of disgust to the melting down of the Frenchman, as well as the fleshy and awkward wiggles of a bottom. As this last example illustrates, Sartre's reversals are often profanatory: instead of dealing with the beautiful, the graceful, the nude at an appropriate esthetic distance, as philosophers traditionally have done, Sartre distrusts *Aufhebung*, if in a different fashion from Kierkegaard. He focuses on the obscene, the awkward (*disgracieux*), the naked as seen from behind. Nothing is sacred for Sartre, not even himself. "I respect no one," he has explained, "and I do not wish to be respected."[44] Sartre is not commenting on his own "highly specialized personal experience"; in his case, as in Daniel's, we have to climb to higher levels of implication, for Sartre would subvert the general doctrine of *respectus humanus*.

As an example of how Sartre makes sow's ears out of the silk purses of our tradition, consider what happens to the human soul. Once Sartre commented on the atheism of his alter ego, Paul Nizan: "He promptly stopped believing in life's little white pills, souls, but he retained the obscure feeling that his father had lost his." Note the *interplay:* instead of simply denying that we have souls, Sartre is playing dialectically with the traditional comparison of the problem of their salvation with the medical problem of healing bodies. But the traditional comparison acknowledged a difference between the soul and anything physical; the soul is what I really am. This difference Sartre has already subverted earlier in the essay on Nizan; he has referred to Nizan's friends (like Sartre himself) as "inflated with that flatulence which we call our soul."[45]

The comment on Nizan's own soul is a further move. Traditionally the soul, as what I really am, is most within myself. But souls as pills have been manufactured in quantity and introduced from outside. The suggestion of quack medicine may seem like the conventional atheism of the materialist who accepts as effective only what is physically present and has no use for what is "obscure" and a matter for "feeling." But now we get a second *reversal* which takes the issue out of the setting of the conventional debate between the materialist and the traditionalist, for a soul that is felt to be "lost" cannot entirely be discounted as a little white pill. What Sartre leaves us with as a soul is an *ambiguous, contradictory*, and *unstable* composite.

Sartre's derisiveness has too often been interpreted as if it were merely vicious personal idiosyncrasy. In the memorable words of the ex-existentialist and Christian philosopher Gabriel Marcel, Sartre is "an inveterate disparager, a systematic blasphemer, . . . a flagrant corrupter," and finally "a grave digger of the West."[46] But more attention might be paid to how Sartre digs graves. His dialectic does not halt at the psychological or spiritual level we have been examining but takes in another level of experience as well, since the soul has a vocation that survives the death of God. Literature is pseudo salvation, not only in Genet's case but also in Sartre's. Once again, the dialectical starting point is a confusion. Sartre views himself as having "confused literature with prayer," of having "given myself to literature when in reality I was entering the priesthood."[47] This confusion on the part of the bourgeois writer Sartre is subverting dialectically; he is mustering the conventional anticlericalism of French bourgeois writers to discredit their conventionally creditable role as *clercs*.

CONFIDENCES

As we have discovered before, Sartre's commentary on social roles is not simply sociological. Prayer is a *modus loquendi*, and Sartre's subversion of literature should be approached at the level of literary devices for communication. Let us return to Daniel's dialogue with Marcelle. The last episode considered was Daniel's climactic physical gesture of taking Marcelle by the shoulders. All he had done previously was "take her by the hand," which is described as "a hand soft [*molle*] and feverish as a confidence."[48] Here the literary procedure seems a conventional comparison. But there are complications. Since "he holds the hand without saying anything," we (as well as Daniel) are given time for the experience to sink in. A hand feeling "soft" would be an agreeable experience one would accept, but it becomes an *ambiguous, contradictory,* and *unstable* experience when the characteristic "soft" is combined with "feverish." The hand is now too warm and too damp, and the experience itself is becoming slightly sickening. A sense of revulsion is taking over, as it will again when he takes her by the shoulders and his fingers submerge "into warm butter."

However, the full thrust of the *reversal* only comes with the phrase "as a confidence." When the "as" signals that a comparison is on the way, we expect it to function in the conventional cognitive manner of a comparison. When an "as" offers us a comparison, we assume that a comparison is needed, that we are dealing with an experience which taken just in its own terms would in some significant respect elude us. We expect that the comparison will help to define the experience by bringing to bear some other, more readily accessible experience. But this conventional *direction* in which a comparison proceeds has in the present case been unexpectedly reversed: it is the definite, physically accessible experience of holding a hand which is compared to the intangible psychological or moral experience of sharing a confidence. Thus the conventional procedure of comparison as a device of communication itself suffers a dislocating reversal. What we conventionally expect of a comparison still remains strong enough to survive this reversal, so that we still compare the intangible moral experience of sharing a confidence to the physical experience of hand holding, with the result that the moral experience becomes physically "soft and feverish." Or, rather, our experience as a whole becomes an *ambiguous, contradictory,* and *unstable* composite of the moral and the physical.[49]

There is yet another dislocation of our expectations. A comparison is a cognitive performance which we expect to enrich our understanding of an experience by rendering relevant to it some experience which belongs to some different area of experience. But taking someone's hand is a commonplace physical gesture with which one acts out the moral experience of sharing something with someone else. Thus it belongs to the same area of experience as sharing a confidence, and this area we are already familiar with, since Daniel and Marcelle are ostensibly engaged in sharing confidences. Hence the intrusion of an explicit comparison of the physical gesture with the moral experience seems a forced comparison, not in the conventional sense that a too remote and irrelevant experience is dragged in by the comparison but in the sense that resorting to the procedure of comparing matters which already belong together tends to force them apart. To go to the trouble of rendering relevant what is already accepted as relevant is to insinuate that it is not all that relevant.

EXPRESSION

The irrelevance in this instance of hand holding as an *objective* physical gesture to sharing a confidence as a *subjective* moral experience will be further accentuated with Daniel's next gesture, when the hand held becomes (as in the episode of the woman about to be seduced) an inert object:

> And then there was this hand that was sweating in his own. He forced himself to press it harder, to extract [*exprimer*] all its juice.

The diet Sartre offers of metaphors and comparisons ("warm butter" for flesh, "sweating" for "juice") is not strictly kosher. But more than the physical revulsion of nausea is being elicited. The looseness of the connection ("and then") with what happened before has allowed not only the hand to become inert but also the perverse *affective* logic of the homosexual to subvert the relevance of the conventional.[50] The usual assumption is that to take hold of a hand is to acknowledge that one feels intimate with the other person; it follows that to press it is to insist upon this intimacy, since hand holding is the accepted outward and visible symbol of the feeling. Daniel would then be employing physical pressure in order to "express" his feeling, which he feels is too intimate for him to find quite the right words to "express" it. But the fact that he "forced himself" to do what should have been in its intimacy a spontaneous impulse has divested the conventional symbolism of its moral significance.

The hand-holding operation illustrates in still another way an *ambiguous, contradictory*, and *unstable interplay* between the physical and moral dimensions of experience. *Exprimer* can refer in French to the physical operation of "pressing" something "out" as well to the moral effort of "expressing" oneself which is involved in sharing a confidence, and the first reference has become primary, since Marcelle's hand has become an inert physical object. Yet even here another irrelevance further subverts the logic of the physical operation in a fashion which is designed to violate the cognitive conventions of making a comparison. The characteristic that juice and sweat share is their dampness,[51] but this comparison is undermined not only subjectively, by the difference between what may be pleasantly thirst quenching and what is not, but also objectively, by the fact that the physical operation of squeezing, which is necessary to extract juice, is quite unnecessary to induce sweating.

Thus the hand holding provides a more succinct illustration than previous examples of how the *ambiguous, contradictory,* and *unstable interplay* can be extended to and subvert the process of communication, including not only such conventional social procedures as hand holding itself (whereby one shares in common with someone else the most available portion of each other's anatomy) and its moral equivalent of sharing confidences in common but also such a conventional literary procedure as making comparisons which bring out what different experiences have in common.

THE ANTINOVEL

When the scope of this subversive activity is extended to the literary genre as such, the novel itself becomes an "antinovel." The dialectic whereby an appearance is kept up we are already familiar with from the case of the Respectful Prostitute. Her incongruous attempt to help keep up appearances those who considered her beneath respect subverted in reality the respectability of Southern Gentlemen, Southern Ladyhood, and Southern Patriotism. Similarly, Genet attempted to play the role of saint and martyr, although he was a criminal, and of a woman, although he was a man.[52] Like *The Respectful Prostitute* or *Saint (seins) Genet, Play Actor* and *Martyr,* antinovels are *ambiguous, contradictory,* and *unstable* composites which, Sartre explains,

> retain the appearance and the shape of the novel; they . . . present fictitious individuals and tell us their story. But this is only the better to deceive us; the function of the antinovel is to pit the novel against itself, to destroy it under our very eyes at the same time that it would seem to be constructed, to write the novel of a novel which is not being created, which cannot be created.[53]

Sartre's own novel, *Nausea,* is an antinovel. Its intent, at least in part, is to discredit the novelist as undertaking a *Recherche du temps perdu,* not only in the paradigm version which Proust finally completed in his terminal volume, *Le temps retrouvé,* but also in *Nausea* itself, which is not a novel that is finally completed within the novel but ends instead with the writer's aspiration to write the novel that will salvage his past, but with the presentiment as well of the irrelevance of this aspiration to his own salvation, which entails the future. In short, *Nausea* is not the conventional novel about writing a novel but allows a margin for the disparagement of the writing of the novel that it is itself.[54] This margin widens when, later in his autobiography, *Sartre* discredits the doctrine of salvation by words.

His subversive intentions are also exhibited when he refurbishes a traditional drama, as Kierkegaard's were shown when he refurbished the *Antigone*. Athenian patriotism had already been discounted in *The Trojan Women*, and Sartre reconstructs Euripides' play as a contemporary antiwar play. (The war at one level is the Vietnam war, with the Greeks playing the role of the Americans and the Vietnamese the role of the Trojans, but there are echoes for the French audience of their own colonial war in Algeria.) The "reversal" (*peripeteia*) has been endorsed as an essential feature of the drama since Aristotle's *Poetics*. But Sartre accentuates the dialectic of the drama more than Euripides had done:

> I have tried to render the play more dramatic by bringing out the oppositions that remain merely implicit in Euripides: the conflict between Andromeda and Hecuba; the double attitude of Hecuba, who sometimes surrenders to her misfortune, sometimes demands justice; the reversal in Andromeda's attitude . . . the erotic preoccupation of Cassandra, who throws herself into Agamemnon's bed, quite aware of the fact she will perish with him.[55]

Sartre is accentuating the opposition first between one individual and another (Andromeda and Hecuba), then between the attitude of each of them at one time and her attitude at another; and the dialectic reaches its climax when the difference of time is no longer a factor (Cassandra).

Interplay goes on at another level. A Euripidean tragedy itself is opposed to traditional Greek tragedy, and its audience listens to another dialogue besides the interchange between the characters (just as the reader listens to Daniel's monologue as well as his dialogue with Marcelle). This other dialogue Sartre identifies as "a half-heard conversation about commonplaces." He explains its dialectic:

> The expressions Euripides employs are the same in appearance as those of his predecessors. But . . . they take on another resonance; they take on another meaning.[56]

The half-heard dialogue is thus a dialectic of the same expressions (in appearance) and another meaning (in reality). We can compare the way a portion of Daniel's monologue on his feelings toward Marcelle was a half-thought-out dialogue, a subversive "subconversation" about the commonplace "kindness."[57] The immediately relevant comparison, however, is between the expressions Euripides employs in Sartre's version and those in the original version. With the Vietnam war going on (and the Algerian war having gone on), they take on another resonance; they take on another meaning.

Sartre explicitly compares the subversiveness of Euripides' drama with certain contemporary antibourgeois plays:

Think of Beckett or Ionesco; it is the identical phenomenon; it involves employing the commonplace in order to destroy it from within. . . . The Athenian public responds to *The Trojan Women* as the bourgeois responds today to *Godot* or the *Bald Soprano*, pleased to hear commonplaces but aware too that they are present at their disintegration.[58]

We suspect that Daniel was similarly pleased when in the course of his reflection he finally stumbled on "kindness," while remaining aware that its commonplace implications were disintegrating under the strain of the destructive feelings he was subsuming under it. Assisted by his deviancy, he was disentangling himself from his "lostness in the one" and regaining some grip on these feelings as his own experience.

The Case

History is another genre, besides the novel and the drama, in which this process of subversion can take place, not only at the level of the participants' particular experiences but also at the higher level of the experience of the genre itself. Just as Sartre's *Nausea* can be regarded as an "antinovel," so Merleau-Ponty offers a brief historical commentary which constitutes in effect an antihistory:

> Conservative historians record, as something which goes without saying, the innocence of Dreyfus—and remain no less conservative. Dreyfus was not revenged, not even rehabilitated. His innocence become a commonplace is not worth much, considering the price of his humiliation. It is not inscribed in history with the meaning which was stolen from him, which was demanded by those who came to his defense. From those who have lost everything, history continues to take away, and she continues to give to those who have taken everything. For prescription, which envelops everything, renders the criminal innocent and dismisses the case of his victims. History never confesses anything.[59]

In the opening sentence conservative historians are trapped in the first of a succession of contradictions with which their genre soon becomes riddled. This first contradiction is between accepting the innocence of Dreyfus and still remaining conservatives. They are thereby deprived of any benefit that might accrue to them from a contrast with the conservatives who were Dreyfus's actual contemporaries and proclaimed his guilt.

Since Merleau-Ponty's initial reference to "conservative historians" seems quite conventional, we think at first that what is in question is their belated verdict that Dreyfus was innocent. But this conventional reference is designed to ease our way into a dialectical development in which it finally turns out that it is history itself which is conservative, so that in effect conservative historians can be contemptuously absolved of the intellectual irresponsibility with which they refuse to confront the initial contradiction. Merleau-Ponty gains this broader scope by taking advantage of the *ambiguity* of the expression "history" and disregarding the conventional distinction any historian would draw. "History" can refer to either the (subjective) discipline or its (objective) subject matter. Observe how Merleau-Ponty maneuvers toward dropping the conventional distinction. He has not identified any "conservative historians" personally. By keeping his reference to them impersonal, by having what they record "go without saying," like the anonymous dicta of Heidegger's *the one*, and by personifying the historical process, Merleau-Ponty allows the distinction to disappear between their conservatism and what the course of history itself preserves when "prescription . . . envelops everything."

The verdict of the historian thus becomes indistinguishable from the verdict of history, and it is this conventional metaphor that Merleau-Ponty would subvert. The metaphor is an extrapolation from the legal sphere. The extrapolation is facilitated here by the fact that the historical conclusion of the Dreyfus case was a legal verdict. The effect of assimilating historical outcomes to the verdicts of a judge is that historical outcomes no longer seem contingent, arbitrary; they seem definite and definitive, as if the course of history were regulated by a body of laws. This extrapolation had itself become a commonplace even before Hegel's philosophy of history. All of us have to come to terms with historical outcomes or be damned.

The extrapolation is a matter of taking legal metaphors as applying to the course of history, but Merleau-Ponty is observing that history's verdicts are the opposite of just verdicts: the criminal becomes innocent, while the case of his victim is dismissed. Here Merleau-Ponty appears to be contradicting the historical outcome: Dreyfus's case was not dismissed, and a just verdict was eventually reached. But the point of the apparent contradiction is to play up the real contradiction between a legal or historical verdict and a moral judgment and thereby to introduce a certain *ambiguous interplay* in the meaning of the expression "innocence." It can refer to an individual's private moral conviction that he is innocent as well as to the public legal verdict that he is innocent. But the moral and legal meanings can neither be kept entirely separate nor can their relation be held fixed. On one hand the two meanings are related, inasmuch as Dreyfus would not have had to entertain any conviction as to his innocence until he was accused. Here a rather more general and distinctively philosophical ambiguity may attach to the expression "innocence," which is assignable to the first stage in a dialectic—that of immediate experience.

But when we distinguished stages in Kierkegaard, we recognized that immediate experience is an abstraction: we become aware of what an immediate experience means only when it has lost its immediacy and we have reached the reflective stage of the dialectic; then our effort to restore what was immediate becomes fruitless. Thus Dreyfus became aware of his moral innocence only when he had to deny his legal guilt. But on the other hand, the eventual legal reversal of the original finding of guilt could not restore Dreyfus's unreflecting moral innocence.

The dislocation involved can be compared with a feature of Daniel's monologue: one attribute (with Daniel "kindness," with Dreyfus "innocence") acquires opposed meanings; the crucial meaning is defined reflexively by the individual's own experience (by Dreyfus's sense of humiliation and desire for revenge), while the other meaning is "the indefiniteness of the commonplace."[60] But this opposition undergoes dialectical development, for the experience of the individual becomes in some sense more definitely his own, once he recognizes that its "meaning" is "stolen" from him by others, if he then also recognizes that he can never as a particular individual be subsumed entirely as a "case" under some general rule, as he must be for the public purposes of the law and of history.

In spite of the dependence of his commentary up until now on the analogy between the proceedings of history and of a law court (an analogy which the reader has tended to accept as unsurprising and legitimate, in view of the fact that history has ratified the eventual legal verdict in Dreyfus's case), Merleau-Ponty finally subverts the analogy. He takes two steps. First of all history is denied the role of the judge issuing verdicts, even of a judge who issues unjust verdicts by rendering "the criminal innocent" and dismissing "the case of his victim." Instead, history itself is hauled into court; it becomes the criminal who is on trial and who should be judged. But unfortunately "history never confesses anything" and so holds up the proceedings of the court and the cause of moral justice indefinitely, in spite of history's usual readiness to change in every other way—as the verdict was at last changed in Dreyfus's case.

OUTCOMES

With history's refusal to confess, no outcome is achieved. More specifically, when we recognize that Dreyfus's innocence, as he had experienced it, has not been "taken up" and "preserved" by the outcome of his case, we are brought back from the *Aufhebung* of "conservative historians," who are reconciled with their erstwhile adversaries, to the extent that Dreyfus's "innocence" has "become a commonplace." Thus we are returned to some acknowledgment of the experience with which Dreyfus had started out as his own. But in the mean time philosophy of history, as traditionally conceived, collapses.

This is Merleau-Ponty's general comment:

> I am not even referring to the part played by chance and the unpredictable. . . . Matters are much worse. It is as if a diabolic mechanism conjured the outcome away at the moment it had just showed its face, as if history censored the dramas of which it is composed, as if it liked to hide itself, only half exposing the truth during brief moments of disarray and the rest of the time striving to thwart the movements of *Aufhebung*.[61]

This "diabolical mechanism," which is so "much worse" a dislocation of "the outcome" than the mere intervention of "chance," is an *ex-sistential reversal*, for the truth that is half exposed "during brief moments of disarray" is opposed to the Hegelian conception of the truth as the continuity which is ultimately "preserved" *(aufbewahrt)* when the movement of *Aufhebung* reaches its outcome. In Merleau-Ponty's version, Hegel's conception would seem only a more sophisticated rendering of the conventional conservative conception.

But Merleau-Ponty is thinking less of "conservative historians" than of conventional Marxists, though he is obtaining at the same time malicious dialectical satisfaction from lumping the latter together with their opponents. Furthermore, he is thinking less of such a past outcome as the Dreyfus case than of the way Communists appeal to a future outcome in order to keep their Marxist doctrine intact for deferred fulfillment, however opportunistically it may be compromised by their present tactics.[62]

The Nazi-Soviet pact was the paradigmatic compromise which was regularly recalled during the postwar period whenever Communists pulled off some dismaying tactical maneuver. The philosophical or ideological issues which the pact posed for the Party under the German occupation were to have been prominent in the novel with which Sartre planned to bring to a conclusion his tetralogy, *The Roads to Freedom*. The only portion of the concluding volume which Sartre has published concerns the escape attempted by two French prisoners from a prisoner of war camp in Germany. Let me fill in the background by citing Simone de Beauvoir's bald summary of the relevant portion of the plot:

> A newcomer at the prison camp, Chalais, was a Communist, and he recognized in Schneider the journalist Vicarios, who had left the Party at the time of the Nazi-Soviet pact and who was a marked man, since the Party considered him an informer. Chalais asserted that Russia

would never enter the war and that *L'Humanité* ordered collaboration. Disconcerted, outraged, anguished, Brunet [Sartre's protagonist at this juncture], on learning that Vicarios was going to escape to confront his accusers, decided to accompany him. Their flight sealed their friendship . . . Vicarios was killed, Brunet recaptured.[63]

My citation from the novel itself begins after Vicarios is mortally wounded by the prison guards. Brunet tells himself;

> Vicarios is going to die; despair and hatred are working their way back through the course of this wasted life and are going to rot it away right up to the moment of birth. This absolute of suffering, no human victory could efface it; the Party is finishing him off. Even if Russia wins, men are alone.[64]

Some existential significance can probably be attached to the fact that Sartre's tetralogy reaches its de facto ending when an individual is alone and his experience is arrayed as his own, not only against the Party as a collective organization but also against the future outcome, a Russian victory, to which the Party is dedicated.[65]

As Sartre worked on the manuscript after World War II, history moved on, without pausing for an *Aufhebung*. And Sartre found himself unable to bring his tetralogy to a conclusion, so we are left with this fragment. Something perhaps comparable seems to have happened to him as a philosopher. And philosophy is the conventional genre for organizing and evaluating experience—not the drama, the novel, or history—which ultimately concerns us here. Instead of reaching a final conclusion in *Being and Nothingness*, Sartre looked forward to a sequel, *Man*, in which an ethical conclusion would be reached. But he eventually resigned himself to never completing this work. Has it been replaced (as some interpreters have suggested) by the *Critique*? But the second and concluding volume of the *Critique* itself has never been completed. The *Critique* was followed instead by the study on Flaubert, but the fourth and concluding volume of this last study is not to be completed either.

DESTRUCTION

Meanwhile Merleau-Ponty died, leaving behind fragments of what was to have been a major work. He died prematurely, it is true. But Heidegger's *Being and Time* was published in 1929, and it has remained inconclusive, breaking off with Heidegger still "on the way" (*unterwegs*). And he did not die until 1976. Instead of arriving at a conclusion in his later works, the way Heidegger has followed has been a "reversal" (*Kehre*).[66] Reversals we have seen take place at various levels. There are the short-term reversals, and I have traced the *interplay* they can produce. There are longer-term reversals, not only of the *direction* in which history proceeds (as Merleau-Ponty's interpretation of the Dreyfus case has just illustrated), but also in the *direction* in which the history of philosophy proceeds as a supposedly progressive development. Heidegger's "step backward" is such a reversal. In the program he originally proposed in *Being and Time,* he planned to proceed in its sequel backward through the history of philosophy—from Kant to Descartes to Aristotle.

In his later works Heidegger does arrive at the Pre-Socratics, though the program has not in fact been carried out as proposed in *Being and Time.* Yet the intended subversiveness of the reversal is indicated by Heidegger's characterization of it as the "destruction" of the philosophical tradition. Compare Sartre's description of how a commonplace can be employed in such fashion as "to destroy it from within." For Heidegger's program is still in some sense philosophical, just as Sartre's antinovel *Nausea* is still in some sense a novel. Thus "destruction" here does not have quite its literal sense. In some measure it is undertaken in opposition to the way Hegel's *Aufhebung* "preserves" at the higher level of his own comprehensive philosophy what remains of final significance in earlier partial philosophies. Moreover, the term "destruction" can be broken up and Heidegger's undertaking interpreted as "de-construction," in the sense that the structure of the philosophical tradition, which its own development has covered up, is "discovered," especially insofar as its most significant movement at any juncture has been conceived as an *Aufhebung.*

In *Being and Time* itself Descartes is viewed by Heidegger (as he was by Hegel as well as by Kierkegaard) as the protagonist in the modern development of the philosophical tradition, and in *Being and Time* a more restricted reversal is actually carried out:

> If the *cogito ergo sum* is to serve as the starting point for an existential analytic of being-there, then it requires a reversal [*Umkehrung*]. The *sum* is accordingly asserted first, and specifically in the sense "I am in a world."[67]

With this reversal we arrive at what we assumed in part I was the starting point for this existential analytic—*being-there* as being-in-the-world. We did not then recognize, as we have since come to recognize in part III, that "in no case is *being-there* unaffected and unseduced by the manner in which things have been interpreted," so that in Heidegger's terms our original starting point can only be reached by starting out with further reversals—the reversal in the direction in which Descartes proceeded (and modern philosophy followed) and that which Heidegger proposed as the sequel to *Being and Time.*

Disgust

The earliest published characterization we have of Sartre as a philosopher (probably his own or supplied by his alter ego Nizan) is the notation "Young philosopher—is working on a volume of destructive philosophy." Although this notation, accompanying Sartre's first publication, appeared in a magazine along with the first French translation of a text by Heidegger, Simone de Beauvoir has assured us that the young philosopher did not then have the slightest understanding of Heidegger. It is all the more striking that Sartre's philosophy was also characterized as "destructive."[68] Sartre's reversal is similar to Heidegger's "destruction" at least to the extent that it is a reversal of the Hegelian movement of *Aufhebung* toward an outcome which "preserves" in a reconciling synthesis what is finally significant in what was previously opposed.[69]

We have already felt Sartre's disgust at the confusion of such an indeterminate "interpenetration of opposites" as the Franco-American *en voie de fusion* or Flaubert's "habitual syncretism." In a political pronouncement of 1974 he repudiated coalition politics insofar as it is committed to a Hegelian style of reconciliation at some higher level of differing points of view. An interlocutor suggested to Sartre that the peasants, the women, and the homosexuals adopt a common program with the working class, and he used the term "melting pot." Sartre demurred:

> Your term "melting pot" bothers me. A melting pot is something you put an assortment of things into, each of which has a quite definite form, and then it all melts, taking another unitary form. . . . Give me some idea of what can come out of the melting pot.

The interlocutor explained,

> Into the melting pot people bring different partial points of view which when put together become fused [*fusionnent*].

Sartre objected,

> I don't agree. Take women, for example. They bring . . . a point of view which is not partial. They say, "Up until now there have only been revolutions made by men and for men. What becomes of that in the melting pot?" I don't myself believe in the melting-pot. . . . The idea is too Hegelian that a thought, whatever it is, is partial, that it must come into contact with a complementary thought, and that the two of them together will form a third thought.[70]

Sartre's demurral is couched in terms of the metaphor which we have seen conveyed in 1945 his disdain for the Franco-American.

At the higher level of philosophy, the kind of disgust that Sartre feels at the lower-level confusions of the Franco-American and of coalition politics becomes the nauseous reversal with which he would disgorge traditional philosophy insofar as its *Aufhebung* is a process of "assimilation" (or, more concretely, an "alimentary" or "digestive" dialectic) in which the reconciling synthesis achieved is the mind's confusion of things with itself and itself with other minds:

> The mind was a spider which drew things into its web, covered them with white spittle, and slowly swallowed them. . . . Assimilation . . . of things to ideas, of ideas by ideas, of minds by minds.[71]

The philosophical essay I am citing Sartre wrote in Berlin during 1933–34—that is, at the very beginning of his exposure to the influence of Heidegger and Husserl. Thus Sartre's distrust of *Aufhebung* does not date from his introduction to America in 1945, and it still survives when he expresses his discomfort with the fusions of a "melting pot" in the political dialogue of 1974.

THE ANTIPHILOSOPHER

Lest it be concluded from the examples provided by Merleau-Ponty and Sartre that existential distrust of traditional philosophy is merely a gut reaction of disgust, which cannot develop into a detailed analysis, let us return to Kierkegaard, whom I have postponed because I wished to show first that a destructive reversal is characteristic of contemporary existentialists too, and not just Kierkegaard's ad hoc reaction, on behalf of intellectual modesty, against the arrogance of Hegel's system building.

Kierkegaard's reaction as an "anti-philosopher" it has become fashionable to endorse, even when no other features of his philosophy are endorsed.[72] Who today, when we are expected to be laid back and let it all hang out—who would uphold a system against open-endedness? Yet Kierkegaard's philosophy is not entirely open. It is, like Hegel's, a *relational* analysis, so that the significance of his reaction against Hegel's system can be appreciated only insofar as it is related to other features of his philosophy where he is also opposed to Hegel. But these other features are usually overlooked. So far I myself have concentrated on his proceeding by stages, as illustrated by the esthetic stage of *Either/Or*.

Although Kierkegaard came to believe that his critique of the esthetic still remained valid, when Hegel's philosophy lost favor, I would be shirking my responsibility to the dialectical method were I to neglect entirely the opportunity, which Kierkegaard's opposition to Hegel provides, to sample the most influential of modern dialectians, especially since Hegel's philosophy, if not its systematic character, has come back into some favor today. I would also be shirking my responsibility to Kierkegaard's own philosophy as the philosophy of an "antiphilosopher." What would in fact be left of it that could still be called a philosophy if its references to Hegel's philosophy were eradicated?

Hegel conceived his systematic philosophy as the ultimate *Aufhebung*, the final outcome, which surmounted the contradictions of previous philosophies and in some sense brought the history of philosophy to a conclusion. Where some of Kierkegaard's contemporaries continued to be committed to the principle of *Aufhebung* and proceeded to more ultimate philosophies, Kierkegaard mocked them by refusing to "go beyond" Hegel. He undertook instead to promote the disintegration of Hegel's system from within, by applying to it the opposing principle of contradiction which subverted ultimate outcomes. But Kierkegaard's own philosophy thereby itself remained fragmentary and inconclusive. This is what we are now left with.

Notes

1. See p. 166 above.
2. A better translation than "repetition" is "recovery" or "recuperation," since the reflexive undertaking is self-appropriation.
3. *Being and Time*, p. 268. Heidegger chooses his words much more carefully than his existentialist successors, and it does him scant justice to lump together (as I shall in this chapter) *Rückgang, Wiederholung, Schritt züruck, Umkehrung*, and *Kehre*. But each term does delineate a reversal, though in a different sense from the others; see chap. 4, nn. 42, 43 above.
4. *Sartre*, p. 166.
5. "Radical" in Husserl carries both an etymological reference to getting back to immediate experience (the "root"—e.g., *Ideas*, p. 20) and a reference to the "transformation" (*Umwandlung*) in our "standpoint" (e.g., ibid., p. 7) which is required for this purpose and which is enforced by the transcendental reduction.
6. Husserl's authorized spokesman, Eugen Fink, stresses how inappropriate it is "to treat the reduction . . . as an easily summarized mental technique, the various forms of which could be easily given" ("The Phenomenological Philosophy of Edmund Husserl," p. 113).
7. *Postscript*, p. 74.
8. *Cartesian Meditations*, p. 157.
9. *Republic* 518D.
10. Besides the original "metamorphosis" (see chap. 2, n. 84), Sartre lines up "First Conversion: Evil," "Second Metamorphosis: The Aesthete," "Third Metamorphosis: The Writer."
11. *Sartre*, pp. 262–63.
12. *Situations*, p. 199.
13. *Postscript*, p. 327.
14. *Search for a Method*, pp. 17–18.
15. "Theses on Feuerbach," p. 199; italics in original.

16. *Perception,* p. 62.

17. P. 141.

18. All these metaphors are used by Husserl with reference to the phenomenological reduction, but they are used by Sartre with reference to various possible contingencies of everyday life. I shall compare their reductions in the phenomenological sequel.

19. For Kierkegaard's conversion, see Lowrie, *Kierkegaard,* 1:168–81.

20. *Postscript,* p. 487.

21. I have applied Sartre's terminology here to Maggie's "project," but the contradictions are sharper and less delicately blended when Sartre deals with comparable decisions: "A few years ago it was pointed out to me that the characters in my plays and novels made their decisions abruptly and at a moment of crisis, that a moment was enough, for example, for Orestes to carry out his conversion in *Flies.* Of course. It is because they are made in my own image; not at all as I am, obviously, but as I wanted to be" (*Words,* p. 198).

22. Kierkegaard gets the metaphor not from Hegel but from Lessing, and he equates it with Aristotle's "transference to another realm" (*Postscript,* p. 90).

23. Ibid., p. 510. In Sartre too a conversion is a matter of "becoming radically other" (*Sartre,* p. 262).

24. *Postscript,* p. 327.

25. *Words,* p. 253. This "long-range undertaking" can only be traced as a dialectical development, but a more adequate interpretation of Sartre's conversion would also take into account its phenomenological character. The metaphor of the "lightning" striking, which I cited earlier, manifests a phenomenological appeal to immediate experience.

26. *Situations,* p. 198.

27. This title is not Kierkegaard's, but it does describe the tracts collected under it. The metaphor of subversion itself goes back to the very start of existentialism. It is found in one of the Latin theses which Kierkegaard defended in the dissertation: "Socrates realitatem subvertit" (*Irony,* p. 348).

28. The notion of traitor Sartre may have taken over from his alter ego Nizan (see *Situations,* pp. 115–16) and Merleau-Ponty. The latter, writing of "Bukharin and the Ambiguity of History," had reported, "The Middle Ages are not over, history has not yet stopped being diabolical, it is still capable . . . of turning opposition into treason." But he added, "Like the church, the Party will perhaps rehabilitate those whom it has condemned, once a new phase of history alters the meaning of their behavior" (*Humanism and Terror,* pp. 68–69). The notion must have attracted Sartre because of the ambiguity and instability of its application, and he employs it in both a pejorative and a favorable sense. Its implications are developed in analyzing not only Nizan but also Genet (*Saint Genet,* pp. 596–99) and Tintoretto (*Situations,* p. 45). It is adopted by a once fervent disciple in interpreting Sartre's phrase "I became a traitor and have remained a traitor" (Jeanson, pp. 333–34); and it is borrowed by André Gorz as the title of his autobiography, in which he admits his immense intellectual debt to Sartre.

29. Daniel is repelled by "flesh that was hostile, flesh that was greasy, nourishing, a larder" (*Age,* p. 206). At the same time we have seen that he is also attracted: "What was she feeling inside her, this heavy female in disarray? He would have liked *to be her*" (p. 207; italics in original). Neither his sense of hostility and repulsion nor his vertiginous sense of attraction is unambiguously homosexual. There are other levels, which Sartre's use of the impersonal allows scope for. The tactile metaphors which we shall later watch Daniel employ indicate that he succumbs in some measure to the "tactile fascination" of the "slimy," which "sucks at me," is "a moist and female sucking, which I feel like a vertigo; it attracts me to it as the bottom of an abyss might attract me" (*Sartre,* p. 344; for other abysses besides the female, see p. 347 above). The sliminess that threatens to engulf Daniel is bifocal: it is not merely Marcelle's physical femaleness but also moral—the "mucky pity" (*pitié bourbeuse*), "the sticky pity" (*poisseuse pitié*) (*Age,* pp. 208–9) that he feels for her female predicament which he

cannot share, however he may at moments identify with her as female. The "greasy," the "mucky," and the "sticky" are all affiliated with the "slimy" in Sartre and are indistinguishably physical and moral (or affective) attributes (*Sartre*, p. 339).

30. Each of them is placed in a reflexive situation. If there is irony of sorts in Marcelle's "When a woman is fucked up [in a moral sense], she can always get herself pregnant [in a physical sense]" (see chap. 8, n. 62) turning out to be self-commentary (and at a higher level, commentary on the interplay between these two senses), there is ironical self-commentary too when Daniel finally forces Marcelle to admit she really desires to keep the child, for he copes with her feeling "guilty" about it by insisting that this desire is "natural," whereas her guilty feeling is a "perversion" (*Age*, p. 207). On his way to visit Marcelle, Daniel was fantasizing about candidates for his own homosexual desires.

31. In *Saint Genet* there is considerable highly abstract dialectical manipulation of the concepts of Good and Evil which is designed to discredit "Goodness." But there is already some manipulation in the back of Daniel's mind at a crucial juncture which I have already examined: " 'Do with me what you like, I'm in your hands.' She fascinated him; this tender fire which was devouring him—he did not know if it was Evil or Goodness [*le Mal ou la bonté*]. Good and Evil [*Bien et Mal*], their Good and *his* Evil—it came to the same thing. This woman was there, and this communion which was repellent and vertiginous" (*Age*, pp. 210–11; italics in original).

32. See p. 350 above. At one point Daniel exclaims to himself, "She is looking grateful [*a l'air reconnaissante*], my God! Like Malvina, when he had slapped her" (*Age*, p. 204).

33. See esp. *Sartre*, pp. 207–8.

34. Something that is subverted in the long run at a higher level is the conception of moral character itself. Daniel's particular character is shown up as a contradictory composite. But Sartre also finds the concept of character in general contradictory, and hence the process of characterization, including such characteristics as "kindness." Thus one feature of the self-deception in which the woman indulges who was about to be seduced in chap. 7 was her characterization to herself of her prospective seducer as "sincere and respectful as the table is round or square." The "qualities" thus assigned to him are in this way "congealed into a permanence like that of things" (ibid., p. 147). She is disavowing the distinction between the moral attributes of a self and the physical attributes of a thing. The issue of characterization and character is more fundamentally the issue of self-identity and can only be dealt with in the sequel, since it is a phenomenological issue with respect to my consciousness of myself (or another's self) as something. But it is evident that the contradictions which emerge in such rapid succession during Daniel's effort to characterize his attitude toward Marcelle are designed to preclude the characteristics in question congealing into a permanence like that of things.

35. *Saint Genet*, pp. 281–82.

36. Ibid., p. 281; italics in original. Sartre implies that this "example" of "one of the thefts Genet committed" is picked offhand. But I suspect that the "briefcase" which was *truqué* appealed to Sartre against the background of a "world" which is *truqué* for Sartre is analyzing someone who is "swindled [*truqué*] even in his inner monologue" (p. 279) and who indeed as a child was already *truqué* (Frechtman translates "doctored," e.g., pp. 35, 42). With regard to the "vertiginous word" (see p. 347 above) with which this operation was performed, Sartre employs the spatial analogy of a "box with a double bottom" (p. 62), and its doubleness contributes to launching the dialectic. Probably the briefcase was *truqué* in a similar fashion.

37. *Postscript*, p. 491. That Daniel's conversation with Marcelle is a pseudo communication is played up by the fact that she identifies his preceding seductive conversation with her mother (see chap. 8, n. 60 above) as a pseudo communication, in implicit contrast with the real conversation they are now having: "Look, Daniel, that's the third time she's told you about her trip, and you always listen as if you were passionately in-

terested. To be entirely frank, that rather annoys me; I don't really know what was then going through your mind" (*Age*, p. 200).

38. *Saint Genet*, p. 279. Earlier (chap. 8, n. 49) I observed how integral is metaphorical transposition to Sartre's existential psychoanalysis. Now we see more clearly that the most significant transpositions are reflexive reversals.

39. *Saint Genet*, p. 286.

40. Ibid., p. 289.

41. The incongruity is accentuated dialectically by pitting "break," which is a rather general form of violence, against a specific attitude on Marcelle's part ("stupid obstinacy"); whereas rape, a very specific form of violence, is pitted against a "consciousness" as such.

42. The warmth is partly to be explained by the fact that Marcelle's room is as hot as a "furnace" (p. 200). Sartre is much given to raising the temperature. Generally it is for the dialectical purpose of effecting an intense transformation, as in the case of the melting pot, but sometimes his dialectical purpose is more specific—the transformation manifests the sloppiness of life. The climactic contrast in *Nausea* between life and art is the diarist's visualization of how "Some of These Days" was composed. The composer is "suffocating with the heat. . . . Above New York the sky burns, the blue of the sky is inflamed, enormous yellow flames come and licked the roofs." It was a "terrible heat wave which transformed men into ponds of melting grease." (Recall that Marcelle's "flesh" was also "greasy" as well as "nourishing, a larder" for new life; see n. 29, this chapter). But "the moist hand [of the composer] seizes the pencil on the piano. . . . He held the pencil limply [*mollement*], and drops of sweat fell from his ringed fingers onto the paper" (pp. 176–77).

43. Olfactory sensations, like tactile sensations (see chap. 7, n. 69), are Sartre's vehicle for a reaction which is intimately affective rather than merely sensory. Daniel is not only repelled by Marcelle's "greasy" female flesh, as amplified by her pregnancy, but he also reacts to her as a "solid, dreary smell" (p. 198). "Solid" is a tactile allusion to a physical attribute of her pregnancy (*grossesse*), but it is not an attribute one would expect of a "smell," any more than the moral attribute of dreariness, and these incongruities become even more dislocating by virtue of the incongruity of their combination.) Later when he has forced the admission, "It's filthy business," we observed how he savors her exposure: "At last, this was it, she was naked. . . . All that was left was a fat pregnant woman who smelled of flesh" (p. 201). Still later he concedes to himself, "It was not strictly speaking a smell, but it might be said that she impregnated the atmosphere around her" (p. 204). The correction enjoins a reversal, since "strictly speaking" she cannot impregnate but has herself been impregnated.

44. Consider too Sartre's admission, "I reproach myself for having been in my articles far too respectful toward de Gaulle. I should not have taken account of the fact that he was respected by a large number of Frenchmen, and I should not have respected this respect" (Contat, 1:352).

45. *Situations*, pp. 101, 85.

46. Contat, 1:455. This salvo was fired on the occasion of the award of the 1964 Nobel Prize, which Sartre refused.

47. *Words*, p. 250.

48. *Age*, p. 204.

49. The feverishness represents another rise in temperature. For the ambiguity, see nn. 29, 30, this chapter. Other examples of such composite experiences are the reaction, to the wiggling bottom ("obscene") and that of the sadist to the humiliation of his victim whose shoulders he is leaning on.

50. For Sartre's comments on discontinuous style see chap. 2, n. 77; for Kierkegaard's loosening of connections, see p. 453 below.

51. The wetness is emphasized by the occurrence of its opposite in the next sentence: " 'I don't know what can be done,' he said in rather a dry voice" (*Age*, p. 204). Recall,

because of the association there too with a *confidence* as well as its existential significance, the "damp voice" (*voix mouillée*) of the "weary women" with whom "all
things" were compared in the nauseous vision as "abjectly confessing their existence"
(*elles se faisaient l'abjecte confidence de leur existence*) (see p. 102 above). In both
instances drawing attention to the mode of expression adds to the propulsion to extend
the implications of dampness metaphorically. This helps prepare us in the conversation for one of the characteristics of what turns out to be "kindness"—"It was more
groping, and more humid, more fleshly." Dampness and wetness are generally associated with the sloppiness of life. In *Nausea* "the stone, that notorious stone, the starting
point of this entire story" (p. 184; the diarist is reminiscing during his nauseous vision)
was "damp and muddy [*humide et boueux*] on the under side" (p. 2). Just as "groping"
is associated with the humidity of "kindness," so in the case of the stone it is the
reflexive, affective reaction that counts. Thus the diarist was unable to throw the
stone (see chap. 7, n. 8 above)—i.e., to exercise the freedom of a *projet*. He goes on
to report, "I held it by the edges, fingers wide apart, so as not to become filthy [*me
salir*]." In the nauseous vision itself the reflexive, affective senses are lined up when
their deliverances are pitted against color as a classification (see p. 195 above) introduced by sight, a distance sense: "Black? I felt the word deflating, emptying of meaning with extraordinary rapidity. Black? The root *was not* black. . . . Black . . . did
not exist. . . . It *resembled* a color, but also a bruise or a secretion, an oozing—and
something else, a smell perhaps; it melted into the smell of earth that was damp, of
wood that was warm and damp, into a black smell that spread like varnish over this
sinewy wood, with a flavor of fiber chewed and sweet. I did not simply *see* this black;
sight is an abstract invention, an idea that has been cleaned up, a human idea"
(*Sartre*, pp. 63–64; *Nausea*, pp. 130–31; italics in original). For Sartre's sense of revulsion
toward "varnish" as well as toward the "sweet" and the "soft," see p. 194 and chap. 11,
n. 4 below).

52. See pp. 222–24 above.

53. *Situations*, p. 136.

54. "A moment would really come when the book would be written, . . . and I
think that a little clarity [see the start of the diary preserved as *Nausea*, cited above,
p. 194] would descend on my past. Then perhaps I could, through the book, recall
my life without revulsion. Perhaps one day, while thinking of this very hour now, this
gloomy hour, . . . perhaps I would feel my heart beat faster and say to myself: 'That
was the day, that was the hour, when it all started.' And I might manage—in the past,
only in the past—to accept myself" (ibid., p. 178). The novel thus ends with what
might be taken as its starting point as a novel, but there is a certain discontinuity, for
it is not clear that the diary we have is the novel that was projected, or even that it is
a novel. The circle between end and starting point ("last" and "first") is never completed, and the distinction of level between life and art is maintained. That what the
writer's life had been in Bouville cannot itself qualify as a starting point for a novel
is probably suggested by the final sentence: "The yard of the New Station smells
strongly of damp wood; tomorrow it will rain in Bouville." To be rather literal, "Mucktown" will become even muckier. The sloppy promiscuity of living (as opposed to the
"arid purity" [p. 174] of the work of art) is a rendering of the indeterminacy where
"at the outset and for the most part" one "finds oneself," until the dialectical method
of definition takes hold and sets up such oppositions as that between life and art (or
between the ethical and the esthetic). For a different and incisive account of the relation between the diary and the novel, see Said, *Beginnings*, pp. 222–23.

55. *Les Troyennes*, p. 6.

56. Ibid., p. 3.

57. Sartre employs the term "subconversation" to designate the suppressed conversation in Natalie Sarraute (see p. 347 above). Thus the two levels in question need not
be the conjunction of a dialogue (such as that between Daniel and Marcelle) and a

monologue (such as Daniel's) but can involve two levels within the social group conversing (in the Sarraute novel) or can involve the audience interpreting (in *The Trojan Women*).

58. Ibid., pp. 3–4.

59. *Signs*, p. 4; italics in original. This passage follows directly on the passage cited above, p. 120.

60. For this phrase of Sartre's, see p. 341 above.

61. *Signs*, p. 3. *Dépassements* is set in quotes, and I take it as a broad reference to Hegel's *Aufhebung* or the Marxist equivalent.

62. The issue is not just substantive Marxist doctrine but the higher-level Marxist doctrine of the unity of substantive doctrine (theory) and practice: the Party ideologist "defers until a later date the identity for Marxism of thought and action which the present period calls into question. This resort to an indefinite future preserves the doctrine as a way of thinking and as a shibboleth at a time when it is in difficulty as a way of life. And this is precisely, according to Marx, the vice of philosophy" (ibid., p. 8).

63. *Force of Circumstances*, p. 194. It is significant for my focus on bipersonal relations in existentialism that this episode, "Drôle d'amitié," was all that Sartre has cared to salvage of the final volume of his tetralogy. In her summary here, as sometimes elsewhere, Simone de Beauvoir blunts contradictions which are sharper in Sartre. The "flight" of Vicarios and Brunet can hardly be said to have "sealed their friendship." Vicarios's final speech is one of recrimination ("It's all your fault," etc.) and illustrates how "strange" their "friendship" was. We are reminded of the *déphasement* which disclosed what "wretched friends" Sartre and Merleau-Ponty were (see p. 124 above), not to mention Sartre's earlier rupture with Camus.

64. "Drôle d'amitié," p. 1039. According to the plot as reported by Simone de Beauvoir (*Force of Circumstances*, p. 195), Brunet did later succeed in escaping with Mathieu's help. (Thus he would seem to have moved on into another bipersonal relation.) He joined the French Resistance, resuming his role as a Party member, but meanwhile "solitude had disclosed to him his subjectivity." Contat and Rybalka suggest that "Vicarios may to some extent be identified with Nizan" (1:233). If so, coinage of the name may itself be significant, suggesting Sartre's identification with him as an alter ego. In his "portrait" of Nizan (*Situations*, p. 90; see p. 125 above), Sartre comments on Nizan's break with the Communist Party over the Soviet-Nazi pact: "A Communist who is alone is lost. The truth of his last months was hatred" (p. 122). After the break Nizan was elaborately denounced, and the ugly rumors that he was a "traitor," etc., continued after his death during the retreat to Dunkirk.

65. An *échec* (a "setback" that thwarts a course of action) has always been a crucial moment in Sartre's dialectic and is to be contrasted with the way the fruition of an outcome is reached by the movement of *Aufhebung* in Hegel. The notion of *échec* itself Sartre could have taken from Jaspers. (He suspects that Bataille took the notion from Jaspers or from Wahl's commentary on Jaspers in *Etudes kierkegaardiennes*: *Situations*, 1:167.) Although Sartre has great disdain for Jaspers, his first contact with existentialism was with Jaspers. In 1927–28 Sartre and Nizan together were involved in the translation and proofreading of Jaspers's *General Psychopathology*. The theme of *échec* is omnipresent in Sartre. If Sartre neglects the "delicate emotions" or "feelings" in favor of more dislocating e-motions (see p. 84 above), this dislocation in question is a matter of being thwarted. Consider typical examples: subjects who are thwarted in their effort to reach objects (*Emotions*, pp. 36, 61); subjects who thwart themselves in their effort to tell their troubles to the analyst (pp. 26–27). Flaubert is analyzed as "*un homme-échec*" (*L'idiot*, 3:13). Of course sometimes the "loser wins," but "the secret *échec* of every triumph is that the winner is transformed by his victory" (*Saint Genet*, p. 570). Even when apparently he is not, the *échec* is indispensable. Thus Sartre's analysis of Genet ends on the following note: "Though Genet is accepted and made much of, he remains in exile amidst his triumph. So much the better—this new

échec and the permanence of his exile safeguard his grandeur" (p. 583). Speaking of Kierkegaard, Sartre generalizes, "Every undertaking, even if triumphantly carried out, remains an *échec*—that is, something incomplete still to be completed. It is alive because it is open" (*Between Existentialism and Marxism*, p. 168). Since Sartre has been commenting on Kierkegaard's predicament as a transcended stage within Hegel's system, his pronouncement seems roughly equivalent to the anti-Hegelian protest of "The Buried Alive" that it is "characteristic of any human undertaking in its truth that it is fragmentary" (see p. 449 below).

66. *Being and Time*, p. 437; "Letter on 'Humanism,' " p. 202.

67. *Being and Time*, p. 211. See n. 3, this chapter. In the sequel, which was not carried out (or at any rate not published), "the *cogito sum*" was to have been "phenomenologically destroyed" (ibid., p. 89).

68. *Prime of Life*, p. 41. No term is more in need of de-construction than "destruction." Later in Heidegger's career, Nietzsche's notion will become crucial, but the relevant construals here are Hegel's dialectical version (the negative moment of an *Aufhebung*) and Husserl's phenomenological version of an *Abbau*. Further analysis must wait upon my attempt in the sequel to distinguish the phenomenological method from the dialectical. But Husserl found a precedent in Descartes's proposal with his doubt "to destroy in general all my former opinions," and the corresponding term in the Latin translation of Descartes's first Meditation, *eversio*, adopts the subversive metaphor. But Descartes's objective, which became perhaps the characteristic objective of modern philosophy, was to replace the opinions bequeathed by former philosophies with something "firm and stable in the sciences," whereas Heidegger repudiates laying down a *fundamentum inconcussum* ("a foundation that cannot be overthrown") and argues instead that insight becomes available, even in the sciences, when there is "a crisis in . . . fundamental concepts"—when the subject matter begins to "totter" (*wanken*) (*Being and Time*, pp. 24, 9–10). The specific concept that Descartes retained as foundational is "substance," and Heidegger's subversion of this concept (see p. 101 above) is somewhere in the background of Sartre's recognition of the *ex-sistential, unselbständigkeit* character of human experience—its ambiguity, contradictoriness, and instability. But another programmatic effort at destruction which is relevant to Sartre, especially in *Nausea*, was that of surrealism.

69. A simple illustration is the contempt Sartre feels for Titian as opposed to Tintoretto. In Titian's paintings "the worst enemies are secretly reconciled by the color of their cloaks. . . . Order reigns" (*Situations*, p. 44). See also the reference to the reconciliation of Left and Right sought by Lamourette (ibid., p. 85), whose name must have contributed to the vogue of the expression *baisers Lamourette*.

70. *On a raison de se révolter*, pp. 113–14.

71. "Intentionality," pp. 4–5. Sartre explains the cogency of intentionality: "Against the digestive philosophy of empirio-criticism, against Neo-Kantianism, Husserl is never weary of affirming that things cannot be dissolved in consciousness." It is not clear whether or not Sartre's attack specifically embraces Hegel's notion of *Auflösung* ("dissolution") as well as his notion of *Aufhebung*.

72. If Sartre as a novelist endorses the antinovel, as a philosopher he also endorses Kierkegaard as an "antiphilosopher" (*Between Existentialism and Marxism*, p. 152). See p. 235 above. Moreover, just as Merleau-Ponty repudiates, on behalf of Dreyfus's original experience as an individual, a Hegelian verdict of history, so he repudiates, on behalf of the individuality of philosophies, the verdict of Hegel's history of philosophy: although Hegel may "think that his system includes the truth of all the others, . . . one who knew them only through his system would not know them at all. Hegel is the museum, that is all philosophies, so be it; but deprived of their finiteness, of their power of impact, embalmed, transformed (he believes) into themselves, but in fact transformed into him" (*Signs*, pp. 81–82; the museum is Malraux's *musée imaginaire*). Like Sartre, Merleau-Ponty is protesting against assimilation: "It is enough to observe how a truth perishes when it is integrated with others" (ibid.).

Part IV

Concluding

—————

But really, Socrates, what do you think that all this amounts to?
Scrapings and remnants of systematic thought, that's what it is, . . .
separated into fragments.—Johannes Climacus

10

Paths That Lead Nowhere

Better well hung than ill wed.—Johannes Climacus

INCONCLUSIVENESS

One reason why an introduction to existentialism has seemed warranted is that existentialists have been preoccupied with the problem of starting out. Kierkegaard explained, "What commonly concerns men least is precisely what concerns me most—that is, the starting out; I do not trouble myself much about the rest."[1] And in a sense he initiated existentialism as a movement by attacking Hegel's assumption that starting out was not really a problem.[2] Hegel had accordingly undertaken to eliminate, along with this problem, any introduction to his system. Consider the version of this system Climacus was opposing when he brought his esthetic "authorship" to a conclusion in *Concluding Unscientific Postscript to the Philosophical Fragments*.[3] Climacus was opposing *Science of Logic*. Having introduced this science by raising the question, "With What Must the Science Start?" Hegel wound up his introduction, "These preliminary reflections about the starting point were intended not so much to lead up to the science as, rather, to eliminate all preliminaries."[4] (Hegel is playing with the etymology of "intro-duction" [*Einleitung*] as meaning "to lead into" or "to lead up to" [*herbeizuführen*].) Rather than an introduction to his philosophy, Hegel preferred to rely on its eventual completion as a system, promising (as Climacus scornfully expresses it, with dialectical *interplay* between *first* and *last*), "for the first time when the conclusion of the whole is reached, all will become clear."[5]

Existentialism makes no such promises. Indeed the difficulty we face with existentialism is to reach a conclusion that would be as warranted as an introduction has been. I have noted that the pivotal work in the development of existentialism as a philosophical movement, Heidegger's *Being and Time*, is an inconclusive fragment, breaking off with Heidegger still "on the way." Heidegger has since adapted his meth-odological idiom to this prospect. Some later essays have been published under the title *Wood Roads* (*Holzwege*), and one of the implications of this title is brought out by the French translation—*Les chemins qui mènent nulle part*. I have noted that there are *chemins* in Sartre which have led nowhere: *Les chemins de la liberté*, his major literary effort, has remained without the concluding volume, as have the *Critique* and the volumes on Flaubert. There may well be a special explanation in each case for the inconclusiveness. Yet existentialists do seem to have some special difficulty in reaching a conclusion.

A wood road or trail leads one into the woods, but when it has been used (as often happens in south Germany) only to get logs out and has been abandoned, one cannot expect to arrive somewhere by following it. The objective to be reached in philosophy is not an outcome but in some sense only the *Erfahrung* of the journey: *eundo assequi*—"to attain something in the going." Seemingly assured conclusions are reserved to the sciences. All you are left with in philosophy is the path along which you are proceeding: "The way is everything. What remains for thought is the way."[6] Thus inconclusiveness is associated with the emphasis on *meth-odos* which I have respected in tracing the dialectic of existence and even by hoisting a title which offers no hope of getting beyond the starting point of this dialectic.

I have respected this inconclusiveness too by concentrating in the preceding chapter on a specific trait of *meth-odos* with which this inconclusiveness is closely associated—the *reversal* in *direction* that returns the individual from communion in the commonplace to his own experience, so he can appropriate it as his starting point. That *Nausea* is a novel which is not concluded within the novel itself is a deliberate device. We are left with the protagonist's own experience in the form of a diary, including his experience of deciding to start the novel, but we are not supplied with the novel which he made out of his experience, or indeed any evidence that he ever made it. This is one respect in which *Nausea* is an antinovel—that is a quarrel with the commonplace at the level of literary form as well as at the level of experience.

ÜBERGANG

Kierkegaard's literary or esthetic works are similarly designed to ensure that the individual is left with his own experience, as the existential starting point which philosophy, like literature, is not allowed to "go beyond." When this point is reached, there is nothing more to be said. We must not be misled by Kierkegaard's title, *Concluding Unscientific Postscript*. Here he is bringing his "authorship" to a conclusion by recognizing there is nothing more to be said, except for a postscript. In this postscript he has something to say about how he has said what he has said already. But one reason there is nothing more to be said is that the conclusion to which we are brought in the *Postscript* is less a conclusion for its individual reader than an introduction. It is an introduction to the problem of reaching a religious conclusion, but as such it is still inconclusive. In fact it cannot even count as an intro-duction in the "commonplace" (*almin-delig*) sense of taking advantage of some continuity with the individual reader's previous experience in order to induce him to go beyond it and "become a Christian." For from this "introduction" there is no "immediate transition" comparable to the "transition" (*Übergang*) which recurrently in Hegel assures the continuity of the development of his philosophy with its outcome as a system.[7] Instead, in Kierkegaard the "leap" by which the religious conclusion is reached is decisive, and this "leap" must be left to the individual himself.

We watched Climacus delineate the dislocating abruptness of this "leap" by denying the possibility of an introduction which would provide the individual with a running start:

> Everyone knows that the most difficult leap, even in the external realm, is when someone leaps into the air from a standing position and comes down again at the same place. The leap becomes easier, the more space intervenes between the initial position and the place to which the leap is made.[8]

It is not just a matter of the individual being deprived of the intervening space that an introduction would usually cover as a preparation for this leap. Indeed, instead of being protreptic in the traditional manner of an introduction to philosophy or to a religious conversion, Climacus's introduction is "repellent" in that it "does not make it easier to enter upon that which it introduces but, rather, makes it more difficult."[9]

If the repulsion were just a matter of the reader's coming to recognize the difficulty of becoming a Christian, it would not concern us here. But it is an "aphoristical" procedure for "separating" individuals, and it indicates the strenuousness of existential striving, which must be left up to the individual himself. Thus, although the problem of "becoming a Christian" is beyond our scope, it is in many respects an extreme version of the problem of "becoming an individual." And we are concerned with existentialism as a radical form of individualism.

Even if we had impatiently hurried on and completed the movement through the stages in Kierkegaard, we would not have been able to get beyond the individual:

> "The individual" is the category through which, with respect to the religious, this age, all history, the human race must pass. And he who

stood at Thermopylae was not so secure as I, who have stood in defense of this narrow passage, "the individual."

Kierkegaard goes on to explain that "this narrow passage of 'the individual' ... no one can pass through except by becoming the individual."[10] The passage is not a common place. If what is conclusive is the entry of individuals, one by one, they canot be corralled by anything as general as a conclusion. If we are still to satisfy the formality of reaching a conclusion, it can only take the form of a more detailed explanation of the inconclusiveness of existentialism. The explanation will be *bifocal*, for the inconclusiveness will be at one level a matter of what has to be left up to the particular individual and at a higher level a matter of Kierkegaard's general opposition to the tendency to conclusiveness which he finds characteristic of philosophy, but especially of the philosophy of Hegel, who thought he had brought even the history of philosophy itself to a conclusion with his system.

UNTERGANG

Before we can consider the individual who is to reach his own conclusion, we should first pay some attention to the operation by which Kierkegaard wrecks Hegel's system, in order to salvage this individual and enable him to reach his own conclusion. So far I have indicated that the wrecking operation is a destructive *reversal* of the movement of *Aufhebung* whose eventual outcome in Hegel is the system and the vindication of his promise, "For the first time when the conclusion of the whole is reached, all will become clear." When Kierkegaard's destructive *reversal* has been carried through, clarity will be achieved instead by maintaining the juxtaposition of contradictions. Climacus' title is probably designed to juxtapose "concluding" with "unscientific," in order to display a contradiction in Hegel's terms, for "unscientific" implies a procedure which is not "systematic" as well as not "objective," that is, one which contradicts the procedure by which Hegel proposed his clarifying conclusion.

Yet inasmuch as we are dealing in Kierkegaard with the wrecking of Hegel's system, we need to examine the Hegelian implications of the terms which Kierkegaard salvages, along with the individual, including such terms as "salvation" and "wreck," as well as those whose Hegelian cogency he would subvert, such as the already familiar term "objective." And if we are then to see how Kierkegaard's wrecking operation subverts, we should also reexamine other traits of existential dialectic, insofar as they are involved in this operation, besides the principle of contradiction and the *reversal* as a *dynamic* version of this principle.

Put in humdrum fashion, Climacus criticizes Hegel in the *Concluding Unscientific Postscript* for attempting to explain Christianity philosophically. But put dialectically, Climacus's procedure is *definitional* or *relational* in the concrete sense of "determining a location." Thus the issue he raises is not "whether Christianity is right";[11] it is the issue of the relation between stages. We are prepared for this *meth-odological* issue by having recognized earlier that proceeding by stages itself takes on a significance for Kierkegaard it did not have for Hegel, since there is no longer a system in Kierkegaard to supersede the stages.[12] The specific *meth-odological* issue in the *Postscript* can to a certain extent be reduced to the issue of the sequence of stages. Hegel's philosophical explanation of Christianity is the movement of *Aufhebung* by which he "goes beyond" the stage of religion to philosophy. Insofar as the movement of *Aufhebung* can be visualized as triadic, it involves the "destruction," the going under (*Untergang*) at the second moment of what was available at the first moment, as well as the "salvaging" of what is "preserved" with the "going beyond (*Übergang*) to the higher level reached at the third moment. This is how Hegel (from Climacus's point of view) confuses religion with philosophy: in his philosophy Hegel "salvages" from Christianity precisely this notion of "salvation," which he reads into the final movement of "preservation" that is the outcome of the *Aufhebung*. But in Kierkegaard this movement is subverted by the attack on Hegel's philosophy as "esthetic,"[13] for this attack in effect reallocates Hegel's philosophy back to the first stage.[14]

With this reallocation, the movement of *Aufhebung* becomes *illusory*.[15] What is in question is no longer salvation but the movement of seduction, of being "led away from oneself," which is so prominent in existentialism that it could compose the theme of my interpretation in part III.

THE WRECK

Since the final movement of *Aufhebung* in Hegel has been subverted, the preceding, contradictory, negative, and destructive moment of "going under" becomes climactic in Kierkegaard. Thus the epigraph, *Periissem nisi periissem*, that he employs for the last stage—the religious stage—is ambiguously contradictory.[16] It may carry a reference both to the illusory movement of *Aufhebung* as in fact esthetic se-duction, inasmuch as it can mean in Latin "I should have been lost had I not been lost" and to the destructive moment in this movement (which we are brought back to), inasmuch as it can also mean "I should have been destroyed had I not been destroyed."

Our examination of the religious stage with its problem of "becoming a Christian" has been precluded by the "patience" which the dialectical method imposes on us.[17] But now that Hegel's philosophy is reallocated back to the first stage, we can reexamine the problem of becoming a philosopher, which had been formulated in the unfinished *Johannes Climacus* and is in effect recapitulated by Climacus in the *Concluding Unscientific Postscript*. The *recapitulation* illustrates at once the destructive character of the *reversal* and Climacus's retention of a Hegelian metaphor to characterize it:

> "For the first time when we have reached the conclusion of the whole, all will become clear." . . . Climacus refrains in youthful modesty from drawing any conclusion with regard to the lack of a conclusion [in Hegel] and starts out. . . . He reads and reads and understands a little, but above all he hopes for the clarifying reflection which the conclusion will provide for the whole. And he finishes the book but has not found the problem presented. . . . And yet . . . he has but one desire —to become a thinker. And, alas, the famous man has it in his power to decide his destiny, for if he does not understand him, his one desire must suffer shipwreck. . . . So he starts again.[18]

Climacus's reference to the "shipwreck" of his "one desire" reproduces the play on the words *zu Grunde gehen* with which Hegel often exhibits the *interplay* between the second moment (the destructive moment) and the third (the reconstructive moment of salvation) in the movement of *Aufhebung*: something "goes aground," "goes under," "founders," is "wrecked," but is then transformed by "reaching its ground," for it "goes beyond" itself and becomes at a higher level what it is "fundamentally" or "essentially."

Eremita employed the Hegelian metaphor in the case of one of the "brides of grief" who were "led astray." Recall the predicament of Donna Elvira as Don Giovanni's victim:

> If I were to imagine someone on a ship in distress, unconcerned for his life, remaining on board because there was something he wanted to save and yet could not save, because he was perplexed [*raadvild*] about what he should save, then would I have an image [*billede*] of Elvira; she is in distress at sea, her destruction [*undergang*] impends, but this does not concern her, she is not aware of it, she is perplexed about what she should save.[19]

How could she know, since she has been seduced by an unreflecting seducer?

When, however, we move from Don Giovanni on to his dialectical opposite, the reflective seducer of the "Diary," the prospect of a dialectical development can be entertained with the methodological behest: "Patience—quod antea fuit impetus, nunc ratio est."[20] This citation from Ovid marks the moment in the seduction of Cordelia which corresponds to the *Übergang* in Hegel's *Logic* from the stage of immediacy ("impulse") to the stage when contradiction is encountered and exposes to the reflection that it induces the "ground" for the necessary development of something into what it is (its "essence"). Thus the seducer recognizes that Cordelia is capable of a dialectical development that meeting someone in the common place, provided by the institution of marriage, would not satisfy, nor would even a "commonplace" seducer:

> But if she falls to me, she will save the interesting out of the shipwreck. In relation to me, she must *zu Grunde gehen*, as the philosophers say with a play on words.[21]

Seduction will be her destruction as a woman. Yet it will also be her deconstruction that exposes her structure; she will become what she essentially is (esthetically) as a woman. Until she is seduced, she remains at the stage of immediacy: she is a woman but "she is perplexed [*raadvild*] about what it means to be a woman."[22] When she is seduced, being "led astray" from herself will open up room for her to reflect on herself, so that she can reach the higher level where she will know what to save out of the shipwreck—knowledge. Not that she can be saved herself: "She has lost everything."[23] So in this sense of *perire* the *Aufhebung* is illusory.

THE FLOWER

"She has lost everything" esthetically, inasmuch as a woman belongs properly to the stage of immediacy:

> This being of woman (the term "existence" would attribute too much meaning, for she does not come to be [*bestaaer*] out of herself) is properly described as charm, an expression which is reminiscent of plant life; she is a flower, as the poets are wont to say, and even the spiritual in her is present in a botanical fashion. She is entirely determined by nature [*naturbestemmelse*] and thence only esthetically free. In a deeper sense she first becomes free by her relation to a man, and when he courts her properly, there can be no question of choice.[24]

But when deflowered, she is a flower which "has lost its fragrance"—that is, its immediacy.[25]

She has also "lost everything" dialectically, inasmuch as she no longer can pose any "opposition" (modstand). Her only prospects for Aufhebung and "salvation" are contradictory outcomes which cancel each other out. On one hand she could be "transformed into a sunflower [heliotrope]"—that is, with the disappearance of any opposition she could remain entirely oriented toward her seducer, who has illuminated her with respect to what it means to be a woman as a "being for another"—for a man.[26] But after such knowledge, what forgiveness—for a woman? None. Her relativity precludes self-knowledge. On the other hand, the opposing prospect is to transform her into her opposite—that is, "to transform her into a man,"[27] who can reach the stage of reflection and enjoy the knowledge of what it means to be a woman.

But this outcome for the seducer is also contradictory. He complains, "Why cannot such a night be longer? If Alectryon could forget himself, why cannot the sun be equally sympathetic [and forget to rise and shine]?" In the myth (and we are supposed to remember that the seducer has arrived for the seduction proclaiming, "I myself am a myth about myself") Alectryon was assigned to watch but fell asleep, so that Ares and Aphrodite were taken by surprise by the arrival of Apollo as well as Hephaestus. If Alectryon is imagined to "forget himself," instead of merely falling asleep, it is to point up the contradiction whereby one must in Hegel forget oneself as finite (including the passage of time),[28] in order to enjoy an esthetic experience, which is ideal in its mythical significance. But with the passage of time that night, "she has lost her fragrance," so that the seducer has to admit to himself, "I do not wish to recall my relation to her."[29] Yet if the immediacy he was sniffing is thus incompatible with its recollection, the "Diary" itself becomes a contradictory undertaking on the part of the seducer, and not the carrying out of an Aufhebung, for in the "Diary" the "experience is recorded, of course after it has happened—sometimes perhaps a long time afterwards."[30]

To accord and deny an Aufhebung is to parody not only its positive as well as negative moment but also Hegel's attendant confusion of knowledge (the final philosophical outcome) with salvation (the content of the religious stage which the philosophical outcome ostensibly "preserves"). The confusion is clarified when Hegelian knowledge is shown up to be merely "esthetic"—that is, merely knowledge of the "interesting," of the interplay between levels (immediacy and reflection), since the higher level of the outcome is never really reached. The knowledge Cordelia is supposed to be able to salvage through reflection is at the cost of her salvation. Similarly, the knowledge which the seducer himself undertakes to gain through the seduction, and to salvage in the form of the "Diary," is in fact his being "led astray" from himself by the process of reflection that was involved in the process of seduction and in the process of composing the "Diary." The knowledge of what it means to be a woman is for him also merely a distracting illusion. It is not his salvation, his self-knowledge, for he has not brought himself to his own conclusion. He too is "lost."

REFLECTION

I have suggested that Climacus's title is probably designed to juxtapose "concluding" with "unscientific" in order to display what would be a contradiction in Hegel's terms. But in Climacus's own terms, one sense in which *Postscript* is conclusive is that the mature Climacus is finally drawing a conclusion with regard to what the youthful Climacus had lamented was Hegel's "lack of a conclusion." He is concluding that Hegel's request for "patience" is not entirely justified by the exigencies of a dialectical method. It is justified as a requirement for proceeding by stages, but not for the indefinite postponement of any conclusion until the system is completed.

The inconclusiveness of Hegel's philosophy is exhibited by Kierkegaard's relocating it from the last stage in Hegel (where it is the "whole" reflection reached by subsuming what should be "preserved" from the preceding stages) to the first stage in his own philosophy, where its inconclusiveness is the inconclusiveness of the process of reflection.[31] Remember the *bifocal* character of Kierkegaard's analysis: reflection initially constitutes a point of view and thereby fosters the illusion that one has reached "a definite position"; this illusion is exemplified at a higher level by the movement of *Aufhebung* that constitutes Hegel's philosophy.

At either level this movement is illusory. The movement of reflection is not an *Aufhebung* but the backward movement of recollection: "The movement turns back upon itself and again turns back...."[32] In other words (to regain the philosophical level), the process of reflection, since it continues indefinitely, does not remain a first stage in Hegel's philosophy, as in Kierkegaard's, but subsumes with its reiterated illusory movement of *Aufhebung* what in Kierkegaard's philosophy are distinguished as later stages.[33] Kierkegaard's *de-finition*, delimitation, of the first stage in his philosophy as merely "esthetic" is not a reflective but an ethical delimitation. Thus when he attacks Hegel for "not leaving any place for an ethics,"[34] he is attacking him for not confining reflection within the boundaries of the esthetic stage by bringing reflection to a conclusion ethically, which is the only way in which it can be brought to a conclusion.

Although I cannot trace here the internal development of the ethical stage in *Or*, as it is presided over by Judge William, some of its defining characteristics can be anticipated as contradicting characteristics of the esthetic stage with which we are familiar.[35] But they can only be sketched summarily, for the contradiction *Either/Or* itself is not evenly balanced. If a defining characteristic of the esthetic stage is indefinitely continued reflection which evades contradictions by indulging the illusion of transcending them with an *Aufhebung*, the preeminent contradiction it evades is the contradiction which would bring its own transcending movement to a halt and expose its illusory character. This esthetic illusion is clarified as an ethical confusion; the ethical stage is separated from the esthetic as its contradiction, but only during the ethical stage.[36] Where the esthetic stage exhibits in retrospect the inconclusiveness of the process of reflection and the indefiniteness of a mere point of view, the ethical stage exhibits the process of reaching a "definite position" as a conclusion, by making a choice which is decisive.

The higher-level ethical distinction between the ethical and esthetic stages respects the dislocating and contradictory "doubleness" that is "characteristic of existence," inasmuch as "life must be understood backward, but . . . it must be lived forward." In that reflection has to be employed in understanding one's life, one's arrival at the ethical stage of choice presupposes one's previously having passed through the esthetic stage of reflection.[37] But the process of reflection has to be broken off and *reversed* by a choice that is acted upon, so that a conclusion is reached. The dialectic is *bifocal*: whatever is chosen in particular, the choice is preeminently a reflexive choice of oneself.[38]

Since the process of reflection is inherently the movement of recollection (*Erinnerung*), it is an "internalizing" as well as backward movement and thus a process by which one abstracts from the actual external circumstances that one encounters as one's life moves forward. This process of abstraction is analyzed by the Judge in *Or* as the maneuver with which these actual external circumstances are "dissolved" into possibilities when they are reflected upon instead of acted on and thereby rendered actual.[39] Even a choice remains only a possible choice as long as it remains a matter for reflection.

ACTION

The confusion characteristic of anyone (including Hegel with his philosophy) who continues indefinitely at the esthetic stage of existence is a failure to respect "the doubleness" of existence. His failure too is dialectically *bifocal*: whatever he is reflecting on in particular, he is also (at a higher level) relying on reflection as a means for "keeping existence away."[40] In contrast, the individual who chooses and acts on his choice is bringing himself into actual existence. He is respecting the "doubleness" of existence with a double movement: he has carried out the esthetic movement of reflection, but he is also carrying out the contradictory ethical movement of acting upon a choice, and with his action he is *reversing* the internalizing movement of reflection and "striving" to "reduplicate" himself—that is, to reach a "conclusion" that "reproduces" concretely (i.e., under the actual external circumstances of his life) a possibility which remained indefinite and abstract as long as he was merely reflecting upon it.[41]

In spite of the fact that the individual's arrival at the ethical stage presupposes his previous passage through the esthetic stage, the either/or that separates the two stages does not blur into a Hegelian both/and. As long as reflection continues its inconclusive movement, the possible choice that is not acted upon undergoes dissolution into still further possibilities, which become ever more abstract and remote from the external circumstances of the individual's life. Meanwhile the forward movement of his life also continues: "The ship is all the while making its usual headway." Thus the contradiction widens between the possibilities he is reflecting upon and the external circumstances of his life, until the possibility of overcoming the contradiction and reaching some conclusion for his life itself finally eludes him: "If he forgets to take account of the headway, there comes at last a moment when there is no longer any question of an either/or . . . because others have chosen for him, because he has lost his self."[42]

Of course there would never have been the possibility of finding a self if the individual had not previously passed through the esthetic stage of reflection. The internalizing movement of reflection is a necessary preliminary, if one is to start to "separate" one's experiences "off" as one's "own"—and ultimately one's self—from the immediate pressure of actual external circumstances, so that one can gain autonomy for this self when it is chosen. But one only gains autonomy for this self when it is actualized by being chosen. At the same time, the choice includes these actual external circumstances, though the pressure now comes from within:

> At the moment of choice, the individual is in the most complete isolation, for he withdraws from his environment, and yet at the same moment he is in absolute continuity with it, for he chooses himself as product.[43]

But "he can just as well be said to produce himself," even though "as product he is pressed into the forms of actuality," until "he has his place in the world" and is "a definite individual."[44]

In delineating this contradictory fashion in which the individual "chooses himself," Judge William plays with the concept of concluding:

"At the moment of choice the individual is at the conclusion [*slutning*], for he concludes himself together [*slutter sig sammen*] as a personality."[45] Thus "concluding" illustrates how a *bifocal* concept can be refocused. At the personal level it refers both to a particular choice one makes and to the implicit higher-level choice of oneself. But at a still higher level, it refers to what is philosophically implicit in this choice of oneself—the delimiting of the ethical stage from the esthetic stage as having been taken up with inconclusive reflection upon abstract possibilities.[46]

MARRIAGE

"Environment" (*omgivelser*) may have been misleading, for at the personal level the particular choice that is significant is of someone rather than something. Choice is *bipersonal*: one chooses oneself in relation to some other individual.[47] The delimitation of the ethical from the esthetic stage is concretely exhibited by Judge William taking marriage as paradigmatic for the ethical stage not only in *Or* but also in the *recapitulation* of this stage in *Stages*. We have been able to anticipate characteristics of the ethical stage, as the stage in which the individual "finds" himself by bringing himself to an actual "conclusion," insofar as it is opposed to the esthetic stage with which we are already familiar, as the stage where the individual is "led astray" from himself by possibilities. We are similarly able to deal with marriage insofar as it is opposed to seduction, with which we are already familiar as the paradigmatic performance at the esthetic stage. In the Judge's own words, "Marriage implies a conclusiveness" which "must have been present from the start," while "the other possible consequence of love's immediacy is . . . seduction."[48]

The paradigms also exhibit succinctly the dialectical character of Kierkegaard's opposition to Hegel. Marriage takes on its dialectical significance for Hegel, as for Kierkegaard, as a *relationship*; and Hegel claims, as does Kierkegaard, that it is "essentially an ethical relationship." But this relationship is subordinated in Hegel to the family as the social institution which is located as the first stage in the development of his social ethics that culminates in the state. Kierkegaard's readjustment of the relations involved is a *reflexive* or *subjective* reorientation which has already been suggested by his modern version of the ancient *Antigone*. This was the tragedy Hegel so much admired for its conflict between family loyalty and political authority—the conflict which constitutes "the supreme opposition in ethics."[49] But Kierkegaard does not mention Creon by name in his interpretation of the *Antigone*. His indifference to the claims of political authority in ethics is to be understood in conjunction with his denial that Hegel has a place in his system for an ethics, for what Kierkegaard is denying is that Hegel's social ethics is an ethics.[50] In Kierkegaard an ethics has to do not with the social community but with the "conclusiveness" with which the individual chooses himself, granted that this choice is *bipersonal* and takes place in relation to another individual.

In fact ethics is not familial for Kierkegaard, just as it is not more broadly social. Antigone's childlessness is no longer a matter for complaint in Kierkegaard's *Antigone*, as it was in the ancient tragedy. This may have less to do with the impotency sometimes attributed to Kierkegaard than with his opposition to a more philosophical *Aufhebung*—to the movement by which the *subjective* is transcended toward an *objective* outcome. For the reason marriage is subordinated to the family in Hegel is that

> the relation between husband and wife is not yet objective. . . . The unity of the parents is only attained with their children, in whom they are confronted with the completion of their union. . . . Both have their love objectified for them in the child.

Until its completion with this outcome, the unity in marriage of husband and wife is only subjective—"only a unity of inwardness and disposition."[51] Thus Kierkegaard's selection of marriage as well as seduction as paradigmatic relations also illustrates his dialectical preference for a *bilateral, bipersonal* relation, with a *reflexive* emphasis on the *subjective starting point* for the relation, as opposed to Hegel's triadic relation, where the emphasis falls on the *objective outcome* at the third moment.[52]

THE HERMIT

Even in theology Kierkegaard tends to neglect the third person, whose role in the Trinity is so crucial in Hegel, not only to the *Aufhebung* of the relation between the first two persons but also as an "imaginative representation" (*Vorstellung*) of the role the absolute spirit plays insofar as it can be regarded as the agency of the social community:

> God the Father, putting aside his isolation, . . . begets a Son (his other "I"), but in the power of his love beholds in this Other himself, recognizes his likeness therein, and in it returns to unity with himself. . . . This unity is the Holy Spirit, which proceeds from the Father and the Son, reaching its perfect actuality and truth in the community of Christians.

Kierkegaard, in contrast, never puts aside his own isolation, never begets a son, for he is reluctant to associate perfect actuality and truth with any community.[53]

In fact at the time Kierkegaard was extolling marriage in *Or*, he was in the dialectically opposed situation of breaking off his engagement to Regina. That marriage is not in fact the last word dialectically that it almost seems to be in *Or* is betrayed by the editorial pseudonym, Eremita, which indicates that isolation is in prospect for the individual and that this prospect has some as yet undefined religious "implication." I cannot here examine in its own terms the religious stage thus foreshadowed. But when the religious stage is treated in *Philosophical Fragments*, the paradigm of marriage is discounted by its epigraph, "Better well hung than ill wed."[54] so that it is perhaps feasible for me at least to suggest what happens to the paradigm.

Kierkegaard presumably reserves for himself an autobiographical reference to his breaking off his engagement. But both marriage, as the establishment of an ethical relationship, and breaking off the ethical obligation to establish this relationship have dialectical significance.[55] Marriage is paradigmatic for the externalizing, objectifying movement by which the individual transcends his subjectivity and is "brought into systematic relation with the whole world,"[56] in the fashion illustrated by Hegel's social ethics. One sense in which Kierkegaard was "well hung" was that breaking off his relation with Regina involved an opposing dialectical maneuver which he describes as the "teleological suspension of the ethical." The ethical movement is suspended by reference to a higher religious end: "He who goes without marriage with one stroke cancels out and eliminates the whole of earthly existence and can retain only eternity and spiritual interests."[57] Thus the religious stage foreshadowed by Kierkegaard's adoption of the pseudonym Eremita is reached by a "cancellation" and "elimination," without the compensating ensuing "preservation" which would take place if the procedure were a Hegelian *Aufhebung*. The contradiction between the "earthly" and the "spiritual" is maintained, not transcended, as in Hegel.

Separation

In the retrospect provided by the ethical interpretation of marriage as the individual's bringing himself to a "conclusion" in the form of a "systematic relation with the whole world," we can more readily appreciate the seductive character of reflection, as illustrated by the opposing fashion in which "the bride of grief" is "separated," by reflecting upon her grief, not only from any relation to others (including the man she would have married) but also from her own past life. The stage in the process of reflection that composed the essays on "the brides of grief" was demarcated at a higher level by the comparable "destiny" of the Symparenkromenoi, who sponsor these essays.[58]

The Symparenkromenoi received further delineation. The contradiction between the length of the essays and their characterization, "devoted to the aphoristical," forced us once again to recognize that the *external* is not the *internal* and transferred our attention from the external form of a *modus loquendi* to a *modus vivendi*: "aphoristical" became another metaphor to characterize the "destiny" of the Symparenkromenoi as the same as the modern Antigone's; the process of reflection that "buried" them "alive" is a process which "separated" them "off" from others as "aphorisms in life." Their lives, like hers, remained inconclusive fragments. Since we were originally confronted with the predicament of the brides and of the Symparenkromenoi, we have climbed with Climacus to still higher levels of "implication" and have identified the inconclusiveness in question as the inconclusiveness of reflection that is characteristic not only of the esthetic stage but also of Hegel's philosophy which is assigned to this stage by Kierkegaard. We have not yet, however, done justice to Kierkegaard's recurrent characterization of this inconclusiveness as fragmentation, although this is played up by the subtitle of *Either/Or, A Fragment of Life,* and by the title *Philosophical Fragments* and its replay in *Concluding Unscientific Postscript to the Philosophical Fragments,* which is at the same time decked out with the epigraph,

> But really, Socrates, what do you think that all this amounts to? Scrapings and remnants of systematic thought, that's what it is, as I said a while ago, separated into fragments.[59]

Is this really what existentialism as founded by Kierkegaard amounts to, now that we must reach some conclusion? Kierkegaard started out with the "constant reference" of his dissertation to Socrates, for he conceived himself as assuming an ironic Socratic role in relation to Hegel. This conception involved a *reversal* of Plato's undertaking in relation to Socrates; Plato had gone beyond the inconclusive "Socratic" dialogues to complete a system. Kierkegaard instead exploits, as his present epigraph illustrates, the procedure of "separating" one thing from another which he apparently credits to Socrates and which Plato, like Hegel, regarded as requiring supplementation by the procedure of "synthesis."

REMNANTS

I have already tried to illustrate the dialectical shift to "separation" in Kierkegaard as a readjustment of the relation between discontinuity and continuity in Hegel—a shift which accents the "destructive" or "eliminative" moment of *Aufhebung,* when fragmentation by contradiction takes place, at the expense of the opposing higher-level moment of *Aufbewahrung* in Hegel, when continuity is "preserved," so that eventually a system is completed in which the individual subject by transcending himself is (in Climacus's phrase) "brought into systematic relationship with the whole world." But we still face the question dramatized by Climacus's self-ironizing epigraph: if the "Socratic" dialogues themselves are Platonic compositions, which can hardly be detached from the later positive development and completion of Plato's system, what does Kierkegaard's fragmentation of Hegel's system leave us with besides "remnants" of this system itself?[60]

I have not yet taken the textual trouble to show how much of Kierkegaard's *Either* (at least what might conventionally be considered philosophically significant) can already be found in Hegel's *Aesthetics*. But I have suggested that other existentialists are dependent on the traditional philosophies they would subvert. Heidegger's *Being and Time* formulates its problems in terms of the philosophical tradition, and if we subtracted from Sartre's *Being and Nothingness* those portions that are expositions of his predecessors, what survives would hardly add up to a philosophical position.

Yet if this is all that an existentialism amounts to, we face the paradox which has dogged us from the outset: Why should a philosophy that places such an emphasis on the individual's initiative and authenticity remain so indebted to other philosophers' formulations? We have obtained a general explanation of this paradox. The problem of starting point itself acquires methodological prominence in existentialism by virtue of the individual's striving (which was acknowledged in part I) to start out with his own experience. Striving is needed, and the problem of starting point acquires its methodological prominence dialectically (as was acknowledged in part II) because "at the start and for the most part" the individual's experience is inauthentic, not his "own" (as has been acknowledged in part III), but alienated—the experience of "others."

Among these others previous philosophers are prominent, since they have consolidated a tradition of interpreting and organizing experience, which has thereby acquired a certain *orientation,* so that it is only when the traditional organization is fragmented that the individual can recover his own experience and his own sense of *direction.* But this general explanation is insufficient. The fragmentation is not indiscriminate disarticulation, and it is not enough to deal, as we have so far, with the fragmentation simply as a reinstatement of the negative, destructive moment of separation and contradiction in the Hegelian dialectic. It is necessary to trace the process of fragmentation in detail, in order to discover more precisely what is at stake and eventually the criteria over which Kierkegaard is quarreling with Hegel and which control their respective dialectics.

THE BLOW

Let us restrict our attention for the present to Kierkegaard, since the purely dialectical character of his method renders more readily ascertainable the junctures at which he is introducing contradictions that subvert the organization of the system. We have to accept a further restriction—to the stage when it is Hegel's "system of the arts" that undergoes fragmentation. This restriction does not detract entirely from the methodological scope of the process of fragmentation, for it must not be forgotten that Kierkegaard's strategy for attacking Hegel's system as a whole is to attack it as merely "esthetic."

We are prepared for this strategy by the preface to *Either/Or*. Eremita elaborately draws our attention to a desk which is for sale and which "fascinated" him. When he finally yields to temptation, he warns himself that with so extravagant a purchase "a new period of your life must start";[61] we are being put on notice that this period will be "esthetic," since he has "no use for such a piece of furniture."[62] Nevertheless, he does use one of its drawers to keep his money in. Later, when he is about to leave on a journey which needs financing, the desk presents a problem:

> Every attempt to open the drawer failed. . . . I became angry. . . . A hatchet was fetched. With it I dealt the desk a shattering blow, shocking to see. Whether in my anger I struck the wrong place, or the drawer was as stubborn as myself, the result of the blow was not as anticipated. The drawer was closed [*lukket*], and the drawer remained closed. But something else happened. Whether my blow had struck exactly the right juncture, or whether the shock to the whole organization of the desk was the cause I do not know, but I do know that a secret door sprang open. . . . This disclosed a hiding place that I naturally had never discovered. Here . . . I found . . . the papers which compose the content of the present work. . . . My mind found its doubt reinforced that the external is not the internal.[63]

Before this episode took place, Eremita had become "familiar with the desk's rich content, its many drawers." Let me insinuate the suspicion that he was parodying the all-inclusive completeness of Hegel's system as having a place to put every sort of experience. If so, his metaphor was a reexposure of the system to "the external influences" from which it had been withdrawn in becoming a system.

Reconsider the episode. Eremita leaves the question open as to whether his "blow had struck exactly the right juncture" or whether "the total shock to the whole organization was the cause," but Hegel's esthetics was in fact "the right juncture" for a hatchet job on his system, for since the system as a whole is to be dislocated as "esthetic," a "blow" to Hegel's esthetics would also constitute a "shock" to the system. After all the system is organized and oriented in its development by the presupposition that the contradiction between the *external* and the *internal* can be transcended with an *Aufhebung* and its *Aufbewahrung*. Hegel's esthetics is that juncture in this development at which this presupposition gains its initial plausibility. Let me quote again Hegel's explanation: "The most general thing which can be said . . . about the ideal of art comes to this: the true [the internal content] has existence only as it unfolds into external reality [the artistic form]."[64] Thus it is during the esthetic stage that the *internal* becomes accessible to *external* perception aisthēsis). Eremita is probably parodying the plausibility of this presupposition by taking the desk, which he admires so much esthetically, both as a work of art and as a model for Hegel's system. At any rate the "stubborn" drawer, the "secret door," and more definitely the "hiding place" itself where the papers were "contained" demonstrate, as Eremita observes, that the *external* is not the *internal*—the contradiction that will be vindicated further by the content of the papers themselves.[65]

THE ORGANIZATION

If we are to be prepared to recognize the relevance of the episode with the desk to the fragmentation in *Either* of Hegel's esthetics, it would be well to pause and note how Eremita manipulates the fundamental distinction which is involved initially in the "organization" Hegel ascribes to the work of art as such. Thus Hegel distinguishes between the content (*Inhalt*) and the manner and mode of representation (*Darstellung*) and explains the distinction as follows:

> In a work of art we start with what is immediately represented to us and then ask what its meaning or content is. The former, the external, has no immediate validity for us; we assume behind it something inward, a meaning, through which the external appearance takes on spiritual implications. . . . The work of art is to be meaningful and not to appear exhausted by these lines, curves, surfaces, carvings, hollowings in stone, these colors, notes, word sounds, or whatever material is used; instead, it should unfold as inner life, feeling, soul, a content and a spirit, which is just what we call the meaning of a work of art.[66]

This distinction between the *inner* meaning and the *external* appearance will undergo successive readjustments as the system develops out of the relations between successive arts, but Hegel will continue to apply the distinction to these arts, and its continued application will help ensure the continuity required for their systematization.

In the course of this development the recurrent moment at which Eremita's blow is aimed in order to disrupt the continuity is neither at the *internal* meaning nor at the *external* appearance but at the third moment when this contradiction is transcended. This is how Hegel himself distinguishes these moments:

> Recalling what we have already established about the concept of the beautiful and art, we find two things: first, a content, an aim, a meaning; and second, the expression, appearance, and actualization of this content. But third, both aspects are so interpenetrated by each other that the external, the particular, appears exclusively [*ausschliesslich*] as the representation of the inward. In the work of art, nothing is present but that has an essential relation to the content expressed.[67]

Here the internal content comes first, in order to emphasize the extent to which its need to find external expression impels the dialectic. In the setting of Hegel's system, "the concept . . . releases to actual autonomous [*selbständiger*] objectivity" in the work of art what it "included in itself [*in sich schloss*] as ideal subjectivity." In other words, "the Ideal exists in externality, self-enclosed [*mit sich selbst zusammengeschlossen*], free, reposing in itself [*auf sich beruhend*]."[68]

Admittedly "this conclusiveness [*Abgeschlossenheit*] is not in fact lacking in a particular character [as character would be envisaged in the ethical sphere], but the particularization, which is dispersed in this sphere of the external and the finite, is purified here [in the esthetic sphere] into simple determinateness [*Bestimmtheit*]."[69] We have often watched dialectic, as a method of definition, move from the "indefinite" or "indeterminate," to the "definite," the "determinate," as a "destination." The crucial difference between Kierkegaard's dialectic and Hegel's is Kierkegaard's insistence that one remains at the esthetic stage "indefinite" or "indeterminate"—that "conclusiveness," "determinateness," or a "destiny" is a distinctively ethical achievement. Thus Eremita would separate the ethical from the esthetic stage by dismantling the illusion that the work of art is an *Aufhebung* and *Aufbewahrung* by which "inclusiveness" and "conclusiveness" (and hence autonomy) are achieved.

Earlier I suggested that it is perhaps not a terminological accident that the aphorism which parodied the illusion of *Aufhebung* and *Aufbewahrung* employed the metaphor of a castle (*slot/Schloss*) for the place where esthetic experience was "preserved" or that Kierkegaard extended this metaphor of "enclosure" to Hegel's system as a whole,[70] since he views this system as a final indulgence in the illusion that esthetic experience (i.e., experience as expressed in the work of art) can be "inclusive" and "conclusive."

THE AUDIENCE

The aphorism itself first described the movement from the *external* (the moment when the mind received an "impression" from outside and was in Hegel's terms "exposed to external influences") to the *internal* (the moment when the "internalizing" movement of recollection reached the level of "imaginative representation." At this level there was still a contradiction in Hegel himself between the *external* and the *internal*, but it was in some sense overcome when the "imaginative representation" was externalized in the work of art. This movement too was called in question at the start of *Either,* when Eremita doubted not only "that the external is the internal" but also that "the internal [is] the external." This ensuing movement was also described in the aphorism: the "image" was externalized in the "picture" which the artist wove into the tapestries of the castle.

In my original interpretation of *Either,* I focused primarily on the first version of the esthetic contradiction. Now that we have reached the level of works of art in Hegel's "system of the arts," the focus will shift to the second contradiction. Matters are somewhat more complicated in Hegel than in the aphorism. We have seen that at the third moment in Hegel, when the contradiction is overcome, "the external . . . appears exclusively as the representation [*Darstellung*] of the inward." But it so appears to an audience, for whom Hegel is the spokesman when he explains, "The external has no immediate validity for us," since "we assume behind it something inward, a meaning, through which the external appearance takes on spiritual implications." We have recognized from the first aphorism that Eremita is initially the spokesman for the artist (or poet), as opposed to the audience and the critic, and this was why my original interpretation of *Either* was focused primarily on the process of "internalization."

Now, however, we must follow out the implications of the artist's opposition to the audience and the critic. What is at stake in not just an issue in esthetics. When Kierkegaard attacks Hegel for "not leaving any place for an ethics," he means (as I have stressed before) an ethics which is individualistic; the "social ethics" which Hegel did find a place for Kierkegaard denies is an ethics. It is not just a matter of its norms being social. As such they are an objectification, and social ethics is assigned by Hegel himself to the stage of "objective spirit." In Hegel this stage precedes esthetics as the first in the development of "absolute spirit,"—that is, the first stage when spirit is released from the limitations of a particular society.

Up until now it may have seemed that, when Kierkegaard attacks the system as "esthetic," the esthetics in question might be the same as

Hegel's (aside from parody), so that the attack could be visualized simply as a matter of Kierkegaard reallocating philosophy back to what was the esthetic stage in Hegel himself. Needless to say, so simple a procedure would be undialectical: in a relational analysis a reallocation must alter other relations. We have already traced the altered relation between esthetics and ethics. But esthetics within its own sphere is a relational analysis, as is most obviously illustrated by Hegel's "system of the arts." Thus Kierkegaard's reallocation involves the altered relations within esthetics which we are now beginning to examine.[71]

In other words, Kierkegaard is not just finding a place for the ethics that Hegel left out of his system on the assumption that the experience of "inclusiveness," "conclusiveness" (and hence autonomy), could be enjoyed initially as the experience of the work of art and ultimately as the experience of the system as a whole, whereas Kierkegaard felt that the experience so characterized was a distinctively ethical accomplishment. Kierkegaard's finding a place for this ethical experience depends correlatively on his having first reappraised the characteristics of esthetic experience. As we were encouraged to expect from Eremita's doubt and from the episode with the desk, the contradiction between the *external* and the *internal* cannot be overcome (even transiently, as it is in Hegel) in esthetic experience, which yields in Kierkegaard only the "imaginary illusion" of "inconclusiveness," "conclusiveness" (and hence autonomy).

The pivotal alteration in relations for our purposes is the shift to the individual, who provides in Kierkegaard the point of view from which the work of art is appraised. When Hegel analyzes the concept of the beautiful and art, he starts with what is immediately presented to us, "the external," which we recognize "has no immediate validity for us," etc. The "us" I have identified as the social entity encountered previously in Hegel's ethics, now transformed in esthetics into a critical audience.

Eremita's shift in the first aphorism to the point of view of the poet, as an individual who is alienated from his audience and critics, subverts Hegel's orientation toward the third moment of his dialectic and the other relations that hold at this moment. Hegel's orientation becomes more evident if we drop down to the level of his dialectical interpretation of a specific art form, Greek tragedy:

> The true development consists only in transcending contradictions as contradictions, in the reconciliation of the powers animating the action, which mutually strive to negate each other. Only insofar as unhappiness and suffering are not the outcome but the satisfaction of the spirit, only insofar as for the first time with such an ending the necessity of all that happens to individuals can appear as absolute rationality—only then can our attitude [*Gemüt*] be truly at peace ethically: shaken by the lot of the heroes, reconciled to what is really at issue.[72]

Reason here, as in Hegel's philosophy of history, is displaying its "cunning." The real story, in a drama as in history, is social and objective; it is going on behind the backs of the participants as individuals. Happiness and suffering may be the lot of Antigone, but the audience is satisfied with an outcome she never envisaged. We experience the *Aufhebung* and its *Aufbewahrung*—the transcendent ethical peace of the final reconciliation. We see in retrospect the rational necessity of all that happens to Antigone (e.g., the necessity of the Greek *polis* emerging as a social entity and asserting its authority with Creon); she does not but remains passionate, clinging to her partial, fragmentary point of view, as will Kierkegaard himself in relation to the development of modern society.

THE WHOLE

In Hegel's dialectic, which like Kierkegaard's is *bifocal*, this transcendence of the individual's point of view is integral even to whatever satisfaction is accorded to the individual himself:

> Whatever validity a content may have in itself, we are not satisfied with its abstractness and crave something further. At the outset this is only an unsatisfied need and for the subject something insufficient which strives to transcend itself [*sich aufzuheben*] and advance to satisfaction. In this sense we may say that the content is at first subjective, something merely inward, with the objective standing over against it, so that now the demand emerges that the subjective be objectified. Such an opposition between the subjective and the objective over against it, as well as the imperative that it be transcended, is simply a universal characteristic [*Bestimmung*] pervading everything.

Thus the operation of this dialectic can be detected at a low level:

> Such a satisfaction through the resolution of . . . opposition we find most readily in the system of bodily needs. Hunger, thirst, weariness; eating, drinking, satiety, sleep: these are examples in this sphere of such a contradiction and its resolution. Yet in this natural sphere of human existence the content of its satisfactions is of a finite and limited kind; . . . and so a new need arises restlessly and ceaselessly: eating, satiety, sleeping are no help; hunger and weariness begin again on the morrow.[73]

The movement of transcendence then takes us into the higher sphere of our spiritual needs as a more significant illustration of the operation of the dialectic: "The world of our spiritual aims and interests depends on the demand to carry through into objectivity . . . what at the outset was only subjective and inward." This demand shows itself . . . as an unrest, a grief, as something negative. This, as negative, has to transcend itself. . . . . This deficiency in the subjective itself, and felt by itself, is a lack and a negation in itself, which it strives to negate again.

This striving can have as its outcome a system (in contrast to the "finite striving" endorsed by the subtitle of Eremita's reflection on tragedy) because

the subject with respect to its concept is the whole, not the inner alone, but equally the actualizing of this inner through and in the outward. . . . Only by transcending such a negation in itself does life become affirmative. To go through this process of opposition, contradiction, and the resolution of the contradiction is the higher privilege of living beings. . . . Life proceeds to negation and its grief, and it only becomes affirmative for itself by effacing the opposition and the contradiction.

The "whole" toward which the subjective can be transcended is itself found at different levels as a partial whole. As Climacus interprets Hegel, the individual subject can through marriage be "brought into systematic relation to the whole world." This relational system of "social ethics" is one partial "whole," as is "the system of bodily needs" just cited; another is the systematic relations holding between the different arts. Here too contradictions differentiate the different arts but are transcended to compose this system.

THE OBJECTIVE ARTS

The broadest contribution of the contradiction of the *external* by the *internal* to organizing "the system of the arts" is the differentiation of the *external* or *objective* or "spatial" arts of architecture and sculpture on one hand from the *subjective* arts of music and poetry on the other. Put less elliptically, the *objective* arts belong to that stage in the development of art with respect to which the distinction between the *objective* and the *subjective*, the *external* and the *internal*, cannot be drawn; whereas the *subjective* arts belong to the later stage where the distinction is drawn. Architecture is dialectically the most primitive form of art in this development:

The meanings implanted in architecture it can in general indicate only in the externals of the environment it creates [as an enclosure]. . . . Architecture does not produce structures whose meaning is the inherently spiritual and subjective.

Put positively, the meaning expressed is some three-dimensional organization of (our experience of) space, which is inherently physical and objective. Next in the development comes sculpture, which "corresponds as content to the objectivity of spirit in repose, insofar as spirit has not separated itself . . . from its existence in body and therefore has not withdrawn into its relation to itself in its own subjectivity."[74]

This reflexive withdrawal is the *subjective reorientation* of the dialectic, which Eremita opposes to Hegel's *objective* orientation, and it operates as disruptively at the level of the "system of the arts" as it does at the levels of the buried lives of Antigone and the Symparenkromenoi and at the level where Eremita is a hermit. The most obvious fashion in which the continuity of the development of Hegel's dialectic is disrupted and the system itself fragmented is indicated by Hegel's own admission that "the general transition from sculpture to the other arts is produced . . . by the principle of subjectivity breaking into the content and artistic mode of representation." Thus the most obvious fashion in which Eremita asserts this principle is by leaving out of his esthetics the objective arts of architecture and sculpture. For insofar as an art is *objective*, its *external* form is not contradicted by any *internal, subjective* content.[75] Thus it cannot (this is Eremita's implicit claim) significantly convey our *ex-sistential* experience as the experience of this dislocating contradiction.

Yet we should not underestimate the ingenuity of Eremita in designing structures in the space of the imagination. It would have been undialectical of him simply to leave the *objective* arts out, so he smuggles a specimen in. The elaborate fashion in which he has drawn our attention to the place of the desk as an admirable esthetic object which should be the starting point of a "new period" in his life (I have suggested its esthetic stage) indicates that he is for purposes of parody starting his esthetic where Hegel started—with an *external* or *objective* art, granted that the desk is a deliberately inconsequential specimen and is confined to the preface rather than accorded a place in the esthetics of *Either* proper. But the desk does not remain a specimen of *objective* art in Hegel's sense. By intruding a distinction between what it is externally and the "hiding place" behind the "secret door," Eremita is finding his initial "doubt reinforced" regarding the Hegelian presupposition that the contradiction between the *external* and the *internal* is transcended in esthetics.

THE SUBJECTIVE ARTS

If in Hegel himself the contradiction, before it is transcended, serves in its broader esthetic application to oppose the *objective* or "spatial" arts of architecture and sculpture to the *subjective* arts of music and poetry, it is more narrowly reapplied within the *subjective* sphere of poetry as a distinction between the relatively *objective* art of epic poetry and the *subjective* art of lyric poetry:

Epic sets forth what is itself objective in its objectivity.

This world which is to be made objective for apprehension ... is not conveyed by the bard in such a way that it could betoken his own imaginative representation and living passion; instead the reciter, the rhapsode, speaks mechanically and from memory. . . . For what he narrates should appear in manner and matter, as an actual course of events should appear, in its content and in the manner of its presentation, as reality completely enclosed [*abgeschlossene Wirklichkeit*] in itself and remote from him as a subject. . . .

Lyric as the opposite of epic poetry composes the second type of poetry. Its content is the subjective, the inner world, the mind that meditates and feels, that instead of proceeding to action remains alone with itself as inwardness, and that therefore can take as its sole form and final aim the self-expression of the subject. . . . And since it is the inward which is to give life to the delivery, the expression will turn toward music.[76]

In his *subjective* reorientation, Eremita is sensitive to both of Hegel's applications of the contradiction between the *external* and the *internal*. Not only does he eliminate the *objective* arts (aside from the parody with the desk in the preface) in favor of the *subjective* arts, but he also eliminates the relatively *objective* art of epic poetry (Hegel's first type) by starting out his esthetics with lyric poetry (Hegel's opposing *subjective* type).[77] The "aphorisms," Eremita carefully explains in the preface, are "lyrical outbursts," and by entitling them "Diapsalmata" he (like Hegel) is indicating a turn toward music.

The epic only survives in *Either* as a point of reference for the interpretation of other forms of art, especially tragedy. Its function as such can be best understood by observing Hegel's interpretation of the epic where it is most relevant to Eremita's individualism. In dealing with "the specifically epic way of representing individuals," Hegel stresses "the objectivity of an epic character," which "implies" that they are "whole men." Here we note the sharp contrast with the fragmented character of Eremita's modern *Antigone*, but the contrast cannot be adequately appreciated unless we also take into account Hegel's distinction between the epic and the dramatic representation of character:

In drama the inner will, what it demands and intends, is the essential determinant which remains fundamental to everything that transpires. The things that happen appear to be entirely the result of a character and his aims. . . . Therefore even if in drama external circumstances are operative, they still only count through what the mind and will make of them and the manner in which a character reacts to them. But in epic, circumstances and external contingency count just as much as the character's will, and what he achieves passes before us just like what happens from without, so that his action must prove to be conditioned and brought about just as much by his entanglement in external circumstances. For in epic the individual does not act freely for himself and on his own.[78]

So conceived the epic figure cannot qualify as an existential individual. Hegel goes on to explain the objectivity and wholeness of the epic figure:

> He stands in the midst of a whole [e.g., Homeric or feudal society] whose aim and existence is in overall connection [*Zusammenhang*] of an inner with an outer world, which provides the immovable actual foundation [*Grund*] for every particular individual. . . . What epic should represent to us is what is truly objective. . . . In this sense we can maintain that what rules in epic (though not, as is commonly supposed in drama) is fate. In drama . . . the individual makes his fate himself, whereas an epic character has his fate made for him.[79]

Much of this we have heard before, for the passage suggests the extent to which what is found in Eremita's esthetics are often the "remnants" of Hegel's "system of the arts." But the fragmentation is not haphazard but a *reorientation* which is dialectical, in that it is a process of definition or, rather, of redefinition, and as such a reallocation of the "boundaries" which Hegel had drawn between the tragic and the epic. For when Eremita argues that "in ancient tragedy the action itself . . . is as much an event as it is an action," he is making the point we have now seen that Hegel made in opposing epic to tragedy. When Eremita transfers this characteristic to ancient tragedy as an "epic moment," he is moving ancient tragedy as a genre closer to the epic than it is in Hegel. And this reallocation permits his own sharper contradiction with modern tragedy, which as opposed to ancient tragedy "has no inheritance from the epic."[80]

PLASTICITY

The process of redefinition involves a shift too in the criteria controlling the dialectic. Hegel's criteria are implicit in his recognition that "the truth is the whole"—that is, that contradictions are to be transcended at the moment of *Aufhebung* when continuity is preserved (*aufbewahrt*), until eventually a system is brought to a conclusion. These criteria of continuity and conclusiveness are challenged by Kierkegaard's reassertion of the principle of contradiction. The challenge was illustrated in the preface by the desk. Admittedly the intrusion here of a contradiction between the *internal* and the *external* can only be a spatial metaphor: the "hiding place" concealed within the desk is no more subjectively inward than the external features of the desk that are visible without.

Yet the spatial metaphor is not just a facetious and clumsy extension that goes with the erection of contradiction into a universal principle. For if a metaphor is significantly employed by a dialectician, the extension of meaning that it conveys will display the characteristic movement of his dialectic. *Aufhebung* is the prime example in Hegel, since it is a spatial metaphor for the procedure whereby spatial representation as such eventually becomes essentially irrelevant. As this example illustrates, Hegel still employs spatial metaphors, but he prefers those which bring out the character of this metaphorical movement of *Aufhebung*, whereby contradiction is transcended and continuity prevails, until a development is concluded.

Even though Eremita's reorientation of Hegel's dialectic increasingly discounts the *external,* the *subjective,* and the spatial in favor of the *internal,* the *subjective,* and (as we shall soon see) the temporal, he employs spatial metaphors more frequently than Hegel and prefers those which bring out the increasing discrepancy between the *internal* and the *external* that accompanies discounting the *external* and the concomitant disruption of the continuity of development into fragments. Thus discounting the external is conveyed by the spatial metaphor of "Shadowgraphs," which is the title of the next essay after "The Ancient Tragic." Eremita can be interpreted as adopting this metaphor in opposition to one of Hegel's subordinate criteria, "plasticity," whose application helps maintain both the objective orientation of his dialectic during the esthetic stage and its continuity as so oriented.

"Plasticity" refers literally in Hegel to the three dimensionality which is essential to sculpture as a spatial work of art. "The aim of sculpture" is objectivity—that is, "the complete harmony [*Übereinstimmung*] of the internal with the external."[81] Once the contradiction between the *internal* and the *external* develops with the subjective arts, the *Aufhebung* of this contradiction cannot finally be reached within the sphere of the arts. But "plastic" becomes Hegel's favorite metaphorical way of commending their approximation to this *Aufhebung*, since his dialectic continues to be objectively oriented. Thus the hero of a Greek tragedy is treated by Hegel as a "plastic figure" by virtue of the three-dimensional "solidity" with which his "subjective" character is so thoroughly "objectified" by his actions that the distinction between *internal* and *external* can hardly be introduced, any more than it can in Greek sculpture.[82]

Let me cite one instance of Hegel's usage, where he claims that "the characters in the tragedies of Sophocles . . . may be compared in their plastic conclusiveness [*Abgeschlossenheit*] to the figures of sculpture." The strength of Hegel's commitment to this comparison is illustrated by another passage where the climax of an *Aufhebung* is reached:

> At this height, where the mere contingencies of unmediated individuality vanish, the tragic heroes of dramatic art . . . have risen to become comparable to works of sculpture, and so in this respect the statues and images of the gods [*Götterbilder*] . . . explain the exalted tragic characters of the Greeks better than all other commentaries and notes.[83]

PAINTING

At the level of the "system of the arts," the extension of the criterion of "plasticity" from the *objective* art of sculpture to the *subjective* art of tragedy helps transcend the contradiction between the *external* and the *internal* that would otherwise separate the *objective* from the *subjective* arts and disrupt the continuity of development which allows all the arts eventually to compose a system. But this metaphorical extension of the criterion of "plasticity" is not sufficient of itself to assure the continuity of this development. Continuity depends in Hegel on his not omitting any of the arts themselves. If we would understand this continuity in order to understand how Kierkegaard disrupts it, we must not skip to tragedy (as we have done up until now, since we were following Kierkegaard's sequence) without considering the art which is transitional in Hegel from the *objective* to the *subjective* arts.

This transition is crucial to Hegel, if the continuity required for the arts to be systematized is to be maintained. We have seen that the transition supervenes after sculpture: "The general transition from sculpture to the other arts is produced . . . by the principle of subjectivity breaking into the content and artistic mode of presentation." But the specific transitional art is painting. On one hand it is no longer an *objective* art in the full three-dimensional sense; on the other it is still a "spatial" art, for "a surface" is the "medium of its representation." Furthermore, painting can employ the devices of perspective to create the illusion of three dimensions, so that Hegel can carry over his criterion and take note of "the plastic, sculpture-like character" that painting can exhibit.[84]

Nevertheless, the transition emerges as a necessary dialectical development when the distinction between sculpture and painting as external forms is taken in conjunction with the internal content which sculpture cannot express and which can only receive expression with the development of painting. On one hand the limitations of sculpture are to be recognized:

The sensuous material in which the incarnation of spirit is presented is made adequate to spirit only in its external shape as such. The inner subjectivity, the vitality of disposition, the soul of the feelings that are most his own, are not revealed by a figure that has no look [*blicklose Gestalt*], nor can this figure convey a concentrated expression of the inner life, or of spiritual movement, or discrimination from the external world or discrimination within. This is the reason why the sculptures of antiquity leave us somewhat cold.

The development of painting makes up for this inadequacy of sculpture:

A man's glance [*Blick*] is what is most full of his soul, the concentration of inwardness and of feeling subjectivity. . . . And it is just this fullness of soul that sculpture must neglect. In painting, however, the subject in its entire inwardness of feeling or in its varied contact with external things and the particular interests, feelings, and passion which they evoke finds expression by means of variation in color.[85]

SHADOWGRAPHS

Given Eremita's undertaking to disrupt the continuity with which Hegel's "system of the arts" develops, painting is the art form which must be displaced most carefully, since it is transitional from the *external* or *objective* arts to the *internal* or *subjective* arts. Indeed the very concept of maintaining continuity with a transition (*Übergang*) is indispensable to the development of Hegel's system as a whole and must itself be undermined, with an eye both to the discontinuity of ethical choice with esthetic reflection and to the ultimate discontinuity of the "leap" which will be required for arrival at the religious stage.

The care Eremita displays is apparent in his dignifying "shadowgraphs" as if they constituted a respectable art form which could be compared with the conventional forms that Hegel's system embraces. "Shadowgraphs" lack the perspective with which a painting can give the illusion of an objective, full-bodied rendering of the three-dimensional, so that "plasticity" can be carried over as a criterion from the preceding art of sculpture. What "shadowgraphs" also lack (as compared with paintings) is "the variation in color" with which it is possible, according to Hegel, to express the subject's "varied contact with external things." *Skyggerids* means literally a "shadow outline" or "shadow sketch," and a shadowgraph is in fact only a shadowy outline.[86]

Furthermore, Eremita's "Shadowgraphs" are only marginally specimens of visual art and even then are merely a metaphor for literary sketches which in Hegel's "system" would have to be assigned to the still more subjective genre of poetry. In short, Eremita's disruption of the continuity is wider than we have yet recognized. Let us watch the widening of this gap. The distinction between painting, as a relatively *objective* stage in the development of the *subjective* arts in Hegel, and the more developed subjectivity of the poetic stage is redrawn by Eremita, who uses the same idiom that he used in redrawing the longer-run distinction between the esthetic and the ethical. It is a matter of de-finition, of demarcating "boundaries." Eremita recalls how "Lessing in his renowned essay, *Laokoon* settled the disputed boundaries between poetry and art." In the *Laokoon* itself "art" referred of course to sculpture, which Eremita with his subjective *reorientation* is leaving out. But Lessing's distinction Eremita accepts:

> The result [of this settlement], unanimously endorsed by all estheticians, has been to consider that the difference between them is that art involves definition [*bestemmelse*] in terms of spatial relations, poetry in terms of temporal relations; art represents repose; poetry, movement. In order therefore for a subject matter to lend itself to artistic representation, it must have a quiet transparency, so that its inner essence reposes in a corresponding outer form.[87]

At this juncture, the contradiction between the *internal* and the *external* has not yet emerged. But move on:

> Grief can be represented by art, but there is a stage in its development when it becomes essential to establish an opposition between the internal and the external which makes its representation impossible for art.

This stage is reached when the emotion "conceals itself in its secret hiding place," as with the "brides of grief" who have become "wedded" to their grief by reflecting upon it:

> In reflective grief, the external contains at most a hint which may leave a clue, sometimes not even that much. Such grief does not let itself be represented, for the equilibrium between the internal and the external has been destroyed [*hævat*] and does not lend itself to spatial definition [*bestemmelse*].

Moreover, reflective grief itself undergoes a process of development:

> Reflective grief cannot remain an object for representation by art, partly because it never is but is always in the process of becoming, and partly because it is indifferent to and unconcerned with the external and the visible.[88]

"Cannot remain" is Hegel's recurrent terminology for indicating that the development of the content will require a corresponding development of the form in order for the content to receive the appropriate expression.

The Inner Picture

The stage that is being ushered in entails development in the relation between *internal* and *external* in other senses, for the process of development is *bifocal*. At one level an art form is developing, but at another the point of view from which this art form is appraised is no longer, as it was earlier in *Either*, just a matter of the sufferer expressing himself. Unlike the poet-sufferer of the first aphorism, the reflective sufferer is now "indifferent to . . . the external." With his indifference the dialectical development would be stranded, did it not shift to the point of view of the observing audience. Later we shall see that this shift is undertaken not merely in order to latch on to the development in Hegel but also to formulate Kierkegaard's own problem of communication.

For the present all we need to recognize is that the spokesman for the Symparenkromenoi assigns them the role of audience, when he takes the next step of identifying the art in question as pictorial: "It is this reflective grief which I now propose to draw to your attention [*drage frem*] and as far as possible render visible by means of some pictures [*billeder*]." But then we are forced to recognize that they are not really "pictures." Eremita is taking dialectical advantage, as he has before, of the ambiguity of *billede*, which can mean either an (external) "picture" or an (inner) "image." Thus he goes on to explain,

> I call these [pictures] "shadowgraphs" . . . partly because, like other shadowgraphs, they are not directly visible. . . . Not until I look through the external do I discover that inner picture ["image"] which I desire to show you.

This loss of the direct visibility that we associate with any visual art forces us to accept *reorientation*:

> Direct your attention, then, beloved Symparenkromenoi, to this inner picture; do not allow yourself to be distracted by the external, . . . for it shall be my task to draw it aside [*drage . . . tilside*], in order to afford you a better view of the inner picture. . . . For . . . we are . . . old enough not to be deceived [*bedrage*] by appearances or to continue in this deception.[89]

Once the "clue" left behind by the "bride" has been exploited for whatever "hint" it may yield, it must be discounted as merely an external appearance. The byplay with *drage/bedrage* is carried over to a higher level with the implicit discounting of the shadowgraphic art form as itself also an external appearance, since what we are being offered are not pictorial but literary sketches. Thus a comparison is made with old books where a figure is drawn that could represent almost anything, which bears on its breast a plate in the form of a heart or the like, to which it points, whereon one may read a description of the picture.

Similarly, the shadowgraphic "artist" must at some point "renounce representing reflective grief and leave it to be treated by poets and psychologists."[90] This is in fact the treatment that we are being offered.

It is accordingly necessary at this juncture to keep in mind not only Hegel's "system of the arts" but also certain features of his psychology of the poetic imagination. The *ambiguity* with respect to form, whereby *billede/Bild* can refer either to an (external) "picture" or an (internal) "image," corresponds to an *ambiguity* of the content, since the most to be hoped for externally in the case of reflective suffering is a "hint which may leave a trace." Not enough for a "picture," in the strict sense of a painting; perhaps enough to suggest how one might with imagination sketch an "outline."[91]

When the spokesman for the Symparenkromenoi proposes "to draw it [the external] aside, in order to afford you a better view of the inner picture," he is playfully contradicting the metaphor of "placing before the mind" which Hegel found etymologically in *Vor-stellung* ("imaginative representation") and which Kierkegaard has probably reproduced with his earlier *drage frem.* Previously we recognized that *Vorstellung* is the stage at which the mind becomes conscious of the distinction between the original visual "perception" (*Anschauung*) which was external in that it took place while we were still "outside ourselves in the medium of space and time" and our mind had "no other content besides what is perceived," and an "image" (*Bild*) as the "internalization" of this perception insofar as it is retrieved by the "imagination" (*Einbildungskraft*) which is the mind's ability to externalize an image wthin itself.[92]

At the present juncture, however, the image has already been externalized by the spokesman in the shadowgraph, so that the psychological development which has just been traced has to be reapplied to the audience perceiving the external work of art, who must "internalize" its perception and reproduce it imaginatively. In Hegel this psychological transition correlates with the transition from painting as a visual art to poetry, where what can still be perceived externally (the marks on the page) must be transformed; the "imagination" must take over, if the "inner picture" or "image" (to revert to the idiom of *Either*) is to be represented.[93]

POETRY

We shall see that Hegel introduces his treatment of poetry with a recapitulation. So let me review what has happened so far in *Either* to Hegel's "system of the arts." Painting has survived only by virtue of Eremita's taking the quotation from the *Laokoon* as referring to visual art as such (rather than specifically to sculpture) and only for the purpose of developing the metaphor of "picture," with which we have been watching him play. But the "picture" in question is deprived of any appearance of "plasticity" such as a painting can still achieve in Hegel (though the criterion itself is sculptural) and is reduced instead to a shadowy "outline" whose appearance is in turn to be discounted, until "shadowgraph" becomes merely a metaphor for a literary sketch that solicits "imaginative representation."[94]

Eremita's depictorializing procedure is consistent with his previous elimination not only of the external, objective arts (architecture and sculpture) in Hegel's system but also of the relatively objective subjective art (epic). The "remnants" of Hegel's "system of the arts" with which we are then left are the subjective arts of music and lyric and dramatic poetry. (Music is the art which follows painting and precedes poetry in Hegel's lineup.) With music the contradiction between the *external* and the *internal* is not found in *Either*, since the sound perceived is the meaning. Retaining the distinction between music and poetry enables Eremita to nail down the distinction between immediacy (perception) and reflection (imaginative representation). But the distinction itself remains ambiguous, since lyric poetry is only metaphorically lyrical, and the "Diapsalmata," which occupy the place of lyric poetry in Eremita's esthetics, are in fact poetic "aphorisms." His reflections on *Don Giovanni* are likewise literary in form. In short, Eremita's application of Hegel's "principle of subjectivity" is the *reorientation of esthetics* toward what were already in Hegel the more subjective arts. Indeed poetry is the juncture in Hegel's "system of the arts," as "imaginative representation" is the psychological juncture, at which the contradiction between the *external* and the *internal* emerges, as Hegel himself points out, when he acknowledges that poetry is a *recapitulation*:

> However completely poetry reproduces the whole of beauty once again in a more spiritual fashion [than all of the preceding arts], spirituality still constitutes at the same time the deficiency of this final sphere of art. . . . The fusion of spiritual inwardness with external existence disintegrates to an extent that starts to be no longer compatible with the

original concept of art [as instanced by the preceding arts of sculpture, painting, and music].[95]

Thus poetry is at once the final stage in the development of the "system of the arts" and the stage in which art itself starts to disintegrate (*aufzulösen*), so that we are forced to recognize that the system cannot be brought to a conclusion.

This juncture in Hegel is in effect Eremita's starting point—the stage to which his entire esthetics belongs, as an attempt to define the poet. (Remember that he starts out in the first aphorism by asking, "What is a poet?") Thus we can grant that Eremita is carrying through a *reorientation* of esthetic experience toward its disintegration. But since poetry is the juncture at which disintegration starts in Hegel himself, with the emergence of a contradiction between the *internal* and the *external*, and since his "system of the arts" thereby betrays its inconclusiveness as a system, we have to repeat Climacus's Socratic question, Do the fragments produced in *Either* by Eremita's reassertion of the principle of contradiction really amount to anything more than "remnants" of Hegel's "system of the arts"?

Notes

1. *Present Age*, p. 106.
2. See chap. 1 above.
3. One of Kierkegaard's motives for rescuing the pseudonym "Johannes Climacus" for *Philosophical Fragments* and its *Postscript* may have been that the work *Johannes Climacus* itself had remained a de facto fragment.
4. *Logic*, p. 78. Kierkegaard is alluding to Hegel's elimination of prefaces as "preliminary" when he ironizes, "No preliminary consideration . . . is needed; one passes on at once to the main course. At the conclusion of the system it will be seen that the method is correct" (*Papirer*, V B 14). Observe how Kierkegaard brings together the preliminary and the conclusive, as I did in my preface, where I also had in mind Derrida's merely prefatory, preliminary, and hymeneal performances.
5. *Postscript*, p. 16. If we take, as Kierkegaard frequently does, Hegel's reference to "the conclusion of the whole" to be a reference to the outcome of social history, then Merleau-Ponty's handling of the Dreyfus case, which was considered in the preceding chapter, could be interpreted as a quarrel with this Hegelian perspective whereby "all will become clear in the end" (ibid., p. 34). If we take Hegel's reference as simply to "the end," then Kierkegaard is challenging the Hegelian perspective by bringing forward the problem of starting point. If we take it as a reference to the system as such, then his challenge is that "each stage" must "be made clear by itself," as we saw in chap. 6.
6. *On the Way to Language*, pp. 66, 12.
7. *Postscript*, p. 340. The contrast with Hegel holds even though the discontinuities in the development of Kierkegaard's esthetic production are more complicated than I am able to trace here. The earlier works, starting with *Either/Or*, are in a sense introductory to *Philosophical Fragments*, to which *Postscript* is a postscript in spite of the fact that it also includes a recapitulation of all the pseudonymous works. Kierkegaard

is proceeding in accordance with the methodological principle that "each stage" must "be made clear by itself." (Remember that definition [see chap. 4, n. 18 above] can proceed by the demarcation of stages.) Thus it was "necessary . . . to fix *definitely* the preliminary stages," and so *Fragments* had to be deferred until "the matter of existential inwardness had . . . been so *definitely* specified that its Christian-religious mode could be brought forward without risk of immediate confusion with everything else" (*Postscript*, pp. 251, 241; italics mine).

8. See p. 368 above.

9. *Postscript*, p. 340. This effort to repel is presumably opposed to the traditional rhetorical effort to "conciliate" one's audience with a *captatio benevolentiae*, though Kierkegaard's procedure is ambiguous, for he admits that "Christianity repeals in order to attract" (*Papirer*, IX A 310). See chap. 6, n. 24, for Kierkegaard's apparent adoption of this procedure in *Point of View*; and chap. 12, nn. 21, 50, for other illustrations. At the personal level Kierkegaard had been concerned to deal with Regina —most pointedly in his "Diary of the Seducer," which "was meant to repel her from me," or as it is put in *Fear and Trembling*, "When it is time for the child to be weaned, the mother blackens her breast" (*Papirer*, X5 A 146). See the way in which, in Sartre's interpretation, "Genet repels" (*Saint Genet*, p. 586; see chap. 4, n. 17 above). I have already observed Sartre's effort to discomfit his reader, and he regards as Nizan's "greatest literary merit" his "having wished to offend [*déplaire*]" (*Situations*, p. 84).

10. "A Word about My Activity as an Author in Relation to 'The Individual' " (published in *Point of View*, pp. 130–31). We have already watched Kierkegaard identify "narrowness" as itself the way (see p. 346 above). Now narrowness becomes explicitly the principle of individuation. As such it can be opposed to the infinite scope of the esthetic, which was displayed in the "Diary" by Cordelia's inculcated "infinite audacity for far horizons."

11. *Postscript*, pp. 200, 203.

12. See p. 284 above.

13. The charge of "esthetic" is not directed merely against Hegel, who here as elsewhere is for Kierkegaard (as he was for himself) the summation and consummation of modern philosophy: "What is it to be a poet? It is to have one's own personal life, one's actuality in entirely different categories from those of one's poetic production; it means to be related to the ideal in imagination [*phantasie*] only, so that one's own personal existence is more or less a satire on the poetic and on oneself. In that sense all modern thinkers, even those of standing, are poets" (*Papirer*, X1 A 11). Later in this chapter we shall see the respect in which for Kierkegaard the esthetic is reducible to the poetic.

14. The procedure for dealing with philosophical problems by reallocating them had of course been encouraged by Kant's reallocating problems from his first to his second *Critique*. But it takes on additional significance with Kierkegaard's opposition to Hegel, since there is no system to supersede the stages to which problems are allocated. Recall how Kierkegaard plays up the methodological significance of the procedure with his spatial metaphor for the process of de-finition—"boundary" disputes (p. 268 above.)

15. The reallocation of Hegel's philosophy back to Kierkegaard's first stage means that Kierkegaard is in some sense "going beyond" Hegel. But since he sneers at contemporaries who were supposed to have "gone beyond" Hegel (see chap. 11, n. 15 below), it must be remembered that his reallocation renders the movement of *Aufhebung* itself illusory not only in their case but also when Hegel "goes beyond" one stage to another, and finally "beyond" all stages by completing his system.

16. *Stages on Life's Way*, p. 187. *Per-ire* incorporates the metaphor of "going" along a way.

17. See p. 283 above.

18. *Postscript*, pp. 16–17.

19. See p. 313 above. *Raadvild* is ambiguous, quite aside from the interplay with its cognates (see p. 309 above). It also has the practical implication of being "unable to decide" and so indicates an ethical shortcoming.

20. "What before was impulse is now reflection" (*Either*, p. 344).

21. Ibid., p. 348. The metaphor of "shipwreck" is common in *L'idiot*, though it is used to expound Flaubert's own point of view. Thus "the final shipwreck is the truth" (3:501; see also pp. 178, 192, 281). In Sartre it is frequently the function of an *échec* to reveal the truth.

22. *Either*, p. 377.

23. Ibid., p. 439.

24. Ibid., p. 426. Kierkegaard's conception of woman can hardly be understood except as a transplantation from Hegel. In the *Philosophy of Right* his comments are partly prompted by Schlegel's *Lucinde*, to which "The Diary of the Seducer" is in effect a commentary. But Hegel also illustrates how dialectically indispensable the analogy to plant life is to putting woman in her proper place: "Women can indeed be educated. [The seducer conceives Cordelia's seduction as educational in the dialectical senses of "leading" her "forth" into full bloom and of leading her up to the level of knowledge (see p. 403 above).] But they are not made for the higher sciences, philosophy, or certain artistic activities, since these demand a capacity for the universal. Women may have whimsical thoughts, taste, elegance, but they cannot reach the ideal. The difference between men and women is that between animals and plants. . . . Women correspond to plants because their unfolding is more placid and the principle that underlies it is an indeterminate unity of feeling. . . . The education of women takes place—one does not know how—through the atmosphere of imaginative representation, through living, rather than through acquiring knowledge, while man attains his status only by the strenuousness of thought and much technical exertion" (*Philosophy of Right, Zusatz* to 166). The correspondence should be followed out by consulting not only Hegel's philosophy of nature but also his philosophy of religion, where in treating "immediate religion" or "natural religion" he distinguishes the "religion of animals" which is associated with "struggle" and "guilt" from the "innocence" of the "religion of flowers which is merely the selfless imaginative representation of self." Derrida quotes the relevant passages (*Glas*, pp. 8–9). Kierkegaard may be mocking Hegel when he refers to "fragrance" (as the immediate form taken by the esthetic attraction of a flower as itself life at the level of immediacy), since Hegel denies that smell is an esthetic sense (see chap. 7, n. 69 above). Yet the selflessness of women in Hegel should be kept in mind when Kierkegaard assigns her to the level of immediacy and explains that she does not properly speaking ex-sist, for it is not "in and through herself" that she "emerges outside" herself (as the etymology of ex-sistence requires) to become what she is but only in relation to and through a man. This putting in her place as the Second Sex is not restricted in its significance, as the translator seems to suggest, to her having been manufactured from Adam's rib. The man's role is to court (*at frie*) her, and this is to "liberate" (*at befrie*) her, by bringing her *out* of herself. Since this is something she cannot do for herself, there can be "no question of choice" on her part. Moreover, choice in the significant ethical sense presupposes reflection and so is "unfeminine" (*Either*, p. 426). (Is the fact that Cordelia's last name is "Wahl" a summoning of Regina to what she is generically incapable of?) The freedom credited is "esthetic" in the sense Hegel attributes to the work of art, where "ideal subjectivity" is released "to actual objectivity," so that "the Idea exists in externality, . . . free" (see p. 417 above). Then the "choice" would be Kierkegaard's choice of her.

25. *Either*, p. 439.

26. Ibid., pp. 439, 426. Clytie was salvaged by Apollo's turning her into a sunflower.

27. Ibid., p. 440. In 1842 Kierkegaard had envisaged the possibility of "ending my Antigone [which became "The Ancient Tragic"] by transforming her into a man" (*Papirer*, III A 207).

28. Cf. the aphorism on the aphoristic procedure as a dialectic of forgetting and recollecting an experience (p. 247 above).

29. *Either*, p. 439.

30. Ibid., p. 309.

31. "The lack of the conclusion has retroactive [*tilbagevirkende*] power to make the starting point doubtful, hypothetical, and unsystematic" (*Postscript*, p. 17). At one level Climacus is recognizing that Hegel's system lacks the conclusion which must be reached for it to be a system and hence poses retroactively the problem of starting point. This dialectical development may be suggested by the fact that the youthful Climacus "starts again." But at another level a similar dialectic is a feature of Kierkegaard's "esthetic production" as esthetic, for it ends up inconclusively with a question mark at the final stage of *Stages*, "Guilty/Not Guilty?" which "does not relax the tension of the conflict with a reassuring outcome" (*Postscript*, p. 257). The retroactive power of this lack of conclusion is discernible in the way Eremita started out in *Either* by doubting the contradiction between the internal and the external—the contradiction Hegel considered he had overcome when he reached the "final conclusions" (see my preface above) with his system. At still another level (to be specified in chap. 12) the inconclusiveness of the "esthetic production" comes to involve the reader whom "Guilty/Not Guilty?" leaves "in the lurch by not allowing him any outcome" (*Postscript*, p. 257), so that retroactively *Either/Or* as the starting point of this production remains hypothetical for him—an "experiment" (ibid.). Because of its inconclusiveness, the "esthetic production" had to be brought to a kind of conclusion in *Postscript*, which is accordingly not strictly speaking an esthetic work but is also not a system—merely a postscript.

32. *Postscript*, p. 34. The title *Postscript* may itself be an allusion to Hegel's conviction that "philosophy always comes too late. . . . Then has a form of life grown old," which cannot be rejuvenated [by philosophy] but only understood" (*Philosophy of Right*, preface). Hegel was thinking of the history of society rather than of the individual. That Climacus himself comes too late is played up with respect to his relation to Eremita's and other pseudonymous writings (*Postscript*, p. 225). Probably this byplay also indicates the higher-level location of his recapitulation.

33. The indefinite reiteration will be illustrated in chap. 12 by "The Rotation Method." Kierkegaard acknowledges that "bad infinity" is "a category which the Hegelians are always shooting at," but he argues "that the Hegelians themselves bring it forward again, only in another form" (*Papirer*, II A 381).

34. See, e.g., *Postscript*, p. 110.

35. Kierkegaard claims that "the second part of *Either/Or* answers and corrects every misdirection in the first part" (ibid., p. 264).

36. "An either/or separates enduringly what was separated when he chose" (*Or*, p. 179). Thus the either/or is recognized in retrospect to be a relation of mutual "exclusion," which is the opposite of "mediation"—the both/and reconciliation of opposites and Hegel's distinctively philosophical effort of in Kierkegaard's view.

37. See p. 166 above. Precisely because the esthetic stage is reflective, one can pass through it merely by reflecting upon it. The seduction of Cordelia presumably never took place, but Kierkegaard did consider the possibility of seducing Regina, though it was apparently a very passing thought (see *Papirer*, VIII1 A 251).

38. For the similar distinction of level in Sartre, see p. 216 above.

39. This moment of dissolution can become the vertiginous moment we have encountered in Sartre and Henry James, unless one's soul has become itself "too dissolute in the etymological sense of the word" (*Or*, p. 160).

40. *Postscript*, p. 226.

41. This dialectic develops into Kierkegaard's claim on behalf of his effort to carry through a relation between his *modus loquendi* and his *modus vivendi*: "There have been, I suppose, many more penetrating and more gifted authors than myself, but I would certainly like to see the author who has reduplicated his thinking more penetratingly than myself in the dialectic raised to the second power. It is one thing to be penetrating in books, another to double [*fordoble*] the thought dialectically in existence. . . . The dialectic in books is merely the dialectic in thinking, but reduplication of such thinking is action in life. But every thinker who does not reduplicate the dialectic of this thinking continuously constructs an illusion [*sandesbedrag*]. His thinking

never gains the decisive expression of action" (*Papirer*, VIII¹ A 91). Reduplication is thus the movement Kierkegaard would oppose to the positive movement of *Aufhebung*. Indeed in an early journal entry, he uses an equivalent Danish expression for what he will later identify as reduplication: "I still accept [*antager*] *an imperative of the understanding* . . . , *but it must be taken up* [*optages*] *in my life*" (ibid., I A 75; italics in original).

42. *Or*, p. 168.

43. Ibid., p. 255. The contribution reflection makes to the individual's "isolation" as an Eremita has already been traced in chap. 6, where reflective withdrawal from his environment was recognized to involve his effort to appropriate his experience. But the process must now be recognized to be inconclusive, since his reflection subjects these experiences to continual reinterpretation. It is this process of reinterpretation that will receive illustration in chap. 12 as "The Rotation Method."

44. *Or*, p. 256. By virtue of the reflexive character of the operation, the discrepancy between the internal and the external survives intact: "The real action is not the external action but the internal action with which the individual eliminates [*ophæver*] the possibility and identifies himself with what is thought in order to exist in it. This is the action" (*Postscript*, pp. 302–3).

45. *Or*, pp. 255–56. A contrast is intended with esthetic dissolution. (see n. 39, this chapter).

46. When Judge William recapitulates the ethical stage of *Or* in *Stages*, what was "choice" undergoes a dialectical development into "resolution" *(beslutning)*, which suggests the "conclusiveness" of the choice. *Slutning* means a "conclusion" of the sort which can be reached while reflecting, and *beslutning* means a conclusion reached by a choice. I bring out the interplay by translating it as "resolution," which could be opposed to *raadvildhed* as similarly ambiguous (see n. 19, this chapter). There is comparable interplay in Heidegger: "Resoluteness [*Entschlossenheit*] is a characteristic mode of the disclosedness [*Erschlossenheit*] of being-there. . . . In resoluteness we have now arrived at that truth of being-there which is most original because it is *authentic*. . . . A 'there' is disclosed" (*Being and Time*, p. 297; italics in original). There is some implication here that resoluteness, which would usually be regarded as a moral accomplishment, cannot ultimately be distinguished from disclosure, which would usually be regarded as a cognitive accomplishment. In Kierkegaard too, although the ethical stage of choice (or resolution) is separated from the esthetic stage of reflection, it is the choice itself which effects the separation, by bringing reflection to a conclusion, and thereby assumes a cognitive as well as an ethical function. Hence the Judge's injunction "Choose yourself" can supplant the Socratic "Know yourself" (*Or*, p. 279). In chap. 7 we saw that in Sartre cognitive confusion is associated with ethical lassitude, and lucidity with initiative.

47. The Judge deals with acting upon the choice as a carrying out and explains that " 'to carry out' [*at udrette*] refers to a relation between my action and someone outside of [*udenfor*] me" (*Or*, p. 300).

48. *Stages*, 108.

49. *Philosophy of Right*, par. 166. Hegel relates this opposition in turn to "the opposing natures of man and woman." Kierkegaard will develop this opposition (as we shall see later), but the conflict that Hegel confines within ethics becomes eventually for Kierkegaard a conflict between ethics and the religious.

50. "The derelict Hegelian ethics, with its desperate effort to make the state the supreme court in ethics, is . . . an unethical flight from the category of the individual to the category of the human race." Climacus adds that "the ethicist [the Judge] in *Either/Or* has protested against this. . . . Again in *Stages* . . . the point of view of the ethics which he champions . . . is quite the opposite of the Hegelian" (*Postscript*, p. 450). In both cases the Judge is defending marriage.

51. *Philosophy of Right*, par. 173; see also 176.

52. It may still seem that with marriage there is a risk of the subjective becoming the objective, of the inward becoming the outward, and of Kierkegaard becoming a Hegelian. But the contradiction survives intact, although Kierkegaard's more extensive clarification awaits his recapitulation of *Or* in *Stages*. Having observed that once Hegel has adopted "the principle that the internal is the external," his philosophy is in effect "completed" *(faerdig)*. Climacus, who is commenting on *Stages*, identifies the completion of Hegel's philosophy as simply esthetic or (at a higher level) "deceitfully esthetic" by virtue of its "lumping everything together—including the ethical and the religious" —as esthetic. Climacus protests, "Already the ethical posits one kind of opposition between the internal and the external, inasmuch as it regards the external as a matter of indifference. The external, as the material of action, is neutral, for what the ethical accentuates is the intention; the outcome [*udfaldet*], as the externality of action, is indifferent, . . . and it is just immoral to be concerned about the outcome" *(Postscript,* pp. 263–64). This protest indicates how Kierkegaard would translate the problem of starting point into ethical terms and would add, "I do not trouble myself much about the rest," and it suggests how he could continue to cling to the significance of his intention to marry Regina, even after she had married the commonplace suitor whom he had disposed of in "The Diary of the Seducer"—in fact had "gone beyond" in the best Hegelian style.

53. *Encyclopaedia*, pt. 3, par. 381. "The church exists," according to Kierkegaard, "precisely because we are not truly spirit or pure spirit. 'The congregation' is an accommodation, a concession in view of how little we are able to endure being spirit" *(Papirer*, X⁴ A 226). The *"sine qua non* of Christianity [is] isolation, the single individual" (ibid., XI² A 14).

54. This phrasing reproduces the German translation of Shakespeare's "Many a good hanging prevents a bad marriage" *(Twelfth Night,* act 1, sc. 5).

55. Kierkegaard's emphasis on the ethical obligation incurred by the engagement as an intention ("An engagement is a promise, a broken engagement is a broken promise" *Postscript,* pp. 236–37) illustrates the "subjectivity" of his ethics (see n. 52, this chapter) as compared with Hegel's, where even the social institution of marriage lacks ethical significance, as "only a unity of inwardness and disposition," until love is "objectified . . . in the child" *(Philosophy of Right,* par. 173).

56. *Postscript*, p. 3. This "systematic relation" must be visualized in the dynamic terms of Hegel's philosophy of social history. Thus Kierkegaard can write in his *Journal,* "In the forward movement of history—I mean marriage—there accompanies woman all the frivolities of finitude . . . puttering around" *(Papirer*, XI¹ A 141). Note the brusqueness with which Kierkegaard abbreviates the world-historical dimension in Hegel to a bipersonal relation in a fashion which I took advantage of in my preface.

57. We are familiar with the "suspension" of Socrates as the ironist whom Aristophanes was being ironical about. With the "teleological suspension of the ethical," the particular individual does not reach the universal requirement (marriage) which the ethical imposes but remains an "exception" to the ethical rule.

58. This stage was the juncture where at the end of chap. 6 I temporarily halted my interpretation of *Either* with the first of the "brides," Antigone. We are now prepared to take up the interpretation again by watching further "implications" develop in the second of these essays, "Shadowgraphs."

59. *Postscript*, p. 2 *(Hippias Major* 304A). The phrase "a while ago" indicates a recapitulation in the Socratic dialogue but when quoted by Climacus transfers the recapitulatory reference to his own *Philosophical Fragments*. This kind of interplay between texts is characteristic of the *Auseinandersetzung* ("confrontation") in which Heidegger engages with previous philosophers. The first sentence of *Being and Time* is a quotation from Plato's *Sophist*: "It is clear that you have long been confident of what you really mean when you used the expression 'being.' We, however, who used to think we understood it, have now become perplexed" (see p. 304 above). "You" refers

(I suspect) not only to Theatetus but also to Husserl, whose commitment to the absolute being of consciousness was implemented by his transcendental reduction bracketing the world. The "I" then would refer to Heidegger himself, whose preoccupation with the meaning of being is initially in *Being and Time* with "being-in-the-world." This suspicion is strengthened by Heidegger's smuggling into the translation terms with Husserlian connotations—*"vertraut"* and *"Ausdruck."*

60. I consider raising the general question of Kierkegaard's relation to anything as diffuse as romanticism unprofitable. But the "fragment" had been a romantic genre, closely associated with the "aphorism" and popularized by Friedrich Schlegel (see chap. 6, n. 37 above). "In his imagination," Schlegel admitted, "this whole existence was a pile of unrelated fragments," and he emphasized that "each fragment was single and complete, and whatever else stood next to it actually might just as well not have existed at all" (*Lucinde*, p. 78); whereas Kierkegaard is fragmenting Hegel's system, and his fragments are significantly related to it as well as to each other.

61. *Either*, p. 5. "A new period" starting is not inconsistent with Kierkegaard's pronouncement, which we examined at the beginning of chap. 7, that he had taken "care to find a man where he is and start there," in order to "bring" him "to a definite position." This pronouncement referred to esthetic experience as indefinite and confused, before it finds any expression in a work of art. Eremita's pronouncement refers to *Either* as the stage where esthetic experience does find expression in various definite forms—aphorisms, opera, tragedy, comedy. It is only with the ethical redefinition of the esthetic in *Or* that the essential indefiniteness of these esthetic forms is exposed, as compared with the conclusiveness with which self-choice organizes experience.

62. In launching his esthetics Hegel distinguished between the beautiful and the useful.

63. *Either*, p. 6.

64. *Aesthetics*, 1:153.

65. "The esthete's external conduct [i.e., his apparent pursuit of enjoyment] has been in complete contradiction of his inward life [i.e., despair]. This was the case with the other [Judge William] as well to a certain extent, inasmuch as he concealed under a rather insignificant exterior a more significant inwardness" (*Either*, p. 4; cf. *Postscript*, pp. 226–27).

66. *Aesthetics*, 1:19–20.

67. Ibid., p. 95. Kierkegaard may be toying with the Hegelian teleology by playing with the metaphor of aiming. Eremita left the question open in his preface as to whether or not his "blow had struck exactly the right juncture," but he then transferred the papers to his pistol case. When he reached his destination in the country, it may be relevant that his host interprets his trips to the woods with the pistol case to read the papers as attempts to improve his marksmanship (*Either*, p. 4).

68. Ibid., pp. 110, 157.

69. Ibid., p. 176.

70. See pp. 247, 249 above.

71. The crucial illustration is the effect of reallocating philosophy from its final location after religion in Hegel back to the esthetic stage in Kierkegaard, for not only are their external relations thereby transformed but also their intrinsic characteristics.

72. *Aesthetics*, 2:1215; italics in original. I previously cited this theory of tragedy at the end of chap. 3 for a similar contrast with the theory implicit in Sartre's *Condemned of Altona*.

73. Ibid., 1:96, 98.

74. Ibid., 2:632, 710.

75. Ibid., p. 792. Thus "the subjective as such is excluded from sculpture which belongs only to the objectivity of spirit" (p. 711).

76. Ibid., pp. 1037–38. After acknowledging that "the expression will sometimes turn toward music," Hegel adds, "and sometimes allow, sometimes necessitate, a varied modulation of voice, song, and musical accompaniment." Although Eremita takes this

turn in his "Diapsalmata," they are not merely "varied" but contradictory (see p. 253 above).

77. There are references to the epic in "The Musical Erotic" as well as in "The Ancient Tragic." The myth of Don Juan is credited with an epic character (*Either*, p. 55) before its transformation into an opera. Indeed even after its transformation it can be said that the distinction between subject and object cannot be drawn, any more than it could be in Hegel with reference to the epic, so that it can take the place of the epic as belonging to the stage of immediacy. Thus the Hegelian triad—Lyric ("Diapsalmata"), Epic (Don Juan), and Tragic (Antigone) is perhaps still discernible in *Either*, but the Hegelian (and Greek classical) historical sequence is disrupted by the Lyric coming before the Epic, so that the individual's subjective experience is brought to the fore from the start. Kierkegaard was bothered by the fact that "the history of poetry seems to indicate starting with the epic" (*Papirer*, I A 225), until he came to recognize that his own dialectic traced the existential history of the individual rather than social history.

78. *Aesthetics*, 2:1070.

79. Ibid.

80. *Either*, p. 141.

81. *Aesthetics*, 2:718. Kierkegaard's fragmentation of Hegel's "system of the arts" requires the suppression of sculpture in order not only to maintain the contradiction between the internal and the external but also to reinstate contradiction between part (if each part is to acquire its own integrity as a fragment) and whole; and he must accordingly reinstate contradictions where transitions are available in Hegel, who explains, "By virtue of the fullest richness of the transitions, the part remains in firm interconnection not only with the adjacent part but also with the whole. The shape is thereby fully animated at each juncture . . . so that the whole can be recognized in fragments, and such a separated part preserves the conception [*Anschauung*] and the satisfaction of an undisrupted whole" (ibid., pp. 725–26). Hegel is of course thinking of fragments of classical statues, but I am also thinking of these statues as illustrating for him at another level the norm at which all art aims. Perhaps he even felt (as indeed his phrasing suggests) some analogy between what the spectator must attempt—to reconstruct from his contemplation of fragments the classical statue as a whole—and his own aim at the higher level of esthetics to reconstruct the relations between the arts to compose a system. At any rate Kierkegaard could find in classical sculpture a model for Hegel's system in the respect that Hegel himself picks out in the present passage. Hegel's terminology can be requoted to argue that "the whole [Hegel's system] can be recognized in [Kierkegaard's] fragments" but that the "interconnection" is no longer "firm" but loosened (see chap. 11, n. 28 below)—in fact disrupted. Hegel's more specific criteria of "fullness" and "richness" will be considered in the next chapter.

82. *Aesthetics*, 2:1195.

83. Ibid.

84. Ibid., pp. 805, 838.

85. Ibid., pp. 797, 732. In the "Diary" the seducer is equipped with an enormous array of devastating glances—side glances, upward glances, etc.—which seem to indicate how full of soul he is, how irresistibly concentrated is his inwardness and subjective feeling.

86. The implicit opposition between the spokesman's reliance on the shadowy and the painter's reliance on color can only be understood in terms of Hegel's adoption of Goethe's theory of color. Hegel treats painting as the stage where "nature with light starts for the first time to become subjective," and he stresses that "the painted form is made by light and shadow." For he assumes that color is "light darkened" and that "the principle of color" is "the real material for painting" (*Aesthetics*, 2:808–10). Hegel is correspondingly disparaging of the mere sketch: "It is color, coloring, which makes a painter a painter. We readily linger over draftsmanship and especially over sketches as over something clearly indicative of genius, but no matter with what richness of inven-

tion and wealth of imagination the inner spirit may directly emerge in sketches from the, as it were, more transparent and thinner veil of form [cf. the shadowgraph], still painting must paint if it intends to render its subjects in their living individuality and particular detail and not stop . . . to present only an abstraction" (p. 838).

87. *Either*, p. 167.

88. Ibid., pp. 167, 168, 170. While suppressing sculpture, the spokesman seems to be accentuating the distinction Hegel had drawn between painting and sculpture, just as while suppressing epic he accentuated the distinction Hegel had drawn between tragedy and epic. In painting, according to Hegel, "the subject pervades the external thing as the object belonging to itself [at this juncture the spokesman resorts instead to "Shadowgraphs"], yet at the same time it is that identity, returning into itself [*in sich zurückgehende*], which by virtue of this self-enclosure [*Beschlossenheit*] is indifferent to the external and lets it go its own way" (*Aesthetics*, 2:803). Or again: "In painting [as opposed to sculpture] the content is the spiritual inwardness, which can come into appearance in the external only as retiring into itself [*hineingehende*]" (p. 805). Cf. the spokesman's phraseology: "Retiring . . . within, it finds at last an innermost enclosure [*et indelukke, et inderste*]" (*Either*, p. 158).

89. *Either*, p. 171.

90. Ibid. This idiom of a residue, of something remaining over which requires expression by another art form, is one way in which Hegel manages his transitions. The content develops to a juncture where it "cannot remain an object of representation" for the presently available art form. But in Kierkegaard the transition (if it can still be described as a transition) is more disruptive than in Hegel. Derrida would seem to be offering a comparably fragmented version of a Hegelian transition when he begins *Glas* with the question, "What remains today, for us, here, now, of a Hegel?" and then offers us, instead of an *Aufhebung*, interplay with Jean Genet's question, "What has remained of a Rembrandt torn into small squares, quite regular, and shoved into the holes of a shit house?"

91. Inasmuch as I am concerned with "Shadowgraphs" as an art form, I am largely neglecting their content. But the spokesman also justifies their designation because "they derive from the darker side of life" (*Either*, p. 171). With respect to this content there may be some association with the ancient Antigone who was fated to live among the "shades." But shadows appeared in many guises in romantic thought. Kierkegaard himself refers to the individual as having "a multiplicity of shadows, all of which resemble him and for the moment have an equal claim to be accounted himself" (*Repetition*, p. 40). Thus we might suppose that Kierkegaard's pseudonyms were his "shadows" and, conversely, that Antigone is in some sense his pseudonym (see p. 503 below).

92. See p. 106 above. Drawing the external "aside" (as well as the emphasis with respect to content on "the darker side of life") may also be designed to upset the balance which Hegel seeks to establish between "on the one side" and "on the other side" (see p. 249 above).

93. The contrast with poetry can be extended back to other preceding arts, as Hegel indicates: "Sculpture, painting, and music" work "the spiritual content entirely into a natural medium and make it intelligible to sense perception and spirit alike" (*Aesthetics*, 2:968).

94. As the process of reflection continues, whatever objectivity still attaches to the literary form itself proves unreliable. See p. 313 above, where the letter itself crumbles away. With respect to content, the loss of objectivity is more drastic in the next and last of the triad of tragic essays on suffering. The seduced and abandoned women of "Shadowgraphs" can only carry their grief so far, since they cannot reach that superlative pitch of reflection which is reserved for "The Unhappiest Man." When his grave was opened, there was no "trace of his body" (*Either*, p. 217)—i.e., nothing objective. This loss of objectivity is reemphasized by a comparison with the efforts of the "crusaders to seek the holy grave," for Hegel had disparaged this preoccupation with the

external: "Christendom found the empty grave" (the Holy Sepulcher). But "what it was seeking was to be sought in subjective consciousness and in no external thing" (*Philosophy of History*, p. 393). In "The Unhappiest Man" the external, which in "Shadowgraphs" could still be rendered by a "shadow," only survives as metaphorical play (e.g., "the shadow of memory" and "the shadow of the grave," p. 227). "The Unhappiest Man" is of course Kierkegaard.

95. *Aesthetics*, 2:968. We have not yet reached the climax of this process of disintegration, which will arrive with comedy in *Either* as well as in Hegel.

11

Finish

A completely finished work retains no relation to the poetic personality.—Symparenkromenoi

COMPLETENESS

There is no one with soul so dead but he is happy to join in the subversion of the commonplace. However, the excitement wanes when the common place is a philosophical system whose "many drawers" provide a place for every kind of experience. Thus when I moved up from lower-level commonplaces, I acknowledged that today everyone nods understandingly, but without much interest, when Kierkegaard attacks Hegel's system. Not just existentialism but other prejudices—whether positivistic theorizing or Wittgensteinian contempt of theorizing—conspire to disparage the very idea of anything more pretentious than a conceptual scheme, a temporary paradigm. To relieve the banality of Kierkegaard's attack, I risked the yawns that are elicited by close textual analysis in order to elicit as well some of the more specific criteria which Kierkegaard found implicit in Hegel's being systematic.

In following out what happens in *Either* to the "organization" of Hegel's "system of the arts," I have concentrated so far on its fragmentation, its disintegration, as a challenge to his criteria of continuity of development until the system is brought to a conclusion. I have neglected what happens to another criterion that can hardly be separated in Hegel from conclusiveness—the completeness which his system is also organized to achieve. His "system of the arts" is similarly organized to achieve completeness in a shorter run, insofar as this is possible within the sphere of esthetic experience. Eremita's subjective *reorientation* of the esthetic stage is not just the disintegration of the "organization" of this "system of the arts" but even subverts the criterion of completeness itself. Since this is a rather vague and elusive criterion, we must try in the present chapter to track down subordinate criteria that are closely connected with it. Only then shall we be able in the next chapter to discern the motivation that lies behind Eremita's fragmentation of Hegel's system.

442

In the preceding chapter we considered Eremita's handling of the criterion of "plasticity," which was initially in Hegel that version of conclusiveness achieved by classical sculpture. Hegel's extension of this criterion from an *objective* art to the *subjective* art of tragedy helped maintain not only the objective orientation of his dialectic but also its continuity. But it should also be observed that completeness is also at stake: "plasticity" is a criterion of what art should be to be completely art—the "complete harmony between *internal* and *external*." On one hand (ancient) sculpture accorded this harmony complete external representation, in that the harmony is rendered in all three dimensions. On the other hand, insofar as completeness of representation is not satisfied by a specific art (as it is not by sculpture), the dialectical development is impelled onward until more satisfying art forms emerge, just as it is a criterion which eventually exposes "the deficiency" of the "final sphere of art," so that it impels the dialectical development onward and upward until other forms of experience emerge beyond the esthetic.

We have seen that in *Either* "plasticity" has been discredited as a criterion in favor of the shadowy. But another subordinate criterion for completeness of representation is also discredited. Like "plasticity," it is a criterion which derives its relevance in Hegel from the generally *objective* orientation (in Kierkegaard's interpretation) of his dialectic, so that it can be extended analogically even to the *subjective* art of tragedy. If Eremita takes the trouble to discredit it explicitly, this may be partly because it derives from the relatively *objective* art of painting, which does not simply disappear in *Either* like the *objective* art of sculpture but is employed by Eremita as a point of reference for developing his more *subjective*, shadowgraphic method of representation.

That Kierkegaard finds explicit discrediting of the criterion rather crucial for reasons that have to do with his own philosophy is suggested by the fact that his parody of this criterion adds up to the longest sentence which he ever published, although Hegel himself only employs the criterion once, and in a brief passage. Interpreters of Kierkegaard have overlooked the passage in Hegel. Yet it should be helpful in making an accurate assessment of what is specifically at stake in Kierkegaard's opposition of "fragments" of experience, which are so often in the form of "remnants" of Hegel's philosophy, to the criteria of completeness and conclusiveness that Hegel's philosophy would satisfy by becoming a system.

The criterion in question is *Ausmalung*. The term itself ordinarily refers in a neutral sense to the process of "painting" itself. But etymologically the term means "painting out," and Hegel uses the term once as a criterion by lending the prefix a stronger sense, so that "finish" is involved in the technical sense that can be interpreted dialectically as the requirement of carrying "out" completely the externalizing of the internal in the details with which a painting is executed.[1] Hegel ordinarily tries to avoid getting into the details of the more technical arts, and this technical usage does not explicitly occur in his account of painting itself.[2] But *Ausmalung* (like "plasticity") is introduced analogically as a criterion with respect to the treatment of character in tragedy. "An essential requirement," Hegel is arguing, "of the *pathos* of the tragic hero is its *Darstellung* and its *Ausmalung*"—that is (I would paraphrase), its "representation externally and the finish exhibited in the pictorial rendering of details."[3]

REPRESENTATION

Since *Ausmalung* is used here so tersely, we should pause before continuing with the quotation and consider first the reinforcing implications of the accompanying quasi-technical terms *Darstellung* and *pathos*. They gain these implications from the general teleological movement by which art is defined for Hegel as the *internal* arriving at *external* expression: "The aim of art is . . . to bring out in execution [*herauszuarbeiten*] what is inherently rational and to give to it its true outward form [*Aussengestalt*]."[4]

This general objective orientation of Hegel's dialectic has already been dealt with. We have seen that "even our physical life, and still more the world of our spiritual aims and interests, depends on the demand to carry through into objectivity . . . what at the outset was only subjective and inward." But the problem of "objectivity of representation" becomes acute in esthetics when the *objective* arts are left behind and we reach the *subjective* art of dramatic poetry. Here Hegel reformulates the problem as follows:

> Of all the arts poetry alone is lacking in an outward manifestation which is completely real and perceptible. Now drama does not involve . . . our imaginative representation and heart in the expression of an inner and subjective world [as lyric poetry does]; its effort is, rather, to confront us with a present action in its actuality. Thus it would lapse into contradiction with its own aim if it had to remain restricted to the means which poetry as such has at its command. For the action confronting us is entirely affiliated with the inward and in this respect can be completely expressed in words; on the other hand, however, action also moves outward, into external reality, and therefore its portrayal requires the whole man with his bodily existence and behavior. . . . The surrounding scene is either architectural . . . or else outer nature, but both of these are interpreted and carried out pic-

torially [*malerisch*]. Then the sculptural figures [*Bilder*] come on this scene animated . . . ; they make their willing and feeling objective both by expressive recitation and by pictorial play of features and inwardly motivated positions and movements of the rest of the body.[5]

If this sculptural and pictorial performance is to be commended, it is necessary to lament the esthetic inadequacy of the modern experience of reading a drama:

> Unlike the Greeks, we are accustomed to read a drama as well as sometimes to see it actually performed as a work that is a living whole. And this has further misled dramatists themselves into intending their work to some extent merely to be read, in the belief that this has no influence at all on the nature of the composition.

Hegel recommends a strong countermeasure:

> In my opinion, indeed, no play should actually be printed but should remain, more or less as was the case in antiquity, in manuscript for the theater's repertory and get only extremely insignificant circulation. If that happened, then at least we would not see so many dramas appearing which have indeed a well-formed style, fine feelings, excellent reflections, and profound thoughts but which fail precisely in what makes a drama dramatic, namely, action and its living movement.[6]

But Eremita's modern and reflective version of the *Antigone* and his "Shadowgraphs" are designed to be read and reflected upon inwardly, not to be acted out. They deliberately fail with respect to "objectivity of representation" and visual impact. Eremita is redefining, redrawing "boundaries" in esthetics. Reflection reigns supreme. Or, to put the matter more dialectically, the movement of burial by reflection has displaced what Hegel calls action's "living movement," so that the problem of reaching a conclusion by an action, and the "living movement" with which an action can maintain "continuity" with the "environment," may be left intact to the ethical stage.

PATHOS

Now let us turn from the problem of representation to the pathos that is to be represented. The problem of pathos is also posed for Hegel in terms of the movement, which Eremita would subvert, whereby the *subjective* becomes *objective*, the *internal external*. In Greek *pathos* ordinarily meant "suffering" or "passion." So far I have focused on these meanings in Kierkegaard without paying attention to Hegel's usage. We learned from the epigraph of *Either* that Eremita is pitting the "passions," which fragment life because "almost every passion has its own dialectic," against the rationalistic dialectic with which Hegel's philosophy becomes an integrated system.[7] As this opposition develops, there is considerable "crossing of the threads," so that it is almost impossible to follow out more than one thread at a time.

One nearly continuous thread that I did follow out was the disruptive theme of suffering which was announced in the first of the aphorisms of *Either*, which was developed by the Symparenkromenoi, and which will culminate in "A Passion Story" at the religious stage of *Stages on Life's Way*. We have seen that the predominance of this theme was a feature of Eremita's subjectively oriented fragmentation of Hegel's "system of the arts." During the stage in the development of suffering when the Symparenkromenoi took over, suffering became the content that could not be expressed in the form of painting as a relatively *objective* art and so imposed the transition to the *subjective* form of "shadowgraphs," which was itself merely a metaphorical characterization of the even more subjective literary form which was adopted in the essays with this title.

Although *patho*s means "suffering" (*Leiden*) in Greek, as *passio* does in Latin, Hegel forces another meaning on the term. The reason he gives for introducing the Greek term itself into his German text is that "passion [in its modern sense of *Leidenschaft*] almost always carries the implication of meanness or baseness." This is an implication which Eremita is also protesting against, but his protest is more specifically directed against something with which we are now prepared to deal—Hegel's dismissal of merely "subjective pathos" as opposed to an "objective pathos." Hegel explains that "the former is more involved with a contingent and separate particular passion [*gehört mehr der zufälligen besonderen Leidenshaft an*]." And he points out rather disparagingly that "poets who intend to move our *subjective* feelings . . . make special use of this [*subjective*] kind of pathos." He adds, "But however far in that case they may depict [*ausmalen*, which here is employed in its usual neutral sense] personal suffering [*Leiden*] and impetuous passion [*Leidenschaft*] or an unreconciled inner discord of the soul, still the truly human heart is less moved by this than by a *pathos* in which is developed at the same time some objective content."[8]

Here Hegel's handling of *pathos* illustrates his criterion of "objectivity of representation." He finds "objective pathos" characteristic of the "plastic figures" of Greek tragedy—"stable figures who simply are what they are without any inner conflict." In introducing "objective pathos," Hegel cited Antigone's character as an example, and the distinction which Eremita further develops in sketching his modern Antigone is drawn by Hegel as distinguishing the modern tragic hero from his ancient counterpart:

Since no stable aim animates his soul, . . . he may vacillate inconclusively [*unentschlossen*]. . . . From this vacillation the plastic figures of Greek drama are far removed; for them the link between the subject and what he wills as his object remains indissoluble. What impels them to action is precisely an ethically justified pathos which they assert . . . with solid and well-formulated [*gebildeten*] objectivity of language.[9]

This modern inconclusiveness we have encountered as characteristic of reflective suffering in "Shadowgraphs," for it is taken by Kierkegaard to be characteristic of reflection itself.

AUSMALUNG

We shall soon find an illustration of the difference between the "solid and well-formulated objectivity" that Hegel commends in the use of language and Kierkegaard's *modus loquendi*. First, however, we can at last examine the criterion of *Ausmalung* as another requirement which is posed by Hegel in terms of the movement, which Eremita would subvert, whereby the *subjective* becomes *objective*; the *internal external*. It is a requirement with respect to the completeness of (external) representation, and it is backed up by further consideration of the (*inner*) *pathos* to be represented:

> An essential requirement of . . . *pathos* is its representation [*Darstellung*] and finish [*Ausmalung*]. And indeed a soul must be rich in itself, if it is to turn its inner wealth into pathos, and not one which can remain merely concentrated within itself but is able to find expression outside itself and elevate itself to complete formulation [*sich zur ausgebildeten Gestalt erhebt*].

In other words, if *pathos* were merely the "subjective pathos" which we have seen that Hegel disparages as involving "a contingent and separate passion," it could not elevate itself by an *Aufhebung* to the "complete formulation" which "finish" entails with respect to the execution of details. It could only remain, according to Hegel, "compressed in itself and externalized only aphoristically."[10] It is this specific limitation of Hegel's which seems to have been on the mind of the spokesman for the Symparenkromenoi when he identified his "association" as composed of those who "think and speak aphoristically."[11] We can accordingly approach his subversion of "finish" as a procedure to which he opposes his own procedure as aphoristic as well as shadowgraphic.

In picking out his subversion of "finish," I am not restricting our attention to a mere detail that has only to do with the execution of details. As I have already admitted, there is no more tedious banality in the history of modern philosophy than the reiteration by historians that

Kierkegaard's philosophy is a protest against Hegel's system. Instead of contenting myself with this blanket protest, I am taking advantage of the agility we have acquired in climbing levels while respecting Kierkegaard's criterion of *konsekvens*, so that we can now descend to the lower level of what might seem merely a stylistic issue without losing our sense of its implicit relevance to the whole. For we now see that the criterion of completeness itself is at stake at this low level, as it is at the higher level of the sytsem as a whole, and that this criterion involves at both levels (as well as at intervening levels) the characteristic movement of the Hegelian dialectic whereby the contradiction between *subjective* and *objective*, *internal* and *external*, is to be transcended.[12]

BABELING

Although Hegel's own reference to "finish" is terse, the symparenkro-menous attack on "finish" is central to the longest sentence in *Either*, and the prefatory clauses alert us to its repercussions for contradicting Hegel's system as a whole:

> Since it is contrary to what our society strives for to produce interconnected, coherent works [*sammenhængende arbeider*] or larger wholes, since it is not our intent to work upon a Tower of Babel which God in his righteousness can descend on [*stige ned*] and destroy, since we, conscious of the fact that this confusion of tongues happened rightly, recognize. . . .[13]

Here as elsewhere the largest "whole" in question is Hegel's philosophical system, which is to be deprived of its pretensions (as was the Tower of Babel) to reach to the highest level, thereby usurping the place of re-ligion. But since Kierkegaard regards this philosophical system as "es-thetic," the "blow" is being aimed at one of Hegel's "larger wholes," his "system of the arts." Up until now we might have felt that one of the "arts" embraced in this system was being entirely neglected—architecture. Now it may be that the system in its completeness is being encapsulated, for the Tower of Babel itself is a specimen of architecture (Hegel's *first* art form), but the fate of the tower and its builders also provides (as *objective* references in Eremita's dialectic so frequently do) a metaphori-cal reference to the *subjective* genre of linguistic expression, including poetry, which is Hegel's *last* form and which he locates as "the opposite of architecture."[14] The Tower of Babel is a metaphor for "the confusion of tongues," and this metaphor keeps recurring in Kierkegaard, since he discerns in Hegel's system the confusion of religious with philosophical language.[15] Thus the divine intervention envisaged is opposed to the movement of *Aufhebung* with which Hegel constructs this system: a *stige* is a ladder; the verb *stige ned* means the opposite of "climb up" à la Climacus and probably suggests a divine precedent for the spokesman now to "descend" (with us following) to a low-level issue involving the use of language. Similarly, "destroy" asserts the negative, contradictory moment of an *Aufhebung* and suggests a divine precedent for the subversion of Hegel's system.

At the same time, piling up language in so long a sentence is contradictory; this *modus loquendi* is inconsistent with the content—the disavowal of any "intent to work upon a Tower of Babel."[16] After all, the spokesman babbles on for 250 words, even though he is attacking, on the grounds announced in the prefatory clauses I have already cited, the completeness, the conclusiveness, sought by "finish":

> We . . . recognize as characteristic of all human striving in its truth that it is fragmentary, and that it is precisely this which distinguishes it from Nature's infinite coherence; that the wealth of an individual consists precisely in the proficiency with which he *squanders the fragmentary*, . . . not the irksome, *meticulously detailed workmanship* with which the *execution* is carried out. . . .[17]

Let me interrupt the spokesman again, for although we are less than halfway through his long sentence, we have not only reached the brunt of his attack on "finish" but also realize that the sentence as a whole is in its external stylistic form a parody of "finish" as an external stylistic form. Instead of being "compressed and aphoristic" (the style which we have seen that Hegel condemns but which we have been led to expect the Symparenkromenoi would find congenial), the sentence is an exhibition of "finish," becoming "meticulously detailed" in the way its "execution" of the attack on "finish" is being "carried out." Evidence for this meticulousness with which the spokesman is refusing to be "compressed and aphoristic" is the detail of exactly 250 words. He must have counted.

ACCUMULATION

I shall return later to other features of this parody of "finish," but the feature which is relevant now, in order to understand the claim just made "that the wealth of an individual consists precisely in the proficiency with which he squanders the fragmentary," is the subversion of a metaphor which Hegel employed when he required the tragic hero to have "a soul" which "must be rich in itself, if it is to turn its inner wealth into pathos." We have dealt with *pathos* itself already and have begun to deal with "finish" as a requirement for the completeness which *pathos* is to be expressed externally, but we have not yet dealt with the "wealth" which must first be turned into *pathos*.

Hegel is fond of the metaphor of "wealth," which is still another version of his criterion of completeness. As our first example, let us consider Hegel's most famous starting point, even though it has to do with what is in a sense outer "wealth" rather than the "inner wealth" the tragic hero has accumulated by the time this much later stage in the dialectic is reached. Earlier we saw that the "doubt" which was Eremita's starting point in *Either* was a dialectical duplication of the Cartesian doubt that had been the starting point for modern philosophy in Kierkegaard's as well as Hegel's interpretation of its history. Now let us consider Hegel's own starting point in the *Phenomenology*. The evidence of the senses is initially admitted, and then a reversal takes place which is comparable to the Cartesian doubt:

> The concrete content of sense certainty allows it to appear immediately as the richest knowledge, indeed as knowledge of infinite wealth— a wealth to which we can as little find any limit, when we traverse its extent in space and time, where that content is spread out before us, as when we take a fragment [*Stück*] from the abundance [*Fülle*] and by dividing it up seek to penetrate it. . . . This certainty, however, is in fact the most abstract and the poorest truth.[18]

Hegel has wrapped up the Cartesian starting point with interplay between the metaphor of wealth and its opposite.

The metaphor may attract Hegel because he is a bourgeois philosopher for whom experience, like wealth, can be accumulated. Thus what I previously described as the fitting together of his system can be redescribed as a process of accumulation. The redescription has the advantage of suggesting the continuity of a cumulative process. The metaphor of "wealth" enhances this advantage, for it lends itself to the *bifocal* employment which the citation from the *Phenomenology* illustrates. Like (sense) experience, wealth can be divided up into its components or can refer to the sum total. The retention in ordinary usage of the singular "experience" implies some considerable continuity between successive particular experiences, permitting their integration into a coherent whole. The process of integration in Hegel is of course a process of "internalization." Sense experience is "recollected" to become "imaginative representation," etc. Somewhat similarly, though at a much higher level, the tragic hero achieves integrity: the process of "internalization" is carried to a juncture at which the "wealth" of his accumulated experience can be described as "inner wealth."

At a still higher level, the prospect of accumulating and integrating experiences, including the esthetic experience of the way a tragic hero accumulates and integrates his experiences, is a motivation for Hegel's sustaining the application of his dialectic continuously through successive stages. These can accordingly be arranged in the dialectically appropriate succession by virtue of the increasing richness of the experiences accumulated. Thus when Hegel arranges the arts in the succession of stages with which we are familiar, a metaphorical rationale for the arrangement is that "architecture is most impoverished generally in the expression of its content, sculpture is richer, while painting and music are most widely extended in their scope." The rationale itself is *bifocal*: the point of view of a "climb toward ideality" (the internalizing movement) is combined with the point of view of "an increase in the many sided particularization of the outer materials."[19]

The dialectical combination of these points of view is assumed when the symparenkromenous attack on "larger wholes" becomes associated in the long sentence with the attack on "finish" as a procedure for handling stylistic details that does justice to the *pathos* into which the tragic hero has turned his "inner wealth." But although Kierkegaard's dialectic, like Hegel's, is sustained through successive stages of experience, "wealth" of experience is to be disposed of in the opposite way. In Kierkegaard's dialectic discontinuities are to be accentuated instead of continuity; thus when the symparenkromenous individual lives, thinks, and speaks aphoristically, he does not continuously accumulate "wealth" of experience but "squanders" it in "separate," "fragmentary" experiences, as has been illustrated by the essays in *Either* which take the different arts up separately, rather than integrating them, as in Hegel, into a coherent system, as well as by the subversion of the criteria which control in Hegel the development of this system.

STORAGE

Now that we have brought out the general implications of these criteria, we can return to the particular details of *Ausmalung*. In the fashion in which Hegel envisages the tragic hero disposing of his wealth, there is a contradiction which is at once transcended:

> The essential requirement of . . . *pathos* is its [external] representation and the [external] finish exhibited in the painting of details. And indeed a soul must be rich in itself [*in sich*], if it is to turn its inner wealth into pathos [*in ihr Pathos den Reichtum ihres Inneren einlegt*]. . . .

Hegel has employed the verb *einlegen* to describe the way in which the wealth is turned into *pathos*. I was unable to translate this verb literally. *Einlegen* means to "lay in," "enclose," "store up," "deposit," "earn," and

these meanings are of course consistent with the implications of accumulating "wealth" of experience.[20] The metaphor is an entirely traditional
description of psychological accumulation. The imagination had been
traditionally the "storehouse" of images initially acquired through perception, though one novelty of Hegel's bourgeois psychology of experience
(or psychology of bourgeois experience) is the detail with which it elaborates on acquisitive metaphors.[21]

Since Hegel has emphasized with respect to *pathos* that the "wealth" is
"in" the soul, and since *einlegen* with its prefix meaning "in" comes after
"inner," the overall impression has been given that turning this "inner
wealth into pathos" is an inward-turning movement, which as such would
contradict the "essential requirement" of *pathos* that it be provided with
(external) representation and exhibited (externally) in complete detail.
But the contradiction is transcended when the rest of the sentence supplies a final impression of a soul that is so rich in its accumulation of "inner wealth" that it can well afford a lavish outward display of this wealth.

> Thus the "soul" in question is not one which can remain merely
> concentrated within itself [*nicht nur konzentriert und intensiv bleibt*]
> but is able to find expression outside itself [*sich extensiv aussert*] and
> elevate itself to complete formulation. [*sich zur ausgebildeten Gestalt
> erhebt*].

This pronouncement might well have caught Kierkegaard's attention because once again the contradiction between the internal and the external
is played up and then transcended—between the "within itself," the "inner," the "laying in," the *intensiv* on one hand and the *extensiv* on the
other, with the *aus* of *aussert* and *ausgebildeten*, renewing the outward
orientation of *Ausmalung* itself.

At the end of the chapter on the character of the tragic hero, Hegel
sums up the argument we have been examining, while adding "fullness"
as a supplementary metaphor for completeness: "Above all, it must be . . .
the pathos of a soul that is rich and full, whose inner individual world
the pathos so pervades [*durchdringt*] that its pervasiveness no less than
the pathos itself comes to be represented [*zur Darstellung kommt*]."[22] This
metaphor of "fullness" the spokesman for the Symparenkromenoi undertakes to counter with the "finite striving" which he is opposing to Hegel's
system:

> Our society requires at every single meeting a renewal and rebirth,
> to the end of its inner activity may be renewed by a new description of
> its productivity. Let us then describe our intent as an effort at frag-
> mentary striving or in the art of writing posthumous papers. A com-
> pletely finished [*fuldstaendigt fuldfort*—the double reference to "full"

does not come through in the translation] work retains no relation to the poetic personality; with posthumous papers, one continually feels, because of their being broken off, the desultoriness, a prompting to poeticize about the personality. . . . The art then is to produce artistically the same effect, the same appearance of artlessness and contingency, the same anacoluthic flight of thought. . . .[23]

The opposition to fullness is largely conveyed with metaphors for discontinuity—"fragmentary" and "posthumous"—which we examined earlier with reference to Antigone and the Symparenkromenoi.

ANACOLOUTHON

The stress on discontinuity is also conveyed with new metaphors. *Desultorisk* is not Danish but Kierkegaard's importation, and it reinforces "broken off," since it refers in its etymological sense to something which has "sprung apart." Similarly, the etymological sense of *anacoluthon* is "not following," so that the term is a denial, at least overtly, that the criterion of *konsekvens* is being respected. It refers to a disruption in the continuity of the stylistic construction.

The long sentence preceding was indeed an "anacoluthic flight of thought," as we can see if we pick it up at the juncture at which "finish" is dismissed, in order to discover the stylistic alternative which is next envisaged:

not the irksome, meticulously detailed workmanship with which the execution is carried out, or the prolonged apprehension, but the production and enjoyment of the glimpsed transitoriness which for the producer involves something more than thorough execution, since it is the appearance of the Idea, and which for the recipient involves something more, since its fulguration awakens his own productivity—since, I repeat, all such sustained execution and prolonged apprehension is contrary to the intent of our society (and indeed, since even the period just read must almost be regarded as a deliberate attack upon the interjectory style, in which the Idea breaks out without breaking through—a style which in our society has an official status), then, after having called attention to the fact that my procedure still cannot be called subversive, since the connection which holds this period together is so loosened [*det baand, der sammenholder denne periode, er saa lost*] that the intermediary clauses stick out in a sufficiently aphoristical and self-assertive fashion that I shall merely recall that my style has made an effort to appear what it is not—revolutionary.[24]

"Prolonged apprehension" (*opfattelse*—Hegel's *Auffassung*) is opposed by "glimpsed transitoriness," which reminds us of the unsteady vision which we would have, according to Heidegger, if we did not dim it down and the "flickering" character our experience would display, according to Sartre, were it not for our *esprit de sérieux*. We are reminded too that in *Either* itself the aphorisms were "provisional glimpses of what the longer essays develop more connectedly," as we saw to be the case when the "glimpse" of *Don Giovanni* developed into the essay on "The Musical Erotic."[25] But now we have to recognize once again that in opposition to the opera as an "interconnected" or "coherent whole," the significance of the "aphoristical" is being renewed in "The Ancient Tragic." The "glimpsed transitoriness" is opposed not only to the progressive illumination which "prolonged apprehension" is supposed to yield in Hegel but also to "sustained execution" (i.e., *Ausmalung*). Here the progressive externalization of the *internal* in Hegel is once more subverted: the "glimpsed transitoriness . . . contains something more than sustained execution," since it is "the appearance of the Idea" that is glimpsed, whereas the "sustained execution" lingers with the *external*.

At this point the "flight of thought" becomes anacoluthic. Although the external issue of style would seem to have been disposed of with the criticism of "finish," the style of composition that has been employed in this criticism becomes itself a matter for commentary: "and indeed, since even the period just read must almost be regarded as a deliberate attack upon the interjectory style, in which the Idea breaks out without breaking through—a style which in our society has official status. . . ." The style consciousness of this self-commentary is probably a further illustration and parody of "finish." The ostensible argument is that the periodic or continuous style, which has been employed up to this interruption, contradicts the interjectory style, which should have been employed to be consistent with the fragmentary, glimpsed, transitory character of the experiential content that has been endorsed.

DISINTEGRATION

But the attack is not simply a feigned one on the interjectory style but a parody of Hegel's attack on the interjectory style. For Hegel had attacked not only the aphoristic style but also "interjections," on the ground that "the individual spirit, whose pathos is represented, must be a spirit which is full to running over [*erfüllter*] and able to express itself expansively [*sich auszubreiten und auszusprechen*]"—that is, in a fashion which could be rendered adequately only by *Ausmalung*.[26] What the spokesman is ultimately attacking is not Hegel's style but the continuity of development achieved by the movement of *Aufhebung* when it transcends the contradiction between the *internal* and the external in the fashion which

Ausmalung would exemplify. In Hegel the continuity achieved is a transition (*Übergang*) which is a breakthrough (*Durchgang*); in Kierkegaard the "Idea" whose appearance is glimpsed "breaks out without breaking through" (*bryder ud, uden at komme til gjennembrud*), and the interjectory style finds here its justification for an aphorism as an "outburst" (*udbrud*).[27]

The long sentence winds up by retracting the self-criticism:

> after having called attention to the fact that my procedure still cannot be called subversive, since the connection which holds this period together is so loosened that the intermediary clauses stick out in a sufficiently aphoristical and self-assertive fashion that I shall merely recall that my style has made an effort to appear what it is not—revolutionary.

In short, the style has not been the periodic, continuous style that it appears to be, for the interruption to make this charge has itself been anacoluthic. But this retraction merely renews the attack on Hegel's philosophy where the movement of *Aufhebung* reestablishes continuity and coherence at a higher level when a connection is recognized which holds together what had previously appeared separated and contradictory at the lower level. The "breakthrough" is the "resolution" (*Auslösung*) of a contradiction. Just as in the earlier clause, the Hegelian metaphorical movement of "loosening" is now borrowed, but without the prefix retaining its force. For it is no longer the "resolution" of contradiction which is in question, as in Hegel, but its opposite—the "loosening" of connections that leaves intact contradictions which threaten disintegration.[28] With this loosening the continuity is interrupted, and the style becomes obtrusively "aphoristical." If stylistic appearance is then discounted in the last clause, it is not only because the moment of "resolution" in Hegel is a discounting of some previous appearance of contradiction but also because it is not (as it might appear) the stylistic procedure of the Symparenkromenoi which has been subverted; what is still being subverted is the procedure of *Aufhebung* and *Auslösung* by which Hegel composes "interconnected" or "coherent works" and arrives at "greater wholes."

METAPHOR

Since we have devoted so much attention to the metaphorical details of this long sentence, there may be some compensation in recognizing that they do not simply constitute a parody of "finish." We have seen that in Kierkegaard the different conception of the relation between the *internal* and the *external*, the *subjective* and the *objective*, imposes a procedure of representation which differs from Hegel's "objectivity of representation" and that the difference was implicit in Kierkegaard's adoption of "Shadowgraphs" in lieu of painting, which in Hegel was the transtional art form that assured the continuity between the *external, objective* arts and the *internal, subjective* arts. The difference can be further illustrated if we examine more closely the particular metaphors Kierkegaard employs as adapted to his shadowgraphic procedure of representation. For this procedure is dialectical, and I noted earlier that the characteristic movement of a dialectic may be exhibited by the particular metaphors the dialectician favors. "Shadowgraphic" itself, as a metaphor for literary "sketches," we were able to contrast with the criterion of "plasticity" that Hegel extended metaphorically to the treatment of character in Greek tragedy, where the "figures" display such three-dimensional "solidity" that the distinction between *internal* and *external* can hardly be intruded, any more than it can in Greek sculpture.

But there is an additional contrast to be worked out before we review other particular metaphors Kierkegaard actually employs. Recall how the shadowgraphic procedure of representation operates: what the spokesman for the Symparenkromenoi proposed to "draw to the attention of" (*drag frem*) his audience was not the external as such (a shadowgraph makes "by itself no impression," unlike a painting); the inner "picture" or "image" can be represented "through the external," but only when he "draws aside" (*drage . . . tilside*) the external so that his audience is not "deceived" (*bedrage*) by the external or does not continue to remain deceived but, instead, comes to acknowledge the contradiction between the *internal* and the *external* that holds of reflective grief.

Now this shadowgraphic dialectic not only subverts the pictorial procedure of *Ausmalung*, which Hegel recommends as a literary procedure, but also explains Kierkegaard's favoring metaphors as such rather than similes or comparisons, which are preferred by Hegel. The transposition which a metaphor involves "is always," Hegel explains, an "interruption of the continuity in the process of imaginative representation and a constant scattering [*eine Unterbrechung des Vorstellungsganges und eine stete Zerstreuung*], because it arouses and brings together images which do not immediately belong to the matter in hand and its meaning and therefore draw the mind away. . . ." He accordingly praises the Greeks for not indulging "too frequently in metaphors."[29]

I have stressed the existentialist indulgence in metaphors. Our most recent example is the parade of metaphors in the long sentence and the following paragraph. In the spokesman's own terms, he squanders where Hegel would accumulate without significant interruption, and the reference to squandering *(ødselhed)* may echo Hegel's "scattering" as well as the earlier destruction *(ødelseggelse)* of the Tower of Babel,[30] which was itself a metaphor for Hegel's system.

Now we can consider some of the particular metaphors the spokesman employs in the long sentence and following paragraph: "burial alive," "posthumous," "fragmentary," "broken off," "interjectory," "breaks out," "sprung apart," "not following," "stick out," "subversive," "revolutionary." These metaphors characteristically have to do with a particularly disruptive "interruption of the continuity" in Hegel's terms—with a "dislocation," as I originally described the spatial metaphor implicit in *ex-sistence.*

The contrast with Hegel can perhaps be pursued a little further in a way that supplements the contrast between the shadowgraphic procedure and Hegel's procedure of pictorial "finish." What is instanced by most of the metaphors just listed is the harsh disruption of relatively stark spatial relations Hegel visualizes metaphors in a smoother fashion which analogizes them to painting, describing them as "pictorial, depictive, and illustrative" *(malerisch schildernd und versanschaulichend).* But the contrast is more easily brought out by Hegel's preference for similes and comparisons over metaphors. Where Eremita eliminates epic as the relatively *objective* form of poetry, sculpture as an *objective* form of art, and painting in favor of shadowgraphs, Hegel extols epic similes as "pictures [*Gebilden*] which Homer sets before us like works of sculpture, peaceful [*ruhende*] and plastic, designed for contemplative [*theoretisch*] reflection."[31]

REPOSE

When Kierkegaard atttributes an esthetic point of view to Hegel's philosophy as a whole, he is thinking of it as contemplative reflection which fails to confront the ethical problem of action. I have been urging that relations within esthetics as well as well as the relations between esthetics and ethics are altered in Kierkegaard. Thus even if we remain within the scope of esthetics, the same contrast can be drawn. Hegel's esthetics is a dialectic where at the third moment

> the highest purity of the ideal can . . . only consist in the fact that the gods, Christ, Apostles, saints, penitents, and the devout are set before us in their blessed repose [*Ruhe*] and satisfaction, . . . untouched by the world with the stress and affliction of its manifold complications, struggles, and oppositions. In this sense it is especially sculpture and painting which have found forms [*Gestalten*] that are ideal for individual

gods, as well as for Christ as savior of the world, for individual apostles and saints.[32]

Even though my original reference was to Hegel's discussion of epic similes, while the present reference is "especially" to "sculpture and painting," the contrast can be carried over to the case of tragedy, where we have seen that the third moment is a moment of repose for the audience: "Only as far as unhappiness and suffering are not the outcome but the satisfaction of the spirit, . . . only then can our attitude be truly at peace ethically [*sittlich beruhigt*]." But the Symparenkromenoi do not attain this peace, and we have heard their spokesman appeal to the *Laokoon* to distinguish from the "repose" that (visual) "art expresses" the "movement" which "poetry expresses." With the brides, their "grief will find no rest [*ro*] but will be compelled to wander back and forth in their reflection."[33]

Hegel's interpretation of comparisons accords briefly to the characters in a tragedy the kind of repose he reserves eventually to the audience. When they undertake a comparison, they are transcending passion and suffering in the process of representing it:

> While feeling lingers because it is immersed in its object and cannot get free of it, . . . comparisons have the aim of showing that the individual has not merely plunged himself immediately in his definite situation, feeling, or passion but, as a high and noble nature, also transcends [*darübersteht*] all this and can loosen and detach himself from it. Passion restricts the soul and *imprisons* it in itself, narrows it and concentrates it within limits, and therefore makes it inarticulate. . . . But greatness of mind, force of spirit, elevates [*erhebt*] itself above such limitations, so that the spirit soars in fine, tranquil peace [*Ruhe*] over the particular pathos by which it is moved. This freezing of the soul is what similes express. . . . It is only a deep composure [*Gefasstheit*] and strength which is able to objectify even its suffering, to compare itself with something other, and thereby to contemplate itself in the alien object confronting it.[34]

In contrast, the spokesman for the Symparenkromenoi regularly employs the metaphor of the imprisoned or captive soul in representing the predicament of the "brides of grief."[35] They have become too wedded reflexively to their grief to objectify it for the contemplative purpose that Hegel commends.

Only indirectly through shadowgraphs can their grief be glimpsed. And when the metaphor of captivity is extended from the "brides" to their audience, the spokesman apologizes, "Too long, perhaps, I have kept your attention captive with these pictures."[36] Any prospect of understanding the "grief" of the "brides" can only be reflexive, as the final reflection of "Shadowgraphs" reminds us: "Only he who has been bitten by a serpent knows the suffering of having been bitten by a serpent."[37]

It is not feasible to survey the various comparisons that Hegel cites in the hope that we might thereby determine his particular preference more exactly and contrast it with the kind of metaphor which we have seen is preferred by the Symparenkromenoi. But a particular comparison can be placed along side of the final reflection in "Shadowgraphs," since it is the one Shakespeare's Cleopatra undertakes when she is bitten by the asp. More important, it leads up to Hegel's final reflection on the general dialectical function of comparisons. I cite the passage in the setting provided by Hegel's commentary and conclusion:

> In this objectifying and comparative expression resides the peace and composure [*Ruhe und Fassung*] of the character in himself through which he calms the suffering of his own downfall [*Untergang*]. This is the way Cleopatra speaks when she has already put the deadly asp to her breast:
>
> Peace, peace,
Dost thou not see my baby at my breast,
That sucks the nurse asleep?
As sweet as balm, as soft as air, as gentle.
>
> The bite of the serpent relaxes her limbs so tenderly that Death is himself deceived and supposes himself to be Sleep. This image [*Bild*] may well be accepted as itself a valid image of the mild and pacifying [*beruhigende*] nature of such comparisons.[38]

There is no relaxation, no pacification in "Shadowgraphs," only more reflexive and more restless suffering.

REDUPLICATION

The particular stylistic details to which I have tracked down Kierkegaard's opposition to Hegel can be added to the evidence assembled earlier that existentialism is not reducible (as it has tended to become in Anglo-American interpretations) to an ethics—to the conclusiveness with which the individual should choose and act.[39] Existentialism is taken up with the *modus loquendi* as well as the *modus agendi*. For existential reflexivity is consciousness not only of one's responsibility for one's choices and actions (such an emphasis has been a commonplace of philosophy) but also of the responsibility one should take for one's thinking as actualized in one's words. As Climacus explains in the *Postscript*,

> the reduplicated presence of the thought in every word, in every parenthetical expression, in the digression, in the unguarded moment of developing an image or a comparison: this is what must be watched, if

anyone wishes to take the trouble to find out whether an individual is lying or not—provided one first watches oneself.

"Reduplication" here is the reflexive responsibility for "including in an expression as its content a consciousness of what the expression directly expresses."[40] The repetition of the prefix *ud* ("out") in the noun "expression" (*udsagnet*) and in the verb "expresses" (*udsiger*) plays up their external *orientation* to bring out the need for a concomitant "internalizing" or "recollective" movement on the part of consciousness, in order to maintain the "presence" of the "thought" conveyed by the "expression."[41]

Even the expression "existential" itself, we saw at the outset, has become irresponsibly used—a casual commonplace. Confronted by such commonplaces, this introduction to existentialism has become a higher-level "recollective" and "recapitulative" reintroduction. What eventually had to be brought to the fore was existentialism's explanation for the irresponsible use of expressions—man's dislocation "outside" of himself. The specific process by which the dislocation of the *modus loquendi* comes about we have watched Heidegger analyze by reference to the "outspokenness" (*Ausgesprochenheit*) of language, whereby it tends to become "talk." This analysis prepares for the *reversal* that would rescue the individual from the commonplace and restore a sense of the responsibility that he is to take for his *modus loquendi*. My *recapitulative* interpretation has attempted to watch for the thought present even in the development of images and comparisons, on the assumption that the existentialist can permit himself no unguarded moment. Thus Heidegger displays scruples comparable to Kierkegaard's with respect to the use of language; he demands "rigor of thought, carefulness of statement, frugality with words," and his own way of posing and meeting this demand is with an image and a comparison:

> Thought by its speaking [*Sagen*] leaves inconspicuous furrows in language. They are more inconspicuous than the furrows which the farmer's slow tread traces through a field.[42]

In Sartre too we find that the *modus loquendi* is compared with a *modus agendi*: "To speak is to act." Sartre's emphasis on choice and responsibility for one's actions has been reemphasized in three dozen Anglo-American expositions, but without attaching sufficient significance to the fact that the choices he has actually expounded in detail are the choices of writers (Baudelaire's, Genet's, Flaubert's, Sartre's own), including in each case the reflexive choice to become a writer, for (Sartre explains) "a writer is someone who has chosen a certain mode of higher-level action that could be termed 'action by disclosure.' "[43] But this mode of action brings into view a new responsibility of the writer—his responsibility toward his reader.

Notes

1. During the history of painting the criterion of "finish" has varied considerably as to what it concretely requires. In Hegel's dialectic one would guess that it refers to both content and form—i.e., to both the provision of details and the meticulousness with which they are executed. The following could be taken as examples: "The most fleeting appearance of the sky, the time of day, the lighting of the trees, the appearances and reflections of clouds, waves, lochs, streams; the shimmering and glittering of wine in a glass, a flash of the eye, a momentary look or smile, etc." (*Aesthetics*, 2:813–14).

2. Hegel does employ a rough synonym which refers more technically to "finish"— *Fleiss*. He is discussing paintings which achieve their effect "by the exactitude with which the execution [*Ausführung*] of every smallest detail is carried out. Yet this is a matter not of assiduity of composition but of spiritually *rich* finish, which *completes* each detail by itself and yet retains the *whole connected* and *flowing together*" (ibid.). I have italicized criteria which are associated with *Fleiss* and which we shall see Kierkegaard is eager to subvert. It is because *Fleiss* is restricted to painting that Hegel employs *Ausmalung* instead in the passage I previously quoted, where he is discussing "the beauty of art" in general and canvassing opera, epic, comedy, and tragedy. If he employs a metaphor from painting, it is because emphasis on "particular detail" is more obvious in painting. See chap. 10, n. 86 above, where Hegel extols painting in this respect.

3. *Aesthetics*, 1:234. Knox translates *Ausmalung* as "graphic amplification," which has a certain appropriateness in Kierkegaard's interpretation of the procedure as rhetorical. This appropriateness is of course just a coincidence.

4. Ibid., p. 289. Sartre is as contemptuous of "finish" as we shall see Kierkegaard is, but in a somewhat different sense, though he also associates it with objectivity of representation (without any allusion to Hegel's treatment of this topic). Such objectivity he ties in, as does Kierkegaard, with the artist's elimination of any reflexive reference. On one hand "Titian applied himself to finishing [*lécher*] his painting, scraping and polishing with lacquers and varnish, sparing no effort to conceal his work" (*Situations*, p. 45; cf. the contempt for "varnish" in *Nausea*, p. 194 above). On the other hand Tintoretto "left too much evidence of himself in his work." The Venetians "wanted painting which was licked, finished [*du léché, du fini*], above all else impersonal. . . . Venice imposed upon her painters the Puritan maxim: *no personal comments*" (ibid., p. 47; the italicized phrase is in the language of Puritanism—English).

5. *Aesthetics*, 2:1181.

6. Ibid., pp. 1183, 1184–85.

7. See p. 236 above.

8. *Aesthetics*, 1:232; 2:1173.

9. Ibid., 2:1209, 1214.

10. Ibid., 1:234; 2:1173.

11. See p. 281 above.

12. Expositors of Hegel have worried about the criterion of completeness as it applies to the system as a whole (e.g., to its closure when the end of history is reached) without attention to its implications for lower levels or earlier stages.

13. *Either*, p. 149.

14. *Aesthetics*, 2:968. The symbolic stature of the Tower of Babel in Kierkegaard is due as much to Hegel as to the Bible. Hegel starts out his treatment of "symbolic

architecture" (the first form of architecture, as architecture itself is the first form of art) with the Tower of Babylon. Hegel assigns to its construction the function (to which Kierkegaard would take strenuous exception) of symbolizing social concord: " 'What is holy?' asks Goethe . . . , and he answers, 'That which binds together [zusammenbindet] many souls.' In this sense we may say that the holy with the aim of this concord [Zusammenhalt], and as this concord, has been the first content of independent architecture. The readiest example of this is provided by the story of the Tower of Babylon. . . . An enormous architectural work was erected; it was built in common, and the aim and content of the work was at the same time the community of those who constructed it" (ibid., 2:638). When Kirkegaard refers to the Tower of Babel, he probably has in mind a contrast with the Symparenkromenoi, "who live aphorismenoi and segregati, . . . without community with humanity" (Either, p. 218).

15. We have recognized that Kierkegaard's dialectic is designed to clarify "confusion" (see chap. 7, n. 14 above) with respect to the modus loquendi. As a spatial representation he regularly employs the Tower of Babel (e.g., Postscript, pp. 229, 240). Consider his earliest (1836) elaboration of this theme: "At the moment there is nothing of which we are as afraid as the total bankruptcy toward which the whole of Europe seems to be going, and so we forget what is far more dangerous, the seemingly inescapable spiritual bankruptcy which is at the door—a confusion of tongues far more dangerous than the Babylonian confusion (taken as a representation) or the confusion of nations and dialects which followed upon the Babylonian attempt of the Middle Ages—a confusion in language itself, a revolt and, most dangerous of all, the revolt of words themselves, which, torn loose from the control of man, rush upon one another in despair. . . . One particular idea seems to have become the fixed idea of the whole age —to have gone beyond the man ahead. . . . We always see people leap frogging over others. 'Because of the immanent negativity of the concept,' I heard a Hegelian say to me the other day, as he shook me by the hand and prepared to take a run and jump— when I see a man busily running along the street, I am sure that in his joy he is shouting across to me, 'I have gone beyond' " (Papirer, I A 328). Kierkegaard is mocking the Hegelian word Übergang (see chap. 10, n. 15 above), for this transitional movement is involved in the confusion of theological and philosophical language. The entry ends with the program to "win back the lost power and meaning of words, just as Luther won back for his age the concept of faith." This comparison is prepared for by the earlier allusion to "the Babylonian attempt of the Middle Ages."

16. In the process of fragmentation, discrepancy between form and content emerges along with discontinuity between stages (see p. 283 above and n. 28, this chapter). I cannot trace the emergence of the discrepancy here. Let Climacus's comment suffice on Philosophical Fragments, where the form is fairy-tale but the content Christian doctrine: "My peculiar procedure . . . consists first and foremost and decisively in this contrast of the form" (Postscript, p. 246).

17. Either, pp. 149–50; my italics. "Fragmentary" reminds us of the subtitles of "The Ancient Tragic" and Either/Or itself, which are obviously conceived in opposition to the unity of Hegel's system: "Truth is truly anything but an outcome of a unified striving. . . . The only way there can be any possibility of coming to the truth is for each of us to become separate individuals—social unity [foreningen] is nothing but untruth" (Papirer, XI¹ A 438).

18. Phenomenology, p. 58. I shall be considering shortly the criterion of "abundance" or "fullness."

19. Aesthetics, 2:966.

20. Eremita's reference to the "rich content" of the desk and possibly even putting his money in one of its "many drawers' 'may allude to Hegel.

21. See p. 263 above.

22. Aesthetics, 1:244.

23. Either, p. 150.

24. Ibid., p. 150.

25. See pp. 261, 264 above.

26. *Aesthetics*, 1:235.

27. See p. 261 above. For Hegel's dislike of "outbursts," see also *Aesthetics*, 2:1173.

28. This "loosening" of connections plays etymologically with Hegel's concept of *Auslösung* and ensures discontinuity where Hegel had sought continuity. For "resolution" is ultimately achieved in Hegel by recognizing closer interconnections than have previously emerged. But when *Stages* is reached as a recapitulation of *Either/Or*, the pseudonym is not even an editor like Eremita, who encloses—like a nest of boxes—the authors of the essays within himself, but merely a "bookbinder." In other words, the dialectical advance beyond the treatment of stages in *Either/Or* (see p. 283 above) is that the connections between the essays he has collected are loosened. Thus when Judge William, the ethicist of *Or*, reappears in *Stages*, "he expresses himself essentially and nowhere takes into account what according to the plan of the work he cannot be supposed to know" (*Postscript*, p. 264). He does not know about what has transpired during the esthetic stage in *Stages*, whereas in *Or* he was familiar with the life led by the esthete in *Either* (see p. 549 below).

29. *Aesthetics*, 1:407–8.

30. "Destruction" is a metaphor as prominent in Kierkegaard as it is in the other existentialists considered in chap. 9. If the destruction of the Tower of Babel (as a symbol for the binding together of "many souls": see n. 15, this chapter) is contemplated in *Either*, the destruction of Jerusalem (as a comparable symbol for the religious community) becomes in *Or* a backdrop for the "Ultimatum" delivered to the individual at the end of the work: "Only the truth that is involved in the reconstruction of your life is truth for you" (see p. 246 above, where my translation did attempt to bring out the metaphor implicit in "edifies").

31. *Aesthetics*, 1:404, 415.

32. Ibid., p. 176.

33. *Either*, p. 170. We shall see in the next chapter that the "rotation method" is the corresponding procedure for maintaining the mobility of one's enjoyment.

34. *Aesthetics*, 1:417–18; italics mine. By virtue of this ability "to objectify" their sufferings, "the *dramatis personae* . . . appear as themselves the poets" (ibid., p. 118). Here too the subjective orientation of Eremita's dialectic is a reversal of the objective orientation of Hegel's. For the pseudonymous authors or editors become characters. Thus Eremita himself turns up as a character in *Stages*.

35. *Either*, pp. 169, 174, 182.

36. Ibid., p. 213. The reflexive criterion is Alcibiades' in his report of his frustrating affair with Socrates (*Symposium* 218B), and the borrowing may imply that the bride's predicament solicits a bifocal analysis, for Alcibiades is referring to his having been bitten by Socrates' "philosophical *logoi*." In other words, her suffering is attributable not only to the seducer but also to her philosophical reflection upon it. If this implication is present, the bride of grief at this juncture is none other than Kierkegaard himself. Kierkegaard does in fact identify himself with Alcibiades in his frustration (see chap. 15, n. 68 below) as well as with Socrates and Antigone (see chap. 10, n. 91 above) —the first bride who was the starting point for this dialectical development. Given the lavishness of the costumes available in Kierkegaard's wardrobe of pseudonyms, this implication would not be inconsistent with his identification of Regina as the Cordelia whom he might have seduced, thereby offering her the role of the last of the brides.

37. *Either*, p. 213. The metaphor of "captivity" is not only, like "entombment," a variation on the theme of "enclosure" (see p. 428 above), but may also allude to the procedure of *captatio* (*benevolentiae*) which the spokesman has mentioned. In this case the procedure is caught up in a double contradiction. The "pictures" (or "images") of the brides' suffering cannot keep the attention captive because it leaves "at most a hint which may furnish a trace" and as such is essentially elusive. In any case, attention should not be kept captive by the suffering of others, since the requisite knowledge of suffering is reflexive.

38. *Aesthetics*, 1:420–21.

39. See p. 410 above.

40. *Postscript*, p. 152.

41. At this juncture there emerges what Derrida would identify as the presiding idiom of "presence" and "appropriation" in the Western philosophical tradition.

42. "Letter on 'Humanism,' " p. 224.

43. *What Is Literature?* pp. 16, 17. Sartre is quarreling with "pure stylists" who "think that the word is a gentle breeze which plays lightly over the surface of things, which grazes them without altering them, and that the speaker is a pure *witness* who sums up with a word his harmless contemplation" (p. 16). Cf. Kierkegaard's rebuke, "That being an author is action seems to be quite forgotten" (*Papirer*, VII1 A 123). Thus when Climacus makes "Reference to a Contemporary Striving in Danish Literature" (his esthetic production), he characterizes *Either/Or* as an "action" that he was "resolved to start" (*Postscript*, pp. 224–25). But Eremita got ahead of him (see chap. 10, n. 32 above).

12

The Passerby

That which makes communication dialectically so difficult is that the recipient of the communication exists.—Johannes Climacus

COMMUNICATION

One form taken by the radical individualism of the existentialist is distrust of expression, of "outspokenness," of commonplaceness. We have observed how Kierkegaard copes with this threat by "including in an expression as its content a consciousness of what the expression directly expresses." Exercising this reflexive responsibility is an "internalizing" movement on the part of his consciousness which reverses the externalizing movement of the expression itself whereby its meaning is communicated to another individual.

But at the same time, because of this threat, he faces as an existentialist a problem of communication, which is a further reason for his attentiveness to his *modus loquendi*. This problem is a social version of our persistent problem of philosophical generality. The prospect of reaching a general conclusion in an existential dialectic is complicated by the *reversal* of direction, whose function is to return the individual from communion in the commonplace to the meaning of his own experience. This complication recurs at the higher level of existentialism as a philosophy. Just as one becomes in existentialism an individual who must finally go his own way alone, so the existentialist finally goes his own way alone, by becoming something besides an existentialist. If Kierkegaard becomes a Christian and a political reactionary, Sartre becomes an atheist who is a revolutionary. Heidegger bluntly rejects the label "existential philosophy" itself, even though he started out with an "existential analytic" which is the single most important formative influence on the development of existentialism. Merleau-Ponty also drops the label. Existentialists seem to become individualistic philosophers by leaving behind whatever they may have had in common as existentialists.

What I am suggesting that they do continue to have in common is a problem of communication. Although we shall see that this problem develops in Kierkegaard in conjunction with his fragmentation of Hegel's system, no problem is more of a commonplace today, except possibly alienation; but the problem of communication is merely the form taken by alienation at the level of the *modus loquendi*.

To rescue this problem from its commonplaceness and bring out its distinctively existential traits is to undertake a task similar to the one delineated at the outset, where I granted that various kinds of pressures—social, economic, etc.—have been involved in fragmenting modern society and fomenting individualism but argued that it is still feasible to sift out at certain levels philosophical procedures which are employed in formulating a conception of the individual and determining the respects in which he "has" experiences, or "might have" experiences, that are "authentic"— not the experiences of others but his "own." Similarly with the ensuing problem of communication: granted that various pressures have been involved in fragmenting modern society, alienating the individual from others, and rendering communication between them a problem, it is still feasible to sift out at certain levels philosophical procedures which are employed in recognizing and formulating this problem. When these procedures are existential, they satisfy some motivation to "have" experiences which are our "own" that brings with it a tendency to view social and economic explanations as in some sense external to the experiences they reputedly explain. For we want to feel that our experiences are available to us as ours rather than taken over by these explanations. The intervention of such explanations may seem factors in our alienation which might perhaps be held at bay by implementing existential procedures.

We originally watched communication become problematic at a humbler level—in the conversation between Daniel and Marcelle. It has not yet come up for more philosophical consideration because it is not the starting point for an existential philosophy in the obvious sense that taking the initiative and "becoming an individual" is, as was recognized in part I. It is also not a starting point in the sense that the individual, if he is to take the initiative, has to start *defining* his experience in accordance with certain dialectical procedures which were examined in part II. Nor is it a starting point in the sense that "lostness in 'the one,'" as was recognized in part III, is the confused state of affairs from which the individual has to "take himself back," by reaching a "definite position" which constitutes a new starting point for him.

We could have been satisfied to watch the existentialist take the initiative in this fashion and reach his own conclusion, were he not a writer communicating with a reader. Thus the problem of starting point cannot be conceived as attaining its final reformulation as simply the ethical problem of the *modus agendi*—of regaining an initiative that was lost. For if the reader in turn is to take the initiative and find his own starting point for "becoming an individual" by disentangling himself from communion in the commonplace, then his relation to the writer communicating with him poses a problem with respect to the *modus loquendi* that the writer should adopt.

How difficult the problem of communication is in existentialism as a radical individualism has been suggested not only by Daniel's conversation with Marcelle, by Heidegger's analysis of "outspokenness" and "talk," but also by the shadowgraphic procedure of the Symparenkromenoi, culminating in the pronouncement, "Only he who has been bitten by a serpent knows the suffering of having been bitten by a serpent."

SYMPATHY

This problem of communication can be brought forward as specific to existentialism in contrast to more traditional forms of individualism. John Stuart Mill, for example, recommends with his "principle of individuality" that the individual cherish his own experiences as an individual. In visualizing this individual's relations to others, Mill also resorts to the supplementary principle of "sympathy"—of deriving "light from other minds."[1] In cherishing his own experiences, the individual is being instructed to enlarge their scope by "sharing" the experiences of others. Like Eremita, he is "sympathetic" in the etymological sense, but unlike Eremita his sympathy is not counterbalanced by the detachment of "irony"; he is not concerned to detach from himself the other individual whom Kierkegaard would "repel."[2] There is no dialectical shift in point of view to be carried through from the first to the second individual.

A procedure not very different from Mill's is equally characteristic of Continental individualism, if Kant may be taken as an illustration. Kant supplements the individualistic principle "Think for oneself" with a "second principle of mind" whereby "the man of an enlarged mode of thinking . . . disregards the subjective private conditions of his own judgment, by which so many others are confined, and reflects upon it from a universal standpoint, which he can determine only by placing himself at the standpoint of others."[3] Yet again, as in Mill, there is no dialectical shift to a second individual, conceived as finally separated from the first: only an attempt on the part of the first individual to surmount in his own reflections the subjective limitations of his own particular mind and to arrive at a universal point of view, in which other points of view will coalesce with his own. Thus the procedure commended is an exercise of judgment which is itself conceived by Kant as the subsumption of the particular under the universal.

SELF-REVELATION

Philosophy has usually surrendered the problem of communication to rhetoric or grudgingly accorded it merely marginal philosophical significance. Not so Kierkegaard. *Concluding Unscientific Postscript* is his major work. It is several times the length of the *Philosophical Fragments* to which it is the postscript. Though the *Postscript* is an attack on Hegel, a crucial consequence of this attack is the emergence of the problem of communication. Thus any adequate survey of Kierkegaard's treatment of this problem would take us far beyond his starting point in *Either*. Nevertheless, his treatment does illustrate the relation that can hold between *last* and *first*, for the *Postscript* was planned as the last of the pseudonymous works, and it develops implications which can be detected in the preface to *Either*, once some features of the argument in *Postscript* have been anticipated.

Kierkegaard's dialectical handling of the problem of communication is brought out by a seemingly flagrant contradiction: although he condemns Hegel's philosophy as merely "esthetic" (i.e., as inconclusive reflection) and as leaving no "place for an ethics" (i.e., for the "conclusiveness" with which an individual should choose and act), this "ethical" criticism of Hegel is conveyed in works which are themselves also characterized as "esthetic." *Or* is as much an "esthetic" work as *Either*. So are the *Philosophical Fragments* and *Stages on Life's Way*—to mention only those esthetic works to which I have referred. The *Postscript* is a special case (as I shall explain shortly), which is presumably another reason why it is a postscript.

When we dealt before in *Either/Or* with the contradiction between the esthetic and the ethical, we found that on one hand seduction was paradigmatic for the process of reflection by which the esthete leads others astray, and ultimately himself, into a realm of possibilities, while on the other marriage is paradigmatic for the process by which the individual actualizes himself by acting on a possible choice. "In the choice," the

Judge explains in *Or,* "the individual makes himself a definite individual, for he chooses himself."[4] But since in the instance of marriage he is choosing himself in relation to a second individual, the process of self-definition entails another requirement: "In and by this choice the individual reveals himself."[5] Thus Kierkegaard's existentialism, if it can be regarded as an ethics at all, is an ethics of communication as well as of choice and action.

The ethical emphasis on self-definition as self-revelation is carried over in Climacus's recapitulation of *Either/Or* in the *Postscript.* Where the esthete's performance is secretive, as a consequence of its merely reflective "internalizing" movement, what "sharply underscores the difference between the esthetic and the ethical is that it is the duty of everyone to reveal himself." A *recapitulation,* we recall, is a readjustment of an earlier analysis which brings forward an implication that originally remained in the background: the ethical imperative was originally the duty of everyone to get married, but now in the retrospect furnished by the *Postscript, Either/Or* receives the following interpretation:

> The first part [*Either*] was concealment; he [the author of *Or*] is a husband (A was intimate with every possibility within the erotic sphere and yet not actually in love, for he would then in that moment have been involved in consolidating himself) and concentrates himself, precisely in opposition to the concealment of the esthetic, upon marriage [*ægteskab*] as the deepest form of life's revelation.[6]

HUNG UP

However, existentialism is not an ethics of communication in quite so simple a sense. With the transition from the ethical to the religious stage (from "becoming an individual" to "becoming a Christian"), a new stage is reached in the process of self-definition—"a new determination of inwardness," which had already been hinted in *Either/Or* by its pseudonymous editor, Eremita. Now "the impossibility of self-revelation" becomes "something so fearful thaι esthetic concealment [the reflective withdrawal which had been employed in *Either*] becomes child's play in comparison."[7]

The further individuation involved in this reversal is succinctly suggested by the fashion in which the implications of the epigraph for the religious stage of the *Philosophical Fragments* are adjusted by the *recapitulation* undertaken by the preface to the *Postscript,* where the "teleological suspension of the ethical" becomes in effect the teleological suspension of the author:

> Seldom perhaps has a literary enterprise . . . had a reception more in accord with the author's wishes than my *Philosophical Fragments.* Doubtful and reserved as it is my fashion to be with respect to any opinion of my own or any self-criticism, yet I declare without doubt one thing as true about the fate of the piece: it has aroused no sensation, absolutely none. Undisturbed, and in compliance with his own motto, "Better well hung than ill wed," the well-hung author remains hanging. . . . Better well hung than brought by an unhappy marriage into systematic relationship with the whole world.[8]

It is no longer the prospective bridegroom who remains inconclusively "hanging" instead of being "brought into systematic relationship with the whole world," by getting himself married, assuming his station and its duties, and perpetuating the race (like Judge William), but an author who is congratulating himself over the poor sales of his work in order to ironize over the difficulty of consummating a communication.

The difficulty an existential author confronts is more complicated than the husband's in *Or,* who must choose himself in relation to another individual and reveal himself by his choice. Climacus describes the difficulty:

> That which makes communication dialectically so difficult is that the recipient of the communication exists. To stop a man on the street and stand still in order to talk with him is not so difficult as to have to say something to a passerby in passing, without standing still and without delaying the other, without inducing [*bevaege*] him to go the same way but giving him, instead, an impulse to go precisely his own way. Such is the relation between one existing individual and another existing individual when the communication has to do with the truth as existential inwardness.[9]

The first individual's predicament I delineated in treating the problem of existence: he is caught up in the contradictory relation between the backward movement of reflecting upon his life and the movement of his life forward. "Standing still" is then impossible, for if he responds to this forward movement, he is "persistently striving" to reach a "conclusion" that actualizes under the particular external circumstances of his life a possibility which has remained abstract as long as he was merely reflecting upon it. In his esthetic works Kierkegaard has been reflecting at a higher level upon possible points of view toward life—esthetic, ethical, and religious. He has been concealing himself behind pseudonyms to develop these points of view. This process of reflection, like any other, can only be brought to a conclusion ethically. *Concluding* [*Afsluttende*] *Unscientific Postscript* not only is a matter of reaching a "conclusion" about Hegel's "lack of a conclusion" but also embodies, in relation to Kierkegaard himself, the ethical resolution (*beslutning*) to bring his esthetic works to a "conclusion." Accordingly it is not, strictly speaking, another esthetic work.

As Kierkegaard will later note in *The Point of View for My Work as an Author*, the *Postscript* represents "a turning point" (*vendepunktet*).[10] It is a *reversal* which reproduces, at a higher level, the reversal with which any "existing individual" should recognize (in opposition to Hegel) the inconclusiveness of reflection, whose regressive movement can only be halted by turning himself around and "persistently striving" to actualize some possible choice under the particular external circumstances of his life. The "existential actuality" he thereby acquires is self-differentiating, "subjective," and "incommunicable."[11]

The problem of communication which still remains to be resolved has been presented by envisaging two individuals as on the move. Not "delaying the other" is the existential tact which the first individual should display in communicating with a second individual whose own life is also moving forward, but under different external circumstances. For the first individual, the writer, to communicate "directly" his own "existential actuality" would be to attempt to persuade this other individual, his reader, "to go the same way."

THE SPIRIT OF THE AGE

At this juncture it may be well to distinguish Climacus's effort to avoid confusing the other individual with himself from his effort to subvert more fully developed forms of social pressure, including Hegel's philosophy of history. Earlier I compared the individual's conversion to Christianity, as characterized by Climacus, with Sartre's conversion to atheism. But I neglected a dialectical doubling that takes place. Sartre recalls how at the age of twelve he became an atheist "in a certain fashion," but then atheism turned out to be "a cruel and long-range enterprise," taking up most of his life.[12] Just as his juvenile decision to become an atheist was not Sartre's own choice as an individual but had already been made for him by his bourgeois milieu, where atheism was commonplace, so the difficulty Climacus would have us become aware of in becoming a Christian is that "the decision seems to have been already reached." Just as the progress of culture, etc., in our own age makes it seem easy to be an atheist "in a certain fashion," so Climacus found his contemporaries living "in an age when the progress of culture, etc., has made it seem easy to be a Christian"—in a certain fashion.[13]

However, in Climacus's appraisal what is in question is not just the spirit of the age as such but also Hegel's philosophy as the revelation of this spirit. This is Hegel's own claim on behalf of his philosophy, and Climacus concedes the claim. As Hegel himself puts it,

> philosophy does not stand above its age . . . [but] one spirit pervades both the actual world and philosophical thought, and the latter is only the true self-comprehension of what is actual. In other words, it is one movement upon which both the age and its philosophy are born, the distinction being only that the character [*Bestimmtheit*] of the age still appears to present itself as accidental.

Hegel's philosophy supplies "rational justification" for regarding "the character of the age" as not merely "accidental" but "necessary."[14] The pressure then on individuals to coalesce with others in composing this spirit becomes well nigh irresistible.

This spiritual pressure is not just social but theological. In Christianity, as interpreted by Hegel's philosophy, "God has become wholly revealed."[15] But God in Kierkegaard remains "incognito" and as the most authoritative of authors provides further warrant for indirect communication:

> It is remarkable that, while there is such a clamor for the positive and for the direct form where outcomes are communicated, it occurs to no one to complain about God. . . . For no anonymous author can more cunningly conceal himself, no practitioner of the maieutic can more carefully withdraw himself from the direct relationship than God. He is in the creation and present everywhere in it, but directly he is not there; and only when the single individual turns to his inner self, and hence only in the inwardness of self-activity, does he become attentive and in a position to see God.
>
> Is this not to behave in relation to the individual like a deceitful author who nowhere sets down his outcome in bold type, or gives it to the reader beforehand in a preface?[16]

OUTCOMES

With its explanation of "indirect communication," the *Postscript* renders explicit the procedure which had been employed in the esthetic works themselves. Let us return to *Either/Or*, whose editor eludes the charge of deceit by explicitly promising no outcome in the preface with which he starts out:

> One sometimes comes upon novels in which definite characters represent opposing points of view toward life. They usually end by one of them persuading the other. Instead of the views being allowed to speak for themselves, the reader is enriched by being told the historical outcome that the one has persuaded the other. I regard it as fortunate

that these papers contain no such information. . . . When the book is read, then A and B are forgotten. Only their views confront one another and await no finite decision in definite personalities.[17]

The term "historical" is the giveaway; the "outcome" in a novel cannot ordinarily be construed as "historical." It is fictitious. Eremita is not just editing an antinovel in which he is opposing the conventional form of the novel. He is editing an antiphilosophy and assimilating to a fiction the historical form assumed by Hegel's philosophy.[18] Eremita is protesting against the illusory character of the *Aufhebung* which takes place at the third moment of Hegel's dialectic, but his protest is more specifically an expression of skepticism regarding the confusion in Hegel of philosophical conclusions with historical outcomes. To revert to the jargon at the start of Eremita's preface, he is again expressing his "doubt" as to whether the *internal* is the *external* or whether (in the phraseology so often quoted against Hegel) the "ideal" is the "actual."[19] Dialectical "division" or "doubling" (*Entzweiung*) is being reinstated by Eremita: historical outcomes are not necessary conclusions but contingent facts, including the fact that "these papers contain no . . . information" with respect to "the historical outcome."[20] Eremita has played up the contingency of this fact by regarding it as "fortunate."

When the author of the so-called novel supplies a conclusion in the guise of a historical outcome, he is applying social pressure, as we have seen Hegel's philosophy of history does on a grander scale by providing individuals with a philosophy that is an expression of their age, from which they cannot hope to escape. The reader is then persuaded to "go the same way" and is thus relieved of performing his own subjective act of self-differentiating choice as an individual.

POSSIBILITIES

If such "direct communication" is the attempt to communicate a philosophical conclusion in the form of an actual outcome, "indirect communication" is "a communication in the form of a possibility." In order to "turn the look of the observer [the reader] in upon himself," the author must "repel him by placing the possibility between the example [the character in the novel that exemplifies the possibility] as something they both have in common." Such "a communication in the form of the possible operates with the ideal type—not the differentiated ideal but the universal ideal."[21] A universal ideal possibility induces the reader to reflect and thereby abstract from the particular circumstances of his own life. To this extent he is seduced, led away from himself, though in fact he did not at the start have a self, since what he had was held in place and propped up by these particular circumstances from which he had not yet separated himself. Once he has abstracted himself through reflection from these particular circumstances and thereby gained the freedom to choose, it is up to him to reverse the movement of reflection and to undertake the differentiating choice that will actualize under these particular circumstances the ideal possibility that he has been reflecting upon.[22]

In Eremita's preface the proponents of the opposing esthetic and ethical points of view are denominated A and B in order to indicate that they must, for the purposes of communication, remain abstract possibilities which do not actually exist, in contrast to Hegel's "world-historical figures." These supposedly did exist, if only half-heartedly as the vehicles of a historical development whose outcome remained quite beyond the scope of any possibilities they were able to reflect upon. But for the purpose of distinguishing existentially the ethical from the esthetic point of view, B must also be a differentiated individual with his "place in the world," as we noted earlier when we first examined the preface. Hence B also receives the name "Judge William" and is married. But A as the proponent of the esthetic point of view is without a name, which would imply the attainment of personal identity, and without occupation or wife, which would imply acceptance of particular circumstances for his life.

"While reading the work," Eremita explains, "the reader may perfectly well forget the title." In other words, the reader may reflect on the development of the opposing points of view in terms of particular experiences of the characters under the particular circumstances of their lives. But "then, when he has read the book, he may perhaps reflect upon the title and by reflecting arrive at the level where the general relation of contradiction holds between the ethical and the esthetic points of view. At this juncture a *reversal* takes place: when the title is remembered, "A and B are forgotten," and "only their views confront one other" as the "either/or" which awaits a further *reversal*—the reader's self-differentiating choice in terms of his own experiences under the particular circumstances of his own life rather than theirs.[23]

THE BOX

In *Either/Or* the reader is invited to respect the distinction between his life and those of the characters because Eremita keeps his own distance, with his ironical denial that he is the author of their papers. He is only the editor. This esthetic distance is an imaginary space which opens up as the process of reflection widens the discrepancy between the possible and the actual, between the *internal* and the *external*. For as the process of reflection continues, the possibilities become more remote from the external circumstances of the characters, including the characters who become authors (the Symparenkromenoi and the seducer who is the author of the "Diary").

The reader is further encouraged to reach the level where he finally confronts an either/or by Eremita's reflecting on the work as a whole:

> During my constant preoccupation with the papers, it dawned upon me that they might be looked at from a new point of view, by considering all the papers [i.e., *Or* as well as the various papers composing *Either*] the work of one individual. . . . Let us imagine an individual who had lived through both of these movements [*bevaegelser*] or who had reflected upon both.[24]

What was apparently an external relation between one separate individual and another with "opposing views of life" has been reflexively internalized within one individual, who thereby becomes an unstable composite of contradictory possibilities.[25]

Now the obvious candidate for this one author is the announced editor—Eremita himself. But there are other complications. First of all, Eremita's position as editor in relation to A as author is complicated by the threat that A will displace him as an editor:

> The last of A's papers is a story entitled "Diary of the Seducer." Here we meet with new difficulties, since A acknowledges himself not as author but only as editor. This is an old trick of the novelist, and I would not object to it if it did not make my own position so complicated, as one author seems to be located within another, like the nest of boxes in a puzzle box. Here is not the place to develop what would confirm my opinion.[26]

Eremita's dithering about his own position and his failure "to develop what would confirm [his] opinion" add up to an invitation to the reader to intervene in this development and replace Eremita. The reader then takes over the designated place of the "one individual who had lived through both movements"—namely, the esthetic and the ethical—or, rather, "who had reflected on both" while reading and should now face up to the contradiction by choosing between them.

Earlier I cited from *Either* a lower-level instance in which the relations between individuals were exhibited in accordance with the principle of contradiction whereby the *internal* is not the *external*. On one hand the position of the chairs occupied by the characters in "The Diary of the Seducer" was so arranged that the seducer remained *external* to the relation between Cordelia and her fiancé; on the other the place he imagined he occupied in the space of her imagination was *internal* to the relation between her fiancé and herself.[27] In a somewhat similar fashion, the reader who is only externally related to A and B (as A and B were themselves originally conceived to be externally related to each other as two separate individuals) is maneuvered into internalizing and enclosing within himself their opposing points of view. Just as A, when he acknowledges himself not as author but only as editor of the "Diary," threatens to displace Eremita, who also acknowledges himself only as editor of the "Diary," so the reader is to take the place of Eremita and

> perhaps reflect upon the title. This will free him from all finite [*endeligt*] questions as to whether A was really persuaded of his error and repented or whether B conquered or if it perhaps ended by B's going over to A's opinion. In this respect these papers have no final ending [*ende*].[28]

Hegel had promised, we remember, that "all will become clear in the end" when the "conclusion" is reached, for it will resolve previous conflicts. However, the conflict between A and B is left unresolved in *Either/Or*. There is no outcome. Clarity is achieved by a juxtaposition of opposite positions, but with the "conclusion" left up to the "resolution" (*beslutning*) of the reader, as the individual who must finally assume, on his own authority, as if he were the author, the responsibility for the "ending" which the papers themselves lack.

THE PSEUDONYMS

In adopting an esthetic means of communication, Kierkegaard is not disavowing his ethical criticism of Hegel's philosophy as esthetic. Rather, he is extending this criticism to a further level. He is criticizing Hegel's procedure of composing a philosophy of history instead of employing the "storytelling method" that he himself adopts in composing his own esthetic works. Like Kierkegaard's esthetic works, Hegel's *philosophy* is esthetic in that it embodies a process of reflection which as such is inconclusive but which in these works of Kierkegaard's has the justification that it enables him to abstract from the particular external circumstances of his own life and communicate with another individual. Yet since Hegel's philosophy itself is ostensibly a philosophy *of history*, "the place" is usurped that should have been left to an "ethics" which would bear on the history of the individual. For Hegel is assuming that the process of reflection which is his philosophy is in some sense the explication of what has been actualized under particular sociohistorical circumstances. In failing to see that reflection and action are separate and opposed movements, Hegel is failing to respect not only "the doubleness" which poses the problem of existence for any individual but also the separateness of individuals which poses the problem of communication if each is to proceed in his own *direction*. The ethical movement of action is, as we have seen, this movement of self-differentiation, by which the individual acquires his own separate "existential reality" under the particular circumstances of his own life history.[29] But instead of separating himself as an individual and treating this movement in an ethics, Hegel in his philosophy of history "confuses himself with humanity as a whole,"[30] including his readers. Once it is acknowledged that there can be ethically only separate individual subjects, each with his own life history, it also has to be acknowledged that what Hegel is confusing himself with is only "a fictitious objective subject."[31]

Kierkegaard's esthetic works are produced by fictitious subjects, but their pseudonymity is a denial that these subjects are *objective*. The pseudonymous "authors" and "editors" are not to be confused with actual individuals, not even with Kierkegaard. Because Kierkegaard's philosophy separates the conclusive ethical movement of individual choice and action from the inconclusive esthetic movement of reflection with which this philosophy can be communicated, it also can keep separate the individuals involved in this process of communication:

> The subjectivities must be held devoutly apart from one another and not permitted to fuse together into objectivity. It is at this point that objectivity and subjectivity take leave of each other.[32]

But in Hegel's philosophy individual subjects fuse together into the fictitious objectivity of "humanity as a whole" with which Hegel confuses even himself when he puts absolute spirit in charge of his historical dialectic.

SHADOWGRAPHS

This confusion is indispensable, from Kierkegaard's point of view, to the deceptively "scientific" (i.e., objective and systematic) pretensions of Hegel's dialectic. The clarification of this confusion is sought esthetically by Eremita's subjectively oriented fragmentation of Hegel's "system of the arts" as well as by the way individual writers (the Symparenkromenoi, the seducer, and A) replace the absolute spirit as the finite fictitious subjects who are associated with the different stages of this process of fragmentation. We have recognized that this process was the subversion of Hegel's system with respect to both its development into a complete whole and to the "finish" to be developed in the handling of particular details.

The process was seen to involve eliminating from the system the *objective* arts, relinquishing the *objective* criterion of "plasticity," with the ensuing fading of the relatively *objective* art of painting into shadow-graphs, which in turn only became a metaphor for the way stories are to be told. The "objectivity of representation" to which "finish" contributed was subverted.

Now we shall see that this subversive process is not designed simply in order to do justice to the fragmentary and *subjective* character of any individual's own experience, as opposed to the collective *objective* experience assigned by Hegel to "humanity as a whole." Since humanity is not a whole, the process is also designed (in the terminology of the *Postscript*) "to hold" the reader "apart from" the writer and thus cope with the problem of communication.

In representing his "brides of grief" shadowgraphically, the spokesman for the Symparenkromenoi warned,

> Direct your attention, . . . beloved Symparenkromenoi, to this inner picture [or "image"]; do not allow yourselves be distracted by the external, . . . for it shall be my task to draw it aside [*drage . . . tilside*] in order to afford you a better view of the inner picture.[33]

This procedure for representing the "brides of grief" conformed to the subjectively oriented procedure of reflection which they had employed in wedding themselves to their grief in order to appropriate it. They drew aside the distractingly external when they undertook the "internalizing" operation of "recollecting" an external "picture." Then they undertook the imaginative operation of *Vorstellung*, with which the internalized "image" can be "represented," and to this extent reexternalized within their minds, but to so limited an extent that their reflection could leave behind what is "at most a hint which may furnish a trace."[34]

But at the same time the drawing aside of the external by the spokesman himself is also an indirect method of representation which at most leaves hints behind for the reader to follow up. It is a stage in the development of the procedure of "indirect communication" that is explained later in the *Postscript*.

Thus the first of the "brides," the modern Antigone, becomes so "separated" from others when she reflects that she suffers as well from her inability to communicate with her prospective bridegroom. The problem of communication reaches further stages with the other "brides of grief" and emerges at a higher level with the Symparenkromenoi, who are reflecting upon these "brides" and are likewise isolated by their reflections from the external circumstances of their life, including their relations to others. It is in this sense that their reflections have "buried them alive."

THE COMIC

This "aphoristical" procedure of isolating individuals by reflection
should not be construed simply as a function of the sufferings of the
modern Antigone, of the other "brides of grief," and of the Symparenkromenoi themselves. Separation, disrupting continuity, is a more general
function of Eremita's reflective dialectic as such. Thus, after a triad of
tragic essays on suffering, the dialectic in *Either* shifts to the opposite—
to the comic form and to reflective enjoyment as a content.[35] But it will
continue to display "aphoristical" discontinuity.

Earlier we considered the first two tragic essays, "The Ancient Tragic"
and "Shadowgraphs," but we never reached the comic. The sequence
Kierkegaard is following here is the same as Hegel's. We have seen that
in Hegel, "however completely poetry reproduces the whole of beauty
once again in a more spiritual fashion" than all of the preceding arts,
nevertheless "the fusion of spiritual inwardness with external existence
disintegrates [*auflöst*]. . . ." This disintegration reaches a climax in Hegel
with the final form of dramatic art—comedy.[36] This final moment, when
in Hegel himself the *internal* is not the *external*, Eremita exploits for his
fragmentation and subjective reorientation of Hegel's dialectic. How
crucial this moment is for Eremita's purpose is indicated by his brief
departure from the Hegelian sequence, when he offers certain anticipations of the comic in "The Ancient Tragic."[37] Having announced that
the essay "will be an attempt to show that what is characteristic of ancient
tragedy is taken up within the modern, so that the truly tragic may
appear," Eremita ironically digresses on modernity:

But however much I may strive for this to appear, I shall still refrain
from every prophecy about this being what the age demands, so that
the appearance of the truly tragic becomes entirely without outcome,
more especially since the whole age is oriented in the direction of the
comic. Existence is correspondingly subverted by doubt on the part of
subjects; isolation constantly gets more and more the upper hand.[38]

That this is Eremita's own *orientation* is indicated by the doubt with
which he started out, by the fact that isolation "gets more and more the
upper hand" during the dialectic development, and by his rejection of
any historical outcome for this development.

If Eremita is "sympathetic" as well as ironical, it is not in any organized sense that might seem to become relevant when "The Ancient Tragic"
is attributed to the society of the Symparenkromenoi. For the social
commentary offered in the digression is a denial that the "sym" can
imply that "the buried alive" are significantly "together." That "isolation
constantly gets more and more the upper hand" is

something one can best be convinced of by giving attention to the multitudinous social strivings. These indeed demonstrate the isolation of the striving of the age by the fact that they attempt to counteract it."[39]

One of these demonstrations is of course this very essay on "The Ancient Tragic," for its "Reflection . . . in the Modern" constitutes "An Experiment in Fragmentary Striving." The Symparenkromenoi are not really a society; their attempt to counteract their isolation as individuals in fact contributes toward hastening the disintegration of the age, as its demands for social and political organization are set forth in Hegel's philosophy of history.

When the digression is terminated in order to return to the tragic, the comic is again anticipated as the genre with which to oppose the necessary development that the Hegelian dialectic set forth on behalf of its demands:

> This is sufficient to show that what really holds the state together is disorganized, but the isolation thereby effected is naturally comic, and the comic resides in the fact that subjectivity as mere form would assert its validity. Any isolated individual always becomes comic by asserting his own contingency over against necessary development.[40]

DEFINITION

The comedy of individual self-isolation exhibits a dialectic which is comparable to that of the tragedy of individual self-isolation, in spite of the shift in content to enjoyment from suffering, now that it is assumed that the "*bestemmelse* [here "determination" or "intention"] of everyone is to enjoy himself." For it is still assumed that he will make a reflective effort to *define* this content in order to appropriate it. Thus the first of the comic essays, "The First Love," starts out by playing up the problem of definition:

> This article was definitely intended [*bestemt*] for publication in a journal, which Frederk Unsmann had intended to publish at definite [*bestemte*] times. Alas, what are all human intentions [*bestemmelser*]![41]

The problem of "intention" is fitted to the contradiction between the *external* and the *internal*: "a little contingent external circumstance" is necessary in order that an author's "inward intention [*bestemmelse*] may become outward."[42]

The threat dependency on the "outward" poses to the reflexive *orientation* of existential definition is opposed by transposing the problem of definition into that of appropriation:

Wealth of thought is revealed before authors, but so overpoweringly that . . . it seems to them as if it were not their own property. When, then, consciousness has so come to itself that it owns the entire content, the moment has arrived which contains the possibility of authentic [*egentlig*] creation.[43]

We observed long ago that "having" an experience as our "own" entails determining what it is, how it is to be defined, what it means. But we were then "having" a particular experience and weaving out of it a single "picture."[44]

Since then we have traced Hegel's appropriative procedure for "accumulating" the variety of experiences which constitutes the "wealth" he would "store up" in his system.[45] We have also watched the spokesman for the Symparenkromenoi subvert this procedure by squandering the fragmentary. Thus we need not linger with the comic version of this subversive operation. The first comic essay, like the first tragic essay, "The Reflection of the Ancient Tragic in the Modern," is a review of a play, Scribe's *First Love*. But the reader is less likely to be acquainted with this play than with the *Antigone*, so it seems hardly worthwhile to trace the dialectic. The most obvious contradiction is that "the first love is the true love." For from this premise can be demonstrated that "my present love is my first love," even though it is chronologically my "third love." Here is presumably *interplay* with which we are already familiar between the chronological and the ideal, and probably some reference to the Hegelian distinction between the immediacy of a first stage and the emergence of truth at the third moment where *Aufbewahrung* takes place at the higher level of reflection.[46]

With respect to the content, it is easy to guess how the dialectic of reflective suffering can be transformed into its opposite. In "Shadowgraphs" the factor triggering further reflection on the part of the "brides of grief" was the doubt as to whether or not their seducer had deceived them. Their tragic separation is readily transformed into a comic separation when the doubt becomes mutual—when "the situation is so crazy that it becomes doubtful whether one should say that it is Rinville who deceives Emmeline or Emmeline who deceives Rinville." Indeed in *The First Love* we are confronted with a "quite crazy crisscrossing of the situations," where "four people are mutually mystified."[47]

WEALTH

The "wealth of thought" with which the authors are confronted in the first essay probably echoed Hegel. The metaphor is carried over in the second essay, which is decked out with an epigraph from an ancient comedy, the *Plutus* of Aristophanes, and which introduces us to "The Rotation Method." Eremita quotes (or, rather, misquotes) Marcus Aurelius: "It is in your power to recover [*leve op igjen*]; to reflect on things which you reflected on before, but from another point of view."[48] Such shifting of points of view was in Hegel a reflective procedure for reestablishing connections at a higher level and thereby accumulating "wealth" of experience.[49] Such shifting is now a rotation method which severs connections in order to keep experience fragmentary. Since we are already acquainted with the dialectical opposition to be developed in *Or* between marriage as sustained interconnection and seduction as the prompt disconnection of *Either*, we can take the following warning as a specimen of the rotation method: "As soon as two individuals fall in love with each other and begin to expect they were destined [*bestemte*] for each other, then it is time to have the courage to break it off."[50] Every *coitus* in *Either* is, metaphorically speaking, *interruptus*.

In "The Rotation Method" another metaphorical rendering of Hegel's criterion of "completeness" is closely associated with "wealth." This is the metaphor of "fullness" which we have also encountered at the start of the *Phenomenology*. The final outcome in Hegel of integrating particular experiences in a higher-level, more coherent experience is "pantheism," according to the standard theological accusation against Hegel, and pantheism is identified in "The Rotation Method" as characterized by "fullness" (*fylde*, a Danish term which is often used metaphorically to refer to "abundance" or "wealth"). This metaphorical criterion is subverted by the epigraph from the *Plutus*:

CHREMYLOS: Of everything you get finally too much.
              Of love,
KARION: Of bread,
CHREMYLOS: Of art,
KARION: Of candy.
CHREMYLOS: Of honor,
KARION: Of cookies,
CHREMYLOS: Of courage,
KARION: Of figs.
CHREMYLOS: Of ambition,
KARION: Of cakes,
CHREMYLOS: Of command,
KARION: Of lentils.[51]

What is being made a comedy of with this epigraph, which itself rotates with respect to its external form, is the infinite striving, embodied in the rotation of Hegel's dialectic, to acquire completeness of experience, as if such fulfillment were enjoyment, when in fact it is not satisfying but satiety, and hence boredom, which Eremita identifies as "characterized by emptiness." Thus "fullness" has become its opposite.[52] In Hegel's system, because of its completeness, one is replete; one finally gets too much of every form of experience.

Too Much

"Too much" (*Überdruss*) reminds us that the diarist in *Nausea* finds things are indigestibly "too much" (*de trop*) when he is exposed to their contingent proliferation—their "swooning abundance."[53] I am not suggesting that Sartre is influenced by Kierkegaard here; insofar as influence is in question, Sartre is adapting Heidegger's description of the mood felt when "being-there becomes satiated [*überdrüssig*] with itself."[54] The comparison of Sartre with Kierkegaard does provide another illustration of how the physical component does not perform the same literal function in Kierkegaard's elaboration of metaphors as it does in Sartre's, for satiety never becomes nausea in Kierkegaard.

Yet the comparison survives this difference: too-muchness is as much of a metaphor for Kierkegaard as for Sartre, because completeness of experience, and of its assimilation as knowledge, is a philosophical criterion that both would subvert. What is comic here in *Either* turns into irony in the *Postscript* when Climacus explains that *Philosophical Fragments* is written for informed readers whose misfortunate is that

> they know too much. Because everyone knows it, the Christian truth has become progressively a triviality of which it is difficult to secure an original impression. This being the situation, the art of *communication* at last becomes the art of *taking away*. . . . When a man has his mouth so full of food that he is prevented from eating and is likely to starve in consequence, does giving him nourishment consist in stuffing still more food into his mouth, or does it consist in taking some of it away so that he can start eating? Similarly, when a man has much knowledge and his knowledge has little or no meaning for him, does reasonable communication consist in giving him more knowledge . . . , or does it not, rather, consist in taking some of it away?[55]

One fashion in which Sartre would subvert accumulated experiences, assimilated in the form of knowledge, is with his satirical portrait of the man of experience in *Nausea*:

> That's what I call a handsome face. Worn, furrowed by life and passions. But the doctor has understood life, mastered his passions. . . . As soon as you see him, you can tell . . . that he is someone who has lived. He deserves his face, for he has never for one instant been mistaken

when it came to keeping and using his past to the best of his ability.
. . . The doctor has experience. He is a professional in experience; doctors, priests, magistrates, and army officers know men through and through as if they had made them."

At a higher level, the role of man of experience is assumed by the narrator of the conventional short story:

> The structure of these stories is almost unchanging. . . . The narrator is an older man, . . . a professional of experience—doctor, soldier, artist, or Don Juan. . . . They do not present their memories in their original crude form: they are experiences out of which they have squeezed the juice. . . .[56]

To disrupt this structure is one of the functions of Sartre's antinovel, for "the ideal and universal subjectivity of the man of experience" is no less a form of communion in the commonplace than women's talk.

Kierkegaard's procedure for disrupting the infinite striving in Hegel to accumulate experience, and for avoiding the resulting satiety, boredom, is "the rotation method." This method is a parody of the infinite striving which is embodied in the rotation of Hegel's dialectic (and this parody is suggested by the rotation of the Aristophanic epigraph with respect even to its external form), but it is also opposed, since it respects "the boundary principle of limitation."[57] It is "finite striving." By rotating one severs instead of connecting, breaks off relations instead of continuing them. One is searching aphoristically for a limited experience; one is squandering successive experiences, instead of storing them up—to revert to the metaphors of "The Ancient Tragic."

THE LOCKED BOX

The metaphors are similar because isolation, separation, disrupting continuity are (as I have been illustrating) a more general function of Eremita's dialectic than the difference between tragic suffering and comic enjoyment. It is not only experiences that are being separated from other experiences but also the individual himself, who has the experiences from other individuals. Climacus explains in the *Postscript* that *Either* exhibits "an existential possibility" which "though autopathic, deceptively [*bedragersk*] occupies itself with the suffering of others."[58] As evidence he refers to "Shadowgraphs," where we have seen the spokesman for the Symparenkromenoi attempt to "draw" (*drage*) the external "aside" (*tilside*). Once the distractingly external attribution of the suffering to the "brides" is drawn aside, the "existential possibility" is identifiable as

Eremita—that is, as someone who is "isolated" by his own suffering, and his reflection on it, and who suffers too from this isolation.

If we were allowed to do so, we could again draw the distractingly external aside and see behind Eremita Kierkegaard himself, who though autopathic deceptively occupies himself with the suffering of his pseudonym. Indeed this autopathic stage is in effect reached in the esthetic works themselves with the "new determination of inwardness" that is the religious stage, which the pseudonym Eremita foreshadows, as I have already noted. The individual becomes his most "isolated" when he finally recollects his suffering as "A Passion Story." At this *last* stage the process of "internalizing," self-enclosing recollection is played up with another metaphorical box, reminiscent of the *first* box in the preface of *Either*, although the reminiscence is recapitulative in that the box also incorporates the function of the desk. For it is now the box which encloses the papers composing "A Passion Story" and like the drawer in the desk has to be "opened . . . by force." (Perhaps it corresponds to the other drawer which "remained closed" [*lukket*] in the desk.)[59] But the further development in isolating self-enclosure, with which the reflecting individual would appropriate experience, is now signalized by having "the box . . . locked" from the "inside."[60]

Like the desk, the box is selected as a spatial metaphor because of the interplay that can be managed between the *external* form and the *inner* content. This interplay can be interpreted as comparable to the way in which the shadowgraphs were presented. The external "picture" ("The box was locked, and when I opened it by force the key lay inside") is to be drawn aside to provide a better look at what the external "picture" becomes an "image" of within: "Thus it is that *indesluttethed* is always *indadvendt*." Literally (e.g., with reference to an external physical box) the verb *indeslutte* means "to close up," "lock up," "confine," but the noun becomes metaphorically an image for psychological "introversion" or "reserve"; similarly, *indadvendt* means "turned inward" in an external physical sense but acquires the meaning "turned inward" in a psychological sense—the metaphorical meaning which such turning inward itself produces.

ABSTRACTION

At this juncture is presented the problem of communication which we have seen can paradoxically be solved in much the same terms as those in which it is posed. The process of reflection, which Kierkegaard found characteristically "esthetic," is an inward-turning process that involves the individual's abstraction from the pressures of his external circumstances (including other individuals) as a first step in his attempt to appropriate his experience. The attempt, if initially indispensable, is ultimately self-defeating, inasmuch as the circumstances from which he is abstracting are required for the individuation of his experiences as his own. (This is the Judge's protest against the "esthetic" in *Or*.) But the process of abstraction which renders these experiences less his own can also render them more available for other individuals who are living under different external circumstances than his, insofar as reexternalization is achieved in the form of a work of art. (This is Climacus's claim on behalf of the "esthetic" in the *Postscript*.) The process of abstraction is then transitional from *aisthēsis* in the literal sense of perception, which becomes minimal (as "Shadowgraphs" illustrates), to the esthetic level of "imaginative representation." If the reader in turn participates in this process of abstraction, he can become (in the space of his imagination) the external box which in *Either* encloses within itself as their nest the other boxes that mark earlier, less abstract stages in this process.

To induce this participation, the distractingly external, perceptible "picture" is abstracted from, drawn to one side in the case of the "Shadowgraphs," in favor of the "imaginative representation" of what is within, just as (at the higher level of the "system of the arts") shadowgraphs themselves are the more abstract poetic form which displaces the still too "external" art of painting. Consistent with this process of abstraction is the repudiation of the Hegelian procedure of pictorial "finish" in representing poetic characters. This repudiation respects not only, as we earlier recognized, the incompleteness, the fragmentariness, of any individual's own particular experiences (especially when measured against the completeness, the fullness, the conclusiveness of Hegel's finished system) but also the general requirements to be met if he is to communicate with another individual who is to find his own starting point by reaching a conclusion in terms of his own experience.

Notes

1. *Human Nature*, 2:328–29.
2. See pp. 369, 401 above.
3. *Critique of Judgment*, p. 136. For the persistence of the tradition of "a universal standpoint," see my *Human Nature*, 2:329–33.
4. *Or*, p. 256.
5. *Postscript*, p. 227.

6. Ibid. The verb *aegte* means "marry"; the adjective *ægte* means "genuine," "real," "legitimate." Climacus is probably suggesting that marriage is the way a man consolidates his reality.

7. Ibid., p. 234. The "impossibility" imposes a reversal: "The individual in a higher sphere [the religious] comes back again to the point where revelation, which is the life of the ethical, again becomes impossible, but so that the relations are reversed, and the ethical which formerly helped to bring about a revelation (while the esthetic was the obstacle) is now the obstacle" (p. 231). Let me remind the reader that I am attempting only to clarify the procedure of reversal in relations; I am not attempting to deal with the complexities of this reversal as it will later separate the religious from the ethical stage.

8. Ibid., p. 3. See p. 412 above for the original use of the motto.

9. *Postscript*, p. 247. Considerable scholarly work has been done on "the implicit reader" (and on the relation to the reader that is implicit in the way fiction is composed or in the role assumed by the narrator—see, e.g., Iser, *Der implizite Leser*; Booth, *The Rhetoric of Fiction*)—so that it is surprising that so little attention has been paid to those writers of fiction like Kierkegaard and Sartre who have been explicit about the relation they would assume toward their readers.

10. *Point of View*, p. 41.

11. *Postscript*, pp. 110, 320.

12. See p. 368 above; and *Words*, p. 253.

13. *Postscript*, p. 342.

14. *Philosophy of Religion*, 1:47. The assumption that there is "one movement upon which both the age and its philosophy is borne" is not restricted to Hegel. There is a comparable problem for individualism in the "regularizing activity which in his more recent work Foucault has called a discourse" (Said, "The Problem of Textuality," p. 677; note Foucault's own vacillation as reported by Said in his ensuing discussion). There are of course numerous other versions of the same assumption.

15. *Philosophy of Religion*, 1:84.

16. *Postscript*, pp. 217–18. I ordinarily translate *resultat/Resultat* as "outcome," for "result" is too flat and pragmatic to be associated clearly with a dialectical development. This translation might be appropriate when Heidegger expresses his disdain for "results." Thus his "Plato's Doctrine of Truth" begins, "The knowledge of the sciences is usually expressed in propositions which are then set before man as comprehensive results [*Ergebnisse*] for him to put to use" (p. 173). But Heidegger's procedure is to reattach these "results" to the unacknowledged development of which they are the outcome. He tries to secure this acknowledgment by reversing the direction implicit in the sequence of this development—i.e., by going behind the "use," "results," "propositions," "sciences," until he reaches in Plato the doctrine of truth that this development (modern thought) presupposes. The comparison with Kierkegaard may seem tenuous, but in both instances "results" are deprived of the significance they usually have for us.

17. *Either*, p. 14. The point is reemphasized in the recapitulation of *Stages*: "There was no decision in the finite sense (see the preface [to *Either/Or*]), so that the reader could say 'Well, that is decided' " (*Postscript*, p. 263). Kierkegaard's suspension of outcomes and final conclusions or, rather, his leaving them to his reader takes the prefatory form of the essay which is restricted to being an "experiment" (*forsøg*) (see pp. 39, 269).

18. See p. 506 below.

19. "History," according to Hegel, is "Spirit externalized and emptied out into time" (*Phenomenology*, p. 492).

20. Although there are differences, a comparison could still be made with the "papers of Antoine Roquentin," which "are published without alteration" as *Nausea* (p. 1), for they also could be said to "contain no . . . information" with respect to "the historical outcome." See chap. 9, n. 54 above.

21. *Postscript*, p. 321. For the repulsion of the reader, see chap. 10, n. 9 above, and n. 50, this chapter. The repulsion exploits the tension set up by restoring the distinction Hegel collapsed between the ideal possibility and the actual—the collapse which is usually referred to as his equating the ideal with the real.

22. See p. 409 above.

23. *Either*, pp. 13–14.

24. Ibid., p. 13.

25. Sartre carries out a comparable process of internalization in commenting on the theater as "a place where our contradictions become apparent." For he adds, "Hegel was the first to note this, but the fact goes back to antiquity. Since then there has been only the single change: in the ancient theater the various different terms of the contradiction were each represented by a different character, whereas in modern theater these contradictions have been internalized and can coexist in a single character" (*Sartre on Theater*, p. 267). Sartre may have Franz (in *The Condemned of Altona*) primarily in mind. Franz is a contradictory composite in that he is a German Nazi who is designed to embody the contradictions Sartre felt the French faced during the Algerian war.

26. *Either*, p. 9. It is the place to draw the reader into the dialectic by developing instead the distinction between the actual and the possible: "It is actually as if A had become afraid of his poem. . . . If it were an actual occurrence of which he had become cognizant, then it seems remarkable that the preface shows no joy on A's part in seeing the realization of the Idea which had so often hovered before him" (p. 9).

27. See p. 110 above.

28. *Either*, pp. 13–14.

29. "Existential reality is incommunicable, and the subjective thinker finds his reality in his own ethical existence (*Postscript*, p. 320).

30. *Ibid.*, p. 113. Hegel's confusion of himself with humanity, like his other confusions, is not just his own confusion as an individual but is "characteristic of our age," when men "confuse themselves with the age, with the century, with the contemporary generation, with humanity at large" (ibid., pp. 318–19; cf. pp. 309, 313).

31. Ibid., p. 75.

32. Ibid., p. 73. The devoutness (literally, godlikeness) is explained as follows: "Inwardness is when the expression belongs to the recipient as if it were his own—and now it is his own. To communicate in this mode constitutes the most beautiful triumph of the resigned inwardness. And accordingly no one is as resigned as God; for He communicates in creating, so as by creating to give independence [*selvstændighed*] over against himself" (ibid., p. 232).

33. See p. 456 above.

34. See p. 428 above.

35. In the third of these essays, "The Unhappiest Man" (Kierkegaard) is identified as a Christ figure. The essay is "presented at the Friday meeting" of the Symparenkromenoi; toward the end "the stone is rolled away" (p. 227), and it actually ends with a resurrection: "Arise, beloved Symparenkromenoi. The night is over and the day starts. . . ." The shift to the opposite is thus marked as from "night" to "day." Aside from "the darker side of life" dealt with in "Shadowgraphs," Eremita may now have wished to counteract the impression given by having taken his epigraph for *Either* from Young's *Night Thoughts*.

36. See p. 431 above. In one of its guises this "fictitious objective subject" is the "public" Hegel envisages for his *Phenomenology* in its preface (see my preface above).

37. This reversal of the Hegelian sequence whereby reference to the comic temporarily takes precedence over the tragic can be compared with the reversal whereby the lyric takes precedence over the epic (see p. 423 above), for in both instances the individual is asserting himself in his isolation against the social, while Kierkegaard himself is displaying his indifference to the sequence of social and cultural history.

38. *Either*, pp. 138–39.

39. Ibid., p. 139.
40. Ibid., p. 140. The modern state is viewed by Hegel as a vehicle of the "objective spirit," and its organization of the social content is a necessary development. Eremita may intend a contradiction not only between the presumed necessity of this development in Hegel and the disintegration of the state, which since it has taken place must be a necessary development, but also between the isolated individual asserting his own contingency and his contingency (along with his isolation) having been the necessary consequence of this development. In any case, he is exploiting the close connection in Hegel between contingency and isolation.
41. Ibid., p. 230. The last line ("Alas," etc.) constitutes a commentary on what will turn out to be essentially comic—the dependency of an intention for its actualization on external contingencies which in fact are likely to be its frustration.
42. *Either*, p. 231.
43. Ibid. As previously noted, "come to itself" is the regular formula for the reflexive movement, which is here succinctly tied in with the effort at appropriation and with the possibility of authenticity.
44. See p. 264 above.
45. See p. 451 above.
46. *Either*, p. 252. For the interplay, see p. 265 above.
47. *Either*, pp. 266, 259. Not only does the theme of deception continue, but the discontinuity of the shift from "Shadowgraphs," as dealing with "the darker side of life" (see n. 35), is in a measure counteracted when "the curtain falls [on "The First Love"], the play is over," for then "nothing remains subsisting except the grand outline [*omrids*]; only the situation's fantastic shadow play, which irony directs, is visible" (p. 275).
48. Ibid., p. 288. A comparable procedure had in effect been applied by the "brides of grief" in "Shadowgraphs," where "reflection" can "give it [the grief] now one meaning, now another" (p. 190). For what Eremita is ultimately concerned to bring out in *Either* is the inconclusive character of reflection, rather than lingering with the difference between grief and enjoyment.
49. The metaphor of "wealth," which we recognized Kierkegaard took over from Hegel, is felt appropriate by Sartre too. He interprets "the idea of *experience* as accumulated knowledge" as a "diluted expression of the process of economic accumulation" (*L'idiot*, 3:95; italics in original).
50. *Either*, p. 294. The discontinuity of breaking it off goes on not only with the application of the rotation method to relations between the individual and others within the essay but also at its boundary, where the author's starting point is not a *captatio benevolentiae* but an irrefutable insult which brings his relation to the reader almost to a breaking point: "Starting out from a principle is asserted by people with experience to be a very reasonable procedure, so I start out from the principle that all men are bores. Surely no one will prove himself so boring as to contradict me in this. This principle has the force of being in the highest degree repelling, which is always a requirement in the case of the negative that is properly the principle of motion" (ibid., p. 281). As I indicated in chap. 4, motion is a requirement for dialectic (including the dialectic of personal relations), but there is also a specific reference here to both Hegel's philosophy of nature and his logic. A standard form taken by a rhetorical *captatio benevolentiae* was an appeal to the experience and/or reasonableness of the audience and/or to its acceptance of some principle.
51. *Either*, p. 280. "Finally" in the first line is found not in the Greek but in the German translation, and it helps Eremita to emphasize the finality of the completeness toward which Hegel assumes he is striving. Eremita probably intends Aristophanes' list to suggest the lack of continuity between, the randomness of, the items of experience that Hegel "assimilates" by putting them together in a supposedly necessary dialectical development. See chap. 11, n. 28 above.
52. *Either*, p. 287.

53. *Sartre*, p. 66.

54. See p. 174 above.

55. *Postscript*, p. 245; italics in original. "Taking away" is a negative movement opposed to the positive "taking up" movement of *Aufhebung*.

56. *What Is Literature?* pp. 133–37. "The main characteristic of the story . . . is that it has been already thought out" (p. 132). We are offered "an immediately assimilable teaching. Feelings and actions are often presented to us as typical examples"—i.e., as commonplaces: " 'Daniel, like all young people . . . ,' 'Eve was quite feminine in that she . . . ,' 'Mercier had the nasty habit, common among clerks in the civil service . . . ' " (p. 138). If we move to the highest level, we reach Sartre's criticism of idealism as digested philosophy, to which he opposes as a reversal the regurgitations of his own nauseous philosophy (see p. 388 above).

57. *Either*, p. 288.

58. *Postscript*, p. 226. "Shadowgraphs" would be "autopathic" in the respect illustrated by the "multitude of shadows" that attend the individual (see chap. 10, n. 91 above).

59. *Stages*, p. 183; see also p. 415 above. Kierkegaard's metaphors of self-enclosure resemble, perhaps deliberately, those which Hegel employed of the work of art. But in Hegel they apply to the conclusive self-enclosed autonomy of the work of art as over against its author, whom the work transcends, whereas in Kierkegaard they are transferred back to the author as an individual whose process of reflection is self-enclosing, even though it is also inconclusive.

60. *Stages*, p. 183. This spatial metaphor had been with Kierkegaard since the early entries in his journal at the age of twenty-two, when he was trying to decide what to do with his life (see pp. 7, 40 above). The dialectical advance in reflexivity by the time of "A Passion Story" can be measured by comparing "the box" in which it was found "locked from the inside" with the following portion of an early entry: "I have searched . . . for the principle of my life. . . . What did I find? Not my self, which was what I was looking for (thinking of my soul, if I may so express it, as shut in a box with a spring lock which *external circumstances*, by pressing upon the lock, were to open)" (*Papirer*, I A 75; italics mine). This is the dependency on the external that Eremita treats as comic (see n. 41, this chapter).

Part V

Postscript

————

The writer, if there is anything important about the whole matter, can in no way be accused of having in feminine fashion left what is most important to a postscript.—Johannes Climacus

13

The Legacy

The writer must entrust to another the task of finishing what he has started.—Sartre

POSTPONEMENT

Any philosopher faces some difficulty with sequence. In particular, as I recognized in my preface, he has to balance two options against each other: he can go ahead to do whatever he undertakes to do as a philosopher, or he can climb on his own back and explain what he is doing and why and how he is doing it. In the present work I may have sometimes lost my sense of balance, but at least I have tried to keep the explanation of the why and the how tied in with the procedures employed by the existentialists themselves. I have followed in their paths, even when these paths seemed to be leading nowhere—at least in the usual philosophical sense of moving toward a general conclusion.

We have now arrived at a juncture not entirely dissimilar to that which Kierkegaard reached when he decided his esthetic works had served their function with respect to what he wanted to communicate, so that it seemed the time to bring them to a conclusion with a recapitulatory explanation in the *Postscript*. Existentialism today is a philosophical movement that seems to have played itself out and is perhaps dead. Hence it now seems the time to deal with the issue of its legacy. I shall try to do so in the existential terms that have emerged from its treatment of the problem of communication.

Since an existential dialectic develops by stages without reaching any general conclusion that would supersede these stages, sequence is more obviously crucial than in many other philosophies.[1] When in the first aphorism of *Either* the poet was tempted to abandon any effort at communication,[2] the problem was being held in abeyance; it was being postponed until he had tried to communicate what he wanted to communicate. In other words, only after first treating the problem of "becoming an individual" by breaking away from others could Kierkegaard at last explicitly take up in the *Postscript* the further problem that then arises of communicating with others. It then turns out that his treatment of the first problem must remain merely prefatory, merely introductory for any other individual.

At the same time, as I also anticipated in my preface, this postponement until a postscript is probably designed to subvert Hegel's argument for postponement—his argument that his reader should wait patiently until he reaches a systematic conclusion. Climacus is downgrading "concluding" by giving it not the systematic form of a scientific conclusion but that of a mere "postscript." So "unscientific" a procedure may arouse the worst suspicions, as Climacus admits in his self-ironizing defense of *Concluding Unscientific Postscript*: "The writer, if there is anything important about the whole matter, can in no way be accused of having in feminine fashion left what is most important to a postscript."[3]

The irony is directed too at the fashion in which Kierkegaard regards Hegel as unable to reach a conclusion. Reflection, we remember, must continue indefinitely unless it is brought to a conclusion (*slutning*) by a resolution (*beslutning*), and this resolution cannot be indefinitely postponed, because eventually it will be too late.[4] Indeed, in adopting the denigrating title *Postscript* Kierkegaard may be thinking of Hegel's own famous conclusion at the end of the preface to the *Philosophy of Right*:

> When philosophy paints its gray on gray, then has a form of life grown old, and with gray on gray it cannot be rejuvenated but only understood. The owl of Minerva takes flight only at dusk.
> But it is time to conclude this preface.

Kierkegaard would be ready to exploit Hegel's point that philosophy comes too late for anything to be done with regard to what it is reflecting about. But he would also have found in Hegel's conclusion a reference to a "postscript" which he could latch onto:

> But it is time to conclude this preface [*Vorwort*]. As a preface its function is only to speak in an external and subjective fashion of the point of view of the work which it anticipates. If one is to speak of a content in a philosophical fashion, only a scientific objective treatment is tolerable. Contradicting the writer, if it takes any other form besides that of a scientific treatment of the subject matter, it amounts to only a subjective postscript [*nur für subjectives Nachwort*], to which as a matter of capricious conviction I must remain indifferent.

Climacus's *Postscript* does take another form besides that of a scientific treatment of the subject matter. It pits a *subjective* dialectic against Hegel's scientific *objective* treatment.

EREMITA

In spite of Kierkegaard's postponement until a postscript of his explicit treatment of the problem of communicating with his reader, I have managed to employ the esthetic of *Either* to explain why the esthetic form of the communication should be poetic. Even in Hegel's "system of the arts" a disintegrating separation of *internal* from *external* is involved in the arrival at the poetic form,[5] and this form itself is further redesigned by Eremita to respect the separation he feels in his isolation from other individuals, as well as the inconclusive, incomplete, and unfinished character of the writer's own experience. This redesigning is also carried out, we shall soon see, in order not to impose his experience as if it could be a complete and finished version of the reader's own experience.

In presenting the problem of communication, I have focused on Eremita's esthetic. For communication is not a problem in Husserl's phenomenology or in contemporary existentialists, insofar as their philosophies are phenomenological,[6] and it is accordingly best expounded by reference to Kierkegaard's more purely dialectical method. But insofar as their method is dialectical too, the sequence of their works takes on philosophical significance. And just as Kierkegaard postpones his explicit treatment of the problem of communication until the *Postscript*, so Heidegger does not deal explicitly with it in *Being and Time*, nor does Sartre in *Being and Nothingness* nor Merleau-Ponty in *The Phenomenology of Perception*. The problem emerges for explicit treatment only in their later works.

Although I shall continue to focus on Kierkegaard's dialectic, I shall also furnish side references to the later works of other existentialists, in order to push my demonstration of the coherence of the movement. Almost as dislocating as *ex-sistential* experience with the problem of communication as that posed by Kierkegaard's "A Passion Story," which we began considering in the preceding chapter, is the legacy of Genet's passion story as interpreted by Sartre:

> What is left, when the book is closed? A feeling of emptiness, shadows, and terrifying beauty, an "eccentric" experience which we cannot incorporate into the fabric of our life and which will always remain "on its edge," unassimilable, the memory of a filthy night of debauchery [*nuit crapuleuse*] when we gave ourselves up to a man and came off.

Such a book Sartre distinguishes from those that we can assimilate because they belong to our communion when we meet in the common place. In Genet's books we avoid meeting each other:

There are books which are addressed to all of us in each of us, and we feel that we are the crowd when we enter them. Genet's are brothels where one slips in by a half-open door, hoping not to meet anyone, and when one is there one is altogether alone. It is, however, this very refusal to universalize that gives them their universality: the universal and incommunicable experience that they offer to all as particular individuals—the experience of isolation.

Each reader becomes an Eremita, as in *Either/Or*.[7]

POSTHUMOUS PAPERS

The question of legacy—as to "what is left"—is implicit in Eremita's characterization of the contents of *Either* as "Posthumous Papers." Like "buried alive," "posthumous" is a metaphor for dislocation. But where "buried alive" applied most obviously to the symparenkromenous writer and his character Antigone, "posthumous" applies to what has been written and to the relation that then ensues between the writer and the reader.

An examination of this relation is undertaken in the paragraph following the long sentence in which "finish" is discredited. The paragraph begins with a redescription of the opposing *modus loquendi*:

> Our society requires at every single meeting a renewal and rebirth, to the end that its inner activity may be renewed by a new description of its productivity. Let us then describe our intent [*tendents*] as an effort at fragmentary striving or in the art of writing posthumous papers.

If the metaphor of "buried alive" implies in the case of the writer an interrupted, unfinished life, "posthumous" similarly implies that his work was interrupted and left unfinished:

> A completely finished work retains no relation to the poetic personality; with posthumous papers, one continually feels, because of their having been broken off, the desultoriness, a prompting to poeticize about the personality. Posthumous papers are like a ruin, and what haunted place could be more natural for the buried?[8]

A completely finished work retains no relation to the poetic personality because it acquires from its completeness, as Hegel keeps emphasizing, its own conclusive, self-enclosed autonomy, as over against the writer; whereas with the unfinished work, the details that the writer failed to provide are left to the poetic imagination of the reader.

When I previously cited from the discussion of "posthumous papers," I did not reach the byplay which the spokesman for the spokesman for the Symparenkromenoi goes on to indulge:

> In a certain sense, everything a poet has produced is posthumous; but one would never think of calling a completely executed work posthumous, even though it had the contingent property of not having been published in the poet's lifetime. Also I assume that the true property of all human productivity, as we have apprehended it, is that it is a legacy. A legacy, then, is what I shall call our productions—an artistic legacy, negligence, indolence. I shall call the genius we appreciate *vis inertiae*, the natural law that we worship. With this pronouncement I have now complied with our sacred customs and procedures.

The problem of appropriation is undergoing reformulation here. It is a problem no longer simply for the individual but involves the relation between the writer and the reader. Hence the *interplay* between property (*egenskab*—something that is one's own/what is intrinsic to something) and legacy (*efterladenskab*)—something which is becoming another's.

INHERITANCE

There is also byplay that does not come across in the English translation of *efterladte* as "posthumous," even though our anticipations of the *Postscript* (*efterskrift*) have indicated how Kierkegaard counts on the sequential character of a dialectic in order to play with the term "after." *Efterladte* means "left after" or "left behind." The verb *efterlade* can refer to "leaving" either property or persons "behind," and *efterladte* can refer to the "bereaved" who are "left behind" and are the heirs of those buried—in the present case to ourselves as readers.

Kirkegaard's playing with *efterlade* in the first sense exploits the dynamics of transition in Hegel's dialectic, where what is "left over," what "remains" at one stage, must be taken over for development during the superseding stage. Eremita is parodying such transitions when he explains that visual art must at some point in the development of reflective grief "renounce" the attempt to represent it and "leave it over to be treated by poets and psychologists"—that is, by "Shadowgraphs."[9] But a transition in the second sense of *efterlade* is not found in Hegel, where nothing can be significantly "left over" for another individual to "finish," since the transition which is picked out by Kierkegaard's opposition as significant is the movement of *Aufhebung* by which differences between individuals are transcended. No individual survives this movement, not even the writer who initiated it, for when "the system is brought to a conclusion [*slutter sig af*]," Kierkegaard points out on Hegel's behalf, "there must be no existing remainder [*rest*] left behind, not even such a little dingle-dangle as the existing Herr Professor who writes the system."[10]

The transition in the second sense of *efterladte*, which is found in Kierkegaard, is not a Hegelian transition: there is nothing in the way of a dialectical outcome for the reader to "inherit." Kierkegaard instead "leaves the reader in the lurch by not allowing him any outcome."[11] Thus "it is left [*overladt*] to the reader himself to put things together [in order to satisfy the *relational* requirements of a dialectic], if he so wishes."[12]

Unfortunately, it is here that a little dingle-dangle of a Herr Professor is likely to intervene. This risk we became aware of at the very outset, where I quoted Kierkegaard's prophetic lament:

> I shall leave behind me, intellectually speaking, considerable capital; and yet I know too who will be my heir—that figure so very distasteful to me, he who until now has inherited and will continue to inherit all that is best: the Scholar, the Professor.

The metaphors of "wealth," "capital," "inheritance," are not just metaphors for Kierkegaard. We have watched him maintain the double-edged thrust of the contradiction between the *internal* and the *external* by retaining a reference to the external when the process of "internalization" produces a metaphor. Thus the metaphor of becoming "buried alive" by the "internalizing" process of reflection is underpinned by the ancient Antigone's having been literally "buried alive." Similarly, Kierkegaard's own life was often a literal rendering of what was metaphorical in his philosophy, so that we can sometimes ferret out in some detail of his life "the reduplicated presence" of a "thought" which he carefully developed into an image or a metaphor in his philosophy.[13] Thus he was literally preoccupied with the capital he inherited from his father as well as metaphorically with the "capital" he would leave behind him "intellectually speaking."

The two seem in fact to have been closely linked in his mind. We have watched him uphold squandering metaphorically, and he did in fact live rather extravagantly, using up his inherited capital to support in some style his life of writing and the costs of publishing his writings. He then died—as it were by some providential prearrangement—when there was only enough left to pay for his burial.[14]

When Sartre comments that Kierkegaard employed his own life to formulate the problem of his philosophy,[15] he is referring to the problem he himself finds crucial to any existential philosophy. But the comment can be extended to many of the details of Kierkegaard's life. He may have rejected *Ausmalung* as a procedure for carrying out in detail the execution of a work of art. But he often did carry out in detail in life the execution of the role he felt assigned by his writings. Since we are concerned with his "esthetic production," it may be worth noting the extremes to which he went to sustain the role of an esthete who as such is entirely indolent and committed to no course of action. Only his proof-reader knew the truth. The explanation of "the existence I led by way of seconding my esthetic production" he reserved for posterity:

> I was so busy when I was reading the proofs of *Either/Or* that it was impossible to spend the time I usually spent sauntering back and forth on the street. I did not get through the work until late in the evening, and then I hurried to the theater, where I remained actually only from five to ten minutes. . . . To be seen every night for five minutes by several hundred people sufficed to substantiate the verdict: he hasn't the least thing in the world to do; he is a mere idler.[16]

This appearance of dissolute behavior may seem a trivial detail, but it is not irrelevant to his characterization of "the art" of the Symparenkromenoi as designed "artificially to produce . . . the effect of carelessness and contingency" or to the final addition in the chain of these characterizations—an "artistic legacy [*efterladenskab*], negligence [*efterladenhed*], indolence."

LEAVINGS

The addition of "indolence" reinforces the implication of "negligence" with respect to the way the "legacy" is to be handled, since a punning relation has already been established between *efterladenskab* and *efterladenhed,* and the "negligence" is in turn reduced to the "natural law" of *vis inertiae*. Thus the earlier contradiction of producing "artistically . . . the effect of carelessness" is renewed. The dialectical *ambiguity* of *tendents* is thereby exploited: earlier it seemed to refer to a deliberate "intent"; now in retrospect it seems to refer to the "tendency" to let oneself go. The writer's "striving" which was associated with deliberate "intent" is relaxed in favor of the reader's taking over.[17] At the same time "the effect of carelessness" refurbishes the theme of "looseness" which developed at the end of the long sentence where the "troublesome, meticulous workmanship" which "finish" requires was attacked.

The term translated as "legacy" refers to "something left behind," but in the plural it can also mean "leavings," "leftovers," "remnants," "litter," "excrement." The plural seems pertinent here since a redescription of the symparenkromenous "productions" or "posthumous papers" is under way. This redescription is even more disparaging than the original description, "fragments." The reason becomes clearer if we keep in mind the portion of the long sentence that is relevant to the relation between the writer and the reader. We recall that

> the wealth of an individual consists precisely in the proficiency with which he squanders the fragmentary, that what brings enjoyment to the producing individual also brings enjoyment to the receiving individual, not the irksome, meticulously detailed workmanship with which the execution is carried out, or the prolonged apprehension, but the production and enjoyment of the glimpsed transitoriness which for the producer involves something more than thorough execution, since it is the appearance of the Idea, and which for the recipient involves something more, since its fulguration awakens his own productivity—since, I repeat, all such sustained execution and prolonged apprehension is contrary to the intent of our society. . . .

It is from the point of view of the "receiving individual" as heir, as reader, that "everything a poet has produced" and "left behind" is worthless "litter," "excrement"; and that the previously strenuous effort of the poet or writer becomes mere "carelessness," "indolence," "vis inertiae."

Thus "finish" is discredited, not just because the personal experience of the "producing individual," which the work is to express, was itself fragmentary. Indeed we have watched him retreat into his isolation as an Eremita. But he then loses his authority over his work and becomes pseudonymous. In the process, he loses his authority over his characters too. Eremita's modern Antigone lacks the completeness, the objectivity, the plasticity of the ancient Antigone. Her character remains unfinished, and it is "left" to a reader to fill in the shadowy outlines by reference to the details of his own personal experience—or, put more dialectically, by reference to the details of his own life in relation to some second individual. In other words, it is not only within the perspective imposed by the problem of existence but also within the perspective imposed by the ensuing problem of communication that Hegel's criteria of "plasticity," "objectivity" of representation, "inclusiveness," "conclusiveness," and hence "finish" have to be abandoned.[18] The writer's version of his experience must be left subjective, inconclusive, incomplete, and unfinished, so that it does not impose itself on the reader as a finished version of *his* experience.

Accordingly, the first of the "brides," Antigone, is presented by the spokesman as follows: "She is my creation, but still her outline [*omrids*] is so indefinite [*ubestemt*], her figure so nebulous, that each of you can become enamored of her and love her in your own fashion."[19] Her shadowy figure is the "trace" of a general outline to be shared in common with the reader as an abstract possibility which they both reflect upon.

But the reader is to regard the spokesman as "buried" and himself as his heir. The "execution" which has not been carried out in detail has been "left" to the reader to carry out in terms of his own life, just as Kierkegaard himself carried out in his own life (e.g., with five minutes at the theater) some of the details of the abstract esthetic possibility he reflected on as A in *Either*.

SUSPENSE

In a somewhat similar fashion, the "execution" cannot be carried out by the writer in Sartre. "The object which the writer creates is out of his reach," and it cannot become objective for him. It remains

> in suspense [*en sursis*]—one can always change this line, that tint, this word. Thus the neophyte painter asked his master, "When should I regard my painting as finished?" And the master replied, "When you can look at it with surprise and say to yourself, 'I made that.'"
>
> That is to say, never. It would amount to regarding one's own work with the eyes of another.

In short, an objective work of art can never be achieved by the writer: "Creation can only find its completion in reading." For "the artist [the writer] must entrust to another the task of finishing what he has started."[20]

Their collaboration does not mean for Sartre, any more than for Kierkegaard, that reader and writer are communing in some common place in the fashion Sartre associates with the deliverances of Heidegger's "one." Writer and reader remain "two distinct agents." When the process of creation (like the other undertakings we have encountered at other levels in existentialism) fails to attain an autonomous outcome with the work of art, the failure is congruent with its retaining a *reflexive* character:

> We are less conscious of the thing produced the more conscious we are of our activity in producing it. When it is a matter of pottery or building and we are proceeding in accordance with traditional norms, with tools whose use is codified, it is Heidegger's notorious "one" who is working with our hands. In this case the outcome can seem sufficiently alien to us to retain its objectivity in our eyes. But if we are ourselves producing the rules of production, its standards, and criteria, if our creative élan comes from the depths of our heart, then we shall never find anything besides ourselves in our work.

Thus the subjectivity of the work distinguishes it from artifacts: "The writer cannot read what he writes, while the shoemaker can wear the shoes he has made, . . . and the builder can live in the building he has built."[21] It is the reader who finally produces the work of art, just as in *Either* it is the reader who is to produce his own "bride."

AUSMALUNG

This problem of execution bears on an issue which existentialism has raised from the outset—the issue of the relation between the particularity of the individual's experience and the generality we expect a philosophy to achieve. This issue has acquired considerable complexity. If existentialism were merely a matter of the individual writer's romantic self-expression, generality would not perform the function it does. It is needed not simply, as in traditional philosophy, in order to get beyond and above particular experiences but in order to allow sufficient scope for the inclusion of the particular experiences of anyone who is to become an individual and appropriate these experiences, as opposed to those of the writer's.

Furthermore, the *Ausmalung* that is denied the writer and assigned to the reader is not merely just a matter of his filling out the "outline" haphazardly with particular details. They are ingredients in a dialectical *reversal* which we have seen is to enable the reader to proceed in the direction opposite to the dialectical development with which ever higher levels of reflection are sought in *Either* until finally their abstractness is indicated by ascribing the esthetic and ethical points of view presented to A and B. When the reader has followed through this upward movement of reflection, he must be able to break it off with the *reversal*. For his own particular experiences can finally be appropriated as such only when they become ingredients in the actions with which he reaches his own conclusion. Hence he must have been relieved by the writer from "the prolonged apprehension" which "a fully finished work" would inflict on him and which would distract him externally from exercising his own initiative.[22] He has been accorded instead only a "glimpse" of the possibility.

Originally a "provisional" glimpse constituted an "aphorism," although it also became the starting point for the dialectical development in "the longer essays." Yet now we are entering a perspective within which this development shrinks so that these essays can be characterized as "essays in the aphoristical." They cannot yield more than a "glimpse," since their function is merely to awaken the "productivity" of the reader so that he can carry out separately and finish a dialectical development which is his own. The writer has left him (to revert to the idiom of "Shadowgraphs") "at most a hint which may furnish a trace."

What might have gotten in his way as distractingly external, when he carries out this development on his own, is drawn to one side. In Antigone's case there is "left behind" hardly more than a "name" which is "retained" from the ancient tragedy, as is explained regarding the other "brides":

> Definite names of certain poetic figures are borrowed for the purpose of characterization, but it does not follow at all that only these figures appear before you. The names must be regarded as *nomina appellativa* ["general names" or "common nouns"], and from my point of view I shall not stand in the way if one or another of you should feel tempted to give to a particular picture [or "image"] another name, a dearer name that happens perhaps to be more natural to him.[23]

The reader is being encouraged to fill out the outline by visualizing in particular detail whatever other individual is the relevant character in his own life.

Autobiographically speaking, Kierkegaard is attempting in *Either/Or* to communicate with "a feminine reader," Regina, after having broken off their engagement and left his life disconnected, fragmentary.[24] In her case the relevant character (at least in the space of Kierkegaard's imagination) whom she is to catch a "glimpse" of during the process of communication is Kierkegaard himself. Thus a sex change takes place which I noted earlier was implicit in Kierkegaard's presentation of himself as a modern Antigone, who could not communicate with her fiancé. One may be skeptical as to whether Regina could have carried out in the space of her own imagination the necessary surgery or whether she could have found the dialectical flip-flop of this sex change an entirely adequate clarification of their relation. It could hardly have been much less disconcerting than the prospect which he held out at the end of the "Diary of the Seducer" that afterward, if he had seduced her, he would have wished to change her into a man. Nothing less would have been sufficient to overcome her woman's "loving lack of understanding," for she was assured in the "Diary" itself that a woman cannot reach that level of reflective understanding where dialectical dexterity of this sort can be displayed.[25] At any rate Regina did not display it, for she kept her secrets better locked up than Kierkegaard, in spite of the dialectical fashion in which their relation is structured in "A Passion Story": "He Is Introverted [*Indesluttet*]/She Cannot Be So."[26]

PASSION STORY

The title "A Passion Story" suggests, however, that neither this diary nor the earlier "Diary of the Seducer," to which it is related, can be reduced to autobiography. Kierkegaard is not simply attempting to communicate with Regina. His procedure is *bifocal*: he is coping not only with her personal misunderstanding of him as a particular individual but also with Hegel's philosophical misunderstanding of Christ's passion. In interpreting the relation between these two levels, we must keep as far as possible within the limits of the esthetic stage in Hegel and in Kierkegaard.

The transition in Hegel from the *objective* art of sculpture to the *subjective* arts was traced earlier in a general fashion, but the *subjective* arts are a "religious sphere for Hegel, and the transition is more specifically impelled by the requirements of the content presented by the passion story:

> This sphere of representation is entirely separated from the classical plastic ideal. . . . What is human and bodily is negated and manifested in its suffering [*Schmerz*], whereas in the classical ideal it does not lose undisturbed harmony with what is spiritual and substantial. Christ scourged, with the crown of thorns, carrying his cross to the place of execution, nailed to the cross, dying an agonizing and slow death—this cannot be represented in the form of Greek beauty.[27]

We have seen that the suffering of the characters in a Greek tragedy is not the final outcome but the vision accorded the audience of a reconciling *Aufhebung*. Similarly, the suffering of Christ is only transitional, and not the final outcome of his passion story:

> The process of dying in the divine nature is to be considered only as a point of transition [*Durchgangspunkt*] through which the reconciliation of mind with itself is consummated, and the divine on one side and the human on the other, the absolutely universal and the manifestation of subjectivity, whose mediation is being effected, come together in an affirmative conclusion [*sich affirmativ zusammenschliessen*]. . . . In this respect the resurrection and the ascension are the most suitable events for representation in Christ's story [*Geschichte*].[28]

STORYTELLING

The *Aufhebung* illustrated by these historical events ultimately involves the reconciliation of the divine with the human, religion with philosophy. Thus it does not matter much to Hegel whether the resurrection or the ascension is taken as the final outcome of the passion story. (The transfiguration can also qualify as an "imaginative representation" of an *Aufhebung*.) But the reconciliation itself is an *Aufhebung*—that is, a transition from the "imaginative representations," which in the biblical narrative still are historical events, to the higher level of philosophical thought. Hegel explains this transition:

> When it is a matter not of truth but merely of history [*Geschichte*], as in imaginative representation and phenomenal thinking, we can of course remain at the level of storytelling [*Erzahlung*]. . . . But philosophy should be not the narration of events but knowledge of what is true in these events; and further, on the basis of this knowledge to grasp that which in the story appears as mere event [*Geschehen*].[29]

Such discounting of history as narrative coincides with Hegel's discounting of *Vorstellung* psychologically in favor of philosophical thought, although what I have so far stressed has been Hegel's abstraction from, and the existential retrieval of, the spatial relations which *Vorstellung* involves, by virtue of its locating function of "placing" something "before" the mind.

But temporal relations are also abstracted from. "What is relevant to *Vorstellung*," according to Hegel, "is history," which is "a sequence of transactions . . . that follow each other in time and are as well side by side in space." Indeed every narrative involves this external series (*ausserlicher Reihe*) of occurrences and actions. But *Vorstellung* "leaves the connection in a contingent form and does not go on to its true essence and to its eternal interpenetrative unity." But when philosophy internalizes the connection and grasps its "inner meaning," an *Aufhebung* takes place, and "*Vorstellung* dissolves into the form of thought." Thus biblical history (and most significantly the passion story) takes place at two levels—at the level of religious *Vorstellung* and at the level of philosophical conclusions, where it becomes insight into "timeless events" (*zeitloses Geschehen*).[30]

INCARNATION

I have compared Hegel's treatment of the outcome of Christ's passion story with the last stage of *Stages*, which is subtitled "A Passion Story." It may seem that I should not have pressed on impatiently to this religious stage. But "A Passion Story" is not only a diary of Kierkegaard's "unhappy love" as well as an allusion to Christ's passion story, but it is also prepared for, as the last stage of *Stages*, by the passion story which is the last stage of *Either*—the "Diary of the Seducer." And we are not entirely unprepared for this *last* stage of *Either*, since it is related to the *first* stage—"The Immediate Stages of the Erotic," which is a passion story too: at the last stage, the seducer reflects in his diary on a seduction, while Don Giovanni is an immediate seducer who never takes the time to reflect.[31] Indeed *Either* as a whole is a passion story, as we were informed by its epigraph—"Are the passions pagan . . . ?"

In the "Notice" that precedes the diary of *Stages* the editor, just after discovering how easy it is to date all the entries in the diary, refers to Hegel's philosophy of history,[32] lest we assume that his discovery is merely the flaunting of Kierkegaard's autobiography. But if we remember Kierkegaard criticizes Hegel's philosophy as esthetic, we are not surprised that the editor of the seducer's diary, which is the climax of the esthetic stage, observes in his preface,

> The diary as it progresses becomes more and more sparing of dates, as if the history in its progress . . . although historically actual, comes near to being Idea, and for this reason the temporal determinations [*tidsbestemmelshed*] become a matter of indifference.[33]

This indifference, I am suggesting, parodies what Kierkegaard takes to be the indifference to historical events in Hegel's philosophy, for its development is also the progress of a seduction in which the seducer himself is being "led astray" by his attempt to attain a more elevated insight into "timeless events."

Indeed the editor comments, regarding the seducer's own development,

> His way through life was untraceable [*usporlig*], for his feet were so formed that he left no traces—thus I best represent imaginatively to myself his infinite self-reflection. . . . He lived far too spiritually to be a seducer in the commonplace sense. But sometimes he assumed a parastatic body and was then sheer sensuality.[34]

The theologian who translated *Either* tries to pin this down with a footnote:

> The word "parastatic" came into currency in the struggle between the church and the Gnostics in the second century over the nature of the body of Christ, the Gnostics maintaining that the divine Logos had assumed an apparent or phantom body only, not an actual one, for according to the heretical view, it would be unseemly for the Logos to be manifested in the flesh. It comes as a bit of a jolt to have a word from that context applied here, but the meaning is plain enough: the author of the diary, although a coldly intellectual type, did occasionally take upon himself the characteristics of passionate flesh and blood.[35]

But if the meaning were this plain, we would be up against a seducer in a quite commonplace sense. What is more common than "a coldly intellectual type" who sometimes takes upon himself "the characteristics of passionate flesh and blood"?

INTERPENETRATIVE UNITY

The transposition of the word "parastatic" from its theological context should have given the translator a more *ex-sistential* "jolt," for is there not a dislocating contradiction in what is not an actual body becoming "sheer sensuality"? The contradiction seems hardly resolved in the diary entry on the seduction itself, except by way of parody, for the seducer reports;

> Everything is imagery [*billede*]; I myself am a myth about myself, for is it not as myth that I hasten to this rendezvous? Who I am has nothing to do with it. Everything finite and temporal is forgotten; only the eternal remains. . . .[36]

In fact we are warned in Eremita's preface that the seduction itself may only have been an imaginary possibility the author of the "Diary" entertained.

But in any case the moment of seduction when the seducer and seducee finally come together is a parody of the synthesis of subject and object consummated by Hegel's *Aufhebung*. In spite of the fact that we remain at the level of *Vorstellung* in the "Diary," so that (to borrow Hegel's terminology) it "leaves the connection in a contingent form" which can promptly be broken off (as it will be at the end of the "Diary"), the diarist still makes in effect the Hegelian claim that he has risen to the connection's "true essence and to its eternal interpenetrative unity." Or, to describe the reflexive phase of the synthetic operation in terms of the seducer's own mythology;

> This is the glory and divinity of esthetics, that it enters into relation with the beautiful. . . . My eyes never weary of surveying this peripheral manifold, these scattered emanations of feminine beauty. Each particular has its little share and yet is complete in itself—happy, glad, beautiful. Each has her own share: the merry smile, the roguish glance, the wistful eye, the pensive head, the exuberant spirits, the quiet sadness, the deep foreboding, the brooding melancholy, the earthly homesickness, the unbaptized movements, the beckoning brows, the questioning lips, the mysterious forehead, the ensnaring curls, the concealing lashes, the heavenly pride, the earthly modesty, the angelic purity, the secret blush, the light step, the hovering grace, the languishing posture, the dreamy yearning, the inexplicable sighs, the willowy form, the soft form, the opulent bosom, the swelling hips, the little foot, the dainty hand—each has her own share, and the one does merely have what the other has. And when I have gazed and gazed again, contemplated and again contemplated this multitudinous variety, when I have smiled, sighed, flattered, threatened, desired, tempted, laughed, wept, hoped,

feared, won, lost—then I shut up my fan and gather what was scattered into a unity, the parts into a whole.

SELF-REFLECTION

What the translator should not have overlooked in the preface to the "Diary" is that the seduction itself takes the philosophical form of "infinite self-reflection." This would explain why "who I am has nothing to do with it." Who I am is determined, at least minimally, by my spatiotemporal location. But the "I" that continues reflecting on itself transcends its spatiotemporal limitations and its self undergoes dissolution.

The translator should also not have overlooked the contradiction implicit in according such "infinite self-reflection" expression in a diary (*dagbog*), which as a temporal genre is committed to "imaginative representation." If the seducer's "way through life" was "untraceable," if "he left no traces,"[37] there would be nothing spatial left that would be susceptible of *Vorstellung* and could be traced day by day in a diary. Probably Eremita's theological point is that this contradiction is unresolved in Hegel's system.[38] On one hand the incarnation is pivotal to the Hegelian dialectic at the level of *Vorstellung*, inasmuch as it was the (eternally) internal becoming the externally representable in history, so that man in turn can overcome this contradiction and attain the resurrection of the spirit, ascending transfigured beyond finite limitations to the infinite. On the other hand, when this *Aufhebung* takes us up to the higher philosophical level, it becomes clear in Eremita's dialectic that the incarnation can only have been faked. The body was merely a phantom, and Christendom in Hegel, like Cordelia in the "Diary," has been "led astray" by this phantom. Perhaps Cordelia was not actually seduced physically at all but only offered an imaginary possibility to reflect upon.

Thus the seducer's eventual indifference to dates parodies Hegel's short-circuiting of the biblical story of Christ's passion in favor of its outcome with the transfiguration, resurrection, or the ascension, whereby Hegel's philosophy as "infinite self-reflection" at once transcends the externality of "imaginative representation" and salvages salvation from all forms of externality. What Kierkegaard is concerned with is the salvation of the individual as unique as well as the unique individuality of the savior: the seducer's "who I am has nothing to do with it" mimics Hegel's conviction that any individual is to find in the *Aufhebung* that is the outcome of the passion story an imaginative model for discarding his own individuality:

> The history of the spirit, consummated in one individual [Christ], contains nothing but . . . the individual's putting aside his individual-

ity of body and spirit—i.e., that he suffers and dies, but with a reversal [*umgekehrt*] through the grief of death rises out of death and ascends as God in his glory.[39]

Kierkegaard retains the theological model when the religious stage in *Stages* takes the form of "A Passion Story," but this story is not a "putting aside" of his individual existence, for it is the story of his relation to Regina from a religious point of view, just as the earlier "Diary of the Seducer" was the story of the relation he might have had with her, if an esthetic point of view had prevailed.

In the religious story of the later "Diary" suffering is not a "transitional moment" (*gejennemgangsmoment*) but is "unceasing."[40] In other words, there is no *Aufhebung*. Since the earlier "Diary" was already a parody of Hegel's philosophy as esthetic and the story of his own esthetic relation to Regina, it may hardly have been necessary to press on to Kierkegaard's religious stage in order to illustrate the *bifocal* character of his philosophy. But I have anticipated this later stage in Kierkegaard, and even Hegel's transcending religious *Vorstellung* to philosophical thought, because we might not otherwise be able to see as clearly why Kierkegaard's rejecting, on behalf of the individual, the movement of *Aufhebung* should take the form of employing a "storytelling method" or how this method is designed dialectically "to oppose the abominable untruth which is characteristic of modern philosophy."[41]

Notes

1. See p. 284 above.
2. See p. 246 above.
3. *Postscript*, p. 14. In my preface I stressed how Kierkegaard ironically upgrades prefaces in opposition to Hegel. I quoted from *Prefaces (Forord)*, whose pseudonym's "desire to have written a book" (*Samlede Værker*, 5:207) is frustrated by his marriage, which we have since seen Kierkegaard can interpret as a Hegelian commitment to objectification, actuality, and continuity. Now we shall watch Kierkegaard ironically upgrade a postscript in opposition to Hegel.
4. See p. 409 above.
5. See p. 431 above.
6. For what is in effect Husserl's elimination of the problem of communication, see Derrida, *Speech and Phenomena*.
7. *Saint Genet*, p. 589. See p. 475 above.
8. *Either*, p. 150. Note that the renewal requires interplay between the *modus loquendi* and the *modus vivendi*.
9. See p. 430 above.
10. *Postscript*, p. 111. In Hegel's own terms the writer must "forget himself," as I explained in my preface.
11. Ibid., p. 257. Climacus is referring to the absence of an outcome not in *Either/Or*

but in the recapitulation, "A Passion Story," whose title reembodies the principle of contradiction—"Guilty/Not Guilty?" Climacus explains that "the question mark clearly constitutes a reference to a trial" (ibid., p. 256) and that "the failure of an outcome to appear [as it would in a dialectical development in Hegel] is precisely a determination of inwardness, for an outcome is something outward, and a communication of outcomes is an outward relation . . ." (p. 257). "Failure to appear" (*udeblivelse*) can be used of a failure to appear at a trial in court, but it also incorporates as a root the term *blive*, which I have translated as "remain." Although Climacus is dealing with the story of an individual, it is all the more appropriate to interpret his juridical idiom as an attack on the Hegelian concept of "the verdict of [social] history" (p. 122), as I interpreted Merleau-Ponty's handling of the Dreyfus case.

12. Climacus is referring to the fact that at the ethical stage of *Stages* Judge William is not familiar, as he was in *Either*, with what has transpired at the esthetic stage and so is not in a position to propose a resolution to its contradictions. See chap. 11, n. 28 above. For the relational requirements of a dialectic, see p. 145 above.

13. Previously I stressed Sartre's retention of a literal component in his metaphors, but in his case this component is often physiological.

14. Also thirty bottles of wine. For a brief account of Kierkegaard's financial history, see Thompson (pp. 127–28, 204–6), who draws on Brandt and Ramnel, *Sören Kierkegaard og pengene (Kierkegaard and Money)*. They dispose of the legend that Kierkegaard exhausted the very considerable fortune he inherited by his lavish generosity to the poor. Thompson summarizes, "The fact is that Kierkegaard simply spent his fortune on . . . carriage drives, exquisite furniture, elegant bindings, stuffed lamb, and good wine" (p. 128). But he then goes on to resist the inference: "To say that Kierkegaard squandered his fortune would be to miss the point. . . . Having rejected the world early in life . . . , he used his money simply to sustain that rejection [in the form of his writings]."

15. See p. 159 above.

16. *Point of View*, pp. 49–50. In view of the trouble to which Kierkegaard went in posing as an indolent esthete, it may be that "to say that Kierkegaard squandered his fortune" does not entirely "miss the point" for "squandering" may have appealed to him literally as well as in the metaphorical sense indicated in the passage condemning *Ausmalung*.

17. In this dialectic, the writer's "indolence" is a matter of "doing nothing to cater to a reader's indolence" (*Postscript*, p. 265)—i.e., his "striving" is solicited.

18. Kierkegaard ironizes on Hegel's behalf, when "the system is brought to a conclusion, there must be no existing remainder left behind, not even such a little dingle-dangle as the existing Herr Professor who writes the system." Bringing the system to a conclusion would be the fulfillment of Hegel's promise that "when we have reached the conclusion of the whole, all will become clear" (see p. 404 above). There would then be no residue, either of the writer's or (we now see that Kierkegaard would add) of the reader's own experience, for the system is all-inclusive. Alternatively, if any residue is left over, it will require the renewal of the dialectic to keep up with it, and this renewal is in effect what Kierkegaard had undertaken on his own behalf and would encourage the reader to undertake as well.

19. *Either*, p. 151. *Rids* ("sketch") is the root of *skyggerids* ("shadowgraphs") as well as *omrids*. In a sketch the details are not filled in by *Ausmalung*, as they would be if the portrayal were "finished."

20. *What Is Literature?* pp. 33–34, 40. Thus "the literary object's only substance is the reader's subjectivity. Raskolnikov's sense of expectation is my sense of expectation which I lend him; . . . his hate against the judge interrogating him is my hate. . . . It would not exist without the hate that I feel toward him through Raskolnikov" (ibid., p. 39).

21. Ibid., pp. 37, 34–35.

22. Heidegger handles his reader in a comparable manner. Father Richardson has addressed to him certain questions, the first of which, Heidegger says, "concerns the initial impetus that determined the way my thought would travel." Heidegger admits, "I hesitate with my answers," explaining that "such pointers" as he might offer "will not be taken as directions for the way of independent reflection . . . which each must travel on his own" ("Letter to Father Richardson," in Richardson, p. viii).

23. *Either*, p. 175.

24. Ibid., p. 14. For the name "Regina," see p. 536 below.

25. *Either*, p. 440; *Papirer*, X¹ A 374. The dialectical alternative to raising her to the masculine level of reflective competence would be to return her to the level of immediacy as a flower—the heliotrope who remains perpetually turned toward her former lover. For her dependency on him, see chap. 10, n. 24 above.

26. *Stages*, p. 387. Frater Taciturnus is commenting on the dialectical contradictions displayed by "A Passion Story." Regina destroyed her letters to Kierkegaard, although she preserved his letters to her. To this extent she would seem to have succeeded in frustrating his attempt to "take her into history with me" (cited by Lowrie, 1:191). But as an aging widow she was lavish with reminiscences of not much interest.

27. *Aesthetics*, 1:538.

28. Ibid., pp. 538–39. This coming together of the human and the divine in an affirmative conclusion is of course the brunt of Kierkegaard's attack, as is illustrated by the "Ultimatum" of *Or*—"The Edification Implied in the Thought That as against God We Are Always in the Wrong" (p. 343).

29. *Logic*, p. 588. The affinity in German between "story" and "history" may come through in translation, but the association with "event" is sacrificed. The *Aufhebung* envisaged here is indispensable in Hegel, for "if we place the divine in the historical, we continually fall into the realm of instability [*schwankende*] and unsteadiness which are essentially characteristic of all that is historical" (*Philosophy of Religion*, 1:153). At last we recognize not only that Kierkegaard's commitment to "imaginative representation" is also a commitment to the historical but also that whether we consult Hegel's conception of "imaginative representation" or his conception of history, we find that in Hegel's own terms Kierkegaard's Socrates, Kierkegaard's poet, and Kierkegaard himself are condemned as individuals to "hover"—to be left "in suspense."

30. *Philosophy of Religion*, 1:146–47, 143, 148, 146. Kierkegaard's "loosening" of connections is not merely a parody of Hegel's concept of *Auslösung* (see chap. 11, n. 28 above) but illustrates how Kierkegaard's analysis remains in Hegel's terms at the level of *Vorstellung*," since all its movements . . . bring themselves into relation with each other . . . without in any way yielding up their independence" (*Philosophy of Religion*, 1:155).

31. *Either*, pp. 9, 97, 100–101.

32. *Stages*, p. 184.

33. *Either*, pp. 306–7.

34. Ibid., pp. 303–4. At the last stage of the tragic triad, there was "no trace of a body" (see chap. 10, n. 94 above); now at the last stage of the succeeding triad, there is again no trace. The reference to "his feet" probably recalls the dialectical problem of gaining a "foothold" as a starting point (see chap. 6, n. 97), for this problem is played up by the seducer with reference to the dialectical development he would initiate in reflecting on Cordelia ("I can hardly find a footing," he admits, for he is almost overcome with passion, p. 320), as well as with reference to Cordelia, who is threatened with the prospect of losing her footing (see p. 272 above).

35. *Either*, pp. 455–56. However, even on these occasions he apparently leaves no traces. His performance is so infinitely self-reflective that in neither the "Diary" nor its preface nor even Cordelia's letters do we get any impression of his physique. He must have seduced Cordelia without her becoming aware of what he looked like.

36. *Either*, p. 439.

37. Ibid., p. 423.

38. When the editor of the "Diary" adds to "his feet were so formed that he left no traces" the comment "Thus I best represent imaginatively [*forestiller*] to myself this infinite self-reflection," he is compounding the contradiction, since "self-reflection," when it becomes "infinite" in Hegel, transcends imaginative representation. There would seem to be further byplay in "to myself," for a finite self is intruding at a moment when "self-reflection" enjoys a reflexivity that transcends the finite.

39. *Aesthetics*, 1:534–35. Hegel is probably not alluding to the heretical version of the doctrine, but *parastatic* in Greek refers etymologically to a "putting aside," and as we have already seen, the seducer puts aside all individuality when he reaches the level where "who I am has nothing to do with it." The movement to which Hegel is alluding, the resurrection, provides an imaginative model not only for such discarding of one's particularity as an individual but also for discarding imaginative models: "What belongs to the sphere of imaginative representation" is "absolute spirit qua individual, or rather qua particular. . . . The particular self-consciousness [Christ] is represented as having actually died, but it is its particular individuality which dies into universality—i.e., in its knowledge. . . . The immediately preceding sphere of imaginative representation is explicitly transcended" (*Phenomenology*, p. 475). Findlay summarizes the import of the passage from which I have excerpted: "What is really meant by the passion and resurrection is the elimination of pictorial [i.e., imaginatively represented] particularity and its supersession by the life of thought. An existent entity [i.e., Christ, if we revert to the imaginative level] has become . . . a universal self-consciousness" (ibid., pp. 588–89).

40. *Postscript*, p. 256.

41. *Climacus*, p. 102.

14

The Reorientation

In the world of the spirit the various stages are not like towns on a route of travel.—Johannes Climacus

THE CURIOUS TOP

In interpreting existentialism as an individualism, I have tried to demonstrate that it exhibits a sufficient measure of coherence to be regarded as a philosophical movement. Specifically, I have been able to dismiss Lowrie's protest that between Kierkegaard and Sartre there is "hardly enough likeness to make it easy to define the difference." Lowrie did qualify this protest with what he evidently regarded as an inconsequential concession: "Sartre shows a certain resemblance to Kierkegaard in the fact that he has sought to popularize his views by creating a novelistic literature."[1] But even this concession is misconceived. Popularization is not the issue. That existentialism did in fact acquire a popular vogue, bequeathing to our common vocabulary the portentous term "existential"—this we have known from the outset. But we have discovered that popularization is an aim which is not consistent with the undertaking of the existentialist to disentangle his reader as well as himself from communion in the commonplace. We have also discovered that the problem of communication which is posed by this undertaking Kierkegaard solves by resort to "novelistic literature"—what he himself calls "poetry" or his "storytelling method."

When Sartre defines *What Is Literature?* he, like Kierkegaard, defines it as a means of communication. So defined, the literary work loses its objectivity and autonomy (as it does in Kierkegaard's opposition to its status in Hegel's esthetics), and it dissolves into a movement, composed of a dialectical relation between the writer and the reader, with the last word (again as in Kierkegaard) left to the reader:

> The literary object is a curious top which only exists in movement. For it to emerge a concrete act is necessary, reading; and it remains in

existence only as long as the reading goes on. Otherwise there are only black marks on paper.[2]

Thus "writing implies reading as its dialectical correlative."

This dialectical correlation constitutes a broad resemblance to Kierkegaard, and it survives the differences that can be attributed to Sartre's conversion to Marxism. In the social history Sartre offers in his third volume on Flaubert, the social relation he brings into focus is the relation between the writer and his reading public or, rather, the "disruption" of this relation that he finds the most striking feature of modern literature— its "radical shipwreck."[3] The relation between writer and reader was likewise disrupted in Kierkegaard's esthetic works, where the writer acknowledges that the reader is a "passerby."

What Is Literature? was Sartre's first serious venture into social history, and it is striking that he was not capable of carrying through the more straightforward Marxist social history which he envisaged for the second volume of the *Critique* but instead supplied, in interpreting Flaubert, a social history of the origins of modern literature. Indeed when Sartre protests against Engels's elimination of the individual from social history, he does not retain Engels's example of Napoleon, who had been for Hegel the prominent "world historical individual" of the time. He substitutes Flaubert.[4] As I have also already observed, all of Sartre's other existential psychoanalyses are writers: Baudelaire, Genet, and Sartre himself.

The Writer

Writer and reading are visualized by Sartre as "two related activities" which "require two distinct agents."[5] Let us continue to consider the agency of the writer before we return to the problem of communication. With respect to the writer, the comparison with Kierkegaard may seem to falter: Flaubert, Baudelaire, Genet, and Sartre are real individuals, as contrasted with Kierkegaard's dramatis personae, who are merely imaginary possibilities. But just as Kierkegaard uses a pseudonym in each of his esthetic works, so the individual in Sartre (including Sartre himself, according to his autobiography) acquires a fictitious role by writing. "To imagine," Sartre explains, "is at one and the same time to produce an imaginary object and to render oneself imaginary [*s'imaginariser*]." Thus Flaubert

> becomes double [*se dédouble*] during his narration; as *storyteller* he is *an other*. . . . He cannot raise himself to the level of reflection except by reflecting on an imaginary person who would be . . . a possible

Flaubert. . . . This reflection which takes imaginary form . . . is characteristic of the conduct of Flaubert in relation to himself.[6]

This *reflexive* relation is what renders Flaubert's stories available for the purpose of Sartre's psychoanalysis of Flaubert.[7]

The relation involves *interplay* not only between Flaubert himself, Flaubert as storyteller, and the personae of Flaubert's stories but also between Sartre and Flaubert, who "represents," Sartre reports, "the exact opposite of my own conception of literature."[8] Thus the structure of Sartre's interpretation is comparable to the nest of boxes that composes Kierkegaard's *Either/Or*, where most of the personae (e.g., Don Giovanni and Antigone and the other "brides") are similarly borrowed from other authors,[9] and where the conceptions of philosophy and esthetics are the exact opposites of Hegel's.

That the relation of a novelist to his characters is susceptible of a *reflexive* interpretation does not entail (as we have already recognized in Kierkegaard's case) the novel remaining a romantic matter of the novelist's own self-expression. As Sartre points out regarding Genet:

> while writing for his own pleasure the incommunicable dreams of his singularity, Genet has transformed them into the requirements of communication. There was no vocation . . . or that suffocating necessity to express oneself which writers have invented to cajole their public. . . . This onanist transformed himself into a writer.[10]

Besides the traits I earlier sorted out to distinguish Kierkegaard's and Sartre's existentialism as a philosophy, there is this preoccupation with "the requirements of communication" as requirements which can only be met by literary works.

Not only does Sartre interpret the novel as a means of communication in *What Is Literature?* but in his higher-level "novel" on the novelist Flaubert he also interprets him as having become a novelist because he was confronted with a problem of communication.[11] At this level too there is a "relation" between reading and writing which underlies a "disrelation." According to Sartre, Flaubert as a child had difficulty learning to read, so he felt himself "awkwardly inserted in the universe of language" which other men share in common. Thus it seemed to Flaubert that "the word is never his own." Here language is viewed as functioning not with objective reference to things but as a medium of social communication: "Via the word, it is in his relation to other human beings that Flaubert is afflicted from his earliest childhood."[12] Language is the medium of communion in the commonplace, and when Flaubert becomes a writer, he is becoming engaged at once in the subversion of this communion and in a *reversal* that would enable him to appropriate the word as his own.

The similar explanation Sartre develops for Genet becoming a writer has already been examined. "Our words turn their backs on him," so that he is confronted with "the strangeness of language" and accordingly adopts the "dislocated language [*langue décalée*] of argot," which is the artificial language of those "who feel themselves cut off from reality." Their attempts to communicate then become correspondingly indirect, "replacing the direct references [to reality of ordinary language] with oblique routes" that include references to the words which are ordinarily used but which are being displaced.[13]

LITERATURE

The existentialist takes advantage of this displacement, or engages in it himself, at the level not only of language but of literature. Here my earlier interpretation of existentialism needs to be reoriented. I argued that existentialism is distinguishably a philosophical movement, in spite of its popular vogue and the apparently literary character of many of its procedures, including its reliance on levels or stages. But existentialism is a philosophy one of whose distinctive procedures is its reliance, at some level or stage, on some literary or esthetic undertaking, which is also distinctive in its procedures or which receives a distinctive interpretation from an existentialist.

"Existential" may sound like a rather voracious performance. Indeed when existentialism first came to public attention (at a time when sensibilities were more delicate than they have since become) the impression was widespread that it presented an uncivilized hunger for unprocessed experiences, difficult to digest. Yet in fact existentialism as a philosophy derives much of its support from experiences that have been interpreted and shaped at the esthetic level. It cannot be reduced to a simple *bifocal* relation between the two levels with which we began: the particular experiences of the individual and philosophical generalizations.

A certain kind of generality is achieved at the literary or esthetic level in order to achieve philosophical generalization at a higher level. But the achievement of this higher-level generality does not eliminate *interplay* between levels in the fashion of Hegel's *Aufhebung*, as interpreted by Kierkegaard.

As an illustration of how complicated is the relation between levels, consider Sartre's account of the experience whose ambiguity lent itself in Kierkegaard to a dialectical development that involved all three of Kierkegaard's levels or stages—the experience of suffering (*passio*). Sartre finds it necessary first to introduce a distinction of level within this experience: "One suffers, and one suffers from not suffering enough." Thus even the ordinary experience of suffering incorporates, as a higher-level demand on us, the literary rhetoric of suffering: "The suffering of which we *speak* is never exactly that which we feel."[14] Thus suffering has in Sartre the "storytelling" dimension which we have already encountered in Kierkegaard's "Passion Story." The sense of discrepancy between "the suffering of which we *speak*" and "that which we feel" introduces an evaluation of our suffering by measuring it against "what we call 'noble' . . . or 'true' suffering." Sartre is not operating here with a simple distinction between the suffering we feel (the *modus vivendi*) and our conventional pronouncements about the way we feel (the *modus loquendi*); for the evaluation of our feelings alters these feelings, though without removing our feeling of insufficiency—that is, of the distinction of level itself or of the *interplay* between levels.

Similarly, *interplay* takes place in "A Passion Story," though I did not pause to examine it. The "structure" of the story exhibits "an ambiguity" (*duplicitet*) which is commented on: "In the morning he [the diarist] recollects actuality; at night he deals with the same story, but now it is pervaded by his own ideality." He is thereby suffering *in suspenso*, "hovering" ambiguously between these two levels.[15]

ADVENTURE

But a distinction between levels must be maintained. As Kierkegaard puts it, no individual can become "so poetical" that it is as if "his every word, his every gesture were pure poetry, so that he would therefore require no transformation to go on the stage but could go straight there from the street."[16] Yet the transformation takes place with such extensive *interplay* between levels that we cannot think in terms of any tidy hierarchy. Sartre admits, "Man is always a storyteller, he lives surrounded by his stories and the stories of others, he sees everything that happens to him through [*à travers*] these stories, and he tries to live his own life as if he were telling a story." Sartre does protest against this confusion of the *modus vivendi* with the *modus loquendi*: "But you have to choose; live or tell." Kierkegaard confronts us with a comparable ethical choice when he pits his ethical *Or* against his esthetic *Either*. Yet the confrontation takes place in a work which we have seen is (at a higher level) itself esthetic.

Similarly, Sartre confronts us with his ethical choice by telling a story:

One evening, in a little café in San Pauli, she left me to go to the toilet. I was alone; there was a phonograph playing "Blue Sky." I started to tell myself what had happened since I landed. I said to myself, "The third evening, as I was going into a dance hall called *La Grotte Bleue*, I noticed a tall woman half drunk. And that woman is the one I am waiting for now, listening to 'Blue Sky,' the woman who is going to come back, sit down beside me, and put her arms around my neck." Then I had the violent feeling that I was having an adventure. But Erna came back, she sat down beside me, she put her arms around my neck, and I hated her without quite knowing why. I understand now: I had to begin living again and the feeling of an adventure was fading.[17]

It may fade, but we cannot dismiss this feeling of adventure.

Earlier I characterized Sartre's philosophy as a philosophy of conversion. Recall the feeling of adventure that attended those "extraordinary and marvelous moments" of reorientation when the prior project collapses into the past in the light of a new project" and the "moving image of our freedom" which Sartre found they furnished.[18]

He admitted that "these conversions . . . have not been studied by philosophers," although they "have often inspired novelists."[19] One of the latter is Sartre himself. *Nausea* is a novel about the conversion of its protagonist into the novelist who is its author. Moreover, the protagonist tells a story within this story in order to exhibit the reorientation by which the starting point of "a new project" is reached by storytelling:

> While you live, nothing happens. The scenery changes, people come in and go out, that's all. There are no starting points. . . . But when you tell about a life, everything changes. . . . Events take place in one direction, and we tell about them in the opposite direction. You seem to start at the starting point: "It was a fine autumn evening in 1922. I was a notary's clerk in Marommes." But in reality you have started at the end. It is there, invisible and present; it lends these few words the pomp and validity of a starting point.[20]

Since the time of his admission in *Being and Nothingness* that "conversions . . . have not been studied by philosophers," Sartre himself has studied as a philosopher the conversions of Genet and Flaubert as well as his own. But as I have continued to emphasize, these conversions have all involved their transformation into writers.

SUFFERING

The complexity of the relation between levels can be illustrated if we return to Sartre's account of suffering. Since I have interrupted it, let me quote it from the beginning in order to bring out the complex "logic" of this passion:

> One suffers, and one suffers from not suffering enough. The suffering of which we *speak* is never exactly that which we feel. What we call

'noble' . . . or 'true' suffering and what moves us is the suffering which we read on the faces of others or, rather, in portraits, in the face of a statue, in a tragic mask. It is a suffering which has *being*. It is presented to us as a compact, objective whole which did not await our coming in order to be and which overflows the consciousness which we have of it. . . . The suffering is . . . solidified, cast in the bronze of being. And it is as such that it fascinates us; it stands as a degraded approximation of that suffering-in-itself which haunts our own suffering. The suffering which I experience, in contrast, . . . *is* only to the exact degree that I experience it. . . . I cannot observe it as I observe the suffering of the statue. . . . This enormous, opaque suffering, which should transport me out of myself, . . . I cannot *grasp* it. I find only *myself*, myself who moans, myself who wills, myself who, in order to actualize this suffering which I am, must play without respite the drama of suffering. . . . Each groan, each facial expression of the man who suffers aims at sculpting a statue-in-itself of suffering.[21]

I am citing *Being and Nothingness*, where Sartre reaches the level of generalizations which are philosophical and does not reach down to the level of the concrete experiences of a particular individual who "must play" this "drama of suffering," or sculpt the "statue." Yet I doubt if this citation would carry much weight for anyone attempting to understand Sartre's philosophy if its generalizations did not obtain some support from his dramas and stories. As an example which is easily extracted from one of his novels, take the story told of the transformation of the cleaning woman who is unable to restrain her alcoholic husband from his regular binge:

"Charles, come back, I've had enough, I'm too miserable."
I pass so close to her that I could touch her. It's ——— . But how can I believe that this burning flesh, this face shining with sorrow is ——— ? And yet I recognize the scarf, the coat, and the large wine-colored birthmark on the right hand; it is Lucie, the cleaning woman. . . . Her eyes stare at me, but she seems not to see me; she looks as though she does not recognize herself in her suffering. . . .
Yes, it's Lucie. But transfigured, outside herself, suffering with a frenzied generosity. I envy her. She is there, standing straight, holding out her arms as if awaiting stigmata. . . . I am afraid she will faint: she is too weak to bear this unwonted suffering. But she does not move, she seems turned to stone.[22]

POSTURES

When I emphasize the support Sartre's philosophy obtains from his novels, I am merely reproducing his own emphasis: "One can . . . attack . . . problems abstractly by philosophical reflection. But . . . we want to

live them—i.e., support [*soutenir*] our thinking by those fictional and concrete experiences which are novels."[23] The simple distinction of level that
we initially expected between the abstractness of philosophy and the concrete experiences of living is complicated by the inclusion of experiences
which are "fictional" as well as "concrete." And even this conjunction can
be complicated when it is combined dialectically with the further conjunction of the literary fiction with the experience of some other esthetic
genre—with the experience of the statuesque in Sartre's account of
suffering.

However paradoxical such conjunctions may seem when so bluntly set
forth, they are characteristic, in more casual and confused versions, of our
culture. We lived "surrounded" not only by "stories" but also by other
forms of esthetic experience. The postures we adopt in appropriating our
particular experiences are permeated by fictional and artistic experiences
(novels we have read, statues and paintings we have seen) which lend a
certain level of generality. To this extent our experiences are not our
"own" and would be discounted by Sartre himself as the "continual coming and going between the particular and the general" that constitutes
"communion in the commonplace." (Remember his examples: "a family
intrigue" may be alluded to as "Balzacian" and a "landscape" as a "Corot.)
But being able to recognize that such communion is in the commonplace
implies some recognition of our alienation and by implication the alternative that "the coming and going" can be brought under the dialectical
control that would be our struggling against alienation.

LIVED EXPERIENCE

The criterion "live" with which Sartre indicates that novels are needed
as a support for our thinking also indicates that the interpretation of his
reliance on this support cannot, unfortunately, be carried further here.
For the very term "live" betrays Sartre's debt to Husserl's concept of
Erlebnis ("lived experience"),[24] even though novelistic support would be
entirely dispensable for Husserl, for whom "lived experience" is the subject matter of philosophy itself, which is accorded complete autonomy.
This autonomy philosophy loses in Sartre, just as the novel loses its
autonomy. At each of these levels completeness, autonomy, objectivity,
stability (i.e., such criteria as we examined in Hegel's version) are subverted, in order to yield place to a genre that permits some more flexible
approximation to the reflexive requirement that the more particular
experiences of the individual be "lived." At the same time that stability
is lost, support is obtained from the genre to which place has been yielded.

Sartre takes over Husserl's conception of "philosophical reflection" as well that as of "lived experience." An interpretation of the relation between philosophy and literature in Sartre would have to deal both with the phenomenological character of philosophical reflection in Husserl and Sartre and with Sartre's readjustment of its focus. "Lived experience" is conceived by Husserl as predominantly perceptual, but Sartre's principal phenomenological reflection takes the form of an analysis of imaginative experience as opposed to perceptual experience.[25] This displacement (comparable to the shift in Kierkegaard from *aisthēsis* as sense perception to esthetic experience) is implemented by "lived experience" becoming in Sartre a subject matter for fictional treatment as well as for phenomenological reflection. That the two undertakings, literary and philosophical, are related (and indeed overlap in a fashion that precludes any firm distinction of level that would eliminate *interplay*) is suggested by Sartre's characterization of his analysis of Flaubert as both a "novel" and a "sequel" to his earlier phenomenological reflection on imaginative experience.[26]

Although the displacement cannot be followed out here in phenomenological terms, my original comparison of existentialism with traditional Anglo-American empiricism can be renewed, for the empiricist, like Husserl, assumes that experience is predominantly perceptual. William James can be enlisted for this comparison, since he has often been rated closer to Husserl than any other representative of the empiricist tradition. James defends the claim "Two minds can know one thing" as the doctrine of the "coterminousness," "coconsciousness" of different minds. He is defending "the common sense notion of minds sharing the same objects." And he explains, "Our minds meet in a world of objects which they have in common."[27] In this common place there is no problem of communication. Each individual can identify to others the objects he perceives by pointing.

SUBJECTIVITY

The existential subversion of objectivity I have employed Kierkegaard's *Either* to exhibit, first with the reflective "internalizing" movement from *aisthēsis* as sense perception to the esthetic level and then with the correspondingly subjective *reorientation* of Hegel's esthetics. Kierkegaard would admit that there is a common world of physical objects which can be perceived immediately and pointed out. In this common place the moves of the traveler can be located. But once reflection intervenes, the movement supervenes, which I have also shown can be tracked as Sartre's shift of the focus of reflection from perceptual to imaginative experience and have tied in with his reliance on the fictional experience of novels.

But let us reexamine Kierkegaard's version of this shift, as it is carried through in a passage where Climacus justifies resort to indirect communication:

> What does it mean for someone to affirm that he has reflected his way out of the immediate [as Kierkegaard has in effect done in the succession of his "novelistic" esthetic works, culminating in *Stages on Life's Way*] and then communicates this as information afterward [*efterretning*] in the direct form? Why, it means that the man is talking nonsense. In the world of the spirit [at the level where consciousness has become reflective] the various stages are not like towns on a route of travel, which it is quite in order for the traveler to tell about directly: as for example, "we left Peking and arrived at Canton and on the 14th were in Canton." Such a traveler changes places but not himself, and hence it is in order that he reports it in the direct unchanged form and thus tells about the change. But in the world of the spirit a change of place means a change in oneself. . . . That a man has arrived at this or that distant place in the world of the spirit is demonstrated by the mode of representation itself.[28]

One demonstration is the indirectness of the pseudonymous esthetic works themselves. Another is that spatial references to place, traveling, direction are no longer perceptual but become imaginative and metaphorical, as we have already recognized they become with the shadowgraphic mode of representation. Changes in one's identity cannot be delineated in the same linear fashion in which changing physical locations can be identified. One's moves through successive stages on life's way toward individuation cannot be mapped. And once the reflexive reference to "a change in oneself," a conversion, intervenes, there is no longer any simple designative way in which one can supply someone else with one's own sense of direction. The existentialist is not traveling in James's common-sense world where minds can meet by referring to the objects they perceive in common; he has entered "the world of the spirit" where individuals must pass each other by and can only communicate indirectly and where the works of the writer become "posthumous" and must be "left behind" for the reader to finish.

Concomitant with the subversion of objectivity in Sartre, with his shift from perceptual to imaginative experience, and with his reliance on literary works is his rejection of Husserl's claim that phenomenological reflection is a scientific procedure.[29] This rejection is the juncture at which "novelistic literature" takes on its supporting function in relation to philosophy.

Husserl's claim and its rejection by Sartre cannot be considered here, except insofar as the issues are broader than the differences between Husserl's phenomenology and Sartre's existential phenomenology. We have already encountered in the *Concluding Unscientific Postscript* Kierkegaard's comparable rejection of Hegel's comparable claim that philosophy can be conclusive and scientific. Broadly speaking, existentialism is not just an alliance between philosophy and literature; it is also the disruption of the modern philosophical tradition, which has been by and large an alliance between philosophy and science,[30] just as medieval philosophy was by and large the handmaiden of theology. In modern philosophy a sorting process has gone on fairly regularly whereby those features of our behavior and culture which could be associated with scientific procedures became methodologically significant, while all other features succumbed as mere subject matter. The subversion of objectivity in existentialism and the consequent indirection of its references involve a *reorientation* of philosophy, so that science is displaced and esthetic genres are assigned the supporting role so long reserved for one science or another.

This change in what philosophy is most significantly related to is comparable to the lower-level changes in the relations among art, religion, and philosophy which were involved in Kierkegaard's fragmentation of Hegel's system or to the changes at a still lower level in the relations among the arts which were involved in Kierkegaard's fragmentation of Hegel's "system of the arts." Thus my prolonged examination of the correlated changes in these relations has served a higher purpose than illustrating in detail the *relational* character of an existential dialectic and its *subjective reorientation* of Hegel's *objective* dialectic. At this higher level Kierkegaard neglects Hegel's philosophy of nature and starts out his fragmentation of Hegel's system with the fragmentation of his "system of the arts," and this shift implicates the shift of focus from perceptual to imaginative experience—the shift which I have now anticipated also takes place in the focus of Sartre's phenomenological writings.

Modes of Representation

All these changes of place in the world of the spirit are changes in the interpretation and organization of experience. But the higher level the change is, the less easily it can be reconnoitered. In fact, when philosophy breaks loose from the *orientation* toward the sciences that has prevailed for centuries, the dislocation seems so sweeping as to leave our experience unstable and directionless, with little in the way of reference points to guide us. Indeed this is one reason the issue of *direction* looms so large in an existential dialectic. And it is just possibly one reason Heidegger, in treating reference, resorted to what was then the latest familiar scientific-technological gadget in order to play up the issue.

In any case, in reconnoitering the higher-level change, some reference is needed to the lower-level changes where support is provided for the *reorientation*. At this lower level there are specific differences among our existentialists which will be pinned down in the sequel and which will correlate not only with the different loci where experience (and its traditional organization) is dislocated but also with the specific esthetic experience each existentialist brings to the fore.[31]

The different primary loci were located earlier.[32] In adding other correlations, we can refer to Hegel's "system of the arts," which is organized so that every art has its place in relation to the others as a mode of representation. For in this world of the spirit we have seen how a change in the place of an art does correlate with other changes: the displacement of the objective modes of architecture and sculpture, and the objective subjective modes of painting and epic, correlates with Kierkegaard's reorientation of esthetics toward the reflective subjective modes, which are able to represent indirectly the *reflexive* "change in oneself" by which one can hint arrival "at this or that distant place in the world of the spirit"—so distantly internal that only a "trace" is "left behind" for the reader.

Hegel's "system of the arts" can provide a backdrop too for other existentialists, whose detailed treatment of esthetic experience in their own terms cannot be anticipated here because of its phenomenological component. Of course to the extent that each existentialist treats esthetic experience dialectically, any simple reduction to a single preferred mode of representation is precluded. Instead, we get dialectical conjunctions.

Music

We have watched Hegel's "system of the arts" collapse in Kierkegaard into the relation between the musical and the literary: the musical is an immediate representation (with respect to form) of immediate experience (with respect to content), which belongs to the stage before the opposition emerges between *internal* and *external, subjective* and *objective*; the literary is a reflective representation (with respect to form) of the reflective experience (with respect to content) of this opposition. And it is this opposition (with respect to content) which requires indirection (with respect to the form of the representation).

Our other existentialists also rely on literary forms of esthetic experience, though literature itself is variously interpreted by them. Such reliance is dialectically indispensable, since philosophy is a linguistic genre, and its *modus loquendi* can only be exhibited in terms of an opposing linguistic genre, if the "relation" which "underlies the disrelation" is to be maintained. But although the literary form is to this extent privileged among esthetic experiences, other forms of esthetic experience must be referred to in turn to clarify the relevant characteristics of esthetic experience itself.

The primary locus in Kierkegaard was the reflective self-consciousness, and its primacy was most recently illustrated by his selection of a diary as the literary form to place at the *last*, climactic stage of both *Either* ("The Diary of the Seducer") and *Stages* ("A Passion Story").[33] But the illustration was dialectical, inasmuch as the "reflective seducer" of "The Diary of the Seducer" was played off against the unself-consciousness of the "immediate seducer" of the *first* stage. This unself-consciousness secured musical expression in the opera *Don Giovanni*.

Each of the other forms of esthetic experience adduced can, like literature, be interpreted variously, and the variety should not be regarded as a matter of divergencies in esthetics so much as implications of the more general philosophical differences which I am deferring to the sequel. In Sartre the musical as well as the statuesque upholds a norm which displays the insufficiency of ordinary suffering and the distinction of level toward which our sense of this insufficiency points:

> All the objects surrounding me were made of the same material as I, a sort of messy [*moche*] suffering. . . .
> Now there is this song on the saxophone. And I am ashamed. A glorious little suffering has just been born, an exemplary suffering [*souffrance-modèle*]. Four notes. . . . They come and depart, seeming to say, "You must do as we do, suffer in rhythm [*en mesure*]." . . . But is it my fault if the beer is warm at the bottom of my glass, . . . if I am superfluous [*de trop*], if the most sincere of my sufferings drags and is heavy, with too much flesh.

Music which is interpreted by Kierkegaard as a rendering of experience in its immediacy is interpreted by Sartre as an experience of the way "moments" can be "linked together" temporally in "rigorous sequence." It can accordingly provide him with a model not only for suffering but for storytelling—as "if my own life were the subject of the melody."[34]

SCULPTURE

When the primary locus shifts in Sartre from the reflective self-consciousness to the Other's consciousness of me, the role of his consciousness is analogized to sculpting: "The look of the Other shapes my body in its nakedness, makes it emerge, sculpts it, produces as it *is*, sees it as I shall never see it. . . . He makes me be."[35]

Earlier when I cited Sartre's account of suffering, I recalled how persistent this experience was in Kierkegaard, but Sartre's analogies for suffering are not Kierkegaardian. Although suffering in Sartre has a literary character as "noble" and "true" suffering and as "a drama of suffering" (comparable to Eremita's *Antigone*), Sartre's sufferer, who "aims at sculpting a statue-in-itself of suffering," is aiming at the objectivity his suffering would have for himself could he become its spectator and wield "the look of the Other" whose representation of him "makes" him "be." Being here is objective being ("being-in-itself"), and its objectivity is best conveyed by an analogy to sculpture, which was in Hegel the objective mode of artistic representation par excellence, as indicated by his employment of the sculptural criterion of "plasticity" when dealing with the problem of "objectivity of representation" posed by the subjective and literary art of tragedy.

Need I add that sculpture cannot play the same dialectical role in Sartre as in Hegel, since the relation between subject and object is not the same? We have already recognized that the artist in Sartre retains (unlike the artisan) a reflexive relation to the work of art. This relation is always pivotal in existentialism, and to respect it is to recognize that making something must ultimately be a way of making something one's own. When Sartre's suffering "aims at sculpting a statue-in-itself of suffering," or when Lucie is "turned into stone," or when the Other shapes my body, sculpts it," or when I make a woman in an existential sense, it is not a matter just of making something but of appropriating it. Thus "the 'making' is reduced to a mode of having. . . . If I create a picture, a drama, a melody, it is in order that I may be at the starting point of a concrete existence. . . . The bond of creation which I establish . . . gives to me a particular right of property over it." The dialectic of subject and object is not thereby transcended; if it could be, there would be no desire to appropriate. Instead, the object "must be radically distinct from myself— in order that it may be *mine* but not *me*. Here . . . there is the risk that the being of the created object may be reabsorbed in my being because of lack of independence and objectivity."[36] There is no such risk to the independence and objectivity of the work of sculpture in Hegel.

NATURE

In Heidegger the privileged mode of representation is poetry, not in Kierkegaard's sense, but what would conventionally be classified as nature poetry. I mentioned earlier the "dialogue between poet and thinker who 'dwell near each other on mountains far apart.' " It is a dialogue which Heidegger has conducted on behalf of *being-there* as "being-in-the-world" and particularly with Hölderlin, whom he is citing here. But it is also a dialogue in which the thinker, who is (again as "being-in-the-world") also a dweller and is prominently concerned with "building," as we saw from our earlier sampling of "Building Dwelling Thinking."[37]

Merleau-Ponty puzzled Sartre by informing him that he was planning to "write on Nature."[38] But although some influence of Heidegger was undoubtedly in question, it was not the nature of nature poetry. In Merleau-Ponty the primary locus shifts to the place of the body in the world. Painting then becomes the privileged mode, inasmuch as "the problems of painting are also those of the body." Merleau-Ponty is recognizing the *interplay* involved when "the omnipotence of the eye is restored and represented by a gesture of the hand" on the part of the painter. Hence Merleau-Ponty can argue that it is "by lending his body to the world that the painter changes the world into painting." Since his phenomenology is a *Phenomenology of Perception,* it tends to establish more specifically the credentials of landscape painting as a mode of representation which gives scope for further *interplay* between the ordinary visual perception of the world and the perception of the painter. But since his *Phenomenology of Perception* is still a phenomenology, it is a treatment of the problem of meaning, and since the meaning-endowing act is no longer distinctively an act of consciousness, as in Husserl and Sartre, but an act in which the body is incorporated, language acquires relevance as the embodiment of meaning: "Language is the vehicle of meaning in the way that the trace of a footstep carries a reference to the movement and effort of a body." Merleau-Ponty accordingly deals with painting in terms of its "language" —that is, in terms of analogies between pictorial and literary art.[39]

In spite of what may seem a traditional preoccupation with perception, the reorientation we have explored with reference to Kierkegaard and Sartre holds for Merleau-Ponty too. "Modern painting," he explains, "like modern thought generally, obliges us to accept a truth which does not resemble things, which lacks any external model." The predicament poses the problem of communication which we have already observed in Kierkegaard and Sartre and opposed to James's common-sense point of view whereby "our minds meet in a world of objects which they have in common." Thus Merleau-Ponty finds that "the problem posed by modern painting is to know how one can communicate without the help of a preestablished nature on which the senses of everyone would open up."[40]

But we no longer need to restrict our comparison to the empiricist strand in the modern philosophical tradition. All our existentialists accept Descartes as the starting point for the development of modern philosophy. Descartes's *Discourse on Method* opens with his assertion that "sense," which he specifies is "the ability to distinguish the true from the false," is "common" to all men and ends with an appeal for funds to foster collective scientific research. To the extent that the alliance which once prevailed between modern philosophy and science can be said to begin with Descartes's vindication of a new science of the physical world, the commitments of the partnership can be detected here. A scientific prediction is not uniquely valid for the individual observer who originally proposes it; in principle, its validity can be tested by anyone. It is unencumbered by the umbilical cord of the first observer's mood. And the various stages in the progress of a scientific experiment approximate towns on a route of travel, which it is quite in order for the traveler to tell about directly. Different criteria are being implemented when an existentialist adopts a "storytelling method."

Notes

1. " 'Existence' as Understood by Kierkegaard and/or Sartre," p. 389.
2. *What Is Literature?* pp. 34–35, 37.
3. *L'idiot*, 3:178.
4. *Search for a Method*, pp. 56–57.
5. *What Is Literature?* p. 37.
6. *L'idiot*, 1:219. Sartre employs the same idiom of himself in *Words*, though there *je me dédoublai* is rather misleadingly translated, "I split myself in two" (p. 146). Such reflexive doubling is not restricted to a narrator but takes place whenever anyone engages in imaginative activity: "The object as an image is something unreal. . . . I cannot touch it, change its place; or, rather, I can indeed do so, but on condition that I do it unreally, by not using my own hands but phantom hands which administer unreal blows to this face. To act upon these unreal objects, I must double myself, *make myself unreal*" (*Sartre*, p. 88; italics in original).
7. Flaubert attempts to create a work of art which is comparable in its self-enclosure to the Hegelian system—a work of art which is "unattached to anything external to it and which would uphold itself by the internal force of its style" (*L'idiot*, 2:1618). But in Sartre's interpretation the reflexive relation to Flaubert himself is not superseded by the *Aufhebung* this work would represent to Flaubert, any more than the system supersedes Hegel, according to Kierkegaard. There is an "existing remainder left behind," even though it may only be "such a little dingle-dangle as the existing Herr Professor who writes the system" (see chap. 13, n. 18 above).
8. *Between Existentialism and Marxism*, p. 45.
9. Sartre similarly borrows and revises not only *The Trojan Women* (see p. 380 above) but also Dumas's *Kean* as a vehicle for the actor Pierre Brasseur. Sartre comments on the doubling involved, "While the famous Kean . . . was playing Shakespeare in English at the Odéon, Frédérick Lemaitre took him for a tour around the cabarets. Kean drank and told him the story of his life; Lemaitre drank and listened, thinking, 'There are only two actors in the world, he and I.' Kean returned to England and died soon after. Frédérick Lemaitre thought, 'Now there's only one actor in the world,' and to persuade the public better, he developed the mad impulse to identify himself with the dead man." Hence the Dumas play. "Success went so much to the French actor's

head that he ended up identifying himself completely with his English counterpart; toward the end of his life he made the painful discovery that *Kean* was being revived . . . , but with an Italian actor; and in his rage he covered Paris with notices reading, "I am the real Kean" (Contat, 1:287). Observe the similarity to the title of the play *The Real Saint Genet* (p. 224 above), for Sartre characterizes Kean too as a "myth" and as "the patron saint of actors." Both Kean and Genet faced a problem of their reality, since both were illegitimate, and Sartre identifies himself with them (or, rather, a little lower in the scale of reality) as a "false bastard" (reported by Jeanson, *Sartre par lui-même*, p. 117), because he lost his father when he was still an infant. Sartre indulges in inversions which promote interplay between the imaginary or theatrical and the actual that are quite foreign to Dumas. He warns the audience, "You will no longer know whether you are seeing Brasseur playing Kean or Kean playing Brasseur." Compare too the final lines of the Dumas play (Prince: "You are ungrateful, M. Kean." Kean [*throwing himself in the prince's arms*]: "May Your Highness pardon me") with the lines Sartre substitutes: "And you, M. Kean, you are ungrateful." Kean: "Ah, sir, the fine word of the theater [*le beau mot de théâtre*]. Let it be, if you wish, the final word." As I have emphasized before, the actor displays in Sartre the ex-sistential problem of self-identity as well as the concomitant problem (in a bipersonal dialectic) of identification with another. Thus Kean is "the actor who never stops acting, who even acts out his own life, who no longer recognizes himself, does not know who he is. And who, in the last analysis, is no one." To press this argument Sartre must distinguish between an "actor" in this reflexive sense and an ordinary actor: "*L'acteur* is the opposite of the *comédien* who, when he has finished work, again becomes a man like everyone else, whereas *l'acteur* is acting himself every moment" (Contat, 1:290–91).

10. *Saint Genet*, pp. 481–82.
11. *Life/Situations*, p. 112.
12. *L'idiot*, 1:21.
13. See p. 373 above.
14. *Sartre*, p. 173.
15. *Stages*, p. 383. To interpret Kierkegaard's successive essays and works is to determine the relation between the successive steps taken in a climb. "The Rotation Method," which precedes "The Diary of the Seducer," illustrates the reflexive procedure which is carried over at the first level of "The Diary of the Seducer," whose editor explains, "The poetical was the plus he himself brought with him. This plus was the poetical he enjoyed in the poetic situation of actuality." (In the "Diary" itself the bifocal character of his enjoyment is made clear: "The image I now have of her hovers indeterminately between her actual and her ideal form"; see p. 161 above). When the seducer "withdrew this [poetical enjoyment] again in the form of a poetic reflection," which "afforded him a second enjoyment," he reaches a second level: "The fruit of the first stage is thus the mood from which the Diary emerges as the fruit of the second stage" (*Either*, p. 301). "A Passion Story" is not only a shift from enjoyment to its opposite, since it is "A Story of Suffering"; it is also a higher order of reflection, since its lower level is the recollection of actuality. But in both diaries the diarist's "ideality" takes over at the higher level, by virtue of the reflexive fashion in which the dialectic develops.
16. See p. 68 above.
17. *Sartre*, p. 58.
18. See p. 365 above.
19. *Sartre*, p. 262.
20. Ibid., pp. 58–59.
21. Ibid., pp. 173–74.
22. *Nausea*, p. 27. Just after Lucie "seems turned to stone," the bronze statue of Impétraz is confronted as authoritative. See also the statuette in *Nausea* (p. 5) and the bronze in *No Exit*. As opposed to the "actor" who "does not know who he is" and who, "in the last analysis, is no one," the statue embodies the norm of consolidated self-identity ("substance" in the philosophical tradition—see p. 101 above) whether it is

sought by the individual's own role playing, as in the case of Lucie, who is at one and the same time "standing straight" and "too weak to bear this unwonted suffering," or imposed on the individual by the consciousness of the Other. Cf. Baudelaire, who in Sartre's interpretation "all through his life, out of pride and rancor, tried *to make himself something* in the eyes of others and in his own. He wanted to stand aside from [*à l'écart*] the big festival that society is, like a statue, definitive, inassimilable. In short, it can be said that he wanted to *be*, understanding by that the obstinate and rigorously defined presence of an object" (*Baudelaire*, p. 79; italics in original).

23. *What Is Literature?* p. 217.

24. Sartre translates *Erlebnis* as *expérience vécue* (*Situations*, 1:144–45).

25. *L'imaginaire*, esp. pp. 13–37, 231–86, 372–73.

26. *Between Existentialism and Marxism*, p. 46.

27. *Essays in Radical Empiricism*, pp. 123–24.

28. *Postscript*, p. 250. Hegel's disquisitions on China are usually occasions for Kierkegaard's satirizing his irrelevancy. Here the reference probably takes on the implication of the distance the traveler has traveled in his internalization.

29. Husserl's conception of philosophy as *strenge Wissenschaft* ("rigorous science") "seems to me . . . foolish" (*Situations*, 9:70).

30. I qualify "by and large" because I am not denying that there have been modern renegades who have prayed, "May God us keep / From single vision and Newton's sleep!"

31. In recurring to these lower-level changes, it should be kept in mind that a dialectical philosophy is not just what takes place at the highest level of the divided line (to repeat my earlier comparison with Plato) but also the relation between levels that are involved both in moving up and out of the cave and in determining the significance of the "image" of the cave as compared with the mathematical analogies set up by the line.

32. See p. 87 above.

33. *Nausea* is also a diary, but the primary locus for Sartre at that stage of his development is still the reflective consciousness.

34. *Nausea*, pp. 174, 56, 103, 23, 38.

35. *Sartre*, p. 209; italics in original.

36. Ibid., pp. 305–6.

37. In *Being and Time* "temporality" is "the *ekstatikon* as such" (see p. 125 above), and "dwelling" is the mode of our temporal "being-in." Thus Heidegger derives *in* itself from *innan* as meaning *wohnen* ("to dwell") (p. 54). In "Building Thinking Dwelling," "the old English and high German word for building, *buan*, means to dwell" (*Poetry, Language, Thought*, p. 146), which in turn means "to be on the earth as a mortal" (p. 147). In the terminology of *Being and Time*, the being of *being-there* is brought within the horizon of time by its understanding that it will die.

38. *Situations*, p. 214.

39. *Adventures of the Dialectic*, p. 199; "Eye and Mind," p. 255; *Signs*, pp. 70, 44. Merleau-Ponty's major effort in esthetics travels along a network of these analogies—"Indirect Language and the Voices of Silence" (*Signs*, pp. 39–83). Although this essay is ostensibly an appraisal of Malraux's *Voices of Silence*, a book on painting, it is dedicated to Sartre and a comment on his attempt to define *What Is Literature?* In spite of the privileged status of painting for Merleau-Ponty, philosophy retains its prerogatives by virtue of the reflexivity of linguistic expression: "L'homme ne peint pas la peinture, mais il parle sur la parole" (crudely, "Man does not paint about painting, but he employs language about language" (*Signs*, p. 80).

40. *Signs*, pp. 57, 52. The problem of communication is posed at another level by the fact that "all language is indirect or allusive" (p. 43), since linguistic "signs singly convey no meaning." Meaning is relational or, rather, the dislocation of relations: "Each sign expresses a meaning less than it marks a discrepancy [*écart*] of meaning between itself and the others" (p. 39).

15

The Dead Letter

No pressure is felt from anyone's presence.—The Seducer

The Life of the Individual

Different senses of starting point have emerged in existentialism. I dealt in part I with taking the initiative in order to appropriate one's experience, to become an individual and one's own starting point. But to take this initiative the individual must start out by defining his experience in accordance with certain dialectical procedures which were examined in part II. This effort at definition is required, we recognized in part III, because the individual starts out confused, astray, lost, and has to "take himself back." But then the problem of starting point must be reformulated in terms of the existentialist's relation to his reader, who in turn must take the initiative.

In dealing with the problem of starting point in the first sense, I took into account the distinction of level between "the life of the individual,"[1] as it might be reported in an autobiography, and a philosophical principle. Yet ever since I reached the philosophical level with Eremita's promulgation of the principle of contradiction in the first sentence of *Either/Or*, I have largely neglected autobiographical references. Nevertheless, inasmuch as an existential dialectic is a *bipersonal* dialectic, the problem of starting point, as soon as it is reformulated in terms of the problem of communication, again brings to our attention the lives of individuals.

Since the retention of such personal references is existentialism's most radical departure from traditional philosophy, we should reconsider Eremita's preface and Kierkegaard's other attempts to get started as a philosopher, in conjunction with his references to other individuals in his life. If I am continuing to concentrate on Kierkegaard, it is not just because we have become familiar with his philosophy as the most purely dialectical. His life as an individual is sufficiently different from that lived by most of my readers that there is little danger that they will confuse their lives with his and jeopardize their status as passersby.

Having anticipated the treatment of the problem of communication in the *Postscript*, I am now returning to Eremita's preface (and indeed, as it will turn out, concentrating on its first paragraph). It is not that I am taking advantage of the dialectical relation between *first* and *last* in order to establish some sort of Hegelian circle in the logic of his thought. There can be no circle in the life of the "existing individual," inasmuch as "his thought cannot attain to absolute continuity." When "the existing individual nevertheless thinks, . . . he thinks intermittently . . . before and after."[2] He remains committed to a "storytelling method," since he cannot transcend the level of *Vorstellung* with an *Aufhebung* of the spatiotemporal.[3] But he also remains committed to writing prefaces before his stories, since the problem of starting point cannot be transcended with an *Aufhebung*, and postscripts after his stories, since he cannot reach a final outcome with an *Aufhebung*. Thus our attention to Kierkegaard's *modus loquendi* cannot be restricted, as it has largely been up until now, to the stories he tells or to the fragmentation of Hegel's "system of the arts" that is involved in how he tells these stories.[4] The fragmentation of Hegel's system as a whole is involved in Kierkegaard's resort to prefaces and postscripts. This is the logic of his intermittent thought as opposed to Hegel's absolute continuity, though Kierkegaard may also have been aware of the disdain he was manifesting toward the disdain Hegel had manifested for "introductions," "prefaces," and "first paragraphs."[5]

MISUNDERSTANDING

The shift from the philosophical level back to the personal level of "the life of the individual" can be managed by reminding ourselves of a traditional philosophical concern that lends itself to a final comparison with existentialism. This is the concern with understanding. Descartes's method is the prescription of *Rules for the Direction of the Understanding*; Spinoza seeks the *Improvement of the Understanding*; and when Locke founds modern empiricism by attacking Cartesian rationalism, it is still in an *Essay concerning Human Understanding*. Descartes assumes that rules can be prescribed because the "direction" in question should be the same for all individuals, whose understanding is oriented toward the nature of things. But in existentialism concern with understanding becomes concern with one individual's imaginative understanding of another.

Or, rather, it becomes concern with misunderstanding, since individuals pass each other by (in Kierkegaard's idiom), proceeding in different *directions*, and their "universal experience" is (in Sartre's phrase) "the experience of isolation." The problem of communication initially emerges from the reflexively experienced predicament of being misunderstood, and this predicament is a feature of existentialism from the start. The first aphorism in *Either/Or* is the definition of the poet as "misunderstood by men." His internal suffering is contradicted by the external audience's enjoyment of his poetry. An even worse misunderstanding is the critic's; he inherits the poetry as an objective "outcome," which he understands by applying "the rules of esthetics" that are as such incommensurable with the particularity of the poet's experience as an individual.

Misunderstanding continues at the later stages. In the original preface Climacus wrote for *Philosophical Fragments*, what had been a fundamental dislocation threatening the fragmentation of Hegel's system was revised to a misunderstanding:

> I feel like a poor lodger who has a little room in the attic of a huge building which is regularly being enlarged and beautified [Hegelians are at work finishing the system as an expression of the culminating age of Christian culture], while to his terror he seems to discover that the foundation is cracking [revised to "discover a misunderstanding"].[6]

This passage Kierkegaard discarded. But he salvaged its spatial imagery in the *Postscript*,[7] where the theme of misunderstanding undergoes extensive development, as we shall see later.

EREMITA

When in *Either/Or* Eremita's poet is confronted with misunderstanding, he can accept the dialectical alternative of isolating himself from mankind by becoming a swineherd, confident that he would be "understood by the swine." But in spite of his name, Eremita has to fulfill his function as an e-ditor and has no such easy way out. The starting point of his preface too is an exposition of the problem of communication, though this would be harder to recognize, if we had not taken advantage of the dialectical relation between *last* and *first* and anticipated the retrospect provided by the *Postscript*.

Let me quote again the first sentence of Eremita's preface. But since the rest of the first paragraph is only the development of the implications of this sentence for the problem of communication, let me continue the quotation:

> Perhaps it has sometimes happened to you, Dear Reader, to doubt a little the correctness of the familiar philosophical principle that the external is the internal and the internal the external. Perhaps you have hidden within yourself a secret which you felt in all its joy or pain was too precious for you to share with another. Perhaps your life has

brought you into contact with someone of whom you suspected something of the kind was the case, although you were never able to get him to reveal what he concealed. Perhaps neither case is yours, and yet you are not unacquainted with this doubt.

I pause to note that each successive "perhaps" itself expresses Eremita's doubt. The individual cannot be certain of what is going on within the other's mind; he can only suspect.[8] This is a dialectic in which secrets are hidden, as will be confirmed externally when the "secret door" in the desk springs open, disclosing a "hiding place."[9] The *reflexive* reference of the first "you" to the "secret" Kierkegaard has "hidden" within himself and would go to his grave without revealing is balanced against the second "you" referring in the first instance to Regina as the reader from whom he had "hidden" his "secret." Then a wider audience, which we as his readers constitute, is brought in with the third "perhaps."

THE DEATH SENTENCE

Consideration of the wider audience can be postponed until the end, when we shall have taken into account the bearing of the particular personal experiences, to which Kierkegaard is alluding, on his general treatment of the problem of communication. Of course the intervention of Kierkegaard's pseudonyms forbids our interpreting *Either/Or* (and his other esthetic works) as simply autobiography. We are also cautioned by his rejection of Hegel's reduction of Socrates' significance to his "personal relations" with his contemporaries.[10] This reduction, we can now see, was rendered impossible from Kierkegaard's point of view, since Socrates was committed by his irony to indirect communication—that is, to merely indirect personal relations. Any reduction of the significance of Kierkegaard's "authorship" is similarly, but paradoxically, deflected by the very part Regina played in his life: "Really it was she, my relation to her which taught me indirect communication."[11]

His relation to her involved two familiar stages—immediacy and poetic reflection. There was first the immediacy of an actual personal relation, and at this moment Kierkegaard admits, "I cannot dispose of this relation, for I cannot poeticize it." But we are deprived of direct reference to this moment, since what Kierkegaard makes available to us in the authorship is its poetic transformation into a *bifocal* relation, which is played up by the double title of the story he wrote in his journal:

My Relation to "Her"
Something Poetical

"To Some Extent Poetical" might be a more accurate translation. Regina has not become for Kierkegaard simply "Something Poetical," but to the extent she has become poetical, we cannot get behind what she has become to his actual personal relation to her. We are again paradoxically deflected, for it was the relation to her which had "made him a poet."[12] And she had thereby signed her "death sentence" as an actual person. For one thing, she had become a "muse." But Kierkegaard is also recollecting how she had threatened that breaking the engagement would be "the death of her."[13]

TRANSFIGURATION

Poetic transfiguration we are familiar with in Hegel as the psychological movement of recollective "internalization" from the perception of the actual to its "imaginative representation."[14] The corresponding process in Sartre cannot be traced here, because of the phenomenological character of his psychology. But if we visualize his distinction of levels as comparable to Hegel's, we can recognize the *interplay* which in Sartre as well as in Kierkegaard can enable a person to be transfigured.

Take as a preliminary illustration Franconay impersonating Maurice Chevalier: we *perceive* Franconay, "a small, plump, dark-haired . . . woman," but somehow (in a fashion which Sartre analyzes phenomenologically) we *imagine* Chevalier, who has dialectically opposed traits, inasmuch as he is tall, thin, blond, and male.[15] A similar psychological extrapolation can be carried out with a single individual. When Flaubert attends the soirées of Mathilde (the cousin of Louis Bonaparte), he is dazzled: "her actual body," which he can perceive, "serves as an analogue" on which his imagination superimposes her "glorious body"—that is, the body for which we ordinary mortals have to wait until the resurrection.[16]

Transfiguration can also be carried out reflexively. Sartre finds Flaubert's suspected bisexuality dialectically tempting, and he tells us the inside story: because "woman is the perfect work of art," Flaubert when masturbating (even though he would have been "horrified at being effeminate") "makes himself into a woman" by "stroking his thighs, his beautiful womanly breasts."[17] Kierkegaard likewise transfigures himself reflexively into "something poetical" when he becomes a pseudonym,[18] though here as elsewhere the physiological component is missing which is so prominent in Sartre when transfiguration or any other metaphorical process gets under way.

Before we move on to the reflexive moment in Kierkegaard, we should linger with Regina's poetic transfiguration. One feature is Kierkegaard's derivation of the epigraph for "My Relation to Her" from Vergil's *Infandum me jubes, Regina, renovare dolorem*.[19] This feature of the process of transfiguration can be compared with Eremita's borrowing of names of characters in *Either*. Byplay is introduced with the suggestion of the sovereignty Regina exercises over his life as well as *interplay* between the *modus vivendi* ("grief") and the *modus loquendi* (the problem of communication posed by "something which cannot be told about"). The *interplay* takes place because to tell about the "grief" is to "renew" it in a *recapitulative* fashion that we are acquainted with from the "brides of grief," for when they recollected their grief, they became "wedded" to a renewed, more "internalized," and therefore more grievous grief.

Regina gave him opportunity to indulge in further byplay with her sovereign status. When she was not threatening suicide, she was promising never to marry. Instead of producing her own children, she would resign herself to becoming a "governess." Eventually her husband became governor of the Virgin Islands (then the Danish West Indies), and she went off with him. Kierkegaard never saw her again, but he relished the ambiguity of referring to her as "my little governess."[20]

THE MUSE

Regina herself seems to have been eventually willing to accept her poetic transfiguration at least to the extent of discarding her actual name "Regine" and using instead the Latin spelling "Regina"—perhaps as a sort of pseudonym to match Kierkegaard's pseudonyms.[21] Who can tell? Meanwhile her husband too, even before their engagement, had himself undergone poetic transposition into the "commonplace" suitor who was displaced in the "Diary" by the reflective, poetic seducer, interposing himself (in what he imagined was the space of Cordelia's imagination) between her and her suitor.[22]

In short, Kierkegaard's commitment to indirect communication entails no level at which his indirection can finally be circumvented by his reader. With respect to what he would "leave behind" (however scholars and professors may exploit his "legacy"), he can console himself by prophesying, "After my death no one will find in my papers enlightenment as to what has occupied my whole life."[23] His "authorship" leaves us instead with "something poetical" as a means of communication.

Still, the fact remains that "it was she" who "taught me indirect communication." But how? A signal contribution, inseparable from her poetic role as muse, was a woman's "loving lack of understanding."[24] A woman's contribution to a man's reflective ability to draw the distinction of level between the actual and the ideal is necessarily negative:

Through woman ideality entered life—what would man be without her? Many a man became a genius through a girl, many a man became a hero through a girl, many a man became a poet through a girl, many a man became a saint through a girl—but he didn't become a genius through the girl he got, for through her he became only a civil servant; he didn't become a hero through the girl he got, for through her he only became a general; he didn't become a poet through the girl he got, for through her he only became a father; he didn't become a saint through the girl he got, for he didn't get any. . . . In other words, it is in a negative relation that woman makes a man productive in the realm of ideality.[25]

Her more specific negative contribution is her "lack of understanding."

HETEROGENEITY

But we must remember that a dialectic is relational, as well as Kierkegaard's qualification, "It was she, *my relation to her* which taught me indirect communication."[26] Ultimately the misunderstanding is to be explained by the character of their relation—by the fact that they were dialectically related as opposites. The diarist of "A Passion Story" generalizes;

> Now there is misunderstanding wherever the heterogeneous is brought together, but note that it must be such a heterogeneity as does not exclude a relation, for otherwise there is no misunderstanding. At the basis of misunderstanding it can therefore be said that there is an understanding—i.e., a possibility of understanding.[27]

To acknowledge in this way the personal character of the problem of misunderstanding is not to reduce the problem to the obtuseness of the second person. More than particular psychological idiosyncrasies are in question, and a more general heterogeneity than that between feminine immediacy and masculine reflectiveness. Remember that the problem of communication is dialectical: if it is eventually posed by the fact that the second person is a passerby, it is initially posed by the fact that the first person is striving "to express in his life what he has understood."[28] Indeed he only understands what he is able to express in this fashion:

> The dialectic in books is merely the dialectic of thinking, but reduplication of such thinking is action in life. But every thinker who does not reduplicate the dialectic of his thinking continuously constructs an illusion [*sandesbedrag*]. His thinking never gains the decisive expression of action. He tries to correct misunderstandings, etc., in a new book, but it is of no use, for he continues in an illusion of communication. Only

the ethical thinker, by acting, can protect himself against illusions in communication.[29]

The recipient of the communication requires the same protection.

The Father

So general a dialectic is never enough to keep an existentialist going. Caught up in the *bipersonal* dialectic was a particular problem with respect to the understanding Regina lacked—a particular *infandum* which Kierkegaard could not communicate to her and which had to do with his father. This is probably the "secret" alluded to in Eremita's preface.

Kierkegaard recalls in his journal, not long after his father's death, "the great earthquake, the terrible dislocation [*omvæltning*]." It was

> then that I suspected that my father's old age was not a divine blessing but, rather, a curse; . . . then that I felt the silence of death encroaching around me, when in my father I beheld an unhappy individual who must outlive us all, a cross upon the grave of all his hopes. Guilt must rest upon the whole family.[30]

Kierkegaard's suspicion as to what this guilt was he communicates only indirectly, poetically reshaped in the story of "Solomon's Dream." He included this story as an episode in the diary "A Passion Story," which itself is entitled "Guilty/Not Guilty?" The episode is the story of how Solomon discovered that David's "secret guilt" was "the mystery which explained all."[31] Indirection is built into the story itself as the story of something overheard.[32]

The journal entry itself does allow further probing. Kierkegaard's father felt himself condemned to outlive all his seven children. Five of them were in fact dead before he died himself, and the same year Kierkegaard published his first literary work with the ominous title, From the *Papers of One Still Living*.[33] These literal deaths provided family background for his elaboration of the death metaphors which are so prominent a feature of his *modus loquendi*. "Buried alive" and "posthumous" we have already examined in the symparenkromenous essays. Death metaphors were also incorporated in his relation to Regina. She beseeched him, not only "in the name of Christ" but also "by the memory of his dead father," not to leave her.[34] That this would be "the death of her" was a threat that has been balanced against the fact that she had already signed her "death sentence" by making him a poet. Yet one charge the diarist was sometimes guilty of in "Guilty/Not Guilty?" was "murder,"[35] even though Regina was already ending up in the arms of her "commonplace" suitor. While the space of her imagination was not entirely Kierkegaard's to control, her "crying out 'I shall die' " became her having "parodied him." For Kierkegaard's announcement, "When I left her, I chose death,"[36] took precedence in his own mind, if only because "she chose the cry [that is, the outward, direct form of communication], I chose the suffering [that is, the inward suffering that cannot be communicated directly, as we learned in "Shadowgraphs"]."[37]

THE GRAVEYARD

Since we have observed Kierkegaard's byplay with the name "Regina," we should also observe that the family name Kierkegaard means "graveyard."[38] Kierkegaard experienced difficulty in communicating with his father as well as with Regina, and this experience is communicated indirectly by the graveyard story Climacus tells in *Postscript* by way of explaining his adoption of the method of indirect communication. Once again indirection is built into the story itself, since Climacus overhears what he was not intended to hear.

The dramatis personae assembled for the scene of grief in the graveyard are those "left behind"—an old man and his grandson, aged about ten. They have just buried the child's father, who had surrendered his faith in favor of philosophy. The old man's lament is that "modern speculation, like a change in the currency, had made property values in matters of faith doubtful."[39] Climacus admits that the old man's "grief over the loss of his son, not only by death but, as he understood it, still more terribly through philosophy, moved me deeply."[40] Without recognizing the contradiction posed by his son's loss of faith, the old man invokes "the memory of your dead father" to exact from the child a promise "that you hold fast to the faith in life and death and that you will not let yourself be deceived by an illusion, however the figure of the world may change."[41]

Just as the accusation a woman's "loving lack of understanding" suggests that Regina's behavior was contradictory, if the stage of immediacy to which Kierkegaard confined her meant she was naive enough to believe that love should entail some measure of understanding, so the old man is naively contradictory in his attempt to communicate with the child. On one hand he "cannot presuppose enough maturity on the child's part to understand him." But Climacus interpolates, "What may perhaps for a moment incline some reader to assume that the whole story is fictitious— that an old man should talk in this way to a child—was what moved me most of all." On the other hand Climacus emphasizes another lack of understanding. There was the original "contradiction in the old man's position that he could not understand how the enemy [philosophy] had conducted his campaign." For the son was unable to communicate with the old man, just as the old man cannot communicate with the grandson about his son, though he tries with his protest, "To what purpose all his learning, which made him unable to make himself understood by me, so that I could not even speak to him about his error [*vildfarelse*]. . . ." Again an *infandum*.[42]

CRISSCROSSING

Even though the story is "to some extent poetical" and extrapolates from particular experiences of Kierkegaard with his father, it reaches a certain measure of generality, which is indicated by the labeling of the participants "an old man and his grandson" and "the child's father." The distinction of generations (accentuated by the father's death) suggests a distinction of levels, and the *interplay* of contradictions between the levels is designed to induce the reader, like Climacus, to climb to a higher level of misunderstanding:

> The whole affair tantalized me like an intricate criminal case, where much crisscrossing has made it difficult to arrive at the truth. This was something for me. I thought to myself, "You are now bored with life's diversions, bored with girls whom you love only in passing; you must have something that will fully take up your time. Here it is: to discover the misunderstanding between philosophy and Christianity. This accordingly became my resolution [*beslutning*].[43]

This misunderstanding is Hegel's "confusion" of philosophy and religion which we have seen Climacus attempt to rectify by separating the two, reallocating philosophy back to the esthetic stage and reserving the final stage for religion.

We have also seen that not just Hegel's philosophy is at issue but his philosophy as the revelation of the spirit of the age which he claims it is. But since Climacus puts the issue succinctly in the setting of the graveyard story, it may be worthwhile to let him present his "resolution" without interruption for commentary:

> Finally it became clear to me that the misdirection of philosophical speculation and its supposedly warranted justification [*ret*] for reducing faith to a moment [transcended by an *Aufhebung* that moves beyond faith to philosophy] could not be accidental but must be deeply embedded in the whole orientation [*retning*] of the age. . . . as a result of our vastly increased knowledge, men had forgotten what it is to exist and what inwardness means.
>
> When I had grasped this, it also became clear to me that if I wanted to communicate anything in this regard, I must above all give my

representation an *indirect* form. For if inwardness is the truth, outcomes are only junk with which we should not trouble each other. The communication of outcomes is an unnatural form of association between one human being and another, insofar as everyone is a spiritual being, for whom the truth can only be the self-activity of appropriation which an outcome impedes.[44]

POETIC DIALECTIC

In carrying out this undertaking, Climacus visualizes himself as proceeding "methodically, as if a poet and a dialectician watched over . . . every step." This alliance I have commented on with respect to its bearing on the reflexive "self-activity of appropriation" and on the corresponding dispensing with an "outcome" as objective. Climacus has already illustrated the step-by-step procedure by telling the story of the experience in the graveyard, where misunderstandings at the level of personal relations crisscross and provide a personal dimension for the higher-level philosophical misunderstanding which might otherwise be regarded as impersonal. Moreover, the story has cast Climacus himself in contradictory crisscrossing roles: "At one moment it seemed to me that I was the young man whom his father had buried with so much consternation; at the next, it seemed to me that I was the child, bound by the sacred promise."[45]

Climacus's vacillation reemphasizes the *interplay* between levels which carries through to the higher philosophical level. In other words, the fact that Kierkegaard's personal relation to his father furnished the impetus does not imply that he has climbed beyond it and discarded it as a lower-level experience Climacus reports, "The venerable figure of the old man hovered before my mind, whenever I was tempted to transform my reflections into knowledge that was mere learning"—as the son and Hegel had done. We are aware of how the figure of Regina (in the esthetic guise of Cordelia) "hovered" before the seducer's mind, of how in "A Passion Story" the diarist "hovered" *in suspenso* between recollection of his actual passion and its ideal religious significance, as well as how, when Kierkegaard endorsed Aristophanes' imaginative representation of Socrates, that figure "hovered" before his mind. Similar imaginative hovering between particular experiences in relation to his father and their general implications for the relation between philosophy and religion could enter into the composition of "the venerable figure of the old man" as "something poetical," once philosophy had been reallocated back to the esthetic stage. Kierkegaard has indeed proceeded "as if a poet and a dialectician watched over . . . every step" of his movement upward.[46] To employ the terminology of my discussion of the *reorientation* of philosophy in existentialism, the alliance of philosophy with poetry is maintained, whereas in Hegel philosophy had transcended imaginative representation.

I am reminding the reader for the last time that when "figures" in Kierkegaard "hover" as "something poetical," they have reached the level of *Vorstellung*, which Hegel considered appropriate to historical narrative. At this level their original status as particular individuals has not yet been entirely transcended, as it will be when the level of "thought" is reached in Hegel.[47] They remain contradictory composites, comparable to the figure of Christ in Hegel until "its particularity dies away into its universality." Since Christ's transfiguration can qualify in Hegel as a *Vorstellung* ("imaginative, pictorial, or figurative representation") of the *Aufhebung* by which *Vorstellung* itself is finally transcended, since Kierkegaard, like Hegel, puns with the term "transfiguration" in order to elicit the implication that "clarification" is achieved by this movement to a higher level, it may be permissible to try to represent the difference between Kierkegaard and Hegel here by punning with the English terms: "transfiguration" in Kierkegaard, unlike Hegel, does not involve "transcending" the "figure,"[48] just as the "figure" itself, although it is "to some extent poetical," does not involve transcending in an autonomous, conclusive, and objective work of art the experience of the other person with which he had started. To appreciate the *interplay* in Kierkegaard's dialectic, it has to be recognized that it is not only extrapolation from and transcendence of the personal by the poetical but also the *reversal* and descent of the philosophical, as characterized by the movement of *Aufhebung* as conceived by Hegel.

SILENT DESPAIR

Not only does Kierkegaard's philosophical problem of communication emerge from both his personal relation to Regina and his personal relation to his father; he also credits to both his arrival at the imaginative level where they "hover" while he copes with the philosophical problem by writing esthetic works. We have already seen that it was a woman who "had made him a poet." But it is traditional to assign a woman the role of muse, while fathers have only come into their own since Freud, so that it is the father's role which deserves our closer attention.[49]

At least in Kierkegaard's recollection, it would seem to have been in relation to his father that he first both formulated the problem of understanding and arrived at the imaginative means for coping with the ensuing problem of communication. Let me begin with their silence and then consider their conversation.

The first episode incorporated in the diary of *Stages on Life's Way* is entitled "Silent Despair—a Story." The diarist recalls;

> There was once a father and a son. A son is like a mirror in which the father contemplates himself, and for the son the father too is like a mirror in which he contemplates himself in the time to come. . . . The father halted, stood with a grieving face before the son, looked at him steadily, and said, "Poor child, you are going into silent despair." True as this statement was, nothing was ever said to indicate *how it was to be understood.* And the father believed that he was to blame for the son's melancholy, and the son believed that he was the occasion of the father's grief—but they never exchanged a word on this subject.[50]

All the stories that Kierkegaard has told us are efforts to determine how something ambiguous was to be understood, as are also his efforts to climb from one level to another.[51]

The difficulty of understanding was compounded, as the diarist goes on to explain in "Silent Despair":

> Then the father died. . . . The mirror was no longer there; but in loneliness he comforted himself by hearing the father's voice: "Poor child, you are going into silent despair." For the father was the only one who had understood him, and yet he did not know in fact whether he had understood him. . . .

THE WALK

When the father did talk, it was in a way as surprising as the way the old man in the graveyard talked with the child. Kierkegaard's father "hid under his peasant coat a vivid imagination which not even his old age could dim," and the imaginative level which Kierkegaard had first attained with his father he regains by telling a story about it:

> When sometimes Johannes Climacus asked permission to go out, he often was refused, though once in a while the father would suggest instead that his son should take his hand and go for a walk up and down the room. . . . It was left entirely to Johannes Climacus to determine where they should go. So they walked out of the city gate to a nearby castle in the country, or out to the beach, or about the streets. . . . While they walked up and down the room, the father would describe everythey they saw. They greeted the passersby; the carriages rattled by them and drowned out the father's voice. . . . After half an hour's walking with his father, Johannes Climacus was as overwhelmed and weary as if he had been out for a whole day. Johannes soon learned from his father how he, too, could exercise this magic power. . . .[52]

Doubt

If this autobiographical story is close to a particular experience of the contradiction between the *internal* and the *external*, more general philosophical implications are brought out in Eremita's preface. In the first paragraph, after covert allusions to Regina and to the secret of Kierkegaard's father, a transition is made to contradictory evidence yielded by the senses:

> Eventually [*efterhaanden*] the sense of hearing came to be my most valued sense; for just as the voice is the revelation of an inwardness incommensurable with the outer, so the ear is the instrument by which this inwardness is perceived, hearing the sense by which it is appropriated. Whenever then I found a contradiction between what I saw and what I heard, I found my doubt confirmed.[53]

The "whenever" probably refers to a conversation with Regina, though it would be applicable to the contradiction between what Climacus heard as a child in his conversation with his father and what he actually could see walking up and down the room. But whatever the personal reference, Kierkegaard's problem of communication is caught up in the general *reorientation* of philosophy's starting point which he would carry through. Descartes had started out by doubting the contradictory evidence of the senses regarding external things. Hegel had identified Descartes's doubt as the starting point of philosophy as an autonomous discipline,[54] and the dialectical development in the *Phenomenology* had started out with contradictions drawn from sense perception and had gone on to reach the level of scientific thought.

When the editor of "The Diary of the Seducer" starts out his preface in turn with this traditional sequence, he personifies the experience: "One remains imposed upon by an impression until reflection once again breaks loose, and manifold and swift in its movements insinuates itself and cajoles the unknown stranger."[55] The personification receives its justification with the starting point of the diary itself:

> Take care [*forsigtighed*], my beautiful unknown, take care! To step out of a carriage is not so simple a matter. Sometimes it is a decisive step. I could lend you a novel of Tieck's in which you would see that a lady who in stepping down from her horse to such an extent entangled herself [*i den grad indviklede sig*] in an entanglement [*forvikling*] that this step became definitive for her whole life.[56]

The seducer will shortly be appropriating by reflection his impression of this unknown stranger as reflected in a mirror.[57] He is on his way to esthetic knowledge. Eventually his reflection, manifold and swift in its movements, will insinuate itself into the impressions of the "unknown stranger" too and cajole her. When she "goes under," esthetic knowledge will be the compensation she will be left with.[58]

The initial *interplay* with the "unknown" (the "unknown" impression personified as a "stranger"), the impression of an "unknown" stranger in the first line of the diary, indicates that the traditional theory of knowledge is being recapitulated and reoriented.[59]

This *recapitulation* and *reorientation*, which I surveyed earlier, is anticipated in the first paragraph of the preface, when Eremita's doubt (as opposed to Descartes's and Hegel's) is "confirmed" by "a contradiction between what I saw and what I heard." Traditionally the most valued sense had been sight, but the contradictory evidence Eremita is marshaling imposes the *reorientation* of philosophy away from understanding the nature of things to one individual's understanding of another, on the basis of what is said. The traditional philosophical problem of our knowledge of the external world and the nature and limits of this knowledge is displaced by the problem of communication, its nature and its limits.

IRONY

That this problem of the *modus loquendi* was Kierkegaard's starting point is borne out by his other efforts to get started as a philosopher. To these we can finally return, now that we are coming to grips with the preface to *Either* as the designated starting point of his "authorship" and of his application of the principle of contradiction.

Kierkegaard's announced "plan" in the "story" he tells in *Johannes Climacus* is to "strike at philosophy by means of a melancholy irony." He starts this attack by characterizing modern philosophy ironically as "never having been so near solving its problem, which is the revealing of all secrets, as it is now."[60] In other words, the outcome has nearly been reached when the internal will be fully externalized by the Hegelian movement of *Aufhebung*. So near. But Climacus refuses to lend a hand in finishing the system.

In his dissertation Kierkegaard had already endorsed irony as the Socratic *modus loquendi*, and it is the means of communication which he himself adopts in the esthetic works. Recall that Eremita is "sympathetic irony." Verbal irony is a form of disavowal: one does not mean what one says.[61] So too is a pseudonym. The disavowal implicit in Kierkegaard's use of pseudonyms for his "esthetic production" becomes explicit in the

"First and Last Declaration" which he appends as a postscript to the *Postscript.* This explicit disavowal is geared, moreover, to the relation between writer and reader: "In the pseudonymous works there is not a single word which is mine; I have no opinion about these works except as a third person, no knowledge of their meaning except as a reader, not the remotest private relation to them."[62]

When Kierkegaard becomes incognito with his adoption of pseudonyms, the works become imagined points of view, and we are frustrated in our usual tendency to interpret a philosophy as predominantly a theory of knowledge that is making some universal cognitive claims about cognition. We are forced instead to try to get at the philosophical *reorientation* existentialism is introducing. Let us again consider the Socratic point of view implicit in Kierkegaard's irony and pseudonymity. Socrates was the third figure that hovered before Kierkegaard's mind, besides Regina and his father.[63] But he has the advantage of being a philosophical figure. *The Concept of Irony with Constant Reference to Socrates* was that moment in Kierkegaard's career before he went incognito. He wanted to marry Regina, and he needed the graduate degree to obtain an appropriate position. Universities are afflicted with a remarkably unexistential narrowness of mind: they do not permit the student to submit a dissertation under a pseudonym. Yet even here Kierkegaard might be said to outmaneuver us. Not only is Socrates a quasi pseudonym for him, but the dissertation also offers in effect some of the rationale for *Johannes Climacus* and the "esthetic production" later taking an ironical, pseudonymous form.

SOCRATES

The relevance of the dissertation to the way Kierkegaard starts out in *Johannes Climacus* and in *Either* will become clearer if we recognize that the Greek *eirōn,* as applied to Socrates, meant a "deceiver,"[64] that pseudonymity is a deception, that *De omnibus dubitandum est* was originally formulated by Descartes in terms of our deception by the senses, and that seduction in Kierkegaard is not a simple misunderstanding. Remember how the "brides of grief" struggled in their reflections over the question as to whether their seducer had been deceiving them[65] and how in representing their reflections in "Shadowgraphs" it was possible "to draw" the external "to one side," because it was assumed that the Symparenkromenoi were "old enough not to be deceived by appearances nor to continue in this deception"—that is, they were assumed to be capable of rising to the level of imaginative representation.[66] Regina was the "bride" who was hovering here before Kierkegaard's mind:

My relation to her was always kept so vague that it remained in my power to give it the interpretation that I was a deceiver. Humanly speaking, it was the only way to save her, to give her soul resilience.[67]

Socrates was a "deceiver" in that he was "simulating" ignorance when he undertook his questioning of others in response to the Delphic edict, "Know yourself," for unlike them he at least knew that he was ignorant. We have seen that when Kierkegaard interprets this edict to mean "Separate yourself from the 'Other,'" the logic of his interpretation is that only then will a self become isolated and thus accessible to knowledge.[68] What comes to the fore is not the traditional problem of knowledge but a problem of the individual's relation to others.

"The 'Other' for the Greek mind," Kierkegaard explains, is "the state," and Socrates' *Apology*, as a "defense" of himself, becomes ironically its dialectical opposite—an attack on the state. For he defended himself by arguing that he was not teaching anything antisocial, subversive. How could he, since he himself knew nothing? All he did was ask his fellow citizens questions. Such a defense is an attack: this protestation of ignorance, this questioning process is what he must be condemned for. To ask a question is to imply that an answer is available, but Socrates' procedure is ironical, because he gives no answers. He leaves nothing subsisting except the individual's own process of calling into question, Hence his audience is left only with the questions, having lost the social security of the consensus which the conventional answers had ensured and which had held the community together. Thus Socrates's questions are bloodsucking.[69] He was sucking the organic life out of the Athenian state, which is disintegrating into separate individuals.

So employed irony is doubly "aphoristical." If its initial *reflexive* function is to enable the ironist to "separate" himself from others so that he may become himself, its function as a means of communication is to permit the other to "separate" *himself* so that he may become himself. When these dialectically opposed functions are put together, irony can be characterized as a *contradictory composite*, combining opposed "lines of force."[70] It is "the combination of ethical passion, which inwardly lays infinite emphasis upon one's own self, and of education [in this context, Socrates role as midwife], which outwardly abstracts from one's own self. . . . This abstraction makes the first emphasis pass unnoticed, and herein resides the art of the ironist." The *reflexive* emphasis is *reversed:* "The dialectical is seen in the fact that he who communicates truth must work against himself." The individual who must become first-personal for himself must not intrude in the process by which the other becomes first-personal. In identifying himself with Socrates, Kierkegaard is not only becoming third-personal but is also identifying himself with someone who had himself become third-personal:

> Take Socrates: he is not third-personal in the sense that he avoids danger, exposing himself and risking his life. . . . But . . . he speaks of his sentence to death as though he were a third person. He is subjectivity raised to the second power. He is related to himself . . . as a true poet is related to his poetic production.

Kierkegaard's esthetic works[71] are a poetic production which he assigns to third persons—his pseudonyms. As he explains in "A First and Last Clarification," appended to the *Postscript*; "I am impersonal, or personal only in the third person a stage prompter, who has poetically produced the authors."[72]

SCRIPT

A Socratic pronouncement which Kierkegaard cites in the dissertation, in *Either/Or*, and in "A Passion Story" is *Loquere ut videam*.[73] This behest dramatizes the problem of communication as it is posed in the first paragraph of Eremita's preface, where this pseudonym opposed "the sense of hearing" as "my most valued sense" to the traditionally valued sense of sight. The behest brings out the contradiction between the *external* and the *internal* that is at stake in the reevaluation: mere sight yields merely an external appearance; true insight as to what someone really is within comes only when he reveals himself in speech.

But in fact Kierkegaard's dialectic relinquishes dialogue. This is more than a matter of overhearing replacing ordinary conversation, as it does in "Solomon's Dream" and the graveyard scene. Socrates did not write. In existentialism we have in fact been dealing not with a *modus loquendi* but a *modus scribendi*. That the *Postscript* [*Efterskrift*] is Kierkegaard's major work reminds us of this fact. That *Either/Or* is also literature is suggested by the one respect in which Eremita does not hesitate, when he hesitates over a title for what he found in the "hiding place" behind the "secret door," before he finally lit upon *Either/Or*: "I could call them Papers, Posthumous Papers, Found Papers, Lost Papers."[74] The alternative adjectives play up different dialectics which we have watched develop in these papers themselves, but the noun remains "papers." And on the title page of *Either* we read *The Papers of A*; on the title page of *Or, The Papers of B*. The latter are further characterized as *Letters to A* and as such represent an effort of communication. But although B in these letters summons A from his "hiding place" and bids him, "Throw off your mask," he yet admits at the end of his last letter why he has adopted the indirect approach of writing letters: "I know you do not like people to talk to you about your inner history, so I have chosen to write, and I will never talk to you about it." B further explains,

> Your nature is too closed up and introverted [*indesluttet*] for me to believe that it would do any good to talk with you, but on the other hand I hope that my letter would not be without significance. When you labor on your self within the closed [*lukkede*] machinery of your personality, I put in my pleas and am sure that they will become involved in the movement. . . . Since our relation in writing [*skriftlig*] is to remain a secret, I respect all the formalities: I say good-bye as if we were far distant from each other, though I hope to see you in my home just as often as before."[75]

"A secret" is not just a content that has been hidden, and it is not just the "relation in writing" that is to "remain a secret." There is a methodological implication in the distance which separates individuals, rendering them individuals, and the implication can be followed out if we accept Climacus's appraisal that "A is far superior to B as a dialectician."[76] We can then see that the seducer recommends letters as a secretive form of communication on the ground of the dialectic they permit:

> The dead letter often has much greater influence than the living word. A letter is a secretive communication. . . . No *pressure* is felt from anyone's *presence*, and her ideal is something which I believe a young girl would really rather be alone with at some moment, and especially at the moment when it exerts the strongest influence upon her mind. . . . Even if her ideal has found a sufficiently complete expression in a definite loved object, there are still moments when she feels there is a surplus in the ideal which reality lacks. . . . Through a letter, one may be spiritually present in these sacred moments of consecration.[77]

Of course there is still a difference between such reflective seduction via the ideal and reflective communication via the ideal. The seducer is prepared to exploit his victim's "visualization in her imagination [*forestilling*] that a real person is the author of the letter," which "creates a natural and easy transition back to reality." But Kierkegaard denies the reality of his authors by making them pseudonymous. Thus the reader continues to remain alone with his ideal without any pressure from anyone's presence, and the transition back to reality is "left" entirely up to his own initiative.

THE SCREEN

In the rest of the first paragraph of Eremita's preface, the distance separating individuals is further stressed. Eremita moves from the traditional starting point of the senses, where the evidence is contradictory, to the higher level of the imagination. Arrival there removes the contradiction between what is seen and heard, but then it is restored at a different juncture:

> A confessor [*skriftefader*] is separated from the penitent [*skriftende*] by a screen; he does not see, he only hears. Eventually [*efterhaanden*], as he hears he constructs an external appearance which corresponds to what he hears. Thus no contradiction occurs. It is otherwise, however, when you hear and see at the same time and yet see a screen between yourself and the speaker.[78]

The screen suggests in the first instance the indirectedness of the relation between the two individuals ("he does not see, he only hears"). But when he then hears and sees "at the same time," the implication is that there is no screen, but contradictorily a screen is nonetheless seen. This contradiction did not occur when the screen was an actual physical reality which can literally be seen and the other individual was the confessor's imaginary representation; but now the screen that is no longer externally real is imagined as a metaphor for the externality of the relation between one individual and another and for the ensuing problem of communication.

We could compare Merleau-Ponty's sharp distinction: on one hand something can be "hidden merely like a physical reality which we have not been able to discover" or "which we shall one day be able to see confronting us or which others, better situated, could already see, provided that the screen that conceals it is lifted"; on the other hand sometimes "there is no vision without the screen."[79] This is the fashion in which I must, according to Kierkegaard, visualize my relation to the other.

THE CLIMAX

At long last it has been feasible to interpret as the starting point of existentialism Kierkegaard's application of the principle of contradiction in the first paragraph of the preface to *Either/Or*. The problem of starting point itself will have to be reexamined in the sequel as the phenomenological problem of recovering immediate experience. But the present introduction to existential dialectic will remain indispensable as an introduction to existential phenomenology. This is notably the case with respect to the attempt to recover immediate experience. In making this attempt it is necessary for Husserl to determine the levels he has reached,[80] and this is a juncture at which existential phenomenology readily makes his method over into a dialectic.

We have gained a certain expertise from climbing to different levels with Climacus, but what about our own climactic problem? Philosophy itself becomes in existentialism a higher-level experience, and we are in the long run committed by our exposition of existentialism to the higher-level philosophical problem of communication between philosophers who are indulging different conceptions of experience.[81] Philosophy was most sectarian after World War II, with each sect spending much of its time digging its own rut deeper. I am not suggesting that this introduction will have coped with the contemptuous lack of understanding most Anglo-American philosophers felt toward existentialism. They are still smiling.

I am reminding you of the episode in the "story" Kierkegaard told about Climacus long before he assigned to him the "authorship" of the *Postscript*:

> While he was laboring to climb up . . . , he was afraid of losing the numerous implications which he had already formulated but which still had not become entirely clear to him and necessary. When we see someone carrying a large number of breakable articles stacked one upon the other, we are not surprised that he walks unsteadily and every moment tries to keep his balance. But if we do not see the stack, we smile, just as many people smiled at Johannes Climacus without suspecting that . . . his soul was uneasy lest a single one of the implications should fall out and the whole stack fall apart.[82]

Let them smile.

I only hope some readers have been able to see enough of the stack, so that they have become as uneasy as Climacus himself—especially since I have added to it the yet higher level problem of philosophical communication. This higher-level problem is illustrated by some of the misunderstandings that I earlier conceded have bedeviled the development of existentialism itself as a philosophical movement. Inasmuch as Heidegger has been pivotal to this development, his case is the most striking. On one hand he acknowledged in *Being and Time* his debt to both the phenomenologist Husserl and the existentialist Kierkegaard, but in his contribution to a *Festschrift* for Husserl two years later, he no longer described his method as "phenomenological," and he eventually dismissed Kierkegaard as not even a philosopher but "a religious writer." On the other hand he has discounted existential phenomenology as a misunderstanding of his philosophy.[83]

After the split between Sartre and Merleau-Ponty, the two most prominent existential phenomenologists, Sartre commented that Husserl had "become . . . the distance between us. . . ."[84] But there is also considerable distance separating Husserl from either Sartre or Merleau-Ponty, and this distance will have to be measured in the sequel, as will the distance between Husserl and Heidegger.

DISTANCE

The present problem, however, is the distance separating us today from existentialism. This distance has doubtless increased, now that existentialism has become a "dead letter" and we no longer feel the "pressure" of the "influence" of any existentialist, even though the "dead letter" itself has acquired in French philosophy a vitality that traditionally was reserved for the "living word."[85] But as I argued earlier, distance itself is/was an *ex-sistential* problem. And I have been trying to show that it is/was a problem for the existentialist as a writer. I am not recalling the seducer's resort to writing, for his "dead letter" is a deceptive interlude; he will be present for the seduction, granted that the only pressure he will be bring to bear will be with a phantom body. I am thinking, rather, of the way existentialism's reflexive dialectic is frustrated by writing in *Nausea*:

> The letters which I had just traced were not yet dry, and already they were no longer mine. . . .
> That phrase, I had thought it up, it had been at the start something of myself. Now it was inscribed on the paper. . . . I did not recognize it any longer. I could not even any longer think it. It was there, opposite me; in vain would I have sought for a mark of its origin. . . . The letters now no longer glistened; they were dry. . . . Nothing remained of their ephemeral splendor.[86]

Nothing remains today of the ephemeral splendor of existentialism. The subject, an individual as an origin, that there had been at the start something of myself—all these notions have dried up in structuralism, poststructuralism, and hermeneutical phenomenology.

There was a brief intermission when, as I indicated earlier, existentialism—Kierkegaard, Sartre, and Merleau-Ponty—became for the present generation in French philosophy (and to some extent elsewhere) an introduction in effect to their more difficult predecessors—Hegel, Husserl, and Heidegger. But since then the latter have become better understood and thus have eclipsed their own earlier influence on existentialism.

But in other respect these predecessors have come to be understood (or misunderstood) in terms of the "influence" they have exerted on later developments. Here only brief prognosis is possible, for even what is meant by "understanding" has undergone revision with these later developments. Though so miscellaneous that there is little prospect of regarding them as a philosophical movement (as I have existentialism) what structuralists, poststrucuralists, and heremeneutical phenomenologists tend to share more or less in common for our purposes is a denial of Husserl's phenomenological presumption of the eventual accessibility of immediately given experience—or (as most would prefer to put it) of the accessibility of prelinguistic meanings. With this denial (and with their debt to Hegel) their method or, rather, methods, tend to approximate versions of a dialectic. This dialectic is quite different in some of its traits from what has been set forth here as existential, but there are still recognizable similarities. Thus my introduction to an existential dialectic might have a certain limited relevance as an introduction to these later developments.

PRESENCE

Unfortunately the notion of "introduction" has also undergone revision with these later developments.[87] It is true that the dialectic is still an interpretation of texts and of the relation beween texts, and that we have encountered problems in interpreting the relation between the diaries or passion stories in Kierkegaard and between the diary in *Nausea* and the novel. But these have been reflexive problems involving the diarist and his passions. And to the extent that language is taken for granted in these later developments as a medium of communication, the problem of understanding or misunderstanding is no longer carried over from personal experience as a problem of communication but is lodged impersonally in these texts. Kierkegaard may become "impersonal," but he was initially personal, and what he becomes is, rather, "personal in the third person," in order that his individual reader may be "introduced" to his own first-personal experience and to the philosophical implications of its being his own.

With the later developments I am anticipating, no *interplay* is sought in his fashion with the *modus vivendi*. There is no longer any problem of the "pressure . . . felt from anyone's presence." The author no longer feels that he is "spiritually present" and "involved in the movement" of someone else's thought, and the reader is not seduced into visualizing "a real person" as "the author." There is no longer "a natural and easy transition back to reality"—not even to the reader's own reality.

This carry-over of problems from personal experience and the ensuing problem of communication are the philosophical experiences which are the legacy of existentialism. They have been not appropriated but disowned by its successors. Thus an introduction to existentialism retains its intrinsic justification as an introduction to these philosophical experiences, and it need not merge into what existentialism has become historically (as any philosophical movement does), an introduction to succeeding philosophical movements. To surrender to the success of succession leaves us with no distinction between a philosophy and an intellectual vogue and is one way of surrendering the history of philosophy to the history of ideas—which are the debris that scholars and professors successfully inherit and paw over.

THE INTRODUCTION

One issue that has survived the eclipse of existentialism, in France at least, is the relation between the philosophical and the literary. Just as the history of modern philosophy has been by and large an alliance of philosophy and science, but one whose terms have been constantly subject to renegotiation, so the relation between philosophy and literature does not remain a fixed adjustment. It accordingly lent itself to the dialectical treatment which I attempted against the background of the fragmentation of the fixed adjustments of Hegel's "system of the arts." This treatment might be extended to the further adjustments imposed by later developments.

Hence the "implication" in Climacus's stack that I have been most uneasy about, lest it not become entirely clear and might even fall out, has been the transition from Kierkegaard's personal problem of communicating with Regina to esthetic experience, as the starting point for his philosophy and for the application of its "storytelling method." The transition is not merely a matter of his "Relation to 'Her' " developing into "Something Poetical." In fact, if anyone is unable to make this climb and still supposes that Kierkegaard's "storytelling method" is without philosophical implications and is simply reducible to his particular experience with Regina, let him heed Climacus's report of how he had become "bored with girls" by the time he proposed to disentangle the crisscrossing misunderstandings that led him up to higher levels. Let him also turn back from this introduction of mine and read the love story Kierkegaard himself tells in his own "Introduction" to how he started out to become a philosopher:

Introduction
In the town of H—— there lived some years ago a young student by the name of Johannes Climacus, whose . . . joy it was to live apart, hidden, and in quietness. Those who knew him at all well tried to explain his closed up and introverted [*indesluttet*] nature . . . by saying that he was either melancholy or in love. Those who thought the latter were in a sense not wrong. . . . Feelings for girls were entirely alien to his

heart. . . . Yet in love he was, madly in love—but with thought or, rather, with thinking. No young lover, moved by that incomprehensible transition [*overgang*] whereby love wakens in the breast . . . could be more deeply moved than was Johannes Climacus by that comprehensible transition by which one thought fits into another. . . . It was his delight to start with a single thought and from that to climb up step by step along the way of implication to a higher thought, for implications were his *Scala Paradisi*, and his exhilaration in mounting this ladder was to him more exalting than that of Jacob's angels.[88]

However, this love of wisdom, of its upward climb, and of the quiet life is traditional philosophy.[89] Indeed the appellation "Johannes Climacus" was first applied by Kierkegaard to Hegel.[90] And although it is in *Johannes Climacus* that Kierkegaard asserts (in opposition to Hegelian efforts to finish the system) the problem of starting point, he relinquishes *Johannes Climacus* in favor of *Either/Or*. Quite possibly one reason is a more accurate appreciation of a woman's "loving lack of understanding" and of the problem of communication this contradiction poses. Yet Kierkegaard climbs almost out of Regina's reach in the preface to *Either/Or*, not only because what he is doubting is the philosophical prospect of an *Aufhebung* but also because he is concerned with a wider audience of individual readers than Regina.

I say "almost" inasmuch as the upward climb, with which she becomes "Something Poetical," is precisely not an *Aufhebung*: the "figure" of Regina continues to "hover" before his mind, just as do those of the old man and Socrates.[91] The impetus of particular personal experiences is never transcended in Kierkegaard's esthetic writings; it becomes instead *interplay* with their more general philosophical implications, including those of the problem of communication. If *Either/Or* is Kierkegaard's final starting point, it is not that he is any less sure that he will be misunderstood. But the contradiction now is that the "stage prompter", while keeping his distance, would involve himself in the movement of the closed machinery of another's personality. He starts out not (as he does in the "Introduction" I have just retrieved from *Johannes Climacus*) with a poetic version of himself and his own "closed-up and introverted nature" but by addressing you as his "Dear Reader."

Notes

1. See p. 35 above.
2. *Postscript*, p. 293. For the interplay between thought and existence, see p. 58 above.

3. See p. 107 above.

4. I have in mind particularly Eremita's shadowgraphic procedure.

5. Hegel recommends that anyone who would "keep up with the times and with advances in philosophy" ought "to read reviews of philosophical works, perhaps even to read their prefaces and first paragraphs, for these preliminary pages give the general principles on which everything turns" (*Phenomenology,* p. 43). The disdainfulness of this recommendation is of course clear from my other citations from this preface in my preface. Kierkegaard's opposing preoccupations with the problem of starting out is evident not only in his prefaces but also perhaps in his first paragraphs. Earlier I cited the first paragraph of the dissertation (p. 40 above) and demonstrated the care Kierkegaard had taken with its composition. Later in this chapter I shall consider the first paragraph of *Johannes Climacus* as well as the first paragraph of *Either*. These are his three starting points in the most obvious sense, though the first paragraph of *Either* finally takes precedence.

6. *Philosophical Fragments,* p. 153. Misunderstanding can be a providential arrangement for isolating the individual: "The very moment God chooses an individual, he blocks him off, sets madness between him and the others in order to prevent an understanding between them. . . . He wants men as single individuals" (*Papirer,* XI³ B 199). Long before Kierkegaard was tormented by a woman's "loving lack of understanding" (X¹ A 374), he recognized that "the most sublime tragedy without doubt is to be misunderstood. Accordingly the life of Christ is the supreme tragedy, misunderstood as he was by the people, Pharisees, the disciples—in short, by everyone" (I A 33).

7. In the *Postscript* the major dislocation is transferred reflexively to his own reaction: "In his little compartment [*aflukke*]" he suspected "there was a defect in the foundations," and "whenever he looked out of his little window, he observed with a shudder the redoubling of energetic efforts to beautify and enlarge the building, so that after having seen and having shuddered, he collapsed" (p. 59). We are already acquainted with Kierkegaard's analogizing of the Hegelian system to architecture, which in Hegel himself is essentially an "enclosure" (see p. 420 above) and in Kierkegaard is sometimes metamorphosed into a castle (see p. 249 above). The "little room" or "compartment" is a spatial metaphor which can be compared with Kierkegaard's ironical location of himself as a mere "paragraph" transcended by the further development of the system toward its completion (see, e.g., *Either,* p. 220).

8. The same epistemological uncertainty afflicts the editor who writes the preface to "The Diary of the Seducer" (see p. 310 above).

9. See p. 415 above. The interplay between "hidden" papers as a mode of indirect communication and a "hidden" *modus vivendi* becomes explicit with the Judge's complaint about the esthete, "Your activity is a matter of preserving your hiding place" (*Or,* p. 163). See p. 469 above.

10. See p. 121 above.

11. 77. *Papirer,* X³ 413. If one protests that on the evidence of the dissertation, he learned indirect communication from Socrates, one cannot overlook Kierkegaard's further pronouncement: "How amazing; Socrates was always stating that he had learned from a woman" (IX A 18). I assume the woman Kierkegaard has in mind was Diotima rather than Aspasia.

12. Ibid., III A 164; Lowrie, 1:193–94; *Repetition,* pp. 15, 21. These passages from *Repetition* (which was written when Kierkegaard had escaped to Berlin after having broken his engagement) are obviously interpretable as a poeticized version of his relation to Regina. He is "seeking her again" but only succeeds in recollecting her, and recollection with its orientation toward the past is the opposite of repetition, which is oriented toward the future.

13. *Papirer,* X⁵ A. This was her father's report of her desperation, as reported by Kierkegaard.

14. See p. 106 above.

15. *Sartre*, p. 83. Inasmuch as it involves Franconay's movements as well as opposed traits, this portrayal of Chevalier represents in the development of Sartre's analysis a dialectical advance beyond the portrait as a static work of art which "the painter endowed . . . with a complete resemblance to its model."

16. *L'idiot*, 3:540. Mathilde's "glorious body" is compounded of Flaubert's idealization of both femininity and aristocracy. Only Sartre prefers to the traditional conception of "idealization" the reverse conception of *déréalisation* (ibid., p. 539). He explains "The thighs and breasts of a princess are never sufficiently regal unless one refrains from touching them and limits oneself, as Flaubert does, to desiring a glorious body, an image which is abstract and unrealizable, merely the locus where are about to coincide *woman as such* . . . and the *aristocracy as such*." In other words, what Flaubert was up to was "derealizing the flesh and the behavior of Mathilde by the very desire which was ostensibly aroused by her gracefulness and which was in fact feeding on itself, with the primary aim of *transcending* a reality that was too plebian [*roturière*]" (ibid., p. 540; italics in original).

17. Ibid., 1:694. That he would have been horrified indicates that the shift of level is indispensable.

18. See n. 72, this chapter.

19. "Something which cannot be told about is the grief, O Queen, which you bid me renew [by the telling]." Aeneas is addressing Dido, who has requested an account of the fall of Troy. Kierkegaard may be not only punning with the name of his ex-fiancée, but also referring to his abandonment of her for a higher mission, as *pius Aeneas* abandons Dido. Since Regina had threatened suicide, Kierkegaard may even have in mind the way Dido after her suicide had rebuffed Aeneas when he approached her in the underworld. For Kierkegaard wrote "My Relation to 'Her'" after Regina had rebuffed his effort at a rapprochement.

20. Lowrie, 1:193.

21. I doubt if there is any connection between the change of her name from the French to the Latin spelling and her proclamation after his death (she outlived him by half a century), "The French will never understand him." But the proclamation itself would seem to assume that she did understand him, although Kierkegaard so regularly insisted that she could not. Thus it seem probable that they had rather different conceptions of understanding. Regine, in spite of her apparent effort to become Regina, remained undialectical, if we accept one of Kierkegaard's appraisals: "Now she is—not dead—but happily and comfortably married. I said that on the same day (six years ago)—and was called the lowest of lowest cads. Remarkable!" (*Papirer*, VIII A 447). Her own appraisal was, "As is so often said, 'a happy marriage is life's greatest blessing.' And Schlegel and I are so much to each other that we mutually enrich each other's lives. In a way I owe this to him [Kierkegaard] also. . . ." (Croxall, p. 13). The letter as we have it breaks off here, so that we do not know "how" this way "is to be understood." The letter was written from the West Indies to a relative of Kierkegaard's after his death.

22. See p. 110 above.

23. *Papirer*, IV A 85.

24. See n. 6, this chapter, where I cited Kierkegaard's later, more dialectical version of his earlier, flatter pronouncement, "She loved only me, and yet she did not understand me" (Papirer, III A 147). Kierkegaard often meets "the requirement of existence —to put things together" (p. 145 above), which had not earlier been so dialectically juxtaposed.

25. *Stages*, p. 56. It is the man who retains the positive role of producing in the realm of ideality, as we have already recognized to be the case with both diaries.

26. My italics. When I referred earlier to communication as an "ensuing problem" (p. 466 above), I was not envisaging an undialectical linear sequence where this problem develops in tandem with the problem of existence. Communication is itself a

problem of existence, and it became more desperately a problem when Regina became engaged to the commonplace suitor whose *Aufhebung* had been managed by the seducer in the diary. Thus the sequential relation between the two problems can be reversed in a fashion suggested by an earlier entry in the journal: "Someone is writing a novel in which one of the characters goes mad. During the composition he himself becomes mad and finishes it in the first person" (*Papirer,* II A 634).

27. *Stages,* p. 378. This is of course a specification of the dialectical requirement that a "relation" must underlie the "disrelation." "Heterogeneity" is the same term that Kierkegaard uses of the "disrelation" between Christianity and philosophical speculation (e.g., *Postscript,* p. 339), and this usage illustrates the similarity of the disruption of continuity at quite different levels of his dialectic (see n. 43, this chapter).

28. *Papirer,* IX A 344. For Sartre's similarly reflexive doctrine of understanding, see p. 189 above.

29. *Papirer,* VIII¹ A 91. The illusion is that much is accomplished by the process of communicating his thought, when in fact he and his communicant must actualize what has been thought at the ideal level in self-differentiating actions (see p. 474 above). We should not be misled by Kierkegaard's use of the terms "action" and "expression," for it is not the "outcome" of the action that counts (see p. 411 above).

30. *Papirer,* II A 805. This conviction suggests that Kierkegaard was not an entirely modernized Antigone; the guilt of the whole family in the Oedipus legend (see p. 274 above) retained its fascination for him, in spite of his effort, continued in "Guilty/ Not Guilty?" to appropriate the guilt as his own.

31. *Stages,* p. 237. A "mystery" hardly explains all, and "Solomon's Dream" does not explain all. As an account of Kierkegaard's relation to his father it is clearly "something poetical," like his account of his relation to Regina. Scholarly speculation has carefully weighed the fact that Kierkegaard's father got his servant pregnant and had to marry her before the year of mourning for his beloved first wife was over. Kierkegaard himself never mentions his mother even in his journal. Lowrie comments, in his inimitable fashion, "He who wrote so much about woman, and so beautifully but also despitefully, was able to conceive her only as the counterpart of man, and associated no noble and tender thoughts with woman as mother" (1:24). But "counterpart" as the relation of a woman to a man is a dialectic Kierkegaard never envisaged without drawing a distinction of level.

32. Indirection is also demonstrated by the way the story interrupts the diary. "A Passion Story" is, as I have explained, both a double-entry diary and bifocal in its reference to Christ's suffering as well as Kierkegaard's. In addition, Kierkegaard interpolates several stories. One story he planned but did not include was Abelard's. At the time *Stages* was published, Regina was only engaged to Schlegel. It is possible that he did not wish to offer any insinuation which might have seemed to explain all and would have finally let Regina off the hook.

33. The manuscript of Kierkegaard's belated esthetic work, *The Crisis* (see p. 85 above), bore the comment, which he deleted before publication, "From the Papers of a Dead Man." Though an appraisal of Mme Heiberg's acting, Kierkegaard may have been recalling he first met Regina when she was not much older than Juliet. The deleted comment may also have indicated the dialectical shift that had taken place in his life since his first publication, *From the Papers of One Still Living.*

34. Lowrie, *Kierkegaard,* 1:218.

35. *Stages,* p. 202. See also *Papirer,* VII A 126.

36. *Papirer,* VIII A 100.

37. Ibid., V A 88. The distinction is stressed in Climacus's recapitulative commentary on *Fear and Trembling:* "In the form of direct communication, in the form of a shriek, 'fear and trembling' is of no great significance; for the direct form of communication demonstrates that the direction is outward, culminating in the shriek, not inward into the abyss of inwardness" (*Postscript,* p. 234). He may have Regina in mind when he explains how "the immediate individual often makes himself ridiculous by a

womanish shrieking in the moment, which is forgotten the next moment" (ibid., p. 397; see n. 21, this chapter).

38. The name referred to the area around the church and included not only the graveyard but also the parsonage. Lowrie explains that surnames were not firmly fixed in Denmark when Kierkegaard's father was a boy and Kierkegaard's family had derived their name from their place of residence (1:20). With his taste for byplay, Kierkegaard would have welcomed, in one dialectical fashion or another, the commotion attendant on his own burial (see p. 21 above).

39. *Postscript*, p. 216. For the idiom, see my *Human Nature*, 2:14–15. Kierkegaard was aware not only of property values but also of the fact that he was squandering his portion of the family fortune his father had built up.

40. *Postscript*, p. 213. Probably one factor that "moved" Climacus was the momentum acquired by the death metaphor.

41. Ibid.

42. Ibid., pp. 214, 213.

43. Ibid., p. 216. "Crisscrossing" (like Sartre's *carrousels, tourniquets,* and "whirl-igigs") solicits for its disentanglement dialectical skill. But "crisscrossing" can be due to the skill of the dialectician as a *combinateur (Papirer,* X2 A 285). Kierkegaard compares this skill with "the way the strands are crossed in the spider's web" (*Point of View*, p. 147). Such "crisscrossing" we initially observed in Merleau-Ponty's shifting focus from personal relations to more general issues (p. 120 above). In Kierkegaard the discrepancy may seem almost insurmountable between what one would ordinarily dismiss as a merely personal misunderstanding (whether between Kierkegaard and Regina or between Kierkegaard and his father) and a "misunderstanding between philosophy and Christianity." But this is existentialism. Kierkegaard may have been initially inspired to pile misunderstanding on misunderstanding by Overskou's comedy, *Misunderstanding on Misunderstanding* (*Postscript*, p. 189). Yet there is a certain analogy between the problem of the relation between Kierkegaard and Regina and that of the relation between philosophy and Christianity, for in both instances the relation between reflection and immediacy is involved. In Hegel "faith is said to be an immediacy, and it is asserted that the immediate is transcended by thought." Climacus singles this out as "one of the most confusing propositions put forward by recent speculation," and he adds that faith is a "new immediacy" (i.e., an immediacy after reflection) but "one which can never be transcended" (*Postscript*, p. 310). The confusion is clarified by the reallocation I dealt with in chap. 10, but it could be argued that Kierkegaard's dealings with Regina were also efforts to allocate and reallocate her, i.e., to the esthetic stage, to the ethical stage, to the religious stage.

44. *Postscript*, pp. 216–17; italics in original.

45. Ibid., pp. 216, 214. Kierkegaard regarded his engagement to Regina as a sacred promise (see chap. 10, n. 52 above).

46. *Postscript*, p. 216.

47. See p. 477 above.

48. I have already drawn attention to the initial resistance Kierkegaard felt to poeticization vis-à-vis Regina: "I cannot dispose of this relation, for I cannot poeticize it." Similarly, he resisted the recollective imaginative movement in the journal entry he made after his father's death. Indeed he went so far as to deprive himself of the interplay provided by his usual pun: "Of all that I have inherited from him, the recollection of him, his transfigured portrait, not transfigured [*forklaret*] by the poetry of my imagination (for it did not require that) but clarified [*forklaret*] by many individual traits . . . , I will be careful to preserve . . . securely hidden from the world" (Thompson, p. 91). Thompson is skeptical of Kierkegaard's resistance: "A father who was rather annoying in life is transformed in death into an ideal of father love, ultimately a reflection of divine paternity" (p. 92). But Kierkegaard's father was not merely "rather annoying"; he was something much more formidable, since as a child he had cursed God for his poverty, etc., and then had made a lot of money, which survived the

inflation that reduced many of his compatriots to bankruptcy. Furthermore, the process
of transfiguration he underwent was more complicated than Thompson allows. It can
only be traced when Kierkegaard's Hegelian terminology is taken into account, together with his adjustments in its implications, including that adjustment which "preserves" his father's "transfigured portrait" not only "hidden from the world" but also
from an *Aufhebung* that would "ultimately" absorb it into "a reflection of divine
paternity." Like Kierkegaard himself, his father seems to have been more of a Christ
figure. Cf. the image of him already cited as "a cross upon the grave of all his hopes."
Kierkegaard employs similar imagery of himself in "The Unhappiest Man" (see chap. 10,
n. 94 above), and we shall soon recognize that he sees in himself the mirror image of his
father. However, the traditional typological method of Christian theology (see my
Human Nature, 1:307–11) is relevant to Kierkegaard's bifocal procedure as well as to
Hegel's, and it was a tradition in which more literal meanings sometimes offered resistance (*Human Nature*, 1:338).

49. "I owe everything from the start to my father" (*Papirer*, IX A 68). It is feasible
in an existential dialectic not only to refer to one's life as a whole (see p. 276 above) but
also to owe everything to two different persons, provided the part/whole relation is kept
under dialectical control. Kierkegaard's double debt did create problems with his
dedications (see n. 91, this chapter).

50. *Stages*, pp. 191–92; my italics. The mirror is introduced in the preceding first
paragraph of the story: "When Swift was old he was taken into the madhouse he himself had founded in his youth. There, it is reported, he often stood before a mirror. . . .
He looked at himself and said, 'Poor old man!' " Here reflexive use is made of the
mirror reflection as in the epigraph of *Stages* for the esthetic stage: "Such works are
mirrors: when a monkey peers into them, no apostle can be seen looking out." The intrusion within the reflexive relation of the first paragraph of the father/son relation
of the second paragraph is a striking and significant departure by Kierkegaard from his
characteristic procedure. Interplay between "poor old man" and "poor child" probably
lies behind the old man/child graveyard story. Indeed the development of this interplay
is suggested by the different versions of the Swift and mirror story found in Kierkegaard.

51. The difficulty with eliminating ambiguities would of course in Hegel's terms be
due to the failure in this climb to transcend the level of *Vorstellung*, which would involve arrival at an outcome transcending differences in individual interpretation. The
ambiguities occur at different levels, but with interplay between levels. Thus the
seducer admits initially, "I cannot decide how she [Cordelia] is to be understood"
(*Either*, p. 339). Nor does he allow her to decide initially: "My approach must be as artistic as possible. The starting point must be as vague as possible and open to every possibility" (p. 368). There is a thrust here at the indeterminacy of Hegel's starting point
(see p. 39 above), but Kierkegaard's telling of a story is also a process of seduction for
the reader (see p. 473 above), and we must not forget that a dialectician along with a
poet is watching over every step in the process: "I can tell a story so that the point is
not lost, . . . so that it is not revealed too soon. To keep those who listen in suspense, . . .
to ascertain what they want the outcome to be, to trick them in the course of the
narration—that is my delight; to make use of ambiguities, so that the listeners understand one thing in the saying, and then suddenly notice that the words could also be
interpreted otherwise—that is my art" (*Either*, pp. 365–66). The suspense and the trick-
ery (especially with respect to the outcome) lead us on, eliciting our intervention in the
interplay induced by the ambiguities, in the story, so that we have to ask ourselves how
it is to be understood, and the answer is a decision in terms of our own lives (see pp.
409, 474 above).

52. *Johannes Climacus*, p. 105.

53. *Either*, p. 3.

54. See p. 46 above.

55. *Either*, p. 300.

56. Ibid., p. 309. "A step which is decisive" becomes a metaphor later (p. 367), and
the seducer also offers Cordelia a carriage which will take "flight" (p. 391). The requisite

"foresight" that she will be unable to exercise would be into the dialectical development (*udvikling*) which is recollected in the diary and which is an entangling development. (Note the byplay with the root which *udvikling* shares with *indviklede* and *forvikling*, and cf. the failure of foresight on the part of Sartre's woman about to be seduced, though her failure was due to the entanglement of self-deception.) "Decisive," "definitive," and "step" also suggest that a dialectical development will supervene. *Grad* may suggest a distinction of level. In any case, there may be interplay between her stepping down to degradation and the upward dialectical climb of the seducer's "infinite self-reflection" for which the preface has prepared us. Stepping out perhaps suggests exposure, for with his prompt move to the esthetic level the seducer reaches Tieck's novel, where *Die wilde Engländerin* rejects the prospect of love because of the trauma she experienced as a child from reading a textbook on anatomy. When she is out riding with a suitor, they quarrel, and she dismounts in such a hurry that her clothing becomes entangled in the saddle and ripped off. The intrusion of this esthetic level is later credited, discredited, and credited again with interplay between the *modus vivendi* and the *modus loquendi*: "To see her was to love her—that is how it is described in novels, and it is true enough, had love no dialectic; but what does one really learn about love from novels? Nothing but lies, which help shorten the task" (*Either*, pp. 339–40). I would guess this should be unpacked as follows: novels are incapable of this description, since so immediate an experience (we are supposed to recall that it was Don Giovanni's: see p. 268 above) cannot be described in a linguistic genre; but the illusion of immediacy inculcated by novels does "help shorten" the dialectical development of the seduction, so that their "lies" cannot be dismissed as "nothing but."

57. His first anticipation of the process of reflection reinforces the implicit reference to the role anatomy played in Tieck by comparing his dialectical skill to Cuvier's: "I have already seen the little foot, and . . . therefrom I have learned from Cuvier to proceed with certainty to conclusions. Therefore hurry" (see p. 272 above). For the whole he finally achieves and the additional parts it subsumes besides "the little foot," see p. 507 above.

58. See p. 405 above.

59. The personification of the "unknown" object as a "stranger" finds its justification in that "mind" is in Hegel "the activity" by which we come to know what initially was a "seemingly *alien* object" (*Encyclopaedia*, pt. 3, par. 443, *Zusatz*; italics in original).

60. *Johannes Climacus*, pp. 101–2.

61. See p. 240 above.

62. *Postscript*, p. 551. Kierkegaard can admit that his "authorship" had a "purely personal meaning" (*Point of View*, p. 71). Although his "authorship" also takes a dialectical, developmental form, so that he can claim that "my existence relation transformed itself, corresponding altogether exactly to the demands in the productivity" (ibid., p. 63), the details of the specifically "personal meaning" must as such finally elude us. (Such rather trivial correspondences as his five minutes at the theater are hardly personally relevant.) Thus it becomes an eventually thankless undertaking to write Kierkegaard's biography in Lowrie's fashion, which is an attempt to embrace him. Barbara Anderson has appropriately shifted the emphasis to the problem of communication in her reveiw of Thompson's biography, "The best biography of Kierkegaard must be fundamentally one's own" (p. 306). But she is thinking primarily of the implications of Kierkegaard's reaching the religious stage, where the elusiveness of the individual is beyond recall.

63. Kierkegaard applies the notion of transfiguration to Socrates, as he does to his father. He interprets the Platonic Socrates as one who has been "transfigured from the grave" (*Irony*, p. 68; see also p. 87), and he visualizes Plato's dealings with Socrates in somewhat the same terms as he visualizes his own dealings with Regina: it was "impossible for Plato not to confuse the poetic image with historical actuality" (p. 68). But Kierkegaard is cautious about the analogy David Strauss had drawn between the "conclusion of the *Symposium* and the transfiguration of Christ on the mountain" (p. 69).

64. Kierkegaard cites Theophrastus's definition of irony as the "feigning [*prospoiēsis*] in action and thought for a base purpose," which is expanded in Latin into *simulatio dissimulatioque fallax et fraudulenta* ("deceptive and fraudulent dissembling"; *Irony*, p. 272). Kierkegaard may have read into *prospoiēsis* a reference to poetic production. But he is in any case opposing Hegel, as he usually is when he resorts to Socrates. He notes that *eirōneia* is usually translated as "dissembling," and Capel appropriately refers us to Hegel's discussion of *Verstellung* (*Phenomenology*, pp. 374–83). Kierkegaard reinterprets irony by distinguishing between an objective and a subjective orientation: "Whereas dissembling describes rather the objective act by which the disparity between essence and phenomenon is effected, irony is also descriptive of a subjective satisfaction, for it is by means of irony that the subject emancipates himself from the constraint imposed upon him by the continuity of life, whence it may be said of the ironist that he 'cuts loose.' " (We have watched Kierkegaard do this with his own irony, in relation not only to life but also to Hegel's system.) With this reorientation Kierkegaard is able to distinguish (in opposition to Hegel) irony from hypocrisy (*Irony*, p. 743).

65. See p. 312 above. All the seducees were "led away from themselves." But Cordelia's deception is more intimate. Her seducer is her "unseen partner in a dance which is danced by only one" (*Either*, p. 376). When he asks, "What am I doing?" he replies, "An artist paints his love. . . . I do this too, but in a spiritual sense. She does not know that I possess this picture, and therein lies my real deception" (p. 384). In carrying out this deceptive process of appropriation, he manages some *Ausmalung*: "It is as if behind someone [Cordelia] who with an unsteady hand roughly sketched a drawing there was standing another who continuously brought something bold and well rounded out of this" (p. 414). Such reproduction is a development in the dialectic of communication which we are prepared for by the spokesman for the Symparenkromenoi resketching already fictionalized characters as his "brides of sorrow" and by his metaphor "shadowgraphs." We do not look directly at what he is doing but at the shadows reproduced on the wall. The seducer's position behind Cordelia should also be noted, for it further emphasizes the indirectness of their relation. In fact this is Kierkegaard's own favorite posture: not only does he himself stand behind his various pseudonyms, but their thoughts are also regularly presented indirectly, e.g., as "Thoughts Which Wound from Behind—for Edification" (*Papirer*, VIII A 558). It is not absolutely necessary to suspect Kierkegaard of sexual perversity; his purpose may be only to allow the recipient of the communication room to confront herself, inasmuch as edification is a reflexive effort to reconstruct one's life.

66. See p. 430 above.

67. *Papirer*, III A 166. The "resilience" in question is her ability to take the initiative. For Kierkegaard's effort to repel her, see chap. 10, n. 9 above.

68. Further evidence of the dissertation's relevance to *Either* is Kierkegaard's ability to transpose *Either/Or* into Socratic terms. In an entry in his journal entitled "My Judgment on *Either/Or*" he writes, "There was once a young man as fortunately talented as Alcibiades. He went astray in the world. In his need he looked around him for a Socrates, but among his contemporaries he found none. Then he prayed the gods to transform him into one" (*Papirer*, IV A 43). The transposition presupposes the distinction between ancient and modern which is drawn in *Either*. The ancient Socrates was a "plastic" figure (e.g., *Irony*, p. 89; cf. Hegel's conception of the tragic figure, p. 425 above)—i.e., he was solidly self-identical, separated from others but not split within himself. But the separation between Alcibiades (the esthete) and Socrates (the ethical individual) is now internalized within one man, just as *Either/Or* is to be interpreted as "the work of one man" (see p. 475 above). Alongside this existential problem of conversion can perhaps be transposed the problem of communication as it emerged from Kierkegaard's relation to Regina: "I wonder if Socrates was that cold; I wonder if it did not hurt him that Alcibiades could not understand him" (*Papirer*, V B 4). In discussing their relation in the *Symposium*, Kierkegaard explains how "the elusive and ineffable moment of understanding" was "immediately displaced by the anxiety of mis-

understanding," and in this context he recalls how Alcibiades interpreted Socrates as a deceiver (*Irony*, pp. 85–86), as Kierkegaard ostensibly wished Regina would interpret him.

69. *Irony*, pp. 204, 203; see also p. 73.

70. See p. 115 above.

71. *Papirer*, XI² A 97.

72. *Postscript*, p. 551. He is accordingly only "figuratively the author" of the esthetic works (p. 552). Or as he explains elsewhere, "I stand in an altogether poetic relation to my works, and so I am pseudonymous" (*Papirer*, V A 34). Thus there is a sense in which he is capable of being as poetical about himself (X¹ A 272) as he is about Regina, his father, and Socrates.

73. *Irony*, p. 52; *Or*, p. 280; *Stages*, p. 363. As far as I can discover, there is no such pronouncement in Plato or Xenophon. Capel thinks Kierkegaard may have picked it up from Hamann (*Irony*, pp. 367–68), but it was originally a coinage of the rhetorical tradition and is found in Vives (*De ratione dicendi*), Erasmus, and Ben Jonson.

74. *Either*, p. 13.

75. *Or*, p. 338.

76. *Postscript*, p. 227.

77. *Either*, p. 410. The editor cites a contemporary theological controversy, but Kierkegaard is probably also contradicting Hegel's avowed preference in his biblical exegesis for the word that gives spiritual life as opposed to the literalness that kills. This preference is associated not only with the role Hegel assigns the third person of the Trinity (see p. 411 above) but also with the role he assigns philosophy in relation to religion (see p. 430 above), for philosophy is the spiritual interpretation of the religious content (see *Philosophy of History*, pp. 330–31). That it is legitimate for me to supplement these two previous occasions for a comparison with Kierkegaard by extracting methodological implications from "The Diary of the Seducer" seems borne out by Kierkegaard's own comment, "The principle thing is the method, and not the characterization of Johannes or of Cordelia" (*Papirer*, IV A 231).

78. *Either*, pp. 3–4. This is a second paragraph only in the English translation. Kierkegaard regularly wrote long paragraphs which regularly get broken up by his translators. Though the grammatical convention has changed since his time, I also suspect that his motive may be the same as the motive for Sartre's long sentences (see chap. 5, n. 110 above).

79. See p. 308 above.

80. The difficulties in determining these levels are discussed by Ricoeur, pp. 16, 24.

81. See p. 30 above.

82. See p. 259 above.

83. See p. 24 above.

84. See p. 124 above. Earlier I stressed the general significance of spatial relations for existentialism (p. 103 above) and the specific significance of distance for Kierkegaard as well as for Sartre and Heidegger (pp. 112–13). To the previous illustration from Kierkegaard (p. 109 above) might be added the following from *Irony*, since the problems of both existence and communication are short-circuited by Xenophon's failure to appreciate their reflexive dimension: "Xenophon has no intimation of this secret. Allow me to illustrate my meaning with an image. There is an engraving that portrays the grave of Napoleon. Two large trees overshadow the grave. There is nothing else to be seen in the picture, and the immediate spectator will see no more. Between these two trees, however, is an empty space, and as the eye traces out its contour, Napoleon himself suddenly appears out of the nothingness, and now it is impossible to make him disappear. The eye that has once seen him now always sees him with anxious necessity. It is the same with Socrates' replies. As one sees the trees, so one hears his discourse; as the trees are trees, so his words mean exactly what they sound like. There is not a single syllable to give any hint of another interpretation, just as there is not a single brush stroke to suggest Napoleon. Yet it is this empty space, this nothingness, that

conceals what is most significant" (pp. 56–57). This is the "distance" the ironist puts between himself and his interlocutor by interposing his "nothingness"—i.e., his negation of his apparent meaning.

85. Compare Derrida's appraisal of writing with the seducer's: "Writing in the common understanding is the dead letter, it is the vehicle of death [because it signifies the absence of the speaker], . . ." (*Of Grammatology*, p. xl); the bracketed interpolation is the translator's, and she adds by way of explanation, "Because human beings need to comfort themselves with notions of presence, writing in the 'literal' sense, signifying the absence of the actual author, must be 'rejected.' " But such comfort is often sought by authors themselves: the rejection of the letter, or the literary, or literature (see Sartre's citation of the cliché "Tout cela n'est que littérature," *What Is Literature?* p. 28) as merely conventional is of course itself a literary convention. (Some specimens are nicely analyzed by Barbara Leah Harman in "The Fiction of Coherence".) The seducer in *Either* is complicating matters by upholding the sense of presence to herself which Cordelia can only enjoy as a reader with him absent, but his absence is the most effective way in which he can be present and exercise pressure. It is thus the ultimate in seduction: she is still being "led away" from herself by the "unseen partner in a dance which is danced only by one" (n. 65, this chapter). One point Kierkegaard is making is that there is no "common situation" (see p. 372 above)—i.e., the seducer is engaged in what Sartre conceives as a "pseudo communication" (see p. 371 above). It seems doubtful if this conception could retain much significance once a dialectic of presence/absence, actual experience/literary convention (my *modus vivendi/modus loquendi*) is discarded. Indeed the thrust of Derrida's *dissémination* is a refusal to restrict processes of communication to the relations between human beings (or between the actual author and his readers). They become instead "passageways of meaning" in language: "Regular processes of communication [*communications réglées*] become established as a result of the play of language between different functions of the word and in it between different sedimentations or regions of culture" (*La dissémination*, p. 108). See also the broadening of the notion of communication in "Signature Event Context," which begins, "Is it certain that to the word *communication* corresponds a concept that is unique, univocal, rigorously controllable, and transmittable: in a word communicable? . . . One must first of all ask oneself whether or not the word of signifier 'communication' communicates a determinate content, an indentifiable meaning, or a describable value" (p. 172; italics in original). In effect *dissémination* supplants communication.

86. *Nausea*, p. 95. Derrida would give up seeking "a mark of its origin."

87. See Derrida's "Hors livre," which would be a preface (or an introduction) to his *Dissémination* did not this process (if it can be characterized as such) itself dispose both of the distinction between a preface and an actual work and of the *Aufhebung* which holds for Hegel of the relation between a preface (or indeed the writer himself) and the actual work (see my preface above). It may seem that *dissémination* could be compared with the procedure of fragmentation with which Kierkegaard reverses the *Aufhebung* with which Hegel secured systematization. But there are difficulties. I have defended the individuality and integrity of Kierkegaard's philosophy in spite of the fact that it is the fragmentation of Hegel's system. For when Kierkegaard reasserts the contradiction between the internal and the external that the *Aufhebung* ostensibly overcame, he is pulling Hegel's system inside out; and if the *Aufhebung* entailed that "every particular moment has a different meaning within the system from that which it has outside the system" (*Irony*, p. 66), Kierkegaard's reversal of Hegel's *Aufhebung* is not simply subversive and fragmentational but entails every particular moment having a meaning outside the system different from its meaning inside the system—most prominently the particular moment that the individual himself is. In Derrida's case the individual loses his prominence, and it would be difficult to extend the comparison to include Derrida alongside Kierkegaard, on the ground that both subvert from within the philosophical tradition culminating with Hegel. The most obvious difficulty is that Derrida would subvert the contradiction between the internal and external as itself metaphysical in Kierke-

gaard's version as well as Hegel's. It is not, then, just the outsideness of the "Hors livre" that intrudes. The procedure of comparison too is weakened, for any philosopher with whom Derrida becomes involved (Nietzsche and Heidegger are only ambiguously exceptions) cannot significantly survive except as illustrating the metaphysical character of the philosophical tradition, which not even Derrida himself can step confidently outside of. I must accordingly be diffident even about comparing him with Kierkegaard.

88. *Johannes Climacus*, pp. 103–4.

89. For the tradition of the quiet life, see my *Human Nature*, 2:9, 10, 51, 104, 105.

90. *Papirer*, II A 335.

91. But I should add that after some vacillation in distributing his dedications between Regina and his father, finally rebuffed by Regina and her husband, he dedicated it (*For Self-Examination*, p. 5)

To One Unnamed
whose name shall some day be named

. . . .

the whole production of the author from the start.

Works Cited

The works of the major philosophers cited are listed separately below, followed by a general section which includes secondary and other sources referring to these philosophers, as well as works of other writers cited. All works are listed in English translations except where no translation is available, or no reliable or easily obtainable translation.

DERRIDA

La dissémination. Paris: Seuil, 1972.

Glas. Paris: Galilée, 1974.

Introduction to *Essai sur l'origine des connaissances humaines,* by Etienne Bonnot de Condillac. Paris: Galilée, 1973.

Marges de la philosophie. Paris: Minuit, 1972.

Of Grammatology. Translated by Gayatri Chakravorty Spivak. Baltimore: Johns Hopkins Press, 1974.

L'origine de la géométrie. Paris: Presses Universitaires de France, 1974.

"Signature Event Context." Translated by Samuel Weber and Jeffrey Mehlman. In *Glyph,* vol. 1. Johns Hopkins Textual Studies. Baltimore: Johns Hopkins Press, 1977.

Speech and Phenomena. Translated by David B. Allison. Evanston, Ill.: Northwestern University Press, 1973.

HEGEL

Aesthetics. Translated by T. M. Knox. 2 vols. Oxford: Oxford University Press, 1975.

Encyclopaedia of the Philosophical Sciences. Part 1, *Logic.* Translated by William Wallace. Oxford: Oxford University Press, 1974.

Encyclopaedia of the Philosophical Sciences. Part 3, *Philosophy of Mind.* Translated by William Wallace and A. V. Miller. Oxford: Oxford University Press, 1971.

Lectures on the History of Philosophy. Translated by E. S. Haldane and Frances H. Simson. 3 vols. New York: Humanities Press, 1968.

Lectures on the Philosophy of Religion. Translated by E. B. Speirs and J. Burdon Sanderson. 3 vols. New York: Humanities Press, 1968.

Phenomenology of Spirit. Translated by A. V. Miller. Oxford: Oxford University Press, 1977.

Lectures on the Philosophy of History. Translated by J. Sibree. New York: Dover, 1956.

Hegel's Philosophy of Nature. Translated by Michael J. Petry. 3 vols. New York: Humanities Press, 1970.

Philosophy of Right. Translated by T. M. Knox. Oxford: Oxford University Press, 1942.

Science of Logic. Translated by A. V. Miller. New York: Humanities Press, 1969.

HEIDEGGER

"The Age of the World Picture." In *The Question concerning Technology,* translated by William Lovitt. New York: Harper & Row, 1977.

Being and Time. Translated by John Macquarrie and Edward Robinson. New York: Harper & Row, 1962. (A new translation by Joan Stambaugh is forthcoming.)

Existence and Being. Edited by Werner Brock. Chicago: Regnery-Gateway, 1967.

Hegel's Concept of Experience. Edited by J. Glenn Gray. Translated by Kenley Dove. New York: Harper & Row, 1970.

"Heidegger et Cassirer interprètes de Kant: traduction et commentaire d'un document." Translated by Henri Declève. *Revue philosophique de Louvain* 67 (1969): 517–45.

Identity and Difference. Edited by J. Glenn Gray. Translated by Joan Stambaugh. New York: Harper & Row, 1957.

Introduction to "What Is Metaphysics?" In *Philosophy in the Twentieth Century,* edited by William Barrett and Henry D. Aiken, vol. 3. New York: Random House, 1962.

An Introduction to Metaphysics. Translated by Ralph Manheim. New York: Anchor, 1961.

Die Kunst und der Raum. St. Gallen: Erker, 1969.

"Letter on 'Humanism.' " In *Philosophy in the Twentieth Century,* edited by William Barrett and Henry D. Aiken, vol. 3. New York: Random House, 1962.

"Lettre de M. M. Heidegger." *Bulletin de la Société Française de Philosophie* 37 (octobre–décembre 1937): 193–94.

Nietzsche. 2 vols. Pfullingen: Neske, 1961.

"On the Essence of Truth." In *Basic Writings,* edited by David F. Krell. New York: Harper & Row, 1977.

On the Way to Language. Edited by J. Glenn Gray and Fred Wieck. Translated by Peter Hertz and Joan Stambaugh. New York: Harper & Row, 1971.

On Time and Being. Translated by Joan Stambaugh. New York: Harper & Row, 1972.

"Only a God Can Save Us." Translated by Maria P. Alter and John D. Caputo. *Philosophy Today* 20 (1976): 267–84.

"Plato's Doctrine of Truth." In *Philosophy in the Twentieth Century*, edited by William Barrett and Henry D. Aiken, vol. 3. New York: Random House, 1962.

Der Satz vom Grund. Pfullingen: Neske, 1957.

"The Way Back into the Ground of Metaphysics." In *Philosophy in the Twentieth Century*, edited by William Barrett and Henry D. Aiken, vol. 3. New York: Random House, 1962.

What Is a Thing? Translated by N. B. Barton, Jr., and Vera Deutsch. Chicago: Regnery-Gateway, 1968.

What Is Called Thinking? Translated by J. Glenn Gray and Fred Wieck. New York: Harper Torchbooks, 1968.

What Is Philosophy? Translated by William Kluback and Jean T. Wilde. Boston: Twayne, 1958.

HUSSERL

Cartesian Meditations. Translated by Dorion Cairns. The Hague: Nijhoff, 1960.

Ideas: General Introduction to Pure Phenomenology. Translated by W. R. Boyce-Gibson. New York: Collier, 1969.

Logical Investigations. Translated by J. N. Findlay. 2 vols. New York: Humanities Press, 1970.

Vorlesungen zur Phänomenologie des inneren Zeitbewusstseins. Edited by H. Dussort. Husserliana, no. 10. The Hague: Nijhoff, 1966.

KIERKEGAARD

The Concept of Dread. Translated by Walter Lowrie. Princeton, N.J.: Princeton University Press, 1957.

The Concept of Irony: With Constant Reference to Socrates. Translated by Lee M. Capel. Bloomington: Indiana University Press, 1968.

Concluding Unscientific Postscript. Translated by David F. Swenson and Walter Lowrie. Princeton, N.J.: Princeton University Press, 1941.

The Crisis and A Crisis in the Life of an Actress. Translated by Stephen Crites. New York: Harper & Row, 1967.

Either/Or. Vol. 1. Translated by David F. Swenson and Lillian Marvin Swenson. 2d ed., Princeton, N.J.: Princeton University Press, 1971.

Either/Or. Vol. 2. Translated by Water Lowrie. 2d ed., Princeton, N.J.: Princeton University Press, 1971.

For Self-Examination. Translated by Walter Lowrie. Princeton, N.J.: Princeton University Press, 1944.

Forord. In *Samlede Værker*, edited by J. L. Heiberg, vol. 5. Copenhagen: Gyldendal, 1963.

The Gospel of Suffering. Translated by David F. and Lillian Marvin Swenson. Minneapolis: Augsburg, 1948.

Johannes Climacus. Translated by T. H. Croxall. Stanford, Calif.: Stanford University Press, 1958.

Kierkegaard's Attack upon Christendom. Translated by Walter Lowrie. Princeton, N.J.: Princeton University Press, 1944.

Philosophical Fragments. Translated by David Swenson, revised by Howard V. Hong. Princeton, N.J.: Princeton University Press, 1967.

The Point of View for My Work as an Author. Translated by Walter Lowrie. London and New York: Oxford University Press, 1933.

The Present Age. Translated by Alexander Dru and Walter Lowrie. London and New York: Oxford University Press, 1940.

Repetition: An Essay in Experimental Psychology. Translated by Walter Lowrie. Princeton, N.J.: Princeton University Press, 1941.

The Sickness unto Death. Translated by Walter Lowrie. Princeton, N.J.: Princeton University Press, 1941.

Søren Kierkegaards Papirer. Edited by P. A. Heiberg and V. Kuhr. 20 vols. Copenhagen: Gyldendal, 1909–48.

Stages on Life's Way. Translated by Walter Lowrie. London: Milford, Oxford University Press, 1945.

MERLEAU-PONTY

Adventures of the Dialectic. Translated by Joseph J. Bien. Evanston, Ill.: Northwestern University Press, 1973.

"Eye and Mind." In *The Essential Writings of Merleau-Ponty*, edited by Alden L. Fisher. New York: Harcourt, Brace & World, 1969.

Humanism and Terror. Translated by John O'Neill. Boston: Beacon, 1969.

"Husserl et la notion de nature: notes prises au cours de M. Merleau-Ponty." *Revue de métaphysique et de morale* 70 (1965): 257–68.

The Phenomenology of Perception. Translated by Colin Smith. New York: Humanities Press, 1962.

The Primacy of Perception. Edited by James M. Edie. Translated by William Cobb et al. Evanston, Ill.: Northwestern University Press, 1964.

The Prose of the World. Edited by Claude Lefort. Translated by John O'Neill. Evanston, Ill.: Northwestern University Press, 1973.

Sense and Non-Sense. Translated by Herbert L. Dreyfus and Patricia Allen Dreyfus. Evanston, Ill.: Northwestern University Press, 1964.

Signs. Translated by Richard C. McCleary. Evanston, Ill.: Northwestern University Press, 1964.

The Structure of Behavior. Translated by Alden L. Fisher. Boston: Beacon, 1963.

Themes from the Lectures at the College de France, 1952–1960. Translated by John O'Neill. Evanston, Ill.: Northwestern University Press, 1970.

The Visible and the Invisible. Translated by Alphonso Lingis. Evanston, Ill.: Northwestern University Press, 1968.

SARTRE

The Age of Reason. Translated by Eric Sutton. New York: Modern Library, 1963.

"The Anti-Novel of Nathalie Sarraute." Translated by Beth Brombert. *Yale French Studies* 16 (1955–56): 40–44.

Anti-Semite and Jew. Translated by George J. Becker. New York: Schocken, 1948.

Baudelaire. Translated by Martin Turnell. New York: New Directions, 1950.

Being and Nothingness. Translated by Hazel E. Barnes. New York: Washington Square, 1966.

Between Existentialism and Marxism. Translated by John Mathews. New York: Pantheon, 1974.

The Condemned of Altona. Translated by Sylvia and George Leeson. New York: Vintage, 1961.

Critique of Dialectical Reason. Translated by Alan Sheridan-Smith. New York: Schocken, 1976.

Dirty Hands. See *"No Exit."*

"Drôle d'amitié." *Temps modernes* 49–50 (1949): 769–806, 1009–39.

Emotions: Outline of a Theory. Translated by Bernard Frechtman. New York: Citadel, 1971.

Essays in Aesthetics. Translated by Wade Baskin. New York: Philosophical Library, 1963.

Existentialism Is a Humanism. Excerpted in *Existentialism and Human Emotions.* New York: Philosophical Library, 1947.

L'idiot de la famille. 3 vols. Paris: Gallimard, 1971–72.

L'imaginaire. Paris: Gallimard, 1940.

Imagination: A Psychological Critique. Translated by Forrest Williams. Ann Arbor: University of Michigan Press, 1972.

"Intentionality: A Fundamental Idea of Husserl's Phenomenology." *Journal of the British Society for Phenomenology* 1, no. 2 (May 1970): 4–5.

Kean. In *"The Devil and the Good Lord" and Two Other Plays.* Translated by Kitty Black. New York: Knopf, 1960.

Life/Situations: Essays Written and Spoken. Translated by Paul Auster and Lydia Davis. New York: Pantheon, 1977.

Literary and Philosophical Essays. Translated by Annette Michelson. New York: Collier, 1966.

Nausea. Translated by Lloyd Alexander. 2d ed. New York: New Directions, 1964.

"No Exit" and Three Other Plays. Translated by Lionel Abel. New York: Vintage, 1955.

On a raison de se révolter. With Ph. Gavi and P. Victor. Paris: Gallimard, 1974.

The Philosophy of Jean-Paul Sartre. Edited by Robert Denoon Cumming. 2d ed. New York: Vintage, 1972.

Présentation to *La promenade du dimanche*, by George Michel. Paris: Gallimard, 1967.

The Respectful Prostitute. See *"No Exit."*

Saint Genet: Actor and Martyr. Translated by Bernard Frechtman. New York: Braziller, 1963.

"Sartre et les femmes." *Nouvelle observateur,* vol. 64 (7 février 1977).

Sartre on Theater. Translated by Frank Fellinek. New York: Pantheon, 1976.

Search for a Method. Translated by Hazel E. Barnes. New York: Knopf, 1963.

Situations. Vols. 1–10. Paris: Gallimard, 1948–76.

Situations. Translated by Benita Eisler. New York: Fawcett, 1965.

"Socialism in One Country." *New Left Review* 100 (1976–77): 143–63.

The Transcendence of the Ego. Translated by Forrest Williams and Robert Kirkpatrick. New York: Noonday, 1957.

"The Wall" and Other Stories. Translated by Lloyd Alexander. New York: New Directions, 1969.

What Is Literature? Translated by Bernard Frechtman. New York: Philosophical Library, 1949.

The Words. Translated by Bernard Frechtman. New York: Fawcett, 1966.

The Writings of Jean-Paul Sartre. Edited by Michel Contat and Michel Rybalka. Translated by Richard O. McCleary. 2 vols. Evanston, Ill.: Northwestern University Press, 1974.

OTHER WORKS

Anderson, Barbara. Review of Josiah Thompson, *Kierkegaard. Man and World* 7 (1964): 300–306.

Attwater, Donald. *The Penguin Dictionary of Saints.* Baltimore: Penguin, 1965.

Ayer, Alfred J. *Metaphysics and Common Sense.* San Francisco: Freeman, Cooper, 1970.

Baudelaire, Charles. "L'irrémédiable." In *Les fleurs du mal.* Paris: Pelletan, 1927.

Bauer, George Henry. *Sartre and the Artist.* Chicago: University of Chicago Press, 1969.

Beaufret, Jean. "Husserl et Heidegger." In *Dialogue avec Heidegger,* vol. 3. Paris: Minuit, 1974.

Berger, Gaston. *The Cogito in Husserl's Philosophy.* Translated by Kathleen McLaughlin. Evanston, Ill.: Northwestern University Press, 1972.

———. *Existentialism and Literature in Action.* Buffalo, N.Y.: University of Buffalo Press, 1948.

Booth, Wayne C. *The Rhetoric of Fiction.* Chicago: University of Chicago Press, 1961.

Camus, Albert. *The Fall.* Translated by Justin O'Brien. New York: Knopf, 1961.

Contat. See Sartre, *The Writings of Jean-Paul Sartre.*

Croxall, T. H. *Glimpses and Impressions of Kierkegaard.* Welwyn, Herts.: Nesbit, 1959.

Cumming, Robert D. *Human Nature and History: A Study of the Development of Liberal Political Thought.* 2 vols. Chicago: University of Chicago Press, 1969.

de Beauvoir, Simone. *The Force of Circumstance.* Translated by Richard Howard. New York: Putnam's, 1965.

———. *Memoirs of a Dutiful Daughter.* Translated by James Kirkup. Cleveland: World, 1959.

————. *The Prime of Life.* Translated by Peter Cleveland. Cleveland: World, 1962.

de Gandillac, Maurice. "Entretien avec Martin Heidegger." *Temps modernes* 4 (1945): 713–16.

De Mott, Benjamin. *Supergrow: Essays and Reports on Imagination in America.* New York: Dutton, 1969.

Eliot, T. S. *Four Quartets.* New York: Harcourt, Brace, 1943.

Fink, Eugen. "The Phenomenological Philosophy of Edmund Husserl and Contemporary Criticism." In *The Phenomenology of Husserl,* edited by R. O. Elveton. Chicago: Quadrangle, 1970.

————. "Das Problem der Phänomenologie Edmund Husserls." *Revue internationale de philosophie* 2 (1939): 226–70.

Harman, Barbara Leah. "The Fiction of Coherence: George Herbert's 'The Collar.'" *PMLA* 93 (1978): 865–77.

Hellman, Lillian. *Pentimento: A Book of Portraits.* New York: New American Library, 1974.

Iser, Wolfgang. *Der implizite Leser.* Munich: Fink, 1972.

James, Henry. *The Golden Bowl.* In *Collected Works,* vol. 9. London: Bodley Head, 1971.

James, William. *Essays in Radical Empiricism.* New York: Longmans Green, 1922.

Jeanson, Francis. *Le problème morale et la pensée de Sartre.* 2d ed., rev. Paris: Seuil, 1965.

————. *Sartre par lui-même.* Paris: Seuil, 1958.

Kafka, Franz. *Parables and Paradoxes.* New York: Schocken, 1946.

Kant, Immanuel. *Critique of Judgment.* Translated by J. H. Bernard. New York: Hafner, 1951.

Lalo, Charles. *L'art loin de la vie.* Paris: Vrin, 1939.

Lowrie, Walter. "'Existence' as Understood by Kierkegaard and/or Sartre." *Sewanee Review* 58 (1950): 379–401.

————. *Kierkegaard.* 2 vols. New York: Harper Torchbooks, 1962.

MacIntyre, Alasdair. "Existentialism." In *Encyclopedia of Philosophy,* edited by Paul Edwards, vol. 3. New York: Macmillan, 1967.

Malantschuk, Gregor. *Kierkegaard's Thought.* Translated by Howard V. Hong and Edna H. Hong. Princeton, N.J.: Princeton University Press, 1971.

Marx, Karl. "Theses on Feuerbach." In *The German Ideology,* edited by R. Pascal. New York: International Publishers, 1947.

————. *Writings of the Young Marx on Philosophy and Society.* Translated by Lloyd D. Easton and Kurt H. Guddat. Garden City, N.Y.: Doubleday, 1967.

Mill, John Stuart. *The Later Letters, 1849–1873.* In *Collected Works,* edited by Francis E. Mineka and Dwight Lindley, vols. 14–17. Toronto: University of Toronto Press, 1972.

————. *On Liberty.* Indianapolis: Bobbs-Merrill, 1956.

————. *A System of Logic.* New York: Longmans Green, 1941.

Molnar, Thomas. *Sartre: Ideologue of Our Time.* New York: Funk & Wagnalls, 1968.

Moore, G. E. *The Philosophy of G. E. Moore.* Edited by Paul A. Schilpp. The Library of Living Philosophers, vol. 4. La Salle, Ill.: Open Court, 1968.

Murdoch, Iris. *An Accidental Man.* New York: Viking, 1972.

———. *Sartre: Romantic Rationalist.* New Haven: Yale University Press, 1953.

———. *The Sovereignty of Good.* New York: Schocken, 1971.

Murray, Michael, ed. *Heidegger & Modern Philosophy.* New Haven and London: Yale University Press, 1978.

Olafson, Frederick A. *Principles and Persons.* Baltimore: Johns Hopkins Press, 1967.

Pingaud, Bernard. "Jean-Paul Sartre répond." *Arc* 30 (1966): 87–96.

Pöggeler, Otto. *Der Denkweg M. Heideggers.* Pfullingen: Neske, 1963.

———. "Heidegger Heute." In *Heidegger,* edited by Otto Pöggeler. Cologne: Kiepenheur & Witsch, 1970.

Poulet, Georges. *Le point de départ.* Paris: Plon, 1964.

Ricoeur, Paul. *Husserl: An Analysis of His Phenomenology.* Translated by Edward G. Ballard and Lester E. Embree. Evanston, Ill.: Northwestern University Press, 1967.

Richardson, William. *Heidegger: From Phenomenology to Thought.* The Hague: Nijhoff, 1967.

Rohde, Peter P. *Søren Kierkegaard: et geni i en købstad.* Copenhagen: Gyldendal, 1962.

Ryle, Gilbert. "Plato's *Parmenides.*" In *Collected Papers,* vol. 1. New York: Barnes & Noble, 1971.

Said, Edward W. *Beginnings: Intention and Method.* New York: Basic, 1975.

———. "The Problem of Textuality: Two Exemplary Positions." *Critical Inquiry* 4 (1978): 673–714.

Salvan, Jacques. *The Scandalous Ghost: Sartre's Existentialism as Related to Vitalism, Humanism, Mysticism, Marxism.* Detroit: Wayne State University Press, 1967.

Schacht, Richard. *Alienation.* Introduction by Walter Kaufmann. Garden City, N.Y.: Doubleday, 1971.

Schlegel, Friedrich. *Kritische Schriften.* Munich: Hanser, 1964.

———. *Lucinde.* Edited by Peter Firchow. Minneapolis: University of Minnesota Press, 1971.

Spiegelberg, Herbert. *The Phenomenological Movement.* 2 vols. The Hague: Nijhoff, 1960.

Taylor, Charles. Review of *La philosophie analytique. Philosophical Review* 73 (1964): 133–34.

Thody, Philip. *Sartre: A Biographical Outline.* New York: Scribners, 1972.

Thompson, Josiah. *Kierkegaard.* New York: Knopf, 1973.

Trendelenburg, Friedrich A. "The Logical Question in Hegel's System." Translated by Thomas Davidson. *Journal of Speculative Philosophy* 5 (1871): 349–59.

Wahl, Jean. *Etudes kierkegaardiennes.* Paris: Aubier,

Williams, Charles W. *The Figure of Beatrice: A Study in Dante.* New York: Noonday, 1961.

Index

Topics treated with specific reference to any one of the major philosophers discussed are listed under his name. Topics treated with reference to more than one philosopher are usually included only in the general listing.

ject), 73, 81; *Ereignis*, 75, 137; everydayness, 72, 75, 98, 180, 325, **332**, 335,
338, 339, 345, 348, 367; *Geworfenheit*
("thrown-ness"), 103, 132, 136; and Hölderlin, 1, 2, 65; and Husserl, 24, 26–27,
437–38, 552; obstruction, 149, 165, 180,
306–7, 308; starting point, 1, 5–6, 11,
149, 178, 330–31, 337; *Stimmung* (mood),
169–70, 172–76, 245; talking, 331–34, 460;
transcendence, 81, 92; *Verwischung* (effacement), 307; way, 78–79, 91, **146–48**,
159, 179, 305–6, 399–400; world, 66, 98–
99, 100, 101, 228, 316; *Zweideutigkeit*
(ambiguity), 337; mentioned, 9, 12, 19,
20, 23, 24, 26, 29–33, 37, 72, 258, 260,
511
Hermeneutical phenomenology, 34, 177,
552
Humanism, 49, 184
Husserl, Edmund: intentionality ("consciousness of something"), 74, 176, 189,
194, 196, 211, **228**, 229, 232, 325, 329, 357,
363–64, 391, 395; reduction, 73, 76, 194,
227, 334, 348, 356, 366, 389, 390; starting
point, 27–28; mentioned, 24–25, 26–33,
49, 66, 133, 168, 187–88, 530, 551–52

Identification, **194–96**, 222, 226, 233, 325,
522
Identity, 74, 86, 222, 226, 233, 254, 325, 361,
436, 522, 529. *See also* Self
Imagination, **104–7**, 109–10, 132–33, 144,
151, 160–62, 192, 196, 198–201, 225, 247–
48, 278, **291**, 418, 430, 450, 478, 486, 505–
9, 511–12, 514, 521, 532, 540–43, 559
Individual, individualism, 35–36, 39–42,
45–46, **61–64**, 68–69, 77, 88–89, 94, 119,
120–21, 122–25, 209–10, 234–35, 280, 297,
322, 409, 462, 463, 465–69, 488, 549
Initiative, 1–5, 7, 248, 414, 449, 452, 466,
502, 547. *See also* Conformism
Interplay, 114, 158–61, 175, 192, 197, 202,
229, 244, 251–52, 253, 258, 281, 291, 310,
311, 319, 339–40, 343, 344, 354–55, 359,
361, 375, 386, 406, 437, 485, 516–17, 535,
553, 556. *See also* Levels
Introduction, 399–401, 554, 564
Ionesco, Eugène, 381
Irony, 6, 11, 12, 39–45, 50–52, 68, 467, 479,
494, 545–47

James, Henry, 348
James, William, 116, 521
Janet, Pierre, 73

Jaspers, Karl, 49, 131, 394

Kafka, Franz, 154–55, 256–57
Kant, Immanuel, 7, 37, 186, 467–68
Kean, Edmund, 528
Kierkegaard, Søren: aphorisms (separative
procedure), 245–50, 255, 261, 266, 270,
281–82, 289, 294, 413, 447, 449, 455, 462,
547; and Aristophanes, 107–8, 242, 482,
489; *captatio benevolentiae*, 287, 325,
433, 463, 489; Christianity, 21, 401, 403,
540; *Corsair*, 72, 74; despair, 60, 84, 240,
286, 438, 543; esthetics, 54, 69, **243–44**,
245, 253, 300, 326, 403, 406, 415, 433, 435,
468, 474, 485–86, 509, 545, 548, 563; ethics, 54, 253, **407–13**, 436, 469–74, 476; and
father (Michael Pederson Kierkegaard),
280, 538, 543, 558–59; and fiancée (Regine Olsen), 72, 122, 231, 279, 280, 434,
503, 511, 534–36, 538–42, 546, 554–57,
562, 565; fragmentation, 237, 270, 271,
287, 413–15, 432, 438–55, 462, 487, 503,
533; and Heiberg, J. L., 252–53; and
Heiberg, Mme J. L., 85, 558; hovering,
107–8, 182, 511, 541–42, 546–47, 555; immediacy, 161–62, 261–65, 266–69, 273–76,
290, 292, 383, 405–6, 431, 434, 481, 505,
539, 558–59; implication (*konsekvens*),
258–60, 448, 551, 554–55; interesting,
161–62; internal/external, 239–40, 241–
49, 273–79, 286, 415–32, 436–41, 442–52,
454–60, 475–76, 479, 485, 524; journalism,
5, 72; and Lund, Henrick, 21; and Lund,
Peter Wilhelm, 11; and Martensen,
Hans Lassen, 52; misunderstanding, 25,
245–46, 266–67, 273, 286, 289; music, 245,
261–69, 292, 298, 438–39, 524–25; pseudonyms, 239, 285–86, 514, 545–46; and the
professor, 4–5, 334; reduplication, 459–
60; repetition, 115, 183, 289, 362; shadowgraphs, 427, 440, 484–86, 488–89, 502,
546; and Socrates, 6, 7, 12, 35, 107–8,
119–20, 122, 182, 242, 290, 293, 298–99,
413, 546, 557–63; starting point, 4, 5, 38–
40, 41–48, 50, 51–52, 242, **261**, 268, 271–
72, 288, 298, 300, 404, 415–32, 436–41,
442–52, 454–60, 461, 468, 549, 550, 552,
555–56; transfiguration, 534–36, 542, 546,
559, 561; and Xenophon, 107, 109, 242,
563; mentioned, 11–12, 20, 23, 26, 28–30,
32–33, 34–35, 37, 191

Lacan, Jacques, 35
Lalo, Charles, 70